1990

THE PHILOSOPHY OF
GABRIEL MARCEL

THE LIBRARY OF LIVING PHILOSOPHERS

Paul Arthur Schilpp and Lewis Edwin Hahn, Editors

Already Published:

THE PHILOSOPHY OF JOHN DEWEY (1939)*
THE PHILOSOPHY OF GEORGE SANTAYANA (1940)
THE PHILOSOPHY OF ALFRED NORTH WHITEHEAD (1941)*
THE PHILOSOPHY OF G. E. MOORE (1942)
THE PHILOSOPHY OF BERTRAND RUSSELL (1944)*
THE PHILOSOPHY OF ERNST CASSIRER (1949)
ALBERT EINSTEIN: PHILOSOPHER-SCIENTIST (1949)
THE PHILOSOPHY OF SARVEPALLI RADHAKRISHNAN (1952)*
THE PHILOSOPHY OF KARL JASPERS (1957; aug. ed., 1981)
THE PHILOSOPHY OF C. D. BROAD (1959)
THE PHILOSOPHY OF RUDOLF CARNAP (1963)
THE PHILOSOPHY OF MARTIN BUBER (1967)
THE PHILOSOPHY OF C. I. LEWIS (1968)
THE PHILOSOPHY OF KARL POPPER (1974)
THE PHILOSOPHY OF BRAND BLANSHARD (1980)
THE PHILOSOPHY OF JEAN-PAUL SARTRE (1981)
THE PHILOSOPHY OF GABRIEL MARCEL (1984)

In Preparation:

THE PHILOSOPHY OF GEORG HENRIK von WRIGHT
THE PHILOSOPHY OF W. V. QUINE

*Available only from University Microfilms International.

THE LIBRARY OF LIVING PHILOSOPHERS
VOLUME XVII

THE PHILOSOPHY OF
GABRIEL MARCEL

EDITED BY

PAUL ARTHUR SCHILPP

AND

LEWIS EDWIN HAHN

SOUTHERN ILLINOIS UNIVERSITY— CARBONDALE

LA SALLE, ILLINOIS • OPEN COURT • ESTABLISHED 1887

THE PHILOSOPHY OF GABRIEL MARCEL

OPEN COURT and ✺ are registered in the U.S. Patent and Trademark Office.

Printed in the United States of America

OC783   10 9 8 7 6 5 4 3 2 1

FIRST EDITION

Library of Congress Cataloging in Publication Data

Main entry under title:

The Philosophy of Gabriel Marcel.

(The Library of living philosophers; v. 17)
Includes index.
Contents: An autobiographical essay—Descriptive and critical essays on the philosophy of Gabriel Marcel, with replies—A bibliography of the writings of Gabriel Marcel / compiled by François H. Lapointe.
1. Marcel, Gabriel, 1889–1973—Addresses, essays, lectures. I. Marcel, Gabriel, 1889–1973. II. Schilpp, Paul Arthur, 1897–   III. Hahn, Lewis Edwin, 1908–
IV. Series.
B2430.M254P47 1983   194   83-4063
ISBN 0-87548-369-0

The Library of Living Philosophers is published under the sponsorship of Southern Illinois University—Carbondale.

GENERAL INTRODUCTION*
TO
THE LIBRARY OF LIVING PHILOSOPHERS

According to the late F. C. S. Schiller, the greatest obstacle to fruitful discussion in philosophy is "the curious etiquette which apparently taboos the asking of questions about a philosopher's meaning while he is alive." The "interminable controversies which fill the histories of philosophy," he goes on to say, "could have been ended at once by asking the living philosophers a few searching questions."

The confident optimism of this last remark undoubtedly goes too far. Living thinkers have often been asked "a few searching questions," but their answers have not stopped "interminable controversies" about their real meaning. It is nonetheless true that there would be far greater clarity of understanding than is now often the case if more such searching questions had been directed to great thinkers while they were still alive.

This, at any rate, is the basic thought behind the present undertaking. The volumes of The Library of Living Philosophers can in no sense take the place of the major writings of great and original thinkers. Students who would know the philosophies of such men as John Dewey, George Santayana, Alfred North Whitehead, G. E. Moore, Bertrand Russell, Ernst Cassirer, Karl Jaspers, Rudolf Carnap, Martin Buber, et al., will still need to read the writings of these men. There is no substitute for first-hand contact with the original thought of the philosopher himself. Least of all does this Library pretend to be such a substitute. The Library in fact will spare neither effort nor expense in offering to the student the best possible guide to the published writings of a given thinker. We shall attempt to meet this aim by providing at the end of each volume in our series as nearly complete a bibliography of the published work of the philosopher in question as possible. Nor should one overlook the fact that essays in each volume cannot but finally lead to this same goal. The interpretative and critical discussions of the various phases of a great thinker's work and, most of all, the reply of the thinker himself, are bound to lead the reader to the works of the philosopher himself.

*This General Introduction, setting forth the underlying conception of this Library, is purposely reprinted in each volume (with only very minor changes).

At the same time, there is no denying that different experts find different ideas in the writings of the same philosopher. This is as true of the appreciative interpreter and grateful disciple as it is of the critical opponent. Nor can it be denied that such differences of reading and of interpretation on the part of other experts often leave the neophyte aghast before the whole maze of widely varying and even opposing interpretations. Who is right and whose interpretation shall he accept? When the doctors disagree among themselves, what is the poor student to do? If, in desperation, he decides that all of the interpreters are probably wrong and that the only thing for him to do is to go back to the original writings of the philosopher himself and then make his own decision—uninfluenced (as if this were possible) by the interpretation of anyone else—the result is not that he has actually come to the meaning of the original philosopher himself, but rather that he has set up one more interpretation, which may differ to a greater or lesser degree from the interpretations already existing. It is clear that in this direction lies chaos, just the kind of chaos which Schiller has so graphically and inimitably described.[1]

It is curious that until now no way of escaping this difficulty has been seriously considered. It has not occurred to students of philosophy that one effective way of meeting the problem at least partially is to put these varying interpretations and critiques before the philosopher while he is still alive and to ask him to act at one and the same time as both defendant and judge. If the world's great living philosophers can be induced to cooperate in an enterprise whereby their own work can, at least to some extent, be saved from becoming merely "desiccated lecture-fodder," which on the one hand "provides innocuous sustenance for ruminant professors," and on the other hand gives an opportunity to such ruminants and their understudies to "speculate safely, endlessly, and fruitlessly, about what a philosopher must have meant" (Schiller), they will have taken a long step toward making their intentions more clearly comprehensible.

With this in mind, The Library of Living Philosophers expects to publish at more or less regular intervals a volume on each of the greater among the world's living philosophers. In each case it will be the purpose of the editor of the Library to bring together in the volume the interpretations and criticisms of a wide range of that particular thinker's scholarly contemporaries, each of whom will be given a free hand to discuss the specific phase of the thinker's work that has been assigned to him. All contributed essays will finally be submitted to the philosopher with whose work and thought they are concerned, for his careful perusal and reply. And, although it would be expecting too much to imagine that the philosopher's reply will

---

1. In his essay "Must Philosophers Disagree?" in the volume of the same title (London: Macmillan, 1934), from which the above quotations were taken.

be able to stop all differences of interpretation and of critique, this should at least serve the purpose of stopping certain of the grosser and more general kinds of misinterpretation. If no further gain than this were to come from the present and projected volumes of this Library, it would seem to be fully justified.

In carrying out this principal purpose of the Library, the editor announces that (as far as is humanly possible) each volume will contain the following elements:

First, an intellectual autobiography of the thinker whenever this can be secured; in any case an authoritative and authorized biography;
Second, a series of expository and critical articles written by the leading exponents and opponents of the philosopher's thought;
Third, the reply to the critics and commentators by the philosopher himself; and
Fourth, a bibliography of writings of the philosopher to provide a ready instrument to give access to his writings and thought.

The editors have deemed it desirable to secure the services of an Advisory Board of philosophers to aid them in the selection of the subjects of future volumes. The names of the seven prominent American philosophers who have consented to serve appear on the next page. To each of them the editors express their sincere gratitude.

Future volumes in this series will appear in as rapid succession as is feasible in view of the scholarly nature of this Library. The next volume in this series will probably be devoted to the philosophy of Georg Henrik von Wright.

Throughout its forty-five years, The Library of Living Philosophers has, because of its scholarly nature, never been self-supporting. The generosity of the Edward C. Hegeler Foundation has made possible the publication of many of the volumes, but for the support of future volumes additional funds are needed. On February 20, 1979, the Board of Trustees of Southern Illinois University contractually assumed all responsibility for the Library, which is therefore no longer separately incorporated. Gifts specifically designated for the Library may be made through the University, and inasmuch as the University is a tax-exempt institution, all such gifts are tax-deductible.

P.A.S.
Editor

DEPARTMENT OF PHILOSOPHY
SOUTHERN ILLINOIS UNIVERSITY — CARBONDALE

ACKNOWLEDGMENTS

The editors hereby gratefully acknowledge their obligation and sincere gratitude to all the publishers of Gabriel Marcel's books and publications for their kind and uniform courtesy in permitting us to quote—sometimes at some length—from Professor Marcel's writings.

PAUL A. SCHILPP
LEWIS E. HAHN

*Deceased.

TABLE OF CONTENTS

PREFACE

Gabriel Marcel (1888–1973) certainly needs no justification for being included in The Library of Living Philosophers. His work is as well known in the so-called New World as it is in Europe. The list of contributors to this volume is itself a clear demonstration of this fact. To the contributors I express my sincere gratitude and appreciation—particularly for their almost unanimous forbearance, understanding, and patience when a book that was practically ready for the typesetter in 1973 was delayed again and again because, after Professor Marcel passed away in October 1973, the publisher and I agreed that we should attempt to get the volumes on the still-living philosophers out ahead of *The Philosophy of Gabriel Marcel*. As events proved, we were not to be successful even in that attempt, inasmuch as Jean-Paul Sartre died just as our completed manuscript for the volume on his philosophy had gone to press (too late to have it recalled and replaced by the Marcel book).

Consequently, this volume (Volume XVII in our series) is appearing a decade late. I offer to each contributor to this volume my most sincere apologies for this unfortunate delay.

Marcel's own autobiographical essay is a very moving document. It is the most personal—as distinct from either intellectual or philosophical—autobiography in any of the volumes in our series. As a matter of fact, it is rare for any writer to let a reading audience as deeply into his own innermost as Marcel has done in this log of his life, in which he lets us glimpse not merely some of his hopes and aspirations but also his frustrations and disappointments. As one reads this revealing monograph, one wonders whether Marcel would not have much preferred to go down in history as a great playwright and perhaps even actor rather than as a philosopher. He really does not mince words about this preference. And, in view of the fact that all too few of his plays have appeared in English, one finds oneself at a disadvantage in making any objective judgment about which of Marcel's two areas of literary effort was more successful. Unfortunately, we have in this volume only one essay that deals primarily with Marcel's work as a playwright and drama critic—that by Professor Donald MacKinnon, who thoroughly appreciates what I have been saying here. In addition, E. M. Cioran, in his admirably empathetic portrait of Gabriel Marcel, also clearly sees the difficulty that Marcel himself had in judging the success of his various areas of effort. This was a problem with which Marcel, apparently, never was really able to come to terms and certainly did not solve to his own satisfaction. There are even hints in the Cioran essay that perhaps what Marcel really wanted to be all his life was a musician.

In view of the fact that Professor Marcel wrote almost every reply to the contributors' essays in the form of a letter addressed to the contributor himself, we are following in this volume a procedure we first used in The Library of Living Philosophers volume on Blanshard, namely, to publish Marcel's reply in each case immediately following the contributor's essay. In most previous volumes the philosopher's reply appeared as section III between the contributors' essays and the bibliography. The procedure we are following here makes it easier for the reader, who need not search for the philosopher's reply to an essay.

I am sorry to have to record the fact that two contributors passed away before this volume could appear. Professor Erwin W. Straus of Lexington, Kentucky, died on 20 May 1975. His essay, coauthored with Professor Michael A. Machado of Frostburg State College, Maryland, fortunately was in our possession before his passing. Professor John B. O'Malley of the University of Liverpool in England passed away on 18 May 1976. We were also fortunate in having his essay in our possession before his death. In addition, before Professor Marcel's own passing, we had received his replies to both essays.

Professor Lechner's paper was read at De Paul University in Chicago at a memorial service in honor of Marcel, where I heard it and asked him for permission to include it in this volume, assuring him I would explain in the Preface why there is no reply from Marcel.

In the matter of translations from foreign languages, I am pleased to acknowledge help from the translators of various essays in this volume, each of whom is individually given credit in a footnote on the bottom of the respective essay's first page. However, Miss Susan Gruenheck deserves special mention for having actually maintained on behalf and in place of the editor a personal contact with Professor Marcel in Paris over a period of years. That sort of service is quite beyond measure. Acknowledgment is due also, for financial assistance in paying for such translations, to the National Endowment for the Humanities; to the Council on Research and Creative Work of the University of Colorado, Boulder; and to the Penrose Fund of the American Philosophical Society, Philadelphia, Pennsylvania.

And I certainly want, once again, to express my most heartfelt appreciation to our publisher, Open Court Publishing Company of La Salle, Illinois, for continuing its never failing support of this publishing project of no mean proportions. When publisher and editor work harmoniously together, this is an ideal situation.

The administration of Southern Illinois University—Carbondale has given its steady and unstinted support to this Library and, by relieving the editor of any extra teaching and committee duties, has made the continuation of this series possible. In this connection, the reader's attention should be called once more to the fact that since 20 February 1979 The Library of Living Philosophers has been the contractual property of Southern Illinois University—Carbondale, which also appointed the editor of this series. Although most of the basic editing for this volume XVII was done by the founder-editor of the series, I am happy to announce that future volumes will be edited by my successor, Professor Lewis E. Hahn, who undertook editorial duties on the series as of 15 July 1981. Needless to say, Dr. Hahn, who needs no introduction to philosophers, has the former editor's very best and most sincere wishes for a happy and successful editorship.

PAUL ARTHUR SCHILPP
EDITOR EMERITUS

DEPARTMENT OF PHILOSOPHY
SOUTHERN ILLINOIS UNIVERSITY—CARBONDALE
SPRING 1981

Supplement to the Preface

In putting the Marcel manuscript in shape for publication, I am fortunate in having Professor Schilpp at hand for advice and counsel. I am grateful also for the help I have received in many ways and on numerous points from Dawn Barbercheck and the Philosophy Department secretariat and from my colleagues, especially Matthew J. Kelly, G. K. Plochmann, Garth Gillan, and Robert Hahn.

In addition, my thanks are due to the staff of the Morris Library and especially to Alan M. Cohn and his associates, notably Angela B. Rubin and D. Kathleen Eads, for invaluable aid in running down references. Cynthia Cockerham of the Reference Department of the University of Illinois Library at Urbana-Champaign is another who has provided much needed aid.

To Amy Klatzkin goes our warm appreciation for her expert assistance in helping make our manuscript as accurate and readable as possible. And, finally, a very special debt of gratitude is due my secretary and assistant, Marjorie L. Trotter, who has been most helpful in tracking down elusive references.

Lewis Edwin Hahn
Editor

Department of Philosophy
Southern Illinois University—Carbondale
January 1983

PART ONE

AN
AUTOBIOGRAPHICAL
ESSAY

ARE you thankful enough to God for having given you such a fine life?" At the moment a few months ago when an old friend suddenly posed this question, I felt unable to answer it, although it found an echo deep within me. It seemed to call upon me to take a new look at my life. "Is it quite so?" I asked myself. "Can I say in all sincerity that I have had a fine life?" A few moments later, it was as if an acquiescence rose upward from the very depths of me. Yes, it is true: everything considered, my life has been a beautiful one; my old friend was right. But then why a hesitation before acquiescence? I see two reasons. First, the ineradicable sorrows that have darkened my existence: the death of my mother when I was still a small child; then, a little more than twenty years ago, the disappearance of my companion, following by a few years that of my aunt, who had been a second mother to me. Let it not be said that such griefs are, after all, the common lot. That is a meaningless platitude.

Second, my life has been perpetually harrowed by a searching, often and for long stretches undertaken in darkness and anguish. Nothing could be more false than to envisage it as a progression toward the light. True, I have known stages not only of reward and rest, but also of illumination; quite often they have been followed, however, by the most painful downfalls. This has had to do with more than what might be called purely inner experience. As early as the First World War, I was feeling my attention more and more strongly riveted to external events, as I followed their course with the most anxious care. I know that my own euphoria after the victory of 1918 did not last more than a year. I should add that the circumstances in which I lived through the First War, even though as a noncombatant, led me to view a new outbreak as necessarily catastrophic. I have never lost for one second a sense of the exhausting sacrifices—exhausting far beyond the powers of recuperation—the war had cost my country and more generally what we then called the civilized world.

In the course of this autobiographical essay, I will have the opportunity to return to what was unquestionably an incurable trauma. But I simply want to note here how my life, save for some brief periods, was darkened by an increasingly keen awareness of the menace hanging over humanity.

Despite all these reservations, I see a perspective from which I can vouch for the implied affirmation in the question invoked at the outset. First of all, I feel justified in saying that my work seems on the whole to

---

Translated from the French by Forrest Williams in consultations with the author made possible by grants from the Council on Research and Creative Work of the University of Colorado, Boulder, Colorado, and from the Penrose Fund of the American Philosophical Society, Philadelphia, Pennsylvania.

have fulfilled my most fundamental intent—an intent that did not emerge fully until a fairly late date. Can I also say that this work has been understood? My philosophical work has been much better received, it seems to me, than I had any right to expect. A manuscript such as the *Journal métaphysique,* with its groping movement, could have remained an essentially private matter. Such has obviously not been its fate. To be sure, the way my name became coupled with Sartre's after 1945 contributed to the most troublesome misunderstandings. Nevertheless, the *Journal métaphysique* and the succeeding books, thanks to translations, have enjoyed a readership that I hardly counted on initially.

My theatrical works, which on the whole have been less understood than my philosophical ones, have been quite another matter. Later I shall have to ask why. But without a doubt, this disparity, most disturbing in itself, has had deplorable repercussions on the interpretation of my work viewed *in toto* and as a unity.

Along the way I shall also have to show—and this is an aspect of my life that I shall be broaching for the first time—how on the plane of the intimate (which in my eyes is supreme), both by reason of my marriage and its corollaries and by reason of the adoption of him who was to become in the fullest and truest sense our son, my life emerged at last into plenitude and light.

In this sense, yes, my old friend was right: it is an expression of thanksgiving that I must articulate for myself before leaving this world.

As I wrote a few months ago on some pages not destined for publication, the closer I come to the end of my life, the more it seems to me a skein I must try to untangle. Needless to say, any attempt at a purely chronological, hence linear, presentation would appear to me to be a distortion. In these last years I have often felt myself closer to my remote past than to events of a recent date. It would be worthwhile to inquire into the nature of this perception. If we could elucidate it, perhaps we would by the same stroke see more clearly into the secret structure of what we sometimes call our fate. Certain it is, in any case, that in the technological era in which our lives have been placed, chronological presentations seem to be a matter of course. And it is indeed strictly applicable to that irreversible order in which inventions occur, these replacing those, the newer casting the older into who knows what scrap heap, from which it is uncertain that anyone may ever rescue them.

I can scarcely feel any surprise, therefore, that I am unable to determine with any precision what my first memories are, even though some more or less distinct images remain that I could, if necessary, so designate.

It would surely be better to speak of a certain affective tonality of my first years, those years preceding the death of my mother, after two days of illness, on the fifteenth of November, 1893; I was going on four.

That tonality, which could best be rendered musically, is linked to a certain *côté*, or "way," in the Proustian sense of the word. At its center is the apartment where I was born, at the corner of the rue de Naples and the rue du Général Foy. I remember its having been very light, for it was situated on the top floor; indeed, I recall kitchen windows looking out on the covered playground of a primary school, from which I retain audio-olfactory impressions: the joyful tumult of schoolboys at their games oddly permeated with an odor of laundering. It seems to me that the cook must have been called Françoise. I see once more, vaguely, a blue apron. But for me the important person was my nurse, Marie Girard, from the Morvin region, who was to be intertwined with my life for a long time.

But there was also another *côté:* the house on the avenue Raphaël, on the edge of the jardins Ranelagh, where my grandparents lived. I loved the little garden with the grassy lawn on which I could cavort. My grandfather, who was ill for more than fifteen years and whom my grandmother cared for with a tireless devotion, passed away in 1892. The house was sold, and my grandmother moved in with my aunt on a dreary and anonymous street of the plaine Monceau, the rue Meissonier, about five minutes from that parc Monceau that was subsequently to play an important role for me.

Strange as it may seem, I recall absolutely nothing of those two desolate days, the fourteenth and the fifteenth of November in 1893. What was I aware of? What did I sense? What did I surmise? Impossible to remember. Yet I retain a rather definite memory, it seems to me, of my first hours on the rue Meissonier, of the penumbra of the parlor; I must have been seated on one of the small chairs that are now in my house at Corrèze. I still seem to hear the murmurs of Granny and of members of the family who had come to extend their condolences.

I must, however, move back in time: the house on rue Raphaël, which was sold after the death of my grandfather, lies in the recesses of my memory as a place of intimacy and relaxation for which the large and dreary apartment on the rue Meissonier assuredly never provided an equivalent. I was taken there several times for lunch, and those expeditions from the rue du Général Foy were somehow exalting for me.

I think I remember—but I may be mistaken—that I was ushered one day into the room in which Grandfather lay dying and that my timidity was tinged with fright.

How I can identify with all that Proust wrote on the *côtés:* There was the *côté* of the rue du Général Foy, with its mingled noises of the neighboring primary school, one's gaze plunging from the fourth floor to the large, open street, a trifle dreary, that ran down toward Saint Augustin. There was the *côté* of Passy, which, however, was also to become the *côté* of the cemetery where I was taken at long intervals to visit Mother's tomb and where I was to read so often the lines composed by my father:

> Fleur cueillie au jardin du rêve,
> Par les doigts tremblants de l'amour,
> C'en est fait de ta forme brève
> Et de ton sourire d'un jour.
>
> Où s'exhale sa fine essence,
> Quel lys l'incarne aux purs sommets?
> Le respirerons-nous jamais
> Au seuil auguste qu'il encense?
>
> Si du moins de l'eden caché
> Ton sillage marquait la route,
> . . . mais nos yeux hélas dans le doute
> Se cloreront sans avoir séché.[1]

I do not know exactly when I first understood the meaning of these verses, but I believe I am right in thinking that it was relatively early and that the painful question expressed in them made an indelible imprint on my childhood.

I remember having asked before then, no doubt more than once, where she was and when she would return. I think I also remember that it was in her name that I received a birthday present—thus, three weeks after her disappearance—of toy furniture (dining-room furniture, if my memory serves me).

The ensuing period remains in my mind bathed in gentleness. Granny and Auntie enveloped me in a balmlike tenderness. At first I had a room in the rear of the apartment, rather gray and somber; but it seems to me that its dreariness did not affect me at all. It is possible, although I cannot say for certain, that my nurse, Mme Girard, slept by me for a while. Sometimes I was taken to visit Papa, who had kept the apartment on the rue du Général Foy. It seems to me that at that time I did not yet feel intimidated by him, although I did later. He would take me for walks—to the jardin des Plantes, for example. It seems to me that I was proud to walk beside a man for whom I felt an inarticulate admiration.

I have a fairly precise recollection of some of our travels, although I cannot recall the chronology completely. There was the trip to London and the little stay at Hampstead Heath with Uncle Hartwig, brother of my grandfather, and his wife, Franziska, whose strident voice so astonished me that one day, in the middle of a meal, I horrified everyone by imitating her and saying, "That's how Aunt Franziska talks." Their three children, Herbert, Daisy, and Lily, were there; Lily lives today, modestly but with great dignity, in a London boardinghouse. Later I was to learn that, on account of some of my uncle's bad business deals, or perhaps because of stock market speculations, the whole family had to contribute to keep him from bankruptcy.

That visit to London was bound to leave its mark: above all, the walks in the parks, but also something less definable, a certain atmosphere, perhaps kitchen odors rising from the lower levels in a vague mist. How curious to realize that I was not to return to London until the years immediately following the Second World War. In the interim, I returned to England several times; but London frightened me by its immensity.

In relation to that trip, I do not know where to place a short stay at the Pavillon Henri IV at Saint-Germain-en-Laye. From that stay, a scent of flowers rises to greet me. I loved flowers; I wanted to know their names. It seems to me that one day at the parc Monceau Papa pointed out several: the fuchsia, the begonia. I loved these names permeated with fragrance or color.

I am almost certain that I was five when the four of us made a journey in Brittany with four stopovers: Pornichet, which I detested; Pont-Aven, which I liked very much and where I was awakened to a feeling for the picturesque; Trestraou, with the walks to Ploumanach and Tréguier, where I recall admiring the cloister; and finally Saint-Lunaire, where I had once stayed as a tot and of which I retain no distinct recollections except, it seems to me, of a lovely young girl who doubtless thought I was cute and whose features stayed with me for a long time. From Saint-Lunaire we went to Saint Malô, whose beauty I believe I failed to appreciate, and to Saint-Briac, where a longtime friend of my father's lived; she was a musician in the fashion common in those days, possessed of a sense of rhythm without any sensibility for harmony to enrich it.

I remember clearly the day on which Auntie, no doubt after thoroughly preparing the ground, announced to me that she was going to marry Papa. I also remember having pained her a little by remarking how much I hoped that she would not become a wicked stepmother like Mme Fichini in *Les Malheurs de Sophie,* a book many children were reading at that time. Certainly, it is quite impossible to recapture a purely emotional state experienced in childhood; but I would be lying if I said that I had to any degree a feeling that this second marriage would be a betrayal of my mother. I do not think I experienced anything of the sort. It is even likely that I felt some satisfaction on learning that we would henceforth be together under the same roof. I will return later to this singular need for a gathering-together of the family, for this was subsequently to become more acute.

I gaze at the child I was then, with the help of photos we have managed to preserve; I strain, not without some difficulty, to reconstruct his characteristics. A hypersensitive child, without question, but also somewhat turned in on himself, awkward, and no doubt deeply anxious. The trauma provoked by my mother's death is not the only explanation. A physical peculiarity must be noted, for to pass over it in silence would be to fail in the obligation to absolute sincerity that I have undertaken. I suffered for a long time from an intestinal sluggishness that was a permanent source of concern for those close to me. Every method then known, even massages, was used to combat it. Someone made the mistake of frightening me by telling me of the fatal consequences that might result from this matter. I developed a sort of obsession that was to survive in somewhat different forms, infecting my imagination. I will not go into detail. Suffice it to say that a psychoanalyst would find much material here.

Exhibitionism is repellent to me; at the same time, since I have undertaken to speak frankly, I had to overcome the repugnance that entering upon this muddy terrain arouses in me.

If I am not mistaken, it was immediately after the marriage of Papa and Auntie that Granny and I left for Homburg, in the Taunus mountains, where I was to meet my German cousins. Auntie, I remember, went with us on the train as far as Metz, where she was to meet Papa. They were going to take a trip together in Germany and, strangely enough, I still recall their itinerary. They were going to Berlin by way of Brunswick and Magdeburg after a stop at Hannover that seemed a nuisance to them; they were going to return by way of Kassel and meet us again at Homburg. Why all these details? They demonstrate the passionate interest I had in geography, which no doubt was identified in my mind with travel. I have preserved a fairly precise memory of that stay in Homburg: I see myself again with Granny, dining in a restaurant to the sound of Wagnerian music. It seems to me I was told it was an excerpt from *Twilight of the Gods*. We took walks, and I always insisted on knowing the exact name of each village; I was disappointed when we did not get to a place with a name. I remember also a trip in the Taunus mountains, which I was to see again so many years later.

Of the immediately succeeding period I remember above all a stay in Switzerland above the lac de Zug. I recall a little girl from Alsace who was with her grandparents and with whom I discussed the works of Mme de Ségur. That same summer we made a first trip to Flims, in the canton of Grisons, to which I was to return much later. It seems to me that I reveled in the walks in the forest; I see again a vertiginous drop above the Rhine that frightened me and a lovely ride to Lax and Fellers. It is undoubtedly significant that I have remembered all these names. This need for designation, for identification, for bearings, surely corresponded to some original trait in my character. This simultaneously topographical and toponymical exigency seems to have been an invariant within me. Even today, it has not left me.

Everything tended to propel me outward, that is, outside everyday Paris, which bored me because of all the efforts made to take me through museums. I remember having felt a particular aversion to the museums of plaster casts at the Trocadéro; I had to be compensated with a visit to the pastry shop. Interest in museums was not to awaken in me until much later. By contrast, the theater was a passion with me. First, when I was five years old, there was a fairy-tale spectacle at the Châtelet, *Les Sept Chateaux du diable;* and the next years, at the Comédie-Française, *Les Fourberies de Scapin* and *Le Malade imaginaire.* No doubt a little later someone gave me a present of Molière in the two-volume Bibliothèque Rose edition, and I read it voraciously. But how I would have loved to know the plays that were not included, the forbidden ones! It was a serious pedagogical error, I think, to set down for me such clear-cut distinctions between the permitted and the forbidden, with the latter automatically acquiring a fascinating attraction.

But I also wanted to speak of the way in which Auntie, on our walks— when I had the delight of going out with her and not with Babet Fink or, later, with Aline Schmoll—always managed to put compellingly within my ken the books she was reading or the plays she had attended with Papa. I was thus aware of a lot of things that children of my age generally had no notion of—all, to be sure, methodically disinfected. And then there were the readings aloud that Papa sometimes gave in the evening. He was a marvelous reader and contributed greatly to my passion for the theater. In his youth, he had studied at the Conservatoire, if I am not mistaken. I am sure that I saw a photograph of him playing in *Henri III et sa cour,* by the elder Alexandre Dumas.

As I have already suggested, family had a large place in my life: above all, my mother's brothers, Edouard and Ernest, and their wives, Jeanne and Aline; my cousins, first Madeleine, who was slightly my elder, and later Denise, then Suzanne; but also, on the paternal side, Uncle Jules and Aunt Caroline and their children. I was especially fond of Georgette, who was three years older than I; her brother Pierre was too much my elder for any possible contact.

But there were also the great-aunts, elderly ladies whom one went to see once in a long while. Two of them, Séphora and Clara, lived in far parts of the city reached by hansom cab: rue d'Hauteville, rue de la Verrerie, and so on. These, too, were Proustian *côtés*. The elderly ladies seemed to be semisubmerged in a noisy *quartier* that was a trifle dismal, hung with a kind of pall of business activity. There was also Aunt Cécile, who lived in our *quartier* and who was hence a little clearer and less foreign to me. But I also remember Granny's friends, who often came to see her; the most striking was Mme Versigny, whose husband had been exiled in the December 2 coup and who had known Victor Hugo well. It was she, I was told, who had taken my mother, as a young girl, to the poet's funeral. I see again her diaphanous coloring; I hear her slightly grating voice. First she had lived on place Vintmille, and I realize that a strange coalescence developed for me between her and the name *Vintmille*. I am surprised at having kept so distinct a memory of all these persons and of many others whom I could name and who made up Granny's circle. And not only persons, but the very places where they lived: rue Lobineau, a tiny old lady; rue Pont de Lodi, someone else again. I try to interpret such specificity. It seems to me that it represents that passionate interest for human beings and for their settings that was very superficially veiled by my studies, as I shall call them, in their most depersonalized and neutral aspects.

It seems to me that at this period I had, on the one hand, a taste for intimacy and for music that could in no way have been expressed in words and, on the other hand, a certain impatience with the everyday, with a certain drab banality, with a quality that attached itself above all to promenades when Auntie was not with me, for she had the gift of never failing to interest me.

Under such circumstances, how could I not have been literally overcome with joy to learn that Papa was to be named *Ministre Plénipotentiaire* abroad and that we were to accompany him? First there was talk of Belgrade, but finally he was assigned, in 1898, to Stockholm. The stay in Sweden was to leave a profound impression on me, perhaps even an indelible one. I recall that on our arrival we stopped at the Hotel Rydberg, opposite the Royal Palace, before moving into 43 Sturegatan. If I am not mistaken, the legation occupied two floors. The chancellery was on the ground floor, and we lived on the floor above.

What memories I have of the streets of Stockholm and, above all, of the environs! Mainly, the Djärgørden, where I went for walks almost every day; but also Haga Drottningholm and, still farther, Djursholm Waxholm, and of course Saltjöbaden and Delarö. And how I would have liked to go even farther! I watched the boats docking that plied the northern regions: Luleå, Haparanda, and so on. The whole north attracted me irresistibly. I recall excursions of my parents on which I was not allowed to join them: what disappointment! I wonder if they could have suspected the thirst in me for travel, for the unknown—that ardent desire to discover. All that, I think, was so much more revealing than the aptitudes I was able to demonstrate in the various school subjects that took up my time. There was no notion then of my going to school in Stockholm. Auntie undertook to teach me. But I also took some private lessons, in English at any rate. German, which I had begun to speak in my earliest childhood, was left to lie fallow during this whole period and until much later.

I knew by name nearly all the members of the diplomatic corps in Stockholm. Here, too, many names have remained with me. I saw a few children: the Bizios, from Italy; the Deprats, from Spain; the Sponnecks, from Denmark. A little Russian boy, from Butzow, held a special fascination for me because he was handsome and because he was reputed to be very much of a musician: it was said that he would be a composer. How marvelous! Yet half a century later I was to find him again, in Paris, his life ruined; it was he to whom the Russian critic Suvtchinsky directed me for the revision and correction of some of my pieces. I learned in this way that Stravinsky held him in high esteem but that, devoured by a passion for gambling, he had disappointed the great expectations he had aroused. I was, moreover, crushed to see that he had no recollection of me at all, although it is true that in Stockholm I was a very nondescript child.

I believe that period was the happiest of my childhood. It was as though I were blossoming in a world filled with possibilities. Alas, at the end of fifteen months, I learned that my father, troubled by the climate and somewhat exasperated by the protocol of diplomatic life in Stockholm, had arranged an exchange of posts with M. Catusse, *Conseiller d'Etat*, and that we were to return to Paris. My consternation was total. I regretted having to renounce the trip to Norway and Russia that we had envisaged for the holidays. To return to Paris would be to return to banality—and worse, for I could begin to discern the menacing shadow of the lycée. It did not seem that my sense of frustration could be compensated for by any advantage whatsoever.

This somber premonition was later confirmed. My lycée years left, on the whole, the most disagreeable memories; and I can say in retrospect that I think they contributed to a retardation of my intellectual development and, in the last analysis, seriously affected my health.

I entered fifth grade in the Lycée Carnot. A former fourth-grade teacher from the same school gave me a little examination to see where I was. From the start, everything was poisoned for me by the compositions and by the absolutely disproportionate importance that my parents attached to rankings. I remember that I was tenth in the first Latin composition out of thirty students. Objectively, this was not at all disgraceful; yet it caused a day of mourning in the rue Meissonier. Bit by bit, however, I was to win first places and to obtain the Prix d'Excellence *ex aequo* with my friend Paul Chalon. But I approached each composition with a feeling of anguish explained by the attitude of my parents, or, more exactly, of Auntie. To-day, with the distance available to me, I judge that she committed a serious mistake whose consequences were very grave. Each time, I felt myself called into question. Is he intelligent? What will he be able to achieve later? Is he worth the trouble we have taken for him? I would not want to assert that these questions were explicitly put by those around me; but I felt them weighing on me, and there is no doubt that they deprived me of confidence and encouraged me to vacillate inside. I can say without exaggeration that only in philosophy courses—that is, only where a superior ability was manifest—could I free myself from this worry.

I must, I think, add this also: I was not unaware of the fact that Auntie and Papa were often in disagreement—in certain instances, flagrantly so. For example, on the Dreyfus case, Auntie was an impassioned Dreyfusite, whereas Papa did not conceal the impatience or disquiet he experienced at the sight of one man, not even an especially appealing individual, threatening to throw the country into the worst of disorders. I must add that in this matter I was wholeheartedly on Auntie's side, and the contrary viewpoint seemed to me incomprehensible and almost scandalous.

But I sensed other discords more mute, more personal, of which, of course, I was told nothing. I heard certain tones of voice; I gleaned certain alarming allusions; and thus a feeling tended to take shape in me that my existence—without my having done anything in particular—was perhaps the cause of great unhappiness, since it was because of me that these two beings, so different from each other, had decided to come together. From then on, the thought that I might fail in my studies became intolerable to me. I had to be able, at any cost, to justify by my achievements the sacrifices that had been made for me.

It is probable that at the time, all this was not so clear to me. I am nonetheless certain, however, that this anxiety contributed to the desolate climate of my student years. It was the underlying reason why my lycée years, until the philosophy courses, seemed like a desert to me. Disciplines that in themselves might well have interested me, such as history, for example, were devitalized or sterilized by the fact that they were subjects for competition.

What compensations were there? Let me try to recall. Unquestionably, there was music; my piano teacher, Mme Hinstin, had the virtue of understanding that one must insist above all on sight-reading. How many works she revealed to me this way! At home, moreover, I seated myself at the piano at every opportunity, and there, too, I sight-read: Beethoven, Schumann (I found his complete works, for my father had a passion for him), Grieg (from whom I was to turn away rather quickly), and then Wagner, followed, to be sure, by post-Franckian French music. It is beyond a doubt that music was a counterbalance for me, I dare say a vital one, to the intolerable burden of my school life.

Another counterbalance was the holidays. Every year we went to the mountains, although because of my grandmother we could not go higher than four thousand feet. I still see myself feverishly hunting through the Swiss hotel guide for possible stopping places. My precise knowledge of Swiss geography and lodgings dates from that time. I was not to accede until later to what was for me the "promised land," that is to say, the high-altitude places of the Engadine and Valais.

There is another point that I would be loath to leave in darkness: my pleasure in family meals when "the others," as we called them, came to dine; that is, my mother's brothers and their wives. I see something quite singular about that, and on reflection it seems to have a profound import. I seem to have suffered almost unconsciously from some sort of insufficiency, some deficiency, about our little family foursome. Deep down I wanted with all my being to be part of an abundant, a substantial, family community. Much later, during my engagement, I cast an envious glance in retrospect on the relations of my wife's family, the Boegners, for all their illnesses and their griefs; anticipating here what I shall speak of later, I will add that my entrance into that family, despite the mutilations experienced because of the deaths of Acquot and Edmond, represented an enrichment for me that contributed in a most positive way to enhancing my thought.

But shortly after our return from Stockholm, an occurrence that I could not have foreseen was to cast a shadow on the life of my own family. I refer to the divorce of Uncle Ernest and Aunt Aline. I was given almost no details of the causes for the rupture. I think I nevertheless realized that he, an entirely conscientious *maître des requêtes* at the Conseil d'Etat, was at the same time a man of pleasure, I would almost say a man about town. His wife, by contrast, did not exactly draw any specific reproach. But my grandmother considered her self-centered and, being a devoted and hence partisan mother, resented Aunt Aline's not having been the wonted companion of my uncle. Aunt Aline was musically gifted, and this created a special bond between her and my father. I believe, without being able to recall exactly, that she accompanied him sometimes at the piano while he sang. This relationship was to continue for some time after the divorce, a fact that did not fail to pain my grandmother. I should add that there was a mutual antipathy between my father and my uncle. Several times I had heard allusions to a painful scene that must have taken place between them at the Conseil d'Etat, where they were both employed. I have the idea that my uncle knew—I do not know how—something that was not to be revealed to Auntie (I continued to call her so, even though she was my stepmother) until later: the fact that before his remarriage my father had had a liaison, from which a son was born.

I should add that Uncle Ernest and Aunt Aline had a daughter, Madeleine, for whom I felt a great deal of affection and on whom I sought to shower my musical discoveries when she came to lunch at the rue Meissonier.

To be sure, all that was marginal by comparison to my school life. Yet it was in that obscure and ill-defined region that were born not only my dramatic writings, but also my philosophical thinking, at least from the moment it became existential—that is to say, liberated from what had all in all been high-level training. Here again, I am anticipating.

Under such circumstances, it can be no cause for surprise that my having been an only child was literally a mortifying trial for me. I have often noted that this ordeal contributed in large measure to making a playwright of me. A serious pedagogical error committed by my aunt was to have consequences that, although favorable at the literary level, were deadly for my personal life. I mean the daily practice of an examination of conscience that my aunt instituted in my life. I was to keep nothing to myself; I was called on to ferret out in my life or my thought everything that could be viewed as a wrong and to communicate it at once to her who reigned more or less despotically over my life. But I would never have thought of using the word *despotic* at the time. Although I have a blurred recollection of several scenes during which I did struggle against what was, after all, a yoke, I think I can say that I never rebelled and that rebellion would have seemed to me the blackest ingratitude. In the light of contemporary psychology, of course, we would today be inclined to say that a rebellion existed, however inhibited or imperceptible, and that consequently the kind of permanent pall that remains in my memory was inevitable. It is likely that my father was rather clearly aware of this state of affairs, but there was a distance between him and me that, alas, has been closed only since his death—and only at a relatively recent date.

As I inquire into a distant past that has left profound traces in me, I always feel on guard against the temptation to schematize my life as a troubled child and overzealous schoolboy between my eleventh and my sixteenth years. As I have already said, I remain convinced that the lycée hobbled and in any event retarded my intellectual development, above all because of the entirely excessive importance my parents placed on everything having to do with scholastic competition. I still hear myself saying one night before going to sleep, "I would rather be operated on for appendicitis tomorrow morning than have to face that written test." I suffered from a lack of self-confidence; even though I had an adequate memory, I always feared that at the crucial moment it would fail me. I feared especially the reproaches at home if I did not rank well or if I received a mediocre grade. More exactly, the intolerable thing was to feel that my parents' judgment of me depended at least to some degree on the results I obtained in tests, whereas I felt, obscurely at least, that these results really had nothing to do with my essential being. But I must add that I had only a vague awareness of this essential being and that on the whole I was a question to myself.

Where outside the scholastic domain, in which I was aware of stumbling at each step, were the zones where I breathed freely? There was music, certainly. My piano teacher perceived that I would never make a performer but that I was gifted in sight-reading, and nearly every lesson was the occasion for an initiation into some great musical work written for four hands.

It seems that during those lycée years, which now appear to have been so burdensome and so dreary, Paris figured for me as an object of aversion. This was true at least in part because friendship had relatively little place for me during that period of my existence. I had comrades, certainly, but I did not seem to relate to them effectively. Perhaps, however, I am the victim here of a faulty memory; perhaps, too, I am exaggerating from a distance the monochrome and sad quality of my assuredly studious childhood. What seems certain is that I was racked by an anxiety to know what I was going to be fit for later. I believe that to an excessive degree I felt the weight of my debt to my parents and above all to my aunt: it was all too clear to me that I was at the center of her concerns, at the center even of her life, and that if my existence were later destined to failure, that failure would be hers—a thought that was intolerable to me. This relationship, this chafing tension, I was later to translate into a play, "Le Petit

Garçon,'' which has never been published or staged but which should be
included if my complete plays are ever collected.

Even though I succeeded, with my aunt's ceaseless prodding, in winning all the prizes almost every year in my various courses of study, it
does not seem to me in retrospect that I showed a truly exceptional bent
toward any subject prior to the course in philosophy. Although I cared
little for Latin, I had a certain predilection for Greek and for a while even
imagined that I could some day make a career as a Greek classicist. I was
poorly endowed for the sciences, and it was only while taking some private
lessons that I discovered in a flash—but, alas, much too late—what
seemed to me the splendor of mathematics. Until then my teachers had
been quite mediocre and had all proved themselves incapable of awakening
in their pupils the passionate interest that mathematics well taught must be
able to arouse in an intelligent child.

Everything changed, to be sure, when I enrolled in a philosophy
course. I distinctly recall having said to my parents from the very first day,
''I know now what I will do later: I will devote myself to philosophy.''
My teacher, M. Colona d'Istria, never ceased heaping encouraging words
on me, and I certainly needed them; interestingly enough, he happened to
be on the jury that later (in 1910) made me an *agrégé* in philosophy. He
was infirm, a deformed dwarf, with a face lighted by blue eyes that shone
strangely when he smiled. He left but a few articles in the *Revue de métaphysique et de morale* on the philosopher-doctors of the eighteenth century and, if I am not mistaken, on Marie-François-Xavier Bichat. He also
published a revised and amended version of the Count de Boulainvilliers's
translation of Spinoza's *Ethica*. His course consisted almost entirely of
lectures. At the beginning of each class he gave a summary of the given
theories, which he viewed in each case in their opposition to each other,
while he recommended the middle ground as the wisest solution and as the
one that took best account of the data of experience. There was certainly
nothing inspiring in a presentation of this kind; but my philosophic appetite
at that time involved no sort of protest against all too reasonable compro-
mises or accommodations.

Certainly for me, that whole year (1905–1906) of philosophy at the
Lycée Carnot felt as if a vise were opening, as if for the first time I were
called upon to think for myself, to be myself, and at the same time, as if
I were extricating myself from the network of competition in which I had
been imprisoned for five consecutive years.

During the holidays preceding my enrollment in the philosophy curric-
ulum, if I am not mistaken, I wrote the first play that may have indicated
the rudiments of what was later to become a dramatic ability. In *La Lu-*

mière sur la montagne one can see a first sketch, still quite juvenile, of *Un Homme de Dieu*. Through the mediation of my music teacher, my parents relayed this play to the critic and poet Fernand Gregh, who gave an opinion of it that was at least clearly encouraging, if not altogether favorable.

Possessing a *baccalauréat,* which I had earned with an honest, if not brilliant, pass, I enrolled as a student at the Sorbonne, firmly resolved not to enter the competition for the Ecole normale. I have sufficiently stressed that every sort of competition appalled me. Moreover, living in Paris in a comfortable milieu, I would have considered it inequitable to take up a place that belonged by right, it seemed to me, to someone from the provinces or in any case to a young man less fortunate than myself.

I certainly experienced keen satisfaction in feeling extricated from the bondage of the lycée; at the same time, I felt a little lost at the Sorbonne, not knowing just which courses were most worth taking. I believe my first classroom presentation was a critique of the Schopenhauerian theory of freedom before that excellent professor André Lalande, whose colleague I was to become forty years later in the Académie des sciences morales et politiques. He was tolerance and good will themselves, but the sort of eclecticism he espoused in developing his evolutionistic empiricism had no attraction for me. Indeed, I think I can say that, among all those whose courses I took, Henri Bergson was the only one whose thought and words took a sure and lasting hold on me. To get a seat in the little hall of the Collège de France, where he taught, one had to arrive an hour early and thus listen to (I would rather say undergo) the preceding class. As I have often said, what was marvelous and perhaps unique in Bergson was that during each lecture he conveyed a sense of proceeding in a sort of interior jubilation in a labor of discovery in which his listeners were to participate. He spoke slowly but with perfect clarity, always careful to make himself fully intelligible; for my part, I would gladly have dispensed with the summary of what hc had said the preceding week, which he felt obliged to give at the beginning of each session. In every instance, I can testify that by a driving light he cut through the gray and indistinct background of notions that were being inculcated at the Sorbonne by academicians whose knowledge and good will were beyond question but who lacked the spark, the genius. Among all those professors (whose names it does not seem to me indispensable to recall), the one toward whom I feel the liveliest gratitude is the excellent historian of philosophy Victor Delbos, author of *Le Problème moral chez Spinoza* and *La Philosophie pratique de Kant*. It was he to whom I was to show, two or three years after my *agrégation,* my first truly personal philosophical notes, not without a good deal of apprehension and even anxiety. He had the singular merit of understanding, perhaps better than I, what sort of thinking was laboriously emerging from these notes, and he proffered at that time indispensable encouragement to me.

After my *licence en philosophie,* which I passed very handily in October of 1907, how did I come to choose as the subject of my *diplôme d'études supérieures* "The Metaphysical Ideas of Coleridge Considered in Their Relation to the Philosophy of Schelling"? It seems to me that it came about as follows.

My attention, I no longer know just how, had been drawn to Bradley, and it was on him that I had originally wanted to write my essay. But it turned out that the topic had already been reserved by a seminarian who then died, if I am not mistaken, without having carried out his project. To the very extent that British empiricism left me indifferent, I felt an interest in the development that toward the turn of the century culminated in neo-Hegelian thought. But reaching back to the origins of this movement, I saw that even before Carlyle, it was the great poet Coleridge who had been one of the first to bring a veritable transfusion of German metaphysical thought into the intellectual life across the Channel. I set to work resolved to devote two years to this task, which, though difficult, promised to be all-absorbing. Those two years were the happiest of my student days. Nevertheless, I have no unhappy recollections of the final year, which I devoted to preparing for the *agrégation,* to which I was admitted in 1910 along with my friend Jean Wahl. But this intense work damaged my health, and I gave up the idea of immediately taking a lycée position. The periods I then spent by the sea in England at least had the advantage of enabling me to perfect my knowledge of English. I had no idea then how useful this would be later. In the summer of 1911, I was appointed to a professorship at the Lycée de Vendôme. I entered the career of teaching with a fervor, keenly desirous of communicating to young students the philosophic flame that burned within me. Alas, I had to lower my sights. During the first month I had before me, eight hours a week, a lone student who proved rather impermeable to the instruction I was trying to give him. Two others joined him later, but it was nonetheless a phantom class. Moreover, I fell ill and had to interrupt my teaching for a trimester. At the end of the academic year I requested leave and spent a year of ease in Switzerland, collaborating in the running of a little experimental school above lac Léman. The school tried to provide highly individualized teaching for children who were behind in their studies. I became greatly attached to them. On my return to Paris, I was firmly resolved to write a doctoral thesis that I envisaged as bearing on the "conditions of intelligibility of religious reality.'' That last year before the explosion of 1914 was surely one of the happiest I have experienced. Free from all constraints, I was able to give myself, in the most relaxed atmosphere, to those activities for which I felt I was made—philosophical research, music, literature—all, I must confess, without even the vaguest foreboding of the immense catastrophe in the offing. During the period just before the war, I knew that sweet enjoyment of life of which, correctly or incorrectly, we have heard so much in regard to the period preceding the French Revolution; I say this not without embarrassment, for I reproach myself today for having been too inclined at that time to underestimate social injustice. My temperament led me too often to align myself with the defenders of the established order. This was in a way all the less forgivable because as a child, during the Dreyfus affair, I had had an opportunity to understand that a certain way of defending the established order was scandalous to conscience. I recall the indignation I felt at the first general strike in 1910. I made the great mistake of not making myself aware of the living conditions of the striking workers. Arbitrarily, I took it for granted that their demands were unjustified or at least that they had chosen the worst of means for making them. But did they have any other means? That is the question I would ask today. I had heard full well at home from my aunt, who was charity itself, of lamentable cases who required help, but I persuaded myself only too easily that those were unfortunate exceptions. Today it seems to me almost inconceivable that at that time I, along with so many others, found it natural that workers were allowed no vacations with pay. In France this situation did not change until after the 1936 elections, which brought a Popular Front government to power.

So far as the international situation was concerned, I had anxiously followed the development of the Balkan crisis and, like everyone else, I was shaken by the Agadir tragedy in 1912. But I wanted to believe, it seems to me, that in an era of advanced civilization like ours, none of the great powers, not even Germany, would dare to initiate an armed conflict.

I see myself again in the Alpine landscape of Saas Fe with my friend Jean Wahl, reading newspaper accounts of the developments in the trial of Mme Caillaux, and I see again the exact moment at which I said to my companion, ''Oh, here is something very differently serious: the Austrian ultimatum to Serbia.'' From that moment to the final outcome, I felt an anguish that never ceased tearing at me. I see us again, Jean Wahl and myself, walking above Brigue, where we were to pass the night, asking about the future. What would this war be like, this war that now seemed inevitable? And what did it hold for us? I knew that I was not able to bear arms, and I could scarcely imagine myself among combatants. But the idea of remaining a mere spectator seemed intolerable. I relive those first days of August 1914, under a cloudless sky. With a few friends I tried, without much success, to make myself useful in a municipal office in Paris. The anguish, properly speaking, had been replaced by an enthusiastic feeling of confidence that today seems almost inconceivable. All the wrong, it seemed to me, was on the side of our enemies. All the right was on the French side. I was heartened by the sight of the patriotic élan of soldiers and civilians facing this trial almost joyously.

Events were soon to set such a state of mind to rights. I recall the stupor with which I read the famous communiqué a little before the end of August, which began with the words "From the Somme to the Vosges. . . ." Thus we were in retreat; yet we did not dare despair.

It was at that moment that my friend Xavier Léon, editor of the *Revue de métaphysique et de morale,* asked me to direct in his stead a little service that he had just established in the French Red Cross. At first it consisted of organizing and centralizing, for transmission to families, information on the condition of the hospitalized wounded in the French Red Cross hospitals, or, more exactly, in those of the Union des femmes de France. We were soon to realize that as such the service was useless; the wounded and the nurses corresponded directly with the families. By contrast, a tragic problem arose as a result of the disastrous battles in Belgium of August 20–22, 1914: the missing in action. Numerous were those who wrote or who came in person to ask for news of the husband, son, or brother who had not written since a certain day. With the help of reference cards, we would then seek among the French soldiers, wounded or not wounded, or among prisoners in the German camps whomever might be able to throw some light on the fate of the sought-after person. I dedicated myself to this work with a fervor that never flickered to the end of the hostilities. Whenever possible, I met personally with the unfortunate enquirers come in search of news, striving to the greatest extent possible to comfort them and to give them the feeling that they were not alone, that I was personally involved in this quest, far too often a hopeless one. At this time I was surrounded by people of good will, principally women, of course, who cooperated zealously and wholeheartedly with me.

I think this task affected my later work. It undoubtedly contributed to the development not only of a sense of and need for personal contacts, but also of a boundless compassion for the distress to which each day testified anew. To be sure, dogmatic pacifism was alien to me; but the war revealed itself under such a desolate aspect that it became an object of indignation, a horror without equal. Yet at the same time I felt with utter constance and with utmost precision what I, a noncombatant, owed to those who risked death or mutilation every day at the front for a cause that was *ours*. A militant pacifism seemed to me, under these circumstances, a kind of betrayal. Hence the perhaps excessive severity with which I judged the famous essay by Romain Rolland, "Au dessus de la mêlée." I could not countenance any Frenchman having the right to remove himself in whatever fashion from the drama in order to view it from above. On the contrary, I felt myself participating, suffering, drawn and quartered. This was the origin of a theatrical fragment I wrote in 1918–1919 under the title *Un Juste*. The idea was suggested by the case of a philosopher who had been a friend of mine and who, not himself conscripted, contributed in 1917, after the April 16 offensive, to sending pamphlets to the front aimed at inciting the soldiers to rise up against their officers. This was directly related to the famous mutinies, which gave rise, as is known, to a repression. I understood the point of view well enough; yet I found it impossible not to condemn it.

I should add that my work gave me an opportunity to reflect philosophically on the act of inquiring and to investigate the nature of the responses to which it may lead. More profoundly, it led me to consider the limits within which any inquiry at all is possible. This in turn led me to reflect on what could lie beyond questionnaire and investigation and on communication involving no such mediation, such as telepathy.

It was certainly more than chance that led me not only to turn my attention to metaphysical issues, but also to realize, during the winter of 1916–1917, that I possessed some mediumistic capacities. I shall not enter into details here. I underwent a most singular and disconcerting experience, whose repercussions on my thinking are evident in my *Journal métaphysique* [part 2]. This experience convinced me of the reality of a number of phenomena that I cannot in all honesty reject and that I cannot account for by mere recourse to an unconscious. I also came to see, on the one hand, that the truth of these phenomena lay embedded in an ore of involuntary fantasy and, on the other hand and more mysteriously, that from the moment I had the imprudence to consider myself assigned to a mission of demonstrating to afflicted after afflicted the reality of survival, I became guilty of a sin for which an intelligent power punished me by plunging me into a sort of pandemonium in which I soon gave up the foolish presumption I had momentarily taken on. But in the end, things transpired as if this intelligent power—a power without features or name— had undertaken to provide an irrefutable proof that would reinstate some of my lost confidence and that would enable me to reestablish an equilibrium between an unwonted pretension and an unjustified dismay. It happened at the end of the spring of 1917: by the mediation of a planchette,

an entity (which I could not identify) told me three months beforehand of
the disaster of Isonzo, the taking of Udine, and the halting of the Austrians
at Trévise. Before a fact of that sort, lazy explanations in terms of chance
or coincidences (which are indeed only refusals to explain) cannot stand
up for a moment.

I recall recounting my experiences to Henri Bergson, who was inclined
to credit all but the prediction, which seemed to him incompatible with his
theory of duration.

Subsequently, I did not pursue experiences of this order, which seemed
to me possibly dangerous to my equilibrium and even to my health. But I
have never ceased to be interested in these phenomena, and later I was to
be named correspondent for the London Society for Psychical Research. I
have also been a member for several years now of the Institut metapsy-
chique de Paris.

Nothing could be more false, I want to stress, than to attempt to minimize the importance of this aspect of my thought or my studies. I am
profoundly convinced that therein lies a key, but it must be acknowledged
that on the methodological level we are still stammerers. As I wrote in an
article that appeared in 1947 in the *Revue de métaphysique et de morale*
under the title "De l'audace en métaphysique," what needs to be censured
is the false sense of respectability that still prevents so many scientists and
philosophers from participating in metapsychical research or, when they
have themselves had such an experience, from trying to draw out the implications.

I shall not elaborate on the echoings within me of the military and political events that followed one upon the other between 1914 and 1918 or on
the immense relief I felt at the end of this nightmare. The relief was unfortunately of short duration. Very soon—no doubt by 1920—I was to become
obsessed by the thought that all could recommence some day if measures
were not taken to make it impossible for Germany to rearm. At the same
time, I felt a certain mistrust for the politics of Poincaré, and something in
me could have wished to believe sincerely that the truth was on the side of
men like Briand who sought pacification and reconciliation. From a distance, I feel myself today much closer to Briand than to Poincaré.

It was in November 1918 that I became engaged to Jacqueline Boegner, daughter of Alfred Boegner, who had been director of the Maison des
missions protestantes and who had died at his post in 1912. I will note in
passing that his son Henri, who had been my classmate at the Sorbonne
when I was preparing for the *agrégation,* had remained, and was to remain
until his death, one of my dearest friends.

The reader will understand if I do not wish to elaborate here on what our union was to Jacqueline and myself. It is enough to say that to the end she was my absolute companion with whom I shared everything. We were married under the sign of music. She was then organist and professor of harmony at the Schola Cantorum. And I had the delight of opening up to her many contemporary works that she did not know and for which she showed a comprehension similar to mine. Much later—something to which I shall doubtless return—I was to benefit from her perfect understanding of musical notation as I put into final shape the melodies that I composed at the piano around a number of different poems. Without her, they could not have materialized.

Not only was she an excellent musician, but she also had the most profound and most scrupulous sense of inner realities; even though she had no philosophical training, she succeeded in associating herself wholeheartedly with my researches.

We spent our honeymoon in Umbria and Tuscany, where I had the joy of showing her so many works of art and so many landscapes that her innate artistic sensibility enabled her to appreciate deeply. In 1919, I resolved to seek a position as professor of philosophy in a lycée near Paris. I was assigned to Sens, where we passed three years in a most agreeable apartment facing the shaded avenue that circled the town. My skeletal classes demanded little work. We shared lengthy readings aloud, particularly of *A la recherche du temps perdu;* we often played pieces for four hands; and we even tried to create a little chamber music ensemble out of elements that were, unfortunately, quite mediocre.

Every week we went to Paris, where my aunt was happy to welcome us in the apartment on the rue Meissonier. My grandmother, her mind enfeebled by age, died in January 1919. My father, who had been affected terribly by the war, by its ravages, and by the responsibilities he had had as the director of the Musées nationaux, plunged into a painful silence in which it was difficult to make contact with him. He went into retirement and experienced the first blows of an illness that was to carry him away several years later. I shall never forgive myself for not having succeeded more in helping him, in sustaining him, during those years that were undoubtedly so cruel. Certainly, my aunt did everything possible to help him, but I think I had a duty that I did not manage to fulfill as I should have. What I most wish to say is that life has led me to render him in retrospect an ever wider and ever more sincere homage. Doubtless he had his defects; in his private life he even committed some misdeeds. But he was unquestionably one of the men of the highest integrity I have ever known. He discharged the important duties that fell to him with unflagging conscientiousness, no less in the directorship of the Beaux-Arts than subsequently in the administration of the Bibliothèque nationale and still later in the national museums. But even apart from this conscientiousness, which was so admirable in him, he had an impassioned interest in all the manifestations of the spirit in the realms of art and literature. He knew all the museums of Europe and had an extraordinarily visual memory that enabled him to speak in detail of such-and-such a painting in the Prado or in the Hermitage. To him we owe an *Histoire de la peinture française au XIXe siècle,* the chapters of André Michel's *Histoire générale de l'art* devoted to English painting, and monographs on Daumier, on Millet, and so on. I do not know that he wrote anything on music save a speech on César Franck at a dedication of his monument on the square de Sainte Clotilde. He would have liked to write the Schumann volume in the series Musiciens célèbres, which he was directing for the publisher Laurens, but he generously ceded this title to Camille Mauclair, whose beginnings as a critic he had presided over. Schumann was without a doubt his favorite musician: I still hear him singing in a beautiful baritone voice some of the loveliest *Lieder,* and he expressed the wish that the score of Schumann's *Faust* be placed in his coffin. This holds for me a profound meaning: I believe that the sublime song of Pater Mariamus expressed for him the essence of his aspiration. It does not appear to me fortuitous that at the moment of his passing he murmured the name of my mother, whose death, I am convinced, was an inconsolable grief for him.

If my father's mind moved with ease and agility in the region of the relative—a relativity whose limits he had accepted once and for all—my aunt, by comparison, was driven by a need for the absolute. This absolute she conceived entirely at the level of conscience and moral activity, for she too was agnostic; yet I would say that she never really embraced agnosticism. She reached the point of telling me that for her only Christianity could give sense and meaning to life, but unfortunately her intellectual demands would never permit her to join the believers. She did indeed request much later that prayers be said after her death and that a Biblical text be read by a pastor, but that was only the expression of a sort of nostalgia, an unfulfilled wish. It would be completely inaccurate, however, to imagine her frozen in a morose puritanism. Her vitality was no less than my father's, but she was as if of another essence. I have never known anyone to surpass her solicitude for those for whom she felt herself in any way responsible. No one carried further or into greater detail the accomplishment of every task that seemed urgent to her. Never did she put off until tomorrow what could and had to be done today. In this sense, she provided an example by which I have tried to be inspired in every situation, although I have always felt myself deficient. My attachment for her has always had something fervent in it, and doubtless it is significant that even today, when I close my eyes, I can see her in one moment or another of her life always with such precision of expression and of movements as to fill me each time with a tender astonishment. She will be with me to the end, and I have felt myself and know myself indebted to this fervent and admirable soul.

During the three years at Sens, I wrote several of my most important plays, and I think I am not mistaken in saying that the presence of my wife proved extraordinarily beneficial. She effected a relaxation of my spirit, rendering me more supple and more open to concrete reality. And when I speak of her now, I evoke at the same time those close to her, to whom she was so fervently attached and whom she helped me to understand and to love. Her sisters (who, with a sole exception, were all to meet untimely deaths) also remain infinitely precious presences whom I aspire to find once again with her in that society of the beyond whose felt nearness can alone render bearable the more and more inhuman world that solidifies around us.

Have I said that my father-in-law was of Alsatian origin and that part of his family remained in Strasbourg and in the vallée de la Bruche, never consenting to make contact with the Germans, whom they considered occupiers or invaders? I think again with emotion of that summer of 1919 when the whole family could come together at Rothau, in liberated Alsace, on a square watched over by loyal ones still animated by their hope—a hope that had become a reality. How I loved our walks, which were to be repeated for several years, in the woods that extend between Saint Odile and the Horwald forest or in the chain of the Nolles mountains that prolong Mount Donon in the direction of the Rhine plain! I had not cared much for the French Vosges when I saw them from Gérardmer in my childhood. But here they were a revelation, and wooded Alsace remains for me a part of that internalized world to which the environs of Stockholm and the Italian lakes already belonged, an internalized world that was to be enriched by so many new provinces. I will come back to this later.

At the end of three years, I decided to ask for an indefinite leave. It seemed to me that I was wasting my energies at Sens. I also thought—although this was to prove illusory—that once located in Paris I would have a better chance of getting my plays produced. Three of them had already been performed while I was a professor at Sens: *Le Coeur des autres,* at the Théâtre Grévin, by the Canard Sauvage company; *La Grâce,* at the Théâtre des Mathurins, by the Grimace company; and *Le Regard neuf,* at the Ambigu, under the patronage of the Escholiers. It was *La Grâce* that first put me into contact with François Mauriac, who reviewed the play in the *Revue hebdomadaire* and paid tribute to the extremely daring attempt I had made to show a conversion on the stage.

I recall with amusement the scandal provoked among certain right-thinking persons by scenes in *Regard neuf* that today would appear utterly inoffensive. On the whole, these plays were well received by the critics. But they needed to be played in a regular theater, and this unfortunately did not happen.

This same time also marked an important event in my private life. Fearing that we would have no child, my wife and I decided to adopt a little boy. The adoption was a source of joy and of spiritual enrichment. My son, Jean Marie, was later to become a remarkable photographer and a filmmaker profoundly concerned with human truths. Exceptionally sensitive to music, he was to become as well an excellent specialist in sound recording.

The years immediately following our move to Paris have left a recollection that, if not blurred, is at least difficult to make precise. Since I had stopped teaching, I had taken on the functions of drama critic for the review *Europe nouvelle*. In addition, as reader for the Editions Plon and the Editions Grasset, I read a large number of manuscripts. It was a profound joy from time to time to discover a new talent and to call it to the attention of those having the power to disclose it to the public. It was thus that I came to act as a kind of arbitrator between two readers who had seen Bernanos's manuscript of *Sous le soleil de Satan* and who had rendered contrary judgments. In my report, I stated that without question his was a powerful, fresh work testifying to an absolutely original creative faculty and that its publication was mandatory. I was not called on to give an opinion on Julien Green's *Mont Cinère,* which appeared about the same time, but here too I knew at once and for certain that we were confronted by a revelation; this was the beginning of a friendship between Julien Green and myself that still abides.

During those years it seems to me I absented myself from philosophy, to which I was to return a little later. The theater occupied the best of my thinking, and I chafed under the difficulty I had getting produced. Fortunately, *La Chapelle ardente* was presented at the Vieux Colombier sponsored by the eminent critic Henry Bidou, who told me he considered it a masterpiece. But it did not meet with the degree of success I had hoped for. Admittedly, the casting left something to be desired. I had requested Mme Falconetti for the part of Mireille, but her consent came after the part had already been given to an actress who, though certainly conscientious, lacked brilliance. Mme Jeanne Lion, who played the principal role of the mother, had the singular merit of writing me several months later that she feared she had betrayed my thought. This was no doubt true, but the fault lay with Gaston Baty, the director, who was inclined to see a clinical case in that painfully human character. Georges and Lidmilla Pitöeff said that they had found the play tedious, and this impression, resting on a lack of comprehension, mortified me.

When I think of that distant epoch, I find that it was all in all happy. Our union, my wife's and mine, was perfect, and it was illuminated by the presence of him who immediately and in an almost unhoped-for way had become our child. Yet it seems to me I did not enjoy that true happiness as I should have, because I was consumed by the playwright's craving for an audience.

Even though the situation today is quite different, as I will note later, I still have the painful impression that except in the cases of *Un Homme de Dieu* and *Rome n'est plus dans Rome,* the audience I so ardently desired has been denied me. Only two or three times was I fortunate enough to have in the service of my principal works the truly great actors who could have made them come across. I think above all of Pierre Fresnay, who refused to play two of my plays bearing on subjects that he felt were too burning; this was the period during which he followed the taste and the injunctions of Yvonne Printemps. Certainly, I still find it difficult to accept that this is the way it was; yet to some extent I think I discern a kind of spiritual economy about my life, an economy in which my freedom has been directed toward necessities or solicitations in another dimension. I sometimes think it was perhaps fortunate that the great success I so ardently desired for my dramatic works did not happen. Can I be sure that I would have resisted the temptation to try to please that public that first I would have conquered but that subsequently might have managed to make me leave the personal path, the difficult path I had chosen? It seems to me that I would have resisted the temptation, but I cannot be certain of it; in particular, I might have been tempted to write especially for such-and-such an actor of great renown. The frustration I suffered, and indeed suffered most cruelly, has perhaps been compensated for by the fact that none of my works has ever been falsified by an anxiety to please anyone else. I believe, moreover, that all my work, philosophical as well as dramatic, is destined to a sporadic audience; that is, it has shown itself capable of moving and often of absorbing readers very different from one another, living in the most diverse countries—beings whom it is not a question of counting precisely because they are human beings and belong as such to an order where number loses all meaning. One of these was my very dear friend Charles Du Bos, whose name I cannot evoke without turning my gaze to those years.

I met him through Jacques Rivière, then director of the *Nouvelle Revue française,* whom I had found again after the war. He had been my friend at the Sorbonne when I was preparing for the *agrégation.*

Perhaps it is worth describing the circumstances in which Charles Du Bos and I met. He came to see me one Sunday, hand outstretched, and told me that at Potigny—where so many famous symposia had taken place under the presidency of Paul Desjardins—he had come across my play *Le Quatuor en fa dièse* and had been immediately struck by the musical epigraph, which was none other than a phrase from the sextet of Ernest Chausson. It was thus under the sign of music and of that composer that we made contact, and our friendship deepened during the years that followed. I regularly attended the talks he gave before a public small and select—but, alas, without his having wished it, too exclusively worldly— at the home of Mme de Lestrange, on the quai Voltaire, then at the home of Mme Ridel, on the quai de Passy, and later in the apartment he acquired at Versailles, on the rue des Reservoirs, where he gave his "lessons" on Goethe. I shall not try to draw here a portrait of Charles Du Bos; I do not feel capable of fixing for the reader those features lighted by marvelous blue eyes, which remain for me as on the first day. He and I were certainly as different as possible. Alongside this being so marvelously refined, with whom culture was virtually cosubstantial, I gave something of the effect of an illiterate. No doubt it was on music that we communicated most directly, but his appraisals of literature and of painting bore for me a special authority. I must add that those who did not know him would never suspect what there was in him not only of exquisite delicacy, but also of humor and of sparkling vivacity. He is one of the most marvelous men I have ever known, one of those who testify the most directly in favor of human beings not as they are, but as they can become when they do not refuse grace. This word *grace* is in place here. I found myself associated with the movement that was to prepare the return of Charles Du Bos to the faith; I say truly the return, for he had been a pious adolescent.

Charles Du Bos, along with Robert Garric and the great Arabic scholar Louis Massignon, was indeed one of those men, actually very few in number, who triumphed over my resistance to Catholicism. It is certainly true that for many long years I had had the feeling, perhaps even inarticulate, that a mind essentially turned toward reflection could not adhere to Christianity today save in its Protestant forms. I have already said that my entrance by marriage into a Protestant family for whom any narrowly confessional faith was entirely out of the question undoubtedly contributed to the development of my sympathy for the Reformed Church. It is therefore somewhat paradoxical that in 1929, in circumstances I shall relate, when I posed to myself the question of an explicit adherence to Christianity, I opted in fact for Roman Catholicism.

After the publication in the *Nouvelle Revue française* of a "Note" of mine on Mauriac's *Souffrance du chrétien,* which had just appeared, Mauriac wrote me a letter in which he explicitly asked me whether I ought not to join the ranks of the Catholic Church. I have often had occasion to say this and to repeat it: I was at that time in a period of calm and equilibrium, which perhaps had not been the case a few years earlier. And I remember distinctly the manner in which I greeted the invitation addressed to me by the author of *Désert de l'amour.* It seemed to me that he was but a spokesman and that the call came from much higher up. It was as though a more than human voice were questioning me and putting me into my own presence. "Can you really persevere indefinitely in that equivocal position of yours?" this voice asked me. "Is it even honest to continue to think and to speak like someone who believes in the faith of others and who is convinced that this faith is everything but illusion, but who nevertheless does not resolve to take it unto himself? Is there not a sort of equivocation here that must be definitively dispelled; is it not like a leap before which you are obliged to decide?" It seemed to me that I could only reply to this last interrogative with an assent. But what confessional form should my adherence take? Normally, if I may use that term, it would seem that I had to rally to Protestantism. And yet I opted for the Roman Church. For what reason? Essentially because it seemed to me that Protestantism was in fact divided among a variety of sects that were not at all in agreement on the essentials and that a choice in favor of one of them would have a fundamentally arbitrary character. It then seemed to me that I could not give my adherence save to the Church that presented itself as corresponding to the richest and most global vision. To be sure, I had to muffle, at least provisionally, all those who in the Roman Catholic religion seemed to me either adulterated by superstitions or tainted by a legalism to which my thought was, and always has been, refractory.

Both Charles Du Bos and François Mauriac were very happy about my decision; Du Bos put me in touch with his friend Abbott Altermann. I note in passing that the latter was a converted Jew; I later learned, not without emotion, that his father had once been a teacher of my mother's.

I must add that my wife, although Protestant, offered no objection to my conversion to Catholicism and even took joy in it, for in certain respects—that is, in her love for the liturgy and for Gregorian chant—she found in the Catholic religion substantial elements for which Protestantism offered her no equivalents. Indeed a few years before her death, she was herself to adhere to Catholicism, in which she found a sustenance that never failed to support her during the terrible illness that was to carry her away. I am inclined to wonder today whether she did not penetrate the very essence of Catholicism much more profoundly than I, and during the long, desert period of more than twenty years that has gone by since her death, I have always thought of her as the most active and most beneficent of intercessors.

I apologize for this parenthesis, but it was too important to be omitted. I must also add that her family, even though for the most part remaining Protestant, viewed my conversion as in no way a defection and, in the truest ecumenical spirit, rejoiced that I had become a member of the Great Christian Family.

As the journal in *Etre et avoir* testifies, I knew moments of joy and expansion in my baptism and my first communion that I still cannot think about today without emotion. Yet as I evoke that period, I cannot keep from thinking that the worthy Abbott Altermann probably made a mistake in abridging my religious instruction. I am inclined to think that he ought to have assigned me a probationary period of perhaps not longer than a year. Certainly, I loved my meetings with Abbott Altermann, and I marveled at the facts he related to me, in particular those concerning the truly miraculous life of Father Lamy in the *banlieue* of Paris. I am still profoundly affected by what I would call "the Christian marvel," which my experiences and research in the metapsychical domain had in fact readied me to recognize. And I feel some irritation with those in the very bosom of the Church who, often from a fear of appearing naive or simply from a surprising attachment to rationalism, seem eager to reduce, or even sometimes to deny explicitly, the aspect of the marvelous in the Christian given and in the life of the saints.

On the other hand, the essentially Thomist dogmatism I found in Abbott Altermann aroused my unalterable protest. At the time, I made several attempts to understand St. Thomas's thinking better and to read some of his contemporary disciples. But I am obliged to acknowledge that this effort was not crowned with success, and the most elementary fairness forces me to add that I did not carry it out with the requisite earnestness and tenacity. It was at this time that Charles Du Bos and I had weekly meetings with Jacques Maritain, who took great pains to help us understand Thomist thought better and to appreciate it more. All three of us showed good will, but the result was meager indeed.

In 1934, in an article written for the *Revue des jeunes* on Jacques Maritain's *Degrés du savoir,* I ventured to express the idea that in remaining so attached to the use of scholastic terminology, Maritain risked rendering a disservice to Christianity by supporting the notion that it remained bound to a medieval mode of thought and thus seemed unable to accommodate the conquests of science and modern philosophy. This observation hurt the author, who asked me—or rather saw to it that I was asked—not to publish the article. I assented with a smile.

My meetings with Abbott Altermann terminated the day I allowed myself to say, "After all, we do not know what God thinks of the Reformation." In reply he exclaimed, "I, *I* know!"—he stopped abruptly, conscious, I think, of the enormity of such an assertion. Consequently, I ceased seeing him. But what I want very much to say in tribute to him is that he retained no animosity toward me; many years later, after the death of my wife, he paid me a visit that is precious in my memory. He was an ardent and noble spirit, but there were certain excesses in him that one notices rather often in converts.

This autobiography is not a history of my thoughts. I do not, therefore, need to specify the effect of my conversion on what I dislike calling my "philosophy." I leave that inquiry to my commentators, though not without noting that it presents serious difficulties: is it to be feared that there can be no accord here between believers and nonbelievers? All that I can say is that in recently reading *Etre et avoir* for the first time after many years, I was struck by the fact that some of the most essential themes of my work appear rather abruptly and distinctly during the months immediately prior to my conversion. Still, I acknowledge that it would not be too difficult to show these same themes prefigured in many of my earlier writings, particularly in my plays.

When I try to recall what my life was like up to 1935 and 1936, no external event clearly stands out. Our hearth was brightened by the presence of the child whom we had adopted in 1923 and to whom we devoted a tender care quite identical to what we would have felt for one born of our flesh. This adoption was such a success that I must judge it to have been presided over by Providence; to my last day I shall give thanks to Him who, under often nearly inscrutable conditions, guides our destinies.

Meanwhile, in 1927, if I am not mistaken, Charles Du Bos asked me to take his place as editor of Plon's series of foreign authors, among which several important works had already appeared, including the Goethe-Schiller correspondence. I eagerly seized this opportunity and felt a need to stress the import of the series more than Du Bos had done. The publisher and I decided to call it Feux croisés and to add the subtitle Terres et âmes étrangères. I began, of course, by including several books Du Bos

had already secured, such as Alexis Remizov's *Sur champ d'azur*. I
wanted to inaugurate my editorship with the admirable *Passage to India*,
by E. M. Forster, but the translation seemed to me defective. Hence, I
addressed a certain number of comments to the translator. A personal acquaintance of Forster's, he appealed to the author to defend him against
my intervention. Forster, who had little knowledge of French, asked me to
leave the translator alone. I submitted, but I felt that under such conditions
the work could not be included in Feux croisés. A number of years later it
was to be included, the translator having in the meantime made noticeable
improvements.

I will not weary the reader with an account of the works that appeared
in Feux croisés. I certainly made mistakes in one direction or another, but
on the whole this series was generally considered one of the best of its
kind in those days. English letters certainly occupied a preponderant place,
particularly the novels by women, who provided so many works of the
first rank between the wars. I think especially of Rosamund Lehmann,
Sheila Kaye Smith, Elisabeth Bowen, and Margaret Kennedy, not to mention Virginia Woolf, whose work was published by Stock. But outside the
Anglo-Saxon register, where Aldous Huxley occupied a foremost place, I
had the joy of making available the great novelist Jacob Wasserman and
later Kazantzakis and many others.

I shall never forget the delighted thrill with which, in a bookstore such
as Galignani, I would leaf through such-and-such a new book whose interest and novelty I sensed by means of I know not what antennae. It was
akin to the joy in exploration that I experienced during so many walks in
times—alas, past—when walking was for me a ceaselessly renewed delight.

This is the place to call to mind our holidays, which we so loved. We
spent at least part of our vacation each year in a different place. Until
about 1930, the remainder was spent in Alsace, where my in-laws passed
some time in an apartment in a large house, pompously called a château,
at Rothau, in the Bruche valley. I came instantly to love that spot where
my wife had come so often with her family, long before Alsace became
French again—not the spot itself, but the innumerable walks radiating
from it, in those Vosges woods of which I have never thought without
emotion. Alas, the Struthof meadow, where the view of Mount Donon
and of the hauts de Chaume was so beautiful and where we sometimes
climbed to take our breakfast, was to become one of the most abominable
extermination camps during the Second World War. But at the time of
which I am speaking, the whole Ban de la Roche had preserved its idyllic
charm, and the community piously cherished the memory of certain pas-

tors who had been veritable pioneers in the social realm in the nineteenth century.

I also loved the visits we paid each year to the high mountains in France, between 1925 and 1930, and later in Switzerland (Engadine and Valais), and then in the Dolomites. I was certainly never a sportsman, but until the accident in 1953, which sadly changed my life, I was an indefatigable walker. I am convinced that walking was for me far more than a mere distraction; it was also necessary to the progress of my health, as can be seen in certain notes in *Etre et avoir* and *Présence et immortalité*. My preference was for hiking in the high mountains, the air at high altitudes positively bracing me. My wife accompanied me during these pilgrimages, though I fear they may have imposed excessive demands on her at times; nevertheless, on this point as on so many others, we were in perfect rapport. Together we delighted in the landscape that opened up to us during our long walks. There is no doubt that music and landscape have held for me the greatest of delights during the better part of my life.

I mention music. In all these years I have not ceased to read scores untiringly. Together my wife and I played four-handed many wholly modern works, and I cannot stress sufficiently that such executing, however imperfect, enabled me to penetrate works that might otherwise have remained foreign to me. I think, for example, of Debussy's *La Mer,* which I did not understand when I first heard it at the Concerts Colonnes.

In those days I improvised quite often, but it was only much later, after the Second World War, that a friend urged my wife to set down some of my improvisations, thus beginning a series of musical compositions that followed one after another in 1945 and 1946. I shall come back to this, for it was one of the important moments of my life.

When I recall that period, how can I not think that it was essentially a happy one? And yet, had I been asked at that time, I think I might have hesitated to declare that I was happy.

On the strictly personal level, I could not reconcile myself to the ill will shown me by theater producers; I could not understand the nature of the obstacles I encountered, and even now I have some difficulty explaining it to myself. It was as if my plays aroused apprehensiveness or distrust not generally among the actors themselves, but among producers, who were probably convinced that the plays of a philosopher could be nothing but flops. They did not seem to understand that even if I was a philosopher, my drama was not philosophic—that it was in fact exactly the opposite of what is known as the drama of ideas and of those thesis-plays that have always horrified me.

It was chiefly between 1925 and 1930, it seems to me, that this defeat at the hands of producers brought on an extremely painful fever. Subsequently, the situation was to change, perhaps because of the comparative notoriety engendered by the publication of my *Journal métaphysique* in 1927, the very year in which Heidegger's *Sein und Zeit* appeared. In retrospect, I am indebted to Jean Paulhan for having urged me to publish those journal notes, which in my own mind at first were only a preparation for the more categorical work I intended to publish some day. Little by little I came to understand that the work in question was not to be written and that something in the very nature of my thought probably excluded any such possibility. However that may be, from 1930 on I had the satisfaction of feeling myself recognized, understood, and thus encouraged.

In contrast, external events caused me increasing anxiety. I believe I have already mentioned that my euphoria following the end of the 1914–1918 war did not last. Already the fact that first the United States and then Russia had withdrawn from the League of Nations caused me to lose all confidence in the efficacy of an institution that at the outset had aroused so much hope. To be sure, if I saw clearly on some matters, on others I was as mistaken as everyone else. I do not believe that I understood at first the political error of the reoccupation of the Ruhr. Like so many others, I was haunted by the thought that Germany was preparing her revenge. I feared that Briand might let himself be tricked by appearances. Poincaré's attitude at the time seemed more reasonable, even if, from another point of view, I was inclined to disapprove what was too exclusively legalistic in his position. This amounts to saying that at bottom I was not fully in agreement with myself. But the anguish in me did not cease to mount, and from the beginning National Socialism awakened in me the keenest apprehension. I recall in 1932 asking Henri Lichlenberger, a famed and authoritative expert on Germany who had just returned from there, whether he was not very troubled by what was taking place across the Rhine; he gave me the stupefying answer that his German friends had reassured him that National Socialism concerned only internal politics. Not only did I refuse to accept this astounding statement, but I was bewildered. How could a specialist in Goethe and Wagner be deceived by such an assertion? I also recall my consternation when, at the Disarmament Conference, André Tardieu refrained from denouncing, as he should have done, the alarming progress of German rearmament at about that time.

Naturally, it is impossible for me to state the exact place this concern occupied in my life. But I think I can say that it tended to color what I might call my feeling, rather than my vision, of life. How could I have felt wholly happy in a world so menaced?

No doubt it was largely because I was obsessed with the external menace that I regarded the elections of May 1936 and the coming to power of the Popular Front as a disaster. I simply could not forgive Blum for having said several years earlier that Hitler would never come to power. Such blindness seemed to hold no promise of his being an effective leader of government.

To be completely honest, I must add something that I admit is not to my credit. My exasperation with the occupation of the factories in the summer of 1936, and in a general way with the disorder that was mounting everywhere, contributed to my misunderstanding what was fundamentally just in certain demands that the Popular Front aimed to satisfy. I think particularly of the right to paid vacations, which today seems to me the most elementary justice, so much so that I cannot understand how it was ever considered natural for workers to be deprived of them. I am more than ready to recognize today that the sense of order I had inherited from my father masked an egoism that was largely camouflaged by rational argument. Since then, I think I have made considerable headway, which is not to say that I have ever ceased to feel myself a bourgeois.

Recalling the events of 1936, I feel I must mention the lectures I gave in Budapest the day after the remilitarization of the left bank of the Rhine. When I arrived in the Hungarian capital on my first visit, I found myself besieged by journalists eager to know the reactions in Paris to the major event that had just occurred. I tried to put on a bold front and to assure my questioners that the French government had not been taken unawares. But deep within me I was gripped by a cruel anxiety. I wondered whether I was not risking being trapped in Budapest in the event that France and England replied with force to Hitler's provocation. The few days I passed in that city thus left a very painful memory. I was indeed rapidly reassured, but I soon realized that the Allies had inexcusably let pass their last opportunity to strike a really decisive blow against the Hitlerian undertaking. In a lecture I was to give some twenty years later in Germany on "Truth and Concrete Situations," I was to cite this abstention as a particularly striking example of the essential political error or misdemeanor of not seizing the *kairos* when it presents itself.

During that visit, which lasted scarcely a week, I was exposed to repeated efforts of Hungarian propaganda: writers and journalists outdid themselves to demonstrate that the Allies had made a serious mistake and had even sinned against justice in giving Transylvania to the Rumanians. I was impressed by the arguments that unfolded before me, but the writers were greatly mistaken in imagining that I could contribute to a revision of the Treaty of Trianon.

It now seems to me that those days of March 1938 formed the bonds between the Hungarians and myself—bonds that were to be strengthened twenty years later during the tragic events in Budapest.

I emphasize these matters to demonstrate that from that period on I had an increasing interest in political events. I think I can say sincerely that I have always been horrified by anything resembling an ivory tower.

Yet I must also admit that the position of the intellectual in such matters has always struck me as extremely delicate. I allude here above all to the innumerable petitions and manifestos I have been asked to sign in the course of my life. Some of those around me systematically refused to sign anything, whereas others signed everything that came along. My attitude lay between these two extremes, and I may certainly have erred either in giving or in refusing my signature. A specific instance remains fixed in my mind. During the very harsh repression by Chancellor Dolfuss of the Socialist agitation in Vienna, Jacques Maritain and his friends sent me the text of a protest that I refused to sign. Why the refusal? Simply, I said, because I did not want to associate myself with an action that risked undermining, however slightly, the moral authority of Dolfuss while he was engaged in a heroic struggle against National Socialism. Was I wrong? How can one know? But what is clear in my eyes is that this refusal expressed something very specific in myself: an unshakable distrust of ideology and of the blindness that so often results. Another example illustrates this tendency of mind. It must have been in 1937 that the Austrian educator Foerster came to Passy to give a lecture to a private group in order to demonstrate that a certain pacifism threatened to play into the hands of the predatory powers. I still see before me the adamant features of Emmanuel Mounier, who was in the audience and who obviously did not admit that this could be true; he even went so far as to reproach Foerster for having denounced the aggressive intent of his own country. In a certain way, Emmanuel Mounier was kindred to my own way of thinking, and all things considered, I still think that he was a man of great good will. But in that situation, too, I discerned the maleficent character of an ideology that drops a curtain between conscience and concrete reality.

If Jacques Bainville was the only one in the movement of Action française (for which I felt not the slightest sympathy) to arouse a feeling of great intellectual respect in me, it was because I felt in him that indefeasible lucidity that one encounters so rarely in political writers.

Nineteen thirty-six was a year of anguish. In 1937, the year of the Paris International Exposition, one could still hope, although quite unreasonably and most precariously, that the worst was not inevitable.

Yes, thus it seems to me to have been; and yet I am almost tempted to scratch out what I have just written when I recall the Sunday following the announcement of the *Anschluss*. I see myself again walking up the Champs Elysées on a magnificent day and scanning with a sort of despair the carefree faces of all those passers-by who seemed to show not the slightest awareness of an approaching catastrophe. Yes, I am certain that on that day I had a distinct foreboding of imminent disaster. But during the months that followed, life resumed its ordinary course. The performances of *Le Dard* absorbed me completely, and I would like to express my deep gratitude to that great-hearted actress Magdeleine Bérubet, who loved the play and staged it so well, first at the Théâtre des Arts, for two exceptional performances, and then at the Petit Théâtre des Deux Masques, which no longer exists.

In this autobiographical sketch I did not wish to introduce anything resembling a history of my works; that would be an entirely different undertaking. But I believe I must pause a few moments over *Le Dard,* which today seems to me one of my most significant plays as well as one of those from which any biographical reference is radically excluded.

For some time already I had been meeting a growing number of philosophers, for the most part Jewish, who had had to leave Germany to escape persecution. Also, my friend Maurice Boucher, professor of German literature at the Sorbonne, had recommended to me a young man who had arrived from across the Rhine after having been involved in a widely publicized court proceeding. Paul Krantz, as he was called, was an Aryan type, with blond hair and blue eyes. He won me over immediately, and I arranged for the novel he had just completed, *Die Miets-Kaserne,* to be published in the Feux croisés series. I formed an idealized view of him that events were to show did not correspond to reality. But that is no matter here. The personage of Werner Schnee was for me the incarnation of the free spirit as I conceived it then, in those years in which the totalitarian menace weighed more and more heavily on me each day. In addition, I had heard of the violinist Adolf Busch, who, if I am not mistaken, had allied himself with the Jewish pianist Rudolf Serkin and had left Germany with him. I fancied that in an analogous manner my Werner Schnee, a singer, had decided to share the fate of his Jewish accompanist, Rudolf Schönthal, who was persecuted and hounded by racists.

But that was only one pole of the play; the other pole was furnished by a great intellectual of the Left, whose name I will not mention and whose humble origins were known; he seemed to me never to have entirely digested his success, as if he had a guilty conscience. That guilty conscience is *le dard,* the poisoned sting.

I wrote my play in the absence of Krantz, who had adopted the alias of Erich Noth. But mentally I tried out all the replies I put into Werner's mouth by asking myself whether Noth could have spoken them. Mistakenly thinking that he had once acted in a play, I read him *Le Dard* on his return to Paris and asked him whether he would consider playing the part. He accepted instantly. I introduced him, therefore, to Magdeleine Bérubet, who agreed to give him a tryout. The first day, she was close to despair. "But he knows nothing," she wailed, "not the smallest rudiment of stage experience!" By the second day, her viewpoint had changed: "Perhaps, after all, who knows? . . ." In the end he was a triumphant success. No sooner did he appear—in his threadbare coat, his features in anguish— than applause broke out. He was the character himself. It was indeed an exceptional case and a rarity in the history of theater.

But I must also say, without making any more of it, that after the war the man Noth became in America turned out to be distressingly dissimilar to the personage I had conceived and whom he had incarnated on the stage.

That summer of 1937 was one of the most beautiful I have ever experienced. Something irrational in us, which should not be confused with Hope, tended to persuade us that the worst was not a certainty. I recall again with deep emotion the weeks we passed *en famille* at Morgat in a house we had rented. Those of my sisters-in-law who were still alive were with us, along with my brother-in-law and his family. I need not elaborate on the place of family bonds in my life, but I do want to say how important that place was. Despite certain differences of opinion, relations with my brother-in-law, Henri Boegner, remained perfect. The German word *Einklang* is the term that best conveys that abiding intimacy. The confessional difference that still existed between me and my wife or her sisters was never the source of any difficulties. Indeed much later, as I have said, my wife was to join me and even to outdistance me.

During that same summer, the International Congress of Philosophy was held in Paris, before which I read my paper on "Le Méta-problématique." During the subsequent exchange of views between Léon Brunschvicg and myself, an argument occurred that caused a considerable stir. The author of *La Modalité du jugement* thought it incumbent upon him to observe that my death seemed to preoccupy me more than he himself was concerned with his own death. I replied that "what counted for me was not *my* death, but that of the beloved," thus accenting one of the points that differentiates my thought from that of the majority of my contemporaries. Nevertheless, I wish to pay homage retrospectively to that philosopher, who only a few years later was to suffer persecution for being a Jew and who, during his ordeals, gave proof of an admirable strength of spirit.

After the congress, my wife and I left for Yugoslavia in the company of Jean Wahl, from whom we parted regretfully in Pola. That journey in Dalmatia and Bosnia remains one of the most beautiful memories bequeathed to me by our many wanderings.

It was during the theatrical season of 1937–1938 that the Comédie-Française, then administered by Edouard Bourdet, put on my one-act play *Le Fanal,* which strangely enough had been inspired by the death of Catherine Pozzi, Bourdet's first wife. I do not know whether this play, though remarkably well acted, was really understood; I doubt it. Some thought they saw an attack on divorce; this was to confuse me with Paul Bourget.

I come to the summer of 1938 and the crisis that culminated in the Munich agreement. I remember very precisely what my feeling was at that time, and I would underscore today what I said then. I thought, on the one hand, that the Munich pact was inevitable but, on the other, that it had to be seen as the consequence of, and *as punishment for,* the unpardonable mistake committed in 1936. I cannot deny that the conclusion of the pact was greeted by myself and by many others with a certain relief. But this emotion was accompanied by shame over the abandonment of Czechoslovakia. It became evident that a trial by arms could not be avoided. We would have to prepare ourselves and neglect nothing, so that France and England might be ready on the day of the inevitable. It was in this sense that my aunt wrote to President Daladier imploring him to ask all the necessary sacrifices of the French people. Her voice was not heard. She was to pass away on the first of January, 1940, full in that *drôle de guerre,* haunted to the moment she lapsed into unconsciousness by the thought of the heroic Finnish resistance. This word *heroic* I am in retrospect inclined to apply to her; the errors she may have made in my education are minimal in comparison to her virtues, her nobility of soul, and her abnegation. She remains one of the infinitely rare beings in whom I was able to recognize something like a call to the Absolute.

I am no longer able to establish exactly what my state of mind was during the winter of 1938–1939. I have the impression that we were too close to the approaching terrible event to be able to foresee it. It was as if we were already in its shadow.

By contrast, what I do recall is the little trip my wife and I took by car to Lyon and in Savoie. My wife was driving; I would have been quite unable to relieve her at the steering wheel. On the return trip, we had an accident near Morestal, in Isère, not far from the estate of Paul Claudel. The weather was bad and the road slippery, or at least I suppose so, for suddenly the car started to zigzag, and I still hear my wife crying out, "Mon Dieu, nous allons mourir!" The car spun around, and we found ourselves off the road, at the bottom of a slope. God be praised, my wife was unhurt, but she was frightened when she discovered that I had no memory of what had just happened. Actually, it was only a passing disruption. We spent the afternoon in a hotel room in Morestal, and even today I relive that feeling of having escaped a mortal peril—that feeling of having been the object of Grace. We returned by train, leaving the seriously damaged car for my son to fetch several weeks later.

If my memory serves me well, it was in the spring of 1939 that the Germans entered Prague, thus sealing the fate of the brother nation we had abandoned. That very evening we were attending Henri Sauguet's *Chartreuse de Parme* at the Opéra. I recall my emotion that evening; who could have minimized the gravity of the event? I was imprudent enough to solicit an echo from Jacques Benoist-Méchin, a composer and writer with whom I had amicable relations and who was later to place himself in the front ranks of the collaborators. I remember that the silence with which he countered my exclamations froze me. Everything was falling into place for the hideous drama we were called upon to experience.

During the months of July and August of 1939 we still knew some happy moments in a secluded corner of the French Alps, at Villard d'Arêne. I did not doubt, as I clambered up the wooded slopes overlooking the Meije glaciers, that that was to be my last mountain hike.

A few days later, at Bourg-Saint-Andéol, on the banks of the Rhône in Ardèche, I had my first encounter with a man who had caught my attention by his writings and who was to become a true friend: Gustave Thibon. This self-taught man of peasant origin, in whom the most solid common sense conjoined with a profound comprehension of the mystics, was later to be the first to make Simone Weil known to the public. I had the pleasure of presiding over the publication by Plon of *La Pesanteur et la grâce*. Earlier, I had also had the satisfaction of having another publisher do Thibon's volume of essays, entitled *Diagnostics,* which marked the beginning of his career.

I always strove to make known works that otherwise risked escaping general attention, and I also strove to create links among beings who in theory had no reason to meet. This was certainly the source of one of the purest joys I knew in my life as a writer. When I consider what have been my reasons for living, one seems to have consisted essentially in this task of "gatherer." It goes without saying, too, that this same state of mind presided over the Feux croisés series, with which I concerned myself actively until about 1960. I have already made allusion to it, but perhaps I have not sufficiently emphasized the attention I gave to the problem of translation. I reached the conclusion that the problem can be satisfactorily resolved only in exceptional cases, where a consonance of mind and feeling arises between the writer and the translator. But in any case a conscientiously undertaken translation requires effort and time out of all proportion to the remuneration, always insufficient, that a publisher is in a position to give.

We were at Merlée, the picturesque old château situated in the heart of the Forèze mountains, where the preceding year we had welcomed an old and good friend, when the news of the German-Soviet accord exploded like a thunderbolt. It revealed the imminence of the catastrophe.

In retrospect, I am astounded that my wife and I nevertheless had the courage to leave by car in the direction of the provinces of Lot and Aveyron. I think that what was uppermost in our minds was to profit from the last remaining days to contemplate further some beautiful landscapes and churches. Crossing the Auvergne mountains, we descended into Mauriac, Aurillac, and Figeac until a telephone call from this last town to our families determined a return northward. Indeed, had we not seen the day before, in a little village in Cantal, the first mobilization posters? Our anguish continued to mount, and we found ourselves back at Merlée several steps lower on the sinister stairway that led to the abyss. I have some difficulty now trying to understand our actions and our behavior. I remember that we returned to Paris but that we left almost immediately, only to learn that war had been declared. I see us again dining with some near relatives above Tonnerre in a hospitable house where my aunt had taken refuge with her adopted son. We wanted to take her with us, but she refused to come along, determined to get back to Paris as soon as possible. The dislocation that was subsequently to become intolerable had already begun. After several more days in the château of Merlée, which was to be one of the poles of our existence until the time we installed ourselves in Corrèze, we regained Paris, to live there the strange period of the *drôle de guerre*. But by the end of September the crushing of Poland was complete; once more that unhappy country had been delivered to predatory powers determined to carve it up.

Naturally, I could not stand the idea of remaining inactive in Paris. I even envisaged taking a position in the provinces, although the idea of

leaving our families was intolerable to both of us. It must have been toward the end of October that I was offered a philosophy course at the
Lycée Louis-le-Grand, where the professor had been drafted. I accepted
without hesitation and indeed found real comfort in being able to bend
myself to a specific task. But what were we thinking, what were we hoping
for, during those months when the war on the western front dwindled to
small actions, seemed bottled up? It is most difficult to reconstruct what
our state of mind was. Were we able to believe seriously in a resolution
of the situation short of a terrible trial by arms, which by all the evidence
could not be avoided? Were we able to imagine that a compromise would
be possible, a sort of armistice of indeterminate duration? I find it difficult
to believe. And yet it is certain that we clung to each reassuring possibility, however illusory it might turn out to be—that we did not have, and
perhaps could not have had, the courage to face the event toward which
we were being borne by an implacable destiny.

The Narwick expedition awakened some hope in us. It had at least the
psychological advantage of ending an immobility that caused only impatience and anguish. My ears can still hear the voice of President Reynaud
announcing that the ore route was closed. But it seems to me that the
arrogant tone in which this hazardous statement was pronounced provoked
some disquiet. The reawakening was not long in coming, and it was cruel.

It was the tenth of May [1940]: the irruption of the German army
across Holland, Belgium, and the north of France, the Maginot line out-
flanked, and so on. Could the flood be stopped? My mind repeatedly
evoked the despair of my aunt, so ardently patriotic. The Lord be thanked,
she had gone to sleep the first of January, not to reawaken. At the level of
daily existence in its most petty aspect, a problem arose that had to be
solved. I now found myself in charge of an enormous amount of furniture,
huge bookcases loaded with books, paintings, and so on. It was impossible
to store any of it in the apartment on the rue de Tournon to which we had
moved seven years earlier. We were forced to contemplate buying a country house, a possibility we had been considering for a long time. We
searched the environs of Paris first, but soon realized that nothing suitable
could be found for what we could pay. A postcard during Christmas vacation from one of my pupils reminded us of that region of Corrèze where
we had sojourned twice for several days. In reply to our inquiry, a real-
estate agency in Brive conveyed a listing that seemed to correspond to
what we were looking for. It was during Easter vacation, and thus well
before the unleashing of the German offensive, that we went to Brive to
see the house in question. My friend Daniel Rops, whom I had told about
our project, was good enough to write Edmond Michelet, whom we did

not yet know, to ask him to help us in our search. Thus it was that we came to know this good man, this perfect Christian, who, after having committed himself wholly to the Resistance, was to know the horrors of deportation to Dachau, where he miraculously survived typhus, and was later to become one of General de Gaulle's ministers and steadiest supporters. It is sweet indeed to be able to pay a tribute of affection and admiration to this admirable man, who, raised to high honors, has remained as I knew him in 1940, when he was but a middleman in groceries. How not to remember that this man, himself a victim of Nazi barbarity, was later to be one of the most ardent and tenacious workers for a Franco-German rapprochement after the war? Like Robert Schumann, whom I knew much less well but with whom I was acquainted, he gave the wonderful example of a man who could remain a militant Christian in politics without becoming intoxicated or distorted by it.

In those days of April 1940, Edmond Michelet was kind enough to place himself and his car at our disposal. We went at once to Peuch. It was a small sixteenth-century manor house, high up on a hill above the road linking the Turenne station to the more important road running from Brive to Meyssac. We could not help being won over by the sixteenth-century façade and by the view that extended to the other side of the little valley, toward gently undulating hills. But the information supplied by the agency was erroneous; everything or almost everything still had to be done, including plumbing in water, wiring for electricity, and so on. These difficulties seemed insurmountable. But Edmond Michelet enjoined us, after we had seen some other places with him, to acquire this house, which was subsequently to play so essential a role in our lives. Nevertheless, we did not decide on the spot. My wife wanted to return with one of her sisters to get her opinion. My son had been called up and was out of reach. It was in the first days of June that we became owners of Peuch, but now the German armies were approaching; it was out of the question to have the furniture that had prompted our decision shipped to Corrèze. We decided to leave two or three days before the Germans entered Paris, and we headed once more to Merlée.

There we were on the exodus route. My wife was at the wheel, and we had one of our cousins with us in addition to our Alsatian maid and her small child. It took us six hours to cover the thirty-odd kilometers between Paris and Arpajon. We were racked with worry. The smallest breakdown and all four of us would have had to leave the car to face who knows what ordeal. At Arpajon, I decided to leave the main highway, and at once all was calm and serene. At one point, we encountered Czechoslovakian troops moving toward Paris. Otherwise the road was deserted;

hopes revived. But at Sully-sur-Loire, where I anticipated stopping, there was nowhere to spend the night. Finally, we stopped in a field and decided to stay there until morning.

I do not believe I have ever experienced to the same degree as I did that night the feeling of existing "by the grace of God." It was as if the anguish had crumbled, making room for a sort of detachment, a trusting in absolute uncertainty.

By way of the provinces of Berry and Bourbonnais, we arrived at Merlée, where we were anxiously awaited. It was there that we heard the June 18 appeal on the radio. It awakened hope in us, but we soon experienced the regret of realizing that by attacking and directly incriminating Marshal Pétain, General de Gaulle was tending to divide the French people at the very moment when remaining united seemed indispensable.

As for the armistice itself, I would be lying if I did not admit that at the time, it appeared inevitable to us and that despite everything, it was a relief to know we were no longer fighting. As for the Marshal, however, from the beginning I deplored his pretension of recreating a sort of moral order that to my mind could only be deceptive, since it was based on defeat.

I recall clearly those mortal days at the end of June and the beginning of July in 1940, when we were waiting in anguish for news of my son and my nephew, both in uniform. The former, attached to the geographical service of the army, was to be discharged several weeks later; the latter, an infantry officer, was taken prisoner.

Some time later I had to go to Clermont Ferrand, the ministry having designated me a member of the *baccalauréat* jury. I confess that I felt full of compassion for those poor young people who were called upon to write examinations under horrible circumstances that would surely disturb, if not paralyze, one's judgment.

My wife and I left Clermont for Corrèze, where we were to rejoin our son, now discharged, and show him our new house, which he had not yet seen. He was immediately captivated by it and, on entering, had an indistinct premonition of all that it would subsequently mean to us.

In the train on the way back to Clermont, my wife gave me news that overwhelmed me: for some time she had been feeling the first symptoms of an illness whose gravity she suspected. She had consulted a doctor at Clermont and was going to have an operation. She withstood the operation well, but a laboratory analysis showed that it was a malignant tumor. We decided to go to Lyon, where we had family and where we knew that my wife could receive the necessary care. I myself would live with a relative, who would willingly take me in.

At all events, my wife's state of health did not permit my considering a return to Paris. Moreover, a friend who had remained there, having made I know not what inquiries, informed me that a return might be risky for me. Thus, it was really an exile that was beginning.

We were in Switzerland, where I had succeeded in taking my wife to try to facilitate her convalescence, when I received the news of my appointment to Montpellier as professor of philosophy for the preparatory course for the Ecole normale supérieure. There was no question of refusing, so we passed the first trimester in Montpellier in rather arduous material circumstances. I ended by falling ill myself and had to give up the course.

Meanwhile, my son having already installed himself at Corrèze, we were able to go ahead with the indispensable work on the house. Furthermore, by means of a Vichy law concerning return to the land, I was able to have the furniture I had inherited sent, so that it was possible to move to Peuch during the first days of July 1941.

Need I say that I followed with anguish the development of the military situation and the progress of the German armies in Russia? Yet I do not believe that I ever despaired completely. At the risk of eliciting smiles from my readers, I will say that certain predictions, though no doubt apocryphal, perhaps bolstered my confidence.

Although I did not participate in the Resistance, for I felt myself unsuited to clandestine battle, I abstained at least from any relation with the Vichy government and turned a deaf ear to any invitation to a gathering under the auspices of the marshal. For a long time I wanted to believe that he was playing a double game and that there was a secret agreement between him and General de Gaulle. But bit by bit I had to disabuse myself, and many measures, such as the statute concerning Jews, provoked my indignation.

I was fortunately able to maintain contact with Lyon and was able to go there on several occasions to give lectures, which were to be collected after the war in the volume entitled *Homo Viator*.

It was Edmond Michelet, I remember, who came to tell us of the landing in North Africa at the beginning of November 1942. Hope thus took on a more definite shape. Naturally, we tuned in regularly to the English radio broadcasts and often managed to hear them, even though they were frequently garbled. I remember saying to myself one day that they were too much like injections that I needed in order to keep going. In general, one felt that life lay in wait for events that would put an end to the atrocious occupation and its sinister corollaries.

We meandered far and wide on foot in the Corrèze countryside, which we came to love more and more and which gave us a sense of having taken root. Thus, in unexpected and very painful circumstances, I was given something in the second half of my life that had always been lacking in my childhood and adolescence: the sense of belonging to a place, to a spot somewhere. I continually meditated on the strange conditions by which we were planted in a region to which at first nothing, absolutely nothing, rooted us. It was a mystery rather comparable to that mystery of adoption of which we had also been the beneficiaries.

We were given the opportunity to shelter under our roof some of our relatives who had been harshly restricted by the rationing; in that corner of Corrèze food was rather easy to come by. Meanwhile, my son had found employment at the Secours national, and my nephew had been repatriated from Germany, thanks to the efforts of a friend in Switzerland. My wife seemed to have recovered her health; the immediate worries had dissipated. But there was all the rest: the immense unknown of a future and nothing to indicate its outlines.

The illness with which my wife's family had already been so cruelly afflicted pursued its course in the person of one of her sisters, a doctor, an elite among persons, who was to pass away at the beginning of 1943. Without going into the detail of these family ordeals, I think I would be remiss in truthfulness if I did not speak here of their reverberations in me. To fail to recognize their impact on my philosophical writings (especially on *Présence et immortalité*) as well as on my plays would be to understand nothing of my work.

It was at the beginning of the fall of 1943 that we decided to return to Paris for good. We had already gone back twice, but only for a few weeks each time. The main motive for this return was the marriage of my son to the daughter of my brother-in-law, Henri Boegner. A happy event for us, which had burgeoned in Corréze without our knowing it during long conversations when my niece had come to Peuch for the holidays. Here again occurred that marvel of something taking root. It was infinitely gratifying for my wife and me to know that the children of our adopted son would be of her blood through their mother.

I have never entered into these essential facts of my existence in any published writing, but I am happy to have the opportunity to recall them here, because they have colored—indeed, they have profoundly saturated—my very substance.

The winter we spent in Paris in 1943–1944 left only a confused memory, as if it had been overshadowed by the luminous days of the Liberation. The announcement of the Allied landings in Normandy certainly caused intense joy, but during the succeeding weeks the rigors of the Occupation mounted, and the shuffling of the liberating armies around Caen only augmented our feverish impatience.

During the decisive week preceding the entry of the Leclerc army into Paris, I noted my impressions almost by the hour. The struggle was joined between the responsible elements, admirably seconded by the Swedish consul, Raoul Nordling, and also by the Communists, who would not hear of any deals and who hoped, by bloody battles and terrible reprisals, to achieve their objective: the triumph of the revolution.

I shall always hear the ringing of the bells greeting the entry of the Leclerc army into Paris. A few moments later, the telephone rang: there is a rumor that the Senate will be blown up—look out! Had the explosion occurred, our house, located fifty yards from the Senate, would certainly have collapsed. To ease our anxiety, we went to the cellar. But on the way down, I remarked to my wife that if the worst should happen, we would certainly be buried. By mutual agreement we went back up to our apartment to enjoy a peaceful sleep. It was as if the joy of the Liberation had silenced every personal worry. The next morning, under a dazzling sun, we set out to find our family on the boulevard de Port-Royal, on the other side of the jardin du Luxembourg. I can see us again threading our way through the deserted streets and skirting the gardens, where the enemy was still dug in.

As it turned out, the anticipated explosion never occurred, and our house remained intact. A strange period began for me. We were still fighting—we even knew several disquieting days during the von Rundstedt offensive—yet it seemed to us that it was all over.

Unfortunately, the day of reckoning had come. Certainly, sanctions had to be taken against traitors; indeed, they had to be brought before a regular court. The spectacle of special tribunals, which were to multiply, could only arouse the indignation of all those who desired justice worthy of the name. A committee of writers formed to carry out a purge in the domain of Letters. Thus I was called upon to sit on a commission with fanatics, whose sectarianism was odious to me. I felt all too clearly that the Communists and their associates were striving to discredit and systematically to dishonor their political adversaries, as if these had been collaborators en masse. Hence at the beginning of 1945 I wrote the outline of *Philosophie de l'épuration: contribution à une théorie de l'hypocrisie dans l'ordre politique.* The text could be published only in Canada. I found myself in the paradoxical situation of having to defend the very people whose behavior during the Occupation I had expressly disapproved against a sectarianism that shrank from nothing to fell its adversaries. Like Jean

Paulhan, I did not delay submitting my resignation from the Comité national des écrivains.

Meanwhile, Sartrean existentialism benefited from the favorable conditions provided by the climate of the Liberation and was flourishing everywhere. Paradoxically, I found myself quite involuntarily deriving some profit from this situation. At the International Congress of Philosophy held in Rome in 1946, I noted with surprise that in Italy, at least, I was considered the ranking leader of what was called "Christian existentialism." And Sartre himself, at about the same time, undertook a comprehensive and in fact inaccurate classification in his lecture "L'Existentialisme est-il un humanisme?" which was subsequently reproduced in innumerable handbooks of philosophy. According to him, he and Heidegger were the representatives of atheistic existentialism, whereas Jaspers and I were representatives of Christian existentialism. A collective volume was assigned to me in the Présence series, edited for Plon by Daniel Rops, and I was asked to agree to the title *Existentialisme chrétien*. I hesitated to give my consent to this proposal until I consulted my friend Louis Lavelle. Although understanding my objections perfectly well, he assured me that I could make this concession to the publisher without compromise. The book appeared in early 1947.

But I was to realize very quickly that my fears had been well founded and that the term *existentialism* engendered the most unfortunate associations of ideas in the mind of the average reader. I have often told a significant anecdote by way of illustration. I had given a lecture in Lille during which I had spoken, by way of criticism, of Sartrean existentialism. In the suburban train going back to Paris, one of the listeners congratulated me, but her companion cried: "Sir, what a horror, existentialism! I have a friend whose son is an existentialist; he lives in a kitchen with a Negro woman!" How many times have sophisticated ladies approached me to say, "But, sir, how can one be existentialist and Christian?" Even invoking the example of Kierkegaard—who can, after all, be regarded as the father of existentialism—was wasted effort. Hence from 1949 on, I passed up no opportunity to oppose the label "Christian existentialism." Eventually I realized that I was surely closer to Heidegger than Sartre was; during the first conversation I had with him in 1946, in Freiburg, the author of *Sein und Zeit* explicitly told me that he did not wish to be represented as an atheist.

Unfortunately, my protests proved futile; even quite recently, during some lectures I gave in Spain in November of 1968, I had to explain once more why I refuse to be classified as a Christian existentialist. In fact, I do not believe I have ever made use of the term *existentialism* in my writings; besides, I suspect that the idea of existentialism implies a contradiction, for I do not see how a philosophy of existence worthy of the name could be an "ism."*

The period immediately following the Second World War left very mixed recollections. On the one hand, there was the immense relief of being done with the nightmare of the Occupation; on the other hand, the spectacle of our dissensions and the reprehensible duplicity that spread among the victors were most painful. Yet it was during the summers of 1945 and 1946 that I was able to compose thirty-five-odd melodies that not only are an integral part of my work, but that convey in the most direct and immediate way what is essential in my work.

During a short visit to my friend Mme Georges Parain, who lived near Saint Etienne, I played one of those improvisations on the piano that until then only my wife had heard. My friend and her mother, both good musicians, insisted that these improvisations be noted down. In this matter I was to benefit from the fact that my wife, as I have said, had the technical knowledge of scales and harmony that I lacked. Under these circumstances I decided to undertake a project I had conceived of many years earlier without having followed through: I decided to set to music certain poems, particularly of Baudelaire's, that awakened in me an especially profound echo. My wife never had to harmonize the melodies born under my fingertips, since they came to me with their harmonic substructures, but she was of inestimable help in resolving the notation and the metrics, for although I heard the rhythm, I was not able to make its character explicit. When I summon up the long hours I spent at the piano with my wife, they seem to me an extraordinary dispensation given the two of us so shortly before her passing.

The terrible threat seemed to have withdrawn. We took a short trip to Holland in February 1947, which she enjoyed immensely. But a few weeks later, the relapse occurred that was to carry her off on the thirteenth of November, 1947. I will not expand on that time, but I feel at least the need to speak of her courage and her lucidity during those summer and autumn months of 1947. She harbored no illusions. Neither the doctor nor I needed to take recourse to lying encouragement, by which she would not have been deceived anyhow. Her faith was profound. She became a convert to the Roman Church, and the bulky *paroissien* ("prayer book") that

---

*The editor is inclined to think that the late Karl Jaspers would have agreed with this statement.—ED.

had accompanied her so long was always on her knees during the weeks in which, despite almost continuous and horrible pain, she was preparing herself to leave the earth.

I cannot say more; perhaps I have already said too much. Yet I must add that without her invisible assistance, I could not have assumed the burdens of the following years.

Since the summer of 1945, I had taken on the duties of drama critic for the *Nouvelles littéraires*. I exercised them for twenty-three years, with brief interruptions brought on by travels or, more rarely, by illness. I loved the craft of the drama critic, and I kept to the end that sort of zeal one needs to write decent criticism. I certainly made mistakes in my evaluations; indeed, all critics must recognize their fallibility. The general rule I gave myself—but which I was not always able to follow, for it is very difficult to apply—consisted in asking myself what the author intended and in comparing these intentions with the result.

I tried to remain equidistant from purely impressionistic criticism à la Jules Lemaître and dogmatic criticism à la Brunetière. No overall study has yet been devoted to this part of my work, which, materially speaking, is the most voluminous, and I have no way of knowing how it will be estimated in the future. That will depend largely on what becomes of the theater, and on this point, at least in the short run, I am not optimistic.

At present, I find myself freed from weekly criticism, which certainly constituted a burden for me. By a timely coincidence, fewer and fewer of the plays that follow one another on the Parisian stage elicit the type of reflection that alone can give criticism its significance and its range. The title of my last play, *Mon Temps n'est pas le vôtre* (written in 1953, immediately prior to the accident that was to have such a baneful effect on my life), aptly characterizes my present situation, one whose bruising quality it would be superfluous to specify.

Curiously, when I try to summon up the period of my life since my wife's death, it strikes me as somewhat becalmed. I say curiously because during this period, as I shall describe, I took numerous trips not only in Europe, but also in Morocco, Lebanon, Japan, and the two Americas. Moreover, it was during this period that my fame was established: translations of my writings multiplied, and various awards brought to my work a sort of consecration. It would be absolutely contrary to the truth to pretend that these successes were a matter of indifference to me. But I rejoiced in them above all to the extent that I was able to associate my family with them. My son accompanied me to Frankfurt in 1964, when I received the Peace Prize of the German publishers. My son and my daughter-in-law were with me when I gave the inaugural address at the Salzburg Festival in 1965.

I must not try to enumerate here the cycles of lectures I have given during these twenty years. I shall limit myself to some general indications in order to place experiences of definitely unequal importance in some sort of hierarchy.

I must certainly accord a special place to the Gifford Lectures that I was invited to give at Aberdeen in 1949–1950 and to the William James Lectures that I gave at Harvard during the last two months of 1961. They held the singular interest of forcing me to effect a work of synthesis that I probably never would have attempted had I not received the necessary impetus from the outside.

Perhaps the same is generally true of other lectures I have given, particularly in Germany and, since 1961, in the United States. I realize that these lectures have in a way taken the place of the *Journal métaphysique* as pursued during the Occupation years in our isolation at Corrèze. Perhaps it is futile to wonder whether it would have been better to be less in demand on the outside or whether a more retiring existence, by choice or by force, would have led me to push my personal inquiries much further. Although it is impossible to reply categorically to such a question, I think that, in fact, communion with others became increasingly important to me, and thus it became necessary for my thinking to find myself in the presence of as varied an audience as possible. I always tried to follow up presentations in large auditoria with discussions carried on in much smaller groups, so that personal contact could be established between the students and myself.

It goes without saying that I sometimes encountered linguistic difficulties, notably in Japan during the two trips I made to that country in 1957 and 1966. The passages I read from my text almost always alternated with a Japanese translation. I was certainly fortunate to find, in the persons of Messrs. Takeno, Jasui, and so on, men who possessed a near-perfect knowledge of the French language and who made signal contributions to the translation of my works into Japanese. But they were relatively exceptional cases. For the most part, I have never known precisely and for certain to what extent my thought was communicated to those immense audiences before whom I spoke in Tokyo, in Sendai, in Nagoya, in Kyoto, and so on.

I also encountered linguistic difficulties during my lectures in Spain in November 1968, and I must pay tribute to the zeal with which Mlle Marie

Aline de la Forest Divonne, who accompanied me during this tour, succeeded in explaining to bewildered reporters the meaning of discourses they had listened to while scarcely understanding a word.

I want particularly to note that many of these trips were opportunities to see towns and landscapes that I shall never forget. Perhaps I have not yet sufficiently stressed the impassioned liking I have always had for journeys—the zeal for discovery that has been one of the moving springs of my life. It would be fastidious to enumerate all the places I have seen, during these past twenty years, that have brought me to feel an admiration I experience each time as an inner renewal. I shall limit myself to citing a few such places that retain for me a special significance.

I think first of Lebanon in November and December of 1948, when I was a member of the French delegation to the General Conference of UNESCO. If, on the one hand, I was exasperated by the bureaucratic Anglo-Saxon spirit that tended to sterilize the conference, on the other hand, I fell in love with that country, one of the most beautiful and enchanting anywhere. And how deep my emotion on noting how much the Lebanese elite remained saturated with French culture! My visits to Baalbek, to Damascus, and to the Valley of the Cedars left a never-fading memory.

I would say about as much for the two trips to Morocco in 1951 and 1963. Here I think above all of the revelation of an unknown world yielded by a visit to Marrakesh and, perhaps even more, by a visit to Fez in the company of an exceptionally enlightened man, Doctor Fauque, the author of the fascinating play *La Tribu,* which I was later to support on a committee as a first work deserving recognition.

No less enriching was the cycle of conferences in Latin America in 1951 on the occasion of the International Congress of Philosophy in Lima, to which I had been invited along with Gaston Berger, who was an excellent traveling companion. After brief stops in Venezuela and Colombia, I spent a fortnight in Peru and had the pleasure of visiting Cuzco and the marvelous Machu Picchu, the ancient Inca city. The extraordinary journey the length of the Urubanba Valley, between the snowy peaks of the Cordillera, and the climb to the ruins, from which one overlooks one of the most grandiose mountain corries I have ever seen, remain indelibly imprinted on my memory. On the human plane, Chile made the most favorable impression on me, if only because I sensed that the redoubtable racial problem, which I had felt acutely in Peru, really did not arise in that country. After a stay in Buenos Aires, where I enjoyed the hospitality of an old friend, now gone, and two days in Uruguay, I arrived in Brazil, where I was to have the pleasure of finding my very dear friend Robert Garric, who was entirely at home in Rio after numerous trips there. It is with pleasure that I summon to mind the memory of that man of high quality, that fine Christian fashioned after the example of Ozanam, creator of the "Equipes sociales," whose life was to end as delegate-general to the Cité universitaire and whose radiance subsists in every country where his warm and inspired words were heard.

The two trips to Japan, in 1957 and 1966, also constituted major events for me. I had been invited by Professor Kojima, who had suggested the idea to me a year earlier and who now introduced me to his country in the most attentive and solicitous manner imaginable. No one will be surprised if I say that Tokyo, where on two occasions I had to spend much too much time for my liking, was at first very disappointing. Even though I finally found some things on which to peg my imagination, that immense and shapeless city, where modern technology tends bit by bit to dissolve everything from the past, seemed oppressive to me. By contrast, I was enchanted by Kyoto, and I can say the same of scenery that figures among the most beautiful I have been permitted to see.

It would be impossible to render sufficient tribute to the delicacy and generosity shown me by my Japanese friends. Yet I would not dare say that I really made contact with the Japanese soul. In order to do so, I would have had to stay there for years and to master the language.

It was in 1959 that I went to the United States for the first time, under rather unusual conditions: I was invited by my Moral Rearmament friends to attend the conference at Mackinac. Here I must say a few words about my relations to Moral Rearmament.

Between the two wars, I had made contact with the Oxford Groups, and for several months we held gatherings at my home during which these or those gave testimonials, followed by a few moments of "silence," which constituted the best of the techniques used by the groups. I thus made contact with men and women of great good will, such as Baron and Baroness de Watteville, Pastor Grosjean, and others. Unfortunately, my wife and I soon realized that it all ran the risk of being falsified by a sort of mechanical pietism. This danger was revealed in a dismaying way during a house party we attended the following summer at Trois Epis, in Alsace. A lady from Colmar, who, one felt, needed terribly to testify publicly to an inner experience she found difficult to put into words and who was expressing herself in a hesitant, stumbling fashion out of the most laudable regard for honesty, was brutally called to order by an American harpy who cried out: "Faster, faster! Testimonials should follow one another like machine-gun bursts!" Shocked and horrified, I decided that very evening to break off all relations with the Oxford Groups while preserving my friendship for such-and-such a person, who was not responsible for this ignoble outburst. I was to see the de Wattevilles again in Toulouse during the Occupation and to admire the strength of soul with which they withstood the most cruel ordeals.

After the war, Moral Rearmament having by then been organized, two or three young people sought me out to give me an account of their activities. I agreed to go to Caux, and there, while keenly regretting the Salvationist aspect of the general sessions, I was led to note with admiration their effective work at the level of individuals and the manner in which, here and there, in circumstances that were often paradoxical, fraternal bonds were created where a spirit of division and hatred had prevailed for so long. Thus it came about that I suggested putting together a book made up almost exclusively of authentic and diverse testimonials. I hoped this would help to give an idea of the movement, which was too often mistakenly judged from the outside and not credited with all that was valuable in it. I added that I would be willing to write an introduction in which I would define my own position. My proposal was accepted, and we went to work immediately. I obtained the consent of the Plon publishing house without any difficulty. When I spoke about our project to my friend Countess de la Forest Divonne, who had attended one of the Oxford Groups' sessions at my home, she quoted a phrase of Henri Gouhier's: "There is nothing greater in history than a change of hope"—hence the idea of titling the collection *Un Changement d'espérance*. This work was to meet with great success and was translated into the principal languages.

Thus it was that I made the trip to Mackinac, Michigan. I found the fine scenery on Lake Huron more in accord with the essence of the movement than the setting (much more familiar to me, but also much more "postcard") of the atrocious palace at Caux. I must add that several years later, in 1966, I was cordially received at the House of Moral Rearmament in Odawara, Japan. Whatever reservations I may have regarding this or that point—particularly regarding the quality, too often mediocre, of the plays or films presented—I must also emphasize the immense and admirable good will that spreads in so many countries and in such differing contexts under the impact of Moral Rearmament.

While in Mackinac, I wrote William Ernest Hocking that I might be able to spend the few days before my return to France at his residence in New Hampshire. He replied by telegram that he and his daughter-in-law would meet me at the Boston airport. His great work *The Meaning of God in Human Experience,* which appeared in 1913 and to which Jean Wahl introduced me, had been a sort of revelation for me; so much so that in 1927 I dedicated my *Journal métaphysique* jointly to Hocking and Bergson. Immediately after the war, I translated an article by Hocking on

"Method in Religious Philosophy" for the *Revue de métaphysique et de morale*. We exchanged some letters on that occasion. He came to France once or twice, but chance had it that we could not meet. Much later, after the Second World War, I encountered an excellent article he had published in an important American philosophical journal that showed how close we were to each other. It was with great emotion, therefore, that I made contact with this admirable thinker, who was at the same time a man of feeling and of great courage. The day we passed together at his retreat in Madison, New Hampshire, remains one of the most memorable of my existence. It was as if we were seeing each other again and, at the same time, as if we had never been apart. This experience was to be very happily renewed during my visit to Harvard in 1961. Hocking remains for me an unsurpassed example of what a philosopher can be, in the fullest sense of the word, in a topsy-turvy world like ours.

Two years after my trip to Mackinac, I was invited to give the William James Lectures at Harvard University. I was quartered in two rooms with windows looking out on the campus. There was perfect calm; it was fall; and I rejoiced at the sight of squirrels darting among the autumn leaves. I remained there the first days of each week to give a lecture and a seminar and then departed regularly for a different destination—now for Maine, now for Pennsylvania, now for San Francisco. It was my first true contact with the United States. Two or three friends contributed in large measure to the agreeableness of my stay. I think above all of Henry Bugbee, whom I had met several years earlier and who had come to join me at Cérizy-la-Salle in 1955 for a meeting with Heidegger during the latter's first visit to France. Ever strengthening bonds of friendship were to grow between us. I wrote an introduction for his very beautiful book *The Inward Morning*. We saw each other often while he and his wife were living near Paris. He took me from Harvard to a state college where he was then professor; I gave a lecture, and then he took me to Philadelphia after a stopover, at Hocking's insistence, to see Pearl Buck. He was subsequently to welcome me on two occasions at Missoula, Montana, where he showed me the impressive mountain landscapes that lend an irresistible attraction to that part of the United States. In 1966, he was to be so excessively good as to accompany me to Washington and Oregon, where I gave some lectures before going for the second time to San Francisco, from which I departed for Japan after a short stop in Hawaii. This little trip in the company of a man of quality left an indelible memory. My gratitude extends not only to him, but also to his wife, Daphne Bugbee, who had been so very kind as to accompany me the preceding year on an exhausting two-week tour from Minnesota to Louisiana, Georgia, and North Carolina.

Another American friend to whom I would like to express my gratitude is Hubert Dreyfus, then a professor at MIT, who welcomed me on my arrival at Harvard, when I was feeling a little disconcerted and lost; his vigorous and resourceful friendship helped me to acclimatize myself to a world entirely new to me.

During these American travels I had opportunities to meet many men whom I was able to appreciate not only for their high intellect, but also for something even more important in my eyes; their nobility, their kindness, and their spirit of hospitality, of which I have scarcely found the equivalent in my own country. These experiences warrant my saying that the best American is perhaps superior to the European of the same social milieu.

This feeling was confirmed during the cycles of lectures I subsequently gave in the United States, the details of which I think I may dispense with. Thus in 1963, 1965, and 1966, I had the opportunity of visiting most of the major American universities, and I always enjoyed a hospitality that left the best of memories. Moreover, I was occasionally able to give some seminars during which it was possible to have a direct and nourishing contact with students.

This is the place to note how much of nature has been preserved in that country. It is difficult to console myself for not having been able to traverse more than a small fraction of the great national parks. Indeed, the love of nature has remained invariant from one end of my existence to the other. I am sometimes astonished to see how, despite the weight and subjections of age, I have remained at bottom insatiable in curiosity and filled with an unquenchable desire to discover and explore.

Unfortunately, during my travels I have often suffered from being the prisoner of a very strict itinerary, which was arranged without prior consultation with me and to which I had to conform day after day. Thus I was often unable to take advantage of opportunities offered by this or that encounter because I could not loosen the vise in which I was caught. As I write these lines, I think, for example, of the doctor I met in Lima in 1951 at the International Congress of Philosophy. He offered to take me for several days into the Upper Amazon territory, where he had spent two years tending the Indians and where he had a little place that he visited regularly. How much such an excursion into an unknown world would have meant to me! But I could not think of it, because I was expected in Santiago, Chile, where I had to continue my South American tour.

My charitable friends would doubtless have me note here that my life has all the same been that of an explorer, since it has been largely devoted to a work of detection within the invisible world. But for that to have been more than a consolation prize, I would have had to be able to pursue much further—notably and principally in the metaphysical domain—the experiment initiated during the First World War. I also would have had to possess qualities of observation and experimentation that in fact I have never had. If I have demonstrated to some extent the behavior of an explorer on the philosophic plane, this has been at the level of reflection, not of experiment. As for dramatic creation (so intimately linked to philosophic reflection), its spring seems to have consisted in a faculty whose nature I have never been able to define exactly, but which is more like intuition or divination than like the capacity of an experimenter or a scientist.

This leads me to say at least a few words about my theatrical activity since 1947. First of all, in the course of the few days preceding my departure for Beirut in the fall of 1948, I found myself completing two plays for which I had already written the first acts without having been able to finish them: *L'Emissaire* and *Le Signe de la Croix,* which were to appear a little later under the single title: *Vers un autre royaume.*[2] I thought at the time that those would be my *ultima verba* in the theatrical domain. I was mistaken.

The Centre dramatique de l'est having performed with great success *Un Homme de Dieu,* which I had written a quarter of a century earlier, the play was presented in June 1949 at the Théâtre Montparnasse and extended to the Théâtre de l'Oeuvre, where it was billed for several months. Jacques Herbetot asked me to give him a play for his theater. Thus I was led to write *Rome n'est plus dans Rome.* This is one of the rare instances in which I discern the exact origin of a theatrical creation. During the summer of 1950, I received an anonymous as well as libelous letter: "The Russians are coming, you are on their lists, look out." I never discovered the origin of this message, which was no doubt simply the work of an ill-wisher. And although an invasion of Western Europe by the Russians seemed a possibility at the time, I did not for one second contemplate leaving France. Yet I could envisage someone different from myself making the decision to leave, and it is possible that the case of Etienne Gilson, a professor at the Collège de France who decided a little later to exile himself voluntarily in Toronto, may have brought about that crystallization that led to the writing of my play. (Although the last part of the play takes place in Brazil, I actually wrote it before the trip I made to that country.) Exceedingly well acted, the play achieved a certain success and was later presented on tour all over France.

At about the same time, the success in Münster of *Un Homme de Dieu* caused several of my plays to be performed in Germany. I must recognize, however, that in a country where my philosophical work has been translated in its entirety, the absolutely intimate and essential relation between that work and my dramatic work has never really been understood. The proof is that the publishing house of Glock and Lutz in Nürnberg, which courageously undertook to publish my selected plays, has not yet managed to publish volume 3, the first two volumes having had insufficient sales.

An analogous remark applies to the United States, where a certain number of my books have even appeared in paperback but where it has not yet been decided to publish my plays in translation, with the exception of three that had previously appeared with Secker in England and that then reappeared in paperback in the United States a few years ago: *Un Homme de Dieu* (*A Man of God*), *La Chapelle ardente* (*The Funeral Pyre*), and *Le Chemin de crête* (*Ariadne*).

Nevertheless, in my Harvard lectures in 1961, I attempted to illuminate as clearly as possible the connection between theater and philosophy, which I consider not only a characteristic of my undertaking, but also the source of its value and its uniqueness. Until recently, the belief persisted that theater was only a second-fiddle form. We see here how bias can prevail over genuine judgment.

Having met Madeleine Ozeray, one of Giraudoux's best actresses, I succeeded against all expectation in getting her to accept the role of Ariadne (Ariane) Leprieur, the heroine of *Chemin de crête,* at the Théâtre du Parc in Brussels. This is without a doubt one of my most significant plays. Intelligently staged, it gained a certain success in Brussels. Unfortunately, this was not the case when it was presented in Paris in 1953 at the Vieux Colombier.

Bedridden after a serious automobile accident in Corrèze in August of 1953, I was unable to attend the rehearsals. I had to be carried on a stretcher to see the last rehearsal before the critics' preview, and I had to admit that this time some serious mistakes in the production threatened to render the play incomprehensible. I have a horrible memory of the occasion and of the atmosphere of chuckling hostility in which it unfolded. To be sure, some understood and appreciated it. The critic of *Le Monde,* Robert Kemp, devoted a long, comprehensive, and enthusiastic article to the play. By contrast, the *Figaro* critic, whose influence at that time was decisive, helped to kill the play, which remained on the boards only a month.

Without exaggeration, one could say that I never recovered from that failure. It must also be admitted that the year of 1953 was catastrophic for me in all respects, because of the physical consequences of the accident alluded to above. Until then I had been an indefatigable walker. Now, as a result of the arthritis contracted since the accident, walking became more and more difficult for me, more and more painful. In the past, the most creative ideas had come to me more often than not while I was walking; thus, in a sense, the collision that threw me unconscious from the car had a direct effect on my creative faculties. I do not believe it coincidental that the play I had finished just before the accident was in fact the last I have written: *Mon Temps n'est pas le vôtre*. This work, which was recently broadcast on the radio by French actors, appears to me today as the conclusion of my dramatic writing. Those who heard it again on January 26, 1969, were unanimous, I believe, in recognizing a prophetic significance, for the state of affairs the play expresses has become much more evident since the disturbances of spring 1968 than it was when I wrote the play in 1953.

I note for the record that between *Rome n'est plus dans Rome* and *Mon Temps n'est pas le vôtre*, I wrote, besides the radio play *La Fin des temps*, two important plays: *Croissez et multipliez* and *La Dimension Florestan*. The latter was in some sense thought out in German, and the best title is the one given to the German translation, *Die Wacht am Sein*. The thinker in question is none other than Heidegger, and he is intended essentially for his language and for certain of his attitudes. But when the play was given a reading performance at Oberhausen in the Ruhr in April 1957, I was careful, on the following day, to devote a lecture to the relation between Heidegger and myself on the philosophic plane, a lecture in which I expressed the admiration I felt, despite our differences, for the author of *Sein und Zeit*. The director of the Oberhausen theater was imprudent enough to send the German text of my play to Heidegger. Several months later I was told that he had laughed; but still later I was to learn that he felt in fact rather resentful. It is interesting to note that, up to now, no German theater has dared to present the play in a regular performance. Only a little theater in Innsbruck had the courage to do so, in 1967.

Written in 1952, *Croissez et multipliez*, without being in any way a thesis play, treats the Christian attitude toward birth control within marriage—a problem that experience has shown was at that time, and has continued to be, even more burning than I had imagined. The play was performed only in Vienna, under another title and in a small theater whose name I have forgotten. I am afraid that the production was quite mediocre. In France it has never even been performed on the radio, the authorities fearing repercussions.

Indeed, Cardinal Feltin, archbishop of Paris, was charged by the Holy Office to write me a letter to inform me that the work had painfully surprised him and that I was under request not to have it performed or republished. I deferred as a matter of form, without expressing anything resembling contrition. In fact, I felt that my promise in no way fettered me, since the terms of the letter showed that the Holy Office had understood nothing of the play. Fortunately, the tide has turned since 1955, and today I feel perfectly free to do as I wish with this play, which my Catholic friends see as one of my best achievements.

Why not observe, at this point, that I had other skirmishes too, I will not say with Protestants, but with certain liberal Protestants, regarding *Un Homme de Dieu;* with more or less fanatic Jews, regarding *Le Signe de la Croix;* and with rigidly orthodox Catholics, for whom the Holy Office made itself the spokesman, regarding *Croissez et multipliez?* I would like to be able to resist the temptation to take pride in this. But in any case I must observe that to stigmatize these works is to attack a disposition central to my being and at the heart of my writings, or at least of all those in which I can truly recognize myself.

Although I wrote no more plays after 1953, it should not be supposed that the need for dramatic creation had left me. Nothing could be more inaccurate. Those who will be authorized, after my demise, to go through the notebooks that fill my drawers will find that I have often written part of a scene and sometimes even more. What I have lacked has been the capacity to organize and to construct, without which there cannot be a dramatic work worthy of the name. In so speaking I firmly oppose the increasingly widespread tendency today to reject everything in drama that may align itself with architecture. After far more than twenty years of drama criticism, I still hold to the conviction that those playwrights who lack this architectural vision cannot claim the title they dare to assume.

I would transgress the framework of this autobiography if I tried to elaborate on the deeper reasons that dictate this belief. But I could not dispense with stating it or with indicating why in recent years I have felt a ravine opening between myself and avant-garde authors. Yes, it is certain that in the theater I feel myself more and more alone and, like most authors of my generation, more and more rejected. The most recent theatrical efforts seem to me to proceed either from a political sectarianism that repels me or from an experimental concern that I admit may perhaps lead to interesting works, but that in itself has nothing in common with the dramatic faculty, properly speaking.

I have referred to my solitude, but here a distinction is needed. It would be not only unjust but quite untrue to deny that every week, if not every day, brings testimony of an almost fervent interest on the part of people dispersed in the four corners of France, in Europe, or in the United States of whose existence I knew nothing before receiving their letters. It is not an audience as generally conceived: an audience that can be counted and that thus lends itself to statistics. I remember laughing once over a letter from a professor at the University of Arizona, who asked on behalf of his students how many existentialists there were in France. I replied that unfortunately there was no tax on existentialists, and therefore his question admitted of no answer. (I refrained, I should add, from sending that letter.)

But when I reflect on it, I believe it is in consonance—let us not say with my destiny, but with the very essence of my work—that my work be called upon to awaken here and there some solitary and anxious spirits, rather than to excite among spectators crowded into theaters who knows what transient and indistinct surge of feeling.

I would be lying, however, if I did not admit that these lines are not completely convincing. I shall always feel some bitter regret at not having seen my plays—with only one or two exceptions—performed by great actors who could have incarnated the protagonists worthily, and I shall never quite know why this joy has been denied me. I try to console myself by thinking that too great a success in the theater would perhaps have damaged a certain integrity, had I become its captive.

The chief question I have to ask myself, when my inner gaze looks at the last twenty years, is the one Arnaud Chartrain asks his mother-in-law, Evelyne, in *Les Coeurs avides:* "What are you living on?" Yes, I have to ask myself what I am living on, and my reply would not be Evelyne's when she says, "I am like the rest, I live only provided I do not ask." As I have said, that which has sustained me has almost certainly been an invisible support, but it has also and conjointly been the constant and often anxious thought of my family and of my son's family, which today numbers six children: three girls and three boys, who are from five to twenty-four years of age. The eldest are two daughters, one of whom has a degree in psychology, is a psychiatric assistant in a Paris hospital, and is already married; the other, after exceptionally brilliant and rapid studies, was received in her first attempt as *agrégée* in philosophy and now teaches at the Lycée de Havre. The other elder sibling is currently doing his military service and does not yet know which direction he will take; the younger three are still children. My son, after having distinguished himself as a photographer, turned to cinema and has made an excellent film for television—semidocumentary, semidramatic—about the Corrèze that we love so well and that has become for us like an adopted country. He has just completed another film, on the fishermen of Brittany, which will shortly appear on television. Very much musically inclined, he has also become an outstanding specialist in high fidelity and is codirector of the *Revue du son.*

But beyond this narrow circle are vaster, concentric ones of many relatives, nephews, nieces, cousins, and intimate friends who are in no sense apart from me. In my philosophical work I have often noted the essential value of certain prepositions—in particular *with* [*avec*] and *at* [*auprès de*]—that affective proximity so marvelously expressed by the great English novelists more than by ours and in general so little attended to by philosophers to this day.*

Need I say that the musician in me and the intimate self are one and the same person? If Schumann and Brahms, among so many others, are an integral part of myself, it is to the exact degree that interpersonal relations hold a privileged place in my life. In Schumann, moreover, I have the feeling of rejoining my father, who had, as I believe I have said, a marked predilection for him. I remember accompanying my father at the piano while he sang the poet's love songs, and I realize today, after all the intervening years, that what flowed through his singing was the indelible memory of the short years of happiness he had experienced with my mother.

I would not want to give the impression, however, that during all these years I have enclosed myself in the restrictive sphere of private life. I have not ceased to follow in anguish the events that have succeeded one another so vertiginously in Europe and elsewhere since the end of the Second World War. I recall having foreseen, at the beginning of 1958, the return to power of de Gaulle. At the time, it seemed to be desirable. Subsequently, I have come to hold serious reservations regarding the style of the regime, regarding the conditions—disastrous, in my opinion—under which the Algerian war was concluded, regarding the attitude assumed by our government at the time of the Six-Day War, and, more recently, regarding the embargo [on the sale of arms to Israel] determined in circumstances that could only scandalize a democrat. I also deeply regret that the course initially pursued by our statesman Robert Schumann was not followed and that at the moment I write these lines, the creation of a united Europe really worthy of the name still appears remote.

I have sometimes been reproached for having made hardly any place for politics in my writings, and I freely admit the lacuna. But having always been severe with professors of philosophy who embroiled themselves in politics without the necessary competence, I decided that I must surely guard myself against errors that I criticized in others. I have always been aware of my ignorance in economic and financial matters, and I regret not having the historical learning that seems to me indispensable. In the broad-

---

*Marcel felt that these prepositions could not be translated satisfactorily or even understood very well apart from his context.—TRANS.

est of terms, I will say that I consider myself a liberal who has become more and more painfully aware of the limits of liberalism but who at the same time has remained convinced of the absolutely maleficent character of totalitarian regimes of any sort. Hence the sympathy and admiration with which I followed the heroic effort of the Czechoslovakians to disengage themselves from Stalinism and its sequels.

I cannot conclude this autobiography without at least alluding to the troubles for which the French universities (like the universities of many other countries) have been the stage since the deplorable events of the spring of 1968. One cannot yet pronounce with certainty either on the ultimate causes or on the scope of these disturbances, but their seriousness cannot be denied. Doubtless the most alarming thing is the incredible deficiency manifested by a very large number of teachers, some of whom literally prostrated themselves before the rioters while others shut themselves up in a contempt that was inevitably inefficacious.

I have neglected to say that for more than thirty years, I have regularly received students in my home in the hope of establishing personal, living contacts with them. In June of 1968, two such students told me very simply that society, being entirely damnable, must first be destroyed, without their knowing just what should be erected in its place. They demonstrated a state of mind that is unfortunately widespread today and that can only be characterized as infantile. Those who thus express themselves are almost always sons of the middle class, and future historians will have to search out carefully how a social class that had resisted so many ordeals collapsed in just a few years.

For my part, I have never experienced anything resembling shame for belonging to the middle class, and this is one of the numerous points on which I am in opposition to Jean-Paul Sartre. Yet I have regretted never being able to make greater contact with the workers' world, for example. This limitation has injured and in a certain way humiliated me. I had a little more rapport with rural people, especially in Corrèze during the war, but I must admit that the contact remained quite superficial. My son has doubtless penetrated much further into their minds, for the films he shot in Corrèze involved local people, not professionals.

Yes, when I consider my life, I am saddened to think of all that has been too much constricted in my experience of people. To be sure, there have been the travels, the thousands of listeners before whom I have spoken, and the innumerable conversations that followed my lectures in so many countries. But they always unfolded on a well-defined plane, too intellectual for my liking. I can say in all sincerity that something in me has always aspired to break that overly limited framework in order to immerse myself in the lives of others. This aspiration constitutes one of the mainsprings of my work.

Since 1952, I have been a member of the Académie des sciences morales et politiques, and I am happy to belong to this body, which has known so many illustrious men. I have been among those who frequently and even recently have tried to aerate the academy, to open as many windows as possible on major problems in their most tragic and pressing forms. I persist in believing—and I said so specifically regarding the embargo on the supply of arms to Israel—that in grave circumstances the Académie des sciences morales et politiques is qualified to formulate views and to take a stand in the arena of public opinion, since it unites in its embrace jurists, economists, historians, and philosophers.

In the lecture I gave in Frankfurt in September 1964, when I was awarded the Peace Prize, I said that the role of a philosopher today was to be a watchman.* This is my profound belief. This role, which the alarming progression of technology renders more and more necessary, is also more and more contested. The Nietzschean idea of the tragic thinker will thus be confirmed, although in a very different sense from what the author of *The Dawn* conceived. At the close of this autobiographical sketch, I have to acknowledge that in this role I have acquitted myself most imperfectly. To be sure, I filled my work with warnings and cautions, for I have never lost sight of the anguished predicament of our world today. And never since the terrible days of 1914–1918 have I ceased to feel, I can say *in my flesh,* the unutterable ordeal that our moral condition imposes on those who love—that is to say, on the only ones who count. In that sense, I believe I can say that my thought has been a committed thinking—not for the benefit of any party or ideology, but for *my fellow beings*.

I have abstained in these pages from relating directly what Christianity has meant to me. This abstention stems from a keen awareness of my own insufficiency, let us even say my unworthiness, as a Christian. In addition, a certitude antedating my conversion has continued intact in me: the testimony of the Christian, where it has occurred in its purity and its integrity, remains the only one to which an epithet can be attributed that everywhere else defies application, that of *absolute*.

By comparison to the unflinching and radiant witness of the saints or of those who, like Robert Garric, approached sainthood, how weak, quivering—in a word, infirm—mine appears: mine a second-order testimony by a reflection rooted in authentic witness. Never have I lost sight of the

---

*The late Albert Schweitzer also insisted on this role for the philosopher, but his strictures fell on as generally deaf ears as did Marcel's.—ED.

gap between what I was in fact and what I should have been in order to have the full right to formulate my thoughts. If others have been reached and sometimes changed through me in spite of this flagrant insufficiency, it is a sign of grace that can be discerned only in absolute humility.

I trace these lines, which will perhaps have the value of a testament, at a time when the susceptibilities of age make themselves increasingly felt. Reading and walking have become ordeals for me, and it is in music that I find my surest recourse against desolation.

Circumstances have made it possible for my sister-in-law, Geneviève, the sole survivor among the children of Alfred Boegner, to come and live with me. And I scarcely know what would have become of me without this fragile woman, whose life has not been spared trials of every sort, but who has been able to preserve through it all an unalterable freshness of spirit. May we together leave this world, which becomes more foreign to us every day and over which violence and mendacity seem to exercise a more and more unchallenged dominion!

Indeed, there are madmen today, even among priests, who exhort us to turn our gaze from the past and look exclusively toward the future. But what we call by that name consists only of phantasms born of desire or of the labored fruit of purely technical projections based on a misunderstanding of real human beings, their misery, and their aspirations. For it is only by meditating on this scorned past that we can prepare ourselves for that life beyond this world whose magnetic pull, too often unsuspected, alone can make beings, persons, of us—souls.

GABRIEL MARCEL

L'INSTITUT DE FRANCE
SPRING 1969

POSTCRIPT

I feel that I cannot omit adding a postscript to this autobiography, whose inevitably incomplete character I fully recognize. The brief trip I made to Dresden and Prague in the last days of April [1969] affected me far too deeply for me not to recall it briefly here.

In reality, the trip took on the nature of a pilgrimage, for in the spring of 1965 (if I am not mistaken), I received a letter postmarked "Dresden" that touched me deeply. A Catholic priest, the Reverend Siegfried Fölz, had written to say that he was making every effort to have excerpts from my work published in East Germany so that readers there could form some idea of my thought. He wrote that he had been quickened by my work and that such a publication would express the gratitude he felt toward me. He did not conceal the difficulties implicit in the considerable censorship to which a collection of this sort would inevitably be subjected. I replied by return mail to thank him and to tell him that I was stunned when I first learned of the bombardment that had turned Dresden into a martyr-city. I was especially moved by the fact that this precious testimonial had come to me precisely from Dresden.

Thus began an exchange of letters between us. Several months later I learned that the obstacles had been overcome and that the book would be published by the St. Benno Press in Leipzig.

The following year the two volumes arrived, very handsomely conceived, in which Siegfried Fölz had brought together some particularly significant portions of the *Journal métaphysique* and several other essays, the whole preceded by a remarkable introduction revealing how deeply my correspondent had penetrated my thought.

I wrote him soon after to thank him and to tell him how much I would like to express my gratitude in person at Pirna, where he had just moved, only a few kilometers from Dresden. I did not delude myself about the difficulties I would have to overcome, all the more since travel has become very arduous for me in these last few years. But then I had the good fortune to find the assistance I needed in two young Americans, Stephen Jolin and Peter McCormick, both Fulbright scholars. These two young men, whose true good will I can scarcely praise sufficiently, declared themselves ready to drive me to Pirna as soon as they learned of my wish; they would relieve each other at the wheel in order not to become over-tired.

We left after breakfast on the twenty-third of April and spent that night near the château of Haut-Bar, above Saverne. We went on, by way of Stuttgart and Würzburg, to Bamberg. I wanted to see this wonderful city again, one of the few left intact in Germany by the war. Unfortunately, the weather was bad, and repairs prevented us from visiting the interior of the cathedral as I would have liked. We crossed the frontier between the two Germanys near Bad Steben. It was a most painful sight. The soldiers who endlessly inspected our papers wore Russian uniforms. We had to wait more than two hours, with no idea of what was happening and with the impression that they might finally turn us back. But this did not happen, and we arrived in Dresden that evening. As I had suspected, the sight of this city devastated by the war was heartrending. With no map, we had the greatest difficulty finding the hotel where our rooms had been reserved.

M. Fölz had already telephoned twice and appeared a few minutes after our arrival. I had at once the feeling that the pilgrimage was a success. The very way in which he thanked me for having made the effort to come to him was enough to show me that he was exactly as I had imagined him.

It was with him that we visited the Hofkirche in Dresden—one of the most beautiful museums in Europe—in the company of M. Loeffler, inspector of monuments, and Frau Hütte, who had supervised the restoration of the church. We were happy to see that Zeinger's fine architectural ensemble had been perfectly restored. The weather was lovely, and children were playing in the French garden, but all around was destruction. The Frauenkirche, for example, was nothing but a mass of debris preserved as a testimony to the crime of the 1945 bombing. That afternoon we reached Pirna, and I was able to talk intimately and at length with him on whose behalf I had undertaken the journey and in whom I see today a sort of spiritual son. One could not easily imagine my emotion, the following morning, when he celebrated mass for us and I received communion from his hands. In the very heart of destruction, it was the indestructible irresistibly affirming itself.

He accompanied us to the Czechoslovakian frontier, which we crossed at Zinnwald in the afternoon. I felt a wrenching within me as I pressed for the last time the hand of him who had become as close to me as the closest, for I could scarcely hope to see him again in this world. But he promised that if he were some day to leave East Germany, it would be to come see me in Paris.

After the desolate scene of Dresden, Prague at first gave the superficial impression of a city not only intact, but extraordinarily animated and almost joyful. Conversations that I had with Czechoslovakians and with Frenchmen brought things into focus, as indeed was my desire. Beneath the appearances, I glimpsed the reality. I was able to give a lecture on "My Philosophical Itinerary" in German at the Philosophy Faculty. It was very warmly received, but I had no way of knowing, as I would have liked, what echo it found among the students who heard me. Since then, unfortunately, the situation has not ceased to worsen. Freedom of thought now appears stifled in that country—for how long?

On the way back we stopped at Rothenburg ob der Tauber, which I had never seen and which, thanks be to God, has remained intact: this little town is a jewel. In the main church, of the purest Gothic style, I had the moving experience of hearing an organist play one of the Bach Preludes that my wife particularly loved and that she had played for me several times. I saw this as a seal providentially placed on an experience that constituted one of the supreme summits of my life. I cannot say more, and

I can scarcely hope that the reader will understand why I felt I had to recall this pilgrimage to Dresden; something in me could almost wish that it had been given to me not to live past it.

G.M.

NOTES

1. In prose translation: "Flower plucked in the garden of dreams, / By fingers trembling with love, / Gone are your form so briefly here / And your smile of before. / Where is its subtle essence exhaled, / In what lily is it incarnated on the pure heights? / Shall we ever breathe its fragrance / On the lofty slope? / If only your wake at least traced / The way toward the hidden Eden / . . . but our eyes, alas, will close / In doubt before they are dry."—TRANS.

2. *Le Signe de la Croix* was republished in 1960 with an epilogue, written in 1951, that it did not originally possess. *L'Emissaire* stands with *Le Dard* and *La Fin des temps* in the volume entitled *Le Secret est dans les îles,* published in 1967.

PART TWO

DESCRIPTIVE
AND CRITICAL ESSAYS
ON THE PHILOSOPHY
OF GABRIEL MARCEL,
WITH REPLIES

1

E. M. Cioran

GABRIEL MARCEL:
NOTES FOR A CHARACTER SKETCH

GABRIEL Marcel's most singular good fortune was never to have been a college professor, never to have been obliged to think on a schedule. Professorship can be the philosopher's tomb, the death of any living thought. Essentials should not be institutionalized: the university rings the knell of the mind. Philosophy should be taught in the agora, in the park, or at home. This was indeed the manner in which Marcel chose to work, because it suited his temperament and his high esteem for spontaneous, unpredictable discussion. For a great many years he invited young people into his home and conversed with them quite freely on any topic whatsoever. Even subjects that on the surface may seem utterly banal were liable to engender an exchange of views. He made a point of getting as many people as possible to participate in the conversation, and what he attempted to do, on each occasion, was to meet the mind of the person speaking. Most often, he was the one who initiated a topic on which he expounded briefly, espousing a certain point of view or assuming at least some attitude toward the issue. At once he would solicit a response. He challenged others to contradict him. In fact, he invited contradiction not only in matters of philosophy, but in all matters. I will go so far as to say that opposition was his daily bread; he could not do without it; he needed it to survive, to function. The author of the *Journal métaphysique,* a work where monologue is indispensable, in real life was addicted to dialogue and was an enemy, therefore, of any haughty, solemn, imperious thought seeking to impose itself or to dominate. He was the exact opposite of a professor: he did not decree; he surrendered to the surprises of his own thought and in

Translated from the French by Maurice A. O'Meara.

that very surrender respected all similar thoughts originating in the person with whom he was conversing. To be a professor is to cloak oneself in rigidity and narrowness, to assume a kind of superior attitude for which Marcel fortunately had no gift. Restraining oneself, keeping constant watch over oneself, was behavior repugnant to him; he preferred to explode and managed to do so effortlessly. Indignation was his natural state of mind, his personal reaction to the injustice inherent in human existence. Diametrically opposed to Stoic thought and indeed to all types of set or established invulnerability, he could be quite fearsome when exasperated by stupidity or arrogance. I shall never forget the time he broke into an argument that took place at an overflowing, elite Parisian party. The discussion concerned a charitable organization that, although claiming to be Christian, deviated somewhat from orthodoxy. A priest who was present was asked to comment. He did so, but in a way that was quite unpleasant and almost nagging, warning all the Catholics present against any involvement with a movement smacking of heresy. He did not even see fit to take into account the charitable works that those who favored the movement in question deemed to be of prime importance. Marcel answered the priest's remarks immediately with an uncommonly violent yet clear rejoinder that utterly devastated the poor priest, who suddenly found himself quite alone at the gathering. That was the day I came to understand that if this explosive philosopher had been in Parlement, he would not have accepted the role of a mere observer; rather he would have had a brilliant or even a tempestuous career.

Having associated with several philosophers in my lifetime, and with a variety of writers as well, I have noticed that the measure of interest they show in others depends on the admiration, allegiance, or flattery the latter display toward them, each being so utterly obsessed by his own work that he seizes every opportunity to refer to it. ''Do you know this or that book of mine?'' is the question most often mouthed in such wretched circles. From the mouth of a novelist this sort of question might be tolerable, but coming from a philosopher it definitely is not, and I must add that I never heard Marcel ask it. Needing others' existence, he was interested in the *being* of each person, in what was unique and irreplaceable in the individual, in the *self* of that person—*le soi du moi,* if you'll pardon the pun. It is a question of knowledge through kindness. So he was at once vivacious and good. This is a noteworthy paradox for those who realize that vivacity and goodness are a rare combination. Goodness is more common among people who are calm, reserved, and slow. Paradoxically, goodness in Marcel took on the dynamics of a reflex. By this I mean that I never knew him to pause to reflect when what was really needed was a good deed; he intervened, put himself out, hurried, and even inconvenienced himself in the extreme to help someone. Always ready to listen to anyone who might come to him in trouble, he sacrificed an incredible number of hours doing a job that required the talents of a confessor or of a diplomat.

The gift for communication is natural in an author or a dramatic writer, and Marcel was both at the same time. His love of dialogue spurred him to write plays, and his passion for analysis inspired him to meditate on theatrical works. He and I saw a considerable number of plays together, some excellent, some of debatable worth, and others depressingly poor in quality. But however poor, however exasperating, any one of them might have been, Marcel was always interested, first because he had to report on it, and then because in each case he wanted to zero in on its intrinsic fault, the fundamental reason for the work's deficiency or worthlessness. I have never ceased to wonder why such a subtle mind was willing to ponder such ordinary works and why he used the resources of his intelligence for such apparently useless tasks. I say "apparently" because one must remember that the theater was for him not a diversion but a living experience. (The German word *Erlebnis* would be quite appropriate here.) From the very opening of the curtain, Marcel was a different man; his curiosity verged on exaltation and outlived disappointment. Hoping that he might suggest leaving at the first intermission, I remember repeatedly assuring him that any further illusion would be hopeless and that the play was so bad even God could not save it. But his professional scruples always won out over my suggestions or hints, and so we endured the ordeal to the bitter end. On saying good-night, he never failed to express his regret for having taken me to such a bad show. To tell the truth, I never had the impression I had wasted my evening, for by lacking from the outset any possibility of moving or even of interesting the audience, a complete fiasco of a play automatically leaves the mind totally free and thus allows it to wander at will.

If Marcel generally shied away from avant-garde theater, it was because most of the plays produced there were deliberately obscure. In any case, such performances demand a loose construction where the interest of the plot lies in the shrouding of the meaning. Mystification is usually the result and sometimes a requirement. Spectators, in order to enjoy themselves, must be prepared to be duped, a role Marcel refused to assume. After spectacles of this ilk, which usually drove him mad, he customarily said in an exasperated voice, "I want to understand; I want some explanation!" More often than not, there was nothing to explain, since in such cases incomprehensibility is of the very essence. The philosopher might readily allow such a thing, if only it were not tainted by trickery and sham.

This attachment to the theater, which is so unusual in a metaphysician, was motivated, I believe, by a deep-seated fear in Marcel—the fear of loneliness. This may indeed appear inconceivable in philosophers, who are commonly thought of as lost in thought and shut off completely from the world. But Marcel was exactly the opposite. He had an immeasurable need to love and be loved; he could not do without a certain climate of affection, without that certain feeling of closeness one has in the presence of another human being. In order to endure loneliness, one must be capable of despising or hating all people and incapable of taking friendship to the point of tragedy. One must also be prone to some kind of cynicism. I had known Marcel personally for more than twenty years, and because we were practically neighbors we had many opportunities to get together; in all that time I never heard him utter a cynical word, despite his natural tendency to ridicule.

Marcel was always ready to face an adversary, for what he really enjoyed, both in his life with others and in his inner life of thought, was challenge. He saw the universe as a constant source of problems to be solved, and he went about solving them in a way that differed from, say, Heidegger's, to cite a contemporary example. When Heidegger encountered a difficulty, he tended to invent a word to cover or mask it, a word that allowed him to avoid the issue; or, even worse, he resorted to the most suspect device imaginable: etymology. This he did brilliantly, but he abused it in that he *played* with the words; he twisted them into the meaning that suited his need; he *exploited* them cleverly, slyly. These verbal acrobatics are so amazing that they easily give the illusion of depth.

This was not at all Marcel's way, as evidenced by his spontaneous expression both in his books and in conversation. His most fundamental concern was the definition, the meaning, of words. Yet it was not a question of some definition designed to suppress a problem or cleverly to evade it; it was rather a gradual definition, forming slowly as the thought progressed; it was a temporary definition that took shape little by little but never fossilized. At the end of the encounter, it might be just as problematic as it was in the beginning. The weight of the problem remained; it had not been lessened by the discussion. After viewing a given concrete situation from several angles, Marcel would often say that he was unable to provide a definitive solution or that he could not pass judgment on the question. This confession of uncertainty, quite natural in matters of metaphysics, is less common in areas of a more or less practical nature. But this uncertainty was merely the reflection, in the mirror of present or daily experience, of his intellectual integrity—the meticulous probing between certainty and doubt, the constant scruple of a mind questioning itself.

Marcel has been accused of inconsistency, and this or that situation where he has changed his mind has been offered as evidence. No thought of opportunism must even be entertained. What was involved here was a studied shifting of position, or, if you prefer, the changing of an *open* mind, always eager to understand another's point of view or even an opponent's opinion. For speculative as well as moral reasons, his was a mind ready to concede any apparently legitimate points. Considering the type of mind with which he was endowed, I have often asked myself how he managed to avoid sinking into that catastrophic state of perpetual doubt bordering on a spiritual shipwreck. I believe that the explanation for his ability to resist skepticism lies here. Skeptics gaily pose a problem for the sake of formulating it, only to renounce it at once in order to pick it apart and expose its fundamental inanity. They delight in problems that cannot be solved; they wallow in them, drunk with the impediment. Absolute skepticism necessarily carries with it an element of morbidity. Like a skeptic, Marcel was aware of what might be termed the *sensual pleasure* of the problem as such. Yet in his mind (as opposed to the mind of a doubter), everything had a deep inner foundation; everything contributed to inner life. Without this he would have fallen into utter confusion. His type of intellect may indeed have converted everything into problems, because the essence of his being required mystery; but this mystery, instead of plunging him into doubt and suffering, saved both his life and his thought. It is not mere chance that Rilke was one of his favorite poets. Just imagine reasoning in which thought, unfolding incessantly, would indefinitely engender question after question, never stumbling, never encountering obstacles, never pausing! Some sort of obstacle is necessary, lest one waver in the quest. *Sonnets to Orpheus* might well represent this limit. This . . . infinite limit.

"Everyone has known times when he has been tempted to posit universal nonsense," wrote Marcel during the Second World War (*Présence et immortalité*). One might say that the basic meaning of his work and of his life was his refusal to succumb to this temptation, which is the most terrible of all temptations, since it is the product of our negative states, of our weak moments, and of all the gaps in our being. Such temptations are also characterized by a certain sick quality that gives them a dangerous, irresistible charm. The person who is alive has a natural relish for being; it is therefore easy for him or her to seek and to find meaning in everything. Imagine this relish diverted, perverted, or merely weakened: what previously had some significance has now ceased to have any, and this disastrous sliding has nowhere to go but down until it ends in the total unhinging of meaning from existence, with no hope of bringing the two together again. Without faith and without the need he always felt for holding onto and creating relationships and convictions for himself, Marcel might not have avoided the lasting obsessive experience of nonsense, especially since nihilism is neither a paradoxical nor a monstrous position, but rather a logical conclusion wrecking every mind that has lost intimate contact with mystery (*mystery* being the prudish term for *the absolute*).

As we know, Proust drew up a questionnaire by which a writer might clarify his or her thought. Among Marcel's replies, I find two particularly striking. In answer to the first question, "What is your favorite activity?" he said, "Writing and listening to music." To the second, "What would you like to be?" he replied, "A composer entirely dedicated to music." Elsewhere he wrote that the art of music had been one of the original ingredients in the making of his being and, I should add, his prime *encounter* in life, at least his prime spiritual encounter.

I often listened to music with him, to everything from Monteverdi to Fauré and the great Russian masters, and I noticed that music uplifted him, projected him into some other sphere, and transported him to a level of being inaccessible to philosophy except in some rare moments of insight. Proust, who should always be quoted in matters of experiences that are revelations, thought that if people had not had the faculty of speech, music would have been the only means of communication between souls. This is approximately what Marcel maintained, in speaking of his improvisations, when he admitted that through them he was able to delve into his most intimate inner self; it was in this state, he said, that "everything would move as if the border between the lands of the living and the dead were disappearing, as if I were entering a universe in which this distinction, I dare say a quite common one, was nearing total eradication."

One reason he never tired of paying tribute to Schopenhauer (a philosopher who has been unjustly neglected, whereas Hegel took all the laurels by glorifying history) was that the philosopher of *The World as Will and Idea* held music in extraordinarily high esteem. Compared with this art, how pale all philosophy seems! The humiliation of being a philosopher was Marcel's secret wound. It is indeed true that people who love music above all else are bound to live with lasting regret if they become anything less than musicians. Philosophers who have drawn so near the ineffable are prone to regret being neither musicians nor poets nor mystics and to regard their lot as a loss. Fortunately for them, not all philosophers attain this level of clear-sightedness, but those who come close inject into their works a soul-rending feeling that redeems and humanizes their philosophy.

I rarely saw Marcel complain or lament. Even when he had to undergo a serious operation, he spoke of it only in passing, as if it were just an unpleasant event and nothing more. Both before and after it, he consistently led the conversation in other directions; he did so not in order to bolster his courage, but because of his strong aversion to the self-centeredness characteristic of sick people. Speaking of courage, one would in his case have to use the word *temerity*. At the age of seventy-six he undertook a two-month lecture tour in both the United States and Japan. He lectured almost every day, and each lecture was followed by a discussion and a reception. All his friends considered the undertaking imprudent. And so it was, for it took its toll of his health. His eyesight suffered. A few days before his departure he had the feeling that he would not come back alive; yet the day before he left he overcame his anguish and embarked unfalteringly on his adventure. When he came home, he seemed rather demoralized, although not for long. He soon resumed his normal activities and even took on new engagements—that is to say, other trips.

His ascetic nature was the secret of his vitality. He abstained from both alcohol and tobacco, which jointly enslave modern people, especially the intellectuals. With his explosive nervousness, it is doubtful that he could have maintained his equilibrium if he had resorted to taking these poisons we often see disguised as stimulants. Another of his fortunate characteristics was his moderation. The French are notoriously obsessed by food. For them, eating is a ritual that borders on vice. It is not at all uncommon to hear people, even people of distinction, say such things as, ''I had dinner at so-and-so's house, and they served a dish seasoned with . . . ,'' with the following details astoundingly precise. Never did I hear Marcel make comments of this kind. He was not a worshiper of the culinary arts, and in this regard he was very un-French. But perhaps I have exaggerated, for I recall the approval he expressed when I mentioned that I had no desire to dine again at Mme X's because all I could think of at her table was the Marquise de Brinvilliers, the famous French poisoner.

Being advanced in years is not really important when one's memory and basic curiosity remain so prodigious. In 1968, after a hike I had taken in the marvelous Célé Valley, I found myself unable to remember the names of the villages I had just gone through; yet Marcel could recite them all from memory, even though he had not visited the area since 1943. On another occasion, in connection with activities of the Bloomsbury group, I was filling him in on the *Autobiography* of Bertrand Russell, which he had not read and which he had in fact deliberately avoided reading because he didn't particularly care for Russell. (He disliked positivism in any form, logical or otherwise.) At one point, my memory playing its usual tricks on me, I drew a blank on the surname of "Ottoline . . . ," but Marcel was quick to add, "Morrell." I could cite endless examples of the power of his memory. This power was the reason for his faithfulness to people and to places. An unfaithful person is one who does not remember or who remembers with difficulty. One might go so far as to say that a good memory is a prerequisite to spiritual or moral life.

His curiosity continued to keep him remarkably open to the world. Despite the usual health problems, he never seemed in low spirits, or at least he never seemed to give in to such feelings; such surrender would be a sure sign of aging. I am certain that he did not feel—indeed, that he could not feel—the "difficulty of being" of which Fontnelle complained. For Marcel was always in the mainstream of life—in the swing of things, in the best sense of the phrase. Such curiosity is the truest sign of life, the sign one really is alive; it constantly uplifts and enriches the world, and simply seeks to find its own match. Curiosity is in fact the intellectual counterpart of desire. Likewise, the lack of curiosity, except when it brings one to the state of nirvana, is a most alarming symptom. In certain Latin American countries it is common to send out death notices that read, "So-and-so has become *indifferent*." Under this formal euphemism lies a deep philosophical meaning.

Who can forget the remark Royer-Collard made to Vigny (whose work he had not read): "Sir, at my age one does not read any more, one re-reads." Here we find one more manifestation of Marcel's intellectual capacity: he read much more than he re-read. He picked up the latest book on politics or the newest novel. With his natural wellspring of enthusiasm, he quickly got involved in the book he was reading; as he got deeper into it, he felt compelled to admit his error, and in so doing he would also give the reasons for his judgment. For more than thirty years he was in charge of publishing a series of foreign novels—an unprecedented task for a philosopher, especially given the average worth of novels on sale today. One day he gave a sigh betraying his feeling. "This is one of the few novels I have been able to read from beginning to end without effort," he explained, referring to a work I no longer remember. The reason for this is, I believe, that although theoretically philosophy is compatible with many things, in practice it is compatible with very few. Philosophy is intolerant because it is too bent on passing judgment and too apt to consider itself in a privileged light. Marcel bitterly opposed philosophy's constant, unwarranted arrogance.

If I were asked to define Marcel's attitude toward life, the basic feeling life inspired in him, I would speak, I believe, of his *radical non-Buddhism*. This statement seems clear enough to me, but I might be able to clarify it further by an example. A few years ago, inspired by a chance visit to the natural history museum, I wrote an article in the *Nouvelle revue francaise* entitled ''Paléontologie.'' In my essay I mentioned I had a particularly tender feeling toward skeletons and a kind of desperate horror of the perishable and unreal nature of flesh. My position on the issue was close to that of Swift or Buddha or Baudelaire—a blend of disgust and funereal obsessions. Marcel was up in arms. He told me that he stood diametrically opposed to this view and that he could not abide anyone's speaking this way of the flesh, treating it as if it were a worthless nothing. A mind like his, which had no trouble imagining immortality, could feel no aversion to life whatsoever, because it is precisely in order to reclaim this life—in a pure form, of course—that he clung to the notion of permanence or of eternity. It is true that he had long meditated on death, but he did so in order to transcend it, to find some principle beyond it, to rise above it. In his view, death could not be the end of everything; his instinct and his feelings told him that he must refuse to conceive of death as an impediment to the assembly of beings beyond time. One may safely say that for him dying was really a victory over death; it was a meeting and a reuniting with loved ones. The concept of faithfulness is again central to this vision, for it banishes despair and deems resignation cowardice. To give credence to absolute death is nothing more than an expression of self-centeredness, an act of despair and treason.

Pascal spoke of the joy one feels when, expecting to encounter an author, one comes face to face with a man. This joy, I must add, is increased even more when the author in question is a philosopher.*

E. M. CIORAN

PARIS, FRANCE
NOVEMBER 1971

---

*Being a ''portrait'' of the philosopher, this essay needed no reply.—ED.

2

Henry G. Bugbee

L'EXIGENCE ONTOLOGIQUE

C OMING home the other evening from an excellent Bach concert, I thought to myself, 'Here is something that restores to one a feeling that one might have thought lost, or perhaps something more than a feeling, an assurance: the assurance that it is an honour to be a man.' "[1]

While meditating on Gabriel Marcel's work once again, I felt it entirely coherent that a particular Bach organ prelude kept coming back to me, upsurging and unsummoned, to preside as if by rightful sovereignty over the readying of this essay. For to reflect with M. Marcel is to be drawn into a sense of humanity in which the honor—the dignity—of being human resounds, as it does in Bach. Even so, the possibility of life in the spirit of consecration seems to come home to us.

It is in terms of nothing less than this possibility that I hope we may approach that moving center of M. Marcel's thought: *l'exigence ontologique*. An almost naïve rationale might be offered for such an approach. *L'exigence ontologique* projects us into a metamorphosis of human concern. If we try to accompany M. Marcel's thought and to follow the ramifications of his development of the theme, we find ourselves called on to move thoughtfully into a consideration of the deliverances of the life of concern as that life may deepen and "come to understand itself." *L'exigence ontologique,* if not stifled or unheeded, involves us essentially in a kind of movement and a kind of becoming "beyond ourselves." And the life of concern becomes imbued with a sense of direction quite distinct from an orientation toward ideals or goals, to whatever extent it may support them. How, then, might one hope for reflective clarity from within such a movement and such a becoming concerning the import of *l'exigence ontologique?* Might we approach our theme from the direction in which it takes us, letting it hold sway at its clearest, even if in so doing it may far outrun so much of our actual lives—even as the possibility of life in the spirit of consecration may occur to us, in a being beyond ourselves? Let us try to analyze such a possibility of life in terms that might be intrinsic to it.

To speak of a possibility in connection with an active undertaking may readily suggest choice, and consecration seems inseparable from this sense of an active undertaking. Yet we may notice that life in the spirit of consecration is not present to us as a possibility relative to choice, not because of the remoteness of such a possibility from our actual lives, but rather because the more near and present to us such a possibility becomes, the less it appears to lie in our power and the less it is accessible to us as a matter of choice. Even definitively, the power of consecration seems to come to us in a way that qualifies initiative in the exercise of powers at our disposal as a *dependent initiative.* So far from being in the first instance a matter of availing ourselves of . . . , it would seem a matter of our being available, at the disposition of . . . , albeit *willingly,* consenting and assenting in . . . , unstintingly and without inhibition. But if the matter can be appropriately considered by approaching it in such terms, how should we interpret the element of dependency that seems to obtain? Might the dependency in question imply a straightforward reference indicating that on which initiative in consecration depends?

It would not seem amiss to speak in terms of a certain spirit of consecration and of such a spirit as subject to a kind of alimentation in us. Surely the beings we come to care for deeply, the place of our dwelling, and the things of the place—indeed all that occupies our attention in eliciting, sustaining, and deepening our concern—would be salient for us in considering how a spirit of consecration may come to be nurtured in us. And since consecration seems so clearly a matter of concern with these beings, and of active concern on their behalf, do they of themselves engender and sustain in us the capacity for consecration? Is our dependency in becoming capable of consecration a dependency on those beings to whom we attend in the openness and availability of really caring for them? In what manner do they thus concern us, and how do they come to concern us so?

They come to concern us in the manner of claiming us, I think, or in response to a sense of ourselves as claimed in a way qualifying our direct relationship with beings, so that they engage us in our response to being claimed by addressing that response. Yes, they come to concern us by claiming us in our concern with them, and they are indeed salient in our concerned attention. Yet their claiming us in such a way is not a matter of their making manifest, as if inherent in themselves, an origin of their standing in and for our concern. It is not by self-assertion on their part that beings come to engage us in the spirit of consecration, nor is it we who confer on beings the standing in and for our concern in which we find ourselves addressed by them. For we are as claimed and cannot originate our own being as claimed. Yet our own being as claimed seems indissolubly bound up with the standing in which we are able to receive and acknowledge beings, in their very being, as speaking to our concern.

Indeed the very possibility of consecration seems to imply an acknowledgment, perhaps most centrally a deeply silent acknowledgment, of our being as claimed. For there is an absolute stillness about the matter—prior to all giving voice. Concern comes to maturity in being unconditionally claimed and in its free and unforced accord in being so—it finds itself in a rooted and grounded mode of being; this becomes its *raison d'être:* to be radically claimed and sustained in being with beings. Such a discovery is enlightening with respect to what has implicitly held true all along in the life of concern, regardless of the extent to which it may have been resisted, lost upon us, or otherwise obscured. To come to at least a measure of clarity in this radical mode of being, responsiveness must develop *reflexively,* for there can be no willing accord with our being as claimed, and no clarity with respect to it, except in the reflexively responsive acceptance and acknowledgment of our being in this manner. At the same time our reflection must partake of the reflexivity of the way in which concern is radically dependent if that dependence is understood to be at the root of our initiative and of our freedom.

Perhaps we are wont to construe this unconditional claiming "from the root" as something initiated within ourselves. Yet we ourselves are embraced in being thus claimed "from within"; at the same time, equally and integrally, all beings other than ourselves, belonging with us in the world, are qualified, intoned, inflected—yes, defined—in their essential mode of significance, in accordance with this manner of our being embraced with these beings. Thus grasped in function of our being claimed, these beings are indeed in the manner of "speaking to us." Their instatement in and for our concerned attention in claiming us to them seems of a shared derivation with the reflexively radical way in which we are claimed unconditionally. As if from a grounding most intimately inward yet infinitely distant from us, we stand forth in the meeting with beings, so too they seem to come to us as if proffered out of an inwardness from which they stand forth. Hence there is a fundamental mutuality about sharing in being with them. A grounding of that mutuality seems to hold good not only for the reciprocity between human beings but also for the very being unto one another of beings with ourselves. Let us now apply this line of reflection to M. Marcel's ontological thought. What is it for beings to be given, and therefore to be responsively received, in the mode of presence?

> Quand je dis qu'un être m'est donné comme présence ou comme être (cela revient au même, car il n'est pas un être pour moi s'il n'est une présence), cela signifie que je ne peux pas le traiter comme s'il était simplement posé devant moi; entre lui et moi se noue une relation qui en un certain sens déborde la conscience que je suis susceptible d'en prendre; il n'est plus seulement devant moi, il est aussi en moi; ou plus exactement ces catégories sont surmontées, elles n'ont plus de sens. Le mot influx traduit, bien que d'une façon beaucoup trop spatiale, trop physique, l'espèce d'apport intérieur, d'apport par le dedans qui se réalise dès le moment où la présence est effective.[2]

In responding *to* beings as beings I respond *upon* or *from* a kind of accretion "from within." My openness or availability to beings is inseparable from a reflexive openness or availability; better than these English expressions is M. Marcel's expression, *disponibilité*.

The preceding analysis of consecration suggests that *disponibilité* is twofold. Reflexive *disponibilité* is the deepening of concern in its radical character; it is ultimately no less than the willing disposition of oneself to being unconditionally claimed. But it is in and out of being so claimed that we can come to "hear" and to heed beings in their grounded claim on us. That hearing and heeding is the manner of our *disponibilité* in the direct engagement of concern by beings occupying our attention; accordingly, *disponibilité* is also coordinate with respect to those beings. We are (1) reflexively ordained (2) unto beings in a (3) consequent grasp of the mutuality of being; therefore the force of *einai* ("to be") is found in to-be-shared-in-with. This is simplicity itself. The sense of life lived in such a vein is that being is shared in as a given, even as a granted dispensation. One can give oneself in that. That is the hang of it.

It seems absolutely precise that M. Marcel has held by the theme that our involvement in being is mysterious; if that involvement is intelligible, it is intelligible *as* a mystery. The pivot of the mystery is the twofold way we are ordained in being: both radically and *unto*—unto all with which we come to share in being. In that radical grounding of the self in becoming reflexively *disponible* as unconditionally claimed, one's very selfhood is the dispensation; one is graced with the ability to be willingly and truly oneself. Yet that reflexive ordination and dispensation is integral with the disposition of concern unto beings granted us to share in being with; those beings are grasped as given in that we, who are infirm, can firmly participate in being with them. They call for recognition as participants in being, and being thus fundamentally shared in is sacred. *Appel et réponse* is the basic mode of our participation in being with other beings. Perhaps it is thus that music can come to be the very language of being, as it does in Bach.

During 1929, when the ontological themes central to M. Marcel's thought were fast emerging, a particular expression occurred to him with a musical fecundity that he noted: "De l'être comme lieu de la fidélité."[3] Twenty-six years later, alluding to that original phrasing of the expression, he remarked: "Tout au plus préciseral-je un peu davantage en disant: l'être est le lieu *des plus hautes fidélités.* . . . La seule fidélité qui vaille est positive, elle se traduit par des initiatives d'autant plus novatrices qu'elle même est enracinée plus fermement aux profondeurs de l'âme."[4]

If *disponibilité* is the twofold receptivity by which we are claimed to participation in being, *la fidélité créatrice* is that sponsored initiative in adherence and commitment by which we place ourselves as participants in being. Being is thus "the place" of fidelity, and it is in actively committing ourselves to beings claiming our concern that we responsively find our placement in being. As *disponibles* we are in the manner of being called upon, and beings claim our receptive attention in the manner of exerting an appeal; correlative with our being as called upon is the possibility of refusal, of betrayal, and of defection. The active acceptance, acknowledgment, and pledging of oneself in commitment to . . . answeringly coordinate with the appeal; this positive contrary of refusal is the free defining and placing of oneself in being. Accordingly, one's sense of being is decisively qualified—both in the vein of freedom and in the vein of commitment—by an *il faut* freely acknowledged and undertaken. In the "highest" fidelity, that of consecration, we come knowingly into the world, and the law of that becoming is the essential complementarity in mutual qualification of freedom and necessity and of initiative and grace.

By the time M. Marcel is well into his most protracted *reconnaissance* of the mystery of being, he writes: "Mais ici il convient de rester aussi concret que possible, et je veux dire par là de rester comme à l'écoute de l'expérience la plus intime. Il ne s'agit en effet au fond de rien moins que d'apercevoir la façon dont il est possible de concevoir l'articulation de la vérité et de la vie."[5] The "discovery" of that connection by taking it up into reflection would hinge on the reflexive recognition of such a connection from within it and by virtue of a "dimension" of humanly lived life "qui est précisément la profondcur elle-même."[6] The coarticulation of life and truth is therefore not analogous to something that can be "exposed to view" or "shown." The connection is exactly the point on which we must reflect, however, at the center of our present undertaking. For one might define *l'exigence ontologique* as the sense of that connection by which the life one leads—with others, and in the cumulative encounter with beings—becomes charged with the underlying constancy and unity of being continuously at issue throughout our various concerns. Hence there are no moments of concern that are alien to or separable from a life rendered one through being ever at issue, for one is inescapably called on to bear witness to how that being at issue might come to the decisive realization of itself. To the extent that our vital needs and their satisfaction, our interests and inclinations, our practical affairs, our relationships of obligation, our haunting anxieties, our hopes and fears, our delights and discouragements are taken up in a life at issue—at issue for us in the mode of our being called on, with an underlying constancy of the sense that this is the way it is with us—then to that extent *l'exigence* draws on these myriad moments and ways of concern; they charge it with aspiration, with "metaphysical disquiet,"[7] and with commitment not to disavow them or exclude them from a hearing. But the hearing to which the whole life of concern comes—under *l'exigence ontologique*—attests to the requirement of a certain detachment, of a relinquishment of attachment to all one cares for without ceasing to care, and of a making over of oneself with all one's cares and all one cares for into the keeping of that claim and that call on care coming from its own root.

Since in the life of the spirit receptivity and active initiative become as basically integral as they are in the matter now concerning us, perhaps it is appropriate to speak of a kind of "movement" in that life—or even of a polarization that may occur in it—within which we come to discover ourselves in a certain way. The image of *dégagement* ("detachment and withdrawal") suggests that we can sense this as a movement, a movement in which we are moved so to move: to relinquish, to suspend, to draw back; to gather, but to gather inwardly; to recollect; and to come near . . .; yet *not* as one turns from something seen in order to look in the opposite direction and then to draw nearer what may appear from that direction. "Le recueillement est sans doute ce qu'il y a de moins spectaculaire dans l'âme; il ne consiste pas à regarder quelque chose, il est une reprise, une réfection intérieure. . . . Le mot anglais 'to recollect one self' est ici révélateur."[8] There is the suggestion of moving into a reflectiveness from having been intent on our affairs, immersed in them, and bent on what we were doing. Perhaps too if we have been insistently bent on what we were doing, then there must be a rather radical "giving over" in order to place ourselves, recollectively, questioningly, and in question, nearer the center of our lives, in concentration, and positioned "comme à l'écoute."[9] The deeper the candor of spirit in recollection, the more our concerns and the beings engaging them come to be weighed by a measure to which we bring ourselves. If in meditative recollection there is the active animation of genuine concentration, then within that concentration things have a chance to discover themselves more nearly as they might really be and maybe even as they most deeply want to be. Then, most incredibly of all, it is so: we, all beings, are affirmed in our being—owned in a standing received as a blessing that has nothing to do with our deserving it or not. It is in this standing that we are given in the mutuality of being, which comes to human recognition as the entitlement of beings to respect. In our being reflexively the beneficiaries of being-as-unconditionally-affirmed, we are unconditionally and wholly claimed as beings of concern; at the same time we are ordained in responsiveness to beings through a union with them in which they address us as beings to be shared with in being-as-unconditionally-affirmed. It is with them that the affirmation can be confirmed. The life of concern thus comes to be animated by the ontological truth at issue in it—a truth continuously open to confirmation in our actual circumstance and relation with beings. *L'exigence ontologique* could not be so fulfilled that it ceased to be relevant, nor could the way of its fulfillment ever be taken for granted or assured.

We have spoken of *recueillement* and of the pivotal *dégagement* in this essential movement in the life of the spirit as a polarization of that life. Yet the crucial point in our analysis of it lies in recognizing that a radical polarization institutes the complementary movement of *accueil* and of *engagement* with respect to beings: the movement toward meeting beings in direct responsiveness to them, in the mutuality of fellow creatures, to live and to confirm the destinate dispensation in which we find ourselves. In the discipline of rhythmic alternation between these complementary movements, each distinctively derives occasion and renewal from the other. All concerns involve a questionableness that calls for qualification, which they can only obtain in a radical way. They must be tried and tested in a reflexive disposition of oneself (the self that lives these concerns) as a being subject to emendation—an emendation that can come only from the depth of one's life. Only in reflexive concentration can concern come to realize that its life is conditional in essence, and therefore no concern can admit of an unconditional endorsement or substantiation. What is unconditional about the life of concern is the unconditional claiming of it and affirming of it in its conditional character by the radical groundedness of that life. Yet the life so grounded is none other than the manifold life of concern with beings as they engage and speak to concern. The renewal and the truing of concern in reflexive concentration is the renewal and truing of concern with beings. Thus the test of detachment in reflexive concentration is in the incarnate life into which we are "returned." Are our ties with beings the ties of attachment, or do they assume the character of a solidarity in being to be acted on? Is life in the spirit lived in contrariety to life in the flesh, or is it only lived as incarnate? Do we find ourselves alienated from the circumstances in which we actually move, so that they appear to be contingent relative to an assumed standpoint abstracted from our involvement in them, or do they occur to us as contributories to the precise form our lives take?

Near the close of the first series of his Gifford Lectures, M. Marcel remarks: "On peut dire d'une manière générale que la difficulté à laquelle nous avons eu continuellement à faire face réside justement dans le fait que le spirituel semble prétendre à la dignité d'existence séparée, alors que plus profondément il ne se constitue comme spirituel qu'à condition de s'incarner."[10] It is exactly in this connection that the twofoldness of the life of concern hangs in the balance for interpretation; more particularly, the meaning of *dégagement* becomes crucial to that interpretation.

In the 1933 essay so central to our study, M. Marcel first writes of the "dégagement *réel;* détachement *réel*" that is effected only in "le recueillement" and by which alone apprehension of the mystery of being is possible.[11] Regarding *recueillement* as an act, he continues: "C'est essentiellement l'acte par lequel je me ressaisis comme unité: le mot même l'indique, mais ce ressaisissement, cette reprise affecte l'aspect d'une détente, d'un abandon. *Abandon à— détente en présence de—* sans qu'il me soit en aucune façon possible de faire suivre ces prépositions d'un substantif qu'elles commanderaient. Le chemin s'arrête au seuil."[12]

Can we draw from these indications further amplification of the meaning of *dégagement?* Taken in their fuller context in the essay and in relation to comparable material of the period in *Etre et avoir,* they suggest that the next step in our analysis is to make more explicit the sense of *abandon à... .*

Initially we spoke of *dégagement* in terms of a "giving over," a relinquishment of attachment to all one cares for without ceasing to care. How is this possible? It certainly cannot be forced as if by a control one exerts over oneself, nor is it compatible with resignation or with a "turning away from" or withdrawal in disillusionment. It is only possible by renouncing a claim, a vested interest, a proprietary demand. My suggestion then is that *dégagement* as a relinquishment of attachment ultimately presupposes the renunciation of such a claim.

The act of *willing* involves far more than the interplay of desire and fear, which can come to hold us in thrall like a compulsion. This does not mean that we will to feel as we come to feel but that in relation to our willing in a certain manner, our wanting comes to be inflected. To become enslaved to our wants and consequent fears in mounting tension is not a matter attributable to desire, as if desire were an inherently suspect mode of concern and autonomous factor governing our actions. That such enslavement may appear attributable to desire, however, must be traced to a kind of appropriative willing in which, however tacitly, a claim is staked to having what we want. If we presume autonomy in an insistent attempt to take charge of our lives, then we cannot find ourselves incarnately in the flow of appeal to concern in which sensory and appetitive elements can participate as embodiments of the life of the spirit. Instead these elements erupt as the signaling and triggering of "self-directed" pursuits; they occur as "drives" and are appropriated as "signs." Being active thus assumes the character of driving to control pursuits into which one is driven. And the mechanisms through which control may be extended become centrally preoccupying, invested with an authority of their own. Where they can be extended, the "self-directed" life tends to follow, so that the means of taking charge define life's destiny. "Nature" then assumes the defining aspect of an exploitable resource, and nothing of Nature can be held sacred.

The substitution of one pursuit for another and the redefinition of ends and goals in the hope that they will lead to the rectification of what is sensed as a predicament are dialectically characteristic of entrenchment in attachment. The predicament only deepens and ramifies in the style of life that construes the issue of concern in terms of a solution to be sought. And it can be in just such a vein that the "distinctively" intellectual, moral, or spiritual life may be embraced—as the stronghold of an individual autonomy defined in opposition to a heteronomous determination or to the threat of it. Significantly, to the extent that these represent recourses in attachment, the "natural" and the "vital" tend to fall into the distinct category of the subhuman. The sterilization of their lived meaning consigns them to the keeping of regimens of health and subsistence, with the attendant possibilities of pleasure to be exploited—or eschewed.

For whatever identifiable concerns our lives may tend toward emptiness, a transference of attachment from those concerns to some alternative recourse, in an attempt to effect independence of them, is the pattern of attachment. Now if our analysis of concern as twofold is not basically misconceived, perhaps we can suggest how in particular "le spirituel semble prétendre à la dignité d'existence séparée."[13] So far as the life of concern involves an attachment to beings, it is bound for emptiness and comes to crisis in despair; mortality assures this. Yet if there is seriousness in despair, there is also a potentiation of concern from the root. Even when all one's manifold concerns in the whole round of life and in all its walks come into radical question, there is something unconditional about the vainness of concern's extroverted quest. Stirred with the sense of what is inward to its own life but still clinging to its directive bent, concern seeks its identity in the form of an inner life. Only when other beings hold forth the promise of confirming it in this, its own unconditional form and the identity to be reached through it, can they speak to its condition. Its separate life in introversion is still attachment's quest, carried out as a pursuit on which "everything" is felt to depend. Yet when concern for beings in time has found itself vulnerable and them wanting, is it not apt to turn in quest of the imperishable and the unchangeable? With the sameness of autonomous intent, concern turns from the manifold relations of engagement with beings and binds itself to a spiritual venture pursued in an effort to attain emancipation from those concerns by which it has come to naught. The aim is to establish a life independent of those concerns. Intimations of something unconditional about the life of concern, from the depth of its own life, are subsumed in the support of *a* concern—that of the distinctively spiritual life—pursued as itself unconditional and contrary to the concerns from which detachment is sought. The twofold life of concern suffers diremption. A dialectic of contraries sets in. On the one hand, concern lives in the mode of an elective emphasis in which intention tends to make itself absolute: concern "owns" only what is intended, sought, or chosen—whatever it is driving at. On the other hand, concern lives in inadvertency as well as in dreaming. Things unintendedly keep coming over it, now insinuating, now erupting, perhaps unrecognized or unnoticed because unsought and unintended, perhaps obtrusive and persistent in their contrariety to its avowed emphasis and intention. On the one hand, there is the sense of being active and of driving; on the other, that of passivity, of inertia, and of being driven. Hence the premium on exercising an autonomy that defines itself in opposition to a looming and opposing heteronomy threatening to take over. Yet concurrent with the striving to subject life to the administration on which hope is pinned, there is the attraction of resignation even if in hopelessness: the rest from striving, the relinquishment into passivity—the moribund.

The dialectical character of the situation would seem the same whether the elective emphasis is on "the spiritual life" (as opposed to "this-worldliness") or on the manifold concerns of "this world" (as opposed to "spirituality"). Since concern tends toward dogmatic entrenchment in either of these autonomous emphases and thus misses its complicity in the correla-

tive heteronomy against which it defines itself, it misses the dialectical
character of its entire life. But what is the correlative heteronomy to the
elective emphasis that does not find itself carnally opposed? What sort of
Doppelgänger threatens the autonomy of concern in an unconditional own-
ing of this world conceived of in repudiation of "spiritual claims"? Is it
not preeminently a far stranger and a far less obtrusive sort of heteronomy:
that of the psychic life itself, hidden and largely alien to the consciousness
of the person whom it inadvertently claims? With the immolation of spirituality and the triumphant embracing of this world as its field of action,
concern atrophies in reflexive sensitivity, and the life of the spirit, en-
tombed in spiritlessness, suddenly threatens the dogma of immersion in the
affairs of this world. The basic disturbances now occurring are peculiarly
psychic in origin; yet they occur in such a way that concern "truthfully"
deplores and disowns them. To fix responsibility for what is going wrong
becomes an ascendant passion. There must be someone or something to
indict, someone or something one might lay hands on and control. The
formula of autonomy is that power is either to be exerted over the situation
or succumbed to; thus things are basically defined as resources to be used
in exerting control on behalf of concern. Objectivity is then required in
dealing with things; subjectivity requires it. Subjectivity, however, short-
circuits the way things acquire meaning and significance in the life of the
spirit, just as "spirituality" does in the alternative elective emphasis.
Therefore the things that come to us naturally are known as "merely natural" and a "matter of course," and we relegate them to the order of the
ordinary and of habituation by way of taking them for granted. Thus the
discovery of the natural in a sacramental order is not only precluded, it
becomes unimaginable.

Only by responding to being called upon in a way that permits beings
and the inexhaustible depth of life to come into mutually confirming accord
can we come knowingly into a sacramental participation in being with
beings. Then too the world is established in its truth—that is, it is revealed
in a decisive way—and temporality comes to have the precise resonance
of forever and evermore. It is in the world so established and revealed that
beings belong, in their very being.

Being is utterly unintelligible apart from a participation in being with
all one's heart, with all one's soul, and with all one's mind. Yet that seems
to require of one no more than oneself, willingly disposed.

L'exigence ontologique is the way in which we are *as* called upon. It
leads to the discovery of ourselves as active agents of an initiative
grounded in receptivity. Perhaps M. Marcel's most fundamental contribu-

tion to the reflective life of the West lies in his having clearly transposed being active from a defining contrariety to passivity into a defining complementarity with receptivity.

It is that musical ear of his that has held him to his task—that of discovering what it may mean to participate in being.

"The truth is that humanity is only truly human when it is upheld by the incorruptible foundations of consecration—without such foundations it decomposes and dies."[14]

Acquiescing now in the lapse of even more than the time allotted for the preparation of this essay, I find that one comment keeps coming to mind by way of an acknowledgment. In talking of participation in being with beings and of beings as "they," the style tends to contradict the style of participation, which is that of *l'appel et réponse*. The language of invocation and of evocation, spoken in the style of participation, is precisely the language in which we can hope for a consonant articulation of the theme here treated analytically.

HENRY G. BUGBEE

DEPARTMENT OF PHILOSOPHY
UNIVERSITY OF MONTANA
SEPTEMBER 1968

NOTES

1. Gabriel Marcel, *Men against Humanity* (London: Harvill Press, 1952), p. 188.

2. Gabriel Marcel, *Position et approches concrètes du mystère ontolgique* (Paris: Vrin, 1949), p. 81 (hereafter cited as *PA*); essay originally published in *Le Monde cassé* (Paris: Desclée de Brouwer, 1933). "When I say a being is granted to me as a presence or as a being (it comes to the same, for he is not a being for me unless he is a presence), this means that I am unable to treat him as if he were merely placed in front of me; between him and me there arises a relationship which, in a sense, surpasses my awareness of him; he is not only before me, he is also within me—or, rather, these categories are transcended, they have no longer any meaning. The word influx conveys, though in a manner which is far too physical and spacial, the kind of interior accretion, of accretion from within, which comes into being as soon as presence is effective" (from the English translation by Manya Harari, "On the Ontological Mystery," in *Philosophy of Existence* [London: Harvill Press, 1948], p. 24 [hereafter cited as *PE*]).

3. Gabriel Marcel, *Etre et avoir* (Paris: Aubier, 1935), p. 55. "Being as the place of fidelity" (*Being and Having,* trans. Katharine Farrer [Westminster: Dacre Press, 1949], p. 41).

4. Gabriel Marcel, "L'Idée de niveau d'expérience et sa portée métaphysique," *Revue des travaux de l'Académie des sciences morales et politiques,* 4th ser. 108 (1955): 140; Marcel's italics. "At most I would say by way of further qualification: being is the place *of the highest forms of fidelity. . . .* The only fidelity that counts is positive; it expresses itself in forms of initiative that are the more innovative the more firmly it is rooted in the depths of the soul" (my translation).

5. Gabriel Marcel, *Le Mystère de l'être,* 2 vols. (Paris: Aubier, 1951), 1:207 (hereafter cited as *ME*). "But at this point we ought to try to keep our thinking as concrete as possible, and by that I mean attending in a listening way for what may come to us from our most intimate experience. For in the last analysis what we have to perceive is no less than the manner in which the co-articulation of life and truth can be conceived" (my translation).

6. *ME* 1:207.

7. For Marcel's development of this theme in careful distinction from that of "anxiety," see *L'Homme problématique* (Paris: Aubier, 1955), passim. The image of divine leavening for "metaphysical disquiet" seems exact (p. 117).

8. *PA,* 64. "Recollection is doubtless what is least spectacular in the soul; it does not consist of looking at something; it is a recovery of inward purchase, an inward renewal. . . . The English verb *to recollect oneself* is revealing here" (my translation).

9. *ME* 1:207.

10. *ME* 1:218–19. "In a very general fashion indeed, one might say that the difficulty we have had, in the course of these lectures, continually to confront lies in the fact that the spiritual seems to wish to claim for itself the dignity of a separate existence, whereas in a deeper sense it only constitutes itself effectively *as* spirit on condition of becoming flesh" (*The Mystery of Being,* vol. 1, trans. G. S. Fraser [Chicago: Henry Regnery Co., 1951], p. 202).

11. *PA,* 62, 63.

12. *PA,* 63; italics in original. "The word means what it says—the act whereby I re-collect myself as a unity; but this hold, this grasp upon myself, is also relaxation and abandon. *Abandon to . . . relaxation in the presence of . . .* yet there is no noun for these prepositions to govern. The way stops at the threshold" (*PE,* 12). But would one really wish to sustain even the attempt to establish a reference for these prepositions by seeking something like a being or beings to be named by a noun? Might it not instead be precisely the reflexive grounding of self that is in question, making the way of "reference to" irrelevant in that connection? One is derivatively oneself in responding *from* and *upon;* it is thus that one is en-couraged, in-spirited, and even so—*radically* blessed.

13. *ME* 1:218–19.

14. Gabriel Marcel, *Homo Viator,* trans. Emma Craufurd (Chicago, Henry Regnery Co., 1951), p. 96.

L'Exigence Ontologique

REPLY TO HENRY G. BUGBEE

I would like to express my thanks to my good friend Henry Bugbee for the in-depth study of *l'exigence ontologique* in my writings. He deserves singular credit for having put my thought in language rather different from my own instead of being satisfied with a literal commentary. The terminology he has adopted is difficult, and I find that it is almost untranslatable into French; the result is that I am not always sure whether we are in complete agreement or not. For the lack of time, I will limit myself to examining several passages that provide me with the occasion for a sort of reconsideration.

The term *concern,* which occurs again and again in the writings of Henry Bugbee, seems to have been borrowed from Tillich, and I am sorry to say that it cannot be translated into French. The words *souci, préoccupation,* and *intérêt* are not truly equivalent, nor do they correspond exactly to the German word *Sorge.* Under these conditions, the expression "being of concern" raises difficulties—more so because it is not very easy to be sure of the exact value that ought to be given to the preposition *of.* The same remark also holds for the phrase "life of concern." Naturally, I think it is quite correct to say that this "life of concern" involves a direction that cannot be confused with an orientation toward a goal or ideal, and I also clearly see that the idea of consecration comes into play here. Nevertheless, we must admit that the word *consecration* is itself rather ambiguous. In French, the verb *consacrer* in the reflexive form—*se consacrer à*—merely means that one gives oneself without reservation to a certain undertaking. This amounts to saying that the sacred or sacral element etymologically implied in the verb is here omitted, left aside, or at least watered down until it practically disappears. It is altogether different if we

Translated from the French by Dr. Girard Etzkorn.

speak of a spirit of consecration. This expression, which sounds rather peculiar to a Frenchman, tends to bring out something that becomes quite distinct the moment we substitute the word *sacralization* for *consecration*. It seems to me that in the course of his thought, Bugbee is really referring to the idea or experience of sacralization. I quote here a few lines from his article that strike me as particularly important:

> Is our dependency in becoming capable of consecration a dependency on those beings to whom we attend in the openness and availability of really caring for them? In what manner do they thus concern us, and how do they come to concern us so?
> They come to concern us in the manner of claiming us, I think, or in response to a sense of ourselves as claimed in a way qualifying our direct relationship with beings, so that they engage us in our response to being claimed by addressing that response.

I feel it necessary here to examine this text from all sides, and to ask myself how I can assimilate or appropriate it. What we are considering here is the bond that unites me to beings whom I hold dear. The words *tenir à* ("to hold dear") seem to me to render best the English expression "to care for." I am not sure I understand exactly what *openness* means in this context, and I'm even less sure what *availability* means; I do not see that we can speak of *validité* ("validity"). What holds my attention most of all in the above text is the use of the verb *to claim*. By this Bugbee seems to mean that we feel *requis* ("needed") by these beings whom we hold dear. Perhaps the French word *requis* is too weak. Rather it seems that here we are dealing with an absolutely silent claim that these persons have on us. The accent is placed on the solidarity that would exist between this claim we feel, the way it is accepted and actively taken into account, and the consecration that would follow.

However, everyone already knows that I feel the need to free myself from the abstract terms I am supposed to use and to step out, as one steps out of a thicket, into the "clearing of an example." Here is an illustration that comes to mind:

Concrete circumstances—there is no need to specify—have put me under the obligation of giving all my attention to a small child who was entrusted to me because his parents were away traveling or had been killed in an accident. Here the use of the word *claim* is perfectly justified;* this child has rights "on" me, even if this were not true in a strictly legal sense. The concrete situation in which this child and I find ourselves has as its consequence the fact that in a certain way I depend on this child.

---

*The English word *claim* is in the original French text.—TRANS.

For example, I will perhaps have to give up a trip I had counted on because it would force me to leave the child behind or to hire professional babysitters, and so on. In this sense we can say that I depend on the child precisely to the extent that he depends on me. The simplest reflection will show that here we have two sorts of dependencies in essence profoundly different. The child depends on me materially, because it is I who must feed and care for him, and so on. I depend on him spiritually, if I may say so, to the extent that his presence implies obligations for me from which I cannot free myself without feeling that I am guilty of a betrayal. We could make this still clearer by pointing out that this betrayal would be understood *in loco parentum* either absent or deceased, but in any case invisible; whatever their condition, I know they would expect me to dedicate myself to their child. I might add that the use of the conditional is not the best expression here; not only *would* they expect this of me, they *do* expect it. However, what should be emphasized here—and this is what Bugbee seems to have seen so clearly—is that in a certain way it is I who, in the above-mentioned example, confer on the parents this right, this *claim* on me. To understand its origin, we must go back to the past to see what our relations were. We might also specify what would happen if I ceased to concern myself with the child and there were no one to take my place; perhaps it might be necessary to put him in a charitable institution, and so on. Hence, it is in terms of a whole complex situation that my dependence with respect to the child can be clarified.

Still referring to this example, which helps me to make my ideas more precise, I would now like to attempt to discern where the sacred or the sacral element fits in. It is a great deal clearer when the parents are dead— after an automobile accident, for example—for it is absolutely impossible to let their wishes be known and *a fortiori* to impose them. The same holds for the child, who is incapable of imposing his will. Here again, let us say that there is no other satisfactory solution to the problem of what will become of the child. Under the circumstances, I would be justified in saying, "It is my sacred duty to. . . ." Naturally this would not be the case if there were any close relatives capable of taking charge of the child, persons known to be good people who could make the child happy. Hence, it all adds up to my considering myself unconditionally bound to accept the child. It is likewise important to recall that on this hypothesis, I am not legally bound to take the child into my care; this means, for example, that no signed contract exists whereby I would be held responsible for the child. Consequently, by acting otherwise, I would in no way be liable to sanctions, or even to reproach, the very thought of which might act as a constraint. It is as though, in the invisible—or, in a more metaphysical language, in being—a hidden web of relationships had been woven between those who had passed away and the child and myself, who now seem affected by what I call a specifically ontological factor. This is also related to the idea I once expressed when I said that being is the *locus* of fidelity—an expression that provoked violent protestations from a Harvard professor, twice divorced and perhaps on the point of separation from his third wife.

Several phrases from Bugbee's essay make me wonder if we are in complete agreement on the relationship between being and beings. For example, I read the following:

> So far as the life of concern involves an attachment to beings, it is bound for emptiness and comes to crisis in despair; mortality assures this. Yet if there is seriousness in despair, there is also a potentiation of concern from the root.

I am not absolutely sure if I understand what the phrase "concern from the root" means. However, here I would like to present more explicitly than in my previous writings the nature of the relationship that for me binds beings and being. There is no question of referring to a theoretical or abstract reflection—which, in my opinion, is obviously useless—but of referring to experience considered in depth. This is precisely the time to bring in the most helpful distinction—about which Henry Bugbee and I have long agreed—between the *empirical* and the *experiential*, although only the latter is pertinent here.

Take this morning, for example. One of my colleagues at L'Institut lost his twenty-one-year-old daughter, who died after a six-month illness. I wrote to him: "A person is speechless when confronted with such an 'abyss.' " Above all, this means that without the slightest hesitation, I refuse all attempts at, if not justification or explanation, at least reduction that consist in reminding us that it is of the essence of finite beings to be mortal or, more precisely, to be subject to all sorts of change ultimately leading to dissolution. But what is the result of this refusal? It seems to me that it constitutes the simple affirmation that the personal being toward whom my love is directed can be reduced only by way of a fiction to the nature or condition of a finite being who is *ascertainable,* or *feststellbar,* for the dispassionate gaze of a pure spectator.

How can I fail to recall here the cry of Valentine in *The Horizon* apropos the death of Bernard: "His death is mine"?

The experience here in question is one of *déchirement* ("being torn apart"), and the French term is completely satisfactory. It is this experience that the Wise Man of the ancients, of Lucretius or Seneca, for example, can neither acknowledge nor understand because he has withdrawn and placed himself—at least so he thinks—above human passions.

It is certain that this *déchirement,* when translated into the language of reason, appears to be a real contradiction. It would be illusory, however, to believe that this contradiction can be resolved dialectically. Consolation, which is a grace, is beyond all dialectics; the dialectician cannot understand it or even admit its existence, and consolation can easily become for him a mere object of derision. And yet, in a world such as ours, when suffering surpasses all estimation, it is the one who consoles who has the last word, unless it were to come from an absolute nihilist. Between consolation and nihilism, there is room only for conceptual games, which could not deceive the heart in any case.

G.M.

3

Sam Keen

THE DEVELOPMENT OF THE
IDEA OF BEING
IN MARCEL'S THOUGHT

T HE idea of being enjoys a mixed reputation in modern philosophy. Whereas existential thinkers such as Heidegger, Sartre, and Tillich have used it as the foundation of philosophy, those philosophers trained in the empirical tradition tend to view it as nonsense, as a category mistake elevated to philosophical office. Marcel's concrete ontology is of special interest because it combines existential and empirical elements. Marcel shares the empiricist's passion for the concrete and was for a long time reluctant to make any use of the idea of being. It was no abstract consideration that finally led him to investigate the idea of being, but the tragic situation of the "broken world" following the First World War in which the "ontological weight of human experience" was missing. Under the impact of this situation he developed an ontology suggesting concrete approaches to that mystery of being that is the source of human dignity.

The purpose of this essay is to trace the development of the idea of being in Marcel's thought. This will involve (1) discovering why Marcel found it necessary to speak of being rather than merely of beings or entities, (2) showing how, after several false starts, he developed a series of concrete approaches to the mystery of being, and (3) exploring one of these concrete approaches to being (fidelity) and discovering how it relates to the religious approach to God (faith).

THE FIRST ATTEMPT

The first stage in Marcel's thinking about being is initiated in the second part of the *Metaphysical Journal*. Previously he had considered whether

love or knowledge penetrated to the being of the other person, but until
this time he had avoided the question of being in more universal terms. To
get at the meaning of the question of being he asks what the positive
implications would be of affirming that there is no being. This, he says,
would be the equivalent of saying that there is only a phenomenal world—
a statement, incidentally, that is a meaningless assertion, since it only
makes sense to speak of phenomena if one contrasts them with something
that is not phenomenal.[1] To deny being, practically speaking, means to say
that "all is vanity," that nothing matters. It is equivalent to the nihilistic
affirmation that nothing can resist the critical acids of experience and
change and that therefore nothing has intrinsic worth. The nihilist takes the
position of one who sees through all those things others find valuable and
who proclaims that finally all is illusion, *maya,* and that there is no ontological foundation to support the aspirations of the human spirit.

One may certainly disagree with Marcel's identification of the rejection
of the question of being with nihilism. To refuse to speak of being could
mean nothing more than to deny that the category of being has any legitimate referent; it could mean that being is a category mistake. Marcel
would deny that the matter is this innocent. The unwillingness to consider
being masks a fundamental refusal to deal with the principle of unity, and
hence with that which gives coherence and meaning to human experience.
Radical pluralism is nihilism! Were the radical pluralist to appeal to some
principal of unification, such as preestablished harmony, the question of
the ontological status of that principle would still remain. It is insufficient
to say with traditional theism that there are only beings and that the Absolute Being provides the principle of unity. The ontological status of the
powers, laws, wills, forces, or whatever by which unity is created among
diverse entities still needs to be explained. We can no more avoid the
question of being than we can avoid the question of the meaning of life.

According to Marcel, to affirm being is to declare that there is a dimension of human experience within which expectations are fulfilled:
"Being is that which does not frustrate our expectation; there is being from
the moment at which our expectation is fulfilled—I mean the expectation
in which we wholly participate."[2] Marcel states this point even more
strongly by indicating that being is inherent in experiences of fulfillment:
"At the bottom we are still dealing with the opposition between the full
and the empty—an opposition which is infinitely more essential than that
of the single and the multiple. Hence, in a word, for me being is defined
as that which does not allow itself to be dissolved by the dialectics of
experience (experience as it reflects itself)."[3] In terms Marcel later used,
we may say being is that which resists the corrosive acids of primary re-

flection's attempt to reduce experience to the level of the objective and the problematic. Being is identified with that upon which the human spirit rests with the assurance that even if heaven and earth pass away, *this* will abide.

The identification of being with that which resists the reductionistic propensity of thought implies a rejection of the rigid separation between phenomena and noumena. If being can be grasped, it is only because phenomena have the power to mediate or manifest the noumena. Thus Marcel's position in this early work (1919) reflects the phenomenological approach to ontology that later became evident in the work of Sartre and Heidegger.

Before we can resume the characteristically Marcelian quest for being via the depths or heights of human experience, we must follow him into the cul-de-sac he entered in seeking to derive the affirmation of being from the structure of thought itself.

A PROBLEMATIC INTERLUDE

The second stage in Marcel's thinking about being begins after his conversion to Catholicism, in 1929, and its articulation is mercifully limited to the early pages of *Being and Having*. By this time Marcel is convinced that he has exorcised the idealistic elements in his thinking that were evident in the first part of the *Journal* and that he has moved to a realistic position. In connection with this change he affirms two principles he believes to be central to a realistic position: the intentionality of thought and the priority of being to thinking. The affirmation of these principles carries with it the implication that the principle of identity is not merely linguistic or formal but applicative to exterior reality as well as to thought. With the adoption of realism Marcel asserts that the principle of identity signifies that thought bears on a real, not merely a notional, other; it bears not on the idea of things but on the things themselves. Thus he commented: "Here I join forces with Thomism, or at least with what I understand to be Thomism. Thought, far from being a relation with itself, is on the contrary essentially a self-transcendence. So the possibility of the realist definition of truth is implied in the very nature of thought. Thought turns toward the Other, it is the pursuit of the Other. The whole riddle is to discover whether this Other is Being."[4]

Marcel thinks that the principle of identity gives him the warrant to solve this riddle by affirming positively that thought can reach being because it is essentially related to beings and because "a blindfold knowledge of Being in general is implied in all particular knowledge."[5] He disallows the obvious objection that thought bears on beings but not on being. Such a radical pluralism ends up in a self-contradictory nominalism, for it makes use of a unity implicit in language without being able to explain the unity.

Marcel is not long satisfied with the affirmation that somehow—he does not specify how—a knowledge of being is involved in our thinking about beings. Indeed he has no sooner asserted this principle than he begins to see difficulties arise. The affirmation of being cannot be derived from the principle of identity unless it can be shown that being is something definite for thought to grasp: "Can I say with the Thomists that the principle of identity forces me to assert Being? I cannot do so unless I am sure that Being is distinguishable from the *apeiron,* from the infinite, which ancient philosophy did not do and even expressly refused to do."[6] If being is identified with the "boundless," then it cannot be thought, and the principle of identity is ineffective as an ontological principle. Therefore it is only when being is identified with the *ens realissimum*—that is, with a definite, thinkable, absolute life or structure—that the affirmation of being can be derived from the principle of identity. However, this still leaves unanswered the question of being, for if, on the one hand, the *ens realissimum* is *an* entity, how can it also be being? On the other hand, if it is not an entity, how can we avoid making of being a predicate or quality that is applicable to all things? If we adopt the course of saying it is a universal predicate, then we have only uttered a tautology, for in this case to say that a thing has being would only be to say that it is. Kant has shown that if being is taken as a predicate in this sense, it is meaningless, for it adds nothing to our knowledge of a thing to be told that it exists or has being. Marcel sees that the ontologist who takes either path enters a blind alley, "condemned to swing between a truism (that which is, exists) and a paralogism which would consist in attributing Being to the *apeiron.*"[7] In some way, which I confess I am not able to fathom, he thinks that the solution to this dilemma lies in "positing the omnipresence of Being, and what I might (perhaps improperly) call the immanence of thought in Being, that is to say, *eo ipso* the transcendence of Being over thought."[8] It is extremely difficult to see in what way the transcendence of being over thought could differ from the transcendence of existence or of a world over thought, which may be a genuine implication of a realistic philosophy. At any rate we are not given the data to solve the questions that arise, and we can only point to the failure, which Marcel acknowledges, to derive the affirmation of being from the structures of thought.

This failure marks the fork in the road where Marcel's thought diverges from Thomism. He refuses to admit that there is any deductive path from the structure of thought to being. Being is not revealed at the end of a process of judgment, deduction, or analogy but is mediated through our encounters with individual beings as they become present to us in love. Love, not knowledge, leads us to being.

In turning aside from a rationalistic, intellectualistic approach to being, Marcel elaborates a new type of reflection—secondary reflection—which searches for being in the concrete realities of experience. His concrete approaches to the mystery of being are nothing more than different modalities of secondary reflection.

We must take care to guard against a possible misinterpretation. Marcel's turning from the problem of being in general to particular beings is not a renunciation of the ontological task of philosophy; it is rather the transposition of the question of being into another register. When Heinemann calls Marcel a "mysterious empiricist," he captures something of his passion for the concrete and the individual. Yet this is only one aspect of Marcel's philosophical concern. Marcel says his thought has always been animated by two concerns that at first seem contradictory. The first of these is expressed most directly in his dramatic works, whereas the second is most evident in his strictly philosophical writings. Of these concerns he says: "The latter is what I shall call the exigence of being; the first is the obsession with *beings* taken in their individuality but also affected by the mysterious relations which link them together. . . . It seems to me that I accepted the view *a priori,* long before I was able to justify it to my own satisfaction, that the more we are able to know the individual being, the more we shall be oriented, and as it were, directed towards, a grasp of being as such."[9]

In order to see the logic behind Marcel's affirmation that the way to being involves grasping the individual being in its concrete reality, we must turn to the third stage in Marcel's ontological thinking, to the beginnings of his elaboration of a concrete approach to being.

THE QUESTION OF BEING TRANSPOSED

The attempt to derive the affirmation of being from the structures of thought fails because it tacitly assumes that being is an object we can discover by primary reflection. Marcel denies that any method seeking to reach being by pure intelligence devoid of love can be successful. Hence if the question of being is to receive a fruitful treatment, we must shift the ground on which the question is asked.

The transposition takes place when Marcel suggests that the question of being is not a *problem,* which means it cannot be considered apart from the subject who asks about being. He calls this "the transition from the problem of being to the question 'What am I?' What am I, I who ask questions about being? What am I like, that I should be led to ask these questions? The transition from problem to mystery."[10] Suddenly the datum that seemed to be before me when I asked the question of being invades me, and I can no longer separate the question of who I am from the question of the nature of being. In transposing the question of being I find that the first philosophical act must be an examination of the credentials of the questioner. As pure problems—questions in which the data are all before the questioner, actually or potentially—the problem of the self and the problem of being cancel one another out. No longer can we speak of the problem of being, but only of the mystery of being. This should be clear if we consider the relation of the questioner to the question asked about being. I who ask the question about being *am;* I exist; in spacial terms, I am somehow included within that about which I ask.

In order to see the real nature of the transposed question of being, we must refer to the description of being Marcel gave earlier: "being is . . . that which does not allow itself to be dissolved by the dialectics of experience."[11] Having rejected the possibility of a purely problematic approach to being, ontology must proceed by seeking to discover what in human experience resists the acids of criticism, despair, doubt, and tragedy. The question of being *is* the question of salvation. It focuses not on the effort to discover the structures of reality in general or of realities in particular but on the immanence of the abiding or the eternal within human experience. Although it starts within human experience, ontology is not necessarily reduced to a study of purely subjective states of feelings about things; it is rather the search for the inexhaustible, in which the authentic self participates. The being we seek cannot be divorced from feeling, but neither can it be reduced to feeling. Only if the self participates in something inexhaustible is there being and salvation.[12] "Being is above all inventories. Despair is, so to speak, the shock felt by the mind when it meets with 'There is no more.' "[13]

It still remains to be determined whether experience provides a testimony to being and whether there are dimensions of experience that constitute a presentiment within human life of an abiding reality. Does experience testify to being or only to the flux and vanity of all things? In answering this question we will (1) examine a range of experiences that reveal the exigence of being and (2) give an analysis of certain concrete approaches to the mystery of being, that is, of "certain data which are spiritual in their own right, such as fidelity, hope, and love, where we may see man at grips with the temptations of denial, introversion and hard heartedness."[14]

THE EXIGENCE OF BEING

Marcel maintains that at the heart of the human condition there is an exigence for being (*l'exigence ontologique*). The word *exigence* indicates neither a wish nor an affirmation that there must be being. "It is rather a deep-rooted interior urge, and it might equally well be interpreted as an appeal."[15] Otherwise stated, the exigence is not reducible to some psychological state, mood, or attitude a person *has;* it is rather a movement of the human spirit that is inseparable from being human. At the extreme limit of thought it can be said to be an "affirmation in regard to which I am, in a sense, passive, and of which I am the stage rather than the subject."[16]

The nature and significance of the exigence of being need not necessarily be clear to the person who feels it. At its primitive or preconscious level it is akin to the inarticulate longing for an unknown good. Perhaps we may say that it is the metaphysical demand arising from a yet unconscious awareness of the vacuum created by inauthentic existence. There are different states of awareness of the exigence of being, ranging from a mild uneasiness and boredom in the midst of a life that provides diversion and labor but neither joy nor vocation, to an active and passionate anxiety expressed in a frantic, conscious search for the meaning of life. The clearest way to characterize what Marcel means by this exigence is to begin with a concrete portrait of the meaning, in social and personal terms, of the loss of the awareness of being.

We live in a world in which the sense of being is increasingly repressed. Marcel sees evidence for this in many of the activities and attitudes of our society. Perhaps the most striking instance is in the tendency to measure the meaning of persons in terms of the functions they perform in society. "The individual tends to appear both to himself and to others as an agglomeration of functions. As a result of deep historical causes, which can as yet be understood only in part, he has been led to see himself more and more as a mere assemblage of functions, the hierarchical interrelation of which seems to him questionable or at least subject to conflicting interpretations."[17] One of the most obvious expressions of the reduction of persons to their functions may be seen in the curious twist given in the present age to the Biblical doctrine of vocation. Vocation has become synonymous with work. The result of this thoroughly un-Christian idea of vocation is that the unemployed and the retired become superfluous and lack a *raison d'être* both in their own eyes and in those of society at large. To be unemployed is to be lacking in that which gives a person value and worth—a function, a job to be performed. The effort of a concrete ontology such as Marcel's, directed toward the reaffirmation of a concept of vocation in which people are called on *to be* and in which work is only one aspect or expression of being, has a particular urgency in a world in which automation promises more unemployment and more leisure.

A second symptom of the loss of the sense of being is the ubiquitous, passionate quest for entertainment and diversion. Marcel gives a critique of the significance of entertainment that is strongly reminiscent of Pascal. A world needing constantly to be entertained is one from which the vital center has been lost, one that is tired and in the ebb of life. No purpose (*telos*) informs its activities. Rather it is occupied with the multiplication of means and techniques designed to serve unconscious and often unworthy ends.

> The need for amusement, as each of us knows from his own experience, is bound up with a certain ebbing of life's tide. . . . The ego is without any doubt faced with a dilemma; to fulfill itself or to escape. Where it does not attain fulfillment, it is only conscious of itself as of an unendurable gaping void from which it must seek protection at any price. Anyone who is absorbed does not know this void; he is as it were caught up in plenitude, life envelops him and protects him.[18]

The craving for diversions is the effort to repress the exigence of being by turning aside from the question "Who am I?"

Christiane, in Marcel's play *Le Monde cassé,* is an excellent example of a person who tries to repress the ontological exigence. She lives at the center of a circle of fast, sophisticated, spiritually unemployed people, all occupied with the trivia of life. She has plunged herself into this life because of a disappointing love affair in her youth with a man who revealed his decision to become a monk at the very moment she was to have declared her love for him. In reaction against this event, which drained the meaning and ecstasy from her life, she enters a loveless marriage with a boring husband whom most of her friends dislike and who takes no part in her social life. In the midst of the titillating excitement of social affairs she senses the emptiness and falsity of her life and says to a companion:

> Do you not sometimes have the impression that we live—if this can be called living—in a broken world? Yes, broken like a broken watch. The resort does not function any longer. In appearance nothing has changed. Everything is all right. But if one puts the watch to his ear . . . one hears nothing. You know,

the world, that which we call the world, the world of men . . . at other times it had a heart. But one believes that this heart has ceased to beat.[19]

All of the tendencies of modern society that converge to identify persons with their functions, to rob them of their dignity, their hope, their purpose, succeed in creating an ontological vacuum but not in destroying the exigence of being. The exigence of being survives because it is a structural condition of human life. This may be seen in the way it manifests itself. Marcel speaks of this exigence variously as *inquiétude,* as the exigence of transcendence, and as hope.[20] There is a certain unrest, dis-ease, or dissatisfaction that always haunts us because we are unsure of the meaning of our own lives. This dissatisfaction is inseparable from the desire to transcend the disintegration and emptiness of the broken world. The exigence of transcendence is not a desire to get beyond the conditions of incarnate existence or to transcend experience but rather a desire to penetrate to a more meaningful and profound dimension of reality. Marcel suggests that there are varying degrees of purity in experience and that the aspiration to pure, rich, full, significant experience is the meaning of the exigence of transcendence. By a "pure" mode of experience he means one saturated with meaning and value, with "intelligible essences": "Let us imagine in an even vaguer fashion whatever sort of thing an intelligible essence might be, and we can easily conceive that the experience most fully charged with these imponderable elements, intelligible essences, might at the same time be the purest."[21]

To have established a demand or exigence of being that is central to the human condition is far from having demonstrated that there is or may be an experience that provides an irrefutable testimony to and assurance of being. Even if this exigence of being is not a mere feeling but the very questing of the human spirit essential to humanness—even if there must be participation in being if human life is not to end in functionalization, despair, and meaninglessness—it does not follow that there *is* being. It may be the case that man is, as Sartre says, a useless passion and that his nature is such that he longs for and demands that which is contradictory. It may be that the exigence of being is nothing more than the impossible longing of the *pour-soi,* the being-for-itself, to be an object, to be *en-soi,* and to be established, founded, and immune to change and decay. Certainly Marcel would not contend that we can pass from what *ought* to be to what *is.* How then can we proceed from the fact of this ontological hunger to an affirmation of the existence of that which fulfills the hunger?

The first step is to observe the relation between question and answer, exigence and fulfillment. The point Marcel wants to make might be seen as a philosophical corollary to the Augustinian principle that one can only seek God because one already has *in some sense* found Him. The hunger for being is possible only because there is a foretaste, the question of being only because there is some indication of an answer, and the quest for being only because there is a blinded intuition. In the terms of Marcel's concrete philosophy it can be said that individuals never cease to be partially informed by their essence; they are never completely lacking in the dimension of depth, intersubjectivity, love; they never exist in a complete ontological vacuum. The conquest of soul, essence, or depth, or the participation in the mystery of being, is never completely absent from any human life.

Thus experience as a whole provides material to develop not only the question of being but also the answer. Taken alone, the experience of disease, discontent, and despair would lead to the affirmation that there is no being. However, we are vouchsafed experiences of fullness, of hope, of love, and of joy. The elaboration of an ontology depends on choosing the correct aspect of experience as the key analogy by which we understand the significance of experience as a whole. The defense of being must begin at the right place—which, as we have seen, cannot be with the structure of thought or the existence of objects—or else it is doomed to failure from the beginning. In defining the starting point of ontology Marcel says in his Gifford lectures:

> Two things seem to me to be of importance. First, we must understand that this enquiry can be developed only if we take a certain fullness of life as our starting point; secondly, we must at the same time note well that this fullness of life can in no circumstances be that of my own personal experience considered in an exclusively private aspect, considered in as much as it is *just mine;* rather it must be that of a whole which is implied by the relation to the *with,* by the *togetherness,* on which last year I laid such emphasis.[22]

Intersubjectivity is the presupposition of ontology, but it is not a sufficient condition for the affirmation of being. There is a certain low degree of intersubjectivity, of the reality of being with others, that is not yet sufficient to provide the basis for ontology. Only in its developed form, in which love, fidelity, faith, and hope emerge, can intersubjectivity justify the assertion that there is being. Hence by analyzing the demands that are interior to love, we can see why love demands being.

Love: The Essential Ontological Datum

Love, in so far as distinct from desire or as opposed to desire, love treated as the subordination of the self to a superior reality, a reality at my deepest level more truly me than I am myself—love as the breaking of the tension between the self and the other, appears to me to be what one might call the essential ontological datum. I think, and will say so by the way, that the science of ontology will not get out of the scholastic rut until it takes full cognisance of the fact that love comes first.[23]

Why does the experience of love lead to the affirmation of being? The answer can only be that love and fidelity imply an absolute vow that can only be made in the light of a recognition of the eternity and absolute value of the other, that is, of the being of the other. The affirmation of love, or the faith of the lover (fidelity, faith, and love are inseparable, as we will see later) is that the beloved is indestructible, eternal. A character in one of Marcel's plays says that to love a being is to affirm, "Thou, at least, thou shalt not die."[24] Within love as it is fully developed there is an exigence for perenniality, an apprehension that the other *is* and that nothing can destroy what truly *is*. It is precisely within the relationship of love that the assurance is given of something that resists, that abides, even if all else passes away. The real meaning of perenniality is in saying, "Because I love you, because I affirm you as being, there is something in you which can bridge the abyss that I vaguely call 'Death.' "[25]

The case for ontology rests on a defense of the integrity of love, faith, fidelity, and hope. If the exigencies interior to these ways of experiencing reality be denied, then there can be no being. Here is the real center of the concrete ontology of Marcel. His concern is with the restoration of the "ontological weight of human experience," or in other words with a justification of the inviolability of the logic of love and faith.[26] It is without doubt true that one may reject love and faith as being only subjective illusions, but in doing so one accepts the logic of a type of thought that is alien; one accepts criteria that are external to the matter being judged. Marcel has affirmed that a "concrete, personalized, thought . . . takes shape only in so far as it discovers the exigencies by which it will be qualified."[27] Therefore in the elaboration of a metaphysical position we must decide the area of experience from which the clue will be taken that will, by extrapolation, help us understand experience as a whole. The logic of the experience chosen is determinative. Marcel has chosen to take as his point of reference the experience of love-blending-into-faith, and it is the exigence interior to this experience that shapes his concrete ontology. We might say Marcel provides a philosophical elaboration of the Pauline insight, "So faith, hope, love abide, these three; but the greatest of these is love."[28]

We have seen that being is a mystery approachable only through individual beings and, further, that beings can only be known as they are approached in love. That love is "the essential ontological datum" will become clearer as we look more closely at fidelity, which is the precondition of all love, and at faith, which is the highest form of fidelity.

FIDELITY: A CONCRETE APPROACH TO THE MYSTERY OF BEING

It is with the study of fidelity that Marcel's own thinking first breaks away from a problematic approach to being. This theme is introduced with a dramatic suddenness following his discussion of being and the principle of identity, and it assumes from the time of its introduction a central place in his thought.

> Being as the place of fidelity.
> How is it that this formula arising in my mind, at a given moment of time has for me the inexhaustible inspiration of a musical theme?
> Access to ontology.
> Betrayal as evil in itself.[29]

The expression "being as the place of fidelity," Marcel says, "gives the clue to my previous inquiries and at the same time heralds a new stage."[30] The emphasis on fidelity is a continuation and an extrapolation of the ideas of love and faith Marcel had been developing from the time of the first *Metaphysical Journal;* however, his developing concern is with approaches to being and not exclusively with approaches to God.

In the study of fidelity the unique emphasis of Marcel's concrete ontology becomes clear. Here we will see how the dual concerns that have always animated his philosophical thinking—the concern for beings in their singularity and the concern with being—are unified. We will also see how, in the words of Kenneth T. Gallagher, the "descent into intersubjectivity is simultaneously an ascent into transcendence."[31] The themes of fidelity and faith show that the category of the personal is at the center of Marcel's thinking. As Ian Alexander has noted, "M. Marcel's vision of the universe may rightly be defined as a 'pluralistic personalism.' The convinced enemy of any Monisms, he sees reality as composed of a multiplicity of spiritual units or 'selves,' of which God is the 'Absolute Self,' and including groups and communities in so far as they constitute spiritual units."[32]

It will be helpful to anticipate the conclusions of our analysis of fidelity. Fidelity gives access to being for three reasons: (1) without fidelity there would be no unity of the self, only successive moments in a process of becoming; (2) only through fidelity can we reach the being of the other, for it is in love that the assurance of being is granted; and (3) in faith, which we will see is the paradigm of fidelity, we reach the assurance that human relationships of love and fidelity are eternally significant.

Marcel's analysis of fidelity centers on an effort to understand how it is possible to make a promise or a vow, to bind oneself to an unknown future. His polemic is directed against the position that refuses people the right to fidelity in the name of sincerity. In its most radical form this is the position implied in the doctrine of the instant. If individuals are reduced to their present states of consciousness and must choose between sincerity and fidelity, between living in the moment and bad faith, the self can have no unity or being. It is fidelity alone that makes it possible for the self to become a unity, because the principle of unity lies in a creative commitment to another person. Fidelity is "the only means we have of effectively vanquishing time."[33]

It would be disastrous to identify fidelity with mere constancy or tenacity in fulfilling to the letter the promises one has made. We cannot, of course, deny that for some persons fidelity is reduced to adherence, as in those innumerable cases where a husband or wife will be faithful solely from the motive of obligation. This is, however, a travesty of true fidelity, for it identifies fidelity with consistency, which may well be a disguised form of pride. Merely to be constant may be a betrayal of fidelity. We have only to remember the parable of the talents in the New Testament to see that fidelity cannot be identified with the preservation of the status quo. This becomes somewhat clearer when we realize that fidelity is given to a person and not to a principle. It is of the very essence of fidelity to be creative and to seek to cooperate with the other person's efforts to become free and creative. "So little is fidelity akin to the inertia of conformism that it implies an active and continuous struggle against the forces of interior dissipation, as also against the sclerosis of habit."[34] In a world where the individual is *homo viator*, faithfulness must either be supple or turn into betrayal.

Although there are emotional and volitional aspects of fidelity, it can be identified with neither of these. Fidelity is an act of the total person taking responsibility for another. As such it is the response to an appeal. If we think of fidelity in terms of love, it would seem there is a scale in which *eros* is at the base and *agape* at the summit. Only as fidelity approaches the unconditional love of *agape* can it be truly open and creative.

As a response to an appeal that arises from the presence of the other, fidelity is "the recognition of something permanent. We are now beyond the opposition between understanding and feeling. . . . The idea of an ontological permanence—the permanence of that which lasts, of that which implies history, as opposed to the permanence of an essence or a formal arrangement."[35] We might say that in pledging oneself, in vowing fidelity to another, one recognizes the being, in contrast to the life, of the other. To say that fidelity is the recognition of something permanent in the other is the same as to say that it is the prolongation of presence. It is only as I treat the other as present, as a thou, that the mystery of the other's being can be affirmed. "Thus if creative fidelity is conceivable, it is because fidelity is ontological in its principle, because it prolongs presence which itself corresponds to a certain kind of hold which being has upon us; because it multiplies and deepens the effect of this presence almost unfathomably in our lives."[36] Being related to the presence of the other, fidelity is closely allied with availability (*disponibilité*). "Creative fidelity consists in maintaining ourselves actively in a permeable state; and there is a mysterious interchange between this free act and the gift granted in response to it."[37]

How is fidelity to be justified? On the purely ethical level one might appeal to the Kantian principle of treating the other person as an end and never as a means. However, this leads us only to a principle of respect and not to the unconditional vow essential to fidelity. We may, on the ethical level, see that an unconditional vow is necessary for human relationships to reach their highest point. But it is only when fidelity reaches its highest point as faith in God that the unconditional vow implied in human love receives its most complete justification. We may now turn to the question we have been skirting thus far: What is the connection between my fidelity to an empirical thou and my faith in God? This question must be stated in its broadest terms if we are to find an adequate answer. It is the question of the relation of the mystery of communion to the mystery of faith, or of the relation of being to God.

FIDELITY AND FAITH

The nature of the connection we seek between fidelity and faith is not easy to specify. Here as in other places Marcel's philosophy moves on a middle ground between phenomenology and psychology. Certainly we would fail if we sought to find a logical connection, for we are trying to discover the relationship between two types of relations and not merely between abstract concepts. Fidelity and faith are states of being whose nature can only be discovered from *within*. Therefore the philosopher can only offer a phenomenology of these relations. We will look at the matter first from the perspective of fidelity and then from the perspective of faith.

The first question we must ask is whether there is anything within fi-

delity itself that seems to demand faith in God as the condition of fidelity
to one's neighbor. The first hint we have, according to Marcel, is the
factor of *unconditionality*. Fidelity demands an unconditional vow, an absolute commitment to the other person. "Love, in the fullest and most
concrete sense of the word, namely, the love of one being for another,
seems to rest on the unconditional: *I shall continue to love you no matter
what happens.*"[38] As an example of this unconditionality we may cite the
pledge of fidelity that is offered in marriage: "for better, for worse, for
richer, for poorer, in sickness and in health, to love and to cherish till
death us do part." When pledged with sincerity, such a vow is absolute.
If conditions are introduced, we have a relationship based not on fidelity
but on desire. (This is not to say that a vow is irrevocable. To continue
to give fidelity to a spouse who has left and married another person might
well be motivated by pride rather than fidelity.) We are here at the heart
of Marcel's argument. Fidelity demands an absolute pledge, an unconditional commitment. The question one immediately wants to ask is, Does
an absolute commitment demand that one be committed to an Absolute
Personal Being—to God? Marcel's answer is that ultimately it does. The
person who makes an absolute commitment to another in fidelity gives
witness to the Absolute Thou even without articulating this witness.
"One might say that conditional pledges are only possible in a world
from which God is absent. Unconditionality is the true sign of God's
presence."[39]

Such a claim seems startling. It is interesting to note that Sartre holds
the same position. He denies that we can follow the path of some of the
nineteenth-century humanists who dispensed with the idea of God but who
found it necessary to maintain certain values as absolute if they were to
live in a stable society. However, Sartre concludes that since there is no
Absolute, there can be no absolute values. If values are not in some sense
a priori and absolute, then they are created by people and by society. What
has been created by people may be changed by people.

Thus we get the first hint of the connection between fidelity and faith.
Fidelity moves toward an absolute commitment that can be fully articulated
only where there is religious faith. "Fidelity can never be unconditional
except when it is Faith, but we must add, however, that it aspires to unconditionality."[40]

The second clue to the relation of fidelity and faith is given us in the
demand, internal to love, for the eternity of the beloved. As we have seen
earlier, love demands that something in the beloved be indestructible, perennial, and eternal. "What cannot be accepted is the death of the beloved
one; more deeply still the death of love itself; and this nonacceptance is

perhaps the most genuine mark of the divine in ourselves."[41] Thus at the death of a loved one, fidelity is joined to faith as one hopes in God for the being of the other. This clue could only be followed by a full discussion of the phenomenon of hope, which is beyond the scope of this essay.

We get only hints about the relation of faith to fidelity by looking at fidelity; therefore we must switch our attention to faith. Marcel readily admits that the connection we seek can be found only from the vantage point of faith, and he denies that there is anything philosophically scandalous about this, since "a metaphysic can only grow up within a certain situation which stimulates it. And in the situation which is ours, the existence of a Christian datum is an essential factor."[42] A certain historical connection between faith and fidelity may be traced even by the philosopher who is not a Christian. A sensitive philosophical analysis would reveal a correlation between the loss of faith in an Absolute Thou (that is, the death of God) and the atrophy of the fidelity of one person toward another. Whether the loss of fidelity and unconditional promises in human affairs—for example, in marriage, friendship, and international relations—is a situation to be applauded, like the withering away of a vestigial appendix, or one to be deplored is a decision that must be made by the philosopher *qua* person and not *qua* phenomenologist. Thus a philosopher may offer to show the connection of fidelity to faith via a phenomenology of faith; the fact that that philosopher may be a Christian does not destroy the philosophical nature of the undertaking.

From the perspective of faith, fidelity cannot be separated from faith any more than love of neighbor can be separated from love of God.[43] The central commandments of Judaism as well as of Christianity are love of God and love of neighbor; thus the vertical can never be separated from the horizontal. Fidelity in human relationships is not something added to faith; it is the way in which the believer is faithful to the Absolute Thou. Marcel states: "My deepest and most unshakable conviction . . . is that it is not God's will at all to be loved by us *against* the Creation, but rather glorified *through* the Creation and with the Creation as our starting point."[44] Indeed it is fidelity and love that give us the only clue to the meaning of God's will. "The more we shall put love at the center of our lives, the more certain we shall be that we act according to God's will."[45]

Faith and fidelity are seen by Marcel as the same reality directed toward different foci. Faith is the paradigm of fidelity pledged to the Absolute Thou. As such it contains all of the temptations to denial as well as the rewards of relationship. Martyrs and saints give the strongest witness to fidelity. "In this connection the study of sanctity with all its concrete attributes seems to me to offer an immense speculative value; indeed, I am not far from saying that it is the true introduction to ontology.''[46]

From the viewpoint of faith, all fidelity is an earnest of faith. Those unbelievers who live in fidelity create a climate in which belief can grow just as small trees create a climate in which a forest of large trees can grow. Their love is like an underground spring keeping the life around them well watered and green and free from despair, from self-hatred, from meaninglessness, by a testimony that they do not articulate. They are, in terms of Christian theology, wordless witnesses to the Word. Their fidelity is a mode of participation in the mystery of being.

From the viewpoint of faith, the concrete approaches to being manifest the immanence of God in human experience. (Here Marcel stands solidly within the tradition of natural theology.) Behind every approach to being and every ethical value lies the hidden presence of God. Needless to say, Marcel would deny that the presence of God can be *deduced* from any ethical or ontological datum. It is the function of Christian witness to lead the inarticulate witness to recognize the crypto-presence of God lying at the heart of fidelity.

BEING AND GOD

To conclude our discussion of faith and fidelity, let us draw together the threads of our inquiry by asking as directly as possible about the relationship between the object of faith (God) and the object of fidelity (being). Some commentators on Marcel's thought have sought to show that his ontological language is crypto-theological and that there is an identity between language about God and language about being. Pontifex and Trethowan, for instance, say that "for M. Marcel, to speak of 'being' is in some sense to speak of God. The reference to 'intrinsic or significant value' suggests that 'beings' are properly so called when the relation in which they stand to God is appreciated."[47] We must ask whether there is an identity of God and being in Marcel's thinking.

The first step in answering this question is to remind ourselves that neither God nor being is in the realm of the problematic or the objective. Since only concepts can be identical, we could only meaningfully ask the question of the identity of God and being if we assumed that they both belonged to the sphere of objective reality, for then alone could we properly form concepts of them that could be compared. We have seen, however, that both belong to the realm of mystery; hence being is inseparable from our participation in concrete approaches, and God can only be thought of—or, more properly, invoked—in faith.

If in the light of this we rephrase the question and ask about the relation between the mystery of being and the mystery of God, we may see the beginning of the answer we seek. Our first step must be to go back to the meaning of the assertion of being. Marcel directs his ontology toward the discovery of that which abides not as a substratum beyond the phenomenal world, but as a support and an assurance within human experience. He focuses upon those elements (presences) within human experience that give, in the words of Tillich, the "courage to be." He expresses this by saying that his effort is directed toward restoring the "ontological weight" of human experience. The nearest we can get to a direct expression of this element that restores the ontological weight to human experience is to say that it is the mystery of love. That which militates against the restoration of the sense of being is despair and isolation. Thus both fidelity and faith give the assurance of being. Both conspire to restore the ontological weight to human experience. The relation between God and being can perhaps best be approached in the metaphor Marcel uses of an orchestra in which each instrumentalist gradually gets a sense of participation in the unity of a musical theme.

> From the moment when we open ourselves to these infiltrations of the invisible, we cease to be the unskilled and yet pretentious soloists we perhaps were at the start, and gradually become members, wide-eyed and brotherly, of an orchestra in which those whom we so inaptly call the dead are quite certainly much closer to Him of whom we should not perhaps say that He conducts the symphony, but that He is the symphony in its profound and intelligible unity; a unity in which we can hope to be included only by degrees, through individual trials, the sum total of which, though it cannot be foreseen by each of us, is inseparable from his own vocation.[48]

Taking this metaphor as our guide may not enable us to give any final answer to the question of the relation of being to God, or of ontological language to theological language, but it will at least allow us to locate one source of difficulty involved in giving an answer. We have presented two perspectives from which an answer may be given. From the perspective of faith, the symphony of being is inseparable from the conductor, and the unity, harmony, and assurance found within human relationships are experienced as earnests of the presence of God. It is from this point of view that Marcel can speak of "the hidden identity of the way which leads to holiness and the road which leads the metaphysician to the affirmation of Being," and also that he can affirm that "the exigence of God is simply the exigence of transcendence disclosing its true face."[49] However, if we adopt another perspective, that of one whose love, hope, and fidelity have not given rise to an articulate faith in God, there is a testimony to participation in the intelligible unity and harmony of the symphony of being, but no testimony to the conductor of the symphony.

We may conclude that for the faithful unbeliever ontological language represents the ultimate expression of those eternal assurances interior to a loving participation. For the believer it represents a necessary but penultimate expression of the assurances of eternal value given within human relationships, which are also understood to mediate the assurance of participation in the Divine Life. Although from one point of view it is ultimate and from the other penultimate, ontological language provides the ground on which the believer and the faithful unbeliever may communicate and witness to one another, for both participate in the same symphony of being. Both ontological and theological language remain necessary even from the perspective of faith, for absolute fidelity to God will have no meaning in a world from which human fidelity has fled, nor ultimately is human fidelity possible unless there remains at least a veiled sense of the holy.

Summary

We have seen that being cannot be approached directly by purely conceptual means because it belongs to the realm of the mysterious rather than of the problematic. This means that I may only approach being insofar as I am totally involved and that to speak of a knowledge of being in itself, apart from participation, is meaningless. If we may use a metaphor that is still dualistic and spacial in its connotations, we may say that the knowledge of being is possible only because it is immanent in the one who participates.

The indwelling presence of being is experienced as the abiding assurance that something of eternal value is being wrought in the empirical conditions of human life. This assurance is not of the nature of an intellectual grasp; it is not conceptual in its essence but is the indwelling presence of the eternal, which the believer identifies with the spirit of God. The nature of the assuring presence that invades one in the environs of the mystery of being remains unclear, although it provides the clarity and illumination that make creative, free, and loving existence possible.

Marcel's ontology does not move toward any systematic understanding of being but rather among those experiences that are the immanent assurances of the presence of being: love, fidelity, faith, and hope.

If being cannot finally be characterized or conceptualized, there are nevertheless certain general statements that can be extrapolated from Marcel's concrete ontology. First, in a very real sense it is true to say that being is a relation that, paradoxically, creates its terms. One may object that a relation is logically between terms that are in some sense substances, and we must grant that in a certain sense the terms creating the ontological relation exist prior to the relationship. However, the relationship is, ontologically speaking, prior to its terms. I and thou are constituted as loving beings by participation in the relationship. Second, we can say that being is a dynamic and not a static reality; it is not a substance that is given but a conquest that has constantly to be made. Third, it is convertible with the good, as in Platonism, and with love, as in Christianity. Finally, ontological language is primarily used in relation to the intersubjective world and refers to the nonpersonal world only analogically or insofar as objects become transmuted into presences. Hence, although Alexander describes Marcel's thought about being as "pluralistic personalism,"[50] it is perhaps best characterized as ontological personalism, for Marcel combines an emphasis on individual beings with an emphasis on the overarching harmony and unity that do not engulf individuals but rather create their individuality. It is by participating in the fullness of being that each individual is constituted as joyful, *disponible,* and free to love and labor in a concrete world.

SAM KEEN

CONTRIBUTING EDITOR,
"PSYCHOLOGY TODAY"
FREELANCE PHILOSOPHER
JUNE 1968

NOTES

1. Gabriel Marcel, *Metaphysical Journal,* trans. Bernard Wall (Chicago: Henry Regnery Co., 1952), p. 174 (hereafter cited as *MJ*).

2. *MJ,* 179.

3. *MJ,* 181.

4. Gabriel Marcel, *Being and Having,* trans. Katharine Farrer (Westminster: Dacre Press, 1949), p. 31 (hereafter cited as *BH*).

5. *BH,* 28. The translator capitalizes *Being* here, as she usually does. There is seldom justification in the French text for this, the exception being those cases where Marcel is speaking of Being roughly as a synonym for God.

6. *BH*, 33.

7. *BH*, 36.

8. *BH*, 36.

9. Gabriel Marcel, *Creative Fidelity*, trans. Robert Rosthal (New York: Noonday Press, 1964), pp. 147–48 (hereafter cited as *CF*).

10. *BH*, 111.

11. *MJ*, 181.

12. The identification of being and salvation seems strange given that ontology has allegedly been the most abstract and least existential aspect of philosophy. However, if one goes back to the beginnings of ontological speculation in Greek philosophy, its true character becomes evident. In asking the question of being, the pre-Socratics were looking for some ultimate that in itself resisted destruction. The religious dimension of this quest is seen in the identification of the prime substance with the gods, as when Thales said all things were full of water and full of gods. The soteriological significance of being is more evident in Plato, where participation in the realm of true being (the forms) is salvation.

13. *BH*, 102.

14. *BH*, 119.

15. Gabriel Marcel, *The Mystery of Being*, trans. G. S. Fraser (vol. 1) and René Hague (vol. 2), 2 vols. (Chicago: Henry Regnery Co., 1950), 2:37 (hereafter cited as *MB*).

16. Gabriel Marcel, *The Philosophy of Existence*, trans. Manya Harari (New York: Philosophical Library, 1949), p. 8 (hereafter cited as *PE*).

17. *PE*, 2.

18. Gabriel Marcel, *Homo Viator*, trans. Emma Craufurd (Chicago: Henry Regnery Co., 1951), p. 85 (hereafter cited as *HV*).

19. Gabriel Marcel, *Le Monde cassé* (Paris: Desclée de Brouwer, 1933), p. 44; my translation.

20. *MB* 2:128, 162.   21. *MB* 1:55.

22. *MB* 2:8.   23. *BH*, 167.

24. Quoted in *MB* 2:61.   25. *MB* 2:62.

26. *BH*, 103.   27. *MB* 2:3.

28. I Cor. 13:13.   29. *BH*, 41.

30. *PE*, 95.

31. Kenneth T. Gallagher, "The Philosophical Method of Gabriel Marcel" (Ph.D. diss., Fordham University, 1958), p. 126.

32. Ian Alexander, "The Philosophy of Gabriel Marcel in Its Relations with Contemporary Thought," (Ph.D. diss., University of Edinburgh, 1948), 2:1.

33. *CF*, 152.   34. *PE*, 22.

35. *BH*, 96.   36. *PE*, 23.

37. *PE*, 24.

38. Gabriel Marcel, *The Existential Background of Human Dignity* (Cambridge, Mass.: Harvard University Press, 1963), p. 74.

39. Gabriel Marcel, "Theism and Personal Relationships," *Cross Currents* 1, no. 1 (1956): 40 (hereafter cited as "TP").

40. *HV*, 133.

41. "TP," 41.

42. *BH*, 120.

43. Marcel never gives the word *faith* an adequate definition. He seems to use it in a general sense to mean theistic faith. In his early writings he does not indicate in any way that faith is limited to Christian faith. However, it is true to say that Christian faith is always the paradigm. In his article "Theism and Personal Relationships," he expresses doubt about the possibility of a general theistic position. "I am sometimes doubtful whether theism can keep up an independent existence in the present world; whether, if it becomes fully conscious of itself, it is not bound to melt into Christianity" (p. 35). As a minimum working definition, faith means a relationship to an absolute Thou who is the creator of the world and who places us under an ethical obligation to our neighbors.

44. *BH*, 135.

45. "TP," 40.

46. *PE*, 27.

47. M. Pontifex and I. Trethowan, *The Meaning of Existence* (London: Longmans, Green and Co., 1953), 150.

48. *MB* 2:187.

49. *BH*, 85; *MB* 2:3.

50. Alexander, "The Philosophy of Gabriel Marcel," 2:1.

The Development of the Idea of Being in Marcel's Thought

REPLY TO SAM KEEN

As far as I am concerned, Sam Keen's excellent paper does not call for any critical remarks. But it does provide me with a chance to reiterate what the quest for being has been in the development of my thought.

Certainly in the beginning, I was much too influenced by the philosophers of freedom to keep from considering being with distrust—a distrust I gradually overcame. I distinctly recall that at the time of the publication of *L'Evolution créatrice,* I challenged the way Bergson seemed to identify being with the static in the last chapter of this work. As badly informed as I was on the great medieval philosophers, I was convinced that the conception of being held by someone like St. Thomas was infinitely more alive than that held by the author of *L'Evolution créatrice.*

It is not without difficulty that I attempt to recall, after so many years, the stages of my philosophical work as they are marked in the *Journal métaphysique.* It seems to me that I hardly applied myself directly to any speculation on being at that time. But I could perhaps say that existence, which has been the core of my search since 1921, was for me a sort of glass through which being first appeared to me.

I have often been asked since then, and again rather recently, how I viewed the relations between "existence" and "being," and I readily confess that this question remains beset with a certain obscurity. My most significant discussion of this difficult subject is in the second section of *Foi et réalité,* which is volume 2 of *Le Mystère de l'être.* I specifically recall saying, in the last part of that section, that to exist is above all to emerge or to arise: "But it is clear that if I can take a position that sets me off more distinctly from others, I should also be able to turn inward and do this by means of meditation. And it seems that this is linked to the

Translated from the French by Colette M. Ferran and Francois R. Ferran.

premonition of a reality that would be mine or, more precisely, that would make me essentially what I am."* And this would move me in the very direction (in the sense of *Richtung*) of being. However, it does not make sense to claim that existence is different from being; to do so would be to objectify and even to materialize concepts, something I have always opposed, even when I was far from waging the war against the spirit of abstraction that I pursued in later years. In reality, it was by basing everything on being (going beyond mere reference to it) that I waged that war, which continues throughout *Man against Humanity (Les Hommes contre l'humain)* and which is the existential background of *Human Dignity (La Dignité humaine)* and of *For Tragic Wisdom (Pour une sagesse tragique)*.

Clearly, it would be advisable to attempt a more precise definition of the words *basing everything* used above. Some time ago, I adhered to a notion I termed *blind intuition,* but I don't mind admitting that I find these words somewhat unsatisfactory. What I meant thereby was something that could be likened to an electrical power source, except that strictly speaking (and however odd or paradoxical it may seem) this power source is nothing over which we have control—nothing that is within our own power. A definite effort must be made here to restate the metaphors that might shed light on this extremely difficult idea. Here is the one that comes to mind as I write these lines. Suppose we were to say, for example, that from the outset each of us is plugged in, so to speak, to a certain current. But this experience, not being in the least the result of some act we know we accomplished, is rather a situation that we have to acknowledge as "prior"; I would venture to say that it is by definition *vorgefunden*. Would it be totally absurd to compare being to this central current?

Perhaps the particularly interesting point in this metaphor is that it allows one to understand that it is possible, at least in most cases, to take out the plug, thereby interrupting the current. This is precisely what every kind of positivist philosophy does. I will limit myself for the moment to these very general remarks, which eventually should be reexamined, modified, and, if necessary, developed further.

G.M.

---

*Translation by Colette M. Ferran and Francois R. Ferran. Cf. René Hague's version in *MB* 2:35.—ED.

4

Erwin W. Straus and Michael A. Machado

GABRIEL MARCEL'S NOTION OF INCARNATE BEING

G ABRIEL Marcel's style of existential thinking has been described as a sensualist metaphysic.[1] This means not only that themes such as embodiment, feeling, and sensation are integral to his thought, but that the theme of incarnation lies at the very center of the metaphysical quest.[2] For Marcel, the human body marks a person's insertion into space and time and institutes that person as a member of the world community. The body is an intricate system of hidden potentialities and relations—hidden only to the extent that they are not immediately evident to reflective thought, for they are recognized at the level of feeling. Only by a persistent and faithful effort of reflection can feeling bring an awareness of its own hidden intent. The human body is a highly sensitive organism capable of emerging into a "full-bodied" and "full-blooded" idea of its situation. The centrality of human embodiment was Marcel's unique discovery. It enabled him to break new ground andd turned him irrevocably in the direction of a concrete philosophy of existence.

A philosophy of life and existence needs a concrete point of departure: not just a logical certitude but an existential indubitable.[3] Marcel finds his starting point in the immediacy of lived existence itself. "I exist" constitutes for him the primary datum. Descartes's "I think" is too pallid to be real. It lacks flesh and blood. It cannot therefore constitute an existential point of departure. The "I think," cut off from its fleshly attachments, quite frankly does not exist. It is a mere mental figment, an abstraction.[4]

Marcel's existential indubitable is an incarnate being. The body is the touchstone of existence. It is an existent "such that, if I were to deny it, any assertion by me that anything else existed would become quite inconceivable."[5] Existence always has reference to one's body: "When I affirm that something exists, I always mean that I consider that something as connected with my body, as able to be put in contact with it, however indirect this contact may be."[6] In other words, existence is always in relation to an incarnate consciousness. The existential indubitable "I exist" turns out to be an embodied self, which, in its very mode of existing, is manifest to the world.[7]

Such an approach to reality contrasts sharply with Marcel's early Hegelian background. Even though Marcel had the subtlety and skill to engage in purely speculative disquisitions, his real interest lay elsewhere. He became less and less enchanted with abstractions and yearned passionately for the richness of concrete reality. No doubt his love for the theater exerted a sobering effect on his mind. But his persistent demand for a concrete approach was also a revolt from within idealism itself. Does not idealism in fact seek to install in the human mind the vantage point of an absolute observer? Is not its primary concern universal thought, or thought in general? According to Marcel, this can only be the thought of n'importe qui, of no one in particular, and therefore it is not anyone's thought at all. The first half of the *Metaphysical Journal* betrays Marcel's painful struggle to be delivered from his early idealism.

His experiences with the Red Cross during the First World War marked a turning point in his life. Marcel was required to supply information about missing persons to their families. He refused to treat the missing persons as cases and their plight as classified information. He regarded them rather as real beings who appealed to him for help, who evoked his interest and concern, and who sometimes even filled him with anguish. Such experiences only deepened his conviction that abstract thought misses the whole drama of existence. Later jottings in his diaries reveal his attempt to come to grips with life as he actually experienced it. Many of them are highly provocative personal sketches of happenings that troubled his thoughts. Marcel's very style of writing seeks vividly to capture the freshness and originality of each living moment as it makes its dramatic impact on his sensitive mind.

But why does human embodiment play such a vital role in Marcel's thought? Since Descartes, philosophy had made problematic the unity of mind and body as well as the relation between the self and the world. It also made problematic the whole sphere of life and experience itself, since the body theoretically operated like a machine. Most of the eighteenth- and nineteenth-century idealists struggled with these problems without being able to heal the breach. In their work, the world of immediate experience has very little to say. It stands mute before the threshold of thought, waiting for the mind to stir and to discover its meaning. Common to all forms of idealism is the unquestioned primacy of thought, consciousness, and mind. For this reason, all existence must be mediated by thought before any meaningful statements about its essence can be made. In reaction to such assumptions, Marcel declared that "a solipsistic type of idealism would never be able to grasp the fact of my existence."[8] From the idealist point of view, even sense experience is simply raw material to be interpreted by thought; indeed, mediation by thought is deemed inevitable. Sensation is merely the passive reception of what is fed into the brain through the intermediary sense organs. It is a conversion effected by the brain after the sensory organs have intercepted the impressions from the outside world. In contrast to the passivity of the sensory process, thought is considered active and constructive.

These unwarranted assumptions led Marcel to question seriously whether we can know anything beyond our own constructions. Not only does the knowledge of physical reality become problematic, but the possibility of arriving at any knowledge of metaphysical reality becomes so as well.

For Marcel, the basic error of idealism consists in dissociating the mind from the integral self and from the world to which the self belongs. Self, body, and world are conceived as if they formed three distinct spheres containing within themselves thoughts, sensations, and existing objects respectively. Ultimately all reality is reduced to two basic divisions: the realm of thoughts and the realm of things. So long as we adhere to these arbitrary categories, there can be no breakthrough to realism.

In the face of such abstractions, an inner conviction led Marcel to affirm that "out there" was a real world of real beings, that these existent beings were somehow linked with his own embodied existence, and that sensations, far from being passive impressions, were manifestations of the body's active intentionality. It was Marcel's task to discover these hidden links. He wrote that his philosophy aimed at restoring "those links which a certain type of ideology has conceived it as its task to break."[9] The primacy of the real asserts itself with full force. The whole order of existence is directly met and affirmed in experience, which, in the immediacy of unreflected awareness, belongs to the order of feeling—a feeling that easily and naturally evolves into a reflective awareness of its own intentionality. Experience thus understood, even sense experience, is much more than raw material to be transcended and worked up. It is not opposed to thought or reflection, but rather shapes and directs it. In this connection, Marcel observed that experience, properly understood in its active and dialectical aspects, cannot fail to transform itself into reflection.[10]

Of course, there were many historical landmarks that enabled the young Marcel to chart his voyage of discovery. From Hegelian idealism he inherited a passionate yearning for a transcendental realm beyond life. Here and there he could discern in the idealist tradition itself some little spark, some faint glimmer, that might one day illumine his path to a realist philosophy.

Bradley's doctrine of internal relations made a profound impression on Marcel's mind. According to Bradley, if things are considered "existences" and not merely "characters," then everything in this well-ordered universe is internally affected by its relations with every other thing. To take Bradley's example, a billiard ball, if considered an existence, occupies and is determined by a definite place and is qualified by the whole material system into which it enters. If this particular determination and qualification is altered, then the billiard ball is also altered. Only if it is considered a character, abstracted from its real situation, can it avoid change. But to conceive of it as a character is not to see it as it really is: an existing entity within a network of relationships. Thus for Bradley all relations are internal, since they affect the very nature of things taken as existences. By the same token, the whole world becomes one unified system of internal relations. This theory led Marcel to the discovery of what he was later to call the "intersubjective nexus" that links one being with another. The nexus in this case is provided by one's body, or, better still, by one's bodily existence. Despite its obvious merit, however, Bradley's monism was characterized by a gross neglect of the individual.

In this respect, Royce's philosophy was far more congenial. Although Royce's outlook is in keeping with the idealist tradition, Marcel felt a close kinship with Royce's attempt to incorporate his idealism in a concrete philosophy of the individual. Marcel clearly expressed his appreciation of Royce: "Faithful to the empirical tradition, which he deepened and enriched, Royce is . . . preoccupied with concrete experience, yours and mine."[11]

Reality, according to Royce, can only be the concrete expression of individual experience, the progressive realization of an act of consciousness that wills and understands at the same time. Real objects are accessible to us only through the ideas we have of them. These ideas are not merely sterile entities in the mind; they also have a volitional aspect. They go after the objects they refer to. The object is presented as a value to be realized. Thus an idea partially or fully realizes some willed end. Being is the "full expression of what our ideas mean and seek."[12] Being is the drama of human consciousness, which it progressively realizes through its ideas of objects. Ultimately, if being is the perfect fulfillment and expression of our individual lives, beyond all fragmentary knowledge of things, then being too must be uniquely individual. Each of us is only the unique expression of the being we partially realize. No one can take our place. In the presence of the real we stand alone.

Royce insists that individuality is revealed only to an act of love.[13] "There is no child like mine," says the parent. Love is the exclusive interest we devote to a being. It makes us declare that the object of our attention is unique. The cry of love is "There shall be no other." Individuality is the result of the selective attention freely directed toward it. As human individuals we progressively realize our uniqueness by acts of loyalty, by subordinating our lives to some cause that gives unity, direction, purpose, and coherence.

Marcel's indebtedness to Royce extends to the discovery of the Thou as the correlate of the I.[14] This aspect of Royce's philosophy gave Marcel the bridge he needed to cross from absolute idealism to a philosophy of concrete existence. Yet Royce lacked a theory of participation; his philosophy states that no human mind can penetrate another—that each stands in the isolation of its own subjectivity.

For a theory of participation, Marcel needed Hocking, whose magnum opus, *The Meaning of God in Human Experience*, greatly stimulated Marcel's social and religious philosophy.[15] Chapter 6, entitled "The Destiny of Feeling," states as its basic thesis that feeling is essentially cognitive— that its essential nature is to terminate in knowledge. Feelings have a "sting of restlessness" about them. They are e-motive, flights to a beyond, as if they needed to escape from themselves. Action is therefore implicit in feeling. Furthermore, feeling is a movement or struggle to grasp its own hidden intent. It begins as a form of activity vaguely aware of itself and comes to rest in its own incipient idea. The passage from feeling to idea, from an unconscious movement to a clear grasp of what the movement is about, is effected quite naturally and spontaneously. All feeling is therefore cognitive. It is "idea-apart-from-its-object tending to become idea-in-presence-of-its-object."[16] Marcel leans heavily on this chapter in working out his own theory of sensation as a form of "submerged," as distinct from "emergent," participation.[17] The former is *sentir*, feeling below the level of thought; better still, it is feeling that has not yet emerged into a conscious idea of its own intentionality.

We are now able to put together the essential ingredients of Marcel's philosophy of concrete existence. The starting point, the central datum, of his metaphysical quest is embodied existence. More precisely, it is the human person who exists bodily. My body, in its very mode of existing, carries with it an awareness of its intersubjective bond with the existing beings around it. The experience of my body is basically the feeling of my sense of community with myself and with the world. *Sentir* is therefore the primordial modality of embodiment. The feeling of community, which mediates every contact with the world, operates under the aegis of its own governing idea, which it can bring to full consciousness through reflection. Body feeling—the feeling of this body as mine—is a continuous process of the participation of the self in its embodied situation in the world, a participation in the range of existence from the prereflective (submerged) to the reflective (emergent). Thus human embodiment, with all its nuances of primordial and sensory feeling, came to play a key role in Marcel's thinking.

Nevertheless, the problem of mediation that Marcel inherited from his idealist forebears continued to haunt his thought. Every contact of the self with the world, however immediate and direct, brings up the question of a principle that is interposed between the knower and the world that is known. For most of his life Marcel grappled with the problem of mediation and virtually admitted it in the process of trying to deny it. Prior to and more basic than any instrumental mediation of the body, Marcel discerned a primal feeling of the body as one's own, which is the basis of the "sympathetic mediation" of one's body for other things.[18] Thus by an inveterate default of language, Marcel seemed to perpetuate the very dualism he was trying to suppress. Looking over his thought in retrospect, one sees that the problem of mediation could only arise if the body were really interposed between the self and the world, that is, if the self were really a disembodied self. Contrary to Hegelian dialectic, which relegates the knowing self to the status of "an intelligible form hovering over the world,"[19] Marcel's embodied self is an incarnate consciousness that carries with it an implied understanding of its felt community with the world. There is no need therefore to mediate existence by thought. At least this seems to be the obvious import of Marcel's conception of the body as "the non-mediatizable immediate."[20] Taking into account his real intent, we can reconstruct his thought and say that really there is no mediation at all. There is only the lived immediacy of participation. Self, body, and world are not three distinct spheres of reality with clearly definable boundaries. They are fluid categories: they flow into one another and only define themselves in relation to one another. The body that is mine is the lived body, which continually engages itself in its existential situation and realizes its community with the world.

Participation is the key to the problem of mediation. In reality, the body is not interposed between the self and the world. It is only in reference to the body's intentional acts that self and world become defined. Participation ensures that as embodied beings, we are not simply spectators juxtaposed to or positioned over other objects in the world. The existing self is not primarily a detached observer, it is a participant. We are constituted as selves only in our intentional acts. We are already engaged in and live off our existential situation before we can stand back and observe what has been going on prior to our thinking about it or taking note of it. Hence participation is the foundation of our experience of existing.

Without specifically saying so, Marcel distinguishes three levels, or hierarchies, of participation. The first level is that on which we establish, through feeling, acting, and sensing, our community with the world. This is a We relationship, an experience of our togetherness in being. The second is the level of communion, the relationship between an I and a Thou, which we freely enter into through creative fidelity, hope, and love. The third is the level of transcendence, where we plumb the depths of our possibilities in the experience of being. All three levels of participation depend on the phenomenon of embodiment.[21]

Embodiment always implies the unique experience of this body as "mine," of my lived body. The possessive index *mine* highlights the principle of intimacy, without which my body would cease to be specifically mine and would be just like any other body. Its unique reference to me prevents it from being considered purely from the objective observer's point of view, as is done in scientific studies of the body. Marcel observes that the purely objective conception of the body fails to take note of the bond that exists between me and my body. This relationship is far more intimate than what the notion of "having" or "using" a body will allow. Both having and using—the language of possession and instrumentality respectively—are secondary and derivative experiences. They become crucial only when the subliminal organization of the body and its functional integrity are temporarily interrupted (as when we "stop to think") or disrupted (as in sickness or disease).[22] As examples of noninstrumental communion between me and my body, we may think "of an ingrained habit, of a perfected skill, and of the ascetic grace of the saint."[23]

At any rate, both possession and instrumentality presuppose the body that is mine, the lived body. Possession in this case cannot be dissociated from the possessor, if only because the body, unlike other possessions, has no independent existence of its own. It cannot be exchanged or disposed of without completely dissolving the bond that makes it mine. To think of the body as a possession is to banish the self to "an indeterminate sphere from which it contemplates, without existing for itself, the anonymous play of the universal mechanism."[24] According to Marcel, possession of any kind is conceivable only because it is modeled on a more original sense of self-possession, which is my body.[25] In the same way, an instrument by definition shares in the same community of nature as my body, whose powers it extends. To conceive of my body as an instrument is therefore to presuppose the lived body. But if the body were nothing but an instrument, it would compromise the self, the principle of intimacy, and would reduce it to the same status as a physical body. My body then is neither a possession nor an instrument; it is what makes both possession and instrumentality possible. The intimate link I feel with my body is truly a unique relationship: it describes a unity that is not an identity. This sense of intimacy, which makes possible the possession of anything else whatsoever, is registered primarily in the modality of feeling. Marcel also speaks of "my body" as an organized system of powers that is inwardly felt before it is outwardly executed.[26] Instrumentality is therefore possible only so far as it extends the latent powers of the body.

Feeling is the basic modality of human embodiment. More precisely, my feelings embody me. To quote Marcel: "My body, insofar as it is properly mine, presents itself to me in the first instance as something felt; I am my body only insofar as I am a being that has feelings. From this point of view it seems therefore that my body is endowed with an absolute priority in relation to everything that I can feel that is other than my body itself. . . ."[27] Marcel's choice of the expression "I am my body" is perhaps not a happy one, but it does emphatically suggest that the self-body relationship is unique and that it manifests itself as an indecomposable unity. Self and body define themselves in reference to each other. Negatively, the expression is an attempt to close the gap that an instrumentalist notion creates. The relationship always retains its irreducible character: to say that I am my body is to point out that my body and I are not mutually exclusive; on the contrary, each implies the other.

There are two distinguishable moments in the experience of *sentir*. There is, first of all, the radical feeling of my body as intimately mine. The sense of bodiliness is brought home to me through forms of internal perception that Marcel describes as coenesthetic. The feeling of coenesthesia places me as an embodied being in such experiences as being tired, hungry, energetic, enthusiastic, and let down. The radical destruction of coenesthesia, if that were possible, would mean the destruction of my body as mine. Marcel calls the feeling of my body as mine an *Urgefühl*, or primordial feeling.[28] *Sentir* further implies that this body feeling (the feeling of my body as mine) lies at the root of all other feelings, such as sensations and activities, that immediately connect my body with the surrounding objects of the world at large. This is obviously true for the sense of touch. I cannot touch your hand without feeling that I am being touched at the same time. But it is also and perhaps less obviously true with respect to sensations other than touch. My body is at the same time what feels and what is felt.[29] *Sentir* in the primary sense has an absolute priority, since, in order to feel anything else, I must first of all feel my body as mine. My immediate contact with my body puts me at the same time in direct contact with the world. Thus I never go "beyond various modifications of my own self-feeling."[30]

Both meanings of *sentir* are crucially implicit in the experience of embodiment, which therefore turns out to be a unified, continuous process constituting the whole person. This process consists of two mutually implicative acts: the internal perception of my body and the external perception of the world. There are no gaps in this process. There is only a continuity of feeling-acting responses originating in my body and reaching out to the world. *Participation* is Marcel's term to describe the crossing over of boundaries between the embodied self and the world. Actually there are no boundaries at all. The inner world of the self and the outer reality of the world belong together; each has meaning only in reference to the other.

This coincidence and mutuality of implication can be described at the general level of feeling; it can also be articulated through the modalities of acting and sensing, which are the carriers of body feelings. With regard to acting, the feeling of my body as mine is carried over into the feeling that the whole world of existent beings belongs to the same system of relations that binds me to my body. In this case, embodiment is the process of realizing my active community with myself and with the world. In its most fundamental appearance, this sense of community is an intentional feeling for objects, which therefore form a network of relationships, with my body as the living center.[31] My body is a living presence that makes itself felt in an all-pervading way. Because it is in my body, it has a certain interiority. It has an inner life of its own. The objects that surround me become existents only to the extent that they share in the nature of my body, that is, only to the extent that they are sensible presences and not merely things.

The body is the living center from which all relations to the world of space and time radiate. According to Marcel, the place where I live has a very special meaning for me. It constitutes my primary center of interest. From here, my body is able to make effective contact with the surrounding world by means of some specific activity. I go to the supermarket to buy groceries. I walk to the library to do research. I drive to the cathedral to attend a wedding. In this way, the body is constantly creating its "network of connivances" with the surrounding objects by bringing them within its own "existential orbit."[32] The process of embodiment is acted out in the modality of feeling. Feeling incarnates me in the world; but the movement that starts out as a feeling generally evolves, by its own inner impulse, into a consciously directed activity and into distinct sense perceptions. Acting and sensing are extensions of body feelings. They show how the self embodies itself in the world by feeling its way around, by bringing its activities to bear on existent objects, and by presenting the world to us in sensation. We need to take a more careful look at these three ways of embodying ourselves.

Feeling is a form of bodily affectivity that enables the body to exercise its attention on objects. It is the modality in which my body is sensed as my body whenever it directs its attention to existing objects in the world.[33] In his carefully worded description of the nature of feeling, Marcel stresses two points. First, he tries to get away from the idea that feeling is the activity of an already constituted subject. There is no subject that feels.[34] Rather, feeling is the activity that embodies me in the world and that thereby constitutes me as a self. By its very nature, therefore, feeling refers to an activity not wholly under the control of the self. Second, feeling is opposed to a calculating reason that tends to override its own competence by demanding that reality be measured by reason's arbitrary standards rather than by the merits of each situation. In other words, feeling is intentional. It makes possible the emergence of the self and presents it to the world. The I that was so long hidden is now embodied, presented, drawn into the sphere of existence, and placed among other existing beings with which it recognizes, however dimly, its own secret links. The privacy of feeling, if it exists at all, is simply the recognition of an intimate self-presence in the very act of realizing one's fellowship with other beings. Marcel remarks that this feeling of intimacy with myself is only an inward resonance of a vaster "concert" to which I belong and which involves me in a "consensus," a feeling with and for others.[35] Therefore I do not exist for myself alone but am always in conjunction with others. It is in relation to my body that all other existents are affirmed. The whole of existence is proclaimed when I affirm my own existence. The affirmation "I exist" tends to merge with an affirmation such as "The universe exists."[36] The terminus of feeling is immediately my body and mediately some existing being in the world. The same principle of intimacy that binds me to myself also binds me to my fellow-beings. Existence always implies coexistence.

Feeling therefore carries with it the import of a global assurance: "I am!" The I in this case is the meeting point of many loyalties. That is why the discovery of self-presence contains a veiled reference to all existence. The assurance "I am!" is extended to include all existing beings with whom I acknowledge my hidden links. My body always secretly intrudes in all descriptions and affirmations of existence. The feeling that embodies me is therefore an act of vitality and generosity. It reveals me as existing in a manner that demands to be greeted.[37] Feeling bursts forth with unmistakable trust and promise as an act of salutation. It is an intrinsic act of admiration. Feeling highlights the existential moment. It endows the common hour with a touch of celebration. What we celebrate is the joy of life, of existence—of my own existence, to be sure, but also, in a global way, of the existence of others.

Feeling enacts my presentation to the world. It crosses me over, embodies me, presents me to the world. It discloses to me not simply the fact of my existence but the radical discovery of presence. This is at bottom an upsurge toward a fullness of life, of plenitude. Feeling is not a comfortable sentiment nurtured in my inmost subjectivity; rather, it is an outgoing, dynamic movement that proclaims my being to the world, a radical act of astonishment that invites recognition and participation by exclaiming, "Here I am!" Marcel links the sense of presence to feeling rather than to vision. This is perhaps because presence is felt even when it is not seen. The description of the body as a felt presence accounts for the polarity between the visible and the invisible, between the reality that is seen and the reality that is not seen but that is present and that must be accounted for. The presential aspects of the body tend to overrun its visible aspects. As a visible form my body is limited to the here and now; as a presence it is carried beyond itself by an overspilling of its boundaries. This explains why, even though I am confined to a definite position in space and time, I can still have effective contact with beings that are far away. Feeling awakens in me the sense of bodily presence beyond all objective descriptions and transcending all changing profiles. The lived immediacy of bodily presence is a nontransparent datum, intensely felt but not in every respect visible. The richness of the experience cannot be adequately represented by abstract schemata. It can only be entered into more fully. It must be lived and relived, evoked and recalled.

The exclamatory awareness of existence dawns on us as a sudden discovery. The birth of a child can awaken in us the wonder of existence. The death of a loved one can become the test of presence. An accident that brings us close to death's door can heighten our appreciation of the gift of life. In any case, we stumble upon existence with a rude shock; the routine of daily life so dulls our sensitivity that we fail to recognize what has been there all along.

Marcel further links the awareness of existence to the recognition of value.[38] To exist is to engage in the experience of presence, and presence is always valuable. It implies that our existence is laden with promise: we are what we are worth, and our "worth is decreased to the extent that our affirmation of existence is limited, pale and hesitant."[39]

Feeling is already implicit action. Marcel incorporates this basic thesis of Hocking's into his own theory of incarnation. The body that feels is also the body that is impelled to act. Marcel describes the body as a unified system of powers. Each power is only a specification of this organic unity.[40] My body is not primarily an object to be looked at but a reality to be participated in. Because it is lived, my body presents itself as a cluster of powers. The most intimate part of my being manifests itself as fundamental abilities that I can at will exercise upon objects around me. The body is felt as "being able to," as "having the power to," and I experience this by exercising my abilities or by resisting them.[41] By a subtle play on words, *avoir* becomes *pouvoir* when I recognize that my body is equipped with all the basic powers for getting around and accomplishing its tasks in the world. The heart of the recognition "I can" hides a suppressed dynamism, which consists in exercising the basic bodily powers of acting and sensing so as partly to reveal and partly to conceal the self. The body is the means for manifesting the personality, for externalizing the body that is indisputably mine. Activity, movement, and instrumental mediation are ways of extending the body's built-in powers to perceive, handle, grasp, and manipulate the surrounding objects in the world. They are ways of developing and perfecting the skills for which the body is adapted. "Such powers are . . . the very notes of an organized body's activity."[42] The body is thus functionally described in terms of its fundamental abilities.

The feelings that embody me are possible only in the context of my body's organic activities in the world. Body actions are a continuation of body feelings. Incarnation is a continuous process of feeling-acting. Feelings are a reflection of body action, and body action is the natural terminus of body feeling. The ontological priority of feeling is in no way compromised by its subsequent recognition at the precise moment of acting. Feelings always result in an action of some kind, and action always presupposes feeling. The two are mutually implicative: one never exists without the other.

Incarnation is a dynamic process of animation that overcomes bodily inertia by acting. Action is "the flesh of advancing process," "the forward movement of existence itself, of my existence"; "action traverses my body."[43]

Sympathetic mediation is sometimes accompanied by instrumental mediation. Sympathetic mediation depicts my body as it manifests my actions immediately. My body's natural affectivity for things already discloses a way of getting to them and of bringing them into its existential orbit. Instrumental mediation makes these objects further accessible by bringing my body's activity to bear on them. The extension of my body's natural powers is carried out by the use of tools and instruments interposed between my body and the objects acted upon. The internal feeling of my body flows into the external activity of my body upon existing objects. Feeling and acting always occur together through an inward tension that, even though existing at the prereflective level, can always rise to an explicit awareness of itself as a self-presence, an I, with all the urgency of becoming outwardly manifest—an inwardness seeking to be revealed. We never come to grips with the coenesthetic perception of the body save through the concomitant kinesthetic activities that the body exercises on objects.

My body is further organized as a body through its perceiving acts. The embodied I—or "the personal body," to use Ricoeur's phrase[44]—can alone be the source and originator of perceptions by investing objects with its own creative intentions.

Our sensations, like body feelings, are acts of participation. Sensation is not merely something that happens to us, something we passively endure or suffer; it is an act of hospitality, of generosity, through which the body actively and directly receives the object in the corresponding sense modality in which it is experienced. Sensations are intentional acts that put the body immediately in contact with objects with which it has affective links.

Nevertheless, sensations constitute a form of submerged participation, since they operate below the level of thought. They contain a latent idea, a rationality, an intelligibility, that is not immediately obvious. Prior to any thought-conscious process, sensation is already a preconscious process. Before we can rise to an idea, thought, or consciousness of the objective order of existence, our senses present objects to us.

This approach asks whether there can be any sensuous grasp of objects without an intelligent understanding of them. Marcel's sensualist metaphysic provides a firm ground for working out his realist philosophy. According to Marcel, the real lies before us and is immediately accessible to our senses. No mental abstractions or constructions could ever help us sink our teeth into the real. *La morsure de réel* takes place in spite of our thoughts, never because of them. Our senses enable us to get a firm hold on reality by immediately presenting it to us.

Rationality and meaning are therefore embedded in our incarnate mode of existence. The task of thought is to struggle to an awareness of itself, not to stand up and assert its right to validate all knowledge while remaining cut off from the stream of its incarnation. The thought process for Marcel is less a construction than a recuperative function, a digging into the hidden roots in human embodiment. The task of secondary reflection is to recapture the lived immediacy of experience, which tends to break up when subjected to the objectifying analysis of primary reflection.

THE ORIGINALITY OF MARCEL'S EXISTENTIALISM

Marcel's conception of the body brings out the profoundly original character of his existentialism. The mainstream of French thought from Descartes to Sartre accords to human reality a specifically egocentric quality. Humanity is conceived of as essentially a collection of beings for themselves, each a *pour soi*. This means that human subjectivity emerges into the consciousness of a fully constituted I. It is completely transparent to itself. It is bathed in its own light. The self enjoys a privileged existence over other beings. It has an absolute priority over them, since it considers itself the luminous source and center around which the world of existent beings gravitates. If people are not spectators beholding an outer spectacle, they are thinkers whose thought is turned inward on themselves and who are able to form a clear and distinct idea of their own subjectivity.

Martin Buber provided an alternative view: human reality is essentially an "I-Thou" relationship in which people and other beings encounter one another actively as subjects. They invoke each other as presences, the being of each flows into the being of the other. The gift of the other to me as a presence is sanctioned by the creative response of my freedom. One might even say that I make the other be, just as the other makes possible the unfolding of my freedom. This ontological communion is the free expression of a truly blossoming spirit. It signals the ability to share the gift of one's intimate being with another in the act of freely receiving the other's to oneself.

The centrality of the body in Marcel's thought makes possible an even more broad-based conception of human reality. The process of embodiment works downward as well as upward: it feeds the hidden roots of our active community with beings, and it nourishes our transcendental relation with being. Human embodiment connects us to both physical and metaphysical reality.

Marcel contends that before the I can emerge as a fully conscious subject, before a communion can flower between an I and a Thou, there is already a community of beings bound together by an intersubjective nexus, which is the body. Personal communion is thus founded on a prior community, just as the self is constituted as a self only in its bodily acts. Prior to there being any I or I-Thou, the experience of the lived body is that of a We-reality, a feeling of active community with all existing beings bound together with my body as the living center. The I and the Thou are therefore derivative forms of the We. Human embodiment is the experience of our togetherness in being. The experience of a shared community enables the I and the Thou to emerge.

Incarnation initiates the awareness that my body and I are somehow one. Together we are partners in being, sharing in a common life venture. But the mutuality exists at a deeper level than mere partnership. My body is experienced as an explosive act of self-revelation. It is the point at which my inward self, so long hidden but always there, now makes itself present. Because my body is intimately mine, it is able to present my self before the world through feeling. Embodiment is primarily a felt recognition that I am me; yet this awareness is not for me alone to enjoy in solitude. It is a yearning to be manifest, an inwardness seeking to become outwardly revealed. I experience my body as the feeling of being presented to the world in a mutuality of my coexistence with it. *Urgefühl* is the recognition of a felt presence, of a radical act of community with myself and with the world. It is the awareness that at the heart of existence, mine as well as others', a strong tie binds us together. My intimate unity with myself is only the inward resonance of my bond with the world.

This is truly a paradoxical relationship, for I am always conscious of being the singular being that I am and at the same time of simulating to myself the other. For Marcel, this inner tension arises from "a borrowed otherness."[45] It is a play before the other, even if that other be myself. A unique act of implied self-discovery and self-revelation lies at the heart of feeling. Feeling, whose very duty and function is to ignore itself,[46] now finds itself caught up in the reflective awareness that "I am myself." At times the I may be a marginal experience at the fringe of feeling and acting. At other times the basic, prereflective sense of being myself may quite naturally and freely rise to full consciousness as an "I am myself" experience. The sense of being myself and the recognition, executed by reflective thought, that "I am myself" spring from the same source—my incarnation—and thus accommodate the transfer from submerged to emergent participation, from experience to reflection, from feeling to the idea of what I feel.

Human embodiment makes reflective consciousness possible. This is because I am not only the subject of my activity but also the stage on which that activity is executed. Human embodiment is what permits there to be a self and not just an I—a self whose essential mark is always to assume the stance of a relation and never of a pure subject. Intersubjectivity makes subjectivity possible. This feature of embodiment accounts both for the horizontal relationship to existing beings and for the vertical relationship to being. The body is our avenue to being as surely as it is the proof of our existence. The body is what permits the I not only to exist but also to be. Because the body is brought into the very center of the metaphysical quest, the natural way to ask the ontological question is, Who am I? The subject I is drawn into the sphere of its own questioning. I am not just the one who questions but also the one who is being questioned. From out of its own exigencies, the embodied self is constrained to ask the question, Who am I? This question clearly addresses two distinct deeds: one is of my own doing; the other is what is being done to me. I who am actively engaged in being am emboldened to ask, "What in effect does it mean to be?"[47]

Commenting on this question, Hocking observes that it implies two distinct acts. There is first of all the act of being: "My being appears to me as something I discover, going on there without having consulted my wishes,—something *done to me.*" Second, there is on my part "an act of consent and collaboration, as if what is done to me, I also do for myself —two deeds merging into one active fact, 'I be.' "[48] The I in this case is sensitized with cosmic pathos. As such it becomes the perennial source of being, of fulfillment, of presence; yet for the most part it remains in the background, hidden, obscure, and elusive. It is the principle of intimacy, of cohesion, of integrity, intimately lived with and felt but impervious to definition. The self is an infinite complex of unfolding possibilities that is accessible to feeling but recalcitrant to an objectifying analysis. It demands to become outwardly manifest, to exist.

My body then presents me as a complex of unfolding relationships both to the outer world and to myself. The passage to existence as well as to being is made through my body. Existence assures me that there is a whole world of beings around me who share with me the same community of nature as my body. The assurance is both "primitive" and "global."[49] It is primitive in the sense that it is the most basic affirmation of all existence. It is global because it is directed not to this or that particular object but to existence as a whole. It is through my body that I become a citizen of the world. My body reinstates me as a member of the human community and of the wider community of beings. The world at large exists to the same degree that I exist within it. This mutuality of implication traverses my body. It is felt and acted out both at the prereflective and at the reflective levels. My body is at once linked to existence and propelled toward being. Because I am in bodily contact with the world, I am also in touch with the deeper reality of my selfhood. The domain of the self extends wherever its relationships are. Nevertheless, Marcel reminds us that both existence and being tend to pass unnoticed when we engage in mere routine activity. Conversely, the moments when we awaken to existence are also the moments when we become deeply aware of the inward experience of presence. It is only in certain gifted moments—or "peak experiences," as Maslow calls them[50]—that we feel the palpitating presence of being as surely as we sense the worth of our existence.

Marcel began his metaphysical journey with the question, Who am I? Then the key changed and the metaphysic of being became a metaphysic of "we are" as opposed to "I think." Ontology must take its starting point in intersubjectivity. The quest for being can be taken up only from the perspective of a human being's felt community with the world. The full flowering of intersubjectivity takes place in interpersonal communion between beings capable of inwardness and presence and therefore able to enter into an I-Thou relationship. Intersubjectivity is the implied understanding of our felt community with the world, the body being the intersubjective nexus that binds us to all beings. Embodiment is not a mere physical fact concerning our corporeal existence; it is a continual process of opening up to the world. There is a close parallel between the movement of conversion, by which reflective thought passes from the objective order of existence to the transcendent order of being, and that by which the self opens into communion out of its prior community with the world. Toward the end of his metaphysical journey, Marcel discovered that the quest for being contained an implicit awareness of the exigence for God. Following the Augustinian tradition, perhaps unconsciously, Marcel viewed us "as bound to God by a sort of fundamental and radical pre-awareness of God as the source of [our] being. . . . The I-Thou relationship is valid only if it posits a supreme God from Whom the 'I' and the 'Thou' derive their being, depth and dynamism."[51] The ultimate meaning of the I lies in its orientation to a principle beyond itself. Just as community reaches its depth in communion, so the ultimate consummation of the I-Thou takes place in our intimate union with God.

Marcel's approach takes up and affirms all that is true and important in the doctrines of Descartes, Sartre, and Buber. The *Cogito* recovers its true ontological status by its participation in the We-reality. The *pour soi* can begin to exist for itself in its integrity only through participation with others. The I-Thou is possible only if it is faithful to its roots in community. The outlook on the We changes: "The We is essentially not a group . . . which has been grouped, not a collectivity which has been collected. The We-reality is essentially a group which groups itself, which constitutes its own existence by affirming its own existence, in an affirmation which imposes a burden of responsibility upon those who make it."[52] Unless the I is a self, being does not affirm itself; yet the I can begin to exist as an authentic *pour soi* only by being with others. The I-Thou is an inescapable dimension of the We; but the We is the ontological ground of the I-Thou.

In Marcel, the I-Thou relationship is reinforced from below as well as from above. Its foundation lies in the We-reality that constitutes our community with the world. Its transcendent meaning lies in the intimate depths of our communion with God.

We might say, then, that Marcel's metaphysical concert is played in a different register from Descartes's, Sartre's, or Buber's. Human reality is not an interminable solo of each person's solitary encounter with the real. Nor is it merely a duet of the I in personal living communion with a Thou. It is rather a vast chorale in which many voices blend. Each part is executed with personal skill; yet it is a part only in the sense that it exists as a function of the whole. It participates in a higher development in which all beings reach their transcendental union with being. The chorale is the perfect expression of the We-reality, and it recaptures on a wider scale the spirit of the Quartet.[53]

SOME CRITICAL REMARKS

In the chapter in *The Mystery of Being* entitled "Feeling as a Mode of Participation," Marcel presents a short imaginary dialogue between himself and a friend:

> "I am out, let us say, for a walk with a friend. I say I feel tired. My friend looks skeptical, since he, for his part, feels no tiredness at all. I say to him, perhaps a little bit irritably, that nobody who is not inside my skin can know what I feel. He will be forced to agree, and yet, of course, he can always claim that I am attaching too much importance to slight disagreeable sensations which he, if he felt them, would resolutely ignore. It is also clear that at this level no real discussion is possible. For I can always say that even if what he calls 'the same sensations' were felt by him and not by me, still they would not really be . . . the *same* sensations. . . . But here we are up against a difficult question, a question that one has a tendency to dodge. What, after all, *is* feeling, and what makes it possible for us to feel?"[54]

If the word *feeling* (*sentir*) were used in the precise sense of coenesthetics, one might accept the story without further comment. Yet Marcel uses this fictitious promenade to raise two questions: "What makes it possible for us not merely vaguely to feel but more precisely to have sensations? How is sensation in general a possibility?"[55] By preceding the discussion of feeling, the story serves to introduce the themes essential to the following discussion. Marcel uses this form not only to emphasize the privacy of such feelings as fatigue, hunger, and pain, but also to say that what is true for the coenesthetics is true for all modes of feeling, external perception included. Critic Richard Zaner comments that "since the *sentir* of the body as mine is fundamental to all the modes of *sentir,* what holds for it must hold for the latter as well."[56]

Unfortunately, the story of the common walk presents a situation diametrically opposed to Marcel's interpretation. In its apparent simplicity it abounds with problems that are taken for granted in everyday life and that are therefore ignored in reflection, secondary as well as primary.

When Marcel, or M, tells his friend F that he feels tired, the two of them presumably have been out together for a long walk. Although the two friends do not share the *same* sensations, they walk together and talk together.

M's friend is for M not a "non-mediatized immediate" but another embodied person located "out there" in an environment accessible to and actually entered by both of them. M's and F's individual views of the ground are private, but the terrain (a word derived from *terra,* "earth") is public, open, and common to both. Although M directs his critical remark—"nobody who is not inside my skin can know what I feel"—to someone outside his skin, M sees this someone "in person," and vice versa. If one of the walkers were short-sighted and had left his glasses at home, his view would be substantially different from his friend's; nevertheless they would move together in a landscape visible to them both. Talking together, each is aware that his partner, visible to him as an embodied person, is talking—a situation inexplicable in physiological or behavioral terms, since optical stimuli cannot produce acoustical stimuli, nor can the striate area of the brain realize what Heschl's gyrus is doing.

During their common walk each of the two friends refers to himself with the pronoun *I.* (In reference to a third person, both would speak of him or her.) But although each one refers to himself alone as I, he has no difficulty understanding that when he hears this word resounding from the mouth of his partner, the speaker refers to himself exclusively. Each sees and hears for himself alone, just as he eats and drinks and feels fresh or tired for himself alone. Yet M and F, you and I—indeed all of us—meet as partners in a world common and open to us through sensory experience. Although your views and my views are just as private as your hunger and my hunger or your fatigue and my fatigue, our sights are "public"; we see and hear the same scene together. When I encounter a friend seated near a window and clearly fascinated by something in the street, I cannot share his private view—at least I cannot until I look out the window and see for myself. To summarize, although our views are private, our sights are public and in common. No one in the practice of life would agree with the philosopher or scientist who wants to persuade us that the sensa are in the brain, that the space in which we move is an a priori form of intuition, or that each of us is a monad functioning through divine foresight in harmony with all the other monads.

During a walk the views follow one another, each in turn filling the boundaries of the visual field within a horizon. The sights present fragments of a permanent continuum even when they are as dissimilar as a narrow street opening into a wide square. Such contrasts among views and sights elicit the acts of searching, wondering, and questioning on the level of feeling.

We should mention here in passing that speech differs from sight in that we human beings have the corporeal power to produce sounds but not to produce light directly. The speaker who hears himself also expects to be understood by his partner, reached by sound, words, meaning, and messages. When M tells F, "I am tired," M is sure that his friend will interpret these words correctly even though they reach his friend "as a message" referring to the speaker.

It is time now to let M and F continue their walk. Of course each one moves his legs for himself and feels the soles of his own feet touched by and touching the ground; each man's muscles function "inside," are private, although the path and the walk are common and synchronized.

Returning to their homes, a new surprise awaits them. They pass the same terrain, but right and left, front and rear, are exchanged. They realize that they have reversed their direction while the landscape has remained and appears permanent, even though the views and the illumination are radically altered. What is easy to enact in the *Lebenswelt* is sometimes hard to understand in philosophical reflection. Obviously there is a striking contrast between the ever-changing actuality of each person's view and the permanence of the scene seen. My viewing is bound to the actual moment—my personal "now"—whereas the visible world (at least heaven and earth) manifests itself in a different order of time as lasting. In the sequence of rapidly changing views, we see the lasting structure of the ground revealed in one of many perspectives. Our wanderers, retracing their path as they walk home, do not expect to hear their words again; the words faded away the very moment they were spoken.

Let us assume that before getting tired, M and F have been out for a long walk. It is the month of October; a cool wind is blowing. On such an occasion we may say, "It is getting cold." We make a clear distinction in English between "It is cold" (to describe the bath or the soup, for instance), and "I am cold"; in French, between "Il fait froid" and "J'ai froid"; in German, between "Es ist kalt" and "Ich friere." Someone clad in a winter mantle and a fur cap may well enjoy the fresh, cold air without feeling cold.

It seems that Marcel, preoccupied with the refutation of the primary reflection, failed to wonder about the characteristic differences experienced in the *Lebenswelt,* where both primary and secondary reflections are rooted. Like many a distinguished scholar doing physiological or psychological research, he neglected to consider the intrinsic problems of objectivity.

Let us assume that the next day one of the friends remembers the walk and the conversation of the previous day. Certainly his memories, even of such public events, are no less private than any coenesthetic feelings. I can tell about my past, but I cannot make it directly accessible to anyone else. Actually, fatigue may be more communicable, at least in some respects. For instance, when during a long plane trip my neighbor stops talking and sits with his head tilted forward, his jaws agape, and his eyes closed, I realize that he has fallen asleep. Yet while his breathing, heartbeat, and temperature continue as they are in sleep, he cannot say, "I am asleep," or, "My body is asleep." Only when he awakens can he ask, somewhat bewildered, "Where are we? Did I sleep a long time?"

Marcel paid little attention to the spectrum of senses and to the particularities of the modes of sensory communication. Perhaps he made concessions, not completely justified, to "primary reflection," for instance, when he said:

> The body that I call my body is in fact only one body among many others. In relation to these other bodies, it has been endowed with no special privileges whatsoever. . . . Let us remind ourselves of exactly what the notion of being an object implies; the body is an object insofar as it can be scientifically known, gives scientific knowledge something solid to get to grips with, and gives a whole range of techniques, from hygiene to surgery, derived originally from scientific knowledge, something equally solid to work upon.[57]

But my body is never a detached body for me, not even when I brush my hair, cut my fingernails, or look into the mirror. My body may be treated as a body among other bodies by an observer, such as a passport officer measuring my height and weight and registering my age and color or a physician taking my blood pressure and examining my x-rays. In both these situations the observer acts in the role of "I see, I measure." Primary reflection does not eliminate my-ness completely, except for the persons studied. Unfortunately, scientists are inclined to forget their own being-in-the-world, that is, their own situation in the *Lebenswelt* as observers.

Two characteristic examples address the problems of objectivity that Marcel overlooked. The first involves R. L. Gregory, of Cambridge, England, who published a book entitled *Eye and Brain: The Psychology of Seeing*.[58] The subtitle leaves no doubt that seeing is meant to be identical with processes within the eye and the brain. Gregory did not distinguish between his seeing eyes and the eyes seen or between a brain observed and an observer's brain. Yet no brain has ever known itself, nor has any investigator known his own brain. If we have the opportunity to study a brain, be it in the laboratory or on the surgical table, the brain seen, touched, cut, and so on, is an object for us. The stimuli that act on the retinae enable us to see the eyes and the brain of another body. Yet this fundamental relation of intentionality, the basic phenomenon of seeing and observing, is by-passed and completely ignored. Instead, the brain is credited with magic powers. At the end of the introductory chapter of his book, Gregory wrote: "Indeed, we may say that the perceived object is a hypothesis, suggested and tested by sensory data. . . . Sometimes eye and brain come to the wrong conclusion, and then we suffer hallucinations or illusions." If a perceived object were a hypothesis, as Gregory claims, then all brains, as objects perceived, would be in themselves nothing but hypotheses.

Forgetting that brains, according to his own interpretation, are parts of the so-called external world, Gregory assigns to them the position of "the thing itself," acting like a *deus ex machina* or a demiurge equipped with incomprehensible power. For although a brain actually functioning within the tenebrous case of the skull should be able to visualize light flooding the wide horizon of open space and activating plant and animal life, it is also a physical agent studied and measured by physicists and physiologists. And according to Gregory this studying and measuring is accomplished by individual brains, each locked up in its own attic, completely isolated, without any possibility of communication, since brains cannot communicate with one another. If Tertullian had had the opportunity to read Gregory's book, he might have said, "Non credo, quia absurdum." Yet such strange and bewildering interpretations pose as scientific objectivity.

The second example of the problems of objectivity involves Hubel and

Wiesel, whose study entitled "Perceptive Fields of Single Neurons in the Cat's Striate Cortex" won widespread approval. They described their method as follows:

> In this series of experiments twenty-four cats were used. Animals were anesthetized with intraperitoneal thiopental sodium (40 mg/kg) and light anaesthesia was maintained throughout the experiment by additional intraperitoneal injections. The eyes were immobilized by continuous intravenous injection of succinylcholine; the employment of this muscle relaxant made it necessary to use artificial respiration. Pupils of both eyes were dilated and accommodation was relaxed by means of 1% atropine. Contact lenses used with a suitably buffered solution prevented the corneal surfaces from drying and becoming cloudy. The lids were held apart by simple wire clips.[59]

Whereas the observers explored the cerebral functions of the cats with the most sophisticated instruments, they preserved for themselves the naïve, familiar attitudes of everyday life. This led to five major inconsistencies. First, they reported that they had used twenty-four cats. How and by whom is such an act of accounting performed? Certainly the bodies of the cats were not fused together; this number, like all measurements, can only be reached through "introspection."[60] If we assume that three cats were studied per week, then the seventh cat, for instance, must have been brought into the laboratory during the third week. The number seven must have been reached by adding the observers' view of the newcomer in retrospect (a kind of introspection) to their views of the preceding six. No doubt a huge quantity of optical and other stimuli acted on the observers' brains in the meantime. How do brains accomplish such masterful strokes of selecting and combining? Does the striate area receive the optical information while the gyrus angularis performs the counting? How are the many preceding impressions united with the last and actual one into the single number seven? Second, if seeing must be interpreted as the intracerebral events occurring in the occipital lobe, how could the two observers (H and W) see each other separately and in addition see the animals together? Third, H and W did not doubt for a moment that in laboratory practice they could observe the same cat under drastically different optical conditions by approaching it from the front, from the sides, and from the rear. Of course in everyday life we do not stop to wonder how we can see things as objects in various situations. But is it permissible to transfer this naïve conviction into the refined interpretation presented by a neurophysiologist? Does the act of seeing in one's own case not also require the "correct interpretation" that one's brain has been activated by optical stimuli? If so, then the animal under observation must disappear from the observer's view and sight and be transformed into a mere sequence of stimuli received by the retinae. In other words, are the cats—or any other experimental animals—objects visible to an observer, or must they be understood as a mere shower of stimuli acting on the brain? If the cats were reduced to a cluster of stimuli, how could other stimuli—such as the isolated light beams used in H and W's experiments—act on the animals, and how could all this be known and recorded by an observer? Fourth, must not observer H be reduced to a mirage of optical stimuli affecting W's brain, and vice versa? Finally, when H and W studied the EEG protocols, following the original exposures of the cat's retinae to stimuli, additional illumination was required. Reading the charts therefore meant responding at a later moment to optical stimulation markedly different from the initial experimental situation. How could the observers' brains relate these optical stimuli to the earlier ones? How can a brain realize that lines visible at this very moment were in fact produced in the past, recorded on a material prepared in a still more remote past?

One may therefore question the validity of experiments performed under conditions so sharply at variance with the natural situation. Actually, in the summary of their paper Hubel and Wiesel wrote: "A light stimulus (approximately 1 sec. duration) covering the whole receptive field or diffused stimulation of the whole retina was relatively ineffective in driving most units." Accepting a strict empiricist theory, the authors regarded this variation as "owing to mutual antagonism between excitatory and inhibitory areas." But an empiricistic theory positing either reaction or single elementary units demands the corresponding assumption of an atomistic structure of time—an assumption that makes any kind of observation impossible, let alone one dealing with a plurality of experimental animals and supplemented by a delayed reading of records and charts. In neurophysiological research the observers, claiming for themselves rights they deny to their Ss, are inclined to an inexcusable confusion of objects and stimuli. Since physical energies are first transformed into stimuli the moment they act upon receptors, stimuli are neither consonant nor dissonant. Photic stimuli are intangible; tactile stimuli are invisible. Stimuli are strictly private; they act only upon one particular organism. Stimuli cannot be seen or used by a third person. A stimulus for a goose is not a stimulus for a gander. The photons that stimulated the cat's retina could never have reached the eyes of Hubel or Wiesel. Within the realm of stimuli, no observation is possible.

To be sure, each of the thousands of spectators watching a ball game receives only that light that enters his or her pupils, just as each swallow of a cool drink is enjoyed by one swallower alone. Yet all the spectators see one and the same performance together. Sight opens the world beyond the boundaries of individual bodies.

The "objectivity" of primary reflection, far from being self-evident, actually conceals one if not the only basic distinction between perceiving and observing and thereby also impairs secondary reflection. Yet it is this distinction that led Marcel to ask, "Who am I?" and to answer, "I am my body," a situation—if this term is permissible—manifested in feeling, which in turn is explained by the idea of participation and active receptiveness.

No doubt the formula "I am my body" presents a semantic imbroglio, for the pronoun *my* in this statement refers neither to possession nor to consanguinity nor to affiliation. Furthermore, the auxiliary verb *am* cannot be replaced by the past tense *was,* even though the body's mode of being is decidedly temporal. Finally, the pronoun *I* cannot be replaced by the corresponding pronouns *you, he,* or *she,* even though the formula "I am my body" is intended to be paradigmatic.

Marcel seemed aware of these ambiguities when he wrote: "My body, insofar as it is properly mine, presents itself to me in the first instance as something felt; I am my body only insofar as I am a being that has feelings." This formulation, vacillating between an active and a passive interpretation, leads to two other aporias: one Marcel directly acknowledged when he wondered whether the body is "at one and the same time what feels and what is felt"; the other he referred to indirectly by stating that "my body is endowed with an absolute priority in relation to everything that I feel that is other than my body itself."[61] But since even this priority demands distinction from everything secondary, how could it be absolute? How could I experience my body as mine without reference to all the other possibilities?

In studying Marcel one cannot help wondering why he by-passed such vital functions as breathing and eating, sleeping and being awake, standing and walking. Certainly my body is mine only between the first cry and the last sigh. Not without reason has the preeminence of breathing been recognized in the Bible (Gen. 1:2), in the Indian mythos (Atman), and last but not least through etymology. Indeed, the term *psychology* is directly related to the Greek verb *psychein* (breathing), and the words *spirit, inspiration, pneuma, anima* (related to the Greek word *anemos,* "wind"), and *animal* all point to that intrinsic performance indispensable to life and— indirectly—to thought. To be sure, without breath there would be no voice; without voice there would be no speech; without speech there would be no language, no questions, and no answers.

One may assume that Marcel had several reasons for disregarding breathing. First, he considered it mainly a topic for primary objective reflection. But even though physiology studies the so-called mechanisms of inhaling and exhaling, of atmospheric pressure, of biochemical exchange, and of cerebral and spinal controls, no one else can breathe for me. In spite of its conformities, breathing is actually the work of my (that is, of an individual) body. Second, the relationship of inner to outer is characteristic of breathing; yet Marcel denies this relation by claiming that "what we normally call the subject [participates] in a surrounding world from which no veritable frontier separates it."[62] Nevertheless, such separation— or contraposition—is quite characteristic of my body as mine. Actually, by breathing I, like everyone else, sustain my vital existence within the world, although in contraposition to it. Each of us participates independently in one shared atmosphere. Therefore the situation of breathing is quite characteristic of my body as mine, for in this exchange, at the same time antithetical and cooperative, I establish my existence in contraposition to the world (the Allon)[63] to which I belong. Third, it is my body that breathes, not I, for I have little control over my breath. Although I am able to vary depth, speed, and rhythm within narrow limits, I cannot suppress breathing completely. Those sentenced to die in a gas chamber cannot for long stop inhaling the fumes that will kill them (a situation, by the way, in sharp contrast to Husserl's contention that "embodied consciousness acts sovereign. . . .") Fourth and finally, while I am asleep, my body continues to breathe. Even though primary reflection reveals that everyone alternates between sleep and wakefulness, I discover for myself alone that I slept last night. Thus "I am my body" involves two drastically different modes of being: (1) I fall asleep, yielding to gravity, suspending all cognizant contacts with the environment, so that nights of profound sleep do not constitute a continuum but rather interrupt the continuity of my personal chronicle; and (2) only emerging from sleep do I resume my relation versus the environment, to which I belong in contraposition. In sleep my breathing does not stop even though my feeling is abolished, together with my awareness of the world. Feeling in Marcel's sense occurs only during the waking hours of the day. Yet wakefulness certainly is an accomplishment of my body. Thanks to inner processes, the bodies of humans and other animals acquire the relation to the world that we call awake.[64]

While awake everyone reaches in sight far beyond the boundaries of his or her body—indeed, as far as the moon, the sun, and the stars. This enigmatic extension has been one if not the only decisive motive for dualistic interpretations, which posit a soul, a mind, or a consciousness transcending the narrow corporeal boundaries. Accordingly, philosophical and later physiological interpretations subordinated the motorium to the sensorium, limiting motor activities to locomotion if not to efferent responses.

Nevertheless, my body is not a curiously shaped *res extensa* lost in solitude somewhere in the vastness of Euclidean space. My body as a chthonic formation is located in terrestrial space, counteracting the fundamental invariant—the omnipresent power of gravity. As long as the earth turns, gravity will persist without change, dominating the earthly nights as well as the earthly days.

The power to rise against the force of gravity enables the organism to establish its "here" in contraposition to the world, thereby transforming the living body into "my" body. It also provides the indispensable condition for locomotion. Facing the encompassing whole of which I am a part, I am enabled to meet partners. Able to move in terrestrial space, I am in open relation to points beyond as potential goals; the intentional relation to visible objects (*Gegenstände*) present from a distance is founded on the capacity of conquering gravity. In our experience as mundane creatures, terra firma constitutes the fundamental, invariant system of coordinates against which even the sun appears to move.

To awaken is often identified in the vernacular with standing and getting up. Yet the action of rising is voluntary: it is not automatic, like the heartbeat or the peristaltic movements; it is not due to coercive mechanisms, as is breathing. Awake, I can get up, but I may choose not to do so. Having achieved my standing, I can sooner or later reverse my decision and return to the ground in coordinate action. Humans and other animals stand up on their own power. They are not raised by the air like a cloud of steam or a blimp; they are not carried by forced air currents like a plane. My body provides me with the opportunity to get up and to hold my stand; yet once accomplished, upright posture still demands my continued efforts. The all-pervading power of gravity never ceases; it remains a counterforce; it requires my constant effort and resistance. Since gravity remains active without cessation, every moment of upright posture is threatened with a fall.

Empowered to counteract gravity, humans and animals are thereby first rendered capable of locomotion. The conquest of gravity provides freedom of motion, "footroom" and "elbowroom." Walking follows standing. Actually, in walking—standing on one leg while lifting the other one from the ground and moving it forward—we have to overcome gravity for the second time. A galloping horse races through space in leaps; even a caterpillar moves by lifting its body in arches from a supporting leaf or twig. The position of my body "here" is the very point of contact from which I counteract gravity. It is therefore not too surprising that Stratton and later Ivo Kohler demonstrated in experiments that antigravity-potency corrected basic optical misinformation as long as the participants, wearing radically distorting prismatic lenses, stood up and moved around.

The words *above* and *high* do not refer to particular regions in space, as Kant once suggested in an early writing. *High* actually signifies a direction: upward against gravity. We should not forget that our antipodes, watching the sky high above their own position (which is determined by antigravity), actually look in a direction diametrically opposed to our view of sky and stars, as seen from an Archimedean point.

One may wonder why the ubiquity of gravitational forces and the corresponding need and ability to overcome them have been so thoroughly neglected in philosophical anthropology, especially since Newton. Probably the very ubiquity and permanence of gravity have veiled its role and importance, as in the following three examples. First, while watching a basketball game, we see the players running over the horizontal, two-dimensional plane of the floor; we completely ignore that invisible below the floor *Gaia* exerts her telluric power. Should one of the players stumble and fall, we consider the accident a result, for example, of a collision with another player. We do not blame gravity for its interference, since we assume that the players keep themselves upright from the start. In everyday life we regard walking, jumping, and running as primary actions; we forget that we must always carry our weight, that with every step we challenge and must conquer gravity. Second, to assess a person's weight on an old-fashioned scale, an equally heavy load must be placed on the other balance pan. When the beam reaches a horizontal position, with both pans pulled down to the same level by gravity, the person can still stand upright, able to counteract gravity though not to eliminate it. This contraposition eludes measurement. Third, "antigravity" requires the recognition and consideration of bodily structures and comportment on a macroscopic level. The upright position cannot be demonstrated under a microscope. It is not a direct function of actin or myosin. No atoms or molecules, no cells or fibrils, are upright, nor is the tibia or the femur, the illeopsoas or the quadriceps femoris, the pyramidal tract or the vestibular system, the medulla or the brain. This situation unfortunately contradicts most scientists' metaphysical conviction that our world of daily experience is but a phantom that must be reduced to the molecular or atomic level for a final account.

Eddington, Crick, and many similar writers obviously forgot that their own research—the exploration of DNA not excluded—was performed on the level of "natural vision" and manipulation. Science itself could never have been founded on the level of "sparsely scattered . . . electric charges rushing through emptiness with great speed,'' although Eddington claimed that such was the character of reality established by modern physics.[65] The antigravity position of humans and animals is an accomplishment of the whole body, or rather of the body architecture as a whole, for not all component parts participate in the same order. When a person stands upright, for instance, both feet are in a horizontal position, and the long muscles of the neck and the trunk pull downward. The apparatus of breathing, the phonetic muscles, the eye muscles (with one exception), and the arms are freed from the direct service of antigravity. Such freedom permits us to use our arms, hands, fingers, and phonetic organs as instruments.

In line with his distinction of secondary from primary reflection, Marcel rejected the postulate "that my body was merely my instrument."[66] Nevertheless, we can use such parts as our arms, our hands, and our vocal apparatus as instruments. If not, it would be hard to understand how a soprano could perform her part or how a violinist could play the score to accompany her.

Thus it seems that in his critique of instrumentality, Marcel did not distinguish sufficiently between tool and instrument. Characteristic of a tool is the combination of a working part (hammer, pen, blade, knife, or saw) and a handle. This combination extends the abilities of the artisan's hands. Instruments, however, such as the flute, the piano, and the typewriter, function in the service of production. They are built to return to a zero position after use; depressed keys, for example, return to their original raised position.

Thanks to the architectural design of my body, the actions of agonists and antagonists are coupled in synergies supported by a reciprocal innervation. When I bend my forearm, for instance, the contraction of the flexor muscles is accompanied by the relaxation of the extensors; alternating between flexation and extension, pronation and supination, the position of my limbs is never final. I have the choice of bending, of stretching, or of leaving the situation unchanged.

We walk in steps; everyone knows it, and everyone does it. Yet it is perhaps not obvious that in so doing we perform a twofold operation. For example, while moving my legs at the hip joints in a repetitive, pendulum-like motion, I progress on the ground in a straight line from one end of a country lane to the other. One thousand steps (*milia passuum* in Latin) transport me over a distance of a mile (a word derived from this Roman technique of measuring distance). Although I move my legs in a temporal sequence, I realize that the single segments just passed are at rest and that all things separating my starting point from my goal coexist simultaneously. As I walk along the road, the pendulum motion in my hips is controlled by proprioceptive feedback, but my progression is directed by sight, which reveals my next position in advance. There is still another remarkable difference. While walking I move one leg after the other and feel a small segment of the ground, now on the sole of the right foot and now on the sole of the left; yet with two eyes I see one world. On the one hand, tactile information is factual, localized, and mutual (in touching I am touched). On the other, the countryside "over there" is presented to my gaze,[67] accessible as a potential goal, opened to my in-sight and fore-sight. It is seen from "here," but the here itself is not seen; my here is established by my antigravity position. Vision then cannot be understood as a purely optical function—as an accomplishment solely of eye and brain.

In Descartes's efforts to debunk sensory experience, he used as one example the familiar observation that a high tower appears small to us when seen from a long distance. Descartes thereby intended to demonstrate the deceptiveness of sensory experience. He assumed that sensory experience was an accumulation, a mere sequence, of sensory data within the thinking substance. But in seeing I find myself, in my corporeal existence within the world, related to visible material things recognized in their constancies of shape and size.

I can represent the Empire State Building or Mount Rainier on a photograph, that is, on a two-dimensional plane a few inches long and a few inches wide. Although my retinae are considerably smaller than a normal photograph, I see the building and the mountain in their "natural" size; that is, I see them in direct relation to my own corporeal dimensions—I climb the mountain; I enter the building. Passing through the door or ascending the slopes, I find myself as a small figure within the wide clearance of embracing space. Hence my experience of the visible world is not a projection of optical data on the screen of consciousness. On the contrary, my sight depends on far more than optical stimuli.

My position at once within the world and in opposition to it, my existence challenging gravity, makes the intentionality of sensory experience—participation and active receptiveness—possible.

ERWIN W. STRAUS

LEXINGTON, KENTUCKY

MICHAEL A. MACHADO

DEPARTMENT OF PHILOSOPHY
FROSTBURG STATE COLLEGE
AUGUST 1970

NOTES

1. Gabriel Marcel, *Metaphysical Journal*, trans. Bernard Wall (Chicago: Henry Regnery Co., 1952), p. 316 (hereafter cited as *MJ*). See also Jean-Pierre Bagot, *Connaissance et amour* (Paris: Beauchesne, 1958), pp. 82–95.

2. Gabriel Marcel, *Creative Fidelity*, trans. Robert Rosthal (New York: Noonday Press, 1964), pp. 11–13 (hereafter cited as *CF*).

3. *CF*, 14–15. See also Gabriel Marcel, *The Mystery of Being*, trans. G. S. Fraser (vol. 1) and René Hague (vol. 2), 2 vols. (Chicago: Henry Regnery Co., Gateway, 1960), 1:108–9 (hereafter cited as *MB*).

4. See *CF*, 65; cf. Gabriel Marcel, *Du refus à l'invocation* (Paris: Gallimard, 1940), p. 91 (hereafter cited as *DR*).

5. *MB* 1:109.

6. Gabriel Marcel, *Being and Having*, trans. Katharine Farrer (Boston: Beacon Press, 1951), p. 10 (hereafter cited as *BH*).

7. *MJ*, 17–22, 269, 274, 275, 314–17; *BH*, 10–12; *MB* 1:135.

8. *MB* 1:106.

9. *CF*, 12.

10. *MB* 1:102.

11. Gabriel Marcel, *Royce's Metaphysics*, trans. Virginia and Gordon Ringer (Chicago: Henry Regnery Co., 1956), p. 32 (hereafter cited as *RM*).

12. Josiah Royce, *The World and the Individual* (New York: Dover Publications, 1959), p. 347.

13. Ibid., pp. 457–60.

14. *RM*, ix.

15. William Ernest Hocking, *The Meaning of God in Human Experience* (New Haven: Yale University Press, 1963).

16. Ibid., p. 68.

17. *MB* 1:140.

18. *MB* 1:124; *MJ*, 246–47, 252, 269, 274.

19. *MJ*, 45.

20. *MB* 1:135.

21. See *MB* 1:249, where Marcel goes so far as to say that spirit "only constitutes itself effectively *as* spirit on condition of becoming flesh" (Marcel's italics).

22. *MB* 1:120.

23. John B. O'Malley, *The Fellowship of Being* (The Hague: Martinus Nijhoff, 1966), p. 25.

24. "Appendix on Existence and Objectivity," *MJ*, 332.

25. "The truth is rather that *within* every ownership, every kind of ownership I exercise, there is this kernel that I feel to be there at the center; and this kernel is nothing other than the experience . . . by which my body is mine" (*MB* 1:120).

26. *MB* 1:122.   27. *MB* 1:125; *MJ*, 243.

28. *MJ*, 247, 310.   29. *MB* 1:125.

30. *MB* 1:125.   31. *MB* 1:173–74.

32. *MB* 1:174.   33. *MJ*, 243.

34. See *MJ*, 311.

35. Gabriel Marcel, *Presence and Immortality*, trans. Michael A. Machado (Pittsburgh: Duquesne University Press, 1967), pp. 194–95 (hereafter cited as *PI*).

36. *MJ*, 323.   37. *PI*, 208.
38. *PI*, 211.   39. *MJ*, 317.
40. *MB* 1:122–23.   41. *BH*, 159.
42. *MB* 1:122.

43. Paul Ricoeur, *Freedom and Nature: The Voluntary and the Involuntary*, trans. E. V. Novak (Evanston, Ill.: Northwestern University Press, 1966), pp. 205, 210.

44. Ibid., pp. 10, 14, 46, 87–88, 92, 112, 125, 208, 214, 220, 228, 272, 295, 297, 320, 468.

45. *CF*, 17; see also *DR*, 27.

46. *MJ*, 173.

47. Gabriel Marcel, *Position et approches concrètes du mystère ontologique* (Paris: Vrin, 1949), pp. 56–57.

48. W. E. Hocking, "Marcel and the Ground Issues of Metaphysics," *Philosophy and Phenomenological Research* 14, no. 4 (June 1954): 442.

49. See *BH*, 119; *DR*, 35, 91–93; *MJ*, 323.

50. See *Toward a Psychology of Being*, 2d ed. (New York: Van Nostrand Reinhold Co., 1968), pp. 71–115.

51. Paul Henry, S. J., *Saint Augustine on Personality* (New York: Macmillan Co., 1960), p. 17; see also *MJ*, 283–84.

52. Carl Michalson, ed., *Christianity and the Existentialists* (New York: Charles Scribner's Sons, 1956), pp. 87–88.

53. *The Quartet in F Sharp* (*Le Quatuor en fa dièse* [Paris: Plon, 1925]) is a play by Gabriel Marcel in which the musical and dramatic modes of expression are beautifully blended. Family tragedy, music, and reflection intermingle before they lead to the final reconciliation between Claire, Roger (her present husband), and Stephane (her former husband). For Marcel, music and the theater were "an unshakable testimony of a deeper reality in which . . . everything fragmentary and unfulfilled on the sensory level would find fulfillment" (Harvard Lectures; subsequently published as *The Existential Background of Human Dignity* [Cambridge, Mass.: Harvard University Press, 1963], p. 21).

54. *MB* 1:128–29.

55. *MB* 1:129.

56. Richard Zaner, *The Problem of Embodiment* (The Hague: Martinus Nijhoff, 1964), p. 35.

57. *MB* 1:113, 127–28.

58. R. L. Gregory, *Eye and Brain: The Psychology of Seeing*, World University Library (New York and Toronto: McGraw-Hill Book Co., 1966).

59. Hubel and Wiesel, "Perceptive Fields of Single Neurons in the Cat's Striate Cortex," *Journal of Physiology* 148 (1959): 574–91.

60. *Introspection* has at least three different connotations. It may signify (1) the personal experience of a subject participating in experiments, as in the Rorschach test; (2) a kind of self-observation reporting personal experiences during an experiment, as in Kuelpe's studies of thinking; and (3) the comprehension of observable data. Whereas the first and second may be avoided in experiments, introspection of the third kind is indispensable.

61. *MB* 1:117.

62. *MJ*, 331–32.

63. See E. Straus, "Psychiatry and Philosophy," in *Psychiatry and Philosophy,* ed. M. Natanson (New York: Springer Verlag, 1969).

64. During the last decades neurophysiologists studied the functions of the reticular activating system regulating sleep and wakefulness. The silent presuppositions, of course, were (1) that the observers themselves were awake and thereby first in a position to study the behavior of animals and human beings as objects and (2) that the criteria used to establish the functions of the reticular systems were presented by the characteristic variations in the comportment of the subjects. The typical curve of the EEG, for instance, had to be gauged in relation to the changing conditions of the subjects.

65. See A. S. Eddington, *The Nature of the Physical World* (New York: Macmillan Co.; Cambridge: Cambridge University Press, 1929) and Francis Crick, *Of Molecules and Men* (Seattle and London: University of Washington Press, 1966).

66. *MB* 1:123.

67. Note that the etymological root of *country* is *contra,* and the root of the German *Gegend* is *gegen.*

Gabriel Marcel's Notion of Incarnate Being

REPLY TO ERWIN W. STRAUS AND MICHAEL A. MACHADO

If I view my situation as an adult subject, my body inevitably appears to be interposed between myself and the world. Only then does reflection enter in. And reflection shows that this mediation, which is an instrumental mediation, is possible only on the basis of something of an altogether different order, which I can no longer reach except a posteriori. In other words, I am led to evoke an anterior and, in a sense, primitive state of immediateness—or, more exactly, of the "nonmediatizable immediate." But it is obvious that language here betrays us, for in reflecting on this initial relationship and in attempting to express it, I am forced to borrow my language from the area of instrumental mediation. Hence, in this case, language is ultimately forced to struggle against itself.

When I say that my body is interposed between myself and the world, the self in question is the thinking self, consciousness, the *cogito*. This is what I call the situation of the adult subject or the adult self, that is, of the "I" that apprehends itself as a thinking subject. But in reflecting on this kind of triad, one realizes that it is possible, as I have said, only on the basis of something altogether different, which is at a point where the thinking self has not yet emerged. In this instance, one could use such expressions as an "emerging self," which is the thinking self, and an "immerged self," which communicates directly with the world.

For me, the situation defined or described by Descartes is secondary to an initial situation that can in no way be expressed in Cartesian language. There remains lived experience, to which one must always refer. Many *Erlebnisse* are indeed of this order of experience and are precisely mo-

---

Translated from the French by Susan Gruenheck.

ments in which the thinking self as such plays no part. Whether these states are of well-being or of ill-being, the thinking self does not intervene. This is what I call the immerged self. I would say that the situation defined by Descartes does not account for itself.

Nevertheless, reflection is not inferior or secondary in importance to an initial situation of an altogether different order. This is extremely important, because all the metapsychic experiments that interest me so much (for example, telepathy—the experience of being "informed," as so often happens, of something happening to someone I love) precisely imply a sympathetic mediation quite different from instrumental mediation. For this reason I said that attempts to explain telepathy as a kind of transmission (or what I call a message) make no sense. The word *participation,* although it does not satisfy me entirely, is nevertheless much more exact. *It is impossible to discard primary reflection. It would be sheer nonsense to try to discard primary reflection.**

It should be kept in mind that I have not worked on these questions in any systematic fashion. Consequently, I have by no means examined all the aspects. My concern was to bring to light an aspect that seemed to me totally neglected and disregarded by precisely those for whom primary reflection was self-sufficient. It is here, moreover, that we find ourselves once again faced with the first subject of my research, in 1912–1914; that is, how is it possible to conceptualize what is given in religious experience? If we start from primary reflection, it is absolutely impossible to deal with religious data. But this does not mean that primary reflection is excluded. It simply means that I have not considered primary reflection by itself. This task has been very well performed (indeed, much better than I could have done it) by scholars and philosophers who have focused on the sciences, whether physical or biological. I think that the problem of a corporeal stratification of thought, for example, should be examined, but I have not studied anthropology and therefore could not deal with it myself.

I have always said that the word *investigation* must be applied in some sense to all of my books. But my investigations concern rather specific subjects; they do not form a general treatise on the human condition.

In making a distinction between tool and instrument, I was not thinking of musical instruments. This presents an interesting problem, and I do not find it troublesome. I grant Professors Straus and Machado that they can in fact distinguish between tool and instrument (as I could have and perhaps should have more explicitly than I did), since there are cases, particularly in music, in which the instrument becomes part of the musician in

---

*Both italicized sentences appear in English in the original French text.—ED.

a way that tools cannot become a part of the artisan. It is obvious that a violin is not a tool. That is absolutely certain. Clearly, the violin becomes an integral part of the violinist, whereas the hammer has quite a different relation to the blacksmith.

One might go further and say that the possessive *my* takes on a different value when the violinist speaks of a violin than when the blacksmith speaks of a hammer. This is certainly true, for one can say that the musician's instrument gradually becomes personalized, whereas one cannot say that a hammer or a shovel becomes personalized in the same manner. The finality of the one is altogether different from the finality of the other.

In a certain sense, one can make use of the body in the same way a musician makes use of an instrument. Athletes, for example, treat their bodies somewhat as instrumentalists treat their instruments. There is probably an analogy here. I was never interested in sports and therefore have not reflected on them. But I think one could say this for sports; it is certainly true of dance.

This is an area of research that I have never undertaken but that appears both valid and interesting. Nevertheless, I think that it will perhaps lead (I say this tentatively) to a reintroduction of sympathetic mediation at the heart of instrumental mediation. All the same, one must try to understand (although this is extremely difficult) how the soul of the violinist, let us say, can pass into the violin. This is something other than the skill of the lumberjack, for example, passing into the axe. There is something else. There is something more. That much is certain. But to understand would require undertaking a whole new area of research. It would necessitate going back to the very history of instruments, for it is probable that the violin, starting at a certain period after its technical perfection, became much more cosubstantial with the artist who used it than it could have been at the beginning. There must have been a kind of refinement of the instrument that gave it an aptitude it did not originally possess and would not possess at all in the hands of a beginner.

I agree that I *by-passed* this research, although I do find it interesting.* It is even interesting to someone from my point of view, that is, precisely to someone who has tried to distinguish between sympathetic and instrumental mediation. But it is a difficult undertaking. One would have to consult a musician who at the same time possessed a great capacity for reflection: the rare combination found in a man like Menuhin, for example.

G.M.

---

*The italicized word appears in English in the original French text.—ED.

5

Alfred O. Schmitz

MARCEL'S DIALECTICAL METHOD

G ABRIEL Marcel makes no formal statement of methodology that could be compared to the systematic statement Sartre makes in *The Transcendence of the Ego*. Instead, Marcel intersperses methodological statements throughout his major works. They occur during his attempts to find solutions to philosophical problems. Moreover, they are for the most part brief. One exception to this is the first five chapters of volume one of *The Mystery of Being*. Here Marcel (1) distinguishes objective (practical and scientific) research from metaphysical research, (2) locates the source of metaphysical research in the human situation, (3) defines truth and intelligibility in their relation to philosophical inquiry, and (4) distinguishes primary from secondary reflection and describes the latter as the mode of reflection peculiar to metaphysical philosophy.

In one respect these chapters of *The Mystery of Being* can be treated as a counterpart to Sartre's *The Transcendence of the Ego*. They constitute a fairly complete statement containing all the essential features of a methodology. But at the same time these chapters can only be taken as an introductory outline, because many of the finer points and deeper implications of Marcel's method are not developed sufficiently. The two volumes of *The Mystery of Being* are based on the Gifford Lectures Marcel gave in 1949 and 1950 at the University of Aberdeen. In these lectures he sought only to give a general orientation to his audience rather than to go into methodological problems. Nevertheless, a more important reason for the lack of a systematic statement of method lies in Marcel's general reluctance to systematize. In the first pages of the initial lecture, Marcel relates the anxiety he felt when invited to give the Gifford Lectures. He felt he was being called on to do what was against the grain of all his reflections: to place his thoughts into a form that would represent the results of his research, his findings. Marcel denies that he has a body of thought that could be organized into a system of interrelated propositions. Early in his career he entertained the fond hope of working out a systematic philosophy, and the notes he began taking, which he later developed into the journal form, were in preparation for this system. This explains the rather abstract character of the earlier part of his *Metaphysical Journal*. Yet he was unable to make the transition from his notes to a systematic work. Something within the very nature of his approach to philosophy seemed to make the task impossible. He encountered a barrier constructed of his own refusal to turn a philosophical question into a technical problem. Marcel therefore sees *The Mystery of Being* as an attempt to indicate the direction in which he has been moving.

The more one reflects on Marcel's work, the more one realizes that the distinction between method and results in philosophy does not fit him very well. This distinction reduces philosophy on the one hand to a product and on the other hand to an instrument of production. Nowhere in this polarity are philosophers themselves an essential factor. Marcel's description of the human condition as "involvement" would contradict itself if it were made into a technical statement of philosophical methodology. For one thing, it would imply that it was aiming at the kind of universal validity that is the goal of any action coming within the scope of a technique designed to deal with problems. That Marcel neither aims at universal validity nor thinks it important for philosophy is very clearly indicated in the latter part of the introductory chapter of *The Mystery of Being*. Here he defines his audience not on the basis of an epistemic criterion, but on the basis of an "existential" or dramatic one. His audience is identified by the kind of demand they make on life.

What then is to be understood by *method* when dealing with Marcel's inquiries? Clearly, if one attempts to confine Marcel to a formal statement about the nature of the relationship between thought and reality, then his rejection of systematic thought is incomprehensible. Marcel rejects the Cartesian notion that thought thinks itself over and against reality and has thus the problem of leaping the gap between itself and reality. Such an image of the relation of thought to reality and the solutions drawn from it result in a distortion of experience. In order to think the image itself or to attain the position from which it would seem a plausible starting point for philosophical problems, philosophers must retreat from the richness and proliferation that characterize immediate experience. They must collapse immediacy into a vague and indefinite Other to be treated as a unit— something that will finally lend itself to being uni-versed. Once this is done, as Nietzsche saw so well, philosophers' own prejudices reemerge as those defining the foundation of the whole. What philosophers do in effect by adopting such a procedure is to essentialize their "global experience of existence." Prejudiced experience then lies under the vague conceptualized Other as a kind of substratum supporting it.

A method defined in these terms seems untenable when seen from the point of view of Marcel's inquiries because it is designed to heal a wound that is not existentially encountered but artificially created and confined within the limits of thought itself. In one stroke thought isolates itself from its situation, without which it cannot even define itself as thought, and then seeks to find its way back. Thought then encounters itself and its ideas, but can no longer be sure that anything else exists. Within the confines of such a method, philosophers become victims of a game thought plays with itself.

Philosophy, according to Marcel, must be defined in terms of a break within the continuum of experience, not in terms of a puzzle thought generates for itself. Philosophy arises as a suffering in the form of a metaphysical disquietude, a loss of the sense of being. In one's role as a moral agent, the loss of the sense of being reveals ontological disunity and one's vulnerability as a finite being. Out of this vulnerability, philosophers posit Being as that in which they aspire to participate, and their questions are directed toward elucidating the conditions for the possibility of such participation. The first consideration is the condition of the world in which metaphysical disquietude can arise. Marcel sees this world as a "broken world."

The "broken world" concept is a descriptive-explanatory one. It describes certain features of the human world, emphasizing the present-day world, and explains the anguish and disquiet it harbors. It expresses the intuition of a situation that is alien to the deepest needs of human beings— the need to participate in the invulnerability of Being.

As a methodological concept, "broken world" refers to the impetus that gives rise to philosophizing. Its significance lies in its explicit denial that philosophy is or ever can be based on mere curiosity or on intellectual interest supported, perhaps, by a taste for contention. If people were indeed *confronted* with a universe, then given the leisure that comes with advanced civilization, they might well entertain themselves with the intellectual pastime of philosophical contention in an attempt to give systematic expression to the nature of the universe. The viewpoint from which it seems as if a system of philosophy were a plausible goal is an illusion created by "primary reflection." It constantly seeks to reduce experience to object categories so that disturbances of the continuum of experience always appear to be amenable to technical solution.

Primary reflection wants always to handle experiential difficulty as a

problem. It wants to universalize its own limited horizon. "Secondary reflection," in causing one to recollect or recover oneself, rejects the uni-
vocality that primary reflection tends to impose on experience. The broken
world is revealed to secondary reflection as the superficial and degrading
unity primary reflection imposes on the diverse situations of life. Once this
occurs, one's own being suffers the same fate, since the unity was lived
as the basis of one's being. The experience of the broken world is the
objective correlate to having one's being called into question. As a first
moment of secondary reflection, it is an alienation from oneself, from others, and from the world. Faced with the strangeness of this alienation, one
seeks to recover the familiar. One means of recovery is to deny secondary
reflection and to cling to the unity imposed by primary reflection. If one
resists this falsifying temptation, one undertakes a movement that will cul-
minate in either despair or hope.

Were the mundane or objective features of life the only ones on which
reflection of any kind could bear, then there would be no doubt about the
kinds of questions and answers with which one could be concerned. Con-
ceivably Marcel would be ready to follow the instrumentalism of John
Dewey if all human experience could be reduced without distortion or degradation to problem-solving activities and the attendant enjoyment. But for
Marcel, the human situation involves a dimension that goes deeper than
the sphere of the problematic as it is constructed by primary reflection.
This is the dimension of the inner life. Although breaks or gaps may also
occur here, interrogation involves something qualitatively different from
that involved when one is, for example, merely looking for a lost object.
In the latter case one questions someone who might know its whereabouts
or help find it, or one attempts to recollect relevant data that have objective
implications. Disquietude of the inner life is not a problem in this sense.
It involves Socratic recollection. An illustration Marcel gives will show
this:

> I am talking to a friend, and somehow I let myself be drawn into telling him
> something which is an actual lie. I am alone with myself again, I get a grip
> on myself, I face the fact of this lie; how was it possible for me to tell such a
> whopper? I am all the more surprised at myself because I have been accus-
> tomed to think of myself, up to the present, as a truthful and trustworthy
> person. But then what importance ought I to attach to this lie? Am I forced to
> conclude that I am not the man I thought I was? And, from another point of
> view, what attitude ought I to take up towards this act of mine? Ought I to
> confess the lie to my friend, or on the other hand would I make myself ridic-
> ulous by doing so? But perhaps I ought to make myself ridiculous, to let my
> friend laugh at me, as a sort of punishment for having told him the lie in the
> first place?[1]

As Marcel points out, once this level of reflection is attained one cannot proceed as if nothing had happened. In cases of this type there is the recognition, for one thing, that the grounds for one's judgments of others have been shaken. But more important, in terms of philosophical method, is the fact that this recognition contains a double realization:

> On the one hand, I am now able to communicate at a broader level with myself, since I have, as it were, introduced the self that committed the dubious act to the self that did not hesitate to set itself up as the harsh judge of others; and on the other hand—and this cannot be a mere coincidence—I am now able to enter into far more intimate communication with my friend, since between us there no longer stands that barrier which separates the judge on the bench from the accused man in the dock.[2]

Thus under certain conditions one can move to a level of reflection where one's own being is called into question. One is forced to question what in fact one lives by or what one is. Marcel uses other examples in various places to elucidate this point. They all involve a double reflection that leads one to become uneasy with oneself when a disturbance breaks the primary structural unity of one's world.

Metaphysical inquiry is definable, for Marcel, in terms of an analogy with the example cited above. It is an activity by which one defines an uneasiness and seeks to transpose it in terms of a creative development of the inner life.

Thus philosophers question on their own account. If they raise the ontological question, it is because their own being is in question. They are not at home in the world, they are alienated from it—from others and from themselves. Whatever reality they possess as beings is obscured by this alienation. Their questions are therefore directed toward uncovering the real and the terms under which they have a share in it.

To experience this broken world requires deposing the *cogito* from the throne of authority. Rather than basing one's inquiry on a presupposition of epistemic isolation, one moves in the opposite direction, remaining "this side" of the *cogito*. For Marcel, consciousness is intersubjective at its core. Although this intersubjectivity cannot assert itself qua intersubjective, it is constantly acknowledged, for example, in the act of publishing one's work. Thus philosophical method is not thinking *sub specie aeterni*. The kind of thinking peculiar to philosophy is to treat one's own experience in a manner that allows one to break the bounds of egocentric isolation and to move in the direction of understanding that experience. Such a movement cannot be construed as an egocentric concern; it can only be accomplished by a self-transcendence leading to an understanding of the experience of others. One moves beyond oneself toward the very basis of

being a person and to the basis of every possible affirmation. Marcel points
to the intersubjective element at the basis of ontology as "the mysterious
root of language."[3] The starting point of ontology is therefore not the
cogito but the "we are." Marcel criticizes Sartre for failing to grasp the
meaning of *philia* or *agape,* thus remaining wholly within the realm of
eros. He writes:

> In the end it is only on the one hand the domain of *eros,* with its formi-
> dable ambiguity, so far as it coincides with want or desire, which is ac-
> cessible to him, or, on the other hand, that of a community of work which
> creates teams united by the knowledge of a task to be done; and it is only
> if you look at it from outside that you can see in this a genuine sort of
> solidarity.[4]

Marcel finds the "we are" to be an even more fundamental relation to
the world. Intersubjectivity is the starting point of philosophy; it is the
infrastructure of the spiritual life, an original human solidarity preceding
the emergence of the ego and the condition for its possibility. Moreover,
being primarily ethical and moral in nature, this solidarity is also the condition for the possibility of objectivity, even in the sciences. Thus objectivity is possible only on the basis of a self-transcending ethical commitment that, in the Socratic spirit, allows the argument to go where it will.

In a broken world this spiritual infrastructure is replaced by an abstract
rational monism defined in terms of technical activity. In such a world
conceptions of truth and intelligibility are determined by the results of instrumental activity and are bound to problem-solving categories. It is a
world that has forgotten where it began. Truth and intelligibility are seen
as functions of universal validity—true for anybody and everybody. For
Marcel, this conception of truth and intelligibility is philosophically untenable. In attempting to reinstate the reality of the spiritual, he transcends
the categories of universal validity as defined by the technical disciplines.
He is directed by the "spirit of truth." His goal is edification. His means
are Socratic and hence indirect. He seeks to revive essential realities by
recalling them to mindful consideration.

For Marcel, philosophers must first put aside the common-sense notion
that facts are somehow just there, to be encountered by anyone who bumps
up against them. This is to treat fact and truth as if they were physical
objects. The spatial analogy places both at a distance from some mind
whose task is to grasp them as one grasps a physical object. But it fails to
explain how a fact can be enlightening at all for someone. The most fruitful way to pursue the questions of fact and truth is to see what is involved
in cases where, for one reason or another, people refuse to face the facts.

In the first place, when people bar themselves from a truth, they must literally shut out something that they would otherwise know or come to realize. Marcel calls this the "reverberatory power" of facts.[5] In the second place, if it were true that facts, like physical objects, were completely outside those for whom they are the facts, it would be difficult to understand why anyone would care to shut them out, since they would have the same contingency as physical objects. Thus facts must get their intelligibility (which can only mean their status as facts) by reference to an understanding. Marcel writes:

> We must not hesitate to affirm that the coherence of a fact, of any fact, is conferred on it by the mind that grasps it, by the understanding self. There is therefore every reason to suppose that if this fact, or this collection of data, should possess the strange power of irradiation . . . it would be from the understanding self that it had borrowed the power, rather than possessing such a power intrinsically itself: the latter supposition . . . is absurd.[6]

Here we encounter the real question: How is the self that confers the power of irradiation on facts distinguished from the self that can blind itself to this irradiation? In answering this question Marcel appeals to dramatic situations. They reveal the tensions present whenever some vital truth is in question. Essentially what Marcel is getting at is the difficulty one encounters, having once moved beyond the ordinary questions of life, of telling just what the truth is. The difficulty arises because the truth resides in the inmost core of a person's life. Suppose, for example, that someone is questioned about the motives behind his choice of vocation. And suppose further that the questioning reveals events in his life that, if they were involved in his choice of vocation, would throw suspicion on his sincerity of purpose. Certainly from an impersonal point of view, if these events can be shown to have had a determining significance, they jeopardize the sincerity of this person. But from the point of view of the person himself questioning his own sincerity, what is to be made of these events?

Anyone who questions in this manner faces a duality between the desiring self and the self that is the spirit of truth.[7] The problem cannot be solved merely by an enumeration and consideration of data in terms of some objective theory of implication. It requires an opening up of the person to the light that these data can cast and that is really what it means for them to become facts. As facts they are frequently, though not always, painful. But whether painful or not, they have no status outside the context of a concrete life. At the same time, there is a relief in opening oneself up to them. This relief is grounded on the emergence of the spirit of truth in opposition to the desiring self. The desiring self is the self that tends to perpetuate illusions. It sees the world as it wants it to be. Consequently, it somehow manages to absorb events into itself without facing them in their fullest reality. It permits the self to live, or to accommodate itself within, a lie. Thus truth, when it comes (the reverberatory power of facts), has the effect of lifting a long-carried burden.

There is then a distinction between truth as common sense conceives of it and truth as philosophers must conceive of it. It must be possible to see a difference between a truth that is concerned with and bound up with things manifested objectively in space and time—that is, a truth correlated with questions of existence or with what is the case—and a truth that has no bearing on questions of this kind. Whereas the former is intimately related to the problem of verification, the latter is not. In opposition to what common sense holds, Marcel claims that objective truth "implies the possibility of verification."[8] His argument rejects approaching the problem in terms of what can or cannot in fact be brought within the scope of experience. Instead, he argues that verifiability enters into the conception of objective truth as a principle of coherence: "That which by definition evades verification is not that which cannot be reproduced but that which is not inserted into a whole that thought can reconstitute, that which is not in a determinable relation to the rest of the content of thought."[9]

Moreover, Marcel holds that the very notion of empirical reality depends on a reflective act of consciousness: "The act by which reflection is defined as such . . . is the act by which consciousness thinks itself as empirical."[10] This allows him to make the claim

> that imaginative thought affirms the identity of the real object and the object represented, it would never occur to it to affirm that they are dual. Hence I think that the problem of the reality of the external world is one that cannot even be raised by imaginative thought. If it is so raised it is as regards the body, and in that field it is meaningless. And even if it were raised on genuine grounds, imaginative thought would clearly prefer idealist theory to the admission of a dualism between the real and what is represented. Furthermore it would object to conceiving this identity (of the real and what is represented) in the interests of what is represented, on the grounds that such a solution seems to compromise the reality of the object (its independence in relation to its *percipi*).[11]

That Marcel accepts a type of coherence theory for ordinary thought does not indicate that he holds a similar position with respect to philosophical thought and its attainable results. He means merely to point out that truth in the realm of metaphysical reflection has no intrinsic relation to the ordinary notion of verifiability.

Marcel's opposition to the common-sense notion of truth is embodied in his use of the term *spirit*. His insistence that objective truth involves the possibility of verification, regardless of the claim of common sense, is a step toward ridding truth of those connotations that are analogous to a thing to be possessed.

The self that is the spirit of truth presents itself in the face of certain realities it finds difficult to accept. Here the spirit of truth manifests itself as the courage to deny what is demanded by want and desire, namely, to see reality as they would like it to be. Marcel uses the example of parents of an abnormal child who, despite their knowledge to the contrary, live as though their child were just like other children.[12] Marcel's analysis of the situation brings out two essential features of the spirit of truth. First, since it involves the courage to face the facts, the spirit of truth is an activity. Marcel takes this to indicate an active element in all judgment. In other words, a judgment in the most vital sense of the term is not an observation from a point outside a certain situation but an active, determining power within the situation. Moreover, there is in reality no alternative but to face the truth that has been blocked out, and this presents a paradox. On the one hand, facing the truth requires courage, and this seems to imply an alternative. On the other hand, there is no real alternative. For Marcel this paradox illustrates the way events can enter into the tissue of a person's life without their real weight being felt; the truth is already there, but the person manages to put it out of action.

The duality of the self enables a layering of capacities so that the self that is the spirit of truth is submerged in favor of the self that is all desire. However, Marcel does not claim that the distinction between the self that is the spirit of truth and the self that is desire indicates a real separation within the self. Nor does he maintain that there is a third self hovering over the other two and making a choice between them. The distinction between two selves is an abstraction used to indicate the existential paradox each concrete individual faces. The paradox is a reflection of the human situation, which always presents the option of accepting or rejecting spiritual reality.

For Marcel the life-world of concrete individuals displays the character of brokenness to the extent that it puts the spirit of truth out of action and conceals the burden it carries. This suppression of the spirit of truth is not an unusual or isolated phenomenon:

> Let us note well . . . that the great majority of human beings grope about during their whole lives among these data of their own existence rather as one gropes one's way between heavy chairs and tables in a darkened room. And what is tragic about their condition is that perhaps only because their lives are passed in this shadowy gloom can they bear to live at all. It is just as if their seeing apparatus had become finally adapted to this twilight state: it is not a

question of what Ibsen in *The Wild Duck* calls the 'life-lie', it is a state of non-vision which is not, however, a state of quite complete non-awareness. It can also be said that the attention of such people is not directed towards the data of their own existence, that they even make a point of directing it else-where, and, indeed, this 'making a point' is as it were the hidden spring that makes their lives tick on reasonably bearably. One might express this in an-other way: all of us tend to secrete and exude a sort of protective covering within which our life goes on.[13]

Marcel's words indicate that he acknowledges the human phenomenon Sartre has labeled "bad faith." But the validity of Marcel's method de-pends on not being obliged to draw the Sartrean consequences from the existence of this phenomenon.

Philosophical inquiry is a dialectical tension between this secretive ten-dency and the demands of the spirit of truth. Its task is the opening up of individuals to themselves and to others by breaking down the barriers im-posed by the secretive tendency. It is not clear in Marcel whether the terms of this dialectic would in every age be a tension between the impersonal categories of primary reflection and the recuperative power of secondary reflection. Given that this secretive tendency is not peculiar to a particular age, the question is whether it is somehow essentially bound up with the goal of primary reflection to reduce experience to impersonal categories. However this may be, it is quite clear that for Marcel primary reflection is the culprit in the present age. Its movement toward technocracy has created individuals who are apparently content to define themselves in terms of their functions in a gigantic social machine. As a result, the personal self attempts to fulfill itself in terms of what can be possessed. This in turn brings about a degradation of those spiritual realities, particularly of faith and hope, that provide the only true sustenance for the individual. Philos-ophers, by means of the dialectical tension, seek to replenish these reali-ties.

There is a tendency to associate Marcel with the Phenomenological movement. Marcel himself has lent support to this tendency by character-izing some of his descriptions and analyses as phenomenological. How-ever, there is little to be gained by making this association, except perhaps to show that philosophers have in the past and continue in the present to engage in what they consider essential analyses. It is only by stretching the imagination beyond reasonable limits that Marcel can be identified with Husserl's goal to make philosophy into a strict science. The most accurate statement summing up Marcel's methodology comes from the introduction to the *Metaphysical Journal*, where he wrote: "One of my pupils once asked me whether my philosophy could not be considered to be a kind of neo-Socratism. The expression struck me very much, and on reflection I wonder whether the description would not be the least inexact that could be applied to me.''[14]

Marcel's concern to replenish and reinstate the realities of Being, as opposed to the technocratic categories of Having, is implicated in his refusal to systematize a philosophy and therefore in his adoption of the informal approach of the journal or diary. It is in the journals that his neo-Socratism is clearly exemplified.

The essence of the journal can be best brought out in connection with some of its implications for the Socratic method. It is a diary Marcel filled over a period of time with fairly regular entries of thoughts directed toward specific questions that troubled him. Presumably the distinctive feature of the journal—what distinguishes it from systematically worked out pieces of writing—is that it is a day-to-day record of an ongoing dialectical process. Therefore, it is not a work initially addressed to a public but a record of a conversation conducted in terms of a question-answer dialectic. It begins for Marcel as notes kept for the writing of a systematic work and ends by remaining just as it began, never undergoing the transition to systematization.

Apparently Marcel grew apprehensive of the inward transformation required of thinkers who move from the things that really bother them to the inward stance they must take in order to write for a professional circle, no matter how small its radius. The stance thinkers must take involves a displacement of the problem into a language in which it loses its existential character. In systematizing, thinkers must move away from the source in their own experience that gave rise to the problem and must place before themselves an anonymous many for whom they must develop the problem and the solution in a language presuming to be objective, at least in the circle for which it is written. This procedure severs the unique relation of the problem to the thinkers themselves. Not only does it presuppose that thought stands over and against a reality it can seize as a whole, but it also presupposes that individual thinkers are only contingently related to the problems they encounter. Marcel's suspicion of his early tendency to systematize a philosophy culminated in his well-known distinction between *problem* and *mystery,* the basic distinction supporting his method.

Marcel's use of the journal form as an application of the Socratic method elucidates ideas that bear mainly on spiritual reality, which Marcel identifies with Being. Dialectic is brought into the service of clarifying and indirectly articulating the spiritual. But only allusions are possible, because here we encounter the realm of mystery where the *involved* nature of thought constitutes an inescapable *"encroaching upon its own data."*[15]

Moreover, it is essential to the method that it not be undermined at the outset by reductionistic tendencies. Therefore it must begin with the assumption that the phenomenon under investigation is real. In what is perhaps his most important methodological statement, Marcel writes:

> When I re-read my notes I observe that one of my usual methods of research consists in reasoning somewhat as follows: Admitting the hypothesis that this given phenomenon is real, what are the conditions under which it is able to be real? When I have determined those conditions by analysis do they not allow me to understand that which in practice is unintelligible in normal experience?[16]

Phenomena such as faith and hope and the ideas corresponding to them do not lose their reality as if they were physical objects beginning to deteriorate after exposure to adverse weather conditions. The phenomena under study in metaphysical inquiry are always realized concretely in relation to an individual self. Nor are faith or hope abstract ideas, such as $\sqrt{2}$, with corresponding theoretical and practical aspects, where practical universality is realized within a theoretical framework that defines ideas operationally. Faith and hope are concretely lived. The question therefore is not so much What are they? but What are the conditions for the possibility of their concrete realization? Once the question is put in these terms it involves the "what" or "who" of the questioning individual—the manner of the individual's participation in Being, and correlatively the question of Being itself.

The journal form is therefore a record of self-interrogation. It is not intended for an audience held together by a universe of discourse that limits the writer's alternatives. It is a movement toward self-clarification. Since it does not have the objectivity characterizing a technical language— the objectivity of a language that has arisen on the basis of an organized group attack on a set of technical problems—the individual reader has only an indirect access to it. To say that the access is indirect is to say that the questions it subjects to inquiry can only be approached if one originates the same inquiry within oneself. This would in turn be contingent on a discovery of the same uneasiness within oneself.

It should be clear that when Marcel says that the reality of the phenomena he seeks to describe is a hypothesis, he is not using *hypothesis* in the sense of a proposition to be verified by primary reflection. Rather, he means that the possibility of its descriptive redemption by dialectical clarification is in question. As pointed out earlier, Marcel conceives of his method as a replenishing and a reinstating of the realities corresponding to certain terms that tend to inflate in a broken world. Although these terms frequently enter into discourse of various kinds, they have a hollow sound.

Other realities seem completely lost; for example, the reality corresponding to the idea of brotherhood or fraternity. To replenish a term and the reality corresponding to it is to describe the conditions for its possibility. Existentially, this amounts to a positioning of the individual questioner.

In *The Philosophy of Existentialism* Marcel criticizes Sartre for failing to understand the nature of a gift. In effect, Sartre refuses to see a gift for what it is; that is, his analysis denies its very reality as a gift by reducing it to a form of appropriation commensurate with his analysis of consciousness. Marcel uses a portion of Sartre's analysis from *Being and Nothingness* as evidence: "to give is to appropriate by destruction while utilizing this destruction to enslave another."[17] Marcel sees Sartre's analysis as being infused with certain misconceptions, coming from Kant and his followers, about the nature of receptivity. They tend to think of receptivity as a passive suffering ascribable only to matter: "As soon as receptivity in a spiritual, or even in a living, being is confused with suffering in a material sense . . . it becomes impossible to conceive the concrete and organic relationship between the individual and the world."[18] Marcel's analysis of the nature of a gift moves in a direction opposite to Sartre's. In so doing it serves to illustrate how the Socratic dialectic, beginning with the "What is?" question and moving toward definition, becomes in Marcel's application an allusion to what ultimately is a mystery. The analysis also reveals the deep importance to his method of the hypothesis that the phenomenon is real:

> What is a gift? Can it be looked at as a simple transfer? The most cursory reflection will show us that it is more than that. Let us suppose that I make someone a present and he comes to thank me for it. If I cut his thanks short by the laconic remark 'It's only a transfer', my words will affect him like a cold douche. To transfer would be simply to move a certain object, a certain possession, from one account to another. Now, even if this is what happens materially, both I and the recipient see it as the expression of something quite different. To understand this, we have only to consider that any gift is in some way a giving of oneself, and that, however difficult it may be to think of a gift of oneself, such a gift cannot on any showing be compared to a transfer.
>
> We should note, in addition, that the gift has a certain character of unconditionalness. It would be no gift at all, for example, to say to someone, 'I am giving you this house, but only on condition that you make no alteration to it except such as I have specified, or receive in it nobody except such people as I shall give you the names of'. We may go deeper and add that to give with a predetermined end in view, such, for example as using the beneficiary's gratitude to secure a hold over him, is not giving. To give is not to seduce.
>
> Here we meet a difficulty. If we say that the gift has no precise end beyond itself, must we thereby deny it significance? The answer to that is that we must probably, as Bergson says, reach a higher level than finality. To give is to expand, to expand oneself. But we must be careful not to interpret that

phrase in a semi-material way, as though it was the overflow of something
that is too full. The soul of a gift is its generosity, and it is manifest that
generosity is a virtue—therefore to be carefully distinguished from prodigal-
ity. Would not a fairly accurate definition of generosity be *a light whose joy
is in giving light, in being light?*[19]

Marcel's description goes further, since what he is interested in, in the
context of this passage, is an analysis of the relation between freedom and
grace. The passage illustrates the Socratic method as Marcel uses it and at
the same time brings out the nature of the object of metaphysical thought
as Marcel conceives of it.

One of Marcel's main concerns about systematic metaphysics seems to
be that it serves the purposes of ideological fanaticism while utterly failing
to recall people to a grounding in Being. The fanatic, by the very nature
of his commitment, introduces the highest possible degree of opacity into
his life. True communication with him is impossible because his relation
to an idea borders on an obsession or fixation. Thus he "ceases to be an
interlocutor, and becomes only an adversary who handles what he calls his
ideas as offensive weapons. The result is that I am forced to find some
defensive armour for myself, and as what is properly called discussion is
shown to be impossible, I feel bound in the end either to meet violence
with violence, or to refuse the battle."[20]

In counteracting this tendency philosophy is necessarily fragmentary.
In philosophy "everything always starts from zero, and a philosopher is
not worthy of the name unless he not only accepts but wills this harsh
necessity."[21] He must approach reality concretely, since it cannot be
summed up as an intelligible whole. He does this in the interests of action,
but of action supported in Being, not in the embodiment of an empty and
abstract universal idea. Action can never be reduced to a mere content of
thought. Marcel thinks of action as an original occurrence, and it is this
originality of action that impresses him:

> To act was, to my mind, primarily equivalent to taking up a position, and it
> was only by a pure fiction that reality could be made to integrate the act
> whereby I took up my position in regard to it. Looking back on it now, I see
> that I was trying to establish a concrete and dramatic type of relationship in
> place of the abstract relationships of inherence or of exteriority between which
> traditional philosophy claimed to make me choose.[22]

Thus Marcel, in equating action with taking a position, sees in human
action a concrete point of origin that by its very nature disallows the attempt to embrace it in a purely abstract and systematic account of the
whole of reality. The vector involved in the human act is qualified by the
original relation to Being of the individual actor. Since an act is always

part of the whole that it posits, the whole cannot itself be universalized in a metaphysical system. Thought itself is action and comes under the same critique, namely, that it is bound up with the vectors of the individual life of the thinker. Therefore the drama of life, rather than abstract thought modeled after the nature of mathematical deductive systems, serves as the basis of metaphysical inquiry.

Marcel claims that his investigations first took root in his plays and were only later worked out in philosophical dialectic proper. The significance of the drama for Marcel is that it provides not only the ground for the emergence of his major concerns but also the medium in which he can move toward the objectivity he seeks. For Marcel objectivity is not something whose form and content are given once and for all; it is the active suppression of the tendency to view the world as one wants it to be, and it is therefore constantly in the process of being realized and strengthened. The objectivity to which he refers is the intersubjectivity that emerges when one ceases to deny the subjectivity of others. But part of what it means to deny the subjectivity of others is to be unaware of that subjectivity and hence of the fact of its denial. Through the medium of the drama, where individual selves encounter one another in conflicts involving the deepest of life-commitments, one can begin to realize the meaning of other perspectives on the world. For Marcel objectivity becomes the same as love, since ultimately others can only be legitimately invoked as "presences." Love as the realization of presence is an acknowledgment of mystery.

Marcel is conscious of the problem of defining the sense in which the type of inquiry he is conducting can be objective for other philosophers. The "objects" of philosophical research are not objects, as ordinarily understood, but presences. And presences, being mysteries, can ultimately only be alluded to, not set out in an objective and clear-cut fashion. Even the meaning of the term *presence* suffers this fate. Nevertheless, these facts do not overly concern Marcel. The task of philosophy is to reinstate the feeling of mystery and to invoke presence. Each is dependent on the other. Truth in philosophical research cannot be equated with universal validity. The philosopher is the person who asks true questions, and true questions are those that involve a

> reciprocal clarification of two unknowns, and it may well be that, in order to pose the true questions, it is actually necessary to have an intuition, in advance, about what the true answer might be. It might be said that the true questions are those which point, not to anything resembling the solution of an enigma, but rather to a line of direction along which we must move. As we move along the line, we get more and more chances of being visited by a sort

of spiritual illumination; for we shall have to acknowledge that Truth can be considered only in this way, as a spirit, as a light.[23]

Thus Marcel speaks of his audiences as "distinguished less by a certain kind of aptitude . . . than by the level at which they make their demands on life and set their standards."[24] Not many philosophers would be willing to accept the severe limitations on the office of philosophy implied by Marcel's method. But placing limitations on philosophy in one way or another has been the rule rather than the exception in contemporary philosophy. This trend may well attest to the validity of Marcel's claim that this world is a broken one. What must be realized is his intense concern about the loss of a spiritual center and, more than this, about the tendency to make up the loss by allowing ideological imperialism to grow within the framework of technocracy so that creative relationships between persons atrophy and the need for self-authentication is in danger of plunging, at the extreme limit of despair, into fanaticism. Therefore, although concerns of this kind may not exhaust the concerns that philosophy might have, to ignore them is to reject the perennial Socratic conscience of philosophy. Marcel has done a great service to philosophy in his efforts to recall this conscience. It speaks through the undogmatic and open character of his reflections and was unmistakably present when he wrote:

> Wherever there is pure creation, having as such is transcended or etherialised within the creative act: the duality of possessor and possessed is lost in a living reality. . . . I am thinking in particular of such pseudo-possessions as *my ideas and opinions*. In this case, the word 'have' takes on a meaning which is at once positive and threatening. The more I treat my own ideas, or even my convictions, as something *belonging* to me . . . the more surely will those ideas and opinions tend, by their very inertia . . . to exercise a tyrannical power over me; that is the principle of fanaticism in all its shapes. What happens in the case of the fanatic, and in other cases too, it seems, is a sort of unjustified alienation of the subject . . . in face of the thing, whatever it may be. That, in my opinion, is the difference between the ideologist, on the one hand, and the thinker or artist on the other. The ideologist is one of the most dangerous of all human types, because he is unconsciously enslaved to a part of himself which has mortified, and this slavery is bound to manifest itself outwardly as tyranny. . . . The thinker, on the other hand, is continually on guard against this alienation, this possible fossilising of his thought. He lives in a continual state of creativity, and the whole of his thought is always being called in question from one minute to the next.[25]

ALFRED O. SCHMITZ

DEPARTMENT OF PHILOSOPHY
CONVERSE COLLEGE
APRIL 1969

NOTES

1. Gabriel Marcel, *The Mystery of Being,* trans. G. S. Fraser (vol. 1) and René Hague (vol. 2), 2 vols. (London: Harvill Press, 1950), 1:79 (hereafter cited as *MB*).

2. *MB* 1:80.   3. *MB* 2:11.

4. *MB* 2:9.   5. *MB* 1:65.

6. *MB* 1:64–65.   7. *MB* 1:69.

8. Gabriel Marcel, *Metaphysical Journal,* trans. Bernard Wall (Chicago: Henry Regnery Co., 1952), p. 29 (hereafter cited as *MJ*).

9. *MJ*, 28.   10. *MJ*, 2.

11. *MJ*, 13.   12. *MB* 1:67–68.

13. *MB* 1:64.   14. *MJ*, xii–xiii.

15. Gabriel Marcel, *Being and Having,* trans. Katharine Farrer (New York: Harper & Row, 1965), p. 117 (hereafter cited as *BH*).

16. *MJ*, 274.

17. Jean-Paul Sartre, *Being and Nothingness,* trans. Hazel E. Barnes (New York: Philosophical Library, 1956), p. 594.

18. Gabriel Marcel, *The Philosophy of Existentialism,* trans. Manya Harari (New York: Citadel Press, 1962), pp. 82–83 (hereafter cited as *PE*).

19. *MB* 2:118–19.   20. *MB* 2:115.

21. *PE*, 125.   22. *PE*, 126.

23. *MB* 1:13.   24. *MB* 1:14.

25. *BH*, 166.

Marcel's Dialectical Method

REPLY TO ALFRED O. SCHMITZ

Professor Schmitz's essay has the merit of seeking to bring out the characteristics of the type of thinking expressed in a journal like mine. He is quite right in saying that on the whole, it is a question of a self-examination and that certainly in the beginning, and often for a very long time afterward, the question of a public to whom one might have to address oneself is not raised. From this point of view, one ought perhaps to compare the *Journal métaphysique* (which appeared in 1927 at the instigation of Jean Paulhan and which I had not intended for publication, at least not in that form) with the journal in *Etre et avoir*. When this second journal appeared, the first had already been published; under these conditions, I might ask myself (without, however, being sure of the answer) whether in writing it I did not have in the back of my mind the idea of an eventual publication of the same type as the first journal.

This question may well pose itself to the student of my thought. But as far as I am concerned, there is no perceptible difference in the mode of expression between the *Journal métaphysique* properly speaking and *Etre et avoir* or, much later, *Présence et immortalité*. All three cases were dialogues with myself. But one should never forget what I once said about the inner plurality I have always observed within me. It is probably because of that inner plurality that I have so often raised objections to myself, which I then found necessary to take into consideration. This means that the other has always been present in me in an increasingly distinct way, and, within this perspective, one could naturally find a certain continuity between the philosophical and dramatic works. But my dramatic works should never be regarded as a certain kind of philosophical dialogue. Nothing could be more false. I would simply like to say that the other, who is as radically independent and autonomous as possible in my plays, already exists as other in my philosophical writings, although in a somewhat anonymous and slightly abstract form.

G.M.

Translated from the French by Susan Gruenheck.

6

Otto Friedrich Bollnow

MARCEL'S CONCEPT OF AVAILABILITY

I

FROM the German standpoint, the name Gabriel Marcel is associated with the recollection of a very specific historical and cultural situation. His books first came to the attention of German readers during the period immediately following the Second World War, when a new exchange of ideas was beginning. In that time of general confusion and collapse, they revealed a liberating prospect. The world's alien and threatening character had overcome people with an overwhelming force; all traditional order had been shaken, and need and despair characterized the prevailing attitude toward life in a period that has quite accurately been termed the age of anxiety. One felt totally abandoned in a world that seemed ultimately absurd.

In this situation, existentialism—in its predominant form in Germany at that time, represented above all by Sartre—appeared to be the only tenable position. There was something invigorating about its uncompromising decisiveness, for it demanded that we renounce any attempt at evasion, accept the anxiety fully, and completely and unreservedly face up to the uncanniness of existence. Only in this way, it suggested, and only after the renunciation of all external support, could there be found, in the innermost core of the individual, an ultimate, absolute, and unshakable reality called *Existenz*. The origin of this existentialism—its descent from Heidegger and Jaspers and ultimately from Kierkegaard—cannot be traced any further here. It must suffice to have recalled briefly the general intellectual climate of the period under consideration.[1]

Translated from the German by Mary Ann Possin and revised by Dr. Richard L. Schacht.

It soon became apparent that existentialism could not be regarded as the final word. It cast us back into the solitude of existence but failed to show how the individual could achieve meaningful relationships with other people and with the world in general. A meaningful life within the confines of existentialism was not possible. The problem thus arose of how existentialism could be superseded in a positive direction.[2]

This was the situation when Marcel's writings began to receive attention. Although many of them had appeared some time earlier, it was only after the war that their significance was recognized. They seemed both to embrace the experiences of which existentialism had made so much and to go beyond existentialism in a liberating way. This explains the peculiar growth of Marcel's influence.

Marcel was born in 1889, sixteen years before Sartre, and his *Metaphysical Journal,* begun in 1914, appeared in 1927. Still, he was initially much less influential than Sartre and seemed to be dependent upon Sartre in. a number of respects in the development of his philosophy. This must be kept in mind when comparing his earlier works, which were written without any regard to existentialism, with his later works, which demonstrate—generally speaking—a surprisingly consistent adherence to his original viewpoint.

In the period under consideration, it was common to hear Marcel's philosophy spoken of as a "Christian existentialism." Sartre, for example, had distinguished between an atheistic and a Christian existentialism.[3] The latter expression was taken up, or at least tacitly accepted, by Marcel himself when he contributed a brief biographical statement to a volume of essays devoted to the discussion of his philosophy, published by Gilson in 1947 under the title *Existentialisme chrétien: Gabriel Marcel.*[4] The expression appropriately captures Marcel's point of view, at least in its historical context. It both indicates his place in the general philosophical and intellectual movement of his time and stresses the distinctive character of his thinking.

There are indeed important points of agreement between Marcel's thought and existentialism in general that we must recognize in order to understand Marcel's philosophical development. In common with existentialism (and with the earlier *Lebensphilosophie,* or "philosophy of life"), for example, Marcel displays an aversion to all abstract thinking, which is carried on in a spirit of cool and composed objectivity.[5] He wages an "obstinate, permanent struggle against the spirit of abstraction," and insists on turning toward the concrete.[6] On the latter point, he explicitly speaks of his "hunger for the concrete," and one of his programmatic essays bears the title "Outline of a Concrete Philosophy."[7]

In *Retrospect,* Marcel recalls the period of writing the *Metaphysical Journal* as one "in which I pursued investigations outside the usual tracks that were to lead to the first existentialist statements."[8] He does, however, use a "category of the existential."[9] And his entire philosophy is grounded in commitment (*engagement*), just as his life in general is characterized by commitment. "We are *engagés* in our existence; it is not in our power to step out of it"[10]—a point he emphasizes from the very beginning of his development. Commitment provides the only possibility of breaking through the "invisible barrier" separating the theoretical thinker from the world and of making genuine, direct contact with reality.[11] For Marcel, "reality" always means, above all, other concretely existing human beings.

On the matter of commitment, Marcel's philosophy is indeed closely related to the philosophy of unconditional commitment as it was subsequently developed, especially by Sartre. But there is a considerable difference. For Sartre, commitment is based on the strength of a solitary decision made by individuals who commit themselves independently and in full freedom. For Marcel, on the contrary, we become committed by being encountered; thus commitment is primarily the response to an appeal directed to us as individuals. This appeal presupposes an openness to receive it on our part, which Marcel terms a *disponibilité,* a state of availability or receptiveness. This is a second basic concept for him, complementing that of commitment; he holds that commitment and availability go together and are closely interconnected. On this point, Marcel's philosophy differs from all other forms of existentialism.

Hence it is clear why Marcel soon protested against being classified among the existentialists: he came to feel that this classification associated him too closely with nihilistic thinking. As early as 1948 a participant in a meeting at which Marcel was present made the following observation: "Marcel appeared indignant at the mere mention of the word 'existentialism.' This much-used word, so debased through constant misuse . . . seemed to make him suspicious. Why would anyone so misrepresent him!"[12] From the very outset Marcel went his own way, determined to circumvent the desperate straits of nihilism.

Marcel later distinguished explicitly between his own position and that of existentialism. Kierkegaard, with Heidegger following his lead, had made anxiety the central phenomenon of existentialist thought—an anxiety conceived of as the "dizziness of freedom that yanks man out of all the refuges of his finitude and, for the first time, brings him to an awareness of his existence." By contrast, Marcel insists that "anxiety is always an evil, since, in the last analysis, it is occupied only with itself" and thus keeps individuals from giving themselves unselfishly to their fellow-beings.[13] It is precisely in the latter direction that Marcel feels it necessary to move: "In my opinion . . . the existentialists whose thinking is founded on anxiety have been the undoing of the age, and it is to be feared that they are leading into a dead end. I am convinced that their regeneration is possible [only] by way of a reflection on hope and on joy."[14]

This quotation clearly indicates Marcel's ambivalent attitude toward existentialism. He expresses his reservations about existentialism, albeit "not without hesitation," and then speaks of the possibility of its "regeneration." This implies, on the one hand, that existentialism in its original form has come to a dead end; yet on the other, in the course of speaking of an existentialism "founded on anxiety," he suggests the possibility of another form of existentialism based not on anxiety but on joy and hope. This is his own starting point. Elsewhere he speaks of an "existentialism as I attempted to define it," and refers to himself as an "existentialist."[15] Hence the German translator of *Christian Existentialism,* a personal acquaintance of Marcel's, asserts: "Existentialism is the philosophy of hope. This is how Gabriel Marcel understood it in his work."[16]

Marcel's "Sketch of a Phenomenology and a Metaphysic of Hope" (1942) can therefore be viewed as indicating the focal point of his philosophy as a whole.[17] The expression "Christian existentialism," however, raises certain problems. Is Marcel's alternative to nihilistic existentialism really possible only on the basis of Christian faith? To be sure, Marcel never made a secret of the Christian foundations of his thought, and in the continuation of his *Metaphysical Journal,* he discusses in detail the path that led him to Catholicism. Still, it remains questionable whether Christianity is an indispensable presupposition of his philosophy and whether his philosophy is to be regarded—as it commonly is, at least in Germany—as an instance of denominational thinking. To my mind, at least, this would unduly delimit his thought, which contains truths that are accessible from a purely philosophical orientation and that are not contingent upon specific theological presuppositions. At any rate, the interpretation attempted here will be purely philosophical.

Of course, the interpretation involves a very special understanding of "philosophically accessible knowledge," for "the secret of being," as Marcel puts it, is fundamentally inaccessible to an objective scientific knowledge based on the answers to "problems" and discloses itself only to those who, in genuine *engagement,* open themselves to a deeper experience of life. In this context the word *experience* must be freed from the restrictions placed on it by its traditional empiricist meaning.[18]

Once experience is thus understood, the question of the scope of

"Christian" existentialism in relation to the above-mentioned basic problem may be put as follows: Is hope (understood as the fundamental category of experience standing in contrast to abandonment to anxiety) possible only on the basis of Christian faith? Or is the Christian concept of hope as a religious virtue only a specific interpretation of a fundamental human experience, which is not essentially bound up with Christian presuppositions? When Marcel states that "hope is closely akin to life"[19] and that hope is "the stuff of which our soul is made,"[20] his own formulations (as on many other occasions) suggest that his claims are intended to have a general validity not limited by specific Christian presuppositions. Indeed, this is how he wishes to be understood. At one point he states: "A student of concrete philosophy, as I understand it, need not necessarily be a Christian."[21] He goes on to say that there is nothing surprising about this, from his point of view, since for a Christian there is "an essential correspondence between Christianity and human nature."[22]

II

For Marcel, the great danger of an existentialism based on anxiety is that it plunges individuals into a radical isolation that offers no possibility of making contact with a supporting reality outside themselves, with the result that their lives remain empty and meaningless. Generally speaking, Marcel implies that an unhappy and despairing mood throws us back on ourselves and shuts us up inside ourselves, so that even if we want to, we cannot escape imprisonment within ourselves, whereas a happy and joyful mood opens our hearts and enables us to establish relationships with the world in general and with our fellow-beings in particular.[23]

Openness and self-enclosedness are thus essentially bound up with happy and unhappy moods respectively. In anxiety, the individual is "occupied with himself" and thus fundamentally incapable of establishing meaningful relationships in life.[24] Marcel therefore strongly states: "Anxiety, in my view, cannot be the end. It is my deepest conviction that only love and joy can have the last word."[25] Joy, which has already been mentioned in connection with hope,[26] thus comes to be of great importance for Marcel in his dispute with existentialism. Indeed, joy is the basis of his attempt to supersede existentialism. Marcel recognized the metaphysical importance of joy quite early in his philosophical development. He speaks of it as "the truly genuine radiation of Being" and as its "fullness," and he states: "Everything that is done in joy has religious value."[27] It reconciles us with life and the world. The attainment and preservation of a joyful mood thus become not only matters of comfort in life but also moral requirements, for only joy renders us capable of fulfilling the demands life makes on us.

Marcel's basic objection to existentialism is that anxiety renders us egoistic. It keeps us from being open to the legitimate claims of life; it makes us—to use one of Marcel's fundamental concepts—"unavailable." As one of the most important concepts developed by Marcel, "availability" (*disponibilité*) is basic to his entire philosophy. We must be "available" both to the appeals of our fellow-beings and to the many demands of life.

The concept of availability played no previous role in the history of philosophy. Until Marcel designated it as a special quality, a peculiar human virtue, nothing like availability had ever been included among the various human virtues in the whole history of ethics. To this extent it constitutes a genuine discovery by Marcel, who was the first to recognize the fundamental significance of the concept and to elaborate on it.

The contrast between availability and unavailability, according to Marcel, is not a simple contrast between a single virtue and a corresponding vice. Rather, he sees it as the most basic contrast between two fundamental styles of human life. In this respect, it is comparable to Heidegger's contrast of human authenticity and inauthenticity. It is only when we are available that we are as we should be. By contrast, unavailability is the basic form of all human offense and is thus comparable to original sin.[28] Most importantly, this basic form of offense is fundamentally construed not as a kind of action, but rather as a peculiar kind of deficiency, a passive inertness, an emptiness. The egoism it produces, in the form of arrogance or the like, is only a derivative consequence of this fundamental shortcoming.

The concept of availability at first appears quite simple. It seems to belong primarily to the practical and mechanical side of life, with little or no influence on ethics or morality. This is perhaps the reason why it received so little attention in ethics. A few simple examples may illustrate the point. A tool, for instance, is supposed to be available—that is, it should be ready to be used and should not be viewed in any other way. This touches on Heidegger's notion of *Zuhandenheit* ("readiness-to-hand"). Perhaps the matter is best explained negatively: something is not available when it already has other claims on it, such as capital that I have already disposed of or a room that has already been rented.[29] Generally, something is available or unavailable in relation to an envisioned use.

Such examples clarify the difficulty of applying the concept of availability to human beings. In speaking of a tool or a substance as available, the concept lies within a utilitarian framework. By the same token, people could be considered available in this utilitarian sense to the extent that they represent a labor force that can be used for this or that purpose. They would be unavailable if they were already engaged in some other job or activity; for example, a store attendant who is waiting on a customer is unavailable to another customer. This brings to mind the notion of the available supply of labor on the labor market.[30]

Yet it is still unclear whether the utilitarian concept of availability applies to human beings as such, for it implies that we are to be regarded in terms of our usefulness—like tools and substances—and this causes problems in the light of the second formulation of Kant's categorical imperative, which states that people are never to be regarded merely as a means to an end. To have a person at one's disposal would be to treat him or her as an object or as a creature incapable of making its own decisions; such treatment would be a violation of human dignity. For this reason we must not use other people merely as means to our own ends, and we cannot allow others to use us in this way without sacrificing our own human dignity.

It is hardly conceivable, therefore, that Marcel construes *availability* in this way, particularly in the light of his passionate rebellion against the human degradation implied in technocratic thinking[31] and his emphatic insistence on the distinction between the dynamic *you* and the mere *it*.[32] In the passage citing the example of available capital, he also explicitly raises the question of the legitimacy of using the term *availability* in a figurative and extended sense.[33]

The essential difference between the two notions of availability is this: availability as a human virtue does not involve being passively and instrumentally used by another person; rather, it involves responding in complete freedom to a directed appeal. It involves, for example, my being receptive to an appeal addressed directly to me as a person, not as an object. This leads us to the heart of Marcel's conception of human beings.

III

Marcel's concept of availability originated in his early philosophical development, when existentialism had not yet acquired a distinctive form in France. This suggests that the concept emerged in its own right, as an original part of Marcel's thought, rather than in the course of his struggle with existentialism. His first penetrating discussion of it, to my knowledge, dates from 1930–31 and is found in the continuation of his *Metaphysical Journal*. Here the concept is closely associated with that of commitment,

which is also fundamentally significant to his philosophy. It is discussed
in connection with the problem of promising or giving one's word; it is
Marcel's contention that we can achieve a firm and enduring existence only
by giving and keeping our word in a spirit of "creative fidelity" and in
spite of fluctuating moods and situations (a highly significant observation
that cannot be discussed further here).[34] To give our word, however, is to
dispose of—or "to commit"—our future,[35] and Marcel raises the question
of the extent to which this is morally justifiable or even possible. We can
only promise something whose fulfillment we can guarantee. Feelings and
moods, for example, are not subject to our control and therefore cannot be
the objects of our promises for the future. Thus Marcel states, "I do not
have the right to make a commitment that I cannot materially support . . .
[without being] imprudent."[36] He then raises the question of the possibility
of a promise that can be made in full responsibility.

At this point the concept of availability becomes important. Giving our
word is permissible only within the limits of our "availabilities." The term
here is intentionally in the plural, for this shows that it does not yet con-
note a general human disposition or virtue for Marcel but rather is associated with a variety of individual circumstances that can be considered collectively. Marcel compares what he has in mind with the writing of a
check: "Compare a check. I know about my availabilities; my commitments are only legitimate or valid if they are made in amounts that equal,
but do not exceed, these availabilities."[37]

He of course acknowledges the limitations of such an analogy; for example, checks fall within the sphere of simple calculation. But because the
future is uncertain and unpredictable, a much stronger guarantee is required. We must make a commitment that involves the "totality of [our]
being."[38] Because of the associated risk, we need a faithfulness, a *fidélité
créatrice* ("creative fidelity"), if we are to shape our own existence. Marcel thus stresses "the great extent to which a total ignorance of the future
is the basis of fidelity"; that is, it is only because the future is unknown
that there is a need for fidelity.[39] Fidelity is "a way of transcending
time."[40] And this venture of fidelity can succeed for us only if, in giving
our word, we do not allow ourselves to be overcome by presumptuousness
and illusions of grandeur but rather are sustained by a firm confidence in
the future—a confidence grounded in a feeling of being at one with an all-
encompassing reality. Marcel speaks of a "transcending act having a counterpart in Being" and characterizes it more concretely as a case of "being
moved by God."[41]

The difference between this formulation and his later formulation of
the problem now becomes clear. Here the question concerns the degree to

which we can commit ourselves, and so Marcel speaks of "availabilities" in the plural. Subsequently, however, the question is reformulated to address the degree to which we are available in relation to our fellow-beings. "Availability" in the singular now becomes the readiness to allow ourselves to be committed by *something else*—by another person or by some challenge. This implies that it is no longer considered a sum of individual circumstances that can be determined quantitatively but rather as a quality of whole persons. It is only now that the problem emerges in its true and fundamental form.

The difference is not quite as great as it may appear at first. For giving our word—which leads us to consider our availabilities—is not the result of a spontaneous impulse occurring in a void; rather, it is a "response" to a claim being made on us from the outside.[42] The further clarification of this relationship marks Marcel's subsequent development.

IV

In its simplest and most obvious form, the concept of availability is associated with the claim of another concrete human being upon us and with that form of love that renders us open to this claim, namely, *caritas* ("charity"). Marcel thus begins his further exploration of the concept by speaking of "charity [*charité*] as a presence, as an absolute availability."[43] What is involved here, as opposed to the quantitative and calculable availabilities discussed previously, is an absolute or total availability, that is, an unconditional readiness to make the appropriate response. Marcel understands this readiness as "presence," that is, as the state of being present in a fully conscious manner.

He first attempts to clarify the nature of availability in relation to its opposite, unavailability, bringing out at the same time its relation to the problem of anxiety and the fatal consequences discussed above. "To be unavailable means to be preoccupied with oneself."[44] He asserts that "this unavailability is inseparable from a certain kind of self-centeredness, which is even more primitive and radical than self-love," the latter being merely a manifestation of the disposition under consideration.[45] Marcel speaks of an "inner inertness" that, roughly speaking, consists of the inability to respond to claims or to appeals.[46] A person who is available, on the other hand, is prepared to be receptive to such claims or appeals—"the opposite of one who is preoccupied with himself."[47]

In a slightly later and more general formulation, Marcel characterizes availability as "the ability to yield to that which we encounter, and in so yielding, to pledge ourselves.''[48] Note that in this statement Marcel once again stresses the intimate connection between availability and commitment. In the same discussion, he also distinguishes the concept of availability from that of mere emptiness: "This word by no means denotes emptiness, as when one speaks of 'available space'.''[49] Availability as a virtue thus does not mean that we should be passive objects at the disposal of other people, to be used by them for some purpose or other, for this would be an inhuman degradation. Rather, it means that we are to respond to an appeal or claim in full freedom—as persons, not as objects. Availability is always grounded in the relation of appeal and response. We should be available not in the sense of mechanical employment but of free response.

Yet the "absolute availability" Marcel ideally requires of us is something we are incapable of achieving. We are constantly hindered by an inner immovability. For example, the misery of another person should move me to sympathy. Indeed, I am certain that "if I had that misery . . . before my eyes, the matter surely would be different; the immediate experience of it would release the well-springs of compassion in me and would burst open the walled-up gates.''[50]

As it is, however, I feel nothing, I remain indifferent; I suffer, perhaps, from my deficiency, but I cannot help it. I remain "unavailable." Marcel speaks of the "walled-up gates" behind which I am enclosed. We can only keep struggling against this immovability; we must try "to reduce in ourselves the extent of our unavailability.''[51]

Marcel compares the obstruction we feel in connection with our unavailability to our relation to our bodies and views the matter as closely connected with the general problem of "having.''[52] We are indebted to him for a profound and highly significant philosophical analysis of this problem, which can only be mentioned in passing here.[53] With reference to my body, for example, I cannot say that I have it—if the word *have* is understood in the sense of possession—since I am much too closely bound up with it, nor can I say that I am simply identical with it. My relation to it fluctuates. In a condition of physical health, I can deal with my body with a certain matter-of-factness without becoming aware of the problematical character of my relation to it. But in the event of illness or of some other difficulty, such as meeting with an obstacle that must be overcome, it eludes my power of disposition and becomes a hindrance. The same is true of my relation to my unavailability: it becomes embarrassing when it stands in the way of my ability to sympathize, and I must attempt to overcome it, that is, to make myself available.

Availability, however, does not refer only to our relation to other people. In his essay on "Relationship and Availability," Marcel resumes his reflection on the matter and speaks in a more general way of "availability proper . . . as it can be realized, not only in compassion, but also in hope and, I would add, in admiration, the great spiritual and metaphysical significance of which would not seem fully to be recognized at present."[54] Marcel discusses hope more extensively elsewhere; here he is concerned primarily with admiration and contributes to our understanding of it by discussing it in this connection. For admiration is likewise something that frees us from our preoccupation with ourselves and that leads us to acknowledge another existence that transcends our own. "There can be no doubt that the nature of admiration consists in tearing us away from ourselves" and in yielding ourselves freely to something else—something that excites our admiration.[55] "Admiration is, to a certain extent, creative, because it is an active reception."[56]

The inability to admire is a further expression of a fundamental unavailability. One who lacks this ability is a "hermetically closed system which can no longer be penetrated."[57] The ability to admire, by contrast, is the ability to assimilate something new. Marcel uses the term "irruption" to describe the way these new impressions can penetrate and enrich us. Thus "admiration is connected with the fact that something is revealed to us"—something new that had not previously been noticed.[58] "The ideas of admiration and revelation are in reality correlative."[59] The former denotes the indispensable state of mind that is required if the world is to disclose itself to us and to endow us with a new abundance; the latter denotes this process of disclosing, which is made possible by the state of mind in question. Availability can thus be given the general definition of receptiveness to the abundance of the world.

This definition gives rise to an even more general one, which was anticipated in the preceding discussion of the connection between availability and hope. Availability is "the ability to abandon oneself to whatever one encounters . . . or the ability to transform mere circumstances into 'occasions' or indeed into opportune situations [faveurs]—i.e., to contribute to the shaping of one's own fate by impressing one's own distinctive mark upon it."[60] Here Marcel is not concerned simply with what we chance to come across—such as another person who appeals to us for help, or something that excites our admiration—but rather with the circumstances in which we find ourselves more generally and with our ability properly to seize upon them and make something of them. What we at first encounter as a mere circumstance—something fortuitous and as a rule unpleasant—to which we are abandoned thus becomes something we are to seize upon explicitly and self-consciously, apprehending it as an "occasion" we may

turn to our advantage and as an "opportune situation" that by good fortune
has befallen us. We are unavailable if, preoccupied with our plans, we
regard the unexpected as merely a troublesome inconvenience interfering
with our purposive actions. We are available if instead we are able to free
ourselves from our preconceived plans and to recognize in the unexpected
new and fruitful possibilities that may lead us in new directions.[61] Clearly,
availability and creativity are closely linked.[62]

Marcel resumes these reflections and elaborates on them in *The Mystery of Being,* one of his most comprehensive later works, in which he
tries in retrospect to sum up the whole of his thought. With the contention
"The self-centered man is not available," he reasserts his earlier position,
adding, by way of elaboration, that such a person "is incapable of responding to the claims of life."[63] In doing so, he develops his earlier
position in a new direction: we are now to be available not only to another
person in need who issues an appeal but to "life" in general. We are
subject to the danger of rendering ourselves inaccessible, that is, of retreating into our shells and "rejecting everything that could broaden [our] experience."[64] Here "experience" and "life" are equated, as Marcel himself points out. Experience is everything capable of extending and
enriching life. But there is in life itself a tendency toward self-isolation,
toward making itself unavailable for any such appeal and shielding itself
from any new experience. The unavailable man "does not want to go
beyond himself, beyond the petty world of his experience. He thus forms
a hard shell, which he is unable to break through."[65] He is imprisoned in
a narrow life governed by rigid habits.

Availability, by contrast, consists of the ability to break through this
shell, to undergo new experiences, and through them to renew and enhance
one's life. So conceived, it is an openness to whatever the future may have
in store in the way of unforeseeable experiences. Availability thus can only
be understood in the broader context of the temporal character of human
life. And here it points to hope as the sustaining foundation of life, for
only on the basis of hope can life unfold in accordance with its distinctive
nature.

V

For Marcel, it has been observed, hope is the fundamental presupposition
of a fulfilled human life. In an important passage, he distinguishes between
two forms of hope, namely, "an absolute 'I hope' and an 'I hope that'."[66]

The latter pertains to a specific concrete incident; Marcel cites as an example the anticipated arrival of a friend: "I hope that Jacques will come for breakfast tomorrow, instead of waiting to come till afternoon."[67] The former pertains to a general human disposition whose nature is objectively undefinable and cannot be represented in determinate images. Marcel speaks similarly of "absolute hope."[68]

This distinction is closely related to the one existentialists following Kierkegaard draw between fear and anxiety. Whereas fear is always the fear of something specific, anxiety cannot be characterized in the same determinate way; people in a state of anxiety are unable to specify why, and in relation to what, they are anxious.[69] According to the existentialists' interpretation, it is "the nothing," the uncanniness of the world itself, that comes to light in anxiety. Although similar, the distinction between the two forms of hope cannot be brought out by using two different words; it must be expressed by using the same word in two different ways. Consequently its meaning cannot be simply or strictly stated.

A more significant trait also differentiates these two distinctions. Whereas fear tends generally to broaden into uncanny anxiety, hope—at first indeterminate—tends to crystallize in concrete forms and to define itself in terms of them. Whereas anxiety tends above all to move of its own accord in the direction of the indeterminate, the restoration and retention of the generality of pure hope above all particular determinations require a considerable effort, namely, the suppression of the willfulness that tends to view the future in terms of its own preconceived ideas, which it is bent upon realizing. Whereas the first form of hope "is restricted by aiming at a particular idea, or by allowing itself to be hypnotized by it," the second form "exceeds the imagination."[70] The latter is fundamentally indeterminate and demands that "I abandon the attempt to imagine what I hope."[71]

The relation of the two forms of hope may now be more clearly specified: it is not a juxtaposition of two forms on an equal footing with each other, but rather a relation of false hope to true hope. Marcel elsewhere refers to the form of hope in which one "clings to a certain idea" as "a paralysis of the soul."[72] The important thing, in his view, is to overcome the enticements of false hope in order to attain genuine hope. Marcel illustrates his point with the example of a person who is ill. So long as he "clings to the idea that he will be well by a certain time," he can be disappointed if things do not work out as he has imagined them.[73] What is necessary is a "purification and transformation" of his inner attitude, which comes about when he realizes that "everything is by no means lost even if he is not restored to health.''[74] He thus comes firmly to believe that he is not falling into a bottomless void but rather remains somehow sustained securely by an all-encompassing presence. This fundamentally unspecifiable ''somehow'' is part of the innermost nature of genuine hope.[75]

This feature is directly connected with another: genuine hope involves the relinquishment of the desire to push impatiently ahead, for it depends on a sequence of events that proceeds independently of our actions.[76] We must, so to speak, ''take [our] time,'' and this requires a tranquility that enables us to let events run their course.[77] Marcel contends that ''hope exhibits all the characteristics of relaxation.''[78] This becomes even clearer when we consider its opposite. Just as the opposite of relative hope is fear (fear and relative hope being the poles of a perpetual oscillation), so despair is the opposite of absolute hope (despair construed as giving up altogether, surrendering completely in the face of an inescapable fate).[79] Marcel refers to this desolate state of mind, in which we simply ''waste away'' (as the saying so aptly puts it), as a ''true spiritual self-devouring.''[80]

In *The Mystery of Being,* Marcel suggests that the opposite of hope is dejection. Perhaps he felt that anxiety and despair were still too active, for existentialism had shown that we could realize our ''existence'' by persevering honestly in our anxiety. By contrast, in complete dejection we simply cease to put up a fight. Marcel thus asserts: ''The opposite of hope is not anxiety, but a state of dejection. It resembles a paralysis of life, which as it were turns to ice.''[81] This state of mind can develop quite undramatically along with a gradual growth of indifference toward life, when in the course of daily routine we slowly trudge, like ''creature[s] of habit fitted with blinders,'' in a kind of inner desolation.[82] In another connection Marcel uses the unusual term *unhope,* saying: ''The word *unhope,* coined by Thomas Hardy in one of his poems, and which Charles Du Bos has rendered by the neologism *Inespoir,* excellently expresses this state of the soul. . . . This unhope . . . is in reality death in life, an anticipation of death.''[83]

This situation too involves paired concepts, this time of openness and constriction, or ''closedness.'' Those who despair, like those who are dejected, are walled up within themselves. Even Stoics, who attempt to live without fear and without hope, remain ''locked up'' within themselves.[84] But the despairing and the dejected are unable to establish any kind of self-transcending relation to a sustaining reality. They are profoundly alone. Marcel asks himself ''whether despair and aloneness are not ultimately identical."[85] Being alone, however, is something a person cannot bear. In his early drama *Le Coeur des autres,* Marcel writes: "There is only one grief, to be alone."[86] And the question thus arises "whether loneliness is the last word, whether man is really condemned to be alone."[87]

Yet what we cannot achieve alone, no matter how hard we try, is given to us as if of its own accord when hope comes over us. With an "absolute confidence," we then have a sense of "security of existence or in existing."[88] Above all, we recover a relation to our fellow-beings, for hope by its very nature involves a consciousness of fellowship. Marcel quite rightly insists that "fellowship is always a part of hope."[89] He thus can summarize the nature of hope in the following formula: "I hope in you for us."[90]

This characterization of the relation between openness and "closedness" becomes particularly important when temporality is taken into consideration. The concept of being self-enclosed, which at first referred to the condition of a person who is unable to make contact with the world, now also indicates a temporal situation. Thus "I will always be subject to the temptation of closing myself up within myself, and thereby of locking up time within myself."[91] Marcel refers to "closed time," or "time as a prison,"[92] in which one is "entrapped like a ship in an ice pack." In contrast to this, he speaks of "open time," in which one is able to open oneself up to a free future. Hope, he says, "presupposes an open time as opposed to the closed time of the narrowly constricted soul."[93]

Although Marcel deals only briefly with the notion of "closed time," it seems to be a notion of fundamental importance. "Closed time" is time in which nothing really new can occur because everything has already been determined by the past. In it, "the future, emptied of its substance and of its mystery, appears as nothing more than an expanse of pure repetition . . . in which the wheels of some unregulated mechanism run on incessantly."[94] Because despair or inertness have destroyed our openness and hence shut us off from the "appeals of life," there remains nothing but the perpetual repetition of a uniform world already in existence.

This conclusion is true not only of despair and of the other forms of dejection but also, analogically, of rationally calculating thought. As Gerhard Haeuptner states, because "the objects at which I aim in my calculations have their existence, not in reality, but for me in my imagination, i.e., as that which is anticipated," I move among the ready-made ideas of a world already in existence; "life completely according to plan," Haeuptner stresses, "means that nothing has existence but yesterday."[95] Only the unforeseeable, as something really new, can take us beyond the already existing world. In this context hope is a trusting openness to the unforeseeable gift of the future. Marcel is thus quite justified in stating that "hope and calculating reason are essentially different, and everything is endangered if these two are confused."[96]

Hope is thus the active supersession of the despair that isolates us. It always presupposes the threat of impending despair; for if we were unshakably secure we would not need hope. In this sense Marcel stresses that "properly speaking, hope can only occur where the tendency to despair arises; hope is the act through which this tendency can be actively and successfully overcome."[97]

It is thus through hope that the "break-through through time"—time in the sense of "closed time"—is achieved.[98] For hope can only exist in "open time," that is, in time open to the enriching newness of a future that is not predetermined. Seen in this light hope is the temporal aspect of the basic human disposition characterized in a general way by "availability." Briefly stated, hope is availability for the gift of the future, which exceeds all expectations and all calculations.

Availability was earlier defined as that basic human disposition in which we fulfill our existence and are as we ought to be. This definition can now be applied to hope as the temporal aspect of availability, and Marcel explicitly construes it in this way. Hope is the indispensable prerequisite of a meaningful, fulfilled life. Marcel asks whether hope in this sense "is not part of life itself" and indeed whether "hope and life are not one and the same thing."[99] He hesitates in giving his answer, for "life" is itself an ambiguous concept and can be understood in a purely biological sense. He thus concludes with an affirmative answer "to the extent that life itself is ontologically related [*prise ontologiquement*]," that is, to the extent that it refers beyond itself to a transcendent reality.[100] Marcel refers to this "ontologically related venture [*enjeu ontologiquement*], . . . which in itself is not part of the realm of life [in the biological sense]," as the "soul."[101] He summarizes as follows: "The soul has existence through hope alone; perhaps hope is the stuff of which the soul is made."[102]

VI

This is perhaps the place to make a brief comparison with the other great philosopher of hope in our time, Ernst Bloch. Marcel and Bloch are united in their opposition to the existentialism that centers on anxiety and foundering. Bloch too sets hope against anxiety as a contrasting positive concept. His major work, *The Principle of Hope,* combatively asserts that "hope drowns anxiety."[103] "What matters," Bloch writes, "is to learn to hope. Hope does not result in renunciation; it is in love with success, not with failure."[104]

This passage reveals the difference between Bloch and Marcel quite clearly. Marcel hardly ever speaks of success. It lies beyond his sphere of interest. This is because, despite his emphasis on commitment, he gives the life of action very little attention. For Marcel, hope is a reliance on a sustaining transcendent ground that catches us and keeps us from falling into the abyss. But for Bloch, hope is a "positive emotion of expectation," which as such is included in a comprehensive ontology of becoming—a standpoint from which the whole of reality is viewed as one great progressing movement, with the individual integrated into this all-encompassing developmental process. For Bloch, the individual—like reality generally—is "not solid," that is, not closed off, but rather open to the newness of an undetermined future. And hope points forward into that "dawn ahead," where human planning loses its bearings in the face of indeterminate horizons. Bloch thus does not set hope in opposition to knowledge, but rather connects hope—once it is distinguished from bad, deceptive hope—with knowledge as *docta spes,* knowing hope.

Although further elaboration is not possible here, this brief reference to Bloch serves to bring into relief the distinctive character of Marcel's thought. Efforts on behalf of the progress of humankind concern him scarcely at all. In fact, for him the idea of progress is highly questionable.[105] The essential thing is the relation of the individual to a religiously understood fundamental reality, which is at rest within itself and thus is not to be construed as developing. Marcel's understanding of the world—his ontology—can thus be characterized as conservative.

This inclination is clear, for example, in Marcel's attitude toward technology. He does not disapprove of it; on the contrary, he regards it quite positively. But he becomes passionate in his struggle against the inhumanity of technocratic thinking.[106] It is true that he resists being labeled an irrationalist, and quite rightly so;[107] yet (to use a distinction that the German language enables one readily to make) the sort of reason he affirms is not *Verstand,* which creates a truly human order, but rather *Vernunft,* which accommodates itself flexibly to an existing order.[108] As a consequence, he is largely unconcerned with the question of an active, reforming transformation of the world.

This is not an objection to Marcel. He and Bloch simply face in different directions. Their assertions thus do not contradict one another but rather are complementary and together yield a more complete picture. A comparison will serve to define their place in philosophy more clearly and to bring out their positive achievements (as well as their limitations) and the points where their achievements should perhaps be supplemented.

In Bloch, hope as *docta spes* is perhaps associated too closely with conscious planning. It is the trust that development will continue, even though we are unable to foresee the end of its course. The darkness is ultimately the as-yet-unilluminated future. Here Bloch shows himself to be a Hegelian, convinced of the meaningfulness and inevitability of development. The possibility of catastrophe or of foundering is simply not considered. He thus has nothing but contempt for anxiety. But Marcel does consider the possibility of utter failure and thus appreciates and grapples with the problems of anxiety and of dread before the abyss. This is why hope for him is associated with the confidence that when the limits of our own power are reached, we encounter a sustaining transcendent reality.

At this point Marcel's concept of availability enters the picture. The one-sided tendency of calculated thinking is here contrasted with the openness of the individual to whatever the future has in store. Availability is our ability to keep ourselves open to these new and unforeseeable possibilities. In place of Bloch's kind of thinking, which is ultimately a monological or one-way affair (that is, looking in one direction only—forward), and despite all his dialectics, Marcel advocates an essentially dialogical attitude, consisting of a creative confrontation of the individual with the "appeals of life." Availability is always the readiness to respond, which gives a positive reception to appeals directed toward us.

At the same time, if availability in the broadest sense is the ability to respond to "the appeals of life," are we not then at the mercy of the various "appeals" that erratic chance addresses to us? Can life under these conditions maintain a steady course and develop progressively? Marcel could first reply that for him availability and commitment are inseparable, that availability manifests itself only in commitment, and that time-spanning "creative fidelity" is an essential part of his philosophy. It is thus in decisive commitment, according to him, that we achieve inner strength. If we were then to object that such commitment is always a subsequent step, always a response to a preceding appeal, and thus always merely a reaction, Marcel would answer that we do not begin as empty zeros but rather are conditioned at every moment by previously assumed obligations—indeed, to such an extent that there arises the question, discussed earlier, of the extent to which we are justified in making new commitments. Previous commitments always mean that there are restrictions on our availability.

This leads to the conclusion that our availability is never absolute but rather is a matter of degree, which should be increased as much as possible.

In discussing the possible sources of unavailability, it would also be well to distinguish between the unavailability resulting from commitments already assumed or projects already undertaken and that resulting from mere inner inertness. Marcel seems to be thinking primarily of the second possibility when he urges that unavailability be overcome and calls upon us repeatedly to free ourselves from our inner inertness. Matters are more difficult, however, with regard to cases of the first sort, for here we must weigh conflicting claims against each other. It would be just as wrong to adhere rigidly to our given word under radically altered circumstances as it would be to yield immediately to every new claim. A middle course is elusive.

Although this conflict complicates the situation, it does not essentially alter it, for each previous commitment is itself a response, albeit one made at an earlier time. We are thus still dealing with a reactive disposition, and we remain essentially reactive beings, dependent on appeals from the outside and capable only of responding, never of being active of our own accord. This leads us to Marcel's crucial limitation. He does not see us as planning beings who responsibly shape their world. He neglects our spontaneity. But both sides of our nature must be considered together. Only by making the active planning and shaping of the world our point of departure can we clearly place availability as the corrective principle in human nature that recognizes the limits of human power and as the *hubris* of the kind of planning thinking that believes itself able to make of the future whatever it chooses (a recognition that is of the greatest importance for right conduct). Moreover, the readiness involved in accepting the unpredictable newness of the future brings about a radical openness that alone can allow us to become creative in the full sense of the word.[109] Hence it is the interplay of these elements—the active, shaping will and the readiness to respond to appeals—that brings about a genuinely dialogical relation between human beings and the world.

These concluding remarks are not intended to be a criticism of Marcel and do not contradict anything he says. They are simply meant to suggest the possibility of a certain supplementation that he did not explicitly provide, perhaps because he felt it was too obvious to require discussion and perhaps because, despite the current myth that everything can be "arranged," he wanted to emphasize the importance of the opposing element—of the grateful readiness to accept the unforeseeable gift of the future. These remarks have simply posed a question in the hope of inducing the long-esteemed thinker to clarify his position further.

OTTO FRIEDRICH BOLLNOW

PHILOSOPHISCHES SEMINAR
TÜBINGEN UNIVERSITY
DECEMBER 1969

NOTES

For the purposes of simplification, the following abbreviations are used in references to Marcel's works. The first page number refers to the original French edition; the second, in parentheses, refers to the German translation indicated.

DR   *Du refus à l'invocation*. Paris: Gallimard, 1940. *Schöpferische Treue*. German translation by Ursula Behler. Paderborn: Schöningh Verlag; Zürich: Thomas Verlag, 1963.
         Creative Fidelity. English translation by Robert Rosthal. New York: Noonday Press, 1964.

DS   *Le Déclin de la sagesse*. Paris: Plon, 1954.
         "Le Crépuscule du sens commun." In *La Dimension Florestan*. Rev. ed. Paris: Plon, 1958.
         Der Untergang der Weisheit; Die Verfinsterung des Verstandes. German translation by Herbert P. M. Schaal. Heidelberg: F. H. Kerle, 1960.
         The Decline of Wisdom. Translated by Manya Harari. New York: Philosophical Library, 1955. ("Le Crépuscule du sens commun" has not been translated into English.)

EA   *Etre et avoir*. Paris: Aubier, 1935. *Sein und Haben*. German translation by Ernst Behler. Paderborn: Ferdinand Schöningh, 1954.
         Being and Having. English translation by Katharine Farrer. Boston: Beacon Press, 1951.

EC   *Existentialisme chrétien: Gabriel Marcel*. Edited by Etienne Gilson. Paris: Plon, 1947.
         Christlicher Existentialismus: Gabriel Marcel. German translation by Charlotte Horstmann. Warendorf, Westfalen: Verlag J. Schnellsche Buchhandlung (C. Leopold), 1951.
         (Not translated into English.)

HH   *Les Hommes contre l'humain*. Paris: La Colombe, 1951.
         Die Erniedrigung des Menschen. German translation by Herbert P. M. Schaad. Frankfurt: Verlag Josef Knecht, 1957.
         Man against Mass Society. English translation by G. S. Fraser. Chicago: Henry Regnery Co., 1962.

HP   *L'Homme problématique*. Paris. Aubier, 1955.
         Der Mensch als Problem. German translation by Herbert P. M. Schaad. Frankfurt: Verlag Josef Knecht, 1957.

Problematic Man. English translation by Brian Thompson. New York: Herder and Herder, 1967.

HV   *Homo Viator:* Prolégomènes à une métaphysique de l'espérance. Paris: Aubier, 1945.

Homo Viator: Philosophie der Hoffnung. German translation by Wolfgang Rüttenauer. Düsseldorf: Bastion-Verlag, 1949.

Homo Viator: Introduction to a Metaphysic of Hope. English translation by Emma Craufurd. Chicago: Henry Regnery Co., 1951.

JM   *Journal métaphysique.* Paris: Gallimard, 1927.

Metaphysisches Tagebuch. German translation by Hanns von Winter. Vienna and Munich: Herold Verlag, 1955.

Metaphysical Journal. English translation by Bernard Wall. Chicago: Henry Regnery Co., 1950.

ME   *Le Mystère de l'être.* Vol. 1, *Réflexion et mystère.* Vol. 2, *Foi et réalité.* Paris: Aubier, 1951.

Das Geheimnis des Seins. German translation by Hanns von Winter. Vienna: Herold Verlag, 1952.

The Mystery of Being. Vol. 1, *Reflection and Mystery.* English translation by G. S. Fraser. Vol. 2, *Faith and Reality.* English translation by René Hague. Chicago: Henry Regnery Co., 1960.

1. For a more complete history, see Otto Friedrich Bollnow, *Existenzphilosophie* (Stuttgart: Kohlhammer, 1943; 7th ed., 1969).

2. For an account of how existentialism can be superseded in a positive direction, see Otto Friedrich Bollnow, *Neue Geborgenheit: Das Problem einer Überwindung des Existentialismus* (Stuttgart: Kohlhammer, 1955; 2d ed., 1960; 3d ed., 1972).

3. Jean-Paul Sartre, *L'Existentialisme est un humanisme* (Paris: Nagel, 1946), pp. 16–17. Cf. Emmanuel Mounier, *Introduction aux existentialismes* (Paris: Société des Editions Denoël, 1947); and Jean Wahl, *Petite Histoire de "l'existentialisme"* (Paris: Editions Club maintenant, 1947).

4. See publication data for *EC,* above.

5. See Otto Friedrich Bollnow, *Die Lebensphilosophie,* Verständliche Wissenschaft, vol. 70 (Berlin, Göttingen, Heidelberg: Springer Verlag, 1958).

6. *HH,* 7 (9).

7. *EC,* 307 (340); *DR,* 81–110 (62ff.).

8. *EC,* 311 (344).

9. *HV,* 199 (198); see also, for example, *ME* 1:91 (112), 163 (127), 105 (128), 2:79 (384), 180 (502). One must proceed cautiously, however, in the documentation of Marcel's use of this category, for he often uses the term *existence* in its traditional sense, especially in his earlier writings.

10. *EA,* 47 (not in the German text).   11. *DR,* 150 (111–12).

12. *EC* (356); not in the French text.   13. *HP,* 186 (185).

14. *HP,* 186 (185).   15. *ME* 2:102 (413); *ME* 1:229 (284).

16. *EC* (360); not in the French text.   17. *HV,* 39–41 (28–30).

18. See, for example, *ME* 2:18–20 (24–26).

19. *ME* 2:165 (485).

20. *EA,* 117 (87); *ME* 2:163 (483).

21. *DR,* 109 (81).

22. *DR*, 109 (82).   23. *HP*, 186 (185).
24. *HV*, 31 (22).   25. *ME* 2:178 (500).
26. *ME* 2:178 (500).   27. *JM*, 230 (323).
28. *ME* 2:182 (505).   29. *EA*, 99 (75); *HV*, 28 (207).
30. Above all in *HH*.
31. See, for example, *HV*, 15–17 (5–7); *EA*, 152–54 (114–16).
32. *EA*, 99 (75).
33. *EA*, 99 (75).
34. For a discussion of "creative fidelity," see Otto Friedrich Bollnow, *Französischer Existentialismus* (Stuttgart: Kohlhammer, 1965), pp. 105ff.
35. *EA*, 56 (43).   36. *EA*, 62–63 (48).
37. *EA*, 63 (48).   38. *EA*, 63 (49).
39. *EA*, 65 (50).   40. *EA*, 65 (50).
41. *EA*, 76 (58).   42. *EA*, 63 (49); *DR*, 71 (54).
43. *EA*, 99 (74).   44. *EA*, 105 (78).
45. *EA*, 100 (74).   46. *DR*, 75 (57).
47. *HV*, 31 (22).   48. *HV*, 28 (20).
49. *HV*, 28 (20).   50. *EA*, 101 (75).
51. *EA*, 100 (74).   52. *EA*, 119–21 (88–90).
53. For a discussion of the problem of "having," see Bollnow, *Französischer Existentialismus*, pp. 81ff.
54. *DR*, 67 (51).   55. *DR*, 68 (52).
56. *ME* 1:151 (185).   57. *DR*, 68 (52).
58. *DR*, 68 (52).   59. *DR*, 68 (52).
60. *HV*, 28 (20).
61. See Gerhard Haeuptner, *Verhängnis und Geschichte: Ein geschichtsphilosophischer Versuch* (Meisenheim/Glan: Hain, 1956).
62. *DR*, 75 (57).   63. *ME* 1:178 (220–21).
64. *ME* 1:178 (221).   65. *ME* 1:178 (221).
66. *HV*, 43 (33).   67. *HV*, 39 (28).
68. *HV*, 62–63 (56); *EA*, 135 (101).
69. See Bollnow, *Existenzphilosophie*, pp. 65–67.
70. *HV*, 60 (53).   71. *HV*, 60 (53).
72. *ME* 2:162 (482).   73. *HV*, 61 (54).
74. *HV*, 12 (55).
75. For a medical view of the matter, see Herbert Plügge, "Über die Hoffnung," in *Wohlbefinden und Missbefinden: Beiträge zu einer medizinschen Anthropologie* (Tübingen: Max Niemeyer Verlag, 1962), pp. 38–50.
76. *HV*, 52 (43).   77. *HV*, 52 (43).
78. *ME* 2:162 (482).   79. *HV*, 49–50 (41–42).
80. *HV*, 59 (51).   81. *ME* 2:159 (478).
82. *ME* 2:162 (482).   83. *DR*, 77 (58).
84. *HV*, 51 (42).   85. *HV*, 78 (73).
86. *EC*, 282 (314).   87. *HV*, 78 (73).
88. *HV*, 62 (55).   89. *HV*, 78 (73).
90. *HV*, 81 (76).   91. *HV*, 80 (75).

92. *HV*, 71 (66).

93. *ME* 2:162. The German translation does not convey the temporal reference.

94. *HV*, 80 (76).

95. Haeuptner, *Verhängnis*, p. 109.

96. *HV*, 87 (83).

97. *HV*, 49 (40).

98. *HV*, 71 (66).

99. *EA*, 136 (102); *ME* 2:163 (483).

100. *EA*, 136 (102).

101. *EA*, 129–30 (96–97).

102. *EA*, 117 (87); *ME* 2:163 (483)

103. Ernst Bloch, *Das Prinzip Hoffnung* (Frankfurt: Suhrkamp Verlag, 1959), p. 126.

104. Ibid., p. 1.

105. *DS*, 2–3, 16 (12–13, 27).

106. Especially in *HH*.

107. *DS*, 5 (14–15).

108. *DS*, 77–116 (113 to end of chap.).

109. The concept of creativity, so important to Marcel, requires consideration in its own right.

Marcel's Concept of Availability

REPLY TO
OTTO FRIEDRICH BOLLNOW

I am inclined to agree with Professor Bollnow that my views on hope do not derive exclusively from Christian theology. The relation of my thinking to Christianity is difficult for me to define. Certainly, my conversion led me to state more explicitly than I might otherwise have done the notion of hope that appears so clearly in *The Phenomenology of Hope,* which I wrote during the Second World War. Nevertheless, I believe Christianity gives a specific character to a relatively special context of data that can also be accessible to non-Christians. To my mind this is extremely important. Since 1947, the period when my thought began to be widely discussed, I have been careful to react against any strictly denominational interpretation of it. Indeed, I have always been happy to find, when the occasion presented itself (as, for example, in Japan and in my discussions with certain Hindu philosophers), that my thought was perfectly accessible to non-Christians. I think, by the way, that this is extremely important in today's world and that I can, in some measure, offer a possibility of reacting against all the implications of increasingly technocratic thinking. Actually, it is technocratic thought in all its forms that is here being challenged and, I would say, transcended. Certainly non-Christians, whether they be Moslems or Hindus, can feel, in the same way and just as much as I, the vital need to arrive at this transcendence. Therefore, credit should be given to Professor Bollnow for having pointed this out, thus enabling the reader to understand why the term "Christian existentialism" has increasingly disturbed me.

I can no longer approve of those of my plays, such as *La Chapelle ardente* (which is of very special significance at this point), that specifi-

Translated from the French by Susan Gruenheck.

cally show the risk contained in all suffering. In all suffering, I risk becoming self-centered and thus locking myself up in despair. I can overcome suffering only so far as I can become free of myself. I can become
free of myself only by a kind of attachment to the other and, above all, by
the most concrete imagination possible concerning the other—that is, by
somehow mentally substituting myself for the other. It is quite certain that
in *La Chapelle ardente,* Aline, the mother, is incapable of putting herself
in the place of Mireille, the fiancée of her dead son. Indeed, Aline's very
pain, her very suffering, implies her lack of openness, for she does not put
herself in the place of her son, who, were he able, would certainly give
witness to a kind of generosity that is foreign to her.

I would probably qualify this notion of suffering today, for I think that
an ingenuous hope may dwell within certain people without the threat of
despair weighing on them. By contrast, when people reflect on true hope,
the threat of despair often appears. In other words, from the moment I
attempt to reflect on hope in its specificity, I realize that hope is not hope
unless it is surrounded by a sort of halo or fringe of possible despair. I
think one has to distinguish between the immediate and that which is mediated by reflection. This, by the way, does not essentially alter the content
of Professor Bollnow's text.

I am always worried when I see the word *disponibilité* translated as
*Verfügbarkeit,** because I think the word *verfügbar* can be applied only to
a thing—specifically, to a thing I can dispose of. But *disponibilité* is essentially active. It implies the state of "being ready to." Thus *Bereitschaft*
would be a more apt translation, I think, than *Verfügbarkeit.*

This receptivity (here I am employing the term *Bereitschaft,* "readiness")† cannot possibly give way to scorn; it cannot simply be a question
of being disposed of. This "readiness" is already something active; it is
already, in a way, an action. Moreover, one must not forget that in other
writings I have insisted that receptivity is never merely passive. I have
alluded to reception in the sense of hospitality, remarking that some people—certain women, for example—know how to receive guests and that
others do not. This makes sense only because receiving is an act or a
certain way of acting. I think this is very important.

One might also say that unreadiness is a lack of life, a lack of vitality.
I think that living persons as such are open. They are apt to lend themselves to whatever arises. And here, as Professor Bollnow has clearly
shown, there is an absolutely direct link between readiness and openness.
On the contrary, unreadiness, to the extent that it is closed, is already

---

*All German words in this reply appear in the original French manuscript.—ED.
†The English word *readiness* appears in the original French manuscript.—ED.

death. Those who are unready no longer belong altogether to the world of the living.

In today's world, we are witnessing a disappearance of joy in favor of what could be called satisfactions. At the same time, we note that these satisfactions contribute very little to joy. Perhaps it is just the opposite. Perhaps these satisfactions contribute to rendering us increasingly unready; they almost always imply a tendency toward envy, because satisfactions are, so to speak, graduated. For example, the person who has only recently been able to afford a small car will envy the owner of a larger car, and so on. Here we are basically in the area of the quantitative, whereas joy, by its very essence, is foreign to any quantification. This is why, for the Christian or the mystic, joy generally refers to eternity.

As far as admiration is concerned, I have always said that I experienced a kind of horror in the presence of people who were incapable of admiration. Admiration is a form of readiness. I remember being shocked when a playwright remarked, "I do not like to admire at all, because I feel that if I admire, I am humiliating myself." This seems to me the most scandalous untruth that could possibly be uttered. I have always felt that in admiring I am not increasing my stature (one cannot speak of it in that sense), but rather opening myself up. I would say that admiration broadens us.

The contrast between my thought and Ernst Bloch's seems to me very well articulated, but I would like to add the following: The only indisputable progress is technical progress. And it is exclusively in the technical field that we can speak intelligibly and specifically of progress. Here the real difference between progress and hope becomes apparent. Hope is, by its very essence, meta-technical. The meta-technical corresponds to the meta-problematical as I defined it a long time ago in my address to the 1937 International Congress of Philosophy in Paris.

I have not been at all concerned with the idea of the establishment of a social order; what I consider important is the foundation of a just order. What is essential for me here is justice. And it is obvious today, if we take into account what is happening around us, that technical progress provides no guarantee for the foundation of a just social order. Technical progress could ultimately lead to a world of robots in some sense bereft of conscience. Naturally, I take the word *conscience* here in the sense of *Gewissen,* not of *Bewusstsein* ("consciousness").

It should also be noted that I have never sought to create a philosophical system. I have concentrated on delving into a certain number of clearly defined problems. The problem of the establishment of a social order is not among those that have concerned me, partly because I do not feel that I have the required competence to make pronouncements on the technical conditions under which this order might arise. This does not mean that I find the question itself secondary; on the contrary, I find it very important. But in this regard, I have always insisted on taking precautions, for with every passing day we are increasingly forced to recognize the absolute necessity for them.

I feel in no way disposed to overlook the element of spontaneity in question here. I can only observe that creative work (for example, artistic creation) cannot be likened to planning. There is something in all creative work that defies this reduction. In my mind, it is most important to understand—or, more precisely, to acknowledge—the value of specifically creative work.

I think we must make a very important distinction between "disposing of the future" and "engaging the future." *Über die Zukunft verfügen* means, I think, to dispose of the future. However, even when we make a promise, we cannot dispose of the future because we do not know, for example, if we will still be alive at the moment when we should fulfill our promise. What we can do is *engage* the future; for example, we can refuse in advance those invitations we could not accept without breaking our promise.

Furthermore, I am somewhat bothered by the word *Verfügbarkeit* used in the plural. I know very well that in French we can say *des disponibilités* or *mes disponibilités,* but this is used almost exclusively in connection with banking. Before making out a check to someone, I will perhaps phone the bank to find out what my *disponibilités* are, that is, what sums are available to me in order to be sure that my check is covered. But I would have thought that this plural was inconceivable or grammatically impossible for a word formed like *Verfügbarkeit(en).*

On further reflection, it seems clear that if we use the word in the plural, *les disponibilités* can be found only in the domain of what is verifiable, of the objective. For example, the banker I phone may tell me, "Sir, you presently have such-and-such an amount in your account, but no more than that," and this is a fact I cannot dispute. But in the case of a promise—that is, in the domain of intersubjectivity—such verification and confirmation is inconceivable. No one can tell me, "Sir, you are in a position to fulfill this promise but not that one. That promise exceeds your possibilities."

I would only like to add that Professor Bollnow's essay is one of the best in the series, and it has the great merit of elucidating certain relationships among analyses that are often treated separately. In this sense, the essay renders a great service to anyone wishing to penetrate my thought.

G.M.

7

Pietro Prini

A METHODOLOGY OF
THE UNVERIFIABLE

AFTER reading the manuscript of my essay on his philosophy almost twenty years ago, Gabriel Marcel told me that he thought the rather provocative title I had chosen, "The Methodology of the Unverifiable," was very apt. But that was 1950 in Paris, in the full summer of existentialism, and in the "Lettre-Préface" he wrote to my essay he observed: "If the concept of the unverifiable has been relegated to a secondary position, it has only happened to the extent that the thought of Léon Brunschwicg—which in certain respects has had the same importance for me as Spencer's had for Bergson—was pushed into the background by the new doctrines that have gained our attention in the last quarter century."[1]

Only a few years later, however, the publication of Wittgenstein's *Philosophische Untersuchungen* in 1953 started the liberalization of the principle of verification that was the extraordinarily fruitful theme of the new trend in linguistic philosophy, not only in Anglo-Saxon circles but in the whole of European thought. Thus the theme of the unverifiable once again stimulated philosophical research. In this new perspective, the relevance of Marcel's philosophy, which had so often been cataloged much too hastily under "the dangerous label of existentialism,"[2] became apparent, revealing the interest in the basic structure on which I had initially tried to make a critical reconstruction of the most original developments of his thinking.

There is in fact a substantial unity of inspiration in the rich variety of his themes. We can see this in the very first pages of the *Journal métaphysique,* in the tenacious and lucidly conscious effort to grasp the processes of a thought that extends beyond the logical domain of mathematics and empirical science but that remains an authentic exercise of knowledge and not just a subjective attitude or purely an effort, an arbitrary *Schwärmerei*. Marcel has always refused to accept as definitive the dilemma believe *or* verify, emotions *or* objective knowledge, which Brunschvicg's epistemological rationalism and the logical positivism of the Vienna circle reintroduced during the first decades of the twentieth century: "Always the same dilemma: objective fact or inner inclination. *All of the one . . .* or nothing but the other. Every time I find it again, I feel as though I am being made to lift a mountain. More than ever, though, I am convinced that this 'dilemma' misses the essentials of religious life and of the most profound metaphysical thinking."[3]

The denunciation of the "over-simplifying" and dogmatic character of the concept of truth as verification or as the public checking of factual assertions has led Marcel to state the problem of metaphysical knowledge in new terms and to indicate some key points of an existential dialectics constantly sustained by an unerring feeling for what is authentically religious and moral.

To understand the original sense of that problem and of this dialectics, it is important to keep in mind what Marcel meant by the "principle of verification" and the criticism he made of it, that is, the perspective of Brunschvicg's epistemological rationalism rather than that of the Viennese, of whom Marcel probably had no direct knowledge. In *Homo Viator* Marcel pictures the initial conditions to which he limited his research and indicates its essential points. First, he felt exasperated by the constant idealistic equivocation between the empirical ego in general and the existing individual, "this undeducible individual," "the real individual that is me, with the incredibly minute details of my experience, with all the specifications of the concrete adventure that is allotted to me, to me alone and to no one else."[4] Second, he constantly rejected the excessive use of the "principle of immanence" characteristic of certain trends within French rationalism during the first decades of the century.[5] In fact, even disregarding retrospective suggestions that could be extracted from later developments in this thinking, it is certain that in the first part of the *Journal métaphysique* he already sets forth in clear terms the problem of the limitations of rationalism as a theory of total verifiability founded on the formal concept of "thought in general," on the Kantian *Denken überhaupt*, stripped of any metaphysical characteristics and reduced to abstract and empty intersubjective identity.

In such a context the doctrine of knowledge is limited within the bounds of what is "valid for everyone," that is, "for anyone" and finally therefore "for no one."[6] At the same time all that transcends the empirical factualism of experience is also excluded, along with everything that does not refer directly to it as its formalized reconstruction. This isolation of knowledge from its very roots—the singularity of the thinker and the transcendence of the Absolute—is the basis for the two-pronged attacks Marcel directs against the rationalists: "Right from the start, my research was explicitly oriented toward the virtually simultaneous recognition of the individual and the transcendent and opposed to any impersonal or immanent idealism."[7]

It is in this light, for example, that we are to understand the theologico-negative theses, with their Neoplatonic flavor, of the first part of the *Journal,* which gravitates around the central affirmation of God as "the absolute Unverifiable," transcending "all possible experience, all existence, all truth."[8] If possible experience is only a web of legal relationships progressively binding empirical data at all levels, if existence is only the *hic et nunc* of these data within perception (the zone of the casual and the fortuitous), if, finally, truth is and is only the objectifying of existence in a given possible experience by means of the logico-empirical procedures of verification, then God is *"beyond any causal nexus,"*[9] *"beyond any existential implication,"*[10] and *"beyond any judgment of truth or falsehood."*[11] In comparison with the tradition of negative theology, the novelty of these theses lies in their close association with the thesis of the *unrepeatable singularity of the believer* in his or her act of faith. The subject of faith is the individual self in its particular situation, whereas the subject of empirical-objective science is the formal impersonal ego, conceived of either as a superindividual consciousness or as a collective ego, an abstract intersubjective identity. In fact, empirical-objective science bases the validity of its propositions on the possibility that given the same conditions, the process of proof that led to the propositions themselves can be repeated by anyone. Its method lies in a series of questions around problems that allow the interlocutors, those who ask and those who answer, to interchange their roles of questioning and answering. If I describe to you a certain fragment of epithelium that I am studying under a microscope, my argument is scientific in that you can invariably check what I state by putting yourself in the position of observation that I am in now. For this reason it is an argument that can always be carried out in the third person, because the one actually speaking is in fact neither you nor I but the impersonal subject of an apparatus of verification, the value of which remains virtually invariable with respect to all systems of reference in which the statement can be repeated.

> When I declare that an affirmation is verifiable . . . I establish a certain number of conditions accepted as universal in their own right because they are recognized as normal and can be found by any subject capable of pronouncing

valid judgments. Thus I have come to the concept of a depersonalized subject; that is, I have come to accept that subject A must be able to interchange with subject B, since both possess this same complex of conditions that preside over any valid experience.[12]

Thus verification implies the possibility of "putting oneself in the place of . . ." as a necessary condition if one is to choose, from among the various observation points, the *positio optima* or whatever presents the maximum guarantee of objectivity. But this is the very condition that cannot be fulfilled by religious experience. I cannot say to the believer, "Your God is an illusion," as, looking at a landscape with a friend whose eyesight is bad, I might say, "Your mountain is a cloud." In the latter case, my friend can move to my position and if necessary use binoculars to correct the weakness of his sight. But in the former, where religious matters are concerned, "this interchange is by definition impossible: I cannot put myself in my friend's position; this is so for many reasons, the most striking of which is that he *cannot be separated from his position,* that he and his position are one and the same thing."[13]

Without a doubt, faith is nothing if it does not overwhelm the believer to the very roots of being, if it does not make a deep mark on one's interrelations with oneself, which is, as Marcel was to say later, one's "being incarnate," one's "being in a situation."[14] Perhaps no one has underlined with more passionate and tragic emphasis than Kierkegaard the fundamental insuperable solitude of the person of faith in relationship with God; the knight of faith, he says, "is completely responsible for himself only, in his state of infinite isolation."[15] In the first pages of the *Journal,* when Marcel did not yet know the works of the Danish theologian,[16] he insisted on this theme of the singularity of the believer as one of the conditions that mystics must never ignore: "The subject of faith is not thought in general. Thought in general, as it reflects on itself (and thus objectifies itself) will appear to itself as a mere abstraction, a mere indeterminate, a formal condition and nothing more. The subject of faith, on the contrary, must be concrete."[17]

Certainly, empirical-objective thought, developing in the field of "human science," has gradually come to acquire a kind of concreteness that cannot be reduced to the formal apparatuses of physical-mathematical structures. In the social disciplines, the category of the "particular," which indicates, in a Hegelian sense, the collective subject (the group, the rank, the class, and so on) has acquired the rights of citizenship within science. Thus the projected structure of the *Wissenssoziologie,* for example, according to Scheler or Mannheim, is based on the idea of a philosophy within the social perspective, where the passions, interests, and choices of a collective take on a logical form. But once again the individual, the single subject, is excluded from this social horizon, as from the others. The old inhibition of Aristotle, which excluded the individual from the realm of science, remains valid for the whole of modern science. But the reason for this inhibition now lies well beyond Aristotle's view of science. Marcel's suggestion seems valuable and worthy of closer analysis; only the relationship to God, he says, only the presupposition of divine transcendence, allows us to conceive of individuality.[18] To derive the concept of the individual as a real unit and not merely as the fragment of a historical-social totality or as the determination of a generic or formal unity, one must refer to an Absolute that is "One" and not "the Whole" (according to the distinction drawn by Parmenides), that is, to the transcendent Absolute that is the logical paradox of any genuinely religious experience.

This bipolarity of the individual and the transcendent also remains outside the range of application of the verification criteria of empirical science in the historical development of the religious event. The very concept of the objectivity of religious history is contradictory. No event can be objectively described by the historian as having really happened, with characteristics distinguishing it from all other events, unless it can be placed within the set of causal relations comprising the unity of experience of thought in general. The objectivity of historical judgment is conditioned by the rigid logical monism of the category of cause; any recourse to transcendence puts itself outside the bounds of objective verifiability and leaves the event existentially uncertain and qualitatively undetermined. But religious history—or "sacred history"—goes beyond any relation of cause and effect; it is a *saltus* that is not deducible from any other form or series of events within experience.

Although often present in the less private manifestations of religious experience, magic and thaumaturgy are nonetheless totally alien to it. The relation between prayer and miracle is the least accessible to the categories of technique and doing. In a religious invocation "everything is constantly questioned; nothing is taken for granted. And this . . . is nothing but an indirect way of defining *hope*."[19] Hope, as Marcel was to say later, "implies a sort of radical refusal of the computation of possibilities": "What is exclusive to hope is that it cannot directly use, or make use of, any technique: hope is the property of the defenseless; it is their weapon, or rather the opposite of a weapon, and in this, mysteriously, lies its efficacy."[20] Thus "sacred history" transcends any possibility of causal explanation and in its most genuine manifestations is itself a miracle "in which faith must not and cannot be dissociated from its object."[21] The world of faith is precisely the opposite of the world of empirical-objective science, especially when the latter is understood as "a sort of huge, inflexible book-keeping."[22] It is the world of the most radical metaphysical contingency. Faith is not possible "unless the metaphysical doubt is in some way imposed on the spirit by the nature, in itself indeterminable, of its object. If a knowledge of Providence were possible, Providence itself would cease to be a religious affirmation."[23] This last is an illuminating remark. But Marcel did not realize that he could have derived from it a more appropriate consideration of the relationship between religion and modern science. Is not modern science, in its development as a kind of knowledge that is problematic, hypothetical, and only probable, a way of recognizing the "metaphysical doubt" and thus of creating a mental disposition not to exclude sacred revelation? Since the great immanent metaphysical systems of modern philosophy have excluded the possibility of revelation and pretended to replace religion, is not the intellectual sobriety of modern science, when practiced in its own domain, a call to reconsider the human and therefore finite condition of reason?

It might seem inevitable that these initial positions of the *Journal métaphysique* would lead to solipsism. For that matter solipsism was a recurrent theme of the 1920s: a renunciation of philosophy in the face of the "publicity" of science, as in the early Wittgenstein, or an attack on the opponent's philosophy, as in many other cases. Marcel manages to keep away from the impasses of religious solipsism—clearly evident in a phrase such as "the faith of others is absolutely not for me"[24]—by orienting his research toward a deeper understanding of the ways and conditions of participatory knowledge, of "knowledge by acquaintance" rather than "knowledge about," and more precisely toward a revaluation of the bodily context of consciousness, "my body," together with its original and inter-subjective structure, the Thou.

In these reflections on bodily self-awareness, Marcel showed a determination to go back to the French sensualist tradition, which permitted him to describe his philosophy as a *métaphysique sensualiste* and which undoubtedly has the advantage of offering an increased credibility to the denunciation of the cognitive inadequacy of empirical-objective science. The paradox resulting from the first of his methodological manifestos—"Existence et objectivité," in the conclusion of the *Journal métaphysique*—is that the objectivity of science does not grasp reality but rather avoids it, whereas subjectivity does not divorce itself from the world but rather, in its original nature of bodily feeling, of *être incarné,* is the prerequisite of any existential judgment and the channel of all our real relationships with the world. This is clearly in opposition to neopositivism, according to which "the subjective does not belong to the world, but is the limit of the world."[25] The world in which the subjective is absent is the world of empirical-objective science, which is in fact a *réseau d'abstractions,* a contest of objects and functions in the shape of a hypothetical legality, where "there is no possibility whatsoever of considering things as existing or not existing."[26]

Marcel recognized that the feeling of one's body ("my body") could not be objectified, and this led him to draw a clear line between the concept of existence and that of objectivity; earlier, in the first pages of the *Journal métaphysique,* both were considered on the same level as factual things to be surpassed dialectically in the act of faith. Existence presents itself as an immediate certainty in the feeling of "my body" and all that is connected to it. To doubt or negate existence as such is senseless, a mere *flatus vocis.*[27] Neither can that privileged existence that I affirm when referring to my body be placed in doubt, because in reality "nothing exists for me that is not in some way connected to me as my body" unless I can consider it an "extension of my body."[28] My organic-psychic consciousness of myself is the center of reference around which all that exists gravitates: "The world exists for me, in the strongest sense of the word *exist,* so far as I have a relation with it similar to what I have with my body, in other words, to the extent that I am incarnate"; "If existence is not there at the beginning, it will not be found anywhere else."[29]

For Marcel, as for Jacobi, existence is not, and never can be, a point of arrival, a *demonstrandum;* it is recognizable only as an irrefutable starting point, as the implication of thought in an original "presence" or "participation." These two expressions, which recur quite frequently in Marcel's language, show precisely enough the peculiar nature of his sensism, which has definitely gone beyond any purely psychological conception of it. They eliminate the equivocation that could result if the affirmation of the existential primacy of the fundamental bodily feeling were interpreted as a sort of dependence of the universe on me and hence as a return to nothing other than a certain gross anthropocentrism, as opposed to a transcendental subjectivism. Marcel clearly refutes the equivocal interpretation: "What I propose here is, first of all, the priority of the existential over the ideal, but with the immediate qualification that the existential must inevitably refer to being incarnate, that is, to the fact of *being alive.*"[30] The reference to Heidegger's expression, which in this case is substantially the same as Marcel's "participation," indicates the character of indivisible unity that links the self with the universe in the existential judgment. The "I exist" is implied in "the universe exists" because "really I belong to all that exists—to the universe that is mine and of which my body is the centre."[31]

In the "I exist" the self is not resolved at all in the "I think" or the "I live" but rather in a complex and ultimately undecipherable "I feel," *j'éprouve*. (In German *Ich erlebe* means the same as *Es erlebt in mir*.) In other words, my existence is the very act of "participating in a universe that creates me as I come in contact with it."[32]

Hence the feeling underlying the existential judgment is in reality an indivisible intersection of intimacy and what is "other than me," of self-relation and relations with others, of "incarnation" and of "participation." This milieu is reconstituted in the immediacy of the existential judgment, and the dialogue with the universe,[33] which objective thought tends to abolish, is thus reestablished. Redeemed from the rarefied atmosphere of logico-mathematical symbols, the universe in its density is conceived of as a range of transcendences, is colored by the varied richness of the "secondary qualities"—themselves real, that is, really "present"[34]—and is consolidated in blocks of duration, as in the scenes of a play.

Such is the world of the existential implications of reason, which Marcel's *métaphysique sensualiste* has proposed to recover as the first condition of our understanding the adventure we live. This world's "concreteness"—or rather the fact that it is composed of a number of concrete entities, an idea that clearly marks one of the limits of Marcel's Bergsonianism[35]—has led Wahl to see a resemblance between the realism of the *Journal métaphysique* and the epistemological pluralism of James and Whitehead.[36] But in fact, in Marcel's presentive sensism there is something original, something that cannot be found in the concepts of the two American philosophers and that caused the *Journal métaphysique* to become one of the classic texts of the philosophy of existence: his very insistence on the antinomic character of a feeling that is both intimate and intentional and that is the singular and opaque feeling of "my body" as well as a highly revealing opening, a participation in the universe, and a permeable presence of the other person. From the recognition of this central datum transcending the contradictions between subject and object, internal and external, Marcel has developed the basic directions of his subsequent research work. It is a question of putting oneself inside this "irrational unit,"[37] into

> a completely extra- or infra-psychological point of view necessary to resolve the central enigmas of psychology itself. . . . The mysterious relationship between the internal and the external, which, far from having to be considered as an abstract relationship between worlds that have no communication what-

soever with each other, is perhaps a central point, an essential fact, without which these same worlds would be nothing but abstractions.

This consideration certainly has its place in Neoplatonism—and particularly in the philosophy of Bergson. But has the latter understood that he was moving toward something that is not psychology—that is beyond psychology?[38]

From here we are led to revise the very roots of that process of introspective involution that conditioned the Cartesian definition of subjectivity as *res cogitans,* that is, the reification of the self as what is "inside" or "under" the bodily covering and in direct relation with itself, in its own "interior world," and in the "internal performance" of its own ideas and states of mind. In commenting ironically on Leibniz's famous phrase by observing that monads have neither doors nor windows because they do not need them, because *they are already on the road, already in the middle of the world,* Heidegger shows clearly enough the gap separating us today from such an obfuscation of a fundamental metaphysical notion. The self is assuredly an ipseity, a relationship with oneself, a process of self-relation. But the "self" of this relation would lose all consistency and would only be a fiction if it were not originally a relationship with others. In order to avoid the metaphors that originated so many mythical positions on the question of "inwardness," the *reditio in se ipsum* can be genuinely understood only as the *prise de conscience* of the original meaning of our active behavior with things, with people, and with God. This unity of meaning, this style or character of our being in relationship to others, is what properly constitutes our individuality as *êtres incarnés.* The gnostic essence of subjectivity, as Ricoeur justly observed, "is to respect the originality of the *cogito* as the sum total of the intentional acts of a subject."[39]

The abstraction of subjectivity from its own nature, which is both sentient and intentional, underlies the image of the world drawn by empirical-objective science. The *cogito,* as established by Descartes at the beginning of modern science, is precisely the "non-inserted" or the "non-insertion in action"—the disarticulation of knowledge from existence.[40] Having broken the indivisible unity of existence, which is our individual participation in the universe through the "fact of feeling," the cognitive relationship is necessarily seen as the opposition of an impersonal subject to an abstract and alien object or to a complex of objects gravitating around it. The objectivity of knowledge thus coincides with its impersonality: "An object as such . . . is given to a thought that leaves out of consideration whatever individuality is in it; the object as such is defined as independent of the qualities that make me myself and not someone else. It is therefore essential to the very nature of the object to leave me out of consideration; if I think of it as referring to me, I cease in this way to consider it as an object."[41]

Thus empirical-objective science, borrowing the basis and the model for its own objectivity from the Cartesian *cogito,* has proceeded along two strongly interconnected lines: the tendency to minimize—indeed, to make disappear—every individual contribution to the act of cognitive synthesis, which becomes neither my view nor yours but the view "of others, no matter whom, and finally of no one"; and the tendency to reduce its object still further "to a set of formal adjustments based on pure symbols, to which no content can be restored unless contact is reestablished through an experience that as such is outside the very conditions of intelligibility that alone are considered valid by science."[42]

These are paradoxical statements, and certainly we could say that they tend to disregard the unquestionably enormous patrimony of information about the world, about this concrete world of ours, that the empirical-objective sciences have progressively built up. Whatever difficulties may be involved in the logical status of science, it has provided modern civilization with a solid basis for its endeavors to transform human and natural reality. And such transformations—which clearly embody in their fullness the very real domain of the needs and threats, the problems and projects, of contemporary humankind—could not be authentic unless they were performed on the basis and under the control of a "real" form of knowledge. Yet in these remarks on modern science, as in other analogous instances I will discuss, Marcel has accepted somewhat uncritically a number of theses, relatively popular in the first decades of the century, regarding the lack of theoretical validity and the purely pragmatic and instrumental nature of scientific procedures. In his defense, he clearly did not so much intend to elaborate a theory of science as to indicate, from the point of view of a concrete anthropology, whatever could not be dealt with by means of the criteria of meaningfulness and validity established by empirical-objective science.[43]

These developments in Marcel's thinking—in the second part of the *Journal métaphysique*—clearly shifted its center from the negative-theological perspective of the "Absolute Unverifiable" to the empirical-sensistic perspective of cosmic participation in the "fundamental situation" of one's own bodily self-awareness. In a way he has rediscovered the original point of reference of modern empiricism: that the truth of any proposition lies in its ability to refer to an immediate feeling. The global and confused certainty of "my body," in Marcel's thought, is in a position analogous to the belief, according to Hume, at the basis of those judgments "which nature, with absolute and irresistible necessity, compels us to pronounce just as we are compelled to breathe and to feel."[44] It is perhaps possible to speak of Marcel's empiricism as a reversal of the trend of contemporary empiricism: if the latter is a conversion or logical reduction of classical empiricism, especially in the neopositivist perspective, then Marcel's empiricism, his "mystical empiricism" (as Wahl called it), is a revaluation of the sensistic basis of modern empiricism. His is a return to that critical concept of belief that surpasses the problematic character of the relations of ideas and in itself welcomes the lively, irresistible, emotional fullness of the daily world of feeling as the constant point of reference and thus the verification of ideas themselves.

At this point the recognition of the central datum of perception allows Marcel to avoid the epistemological impasse of modern empiricism, which is ultimately derived from the psychological reduction of matters of fact to mere contents of consciousness—to states of mind of "internal performances," as Ryle would call them. Old empiricists, such as Berkeley, did not realize that if one abolished the pseudo-concept of representation as a reflection of the "thing in itself," the concept of representation in its merely psychic or mental nature would also inevitably collapse. The false transparency of Berkeley's congeries of perceptions was also in fact a departure from the truth of knowledge by a contact or presence that empiricism attempted to rediscover. To surpass the opposition between internal and external, between subjective and objective, is a *conditio sine qua non* of any theory of real knowledge; the necessity to take this step is imposed by the indivisibility of "incarnation" and "participation" in the fundamental bodily feeling, in "a datum which is not transparent to itself," and in a situation "which can never be rigorously dominated and analyzed."[45]

It is clear, however, that the verification criterion of empirical-objective science as it is commonly used is not applicable to the existential propositions of Marcel's empiricism, even in this new perspective. As we have seen, the object of empirical-objective science is the function of an invariant in the independent variability of the observers, in other words, of "points of view" or of systems of reference. Science in fact values these variables only as a means toward their neutralization. But the existential index of our judgments—that is, their reference to "my body"— does not permit the neutralization of the individuality of whomever expounds them. Since verification consists not only of the factual control of assertions but also of the possibility of role exchange among those who assert, then verification is not possible in the realm of existential judgments. Marcel must be credited with having clearly seen this internal antinomy of empirical-objective science. And it is this recognition that opened the way for him to analyze the problem of communication and intersubjectivity in general, a problem that has occupied the major place in his philosophical works (just as the trauma of incommunicability, misunderstanding, and bad faith is the existential and dramatic backbone of his theatrical works).

His reflections on what we would call his "private discourse," or, as Royce would put it, the "dyadic relationship," the I-Thou, had already appeared in the first *Journal* at about the same time or shortly after those of Martin Buber, about whom Marcel later wrote an insightful critical essay.[46] In the communication of this "private discourse," the existential index cannot be avoided or neutralized. The reciprocity of existences—that is, the original and active coexistence of two "beings incarnate"—is in fact the fundamental structure of the I-Thou relationship. The Thou is transobjective because it is always more than the sum of its own data; it is an unpredictable resource of initiative and wonder—the other person as such, not as a representation or a state of mind or an imaginary projection of the self. The Thou is not something one can talk about with indifference; the I who speaks to it is more than a part of its experience, just as the Thou is more than a "performance" for me or a "look at me" (*le regard d'autrui,* as Sartre would say). Both *performance* and *look* imply the abolition of the very possibility of a dyadic relationship, that is, of a direct one between subject and subject. The essence of the Thou lies in its being the only one who can answer a certain kind of question that I can put to it, just as I am the only one who can answer its questions. In science, once existence has been neutralized, then everyone, at least by right, can answer the questioners' questions, and the questioners themselves must in turn be able to answer as well, since in the domain of objectivity, questioning and answering are only rhetorical or didactic versions of the repeatability of a mental operation. But "private discourse" is very different; there I am open to the other in an appeal or an invocation for an answer that only the other can give. The other's ability to answer is inalienable—it cannot be delegated to a substitute or a representative—because it is the self, the very presence, of the other that is revealed in the process of communication. Here questioning and answering are filled with existential meaning; language becomes action, expression, self-introduction, and manifestation. This sense explains why the answer in the I-Thou relationship is in the form of "witnessing." The nature of its apophasis is one of attesting rather than just enunciating. It means a total commitment to the words spoken, staking one's all, facing all the consequences, as in the sacrifice of "martyrs"—witnesses par excellence of their own faith. In fact we all face the alternative of either being what we really are or of getting lost in the web of our own fictions and misunderstandings with others. This alternative can only be resolved by the sincerity of our intersubjective relations, that is, by the truth of our "private discourse."

In direct communication, therefore, the subject manifests itself as a subject, that is, as an original datum of existence; it is genuinely real knowledge. But this manifestation is essentially reciprocal, and so it can only take place between two subjects who are both acting principles, not terms, of their relationship; in other words, it can only take place between two cosubjects, if we can call them this, both of whom are revealing and revealed at the same time. The subject as acting principle manifests itself by expressing what most originally constitutes its being and by behaving in such a way that another subject will recognize it. If it did not, it would be an object or thing and not a subject. Hence the subject as such—and therefore all that concerns the problems of existence in the forms of incarnation and participation—cannot be the theme of an objective or "public" discourse, in opposition to objects or things that can be "at the disposal of everyone," since they are only terms and not acting principles of relation. Once we have violated its mystery, does not death itself appear as the ultimate negation of existence and hence of intersubjectivity, since in death, according to empirical-objective science, everything happens as though we were inexorably destined to become things at the mercy of everyone's judgment?

In the intersubjective relationship, therefore, direct communication is an expressive bodily contact of reciprocal intentionality between two existences involved in attesting their truth together. The analyses of the experience of loving, to which Marcel dedicated many of his most profound and subtle diary notes, especially in *Etre et avoir* and in *Présence et immortalité*, are the phenomenological counterpoint of these general observations. I will not outline here its intriguing procedures and articulations, as I did in my previous essay,[47] but will limit myself to the two concluding points that clarify the concept of "real knowledge" Marcel gradually developed in his criticism of epistemological rationalism. In the first place the beloved as reached in the experience of love is a totality that cannot be reduced to its parts. All objective determinations, which somehow break and fragment the beloved's individuality, are irrelevant to the lover.[48] Authentic love does not refer to any predicates. For the lover, predicating is always inadequate. It always omits what is most important: the totality beyond all vicissitudes, the eternal in the Thou, or, more exactly, the infinitely renewable and creative within it. From this point of view Marcel observed profoundly, "the *Do Not Judge* of Christian morality must be considered one of the most important metaphysical formulas that ever existed."[49] It is the precondition for asserting the Thou, the true and proper real knowledge of which is love, without diminishing or degrading it. Because the reality of the beloved is essential in love. In this sense perhaps we can truly say that only love is real knowledge, and it is legitimate to compare love to adequate knowledge, because for love, and only for love, the individuality of the beloved is not dispersed, is not reduced to some dust of abstract elements. But, on the other hand, this reality of the beloved can only be safeguarded because it is presented by love as transcending any explanation, any reduction.[50]

By definition, any philosophy of self-consciousness is bound to negate or reject this view of love. If one closes up within one's self-consciousness, affirming the supremacy of the category of subject-object or of the act through which the subject somehow places objects within itself, then the existence of others becomes inconceivable; they "are actually outside the circle I form with myself."[51] To allow the recognition of the other as such, one must pose as a *primum* the very act of communication, that is, intersubjectivity understood as a manner of immediate and intimate participation; the self as isolated self-consciousness is but the repudiation and mutilation of intersubjectivity. This manner of participation is nothing but love, or that attitude toward others that makes us open to their presence as to something more important than ourselves and that therefore reveals them to us with more immediate evidence than we have for ourselves.[52]

> The other as such does not exist for me except to the extent that I have opened myself to him—but I do not feel open to him unless I cease to form a sort of circle with myself, inside which I would somehow place the other, or rather the idea of the other; because, in relation to this circle, the other becomes the idea of the other, and the idea of the other is no longer the other as such, but the other as referred to myself, dissolved, disarticulated, or on the way toward disarticulation.[53]

In relation to the second concluding point, I would like to stress that the real existential character of the experience of loving is not revealed only in its immediate reference to the reality of the beloved (rather than to his or her representation); it is also revealed—and revealed more deeply—through its mediation: the lover and the beloved begin to exist in a reciprocity that is their most authentic way of being. *Love is creative reciprocity*. In it, as Jaspers also notes, "the self is for the self in a mutual creation."[54] "I affirm myself as a person," Marcel says, "insofar as I really believe in the existence of others, and this belief tends to influence my behavior."[55] This formula completely reverses certain naturalistic perspectives through which the ontology of substance can be degraded or put aside. The self is not "a reality that can be isolated," nor can it be comprehended or attested to except "in reference to a certain spiritual economy within which my existence can retain a meaning or a value."[56] This "spiritual economy" comes into existence through the reciprocity of love, in which the self-relation of the lover and the beloved are deeply transformed.

> Loving another being means expecting something undefinable, unpredictable, from him or her; it means, at the same time, somehow giving him or her the means to respond to one's expectation. Yes, though it can sound like a paradox, to expect is somehow to give; nor is the reverse less true: not to expect means to inflict a sort of sterility on the one being from whom nothing is expected any longer, thus robbing him or her somehow, in advance—of what exactly but of a certain capability to invent and create?[57]

Existence then is correlation, or, more exactly, the creative coexistence of the I and the Thou; it is the We operating in the reciprocal dedication of the lover and the beloved. *To exist is to coexist.* To recognize the primacy of the intersubjective leads to the dissolution of the tenacious philosophical myths of monadism and solipsism. The self is communal (social) right from the start, Marcel notes in the third *Journal métaphysique*.[58] The unresolved themes of a science founded on the category of subject-object lose their inhibitory force "if one poses in principle a certain unity of the We, a radical nonisolation of the subject, and finally a primacy of the intersubjective."[59] Because of this primacy, one is actually a We for oneself in one's thoughts, feelings, actions, and plans: *"If the others are not I am not either."*[60] There is a "double falsity in monadism: I am neither *solus* nor *unus*. The We no doubt shows itself to be much more profound than the I."[61]

Finally, this means that "real knowledge" is possible both in its immediate reference to the bodily expressive context of existence and in its communication among subjects who do not neutralize their singularity but instead affirm this singularity in real knowledge, recognizing themselves in a creative community. The difficulty of this existential and affirmative knowledge lies not in one's supposed inability to express the bodily immediacy in words, because the body as "incarnation" is essentially expression and therefore language;[62] nor does the problem lie in the supposed inability to communicate between individual subjects. There is nothing that cannot be expressed or communicated, as far as the integrity of our nature of incarnate and correlated beings is concerned. The difficulty may arise if we reject this nature of ours and therefore reject truth, or the "spirit of truth" inscribed in its very ontological nature. Real knowledge is based on our original act of consensus toward being. It is both the first and the deepest of our moral actions.

The psychoanalysis of the "spirit of abstraction" represented by the *Esquisse d'une phénoménologie de l'avoir,* which concludes the second

Journal, is based on research into the original forms and most profound reasons for this rejection of our nature.[63] Later on Marcel was to say, "If one considers it in its dynamic aspect, my philosophical work appears on the whole as an obstinate, never ending struggle against the spirit of abstraction."[64] Marcel thought that between the real knowledge sought by his "concrete philosophy" and empirical-objective science there was not only a quantitative but also a qualitative difference, a *saltus,* an untraversable chasm. When the abstract world of science claims to include in itself everything that belongs to the realm of being and that constitutes its essence, it is totally overwhelmed by "some fundamental blindness," by "an initial lie."[65] This "lie" comes from the refusal of the original *engagement,* which nourishes thought and outside of which thought itself, as a mere absolute, would be reduced to pure contradiction. The reason operating in empirical-objective science is an evasion, an isolation from reality; in fact it is nothing but the coherent formalization of a certain kind of reflection—a "first-degree reflection," as Marcel calls it, adopting Schelling's famous distinction—which in a way is the constant and most evident mark of a mysterious decadence of existence. By an irresistible tendency, we are stimulated to represent the world to ourselves as a reality from which we can and must detach ourselves in order to grasp it by will and bend it to an ever steadier and more complete possession. There is a metaphysics of the supremacy of *having* over *being* behind "first-degree reflection" as well as behind empirical-objective science. In this metaphysics, the original wonder of the existential and the creative reciprocity of the I-Thou are the object of an obstinate *refoulement,* the aim of which is to allow—at the level of clear consciousness and in the perspective of rational behavior—only what can be included in the realm of an acquisitive relationship: things or human beings, to be dominated, possessed, and exploited. In our times, at least as far as philosophy is concerned, the "initial lie" of the "spirit of having"—what philosophical asceticism has always called "lust"—is finally becoming evident. The exasperated rigor with which the lie's project has been realized in all contemporary forms of mental and practical behavior has produced a world that more and more openly tends to find in empirical-objective science the only source of its evaluations and rules. The category of having is beginning to appear, in the structure of our contemporary world, as a sort of reversed ontology so that the old concept of "nonbeing" of classical philosophy acquires a new and much more realistic content. The world thus produced consists of alienation and worry, in a true and proper "dialectics of the slave and the tyrant," where the owner and the owned are linked together by a reciprocal tension: the owner holds a jealous power of conservation and defense over the owned, and the owned, which is subject to the possibility of being worn out, lost, or destroyed, becomes the center of tumultuous fears and anxieties. Objectification, in the field of science, is simply the logical transcription of this alienating and worrying world. The more we degrade the universe to pure possession, the more the universe appears as an object or as functional machinery. According to Marcel, science is made of a net of objective relations constituting a "system for me" aimed at helping me to make use of my "possession." My body, as an exasperated center of violent desires, is in fact the center of this possession. From this point of view, the claimed disinterestedness of scientific objectivity is only a myth or a mask: the "spectator's" attitude toward the world "corresponds to a form of lust; in fact, it corresponds to the act with which the subject reduces the whole world to himself."[66]

But there is another side of the coin that in a way constitutes the dramatic a posteriori proof of what I was saying: it is the desperation that overwhelms and sweeps away the artificial and passionate world created by our "welfare society." "The structure of our world is such that absolute desperation seems possible in it."[67] The world manifested to us by the schemata of a logic and a technique within which everything must be reduced tends to become utterly degraded; it becomes an area where all mysterious and joyfully creative reality congeals into an inert series of objects and instruments placed in front of me. I can count them and classify them; they are the object of my avaricious desires and the infinite source of my anxiety and of my anguish. In a world of tools and machines, we are reduced to a sum total of "functions"—"étouffante tristesse d'un monde axé sur l'idée de fonction"[68]—so that everything incites us to negate all that is personal and creative within us and within others and to let ourselves be regulated as though we were placed within some sort of mechanism and surrendered to the functioning of a series of rigorous norms imposed on us by the techniques of social, economic, and political power. Here we see the triumph of the categories of *tout naturel* and *n'importe qui:* the world of facileness and anonymity—which carries within itself all its unresolved contradictions and which condemns us to being tossed around by what we possess—sharpens our state of perpetual anxiety, and we assist, helplessly, in the fatal dispersion of all that is ours as we disappear into the chasm of time, at the bottom of which is death.

Today it is possible to judge how serious a philosophy is by considering how it accounts for this negative ontology of the *monde cassé*. In fact the philosophy of the profound is inconceivable unless it includes an inner struggle between the vertiginous negation of being and its vehement affirmation. We are not spectators of this struggle but rather actors in it; on this struggle depends either our reintegration within our own authentic reality or our dissolution. Today philosophy is either nonacademic philosophy or not philosophy at all. As it happened in the Platonic allegory of the cave, to philosophize actually means to commit violence against the irresistible tendency toward the nonbeing, the nonauthenticity, the "false aim" of our lust: "A spirit is metaphysical insofar as its position with regard to the real still seems basically unacceptable to it. Here we must understand the word *position* almost in its physical sense. A false position . . . perhaps needs straightening, perhaps relaxing. Metaphysics is this very act of straightening or relaxing."[69]

Therefore the truth of a philosophy is judged not only by checking the truth of its assertions but also by judging the fundamental attitude on which it is based; in other words, what one sees depends on the way one looks at it, and this is originally nothing but a way of being. For Marcel the ultimate task is to transform the "spirit of having" into an openness to creative participation—a true and proper *metanoia,* with all its religious implications. Marcel calls this transformation "second-degree reflection," which is the path reason follows once it has been reintegrated into its authenticity; at the same time it is a profound *praxis,* or, more exactly, an *umvälzende praxis* of intersubjective existence.[70]

The alternative between first-degree and second-degree reflection is therefore decided by an option, a radical choice. The right way to look at the world must be chosen. Good philosophy, as Marcel understands it, is a healthy *blik,* an attitude or a way of looking, just as bad philosophy is a sort of obsessive *blik,* like that of the psychopath described by R. M. Hare in his essay on theology and falsification.[71] But if philosophy is only a *blik,* is it not incapable of making assertions about reality? And how far can one say that knowledge is an option, a radical choice, without reducing it to a purely arbitrary choice? The problem of the relation between knowledge and freedom is crucial to any "philosophy of the thinking thought" that firmly intends to root itself in the transcendent and personal origins of knowledge.

In fact, this problem haunts many contemporary philosophers of existence—such as Berdyaev, Jaspers, and especially Sartre—as an unresolved and insoluble contradiction. In these philosophies, the radical option derives from the anguish of a total crisis; thought is caught up in this anguish and has no way to get out of it or to dominate it other than by a "decree," a peremptory decision, which in fact implies an acceptance of the crisis rather than a solution to it and hence is beyond rational justification. A similar option is part of a situation of exile, where thought is isolated from being and ends up in a *Zweifel* ("doubt") that in fact is *Verzweiflung* ("despair"), for it has no criterion of orientation or choice. Here is the point of the question: is this state of total abandonment and radical crisis of existence really a *fatum* that conditions us to be inexorably denied any rationality, or is it itself the consequence of an obscure "refusal" with which we detached ourselves from our original participation in being? As we have seen, Marcel's research is oriented toward the latter interpretation and forces a true and proper transformation of the irrational and unresolved problems met by the so-called crisis philosophies. *Verzweiflung* means the active refusal of a crucial certainty. In the various stages of Marcel's research, he gives different definitions of this certainty: in the first part of the *Journal métaphysique* it is the living fullness of the "Act of Faith"; in the second part of the same work it is the global and obscure consciousness of "incarnation"; finally, in *Etre et avoir* and in *Position et approches concrètes du mystère ontologique* it is the all-inclusive certainty of the "I believe," the "I exist," the "participation" on which our reality as subjects is based. But the very possibility of refusal, hanging over our existence like a threat or a permanent temptation from the alienating structures of our contemporary world, changes that certainty from a fact into an act and therefore into a free initiative within the very heart of knowledge.[72]

We must now determine how this power of initiative and choice is exercised within knowledge and within all activities connected with knowledge, such as art, religion, and metaphysics. Since the choice is a radical one, it cannot be made for motives that are alien to our being: "The essence of freedom is that it can be exercised through a self-betrayal. Nothing that is external to us can keep desperation away from us."[73] Undoubtedly, when Marcel underlines the "mysterious and terrible power" of the freedom of refusal and stresses the agony of life as a test of the temptation to betray,[74] he is very close to Kierkegaard as well as to Jaspers, as he himself declared.[75] Nevertheless, the similarity extends only to a recognition of the obscure possibility to negate, which is immanent in the very act through which we are made free. Freedom, in fact, is only the possibility of the existence of opposites, as for instance in Jaspers's philosophy; it is therefore reduced to a mere option independent of an inner motivation. As such, it is isolated in an infinite process of regression, always presupposing itself to be prior to itself, and incapable of becoming determinate except through an absurd *saltus*.

In Marcel's philosophy, on the contrary, the optional moment of freedom—its "negative possibility," such as that in which St. Augustine saw the *liberum arbitrium* of a fallen creature—is merely the condition or the limit of the positive existence of freedom as intersubjective and ontological participation (just as, according to St. Augustine, the *libertas positiva* is an openness to cooperate with the *gratia*).[76] All of Marcel's philosophy orients toward a deeper study of the close link between the notions of participation, motivation, and freedom. The "spirit of truth,"—that is, authentic knowledge—is based on this very link.

> In which way can this freedom, which is no less radical than the immediacy of feeling, be asserted effectively? Above, I came to a definition of metaphysics as a *logic of freedom;* this formula is not quite correct, but it has the advantage of throwing some light on this essential truth: that philosophical progress consists of the series of successive procedures through which a freedom that at the beginning is understood as the mere power to say yes or no becomes incarnate; or, if we want to phrase it differently, it becomes a real power, giving itself a content within which it discovers and recognizes itself.[77]

The positive structure of freedom can only be recognized by eliminating the confusion between the notions of "receiving" and "suffering"; such confusion of notions has always led to a situation of opposition between the metaphysics of being and the metaphysics of pure freedom.[78] This confusion results from the illegitimate use of the scientific-technological category of "cause" in the interpretation of freedom. This same equivocation, according to Marcel, "affects . . . all traditional theological assertions."[79] I cannot think of myself as a "free cause" without becoming somewhat isolated from my actions and alien to myself; a total commitment of my reality as a subject, on the contrary, is typical of an act of authentic freedom. Many philosophers have failed to see this truth; among them, for example, is Maine de Biran. The less I think about myself, the less I close up inside myself; the less I form "a close, hermetic system, which cannot be penetrated by anything that is new," the freer I become.[80] The opposite of freedom is in fact this internal stiffening of the will that wants to "belong to itself," following the ideal of stoic wisdom that Kant translated into the modern notion of "autonomy";[81] thus the will risks closing itself up because of inertia and spiritual atony, which prevent it from receiving the revelations and answering the appeals coming from the presences that transcend it. Genuine freedom consists of opening oneself to participation and leaving behind any opposition between activity and passivity; in it, to receive does not mean to suffer but rather to answer an appeal.[82] If transcending oneself is more than a void dialectical artifice, then it can be understood most correctly and precisely as the act of letting oneself be overwhelmed by a revealing presence and carried away by an exalting admiration. In sum, "nothing is freer, in a true and proper sense, than this acceptance and this consensus. . . . The appeal restores us to ourselves. Not necessarily, of course, since we may always reject it. But our answer, in order to be free, must not of necessity imply a clear consciousness of this capability to reject. I would like to say that *it is free insofar as it frees.*"[83]

This answer is like a new *blik* or interior light appearing within me when I open myself to the presence that reveals to me that "I am not part of myself" and that shows me the world as the context or tangible expression of an inexhaustible irradiation of creativity.[84] My impetus of liberation derives from this *éclat* or *jaillissement* of creative reciprocity in a world of presences. Here the notions of freedom, receptivity, and creativity fuse together:

> Any creation is only possible if it is based on a receptivity that in its very essence is active and somehow prefigures the creation itself. If this is so, then freedom, understood as self-creation, is only conceivable in reference to a being who, if he explores the very depths of his soul, is bound to appear to himself essentially as a sort of gift and cannot in any way attribute to himself those caricatures of nonselfness evoked by most contemporary atheists.[85]

In its true positive character, freedom is thus a liberating interpretation through which we open up to the revelation of a world of creative presences and liberate ourselves from the fetters of unavailability and desperation (within which our paradoxical situation tends to bind us) as beings who can betray themselves and who can reject what makes them exist. This profound way of being free is what Marcel calls "second-degree reflection," the true path of philosophy and the dialectical instrument embodied in it:[86] "The tremendously important function that philosophy should have for us—and here I come to one of Plato's great themes—is that of making us more and more aware of the reality that certainly surrounds us everywhere but that we, as free beings, have the frightening power to reject."[87]

But finally, what sort of knowledge is given to us by our active behavior toward the *inépuisable concret* at the center of human fate and reality? The second-degree reflection transforms the alienating processes of thought—represented by the verbs *to objectify* and *to have*—by means of concentration, of an interior silence, uniting us to what is primary and profound. But what do we actually learn about this being that is us and that transcends us? Marcel answers this sort of question by proposing a distinction between *mystery* and *problem* that has become famous among contemporary philosophers.[88] This distinction takes up some very lively themes of modern religious philosophy, such as Kierkegaard's on the "demoniac" character of the uncontrolled doubting and questioning and Jacobi's on the opposition between *Tiefsinn* and *Scharfsinn* (that is, between profound knowledge and merely formal knowledge).[89]

Mystery is a word taken from religious terminology; translating it into philosophical language risks distorting its meaning by confusing it with the darkness of the unknowable. But whereas this darkness is only a limit to our problemizing—something our thought cannot reach without abolishing itself as thought—"the recognition of mystery is, on the contrary, an essentially positive act of the spirit, the positive act par excellence, the key point, perhaps, around which any positiveness can be defined."[90] In fact the terms *mystery* and *problem* are opposed to each other, the former being a global and immediate way of learning, the latter a divided and temporary one, to be verified over and over again. The problem is something placed in front of me: an operation I must carry out or an unknown quantity I must find on the basis of some known "values" or "data." Mystery, by contrast, is "something to which I am committed and with which I am involved; its essence, therefore, is not to be placed as a whole in front of me."[91] In other words, it is "a problem that involves its very immanent conditions of possibility, overwhelming them and thus surpassing itself as a problem."[92] If we pose a metaphysical question to ourselves with all its serious implications (for example, "What am I?" or "What is the ultimate meaning of my life?"), we immediately realize that it involves the very totality of the questioner. But who can answer these questions?

> Let us reflect on the question "What am I?" and on all its implications. When I reflect on the implications of the question "What am I?" in its global meaning, I realize that it asks, "How qualified am I to answer this question?" Consequently, any answer *I give* must necessarily be questioned. But could someone else give the right answer? One thing can immediately be objected: it is I who judge how qualified the other may be to answer and how valid the other's opinion may be. Am I qualified to judge this? The only judgment I can refer to without giving rise to contradictions is therefore an absolute one, which at the same time would be more internal to me than my own judgment. If I considered this absolute judgment external to me, then the question of how to know its value and how to consider it would inevitably rise again. Thus the question as such is canceled, and turned into an appeal. And perhaps, insofar as I become conscious of it, I am bound to recognize that the appeal is only possible because deep inside me there is something that is not me, something more "internal" to me than my own self.[93]

Marcel once remarked that this section of the second *Journal* must be considered the *charnière métaphysique* of his whole philosophical work. In fact, like other well-known texts of contemporary philosophies of existence, this passage takes up the positivist "challenge" to metaphysics: the charge that metaphysical problems cannot be posed in logical terms. In the perspective of objective knowledge, a problem that involves itself as datum (such as a problem that questions the questioner and the whole logical apparatus of research) is like an equation whose values are all unknowns:

it is a shapeless logical expression and hence nonsense. Thus the attempt to transfer the scientific approach to a problem into the realm of philosophical research has led to the denunciation of the "logical void" of metaphysics. The rejection of metaphysics, though, has another side: the data posed as a condition for the determination or construction of the unknown terms of the problem only provide a temporary, hypothetical certainty and can be questioned at any time. A coherent positivist—if ever there was one—would end up either in a dogmatic atomism of immediate perception (in which thinking would be excluded and abolished) or in an extreme version of Heracliteanism (in which reflection, being incapable of justifying the temporary character of its objects, would be unable either to circumscribe them or to settle them as meaningful entities of a logical relation rather than as arbitrary symbols). Imprisoned in the ever changing immediacy of fact or in the permanent procrastination of research toward a privileged area of evidence or of noncontradiction, the "coherent positivist" would in the end refuse all possible discourse, as did Cratylus, the Heraclitean philosopher Aristotle mentions in the fourth book of his *Metaphysics*.

A sort of paralogism is therefore implied in the positivist denunciation of the "metaphysical quest." This quest rejects the "bad infinity" of an inconclusive succession of problems and takes on its questioning as derivative of an original "intuition"[94] that makes this question possible and in fact justifies it as an absolute question. On account of this original intuition, questioning (*enquête*) about being becomes a quest (*quête*) for being; the curiosity and noninvolvement of the spectator tend to become a total research commitment, a total participation. Instead of hurtling into the deepening obscurity of a world reduced to the cash nexus and becoming alienated in an acquisitive tension, this total commitment attempts to understand the self in the revealing opening of an original experience of presence.

Undoubtedly, Marcel's work retained some of the original obscurities accompanying this concept of intuition, which comprises both the ontological question and the ontological assertion. He speaks at times of a "blinded intuition,"[95] and this arouses the critical reservations of those who see the old unresolved themes of mysticism and fideism emerging from the central point of his philosophy. At other times, using an expression equally unorthodox for philosophers, Marcel refers to the ontological mystery as a sort of "reflexive intuition."[96] This expression is not far from the language Neoplatonists use when they speak of the impossibility of grasping the One except through the reflections of its light on its emanations. Indeed, in *Etre et avoir* he notes: "Everything here seems to take place as if I benefited from an intuition that, properly speaking, could not exist per se, but that emerges only through the modes of experience on which it reflects and that it illuminates by this very reflection."[97] Here the idea of a philosophy of the approach to knowledge and of the way of looking emerges again. The ontological mystery is not an intuition of being as though being were an object, as in classical ontologies; it is rather an internal illumination of our way of looking at reality. But if we avoid the old and evocative metaphor of the light, what could be the criterion to judge the truth of knowledge? What could provide rational motives for the choice of a certain approach to knowledge except, precisely, an act of knowledge, a true and proper *cognitio*? Do we not end up in a vicious circle when we try to found the truth of knowledge on one particular way of knowing? Any *blik*'s philosophy always faces this difficulty because it ignores theoretical requirements, the need for which was first and most strongly asserted by Greek philosophy. Much of Marcel's philosophy is very close to a *blik*'s philosophy, but with Marcel the difficulty mentioned above in fact becomes a critical stimulus that leads him, especially in the 1949 and 1950 Gifford Lectures on the *Mystère de l'être,* to a new appraisal of the theoretical and contemplative aspects of philosophy. Previously, he often insisted on the distinction between *homo spectans* and *homo particeps,* but at this stage the distinction loses much of its value for him, especially since the ambiguous notion of "spectator" could well include proper theoretical activity: "Making a distinction between *homo spectans* and *homo particeps,* I wanted to stress the fact that the latter implied a commitment, whereas the former did not. But I was wrong in leaving aside contemplation, the essence of which is no doubt totally different."[98]

In *Etre et avoir* the spectator is opposed to the saint; the value of life as "service" is exalted and any "spectator's" attitude condemned; this attitude included (or at least did not explicitly exclude) the speculative manner of thinking. But in his Gifford Lectures, Marcel reorients his philosophy toward a theoretical revaluation of an intelligible presence of being, which he understands as "a certain fullness of truth."[99] Whereas the spectator remains indifferent to things or only looks at them superficially, the contemplator exhibits a concentration that is interior participation: "To contemplate is to concentrate in the presence of a certain reality and in such a way that this reality becomes part, somehow, of the very act of meditation."[100] On careful examination this definition amounts to Plato's *metexis*. Hence all that could have been still obscure in the notion of mystery or, more accurately, in Marcel's negation of the identification of mystery with the unknowable, may be cleared. Mystery is not what is basic beyond all problems—not a certainty that is impervious to questions—but rather contemplation itself, that is, true knowing, true knowledge. The ontological mystery is the deeply personal act by which the innermost part of being is revealed; it is a form of intersubjective participation, which implies commitment, creativity, and inexhaustibility. This is a true "metaphysical objectivity," wholly different from the objectivity of first-degree reflection in which, according to Marcel, the scientific processes of invention and verification operate. Indeed, in the ontological mystery, the essence of being reveals itself as an act of creative participation only if one makes oneself available to this participation by doing violence to the spontaneous processes of separation, isolation, and possessive alienation. This concrete universal, which in Marcel's philosophy has the same function Bergson attributes to the "metaphysical intuition" of every genuine philosophy and toward whose acknowledgment Marcel's whole philosophy is oriented, attests to an intrinsic original relationship of participation and contemplation from which every presence takes its own mark of intelligibility, that is, its own individual and everlasting idea. In this sense we witness, in the lectures of the *Mystère de l'être,* a true ontological conversion of the Bergsonian theme of the *moi profond.* Here we do not discuss the *moi profond* (the *moi* emerges, or rather arises, in the expressive sphere of competition and imposition),[101] but rather we grasp its metaphysical acceptance and found it on the theme of the *idée profonde:*

> An idea is profound insofar as it unfolds against the background of a beyond that is only gleaned, and the image that offered itself to my mind was that of a channel, such as the channels between some Dalmatian islands, at the outlet of which one can glean a kind of glittering light.
>
> The experience of the deep is thus tied to a feeling of hope, the fulfillment of which can only be gleaned. But what is remarkable here, I added, is that this gleaned farness is not felt as an elsewhere. It is, to the contrary, something very near, having transcended, in this instance, the distinction between the *here* and the *elsewhere.* This farness offers itself to us as coming from inside, as an ownership of which we must say that it is ours with homesickness—exactly as the lost country is to the exile.[102]

So there is no depth where there is no perception of the continuity of time, or, more accurately, where the perception of time does not have its root in the inexhaustibility of an absolute Presence.

> The dimension of the deep does not intervene, it seems, if there is not a mysterious relation between the future and the farthest past. One could say, for all the obscurity of this notion, that the past and the future are joined in the womb of the deep, that they are bound in an area that re-

fers to what I call the present, what would be an *absolute here* in reference to a contingent here, and this area where the now and the after
tend to blend, as I have said regarding the near and the far, can be
nothing else but what we call Eternity, and this essential word, to which
it is impossible to attribute a representable content, acquires here all its
meaning.[103]

The *idée profonde* then is not the night of the mystics or something
comparable to Jaspers's juxtaposition of the "passion of the night" and
the "law of the day." If all that is alive in Platonism is not recognizable
in the mythical structures of Plato's archaic cosmology but rather in the
dialectical rhythm of the eros as the total striving of the soul toward an
intelligible world (that is, toward a world of "presences" that goes beyond
the events of geneses and corruptions), then we must say that Marcel's
philosophy is genuinely Platonic, or at least very close to the original Platonism represented by Socrates' philosophical character in Plato's first dialogues—a "Neosocratism," then, or a "Christian Socratism," as Marcel
might qualify his thought.[104] Marcel's original and assuredly important
contribution to the best tradition has been the integration of Socratic dialectics as a critical and defining heuristic movement with a dialectics of
secret, existential, and optional motivation. Rather than talk about integration, we should talk about a new synthesis where the existential behavior
toward being and the revelation of being inseparably imply each other.

From this point of view, Marcel is not bound by what in my opinion
is the central difficulty of certain forms of comporary existentialism, which
exhibit now a tendency to assume the extreme attitudes of "humanism"
("We are in a realm where there is nothing but men," says Sartre), now
to extenuate themselves in a hermetic transcendentalism (as happens, for
example, in the strong metaphysical suggestions Jaspers dedicates to the
"reading of figures" in the third book of his *Philosophie,* that is, to the
hermeneutics of an allusive, indirect language symbolic of transcendence
or of the "absolutely else" that is hidden rather than revealed in the
world). We cannot come out of the *Dasein* if we have no knowledge beyond our research; it is impossible to build an ontology while remaining in
the plain analytics of the *Dasein.* This impossibility was the basis of the
charge of "psychologism" or "transcendental anthropologism" Husserl
made against Heidegger in the *Nachwort zu mein 'Ideen'* in 1930. In spite
of Heidegger's protests, it was not a baseless charge, and we may say that
all subsequent works by the author of *Sein und Zeit* were born from the
spur of that critical entreaty. By contrast, I do not believe that such an
objection could be raised against Marcel if we take into account the definitely theoretical, definitely ontological framework in which he placed his

research, recognizing it as tributary to a deep intuition, to an *éclat* of being, that philosophy has the duty to detect in experience as that which exceeds it and constitutes its basis.

Marcel's Neosocratism therefore consists mainly of research, or more accurately of the phenomenological explication of some practical and theoretical structures of experience, where the participatory essence of being reveals its implication in an absolute relationship. The ontological mystery is based on the methods of research that regain—with the same dialectic tension of Socrates' *tì estin* ("What is it really?")—the true meaning of love relations, of freedom, of fidelity, and of hope. Certainly even those who let themselves be influenced by such analyses, undoubtedly conducted with an exceptional *esprit de finesse,* could still limit the justificative range of the metaphysical conclusion. We could see in it, for example, only a compound of biographical and typological assertions about the "person of faith," the "person who hopes," the "person who loves," and so on. The appeal directed to the absolute Thou warrants our obligations to the other, who, on the contrary, "more than the warranters, who would guarantee and confirm from the outside an already established unity, is the very cement that founds it."[105] This appeal constitutes the trust and faith in the ontological permanence of the We that is of the *agape* of human participation, beyond all the denials and proofs to which our state of created being is subject. This intuition and participation compose the fundamental structure of the anthropology inspired by Christianity. But the metaphysical implications—God, the soul, and communal immortality, which after all constitute classical Christian metaphysics—are conditioned by the choice of these "ways of life." Why these and not others? Why love as "creative fidelity," at the expense of disappointment, instead of the eros of Don Juan's aesthetical availability or of the sadomasochistic dialectics in the name of a hopeless lucidity? If the dialectics of "attitude" and of the concrete approaches to the ontological mystery should be understood in the last two ways, it would be bound to a choice that is really a bet, a Pascalian *pari.* The justificative movement would merely elucidate the reasonableness and perhaps the plausibility of the choice but would not eliminate its gratuitousness or its deep irrationality.

Clearly this interpretation reveals a gross misunderstanding. Marcel aims to make us face real situations that we cannot escape without refusing more or less openly our rational responsibilities. Whether in the form of an immoralistic aestheticism refusing every commitment in the name of the everlasting instability of moods or in the form of a formalistic rationalism binding and justifying the fulfillment of a commitment not according to the reality of those with whom it has been made but only according to the constancy of reason (or, as Marcel says, to the soul's glory with itself), the twofold mystification of relations with others cannot be upheld without refusing that original intersubjectivity of which our being consists. Creative fidelity is the ontological statute of our intersubjectivity, and its nature of free act exposes it to the temptations and to the threats of escape and illusion, which constitute the stable texture of a world, like ours, ruled by the categories of having. To refuse this fidelity is to refuse ourselves, that is, the most original structure and meaning of our existence. Yet to recognize it and to carry it out means to acknowledge and to accept all that is implied in it and without which it would be contradictory, namely, according to Marcel's analysis, the premise of an absolute person, without which a commitment is too unstably based to qualify as real commitment.[106]

All considered, this as well as other practical and theoretical procedures of the ontological mystery proposed by Marcel, particularly the phenomenology of hope,[107] establish an analogical reasoning for the participating intuition of being as intersubjectivity, as the original We, and this reasoning repeats in an existential context the classical method of the "proof" of transcendent truths. The creative reciprocity in which the subjective relation is placed—with all the limits of the basic precariousness of the human condition—is neither possible nor understandable outside of its intrinsic reference to an absolute creative reciprocity that can be grasped in the appeal to the absolute Thou. This is, as I have said elsewhere,[108] an "analogy of presence," where the acknowledgment of the transcendent reality is enlightened by the concreteness of the existential method in which the ontological quest expresses itself most authentically. This quest coincides with the infinite appeal of hope or with the appeal to Him who warrants and upholds our commitment to others, renewing us in love's creativity, which is the deep essence of our interpersonal being. Thus an analogical relation of presence is established between the divine Thou and the We, where the Thou is a Presence in which are, and in which are of value, all other presences that make us be and that make us be of value. *Regnum Dei intra vos est*. The eschatological world, which is the ultimate meaning of existence, is already here and now in every genuine action of our deep community.

I do not believe that it is possible to propose again, in this respect, the well-known fallacies of theological rationalism or of metaphysical ontologism. The thing that distinguishes these procedures from the classical proofs of God's existence or of the soul's immortality, regardless of the likeness of the logical structures, is the fact that rationalism and metaphysical ontologism are essentially practical and theoretical; they would be not only unconvincing but incomprehensible in relation to the kind of praxis and of rational behavior represented by second-degree reflection. Nevertheless, this way of philosophizing is quite different from the sort of intuition described by a kind of bad intellectualism (which is an attitude more or less evident in various forms of ontologism) as if this intuition were the vision of an object placed before us, *facie ad faciem,* in an immediate obviousness. Both the rationalist and the intuitionist approaches are perspectives of intellectualist objectivism. A dialectics freed of both, having gone beyond the objective level, can offer itself only as the concrete circulation of invocation and presence and therefore as a true presential inference in the participational act at the center of the mystery discussed deeply in Pascal's *Memorial,* that is, the mystery of the *Deus praesens et absconditus* Who surrounds and pervades us, more ours than ourselves, as we search after having found Him already.

This point of view may perhaps clarify the great contemporary *querelle,* in the semantics of religious language, about the meaningfulness or "connotation" of God's name—a question proposing again, from certain points of view, the old theological debate on God's attributes.[109] I have already observed that the most peculiar mark of contemporary atheism, at least in its most critically conscious forms, is its "semantic atheism," that is, the conviction that it is impossible to attribute a meaning to the word *God* in the context of standards ruling every giving of meaning in a proper use of language.[110] One of the "Death of God" theologians, Paul Van Buren, remarks graphically that "today we cannot even understand Nietzsche's cry that 'God is dead'. . . . The problem is that for us even the word 'God' is dead."[111] And surely the matter would take us far, if we were to go into it deeply. It will suffice for now to say that it is present *ante litteram* in Marcel's work, where he criticizes with great energy the very conception of "divine attribute" and, in a general way, every attempt at "divine" psychology.[112]

> I have always thought that God's attributes, as defined by rational theology— simplicity, unchangeability, and so on—are not of value for us if we do not recognize in them the marks of a *Thou* that we cannot treat as *He* without reducing it to our human and laughable misery. "When we talk about God, it is not God we are talking about," I wrote not so long ago. It will never be said often enough that there is a trap in the theological assertion as such, because those *marks* I have now conjured, if they are borrowed as predicates, turn out to be the poorest of all; if we consider them as contents of knowledge, we must agree that they are, in a way, poorer than those we bestow on the humblest and most ephemeral creature in the world we live in.[113]

The strict dialectics of pure transcendence that Marcel began in the first pages of his *Journal* are forsaken in the later developments of his research. Nonetheless, the deepest reasons of negative theology—at least of the one constituting, as in Neoplatonism, the logical basis of the mystical experience—are also recognized in the new perspective of a "loving knowledge" at the basis of the ontological quest. The absolute Thou cannot be characterized for the same reasons, and *a fortiori,* that every "you" of our participative experience cannot be characterized or reduced to a catalog of registry office data. The impossibility of describing God is the same, analogically, as the impossibility of describing "you," the other, a person as such, that is, the other person as a freedom meeting my freedom. Hence we must acknowledge that the semantics of theological language is founded after all on the much more original semantics of the invocatory language, or "dyadic" language, as Royce would say. Many of the modern analysts of religious language who denounce its alleged senselessness do not take into account the twofold shape it can take: the one I would call "direct" or "primary" speech and the other "indirect" or "secondary" speech. Believers—either expressing immediately a personal experience or participating in the "creed" of a common faith—talk *to* God, or testify their belief to others, before they can talk *about* God. There is a "holy speech" and a "speech on holiness"; the first appeals and testifies (to talk to God or to state God's word), whereas the second constitutes theology and religious science in general. The logical structures that no language can do without are certainly different in the two kinds of religious speech, but the mistake analysts make is to claim that the second, the theoretical speech, can be isolated from the first and that it must draw its meaning from something other than the direct religious experience that expresses itself in it. Perhaps in this instance the doctrine of ontological mystery makes one of the most appreciable contributions to the problem of contemporary thinking. The ontological question is the universal structure of the religious appeal and the basis of the critical mediation of the two modes of religious speech as the criterion of what is truly religious—that is, of what is not idolatry or "inverted anthropologism"—and of the hermeneutical categories that transcribe religious speech in theological language. This ontological question is the point where true universality, or the ecumenicity of the religious experience, is instituted as (according to Jacobi's beautiful imagery) the center where all the beams of deep thought converge.

We might ask ourselves whether the ontological question, to the extent that it becomes radicalized, quite apart from its empirical contents, in the presence of an absolutely noncharacterizable Thou, does not in the end succumb to the impossibility of being confirmed or contradicted by experience. Are not these "metaproblematical" assertions of Marcel's metaphysics directly affected by what modern analysts of religious language call "Flew's challenge" of the impossibility of falsifying religious and metaphysical propositions?[114] In truth all of Marcel's work has been inspired by a critical need to denounce the scientistic misunderstanding of positions like Flew's that stems from unduly extending the standard of the debatableness of empirical scientific propositions to religious and metaphysical assertions.[115] The practical theoretical nature of these assertions assures that they can be neither contradicted nor confirmed within the realm of empirical contents observable by science; indeed, they can only be confirmed by the deliverance of existence from its alienating condition. Love as creative reciprocity is this deliverance. Face to face with it, and only face to face with it, God's name has a meaning. If God did not exist, no love act could be possible. The ontological mystery is understandable and confirmable because being, referring to it, heals the wounds of experience that would otherwise remain open. Outside this reference nothing can prevent our world from appearing and being a "hopeless hell." Thus Marcel's philosophy—which has gradually developed a true "methodology of the unverifiable" that carries to its extreme the differences between scientific procedures and the procedures of metaphysical thought—has in fact opened the way to a final clarification of "verification" or "proof" in relation to the truths that give meaning to existence.

PIETRO PRINI

INSTITUTE OF PHILOSOPHY
UNIVERSITY OF ROME
NOVEMBER 1969

NOTES

1. Pietro Prini, *Gabriel Marcel e la metodologia dell'inverificabile* (Rome: Studium, 1950; 2d ed., 1968), p. 9. All translations of Marcel's work are by the author.

2. Ibid., p. 7.

3. Gabriel Marcel, *Journal métaphysique* (Paris: Gallimard, 1927), p. 200 (hereafter cited as *JM*).

4. Gabriel Marcel, *Homo Viator* (Paris: Aubier, 1945), p. 191 (hereafter cited as *HV*).

5. See Léon Brunschvicg, *L'Idéalisme contemporain* (Paris: Alcan, 1905), pp. 39, 98ff., 167ff.

6. On the problems of "validity" and of the sphere of competence of scien-

tific propositions, see Karl Popper, *Logik der Forschung: Zur Erkenntnistheorie der moderne Naturwissenschaften* (Vienna: Verlag von Julius Springer, 1935), pp. 4ff.

7. *HV*, 192.   8. *JM*, 34.
9. *JM*, 32, 36, 87, 97.   10. *JM*, 15–26.
11. *JM*, 29, 48–49, 53–58.
12. Gabriel Marcel, *Du refus à l'invocation* (Paris: Gallimard, 1940), p. 11 (hereafter cited as *DR*). In the abundant literature on the principle of verification, see essays on "La Notion de vérification," *Revue internationale de philosophie,* 1951, pp. 241–389, contributed by R. Chisholm, G. Ryle, H. Feigl, A. Pap, G. I. Warnock, V. F. Lenzen, T. Czezowski, R. Aron, and I. M. Faverge. See also Ernst Nagel, "Verifiability, Truth and Verification," *Journal of Philosophy* 31 (1934); Wolfgang Stegmueller, *Das Wahrheitsproblem und die Idee der Semantik* (Vienna: Springer Verlag, 1957); and Ch. Perelman and Phil. Devaux, "Dimostrazione, verificazione, giustificazione," *La cultura,* 1968, pp. 1–24.
13. *JM*, 302–3.
14. *DR*, 113.
15. Søren Kierkegaard, *Crainte et tremblement* (Paris: Alcan, 1932), p. 126.
16. Marcel himself states his early ignorance of Kierkegaard; see "Regard en arrière," in *Existentialisme chrétien: Gabriel Marcel,* by Jeanne Delhomme, Roger Troisfontaines, Pierre Colin, J. P. Dubois-Dumée, and Gabriel Marcel (Paris: Plon, Présences, 1947), p. 310. Regarding points of contact between Marcel and Kierkegaard, see Jean Wahl, *Vers le concret* (Paris: Vrin, 1932), p. 255 (footnote); and Paul Ricoeur, *Gabriel Marcel et Karl Jaspers: Philosophie du mystère et philosophie du paradoxe* (Paris: Editions du temps présent, 1948), pp. 116ff., 130.
17. *JM*, 41.
18. *JM*, 86.
19. *JM*, 259.
20. Gabriel Marcel, *Etre et avoir* (Paris: Aubier, 1935), pp. 59, 60 (hereafter cited as *EA*).
21. *JM*, 39.   22. *EA*, 63.
23. *JM*, 97; see also *JM*, x.   24. *JM*, 53.
25. Ludwig Wittgenstein, *Tractatus Logico-Philosophicus* (London: Kegan Paul, Trench, Trubner and Co., 1922), proposition 5.632.
26. *EA*, 9.   27. *DR*, 25.
28. *DR*, 25; *EA*, 11.   29. *JM*, 273, 261.
30. *DR*, 33.
31. *JM*, 265.
32. *JM*, 328.
33. See Louis Lavelle, *Le Moi et son destin* (Paris: Aubier, 1936), pp. 62ff.
34. See *JM*, 266.
35. See *DR*, 21.
36. See Jean Wahl, *Vers le concret,* pp. 3, 13, 23. Regarding the influence of American philosophy on the formation of Marcel's thought, see Gabriel Marcel, *La Dignité humaine et ses assises existentielles* (Paris: Aubier, 1964), pp. 14ff.
37. *JM*, 278.
38. *JM*, 130.

39. Paul Ricoeur, *Philosophie de la volonté*, 2 vols. (Paris: Aubier, 1949), 1:14.

40. *DR*, 20.

41. *JM*, 253.

42. *JM*, 273.

43. For a different approach to the problem of bodily self-awareness (or of "one's own body") and objectification, see Pietro Prini, *Verso una nuova ontologia* (Rome: Studium, 1957), pp. 9ff. and attached bibliography; idem, *Discorso e situazione* (Rome: Studium, 1961), pp. 11–18. For the dissociation between reality and objectivity in the realm of the physical sciences, see Robert Blanché, *La Science physique et la réalité* (Paris: Presses universitaires de France, 1948), pp. 40ff.

44. For an explanation of the theory of belief, see David Hume, *A Treatise of Human Nature* (1886; reprint ed., Aalen: Scientia Verlag, 1964), pp. 394–99, 406–22; and Antony Flew, *Hume's Philosophy of Belief* (London: Routledge & Kegan Paul, 1961).

45. *EA*, 12.

46. For this kind of definition, see Prini, *Discorso*, pp. 19–36.

47. See Prini, *Gabriel Marcel*, pp. 100–129.

48. *JM*, 157ff. 49. *JM*, 65.

50. *JM*, 63. 51. *EA*, 154.

52. See *EA*, 150ff. 53. *EA*, 155; *DR*, 99.

54. Karl Jaspers, *Philosophie*, 3 vols. (Berlin: Verlag von Julius Springer, 1932) 2:58.

55. *HV*, 27–28; *EA*, 151.

56. *HV*, 18, 66.

57. *HV*, 66–67.

58. Gabriel Marcel, *Présence et immortalité* (Paris: Flammarion, 1959), p. 50 (hereafter cited as *PI*).

59. *PI*, 159.

60. *PI*, 22.

61. *PI*, 159.

62. See Max Scheler, *Der Formalismus in der Ethik und die materiale Wertethik*, 3d ed. (Bern: Francke, 1954), pp. 416ff.; Maurice Merleau-Ponty, *Phénoménologie de la perception* (Paris: Gallimard, 1945), pp. 215ff.; and Prini, *Discorso*, pp. 22ff.

63. *EA*, 235, 240.

64. Gabriel Marcel, *Les Hommes contre l'humain* (Paris: La Colombe, 1951), p. 7.

65. *EA*, 35.

66. *EA*, 26.

67. *EA*, 138.

68. Gabriel Marcel, *Position et approches concrètes du mystère ontologique* (Louvain: Nauwelaerts; Paris: Vrin, 1949), p. 258 (hereafter cited as *PA*).

69. *JM*, 312.

70. *EA*, 194, n. 1; *DR*, 89, 217; *HV*, 21–22; Gabriel Marcel, *Le Mystère de l'être*, 2 vols. (Paris: Aubier, 1951), 2:120 (hereafter cited as *ME*).

71. R. M. Hare, "Theology and Falsification," in *New Essays in Philosophical Theology*, ed. Antony Flew and Alasdair MacIntyre, 5th ed. (London: SCM Press, 1966), pp. 99–103.

72. The certainty founded on Aristotelian or Cartesian evidence may, by contrast, be called a fact.

73. *EA*, 138.

74. *EA*, 123; *DR*, 213.

75. *EA*, 123; see also Paul Ricoeur, *Gabriel Marcel et Karl Jaspers: Philosophie du mystère et philosophie du paradoxe* (Paris: Editions du temps présent, 1947), p. 129.

76. Marcel explicitly states this analogy in the opening of his essay "Don et liberté," *Giornale di metafisica*, November 1947, p. 485 (hereafter cited as "DL").

77. *DR*, 40.

78. *DR*, 41ff., 76ff.; *HV*, 203; "DL," 487ff.

79. "DL," 491.

80. *DR*, 68.

81. See *EA*, 188–92, 252ff.; *DR*, 64–65; *PA*, 292–97.

82. "DL," 487.

83. *DR*, 73.

84. See *EA*, 165.

85. "DL," 494.

86. See Prini, *Gabriel Marcel*, pp. 91ff.

87. *ME* 2:187.

88. I have pointed out this distinction in many of my writings; see, for example, Prini, *Gabriel Marcel*, pp. 53–69.

89. Jacobi's words about this interesting subject are deeply clear. See F. H. Jacobi, *Über die Lehre des Spinoza Briefen an den Hevin Moses Mendelssohn* (Löwe: Breslavia, 1789), p. 220.

90. *EA*, 170.   91. *EA*, 145.

92. *EA*, 250.   93. *EA*, 180–81.

94. *DR*, 92.   95. *EA*, 175.

96. *EA*, 142.   97. *EA*, 170.

98. *ME* 1:138.   99. *ME* 2:43.

100. *ME* 1:142.

101. Prini, *Gabriel Marcel*, pp. 145–46.

102. *ME* 1:208.   103. *ME* 1:209.

104. *ME* 1:5.   105. *HV*, 81.

106. *EA*, 139.

107. See Prini, "Filosofia della speranza," in *Discorso*, pp. 134–50.

108. See Prini, *Gabriel Marcel*, pp. 136ff. Also see Marcel's statement in the preface: "The expression you used in the conclusion—'analogy of presence'—seems very apt to me, and I do not hesitate to adopt it. It is certain that I have gradually and progressively oriented myself toward a conception that may well, in fact, come to coincide with Plato's speculation in at least one of its perspectives, namely, that essences are to be considered not so much illuminated objects but rather illuminating presences. I am fully aware, however, of the very serious difficulties that may be encountered in this sort of approach" (pp. 7–8).

109. See ibid., pp. 110–111.

110. See Prini, *Verso*, p. 31; idem, *Discorso*, pp. 99–105.

111. Paul M. Van Buren, *The Secular Meaning of the Gospel* (London: Collier-Macmillan, 1963), pp. xiii, 3, 13ff., 81–106.

112. *EA,* 197, 207–8, 247–48.

113. *DR,* 54–55.

114. "What should happen . . . so that we may say that 'God does not love us' or that 'God does not exist'?" (Antony Flew, "Theology and Falsification," in *New Essays,* p. 99).

115. Regarding this extension, see Karl Popper, "The Demarcation between Science and Metaphysics," in *Conjectures and Refutations* (London: Routledge & Kegan Paul, 1965), pp. 255ff.

A Methodology of the Unverifiable

REPLY TO PIETRO PRINI

It seems to me that I would express myself much less categorically today on the mystery of being than I did in the first part of the *Journal métaphysique*. In reality, I adhered at that time to something reminiscent of what my friend Du Bos noticed in Plotinus: "the flight from the alone to the Alone."* But today, after all the inner changes I have gone through before and since the Second World War, I would be inclined to impute much more importance to what I would call a "concrete We," which could be, for example, the "religious We." When writing the *Journal métaphysique,* I was not aware of this We. I am now not sure that it is possible, in attempting to think concretely of God, to exclude it.

In rereading these already dated texts, I have the feeling that I was nonetheless still dominated at that time by the spirit of abstraction I have never ceased fighting since then, and indeed even then I was tempted to recognize the limits of idealism. All the same, it was as an idealist that I was speaking.

Half a century ago, I was very far from anticipating the phenomenon of pollution, which has, in the space of several years, become so widespread and which numerous nations are going to be forced to combat at the cost of tremendous financial sacrifice. I observe that by a certain abstract way of considering nature as consisting, above all else, of a set of technical possibilities, humanity has become involved in a perhaps catastrophic adventure.

As I had occasion to write in an article in the *Tribuna medica* of Madrid, pollution is seen on reflection as the inevitable and materialized consequence of a specifically metaphysical error. It cannot be merely by

---

Translated from the French by Susan Gruenheck.
*Quotation in English in the original.—TRANS.

chance that we are watching nature become disfigured before our eyes. There is something lacking here that has become, in a few short years, clearly apparent, but we are still far from realizing the means necessary to avoid this slump into which we have allowed ourselves to slide in the process of pretending to conquer nature. Are we not forced to recognize, in short, that the very idea of the conquest of nature implies a fundamental alteration of the relationship between human beings and the world around us? This is one of the points on which I think I am most in agreement with the author of *Sein und Zeit*. Heidegger deserves great credit for having clarified and examined in depth the content of the very notion of human dwelling. But what is striking is that, contrary to what I might have thought at the beginning of my philosophical career, we are in the presence here of a genuine *Feststellung*.

I confess that these passages on the act of despairing (which it is perhaps advisable to distinguish from despair as a state of being) leave me quite uncertain. In truth, I am not sure that we can speak of a refusal in this instance. Let us speak quite concretely. I am thinking of a man who is reduced to despair by an accident in which his loved ones were victims and that he alone survived. We find this person reduced to despair. Can we speak of a refusal here? I think not, and I wonder, moreover, despite certain imprudent statements, whether I have ever asserted it.

I would say that this despairing person finds himself placed by circumstances in what we might call a feeling of impossibility. We could say that it is as if it were no longer possible for him to participate in a certain game governed by rules of which we are not usually conscious. Indeed, in the case of the despairing person, it is as if these more or less implicit rules no longer existed. But then the game, so to speak, no longer makes any sense. Its conditions are canceled. Henceforth, the entire question will be to find out whether, within the framework of what we might call a "qualitative intersubjectivity," it will be possible for anyone to help this despairing person, that is, to get him moving again so that he does not become immobilized by the petrifying consciousness of disaster.

Thus, through his loved ones, through those whom he loves more than himself, he has become a victim. We should not hesitate to acknowledge that in the face of such a situation, our available resources seem absurd. Anything resembling rhetoric, including traditional consoling words, must be regarded as an insult—I would almost be tempted to say a sacrilege. We realize first of all that we must clearly show the despairing person, by the way in which we act toward him, that he is not alone and that others are in communion with him.

But how could he not be tempted to reply that this communion is reduced to a good intention, since others, whatever their good will, cannot put themselves in his place and since his disaster can in no way be theirs.

I can certainly say that since my work during the First World War, tragedy has never ceased to haunt me. I have always come to the same conclusion: the only answer (I dare not use the word *solution,* for this word seems improper) consists in persuading the despairing person that the abyss-situation before which he is placed is not final and that there is a dimension of the real in which the nature of that situation is changed. Here it is advisable to refer him to Swedenborg or to Schelling's *Clara,* which he has surely read, and not to the priest who is inured and cannot rid himself of the ready-made phrases in which he usually takes refuge. I am aware of what proponents of a certain religious purism will be tempted to think in view of such considerations, but I confess that such purism has always worried, if not revolted, me because it operates in an area of abstraction and to that extent fails to understand the intolerable wound that an accident, or anything in the order of an accident, cannot fail to inflict on a creature made the way we are.

Professor Prini has perfectly understood and rendered my idea of freedom, of what it is to be free for a creature like me, but I do not think that we can identify this freedom with secondary reflection. I would rather say that secondary reflection allows us to think of freedom in these terms and consequently to release ourselves from the trap laid for us by the traditional conception of causality and by determinism as it was conceived of up to the beginning of this century.

G.M.

EDITOR'S NOTE: Somewhat later (21 November 1969) Marcel wrote a follow-up letter to Professor Prini, the content of which certainly constitutes an important part of Marcel's reply to Professor Prini. It follows here:

My dear friend:

Several days ago I received the English translation of your essay, which is well typed and as readable as possible. At times I referred to the Italian text and the translation seems to be good. However, I would point out that it seems awkward to translate *Passivité* as "suffering." But, after all, it is not very serious. What is more important is this: on [manuscript] page 42 of the English translation, I read: "It is a sort of new blink or interior light, appearing within me when I open up to the presence which reveals to me that "*I am not part of myself.*" The Italian text reads (p. 42): "Si tratta come di uno guardo nuovo o di un'inhuminazione interiore ohe si opera in me, quando mi apro alla presenza che mi rivela che *non sono parte di me stesso.*" But the footnote [n. 84] refers to page 165 of *Etre et avoir,* where I did not find the sentence

"*I am not a part of myself,*" which hardly makes sense to me. On the contrary, I adhere to the expression on p. 166 at the end of the entry of February 21: "The more I am able to conceptualize my being, the less it seems to me to arise from its own jurisdiction." But perhaps I truly did write the sentence in question, although it would surprise me if I had. By the way, it is only out of a simple concern for accuracy that I have written this to you, since you have understood my thought perfectly.*

If I were able—unfortunately I am tired and this kind of work has become very difficult for me—I would return to the notion of "blind intuition" and would call into question the value of the term *reflexive intuition,* which seems decidedly awkward to me. I would again take up the investigation concerning affirmation: I affirm something because it is, and this only means that affirmation refers to what appears as a pure given, that is, something that does not itself arise from an expressible or merely thinkable affirmation. But doesn't this simply mean that the given that is thought in this way is structurally part of the affirmation itself? In other words, not only does the given solicit the affirmation, but it also claims its independence in relation to the affirmation.

In any case, once again I send you my warmest congratulations for the magnificent work you have done. Surely no one has penetrated more deeply into my thinking.

One further question: what exactly do you mean by "blink philosophy"?†

To you very friendly greetings and my regards to Mrs. Prini.

G. Marcel

---

*The end of the "Note on Having" reads: "Il y a donc un sens où je ne m'appartiens pas, le sens précisément où je ne suis absolument pas autonome" (*EA,* 168). In English, the verb *appartenir* can be translated both as "to belong" and "to be a part of." Obviously, this line should have been translated: "There is therefore a sense in which I do not belong to myself, precisely the sense in which I am not absolutely autonomous." Perhaps there is a mistranslation in the Italian version as well. It is therefore quite understandable that M. Marcel did not recognize the phrase "I am not a part of myself" as his own.—TRANS.

†M. Marcel's copy of Professor Prini's manuscript read "blink philosophy," but it should have read "*blik* philosophy." Prini's point of departure was Professor R. N. Hare's example of *blik* as an attitude or a way of looking at things. See note 71 and the related discussion in Prini's paper.—ED.

8

Gene Reeves

THE IDEA OF MYSTERY IN THE PHILOSOPHY OF GABRIEL MARCEL

IN an important sense, all of Gabriel Marcel's philosophizing moves around a central concern and conviction. To describe his philosophy as simply and directly as possible, one needs a term that is potentially broad enough to encompass the scope of his research but that is not readily identifiable with any of the particular concepts Marcel uses to approach this center. The term I will adopt for this purpose is *personal experience*. Marcel's philosophy is a largely uncoordinated variety of efforts to explore, understand, and elucidate the reality of personal experience.

This exploration proceeds between two poles (or perhaps zones). One of the poles is the purely subjective; the other is the purely objective. Personal experience, then, is intermediary between pure objectivity and pure subjectivity.

The subjective pole figures less prominently in Marcel's writings than either the center or the objective pole, and when it is brought into the discussion it is almost always called subjectivity. Both the center and the objective pole, however, are discussed throughout Marcel's writings and appear under a wide variety of descriptive terms, giving to much of his thought an appearance of dualism, or at least of duality. Some of the more prominent of these terms are:

mystery	*problem*
metaproblematic	*problematic*
unverifiable	*verifiable*
existence	*objectivity*
faith	*opinion*
participation	*detachment*
invocation	*refusal*

concrete	abstract
intersubjective	objective
I-Thou	I-him
being	having

Thus in a sense Marcel's philosophy can be viewed as an exploration and elucidation of two fundamentally different modes, or ways, of being. But although the subjective pole is less prominent, it should not be forgotten, for only in the context of the triadic possibility does the idea of the mystery of personal experience *as central* to being become apparent.

Intimately related to this central idea (the one grows out of the other) is a central conviction: personal experience cannot be adequately accounted for either in the mode of subjectivity (as in idealistic philosophies) or in the mode of objectivity (as in materialistic philosophies). That the subjective pole receives decreasing attention in Marcel's writings reflects the fact that during his lifetime idealistic philosophies became less and less culturally significant and the claims of objectivist or empirical modes of thought more and more blatant. To say that Marcel's philosophy is often negative is to say that much of the time he is concerned to show what personal experience is not and cannot be conceived to be. That is, personal experience is neither merely subjective nor objectively impersonal, and only by a kind of self-betrayal can a person claim that it is either. But Marcel's philosophical efforts are by no means exclusively negative; he also seeks to show, or at least to point toward, what personal experience is and involves positively.

Together Marcel's central idea and central conviction control his metaphysics, his epistemology, and his methodology. Methodologically they mean that if philosophy is appropriate to its central subject matter—to personal experience and especially to the personal experience of the philosopher himself—then it cannot be either rigorously objective, rigorously analytical, or even systematic, nor can it be limited to an elucidation of the philosopher's subjective impressions and feelings. Philosophy itself must be personal. Epistemologically they mean that knowledge, or at least knowledge that counts, cannot be conceived of as either objectively given or as the projection of subjective egos. Knowledge is personal. Ontologically they mean that reality cannot be conceived of or experienced as either a collection of objects or as something purely ideal. Reality too is profoundly personal.

In one sense the idea of mystery, or at least the term *mystery,* is simply one of several inadequate ways to point toward the character and fundamental reality of personal experience. It is not especially more or less important than several other ideas and terms that serve the same purpose.

In another sense all of Marcel's philosophical research attempts to penetrate and evoke mystery. In this sense there is no idea of mystery *in* the philosophy of Marcel because his idea of mystery and his philosophy are the same. But mystery here is not an idea—that is, an abstraction—so much as it is the central character and being of the concrete experiences Marcel seeks to explore.

If Marcel is to be understood at all, one must realize that to write about "the idea of mystery" is to adopt an emphatically non-Marcellian style of philosophy. By engaging myself in the task of writing about "the idea of mystery in the philosophy of Gabriel Marcel," I am forced to confront a problem: if I abstract the idea of mystery from Marcel's own explorations of concrete experiences, can I be faithful to the philosophy I am attempting to explicate? In any case, the alternatives are either to reproduce nearly the entire body of Marcel's writings or to explore the concrete reality of personal experience myself. The former is obviously impossible, and the latter could provide no assurance that I would be engaging Marcel's philosophy. So I am forced back to the task of treating mystery as an idea belonging to Marcel. And this is not so bad, so long as I am clear about what I am doing. With Whitehead I would argue that abstracting is both necessary and good but that the spirit of abstraction becomes perverted when the abstract and the concrete are confused and the abstract made to appear more real and more valuable than the concrete. Marcel seeks to avoid what Whitehead called "the fallacy of misplaced concreteness" by adopting a method of concrete approaches; I will attempt to avoid it by being self-conscious about the process of abstracting and aware of its limits.

The bulk of this paper, then, is a misrepresentation of mystery in Marcel's philosophy in order to say something about the mystery he has found in personal experience. Finally, having indulged in the spirit of abstraction to that extent, I will plunge further and speculate about what reality lies behind Marcel's philosophy. There is, I will claim, a point of identity between the divine and the human. In one sense this will raise the discussion to an even more abstract level; in another it will seek to penetrate more deeply, from another angle, the mystery of being—a mystery that is after all neither Marcel's nor mine but ours.

THE MYSTERY OF KNOWLEDGE AND FAITH

The Unverifiable

"What," asks Marcel in the 1950 preface to the English translation of his *Journal métaphysique,* "is the unverifiable of which so much is said in the first part of the *Journal,* if not mystery itself?"[1] Thus Marcel's idea of mystery must be understood, initially at least, in the context of his early struggles to find a conceptual pathway between purely objective and purely subjective modes of knowing.

Objective knowledge for Marcel is simply the kind of knowledge one can have of physical objects—the kind of knowledge enjoyed by the sciences. In his early works it is frequently called "verifiable" knowledge: knowledge involving a set of general conditions under which anyone can make valid judgments. It is a kind of knowledge involving the depersonalization of the subject and the supposition that one subject is as good as any other, that is, that subject A can be effectively substituted for subject B, and so on.[2]

Early in the *Journal* Marcel sketches a dialectic from the empirical I (*sentio*) to the thinking I (*cogito*) to the believing I (*credo*) in an attempt to establish the reality of unverifiable thought and belief and the heart of his epistemology. Since we can think about the empirical self, there is an apparent dualism between the empirical self and thought. But we know, says Marcel, that it cannot be an absolute dualism, for this would lead to an impossible dilemma: either there are two separate realities that, if they are real, must have something in common and hence must be part of a larger intelligible whole, or else we have to posit one of them as a mere negation. This dilemma leads us to the inescapable conclusion, Marcel claims, that the relation between the two must be thought of as nonobjective and unverifiable. We can only think of their unity as "a function of the freedom that wills it," that is, as something capable of appearing real and nonarbitrary only for the mind that has transcended itself by transcending the apparent dualism.[3]

The necessity of postulating this unverifiable relation between the empirical self and the *cogito* raises at least the possibility of there being another unverifiable relation between the *cogito* and faith. In a sense it is by overcoming the apparent dualism of the empirical self and the *cogito* that thought discovers the bond between the thinking self and the believing self, between thought and faith. The whole person can be neither a completely indeterminate "I think" nor a purely determined empirical datum, neither pure free act nor pure determinate object. Yet thought itself seems incapable of penetrating beyond these alternatives, which are unacceptable to thought itself. The unification of the self, then, depends on thought's transcending or going beyond itself as mere thought. Reflecting on its own discovered limits and seeking to understand the personal subject, thought has to postulate a second act of freedom. Belief or faith appears as the act by which the mind fills the gap between the thinking self and the believing

self and establishes itself as a person by affirming their transcendent connection.[4]

In this context Marcel has written of the "massive assurance" that
certain of the highest human experiences, like faith, imply something that
goes beyond all possible verification but that is nevertheless real.[5] All of
Marcel's probing of personal experiences, especially those involving encounter, presence, creativity, love, fidelity, and hope, has as its fundamental purpose to show that all truly personal experience includes nonobjective, nonverifiable, and nonillusory knowledge.

Mystery and Truth

After the *Journal* an important change in vocabulary and emphasis occurred in Marcel's writings with respect to the relation of mystery and
truth. In the *Journal* the word *truth* was used to refer to the objective
knowledge of what is in space and time. Thus affirmations of faith, including affirmations of the reality of God, could not at this stage of Marcel's
thought be said to be true. But a few years later, writing the beginning of
Etre et avoir, he saw that he could no longer accept the idea of a "beyond
the truth." Such a distinction or gap between truth and being "fills itself
up in some sense from the moment when the presence of God has been
really experienced, and it is partial truths, in the eyes of faith, which cease
to deserve the name."[6] And in *Homo Viator* Marcel makes a distinction
between truths and truth, that is, between particular truths and truth itself
(or, as he likes to put it, "the spirit of truth"). Here, though not explicitly,
it becomes possible to speak of the truth of faith.[7]

This new conception of the relation between truth and faith comes to
fruition in the conclusion of the Gifford Lectures:

> We must emphasize the intelligible aspect of faith . . . for there is a connec-
> tion which it is the philosopher's duty to underline with the utmost sharpness,
> the connection which binds faith and the spirit of truth. Whenever a gap be-
> gins to be created between these two, it is proof either that faith is tending to
> degenerate into idolatry or else that the spirit of truth is becoming arid and
> giving way to ratiocinative reason. . . . The spirit of truth is nothing if it is
> not a light seeking for the light; intelligibility is nothing if it is not at once an
> encounter and the nuptial joy which is inseparable from this encounter. The
> more I tend to raise myself towards this uncreated light, without which I
> would not see [*regard*]—which would mean that I would not be at all—the
> more I in some way advance in faith.[8]

In addition to this new emphasis on the truthfulness of faith, this unwillingness to restrict the notion of truth to what is objective and verifiable,
Marcel ceases to use the term *unverifiable* with regularity. But the kind of

reality (perhaps we can say semicognitive knowledge) that that word pointed to remains a central concern of his philosophy in later works. Thus at the heart of *Etre et avoir* is the distinction, often associated with Marcel's philosophy, between problem and mystery. A problem is something before us blocking our way, something that, in principle at least, can be solved by objective, detached, factual knowledge. A mystery, by contrast, is something in which we are personally engaged, where the distinction between "before us" and "in us" loses meaning. A mystery is something that cannot be solved; it can only be participated in.[9] Thus the reality once designated by the negative *unverifiable* is here more positively designated as *mystery*. And in later works the term *intersubjective reality* often plays a dominant role, explicitly replacing the term *unverifiable*.[10] This shift toward a more positive terminology is extremely important because what primarily distinguishes the mystery of personal experience from objectivity is not some lack or absence within personal experience but rather the positive presence of value. Whereas objective observers hold themselves aloof from value, personal experience always makes a difference to us. When Marcel begins to use the term *mystery* in the *Journal*, the emphasis on value experience is most apparent: "Only that which is capable of interesting me, of presenting a value for me, is mysterious."[11] Thus despite changes in terminology there remains throughout Marcel's work the central concern to establish the reality of a way of being toward others, a reality that is neither purely objective nor purely subjective but something in between—something he calls, in the introduction to *The Mystery of Being*, "intermediary thought."[12]

Faith

This intermediary thought, this kind of semicognitive relation that is neither objective and verifiable nor merely subjective, is called "faith" in religious language. If it is taken to be objective, then religion is reduced to a collection of rational affirmations valid for thought in general and bearing on distinct objects that can be empirically verified. Such a religion, claims Marcel, could be nothing more than an abstract deism, which an atheist could easily refute because its object is not in fact verified. The existence of God is not and cannot be subject to empirical tests. At the same time, if religious knowledge is taken to be merely subjective and religious claims regarded as entirely self-sufficient, faith is nothing more than a sentimental scaffolding, a completely subjective attitude on the part of the believer that is entirely without ontological significance.[13]

Faith, says Marcel, is an "absolute commitment, entered into by the whole self, or at least by something real in myself which could not be repudiated without repudiating the whole."[14] How can the *cogito* transcend itself and go beyond "I think" to "I believe"? It cannot do so by any logical necessity, for here we are in the realm of the nonobjective. Absolute commitment can only be an act that is freely entered into by the whole person. But this free act is not arbitrary like a hypothesis. On the contrary, precisely because it is the most free act, it is the most rooted in being. It is the act by which the self transcends the gaps between feeling, thought, and faith and creates itself as a concrete, active, and living reality and not merely as a thinking subject. That is, it is the act by which the self makes itself what, at a profound level, it already knows itself to be. Thus even though faith is not valid for thought in general, this "transcendent unity" of the self is capable of appearing, and in a sense must appear, as nonarbitrary and valid for the mind that has transcended itself.[15]

Yet despite the fact that faith may appear valid in this sense to the believing subject, it is never certitude. Because it is free, it must always contain an element of uncertainty: "it goes beyond what has been given to me, what I have experienced, it is an extrapolation, a leap, a bet which, like all bets, can be lost."[16]

And yet faith is never merely a free act. It is also a response to grace. All personal commitment involves personal response; it implies that we are grasped by something, that there is a certain "prise de l'être" on us.[17] Similarly, faith or absolute commitment is mysteriously both a free act and a response to divine grace. That is, faith without grace would be mere subjective affirmation, and that is precisely what faith, if it is real, cannot be.

Marcel comes close to subjectivism or fideism when he claims that faith is the act that posits transcendence; when he says that the object of affirmation, God, "is only the translation into the language of knowledge of the privileged act that is faith";[18] and when he says that the "act that thinks faith is also the act that postulates divine transcendence, if the former is abolished the latter could not subsist."[19] But in a sense this postulating of transcendence by faith gives faith a realistic element or reference beyond the subjective self: "As soon as faith ceases to appear to itself as absolutely bound to transcendence it denies itself as faith. Here there is a realistic aspect of faith which is important to underline."[20] To make divine transcendence depend in a subjective way on the act of faith would be to turn it into a sort of projection of the imagination; it would be to deny faith.[21] Thus although the reality of God is only, in a sense, for faith, it is independent of particular acts of faith. Faith must be thought of as "bound to a reality."[22]

Faith, Marcel thinks, can be distinguished from opinion in that the latter can only be formed at a psychological distance. Unlike belief, opinion does not involve personal participation. It implies an "*I maintain that*," which must be maintained against someone else. Thus it may be defined in a general way as "a *seeming which tends to become a claiming*." Thus atheism may usually be seen as a matter of opinion. "The atheist is nearly always someone who could express himself by saying: '*For my part I maintain that* God does not exist'." The atheist claims to have a collection of facts to support his position, but actually he has no experience that God does not exist, and he could not have such an experience. "But the atheist relies not on an experience but on an idea, or pseudo idea, of God: if God existed, He would have such and such characteristics; but if He had those characteristics He could not permit. . . ." The atheist claims that if God existed he could only be a being who was both completely good and completely powerful. But how can the atheist claim this? If we attempt to draw conclusions about divine behavior from historical instances of it, then *ipso facto* we have denied the claim of atheism. The atheist must maintain his position by putting himself in the place of God and relating how he would have behaved in particular circumstances; the absurdity of this is immediately apparent.[23]

Faith, so long as it does not falsify or deceive itself, is very different. Here Marcel makes use of Bergson's distinction between the closed and the open. Whereas opinion and conviction are essentially a closing, faith is "opening a credit"; it is a believing *in* something rather than a believing that. "If *I believe in,* it means that I make a fundamental commitment that affects not only *what I have* but also *what I am*." Put in other words, "*to believe* is essentially *to follow*" or "if I *believe in,* I *rally to*."[24]

If I am concerned to account for my faith or if I am forced to account for it, I may have to treat it as a conviction; I may have to say "I am convinced that God is real." But such statements must be seen as translations of faith into the language of conviction; behind the similarity the attitudes are quite different, the one closed and the other open.

Since faith can only appear valid for those who open themselves to it in a free act, it never appears valid for thought in general. General validity would imply a universal abstract subject and the ability to substitute one person for another. This is precisely what is not possible with faith because faith is an act of personal participation by a concrete person in which the believer is not distinct from that in which he or she participates. In true faith the act of faith and the object of faith cannot be disconnected. "The act by which I think faith must, therefore, be the act by which I deny this dissociation; but by which, in consequence, I also deny subjectivism as well as realism. . . . There is no internal distinction between them."[25] Faith "leads to the affirmation that it is itself conditioned by God."[26] Here the "non-identifiable" is apprehended or experienced as an undeniable *presence*. If I refuse to recognize this presence, I will cease to remain united with him at the level of existence. He will not be for me even though he may actually be for my neighbor who opens himself to him in faith.[27] Thus to open oneself to faith is to have one's very being define itself in mysterious communion with God.

Second Reflection

In a letter written in 1951, Marcel says:

> I cannot even understand how anyone, after reading me, can accuse me of fideism. It must be evident to all attentive readers that the philosophy which I advocate is a philosophy of reflection. Second reflection is more profoundly and more essentially reflection than is primary reflection. Certainly it appears to itself as *oriented towards* or, if you like, as inspired by something which transcends it and which it cannot have the pretention of comprehending but can only recognize.[28]

The trouble is that Marcel nowhere distinguishes between religious faith and the philosophical method of second reflection.

In his early works the term *reflection* was used very broadly to mean any act of thinking. Hence it was necessary to distinguish between acts of the *cogito* called "reflection" and acts of faith, which cannot be attributed to thought alone. But even in the *Journal* there is the idea that reflection can surpass itself without ceasing to be a kind of reflection. Reflection on faith, says Marcel, is capable of reflecting on itself and in this way makes clear to itself its own conditions and limitations. Such a reflection on itself transcends pure thought and negates or destroys itself as a pure act of thinking. But this reflection is not merely a negation. "Reflection is reborn from its own ashes," Marcel says, but it is reborn as faith rather than as thought, or, perhaps more accurately, as faith that includes thought. And this, it is strongly implied, is the "mode of thinking proper to philosophy."[29]

At this point Marcel does not call reflection on faith "reflection." That is, he seems to think that although reflection on reflection may suppress itself as reflection and thus transcend itself, it need not do so, and if it does it is no longer a kind of reflection but an act of belief or faith. He maintains a distinction between *cogito* and *credo* and uses the term *reflection* to refer to the former and the terms *belief* and *faith* to refer to the latter. But he wants to insist that faith need not be merely a blind leap in the dark, and so he calls it reflection negating itself, that is, reflection that is no longer reflection because by definition reflection is an act of thinking and faith an act of believing. Thus he can say that "the value and the supreme significance of religious affirmations reside precisely *in that they transcend all reflection.*"[30]

A term Marcel does sometimes use in the *Journal* for self-negating reflection is *intuitive thought*. Realizing that in talking about reflection on faith and reflection on reflection on faith he raises the possibility of an infinite regress, he seeks to indicate that in the final account faith and reflection on faith are somehow united. Intuitive thought reveals that the distinction between faith and reflection on faith is not finally valid, so that we end up not with the unthinkableness of faith but with the affirmation that if we really dissociate faith from thought about it, we are in an infinite regress that is as unacceptable to faith as it is to thought.[31]

In more recent works Marcel has dropped the term *intuitive thought* and developed the idea behind it into the notion of "second reflection." Ordinary reflection, reflection that is solely an act of thinking, is called "primary reflection," and the kind of reflection on reflection that negates itself and passes over into faith is called "second reflection." This change in terminology does not seem to indicate any basic change in Marcel's thinking.[32] What it does indicate is a change in emphasis. Now he thinks, perhaps as a result of being accused of fideism, that it is important to emphasize the intelligible side of faith, the connection between faith and truth. But he still does not want to make faith a mere act of intellect, and so he continues to insist that faith transcends reflection. Also, although he does not say so explicitly, he undoubtedly wants to allow for approaches to faith other than by second reflection, which is the philosophical approach.

Second reflection is, then, neither a purely intellectual analysis of experience nor a pure transcending of intellect but the kind of thought that negates itself as thought by becoming aware of its own ground and by thus passing over into faith. Therefore second reflection on experiences such as fidelity, love, and hope reveal the reality of God without in any way constituting an empirical proof of the existence of God. At its limit second reflection merges imperceptibly with faith so that the reality of God is actually revealed only to faith. As long as we remain on the level of objective thought in general, the reality of God remains hidden. But if through second reflection we penetrate further into the nature of personal experience, our thought becomes faith, and the reality of God is revealed.

Thus reflection now appears in Marcel's writings as a kind of preparation for and purification of faith. "At certain times," he says, "my own faith seems to be like a stranger: there is a gap between the believing or praying me and the reflecting me." But this gap is no mere accident; it seems to be "implied in what I am." And yet, "the more I consider it, the more I face it, the more I get beyond the opposition; it is as though a new type of unity arose between those two aspects of myself which at first seemed antagonistic." Although this unity is not a sort of Hegelian synthesis, it does make room for a "certain *modus vivendi* between the praying and reflecting me." Consequently, "far from rejecting reflection as one would a temptation, the believer must in some way undertake it." One's faith must be purified so that it can better resist the attacks of reflection, reflection thus "becoming the means, the stimulus which makes this purification possible." And to purify myself is, in the final analysis, to make myself "progressively more capable of giving out this radiance in my own turn."[33]

Thus second reflection in the complete sense is neither pure reflection nor faith but a kind of passageway between thought and faith. At one end second reflection is a kind of reflection (that is, a kind of thinking), but at the other end it merges into faith. When it reaches this latter stage, it has to deny the dualism that allows us to speak or think of it as having two ends at all. Therefore Marcel's second reflection refers to an act through which thought is transcended before the mystery of being without being annihilated.

THE MYSTERY OF BEING

Existence

In the second part of the *Journal* and in an essay later appended to it called "Existence et objectivité," Marcel begins to stress the primacy of being over knowledge, an important theme in his later works. There is a mystery within all cognition and faith because they presuppose a participation in being in which the apparent dualism of subject and object is overcome. Our existence is not primarily a matter of thought or consciousness but something immediately participated in through sensation. Indeed, in the second part of the *Journal* sensation in its unreflected, uninterpreted, lived state is the basic model for religious faith. The problem of sensation is actually "the mystery of feeling," for to feel is not merely to receive something but to experience a power of being, both in ourselves and in what is felt, through immediate participation.[34]

Similarly, my body is something indubitable, the basis for all personal experience, and this is so not merely in a biological or instrumental sense but in the sense that the world only exists for me because I have feelings and can act—and I can feel or act only with my body. Being with my body is my basic way of being with and for others. Thus "incarnation" is the central datum of metaphysical reflection, a fundamental given from which all thought must proceed.[35]

Whereas in the first part of the *Journal* existence is linked to objectivity and to exist is to be an object in space and time, in the second part existence is seen as fundamentally opposed to objectivity. Rather than a product of detached thought, our existence, like our bodies, is something initially and indubitably given. And for us existing things *are,* not through objective, detached, verifiable thought but through the same immediate participation by which we are with our bodies. To exist is to be with; to deeply experience the existence of something is to affirm the beings that we are and therefore to experience worth. Thus the more fully we open ourselves to the existence we are with, the more valuable, the more enriched, is our own existence. The affirmation of existence is, then, neither a matter of assigning a predicate to individual things nor an assertion about abstract existence in general. Fundamentally, existence is something that can only be felt and affirmed on a level where the affirmed and the affirmer are somehow together.

Perhaps because of the confusion inherent in the radically different uses of *existence* in the two parts of the *Journal,* Marcel seemed for a long time to abandon the attempt to refine and clarify the idea of existence and instead gradually replaced the mystery of existence with the mystery of being. In the second part of *The Mystery of Being,* however, he takes up, with considerable care, the relation of existence and being. Here existence is placed between and overlapping being a thing and authentic being.

> The idea of existence (if it is an idea) is itself deeply charged with ambiguity. . . . We are spontaneously led to treat existence as the fact that a thing is somewhere but could also be somewhere else or even nowhere at all, as though it were subject to every vicissitude, every displacement, every kind of destruction. But, if I concentrate my attention on this simple fact: I exist—or again: someone that I love exists, the perspective changes; to exist can no longer simply mean *to be there* or *to be elsewhere*—it can probably mean essentially to transcend the opposition of the here and the elsewhere. . . . Existence will appear at one limit as indistinguishable from authentic being.[36]

Thus at one end of its meaning, to exist is to be an object in space; at the other end, to exist is to participate in the mystery of being. Although there remains a sense of *being* that is not included in the meaning of *existence,* the more fully we can grasp our existence in all its reality, the closer we come to realizing our authentic being.

The Mystery of Being

Being, Marcel admits, cannot be defined or even characterized in any usual manner. To do so would be to treat being as something problematic and objectifiable, both of which it obviously is not. We can, he thinks, approach an understanding of what is meant by being if we think of it as what withstands, or would withstand, any and all attempts to analyze all experience into elements devoid of intrinsic value.[37] Being is that spiritual side of the human person that mysteriously eludes our attempts to understand it but that we know in experience is our reality.

"Ontological exigence" is the thirst for being, the existential need for what is sometimes called self-realization, or the demand to transcend the world of abstract objectivity. This exigence for being is not always experienced as such but may find expression in a variety of ways. Sometimes it is simply a deeply felt dissatisfaction with our present condition in the world; sometimes it is experienced as a need for spiritual adventure, as a need for artistic creativity and expression, or as the search for a vocation.[38] Ontological exigence is never a desire for some object. It is an inner need or urge that cannot be distinguished from an appeal; it is a demand arising within us that our lives find fulfillment.

To realize ontological need is at once to plunge into the realm of mystery. If I ask, "What is being?" I must also ask, "Who am I who questions being? Can I be certain that I am?" At this level the *cogito* cannot help me, for I am concerned with my being as a whole, with the living, feeling, willing, loving, praying, hoping, and so on, as well as thinking, person.[39]

Recognition of the mystery of being is bound up with personal involvement in being. "I" and "am" are not two distinct things that can be analyzed separately. I affirm being only as a living participant in being and only in an affirmation *"that I am rather than I utter,"* an affirmation where "I am, in a sense, passive, and *of which I am the seat rather than the subject."* The dualism of the self that affirms its own being and the being that is affirmed and underlies the affirmation is transcended.[40]

It is by exploring the reality of concrete experience, Marcel believes, that we can if not solve the problem of being, at least begin to penetrate to some degree the mystery of our being. The realm of objective thought, the realm of the problematic, is the realm of abstraction. It is only by abstracting from concrete, personal existence that thought becomes objectively valid. Conversely, the concrete is mysterious. It is "metaproblematic" in the sense that it is prior to or more basic than the abstractions that create problems. Thus a philosophy that would address itself to the mystery of being must approach that mystery through "concrete approaches."

Grace

Marcel has no explicit doctrine of revelation. Frequently he speaks of keeping his own philosophical investigations on "this side of revelation as such," and he never explains what "revelation as such" might be. If he uses the term *mystery* within his philosophy, he does not intend to confuse the mystery of being enveloped within human experience—in knowledge, faith, love, creativity, hope, and so on—with revealed mysteries such as Incarnation and Redemption, to which apparently no amount of second reflection can lead. He insists that a distinction between the natural and the supernatural be rigorously maintained.[41]

Without a discussion of this important theological topic by Marcel himself, we can only assume that, faithful to the tradition of the Roman Catholic Church, he recognizes that at least some important theological doctrines are revealed in some way not accounted for by his philosophy. Bearing in mind the fact that he repudiates the possibility of a natural theology in any traditional, intellectualistic sense, we might say that his efforts are in the direction of developing the philosophical side of traditional theology on a new philosophical base—an existential rather than a purely rational philosophical base.

If Marcel does not shed much light on what he means by "revelation as such," he nonetheless frequently makes use of the term *grace*. Sometimes he even uses the term *revelation* in a sense quite different from "revelation as such." The reason Marcel can legitimately use the term *mystery* in a sense distinct from revealed mysteries—and by implication also the terms *revelation* and *grace* in a sense distinct from "revelation as such"—is that any revelation is thinkable only to the degree that it is addressed to a being who is engaged, that is, who is participating in the mystery of being. To some extent Marcellian philosophy accounts for the reception side of revealed mysteries by asserting that supernatural life must find some "points of insertion" in natural life.[42]

Faith, as we have seen, is both a free act and a response to grace. Ultimately identifiable with salvation, it cannot come from the human side alone but is a gift of God involving "a mysterious and indivisible unity of freedom and grace."[43] Similarly, second reflection, the negation of thought toward faith, "seems to be possible only by the intervention of a transcendent power."[44] Thus illuminating grace is seen as the foundation of both faith and philosophy.

In the *Journal* Marcel develops a dialectic of faith, freedom, and love to bring out the relation of faith to human freedom. According to this dialectic, faith must involve a relation of freedom between God and the person of faith. We know that for faith God must be regarded as independent of the act of faith; faith cannot be a merely subjective affirmation and remain faith. At the same time, we know that faith can be refused or denied. There must then be a relation of freedom between the person of faith and God. But a relation of freedom, Marcel maintains (for reasons that are not clear), must be a relation of love. Therefore side by side with faith must be posited divine love, which is only another way of speaking of grace.[45] This does not mean, of course, that grace is somehow required or made necessary by any human act of faith. It is rather that when there is faith, there is divine grace; if they are real, the two cannot be separated.

In Marcel's view, when we are confronted with grace we can either refuse it or open ourselves to it. But even the act of opening oneself to grace is seen as conditioned or made possible by grace.

> To say that the act of faith is a free act is to put it ambiguously. . . . The truth is that it truly does depend on us to make an open place, that is, to rid ourselves of all the prejudices which bar the path to faith, or even to make ourselves available to grace. . . . But it must certainly be added that this reflection, which thus takes place before grace, implies, without doubt, something in its beginning which is of the same order as grace.[46]

One of the ways Marcel indicates the gap between grace and objective knowledge is by calling grace "unthinkable." "We cannot really think grace," he says, "or rather we can think it only as unthinkable."[47] "Grace remains the transcendent and nonobjectifiable postulate of the act of faith. . . . By the act of faith I posit between God and myself a relation which completely eludes the categories of my thought."[48] To think grace objectively, especially to think of it as a distinct mode of causality, is to deny it as grace.[49]

Thus the question of how we can regard grace as real does not legitimately arise. "Grace implies in every case the absolute irreducibility of the strictly religious mode of intelligibility. . . . To speak of reality in relation to grace is precisely to say nothing at all. . . . [F]or grace is situated beyond the categories of modality."[50] From this point of view, "grace is the absolute fact."[51]

Grace is often manifested as the miraculous. "The miracle," states Marcel, "must be defined . . . as a complex relation of a spiritual order

which is absolutely thinkable only in relation to faith.''[52] From the perspective of rational thought, the miraculous is impossible; from that of the
problematic, it is nonsense; from that of science, it is denied.[53] In all of
this the possibility of miracles is denied because impersonal thinking has
been detached from the mystery of being and substituted for faith, without
which there can be no miracles.

We can better understand grace, Marcel thinks, by meditating on generosity and light. He suggests that a fairly accurate definition of generosity
would be ''a light which would have joy in being light.''[54] The peculiar
property of light is that it illuminates—it is illuminating for others—and
thus goes beyond the usual philosophical distinction between ''for self''
and ''for others.'' Moreover, the term *light* has the advantage of helping
us to understand experiences as diverse as those of the artist, the hero, and
the saint. In each ''radiance'' is involved.[55] Light can be recognized only
by the mediation of whatever it illuminates; in itself it is blinding and
cannot be looked at directly. Similarly, generosity can be recognized only
through the gifts it lavishes. This is also the nature of the light that is
grace. Thus ''light as a physical agent helps us to think of generosity; but
in return as soon as we turn our attention to generosity in its essence, it
gives us access in some way to a metaphysical light which is indeed the
light of which St. John speaks, the light which illuminates every man who
comes into the world.''[56]

By becoming conscious of the light that is revelation, we can more
fully apprehend life, and especially our own lives, as a gift of grace. But
if the receiver is to be certain that the gift is truly a gift and not merely a
loan, it must come with some kind of formal assurance. Consequently a
word giving this assurance may appear as constitutive of the gift itself.
The only possible way a gift such as the gift of life can be guaranteed as
a gift is by revelation.[57] Revelation, then, may be dimly present even
where it is not recognized as such. It may appear, for example, as ''the
light of knowledge''[58] or as a characteristic of a masterpiece of art[59] or of
the ontological quest.[60]

Marcel brings together the three terms *gift, grace,* and *light* in a passage explaining that we must approach the affirmation ''I am,'' which is
the heart of the mystery of being, with humility, fear, and wonder:

> I say with humility because, after all . . . this being can only be given to us,
> it is a great illusion to think that I can confer it on myself; with fear, because
> I cannot even be certain that it may not be, alas, within my ability to render
> myself unworthy of this gift to the point of being condemned to lose it if grace
> did not come to my aid; and finally with wonder because this gift brings with
> it the light, because it *is* light.[61]

Participation

It is fair to point out, as Gallagher does,[62] that a fundamental key to Marcel's philosophy is the idea of participation. To feel, to be incarnate, to believe, to use second reflection, to have faith, to love, to exist, and so on, are all to participate in being. Being is experienced as mysterious precisely because and when we participate in it rather than hold ourselves off from it. At a deep level, we can never simply detach ourselves from the other within our experience without grossly distorting the reality of our situation.

Marcel's idea of participation goes back to his study of the philosophy of Josiah Royce. At the conclusion of his book on Royce, he observes that there are three different approaches to the question of the transcendence and immanence of God: extreme transcendence, in which the evil and tragedy of the world are simply integrated into the divine perspective and thereby denied as evil and tragic; extreme immanence, in which God is bound to the vicissitudes of human experience in a way that destroys his transcendence; and those views that attempt to reconcile these extremes by making individual consciousness merely a fragment of God. The idea of participation in being transcends these three alternatives by orienting "toward a definite rejection of the categories which are inadequate to the proper object of metaphysics, and toward a less systematic but more faithful and more profound interpretation of spiritual life." Such a philosophy, Marcel claims, must acknowledge an order of freedom and love where the relations between things, instead of being integrated into a rational system, "Remain the expressions of interdependent and distinct individuals who participate in God to the degree that they believe in him."[63]

Throughout Marcel's philosophy there is a concern to do justice both to being and to individual beings, or, in traditional terms, to both the one and the many. He tells us that his entire philosophical development has been dominated by two preoccupations that may superficially appear contradictory: "exigence of *being*" and "obsession with *beings* grasped in their singularity and at the same time in the mysterious relations which bind them together."[64] Although it may seem that a philosophy concentrating on the mystery of transcendent being is apt to make an abstraction of the diversity of beings and to regard them as negligible or insignificant and, at the same time, that concentrating on the diversity of individuals is apt to turn being itself into a fiction or at least into an abstraction to which nothing real corresponds, Marcel holds that this apparent dilemma must be rejected and overcome, for "the more we are able to recognize the individual being as such, the more we will be oriented and directed toward grasping being as being.''[65] That is, access to being is gained only through intimate intersubjective participation.

There are many kinds of participation in Marcel's philosophy, involving a kind of scale of degrees from objectivity to absolute participation. At one end participation may refer to the possession of something such as a piece of cake. But it need not always involve something so readily objectifiable. It can, for example, be illuminated by reference to participation in religious or national celebrations. In this case participation is possible through prayer even when one is confined to a sickbed, where nothing is empirically given and even time and place are irrelevant. That is, I can effectively participate in the ceremony even though I remain in bed and even though I pray at a time before or after the public ceremony.[66]

Of course participation need not, indeed most basically is not, conscious. Sensation and feeling as well as the relation to my body that makes it mine involve a basic mode of participation that is below the level of consciousness and may be called "submerged participation." Such participation is also, for example, the basis of the extremely strong tie that unites peasants with the soil, a tie more felt than thought. And here again, objective presence is not important; even if they move to the city, peasants may remain emotionally linked to the soil. Such a bond is more than merely emotional; it is an ontological relationship in which the soil is felt as a presence tied to each peasant's being.[67]

Effective participation is also beyond the traditional opposition of activity and passivity since it is sometimes active and sometimes passive. The relationship of peasants to the soil, for example, can only be understood in terms of both their acts and their sufferings. It is impossible to participate with the whole of one's being in any task or cause without experiencing some feeling of being carried along or caught up in it. Feeling also illustrates the breakdown of the passive-active dichotomy. To feel is to receive, but this is never a merely passive reception; it involves some degree of welcoming or responsiveness.[68]

Participation also accounts for the difference between being a spectator of something and contemplating it. Mere spectators confronted with a mere spectacle are comparable to recording machines. For them a war, at a safe distance, is merely something stimulating to observe; they are not involved in or deeply affected by what confronts them. With contemplation, however, the situation is quite different. It requires an emotional involvement in the situation so that it becomes more than a mere spectacle for those who contemplate it. Rather than being something entirely external, the spectacle takes on internal meaning. At the same time, it is not limited to the emotional or illusory; again the distinction between the internal and the external breaks down. "In as much as I contemplate the landscape, for example, a certain *coesse* is realized between the landscape and me."[69]

Participation in the mystery of being, then, is the opposite of all objective relations, of objective knowing (subject-object knowing), and of objective doing or technique. It is a way of being with in contrast to having.

Although there is some rudimentary participation even in ostensibly objective relations, the supreme degree of participation is that relation in which all objectification is strictly impossible: the relation between the believer and God. In Marcel's view, participation in God is known in the first instance through ontological exigence, the fundamental awareness of ultimacy in being. This participation becomes more complete as we invoke God in such interpersonal experiences as fidelity, hope, and love, whereby the detached self is transcended for communion with others and ultimately with God. In this way, we come to discover that our true being is not something we possess naturally but something we must both choose and create. Our life, in other words, is not simply a datum given to us, but neither is it within our power to create it on our own; it is offered to us as a gift, which to be real has to be received. Therefore our authentic being is not simply ours but God's being, or God's way of being, as well. As we become more truly creative, that is, more truly participants in being, God becomes more manifest to us; we participate in him and he in us.

By responding to God in creative fidelity, we approach our true being; yet we can never fully coincide with it. "One might be tempted to say that between me and my being there is a gulf which I can partially close, but which, in this life at least, I cannot hope to completely fill."[70] The only place where this gulf is apparently filled, according to Marcel, is in the life of the saint, for whom there is no grace at all or (what comes to the same thing) for whom all is grace.[71] But even for the saint God remains the transcendent Thou, neither fully transcendent nor wholly immanent but mysteriously both beyond and deeply within this being.

THE FUNDAMENTAL MYSTERY

Intuition

That some kind of intuition plays a fundamental role in Marcel's philosophy becomes evident when we notice that his arguments are often not arguments at all. For example, when he attempts to show that grace is the foundation of faith, he says that the negation of reflection "seems" to be possible only by grace. What is the basis of this "seems"? Why does it seem that the negation of reflection is based on grace rather than on an act of human freedom alone? It does so only because Marcel has some kind of intuition that this is the case—an intuition he expects his readers to share.

Marcel's difficulties in clarifying this issue stem from his belief that although we have a fundamental awareness of ultimacy, we cannot, or at least usually do not, know it as such. In *Etre et avoir* he says:

> It seems to me that I am bound to admit that I am—let us say at one level of myself—face to face with Being. In one sense I see it—in another I cannot say that I see it since I cannot grasp myself seeing it. This intuition is not reflected and cannot be reflected directly. But in turning on itself it illuminates an entire world of thoughts which it transcends. Metaphysically speaking, I do not see how faith can be accounted for otherwise. . . . I think that there is an intuition of this kind at the root of all fidelity—but its reality can always be put in question.[72]

Later, in reference to recognizing mystery, he says:

> Everything seems to happen here as though I found myself the beneficiary of an intuition that I possess without immediately knowing that I possess it, an intuition which could not be, strictly speaking, *for itself*, but grasps itself only through modes of experience on which it is reflected and which it illuminates by this very reflection.[73]

When Marcel says that this intuition cannot be reflected, he means that it cannot be brought into the realm of objective knowledge and treated as an object or thing. Intuition isn't something we can isolate from its functioning. "Intuition," he says, "is not something that lies at our disposal, something we have, but rather it is a source, in itself inaccessible, from which we set out to think. It is what I have called a blinded intuition; moreover it is also a 'forefeeling' or premonition, and without it . . . there cannot be 'concrete approaches.' "[74]

Some confusion about the role of intuition in Marcel's philosophy is introduced in *Position et approches concrètes du mystère ontologique,* where he seems to reject the use of the term *intuition*. In this centrally important essay, awareness of the ontological mystery requires a certain kind of detachment from one's life that can only be accomplished by recollection. "I am convinced," he writes, "that an ontology, that is to say an apprehension of the ontological mystery, is possible to any degree only for someone who is capable of recollecting himself—and in that way testifying that he is not purely and simply a living creature, a creature who has surrendered to his life and has no hold over it."[75] This recollection is seen as the act by which I pull myself together and at the same time relax, thereby discovering the gap between my authentic being and my life. "I find," he says, "something which I am but which my life is not."[76] But rather than call this awareness of being "intuition," it would be better to say that we are dealing with "an assurance which underlies the entire development of thought."[77]

Despite his rejection of the term *intuition*, it is apparent that the underlying assurance Marcel speaks of here is precisely what in *Etre et avoir* is called intuition. Still, a degree of uncertainty in Marcel's mind about the term *intuition* is evident in the two passages quoted above from *Etre et avoir*, for they were actually written just a few months before *Position et approches*, and the second of them even comes from an early draft of *Position et approches*. Although he uses the term *intuition* again in the preface to the English translation of the *Journal* in 1950, it does not play a significant role in the Gifford Lectures of 1949 and 1950. The important thing to note, however, is that Marcel never questions the reality of the experience or awareness; the question is only whether or not it can properly be called intuition.

Absolute Presence

The content of our awareness of ultimacy is sometimes called a "pure immediate," which has the characteristic of being wholly unspecifiable; "it is not something of which we can say that it is *this* or *that*."[78] That is, it is not an object of any sort and is incapable of being treated as an object. At the same time it is not indeterminate; nonetheless, when confronting it we cannot avoid distorting its nature if we adopt the kind of attitude appropriate for characterizing things. It is, of course, the ontological mystery in which we participate.

Although the content of this awareness is an unspecifiable and uncharacterizable mystery, the awareness does have a certain kind of certainty:[79] it is a certainty that I *am* rather than a certainty that I *have*.[80] The certainty of awareness of ultimacy does not guarantee the correctness of ideas or doctrines about God and does not guarantee the correctness of anything thought or said about God, but it does come as something unquestionably real.

In *Position et approches* Marcel does not even attempt to supply a symbol for the content of this awareness: "*Abandon to— relax in the presence of—*, without it being possible in any way to have a noun follow these prepositions and govern them. The road stops at the threshold."[81] But more often it is clear that Marcel is referring to the *presence* of God in the depths of human being. Thus he concludes the essay "My Ego and Others" with this quotation from Gustave Thibon:

You feel confined. You dream of escape. But beware of mirages. Do not run or fly away in order to escape; rather dig into the place of confinement which is given to you, there you will find God and everything. God does not float on your horizon, he sleeps in your depths. Vanity runs, love digs. If you flee beyond yourself, your prison will run with you and will close in on you in the wind of your flight; if you plunge into yourself, it will open into paradise.[82]

The fullness of our lives can be understood, we have seen, only through the ideas of grace and gift. The bestower of that gift, Marcel says, is "the non-identifiable as such," which is "experienced or apprehended as the absolute *thou*," or, to put it somewhat better (according to Marcel), which is "seen in a light which is hailed as a presence."[83] This is a presence neither of something nor of someone but an *"absolute presence."*[84] Here the distinction between subject and object completely breaks down and is transcended. As "being" absolute presence is at once the presence of God to me and my own true reality; it is the spiritual in human existence.[85]

As "light" the presence of God is at once the light within us, without which we would be unable to proceed on the road to our true being, and the "Light" without which we would never have started toward the Light.[86] Without uncreated light, Marcel avows, we would have no being at all. But we always have being, even though we may only be aware of existing. There is always the presence of God in the depth of human being, even though it may be denied, distorted, or turned against. We *are* always on the road, because a person who is not on the road would no longer be a person.[87]

The Point of Identity between God and Man

The presence of God, we have said, is the spiritual in human existence, our own true being. This is because there is an ontological point in every person where the supernatural and the natural, the divine and the human, meet and are one. There is a point of identity between the two realms, a point where we participate in God and he is present to us. Although this idea is somewhat obscured by Marcel's failure to adopt a single term for it, the awareness of this point of identity occupies a central place in Marcel's thought. Under one form or another, sometimes explicitly and often not, it underlies most of his discussions of personal experience.

In his treatment of the classical proofs of the existence of God, for example, an awareness of the point of identity is the "something essential" that has been left out of the formulas.[88] One commentator has said that intuition of the divine is the "secret soul" of the rational proofs.[89] It is also the reason why at the deepest level the ontological argument is valid.[90] At the same time it is the reason why the classical proofs are of little value: "Those who have experienced the presence of God, not only have no need of proofs, they will probably even regard the idea of a demonstration as an outrage to what is for them a sacred evidence."[91]

For epistemology generally, this point of identity is behind the premonition of what true answers might be.[92] The presence of God acts as the spirit of truth, which is light seeking the Light.[93] It drives us to look for truth and also helps us in our quest for truth. Service to truth implies that truth needs us and hence that truth is a spirit that "is at once beyond and within that which we are ourselves."[94] As "the axis of intelligible light," the point of identity between God and humanity is seen as "a light which is at the root of all and every understanding."[95]

This point of identity may also be seen as the basis of faith and as the "unconditional" that cannot be repudiated without denying something essential to ourselves.[96] At times Marcel seems to imply that God is known in faith not by any kind of awareness but by the fact that faith has to posit the reality of God in order to be realistic. But we must remember that for Marcel faith denies the distinction of subject and object; hence whenever there is genuine faith there is the felt presence of God. As a "grace before grace," the presence of God in us is the basis of our ability to open ourselves to receive grace.[97]

But if the point of identity is the basis of faith, it is also the reason why unbelievers testify to the reality of faith without knowing it.[98] In their seriousness they too testify to their having responded in some rudimentary fashion to the presence of God within them. In this sense faith can never be totally absent from us. Since no amount of estrangement and anxiety can totally separate us from this point of identity, a final estrangement is impossible. Even the most completely alienated slave has some deep awareness of being outraged, of Being outraged.[99] When life is centered on the special or the trivial, it is apt to collapse and leave something else—the "essential"—which is the fundamental awareness of the mystery that is my being and Being.[100]

The "ontological mystery of knowledge" can only be reached by a second reflection that depends on this experience of presence.[101] Marcel teaches that second reflection has its basis in ontological exigence, a "fundamental dissatisfaction"[102] that may be expressed as ontological anxiety.[103] When we become aware of ultimacy, however slight our awareness, we go beyond the objective procedures of primary reflection; we become dissatisfied with the prison of objectivity in which we find ourselves and become anxious about our own being. Second reflection is reflection aware of its own limits and capabilities—and especially of the distortions of reality created by thought—because it is aware, in a more fundamental way, of that ultimate reality in which we are united with God.

From the point of view of the mystery of being, awareness of the point of identity between the divine and the human is a "presentiment" of my authentic being, of that part of me that we might call spiritual and that is beyond the estrangement of the broken world of existence. "The question that should concern us . . . consists in knowing whether I can in some way experience myself as *being* in a sense other than that in which I grasp myself as existing." Just as the word *exist* points to an emerging or arising, so *being* points to a turning inward. "I can turn myself toward the interior, and this is what happens as soon as I recollect myself. But it seems that this act would be bound up with a presentiment of a reality which would be mine, or, perhaps more exactly, which would ground me in as much as I am myself."[104]

We must recognize, Marcel believes, that there is present in history (that is, in existence) a kind of depth that can be uncovered at many different levels, especially at the level of one's own life when one touches a region beyond oneself. This experience of depth, he thinks, is tied to a feeling that a promise is being made of which we can only catch a glimpse. "But what is remarkable . . . is that this glimpsed distance is not experienced as elsewhere: on the contrary, it is wholly near. . . . This distance is offered to us as interior, as a domain which we must say is nostalgically ours."[105]

An awareness of this point of identity between God and humanity is undoubtedly the basis for Marcel's "massive assurance" that concrete approaches to the mystery of being discover something beyond the realm of verification and objectivity.[106] The "fundamental apprehension"[107] or the "recognition of an ontological permanence"[108] at the root of all fidelity makes fidelity and meditation on fidelity significant for both ontology and theology. Fidelity involves an awareness and acknowledgment of the Being in me that is also in others and that cannot be denied without repudiating my true self. Similarly, an awareness of the presence of God is the received assurance at the foundation of all human hope and love.

For ontology, the identity of the divine and the human is the "intersubjective nexus" at the basis of Marcel's ontology of intersubjectivity.[109] It cannot be designated because it is not a this or a that; rather, it involves feeling the depth of being. "If I have insisted on intersubjectivity so much it is precisely in order to emphasize the presence of a felt underlying reality, of a community deeply rooted in ontology without which real human ties would be unintelligible."[110]

Since there is no ultimate difference for Marcel between feeling the presence of God and being profoundly aware of being, he can maintain that there is a correlation between metaphysics and religious life: a "hidden identity of the way which leads to sanctity and the road which leads the metaphysician to the affirmation of being."[111] In this way the saint and the metaphysician are ultimately on the same road and are headed in the same direction; ontology and the religious life are one because both must have their initiation in the same place. Both are possible only if experience and reality are not limited to empirical objects and verifiable facts and only if the thinking self transcends itself with an awareness of transcendence in the strictest sense, that is, in an awareness of divine reality.

All philosophy strives to increase our awareness of the point of identity as a reality that surrounds us on all sides. Philosophy presupposes some awareness, however dimly felt, of ultimate reality. But by the method of second reflection this presence can be brought to a higher level of consciousness and the mystery of being made if not less mysterious, at least more prominent.

In the final analysis, then, personal experience is mysterious not only because it is nonobjective value experience but also because it is ultimately both grounded in and responding to an ontological intersubjective community in which God is present. This is to put very abstractly what can only be experienced in a much more immediate way.

GENE REEVES

MEADVILLE/LOMBARD THEOLOGICAL SCHOOL
JULY 1969

NOTES

1. Gabriel Marcel, *Metaphysical Journal,* trans. Bernard Wall (Chicago: Henry Regnery Co., 1952) p. x (hereafter cited as *MJ*).

2. Gabriel Marcel, *Du refus à l'invocation* (Paris: Gallimard, 1940), p. 11 (hereafter cited as *DR*); *Creative Fidelity,* trans. Robert Rosthal (New York: Noonday Press, 1964), p. 6 (hereafter cited as *CF*).

3. Gabriel Marcel, *Journal métaphysique* (Paris: Gallimard, 1927), p. 45 (hereafter cited as *JM*); *MJ,* 44.

4. *JM,* 45–46; *MJ,* 44–45.

5. *DR,* 11; *CF,* 6.

6. Gabriel Marcel, *Etre et avoir* (Paris: Aubier, 1935), p. 27 (hereafter cited as *EA*); *Being and Having,* trans. Katharine Farrer (London: Fontana Library, 1965), p. 26 (hereafter cited as *BH*).

7. Gabriel Marcel, *Homo Viator* (Paris: Aubier, 1944), pp. 194–96 (hereafter cited as *HV*); *Homo Viator*, trans. Emma Craufurd (New York: Harper Torchbooks, 1962), pp. 147–48 (hereafter cited as *HV* [Eng. trans.]).

8. Gabriel Marcel, *Le Mystère de l'être*, 2 vols. (Paris: Aubier, 1951), 2:178 (hereafter cited as *ME*); *The Mystery of Being*, trans. G. S. Fraser (vol. 1) and René Hague (vol. 2), 2 vols. (Chicago: Henry Regnery Co., 1960), 2:199 (hereafter cited as *MB*).

9. *EA*, 145; *BH*, 109.

10. Gabriel Marcel, *Présence et immortalité* (Paris: Flammarion, 1959), pp. 188–89 (hereafter cited as *PI*).

11. *JM*, 160; *MJ*, 161.
12. *ME* 1:16; *MB* 1:11.

13. *JM*, 41; *MJ*, 40–41.
14. *EA*, 63; *BH*, 52.

15. *JM*, 45; *MJ*, 45.
16. *DR*, 177; *CF*, 135.

17. *EA*, 63; *BH*, 52.
18. *JM*, 39; *MJ*, 38–39.

19. *JM*, 68; *MJ*, 68.
20. *JM*, 85–86; *MJ*, 85.

21. *JM*, 68; *MJ*, 68.
22. *JM*, 39; *MJ*, 39.

23. *ME* 2:69–75; *MB* 2:76–83.
24. *ME* 2:78–79; *MB* 2:86–87.

25. *JM*, 39–40; *MJ*, 39.
26. *JM*, 46; *MJ*, 46.

27. *ME* 2:128; *MB* 2:141.

28. Roger Troisfontaines, *De l'existence á l'être*, 2 vols. (Paris: Vrin, 1953), 2:235.

29. *JM*, 50–51; *MJ*, 49–50.

30. *JM*, 96; *MJ*, 97.

31. *JM*, 73; *MJ*, 72.

32. Kenneth T. Gallagher, *The Philosophy of Gabriel Marcel* (New York: Fordham University Press, 1962), p. 43. See also *ME* 2:6–7; *MB* 2:2–3.

33. *ME* 2:128–29, 130; *MB* 2:141–42, 144.

34. *JM*, 251; *MJ*, 258. See also *DR*, 36; *CF*, 24.

35. *DR*, 19–54; *CF*, 11–37. See also *EA*, 11–15; *BH*, 16–18.

36. *ME* 2:29–30; *MB* 2:31.

37. Gabriel Marcel, *Position et approches concrètes du mystère ontologique* (Paris: Vrin, 1949), p. 52 (hereafter cited as *PA*); *The Philosophy of Existentialism*, trans. Manya Harari (New York: Citadel Press, 1961), p. 14 (hereafter cited as *PE*).

38. *ME* 1:150–53; *MB* 1:52–55.
39. *PA*, 54; *PE*, 16–17.

40. *PA*, 56–57; *PE*, 18.
41. *PA*, 90; *PE*, 45.

42. *PA*, 90; *PE*, 46.
43. *ME* 2:139; *MB* 2:155.

44. *JM*, 51; *MJ*, 50.
45. *JM*, 57–59; *MJ*, 56–59.

46. *ME* 2:179–80; *MB* 2:200.
47. *JM*, 57; *MJ*, 57.

48. *JM*, 60; *MJ*, 59.

49. *JM*, 56; *MJ*, 55–56. See also *ME* 2:127; *MB* 2:140.

50. *JM*, 53–54; *MJ*, 54.

51. *JM*, 56; *MJ*, 55.

52. *JM*, 83; *MJ*, 83.

53. *JM*, 47; *MJ*, 46. See also *EA*, 185; *BH*, 138; and see *JM*, 76; *MJ*, 76.

54. *ME* 2:120; *MB* 2:133.
55. *ME* 2:120–21; *MB* 2:133–34.

56. *ME* 2:122; *MB* 2:136.
57. *ME* 2:122–23; *MB* 2:136–37.

58. *PI*, 189.
59. *ME* 1:17; *MB* 1:11.

60. *PA*, 91; *PE*, 46. See also *EA*, 174; *BH*, 138.

61. *ME* 2:34; *MB* 2:36.

62. Gallagher, *Gabriel Marcel*, p. xi.

63. Gabriel Marcel, *La Métaphysique de Royce* (Paris: Aubier, 1945), pp. 223–24.

64. *DR*, 192; *CF*, 147.

65. *DR*, 192–93; *CF*, 148.

66. *ME* 1:127–30; *MB* 1:137–40.

67. *ME* 1:130–33; *MB* 1:140–43.

68. *ME* 1:133–35; *MB* 1:143–46.

69. *ME* 1:144; *MB* 1:158.

70. *ME* 2:33; *MB* 2:35.

71. *JM*, 60; *MJ*, 60. See also *ME* 2:180; *MB* 2:200.

72. *EA*, 142; *BH*, 107.

73. *EA*, 170–71; *BH*, 128.

74. *MJ*, x.

75. *PA*, 63; *PE*, 23.

76. *PA*, 64; *PE*, 24.

77. *PA*, 65; *PE*, 25.

78. *JM*, 319–20; *MJ*, 329.

79. *PA*, 62; *PE*, 22–23.

80. *ME* 2:130; *MB* 2:144.

81. *PA*, 63; *PE*, 23.

82. *HV*, 34; *HV* (Eng. trans.), 28.

83. *ME* 2:128; *MB* 2:141.

84. *JM*, 321; *MJ*, 331.

85. *PA*, 56; *PE*, 18.

86. *ME* 2:178, 188; *MB* 2:199, 210.

87. *ME* 2:129; *MB* 2:142.

88. *DR*, 230; *CF*, 178.

89. Paul Ricoeur, *Gabriel Marcel et Karl Jaspers* (Paris: Editions du temps présent, 1947), p. 367.

90. *JM*, 34; *MJ*, 33.

91. *ME* 2:177; *MB* 2:197–98.

92. *ME* 1:46; *MB* 1:47.

93. *ME* 2:178; *MB* 2:199.

94. Gabriel Marcel, *Les Hommes contre l'humain* (Paris: La Colombe, 1951), p. 156; *Man against Society*, trans. G. S. Fraser (Chicago: Henry Regnery Co., 1962), pp. 209–10.

95. *ME* 2:125; *MB* 2:139.

96. *EA*, 63; *BH*, 52.

97. *ME* 2:179–80; *MB* 2:200.

98. *DR*, 234; *CF*, 182.

99. *ME* 1:188; *MB* 1:212.

100. *ME* 1:234; *MB* 1:267.

101. *EA*, 166; *BH*, 125.

102. *ME* 1:231; *MB* 1:264.

103. *EA*, 177; *BH*, 132.

104. *ME* 2:32–33; *MB* 2:35.

105. *ME* 1:208; *MB* 1:237.

106. *DR*, 11; *CF*, 6.

107. *EA*, 50; *BH*, 60.

108. *EA*, 173–74; *BH*, 130.

109. *ME* 2:14; *MB* 2:11–12.

110. *ME* 2:20; *MB* 2:19.

111. *EA*, 123; *BH*, 92.

The Idea of Mystery in the Philosophy of Gabriel Marcel
REPLY TO GENE REEVES

Reading the study by Dr. Reeves, I ask myself the main question that quite rightly preoccupies him. I have set aside whatever I may have written on this subject previously in order to face a very real difficulty. When I speak of the ''mystery of being,'' am I entitled to say that I have had an idea of this mystery? Am I not merely putting words together according to a certain pattern? Alternatively, if I *have* the idea in question, doesn't this idea tend to be substituted for the mystery I claim to be talking about?

In order to avoid being imprisoned in this seemingly insoluble antinomy, I must grasp as distinctly as possible what I meant the first time I formulated the distinction between problem and mystery.

It was evident to me that I could not think of the mind working on a problem without thinking at the same time of the limits of that activity; yet to think of those limits is unavoidably to call forth something beyond them. The point, however, is to understand clearly what this beyond may be and, above all, to understand how *not to think of it*. It is only too obvious that whatever spatial representation we choose, we are led into an endless regression. But how is it possible to resist the almost overwhelming tendency toward such a representation? Resistance is possible only by means of what has to be called a conversion, that is, a reorientation of our internal gaze. But on what must this disoriented (or, better, re-oriented) gaze fall? It must fall only on presence, but here one must be careful, for the term *presence* is ambiguous. Only a recourse to living experience can enlighten us by forcing us to distinguish between ''presence'' and ''being there.'' My plays provide numerous examples of what I have in mind here. I think, for instance, of the scene between Christiane and her husband in the first act of *Le Monde cassé*. Christiane tries to reach him, but every-

---

Translated from the French by François R. Ferran and Colette M. Ferran.

thing happens as if Laurent (who is there in the objective sense) were not there at all. He is somewhere else; no one knows where. He is effectively walled up inside himself. He is not with Christiane. He will not be with her until the end of the play, during a period of grace or communion, and there is no way of knowing whether this moment will last. The final scene of *Quatuor en fa dièse* is no less significant. Claire and Roger are at last together, but there again one cannot know if this blessed instant will last.

Such examples also show vividly the impossibility of radically disso-ciating theater from philosophy in my work. I believe that there is not a single allusion to my plays in the study by Dr. Reeves. Moreover, he is far from being the only one to make this mistake; many others proceed as if the philosophical work constituted a sealed compartment, with the plays on the exterior and perhaps secondary.

After this long parenthesis, let me say that the key to the distinction between problem and mystery undoubtedly lies in a certain experience of presence.

But if we now revert to the term involved in the antinomy formulated at the outset, should we declare that this experience completely crystallizes into an idea? I would very much hesitate to say so. In truth, I fear that to resort to the term *idea* is to cause confusion. I will borrow an example not from the theater, but from my musical experience. Only three measures of a given harmonic and melodic sequence are needed before I exclaim, "That is Fauré," even if the measures are from some work by Fauré that I do not know. Here again we are in the dimension of presence. The genius of Fauré takes form in a recognizable way of being or of making himself present. Can I rightfully say that I have an idea of this genius? Am I entitled to answer both yes and no: yes, in that I have a distinct awareness of him that allows me to identify him and to greet him as I identify and greet a beloved face; no, in that I cannot establish the identity of this genius for strangers to whom I wish to transmit a certain content in the same way that I transmit an idea of a philosopher and his system, or, more clearly still, an idea of a theory or even of a scientific hypothesis?

No, it is inconceivable that by words I could give an idea of something of a musical order in its qualitative singularity. I could try to do this only by playing it or by presenting a significant melody—in other words, by participating actively in this music—in the hope that it will evoke (or, perhaps more exactly, that it will release) in the listeners a kind of inner movement by which they will move toward an encounter with what I am trying to have them hear.

I have just used the term *encounter* (*rencontre*); it is absolutely essential here. Encounter can only be accomplished at the level of presence. If it is an authentic encounter, it cannot be limited to coexistence at a particular point at a particular moment. Such coexistence is only a matter of "being there." There is true encounter only if there is a being *with*. It is not without purpose that I have always insisted on the profound value indicated by the word *with* and that I have pointed, in a line of thought possibly deriving from Bradley, to something more than a relation there, to the beginning of a communion. Communion clearly indicates [the French word] *en;* here the English word *within* is naturally preferable to *in*. For what is in question is really a sort of enveloping, or a being invested by. It is in this perspective that the ontological aspect of my thought emerges.

Consequently, the words *mystery of being* translate in a very schematic and therefore inevitably inadequate way the fact that as a thinking being I am involved in a vast communion, a vast *co-esse,* of which I can have, apart from a metaphysical assertion, only a fragmentary awareness through key experiences, to which indeed I must always direct myself if I do not want to bog down in some general, sterile affirmation.

Going back again to the initial antinomy, I wonder to what extent I can say that I have an idea of this universal communion. It seems to me that I can hardly avoid translating this communion into a spatial image, such as a glove, or into a more abstract representation, nonetheless spatial in principle, such as totality. At the same time I retain, fortunately, the power (reflexive) to keep at a distance from these images or representations and to recognize their fallacious character. But then one may rightfully ask what I confront these images or these representations with in order to reject them. Here again we find the paradox of which memory provides such a telling example. When we try to remember a name, we make more or less tentative approximations until something inside us says, "*Touché!* That's it!" It is obvious that each attempt is in itself an operation that cannot be reduced to a comparison because by definition one of the terms is missing. And this is tantamount to saying that there is no relation here.

The solution to the original antinomy would then involve bringing to light the fact, so often unsuspected, that an idea can never be reduced to itself alone (and can never be considered an object) without its ceasing to be an idea: its truth is in being for a moment in the life of thought. We must always resist the temptation to try to strait-jacket this moment. The word *coagulation* comes to mind at this point.

In sum, the word *mystery* takes on meaning only in a philosophy of presence, and such a philosophy can be established only by way of a meticulous critique of coagulated thought.

G.M.

9

John B. O'Malley

MARCEL'S NOTION OF PERSON

TO ask for a philosopher's notion of person is ultimately to query his understanding of what being human means, for this is the radical question we find ourselves asking when we seek adequately to reflect on our existential situation and to comprehend it as a whole. It provides the matrix meaning from which specialised acceptances of the concept of person phenomenologically derive. It is the abiding context within which the particular problems that our existence confronts us with find their setting. It can be lost sight of or simply remain unheeded in our preoccupation with more restricted concerns. Yet the absence of a specifically thematised concept of person from a philosophical idiom may well betoken an omnipervasive concern with (although it may argue a total lack of interest in) the radical question of what it means to be human.

In Marcel's case, this radically human concern has been persistent, pervasive, and comprehensive. "It has been his merit," so we have argued elsewhere, "to have recognised not only that all thinking, all acting, all talking takes place within the personal context but to have further recognised what essentially this context is and its peculiar relevance to the way in which we must understand what takes place within it."[1] His theme, then, has been neither the human mind, held in splendid suspense, nor the world confronting it, fixed in abstract isolation. The main region of Marcel's continuing inquiry has rather been the comprehensive field of human experience: its human quality is its constant focus.

Yet this "humanity," which we have indicated as the core of Marcel's notion of person, is itself no abstract, isolable property. It does not represent a "particular truth"—to borrow Marcel's term—definitively acquired, irrevisably docketted, and filed away for repetitive use within some objectifying system. We could say of Marcel, as has been said of a thinker with such immediately practical interests as Binswanger, that he concerns himself with *homo existentialis*—"man as he really is"[2]—not with *homo natura,* a hypothetical construct drawn from the data of a specialised scientific enterprise. Neither is his concern with a formalised a priori postulate of pure speculation. In the first place, there is for him, strictly speaking, no datum, only what is *being given* for whomever *will accept* what shows itself to such *receptive* vision. ("The characteristic of a meaning," Marcel has perceptively observed, "is to reveal itself only to an awareness that is open to receive it; it is in some way a response to an active and persevering expectation or, more precisely, to an exigence.")[3] In the second place, Marcel has never shown much interest in an absolute ego bereft of a credible link with the concrete ego—"the veritable I"[4]—which, set against such an abstract background, nonetheless and ironically reduces itself to a fictive abstraction. The notion of person—of being human (*menschliches Dasein*)—is operative in, with, and throughout Marcel's whole philosophical enterprise rather than set apart as a fully thematised notion. One might say his philosophy is its thematising, but only if that philosophy is free of illusion, either of such a task being finally accomplished or of its project being fully or exactly predescribable. For the person is both the context of his inquiry and a task to be fulfilled rather than an epistemological specimen to be mounted or dissected. And although the task is of necessity individually assumed and accomplished both in reflection and in the action it recollects and orientates, it is nonetheless a shared task and is universal in its human significance. "The exigency for universality is indefeasible. . . . It is essential to embody it only in the most concrete modalities of human experience, without ever depreciating the least of them but, on the contrary, recognising that the most humble, on condition of its being fully lived, is capable of indefinite deepening."[5]

The trouble with Marcel or (what amounts to the reverse of this critical coin) with us when we try to comprehend him is that his inquiry unfolds at a level deeper than that on which the familiar yet facile dichotomies of scholastic commerce operate. "It would certainly not be proper to deny the legitimacy of making distinctions of order within the unity of a living subject, who *thinks* and strives to *think of himself*," Marcel admits, but he immediately adds the rider: "the ontological problem can only arise beyond such distinctions, and for the living being grasped in his full unity and vitality."[6] And so the notion of person cannot be sought in arid and ultimately vacuous generalisations, either from specialised scientific investigations of what happen to be persons or from uncritically accepted common usage in some anontologically conceived "logical grammar" of the word *person.* "The empirical self-in-general is a fiction. What exists and counts is such an individual, the real individual I am, with the incredibly minute detail of his experience, with all the specifications of the concrete adventure that belong to him to live and to him alone, not to another being."[7] The recognition of this irreducibility of human beings is linked with a simultaneous recognition of their transcendental orientation. "From the beginning my philosophy has been directed towards the so-called conjoint recognition of the individual and the transcendent, in opposition to every impersonal or immanentist idealism."[8] It is precisely in the light of this conjoint recognition that we must understand Marcel's acceptance of the indefeasible claims of universality lodged in the very heart of the individual human being. Indeed, "person-commitment-community-reality"[9] are ideas that can only be adequately understood in reciprocal relationship. The importance of this living nexus to us in our experience of it is the personal—the human style distinctively at work in the living action of single human beings who, however distinctively, manifest the humanity they share together. Thus if to be personal is to transcend the self and its situation ("Its [the person's] device is not *sum* but *sursum*"),[10] then this transcending creates an ontological fellowship ("The more my existence affects an *inclusive* character, the more the gap separating it from Being tends to narrow—in other words, the more I am").[11]

We are now at the very nerve of the personal question as it presents itself to Marcel. The perspective he opens up for us accounts in large measure for the difficulty of doing justice to his thought at this critical juncture. It accounts for our insistence here, as elsewhere,[12] on the peculiar and comprehensive character of the notion of person—or, more precisely (as we shall soon insist), of the *personal* as it emerges from his philosophy. As anyone familiar with Marcel's style of thinking must quickly recognise, the question is metaproblematic. The notion of person, then, is not just another topic of inquiry that can be isolated from the whole complex of Marcel's continuing inquiry, adequately dealt with in methodical isolation, and left to one side as we proceed to another topic. This complexity accounts for the unresolved state in which he leaves the question as well as the hesitancy and provisional character of its treatment in the one paper that he specifically and explicitly devotes to the theme, "*Sur l'acte et la personne.*"[13]

There, Marcel considers the notion of "the person" in contrast to the notion of "act" and the notion of "personality." What is significant about his treatment of these notions is its conjoint existential and ontological bearing. The investigation starts from the notions' "rootedness in living experience" but is directed towards their significance as structures of our mode of being; it concludes with the tentative observation that the greatness of the person might lie "in a certain ontological indigence." How-

ever, we can use the term *structure* in this context only because we have
qualified it simultaneously as "existential" and "ontological." Otherwise,
such a way of speaking would lie dangerously open to a "denaturing" of
the experience to be recollected, which Marcel constantly denounces as the
fruit of "imprudent analysis" and which has led to the "evacuation of the
subject" in current French structuralism. Hence, we find Marcel in the
present instance stressing the strict correlationship of "act" and "person":
"The essence of the act is to involve the agent. . . . What is peculiar to
my act is its being able to be claimed by me afterwards. . . . I am in
solidarity with my act. . . . an act is the more an act . . . the less it is
possible for me to repudiate it without integrally disclaiming myself."[14]
Correlatively, "what is peculiar to the person is to face up (*affronter*),"
which involves the ability to envisage and evaluate his situation: "It is in
the act that is realised the nexus by which the person marries with himself,
but it must be added immediately that he is not outside this marriage. A
being not so married with himself would be, in the strict sense, alienated—
and so incapable of acting."[15] For the person, facing up to his situation
and acting are indissoluble aspects of a single appropriation of himself in
his situation that constitutes him effectively as a person. It is logical, then,
that Marcel query the propriety of evoking either the notion of "nature"
or that of anything like "substance" in this regard.

The unease betrayed in Marcel's hesitancy to evoke these notions receives a sharper outline in the contrast he makes between the notion of
"person" and that of "personality," in the sense of *Prägung* ("mark,
individual imprint"). Personality, in this sense, is "inneity," communicating itself through mysteriously transparent media, such as a tone of
voice or a glance. Person, however, seems to concentrate in acts, where
one might say abstraction is made from any inneity or rootedness. Hence
a philosophy based on person rather than on personality risks relapsing into
formalism.[16] These observations anticipate the remarks on "the existent"
and "the existential" that Marcel made in 1959 on his *Journal* entries of
1943 and 1944. These are worth recalling here. In them, Marcel notes
something of a sea change in his thinking at about the period he comments
on. Earlier, he stressed the opaqueness of existence: the encounter it was
subject to resembled a confrontation. Later, he stresses the exclamative
character of existence and its reflexive awareness, both of which precede
its opacity; as such existence is the subject of a "greeting" within an
encounter that is genuinely a meeting. The difference appears between the
respective resonances of "existential" and "existent": "The existent . . .
is the slackened fire, already almost quenched, whereas the clear sound of
the existential corresponds to the moment of discovery in which existence

is attained or apprehended as thou."[17] The concluding phrase of this note points to the propriety of making a like distinction between "the personal" and "the person" as well as of the former's fitness to provide the distinctive term marking Marcel's peculiar understanding of the notion of person. Indeed, "the personal" is quite capable of embracing in one "syneidesic" insight all that is positive in the contrasted notions of "the person" and "personality." The inclusive openness of the term *the personal* fits in well with Marcel's characterisation of the genuine concept—"that by means of which one thinks"—in its essentially heuristic and dynamic use.[18] We might say, then, that Marcel's is less a philosophy of the person or of the personality than of the personal. For that very reason, it is personal, in the full depth of intensity its unfolding has given this term.

What is essential in this transposition of the notion of the person into the notion of the personal is not the decision to adopt a distinctive terminology but rather the attitude orientating and at work in the inquiry. As Marcel remarks in a similar context (regarding "intimacy," and the personal certainly comprehends what is intimately ours or us): "What counts is not the words, but the inward attitude of which these words are but the sign or symbol."[19] And the attitude—prereflexively disposing us to reflect in a certain style about ourselves and our world—is, in the present case, intimate. Stressing the personal in contrast to the person, we refuse to evade the reality of our existential situation by way of a monadic formalism; at the same time we refuse to acquiesce in our liquidation from the scene of action when that situation is reduced to its atomised elements— which may or may not include our atomised selves—by means of a fatal objectivism. (It would be fatal in Marcel's sense of a self-abdication in the face of a *fatum* that overwhelms our freedom.) So rooting personality in "being personal or personally," we resist its etherialisation into a whimsical fiction. For to speak of our being as personal is in one and the same instant to recognise its rootedness in our encountering of the world and its inhabitants—particularly its human inhabitants—and in the irreducibly distinctive style of our inhabiting that world. Moreover, our interactions with the world and its inhabitants cannot be reduced to a mere epiphenomenal patterning of the relationships we enjoy there. The personal is neither the producer of its world nor its product. If being personally is to be involved—"being 'involved' is the fundamental fact; I cannot leave it out of account except by an unjustifiable fiction"[20]—then this involvement is neither self-annulment nor self-abdication. "We must realise that each of us, to realise what can be called his own fulfilment, must open himself to other beings distinct from him and become capable of welcoming them, without in any way allowing himself to become eclipsed or neutralised."[21]

Involvement and intimacy are indissociable aspects of being personal and together mark the peculiar quality of its experience. The intimacy of a personal being's involvement in the natural and cultural world of its continual encounter marks its essentially self-involving character. Involvement must be personally assumed. The involved character of the intimacy marks the situatedness, the openness, and, one might say, the dialectic mode of its comprehension and fulfilment. Taken together, intimacy and involvement indicate what Marcel described early in his career as "a metaphysical situation of which it is inadequate to say 'it is mine,' since it consists essentially in *being me*."[22] To speak of this situation—which is mine only to the extent that it is, in some mysterious sense, me—as metaphysical is to mark its simultaneously existential and ontological character.

Indeed, my situation is such that I not only continually find myself already in it but, being in it, continually have yet to find myself. At once it is clear that the dialectic of this situation and of its comprehension is no ritual of synthetically transcending (abstract or artificially reified) formalised oppositions. My situation as reflected is a dialogue that reenacts the existential encounter so recollected when, in fact, it is at all adequately reflected. To philosophise in the personal key, which is Marcel's authentic style, involves continual conversation (never degeneratively reduced to impersonal verbal or conceptual commerce) with my situated self, with the world in which I am situated, and with those others I encounter in that shared situation. "The most authentic philosophic thought," Marcel has observed, "is situated at the point where self and other meet."[23] If there I encounter myself as other—that is, as other than myself here and now—I do so by authentically encountering beings other than me as if they were myself, my alter ego, which in the encountering they have become. This means that the point of authentic encounter—the mysterious and nonacquisitive communication of presence—is not superficial to my situation. It is not fixed for me by the adventitiously colliding paths of dumb elements emerging from within an environment into which I happen to be thrown. Rather, it is "located" deep within myself and my situation and equally at the heart of those I encounter and of the world in which that encountering takes place and that makes it ours. This is the "depth" Marcel terms *here* and *elsewhere, now* and *elsewhen,* coincidentally.[24] The point of authentic encounter exists where and when I am present, and from it my presence irradiates, illuminating those I encounter and discovering them for me as it discovers me for myself. "In reality we cannot conceive of an apprehension of the other that is not indeed an apprehension of ourselves and lends its human weight to our experience. . . . The world of others lights up with an ever intenser light the more, and the more heroically, the I dispels its own shadows. . . . Philosophically, the road to the other leads through the depths within myself.''[25] And since presence is always both presence to and presence with, this dialogic openness is ontological and integral to the common style of being human. Hence, speaking of the fundamental experience of ''the openness of man to man,'' Marcel stresses its distance from the restricted experience of a purely individual *Stimmung*.[26]

If we must speak of the personal in terms of the person who manifests it and in whom it is exemplified, it is clear that we should speak in terms of presence, not of substance. This stipulation, of course, makes it difficult for us to speak of the personal and still to remain faithful to the witness of our experience. Yet it does not prevent us from speaking of it altogether. ''Philosophical method,'' Marcel insists, ''is *par excellence* reflexive.''[27] To identify the personal with presence is to underscore the possibility of and the exigency for reflection on the personal. After all, it is the lack of reflexivity in brute animals that leads Marcel, quite rightly, to accord scarcely any meaning to the use of ''presence'' in their regard and none at all in the regard of things.[28] ''The more we apprehend reflection in its complexity, in its active and . . . dialectic aspects, the more we understand that it cannot but transform itself into reflection.''[29] It is equally clear, however, that a presence cannot be crystallized within a formalised analytic system. Even to consider such a system relevant to the symbolic representation of the necessary yet never sufficient conditions within which presence can be manifested demands a prior understanding of the presence in question. Thus the primary task of an adequate reflection (which Marcel calls ''secondary reflection'') is critically to scrutinise the surface readings of ''primary'' or objectifying reflection (''thesis in the natural mode'').

Yet this primary task is not the sole possible reflective task. If it were, its positive character would be merely a negation of negation, since it would ironically appear to be an undialectical view of reflexivity magically producing a spurious self-coincidence by reversing the original reality-negating formulae. Marcel's insight is deeper here than Hegel's or Husserl's, not to mention Kant's. And whereas Sartre leaves his *compréhension* full of unfulfilled promise and Wittgenstein his *Übersehbarlichkeit* unthematised and largely unexploited, Marcel clarifies the issue with his insightful evocation of recollection. Through recollection, as Marcel understands it, ''thought *stretches out* toward the recovery of an intuition which otherwise loses itself in proportion as it is exercised.''[30] Recollection is ''the act whereby I re-collect myself as a unity.''[31] This definition differs significantly from any of Husserl's reductions. It is not an abstraction but rather a concentration, and it is an integrative and comprehensive act. There is certainly a withdrawal, but not from the existential, from

which withdrawal would be meaningless in either the active or the passive
sense and which is entirely different from the Humean type of existence
that is the subject of Husserl's existential epoché. *"In this withdrawal I
carry with me that which I am and which perhaps my life is not."*[32] It is
clear, then, that recollection is an ontological *ascesis* directly ordered towards a reintegration of the personal, itself a prerequisite for authentic
commitment as well as for authentic vision. "Recollection, the actual possibility of which may be regarded as the most revealing ontological index
we possess, is the real place in whose centre this recovery (i.e., of intuition) can be made."[33] Recalling what we have said about the personal and
its dimension of "depth," we see that recollectiveness "defines" the personal as ontological: "No ontology . . . is possible except to a being who
is capable of recollecting himself, and of thus proving that he is not a
living creature pure and simple, a creature, that is to say, which is at the
mercy of its life and without a hold upon it."[34]

Whatever withdrawal is involved in recollection, then, comes from inauthenticity—from a negating of the negative. But it is clear that such a
backhanded positiveness can only be a function of something genuinely
and originally positive in the being who exercises it. This is why we must
not confuse Marcel's "secondary reflection" with his notion of "recollection" *tout court,* though the former is a necessary and integral feature of
the latter. Recollection is a reflection in depth. Furthermore, even secondary reflection can adequately carry out its critical purpose only in the light
of what recollection, in the fullest sense, reveals. But what does it reveal?
Is the revealed merely a naked transcending of my present situation? Certainly Marcel speaks of the "ambiguity of our condition, which is that of
a being involved in the world of things and who participates in it but who
on the other hand transcends this world and knows that he transcends it."[35]
Yet he also notes, when speaking of recollection as a self-integrating act,
"this hold, this grasp upon myself is also relaxation and abandon," and
he significantly adds: *"Abandon to . . . relaxation in the presence of . . .*
—yet there is no noun for these prepositions to govern."[36]

We know quite well what would fill these gaps (if it could be fitted
into them): Being. More specifically, it is Being as I participate in it and
without which I would not be: my being, which cannot meaningfully be
divorced from its situation or, more fundamentally, from Being. The personal re-collecting enacted when we reflect deeply on ourselves-in-situa-
tion reveals the absurdity of reducing the self to a situation and Being to a
Nothingness, for self and Being are etched against the background, respectively, of situation and Nothingness. To reduce the self and Being in this
way is to treat the first member of each pair—self and situation, Being and

Nothingness—as the reverse of the second and thus provides yet another abstract negating of negation. What recollection reveals is mystery and fullness, not emptiness and certainly not muddle. It reveals *clarté* not in the Cartesian sense of a resolved problematic distinction but rather in the sense of an excess (to our constrained capacity for comprehension) of brightness. Mystery is merely the positive designation of the more negatively phrased "metaproblematic." It is the comprehensive, abiding context in which problems actually occur and in which reflection must envisage them if it is to situate them adequately: in the light of Being, which at the same time is participated in by reflection and transcends it. This Being is not the formal ground of a formalising constitution of a formalised universal. It is the source of our exigency for the Universal, which Marcel sees at the heart of the personal and deep within every invocation of the Other and which he alludes to as the Ultimate Recourse. Hence Marcel insists that no technique could discover Being and that we will find no ultimate salvation in any technics.

Marcel, then, has operated a revolution within the Copernican revolution of Kant. He has done this by transcending the dichotomy of the Subject and the Object (the dichotomy simply ceases to be relevant) and by setting the whole theme of the personal in the key of the full and the empty in lieu of the now inadequate key of the one and the many. (For this reason too Marcel avoids Sartre's philosophy of the One-Too-Many.) If talk of transcendence is to have any meaning, there must be, as Marcel has always insisted, an experience of the transcendent. It is, as we have said, the experience of an exigency for Being (remembering always that an exigency is not a desire, which is either quite specific or, if vague, indeterminate in a sense that requires and soon seeks objectification to be effective). The Being that is the source and focus of ontological exigency is not problematic in that way, and this is why its presence is ultimately manifested in belief, hope, and love—all personal ways of invoking a personal Other. Because its presence is absolute, its absence never is. It can only be not fully there for, or not quite recognised by, me. And its being there is experienced as fulfilment: not self-satiation or self-satisfaction but self-fulfilment beyond the achieved satisfaction of any specific need. "Being is expectancy fulfilled to overflowing; the experience of being is fulfilment."[37] Hence its concrete experience—and here Marcel joins with Scheler—is joy. "Joy is not the mark of being but its very upsurge. Joy—fullness."[38]

Such a presentation of personal being—an anthropology that is an ontology rooted in the existential—is necessarily an open reflection. Thus thought "is *inside* existence . . . a mode of existence," and its privileged capacity "to make abstraction from itself *qua* existence" is "for strictly limited purposes"; "far from being a relation with itself, [thought] is on the contrary essentially a self-transcendence."[39] It is an openness to Being that can only be "defined" negatively as that which "withstands—or would withstand—an exhaustive analysis bearing on the data of experience and aiming to reduce them step by step to elements increasingly devoid of intrinsic or significant value."[40] Hence personal being itself—the personal—can only be "defined" as a living affirmation of Being, an affirmation "*of which I am the stage rather than the subject*."[41] Hence too it is inadequate to talk of essence or nature in this context, for either term is necessarily ambiguous. "By essence we can understand either a nature or a freedom," Marcel observes. "It is perhaps of my essence *qua* freedom to be able to conform myself *or not* to my essence *qua* nature. *It may be of my essence to be able not to be what I am*."[42] Thus any talk of essence must in turn be transposed into terms of the essential. Furthermore, this essential cannot in any sense be considered guaranteed in advance, whether in terms of conception or achievement. To use terms other than Marcel's, the essential freedom of the personal is negatively determined by a facticity and a historicity. The meaning of these last two terms is refined in the setting of Marcel's reflection on the personal. Together they represent existential features of what Marcel clearly recognises as a situated freedom. As negative determinants of our being-in-situation, they are called into factual play only by our own positive assumption of our situation. Still, we must remember that in the Marcelian context such positive determining of our situation is itself part of a personal response to the call of Being that issues from its depths.

Nonetheless, we can speak meaningfully of essence in the case of being personal, that is, of the personal project itself, of which all other projects are necessarily so many specifications, either promotive or abortive. "Something is placed in jeopardy from the moment I exist, but [it] can also be saved and it *will be* only on condition of its being saved."[43] It is equally clear that its saving is not merely of individual but also of universal human concern, for the personal though no mere type-instance, is bearer of an ontological significance that only becomes manifest through our action in the world with others. This double sense of essence (personal and universal, the one because of the other) is implicit in Marcel's following recommendation: "Combine the idea of essence with the idea of universe. The essence regarded as the highest point of a certain universe. . . . The idea of 'summit' could perhaps be replaced with the idea of 'the centre'."[44] The essential in the personal is always yet to be achieved. Its achieving is the fulfilling of an exigency at the heart of the personal, and only in its fulfilling is its meaning clarified for us. But what is then manifest is not an arbitrarily posited idiosyncratic goal; rather, it is a project in which I find myself involved, once I recollect myself in living, and to which I appeal whenever I judge my life, as so far lived, to be unworthy of me because unfitting for a person. Recollection is in this sense always a recall to what exigentially I am—a promise and never an acquisition.

The perspective from which Marcel's vision of the personal develops— a vision that opens out into Being, without which the personal cannot exist—is quite different from that of philosophies that try to construct us or to reconstitute us from the fragments to which a reductive analysis has reduced us. With Marcel the live integrity of the real is never destroyed. If he reduces experience to its skeletal outline, it is to find at the end of the process an undifferentiated and therefore relatively empty affirmation in which "I exist" merges with "the universe exists." For him, then, experience authentically lived, as well as authentically recollected, not only maintains but expands that comprehensive integrity despite the differentiations that reflection operates. Reflection is orientated towards a fuller recognition of what is being given to those who will recognise it. Equally, action is orientated towards a fuller realisation of the presence, so recognised, within the world open to receive it. This appropriation of the world, however, is not acquisitive. Authentic action, like authentic reflection, moves in the category of being, not of having; in fact the category of having presupposes that of being even when disposed to ignore it.[45] The acquisitive attitude, which is the translation into action of the objectifying attitude of primary reflection, is destined to a tragic dispossession of itself in seeking to possess; indeed, what it would possess, if possessed, would be effectively destroyed. If the personal is to maintain its self-affirmation as such, even things must be used rather than just acquired; that is, they must be integrated into the deeper, more comprehensive style of human action we call "creative."[46] Apart from that context, the thing becomes the object of a technique and the skill to use it. In such manipulative activity the person is at once more involved (though involved passively) and less self-involving.[47] As for persons, it is clear that they are not fittingly objects of use. Their services may be requested or even demanded, though demanded only for a function they are committed to perform within a community of persons.[48] The *disponibilité* that Marcel views as the hallmark of personal responsiveness is in fact a disposition freely to commit oneself in response to the ontological exigency embodied in human fellowship, which is recognised as the fellowship of Being. The inclusive quality of *disponibilité* betokens the universality of the personal and has its counterpart in Marcel's observation that although "the person only realises himself in the act by which he tends to embody himself (in a work, in action, in the whole of a life) . . . at the same time it is of his essence never to fix or crystallise himself definitively in a particular embodiment."[49]

Embodiment, or incarnation, is a recurrent and central theme of Marcel's philosophy. We have not yet considered it here because we have dealt comprehensively with it and other differentiations of the personal elsewhere.[50] Within the perspective developed here, embodiment marks, at the point of my insertion in the world, the locus of my most intimately personal appropriation of that world and source of my emergence to make it my dwelling. "The world exists for me in the measure that I have relations with it which are of the same type as my relations with my own body."[51] The personal index adhering to embodiment—evident in Marcel's insistence that although in a certain respect my body is *a* body, it is always most significantly *my* body—means that such relations are not interposed between the terms in either case. My body qua mine, which is the root experience and essential feature of embodiment, should rather be understood in terms of my "bodying forth." But that bodying forth derives ambiguities from its twin aspects of "body for me" and "body for others." Just as the second ambiguity argues the need for a mediation of my body to me by the other—but an other who is "thou" for me—so my bodying forth betokens neither a merely passive nor a purely active involvement in the natural world. It is, in Marcel's precise and perceptive sense of the term, receptive. This means that perception itself is receptive and that the sensing in which it is rooted is of the nature of an immediate participation in the world. It is, to use a distinction made earlier, in the nature of a conversation between me and the world, not of a commercialised exchange. Taking the two ambiguities noted above, we can develop an adequately personal reflection on human sexuality, a theme Marcel has never fully treated. Such a development would view sexuality and its fulfilment as a bodily converse between persons, whose intimacy and comprehensivity would provide a fitting prelude to and the most adequate basis for personal communion and fulfilment. Such a natural development of Marcel's reflection would underline the harmonic consistency of his preference for the intimate in the social sphere and the lack of any exclusiveness in his understanding of it.

In fact, the personal key in which Marcel sets his philosophy largely accounts for his lack of concern with the macro-social. He does not lack social concern, but he does remain sceptical of mass salvation. The essential in the social is the personal. This means that his attention is focussed on the point of personal encounter and is taken up with the clarification of its essential themes. Given the comparative neglect of a philosophically adequate anthropological concern among social scientists as well as among those philosophies from which they have borrowed their methodology (a neglect well noted by Marcel's friend, Paul Ricoeur),[52] this emphasis is both intelligible and salutary. What Marcel has to say of the personal may not have manifest relevance to their manifest concerns, but certainly the attitude informing it has. It should warn against the inadequacy both of reducing humans in any sphere to the impersonal and of the severely restricted validity of what can emerge from such a reduced perspective.[53]

The themes of personal encounter are fundamental to all human encountering. They are what Marcel calls "themes of invocation" in which presence is greeted as presence. In elaborating them, Marcel has salvaged them from a theological confinement that has tended to foreclose any adequate interest in them on the part of an increasingly secularised philosophy. Quite summarily they are the themes of believing, of hoping, and of loving—themselves styles through which fidelity, the fundamental style of human commitment, develops its project. By centering his moral concern on fidelity, Marcel escapes the constrictive inadequacies of traditional teleological and deontological points of view and at the same time avoids the inanity of whimsical theories of value and ethics. For fidelity precisely indicates the style of commitment possible to and required of a free being, whose freedom is nonetheless situated as ours is. Absolute in its commitment to the personal, fidelity is open towards any specific embodiment of the human project.[54] For the ideal, in terms of which fidelity anticipates the fulfilment of the project to which it is committed, is not a collective idol but a fellowship yet to be realised and fostered. That is why its realisation issues from the intimate centre of personal encounter. "Universality," Marcel declares, "is situated in the dimension of depth and not of extension. . . . There is no authentic depth except where a communion can effectively be realised; it will never be either between individuals hardened in self-centredness, or among a mass, in a mass state."[55] At the same time, the fellowship in which fidelity finds its concrete expression and effective embodiment is universal in intent. "Every restricted group risks, in each case, enclosing itself upon itself and so becoming a sect or chapel, immediately betraying the universal it is called upon to embody. It must, therefore, hold itself in active readiness or disponibility towards other groups of differing inspiration, but with whom it should entertain fruitful communication."[56] In this clear advocacy of open and inclusive—as opposed to closed and exclusive—grouping, Marcel defines the prerequisites of and existential exigency for genuine, open, and self-critical co-operation.

Believing, hoping, and loving provide the thematic framework in which the personal fulfils its ontological exigency, faithful to its authentic project. Belief, whose commitment is dialectical and open (and thus unlike conviction's), indicates the authentic style of personal vision. Transposed to the sociological plane, the distinction between belief and conviction marks that between ideology and faith, which in turn marks the intellectual attitude informing closed and open social structures respectively. Hope indicates the style of commitment appropriate to belief. It is universal in character: "Hope consists in asserting that there is at the heart of being, beyond all data, beyond all inventories and all calculations, a mysterious principle which is in connivance with me, which cannot but will that which I will, if what I will deserves to be willed and is, in fact, willed by the whole of my being."[57] This universal character sets hope apart from any form of Utopianism. It led Marcel, ahead of Marcuse, to descry the anti-human menace of technicism, the ideological and utopian exaltation of technology. Marcel never denies the purely functional, and therefore limited, role of technology in human life.[58] "The burden of technics has been assumed by man and he can no longer put it down because he finds it heavy."[59] Hope, because it is centred on Being and so emergent from a recollective attitude, is *meta-technical*.[60] It can therefore withstand the despair that issues from the realisation of the radical inadequacy of technics and their ultimately limited ability to "solve" the human question.

The supreme realisation of the personal is in love—ultimately the only adequate response to the ontological exigency. "Love as the breaking of the tension between self and other appears to me as the essential ontological datum."[61] It partakes of all the stylistic character of belief and hope. Loving, I love the other "for what he is, because he is himself, I thus boldly anticipate all experience. . . . The reality of the beloved being is essential in love. . . . Love rises up like an appeal from the I to the I."[62] One cannot, then, help seeing in love, with its transfunctional recognition of being, the source of effective resistance to the "gigantic process of devaluation of what is permanent in man and above man," which Marcel sees as characteristic of the ideologies of our age.[63] Transposed into the more public and less intimate sphere, love issues as the style of action exemplified by fraternity. "The fraternal man is linked to his neighbour, but in such a way that this tie not only does not fetter him, but frees him from himself; . . . [He] is somehow enriched by everything which enriches his brother, in that communion which exists between his brother and himself."[64] Both love, in the intimate sphere, and fraternalism, in the public, run counter to that "spirit of abstraction" that Marcel has always denounced and discerned as the product of hatred, the essence of fanaticism, and the extremity of ideology: "the inability to treat a human being as a human being, and for this human being the substituting of a certain idea, a certain abstract designation."[65] The sad history of oppression and rebellion, of revolution and counter-revolution, witnesses the justice of his evaluation. It is from the uncalculating perspective of fraternity, and not from the quantitatively inclined perspective of equalitarianism, that Marcel holds any hope today for the full recognition of human dignity.[66]

We have shown a radical consistency in all Marcel's reflection on the personal. The consistency is certainly not that of a formalised system, which is why we qualify this term with "radical." It is only by continually recentring one's own interpretative activity on the "ownness" of personal being and its experience that the harmony existing among the differentiated themes of Marcel's exploration of the personal can be comprehended. Yet there is nothing vague about his inquiry and nothing woolly in its approach to the question; hence one should be chary of too quickly describing either metaphorically in aesthetic terms. They are quite plainly philosophical. His inquiry continually refers to what is being given in experience; it is not a self-referring re-creation deriving from experience, which it would seek to reconstitute for the idiosyncratic purpose of esoteric self-expression. If aesthetic allusion is in order, it is only when such experience has been properly understood as a personal mode of existential insight and as therefore relevant to our comprehension of the personal. For Marcel's approach to the personal has clearly sighted the distinctive style of human thinking, which is other than that represented by formal systems, however informally operated. And since bringing this to light has been the burden of the present inquiry, we might conclude it by trying to make explicit what this style of thinking means in terms of the concepts it heuristically and dynamically employs.

It is quite clear that Marcel views his inquiry as continual and never fully achieved. Paradoxically for a philosopher who has always located his inquiry outside the domain of science, this view brings him nearer to contemporary interpretations of scientific inquiry. Contemporary science makes little pretension that it has achieved truth or irrevisible certainty. Nonetheless, the concepts it employs and operationally defines claim the clarity of precise differentiation. Now, the concepts Marcel employs tend to be extremely volatile. They resist being analytically reduced to atomised constituents, which would then be analysable in the same fashion until there was no remainder. On the contrary, differentiations made within them (which are never without remainder) are intelligible only in the light of the original total concept that is being differentiated and that is now enriched by the differentiation. All this is to express in more abstract terms what Marcel has said of the metaproblematic, or of mystery. His conceptual interest is quite clearly intensional rather than extensional, and all this accords well with the "recollective" style he has claimed for, and has exemplified in, his philosophical research.

Two further observations might be made on this subject: the first, with respect to the kind of reality Marcel has been investigating; the second, with respect to the relationship his style of inquiry might be said to have to other styles of inquiry into being. If we wanted to distinguish the conceptual mode of Marcel's kind of inquiry from those he has rejected, we might dub them respectively as "stylising" and "formalising." The topics envisaged by these modes of inquiry differ significantly. That intended by a formalising mode of inquiry is exactly describable, or if not, the open texture of its meaning results from a vagueness either in itself or in our grasp of it. If the vagueness is in our grasp of it, then we revise our concept when closer acquaintance affords us a clearer focus on the topic. If the vagueness is intrinsic, then the classification is in terms of the shifting traits of some family resemblance between members of the class in question. In the case of stylising modes of inquiry like Marcel's, the question is not of vagueness but of profundity. The reality that is its topic is continuously exemplified as it fulfils its eidetic ontological promise—hence the aptness of the comparison with music and its thematic development. Correlatively, the inquiry that seeks to comprehend such a topic is itself dialectical in nature, constantly in need of restructuring itself in its attempt to plumb "the depths of a given fundamental metaphysical situation."[67] But the "metaphysics" is not news from nowhere; it is news from where we are as we encounter the subject of its inquiry, which is ourselves or another like us.

If such is the "nature" of the personal and therefore of human beings, then clearly an inquiry seeking adequately to comprehend it moves on an altogether different plane from that of any "scientific" inquiry that might be brought to bear on it. The metaphysical inquiry would seek to diagnose the necessary, yet never sufficient, conditions for the personal to manifest itself or for personal action to occur. The ultimate validity of their conceptualisation of the human or of the personal would always remain subject to critical appraisal from within the more comprehensive metaproblematic perspective. At the same time, their inquiries would not be otiose. Repetition (or redundancy, which is a form of repetition) plays different roles in formalising and stylising inquiries, as does differentiation. In formalising inquiries, repetition ensures that the pattern of constituent elements is registered and that differentiation is an abstractive and reductive process. In styling inquiries, by contrast, each exemplification or manifestation of the "style" in question yields fresh insight, because it is never exactly repetitive. Similarly, differentiation, which never destroys the integrity of what it discriminates or loses sight of its total context, develops further its potential intensity of meaning.

We may conclude, then, that Marcel's approach to and understanding of the personal offers a basis for an adequate philosophical anthropology that could serve as an integral focus of the various distinctive inquiries operated in the several human sciences. Interweaving the illuminating and the liberating intents of the *Geisteswissenschaften,* such a complex theory of humankind could, on its several and distinctive levels of inquiry, proffer a more adequate understanding of the human condition as we actually experience it. Such an enterprise would well accord with Marcel's designation of the common human task: "To be men; to continue to remain men."[68]

JOHN B. O'MALLEY

DEPARTMENT OF SOCIAL SCIENCE
UNIVERSITY OF LIVERPOOL
APRIL 1969

NOTES

1. John B. O'Malley, *The Fellowship of Being* (The Hague: M. V. Nijhoff, 1966), p. 137.

2. See Danielo Cargnello, "From Psychoanalytic Naturalism to Phenomenological Anthropology (Daseinanalyse)," *The Human Context* 1, no. 1 (1968): 73–76.

3. Gabriel Marcel, *Présence et immortalité* (Paris: Flammarion, 1959), p. 19 (hereafter cited as *PI*).

4. Gabriel Marcel, *The Philosophy of Existence,* trans. Manya Harari (London: Harvill Press, 1949), p. 18 (hereafter cited as *PE*).

5. Gabriel Marcel, *Homo Viator* (Paris: Aubier, 1944), pp. 34–35 (hereafter cited as *HV*).

6. Gabriel Marcel, *Being and Having,* trans. Katharine Farrer (London: Dacre Press, 1949), p. 17 (hereafter cited as *BH*).

7. *HV,* 19.   8. *HV,* 192.

9. *HV,* 27.   10. *HV,* 32.

11. Gabriel Marcel, *Le Mystère de l'être,* 2 vols. (Paris: Aubier, 1951), 2:35 (hereafter cited as *ME*).

12. O'Malley, *Fellowship of Being*, pp. 7–23.

13. In Gabriel Marcel, *Du refus à l'invocation* (Paris: Gallimard, 1940), pp. 139–57 (hereafter cited as *DR*).

14. *DR*, 142,143,145.   15. *DR*, 147,151.

16. *DR*, 156.   17. *PI*, 146.

18. Speech to the Réunion sur la phénoménologie, C.C.I.F. (Catholic Center of French Intellectuals), 20 February 1952.

19. Gabriel Marcel, *L'Homme problématique* (Paris: Aubier, 1955), p. 47.

20. *PE*, 9.

21. "L'umanesimo autentico e i suoi presuppositi esistenziali," *Il fuoco*, January–February 1958, p. 7 (hereafter cited as "UA").

22. *BH*, 20.   23. *PI*, 23.

24. *PI*, 29–31.   25. *PI*, 23, 24, 25.

26. "UA," 8.   27. *PI*, 27.

28. See O'Malley, *Fellowship of Being*, pp. 96–101.

29. *ME* 1:97.   30. *BH*, 118.

31. *PE*, 12.   32. *PE*, 12.

33. *BH*, 118.   34. *PE*, 12.

35. *PI*, 91.   36. *PE*, 12.

37. *ME* 2:46.

38. Gabriel Marcel, *Metaphysical Journal*, trans. Bernard Wall (London: Barrie & Rockcliff, 1952), p. 236 (hereafter cited as *MJ*).

39. *BH*, 27, 30.   40. *PE*, 5.

41. *PE*, 8.   42. *BH*, 106.

43. O'Malley's translation; cf. *MJ*, 291.

44. *BH*, 57.   45. *BH*, 154–56.

46. *BH*, 172–74.   47. *BH*, 173–74.

48. See *HV*, 173–77; *PI*, 169.   49. *HV*, 32.

50. See O'Malley, *Fellowship of Being*.

51. O'Malley's translation; cf. *MJ*, 269.

52. "Philosophical anthropology has become an urgent problem of contemporary thought because all the major problems of that thought converge on it and its absence is deeply felt. The sciences of man are dispersed into separate disciplines and literally do not know what they are talking about" (Paul Ricoeur, "The Antinomy of Human Reality and the Problem of Philosophical Anthropology," in *Readings in Existential Phenomenology*, ed. Nathaniel M. Lawrence and Daniel O'Connor [Englewood Cliffs, N.J.: Prentice-Hall, 1967], p. 390).

53. For further recognitions of the centrality of this question for the human sciences, see Alphonse de Waelhens, *Existence et signification* (Louvain: Nauelwaerts, 1967), pp. 233ff.; Mikel Dufrenne, *Pour l'homme* (Paris: Seuil, 1968); Gerard Radnitzky, *Contemporary Schools of Metascience*, 2 vols. (Göteborg: Akademiförlaget, 1968); and Lucien Goldmann, *The Human Sciences and Philosophy*, trans. Hayden V. White and Robert Anchor (London: Cape, 1969).

54. "The *we* reveals itself, without doubt, as much more profound than the *I*" (*PI*, 159).

55. Gabriel Marcel, *Les Hommes contre l'humain* (Paris: La Colombe, 1951), p. 202 (hereafter cited as *HH*).

56. *HH*, 203.

57. *PE*, 16.

58. See Gabriel Marcel, "The Limits of Industrial Civilization," the first of three essays in *The Decline of Wisdom*, trans. Manya Harari (London: Harvill Press, 1954; hereafter cited as *DW*).

59. *DW*, 19.

60. Gabriel Marcel, *The Existential Background of Human Dignity* (Cambridge, Mass.: Harvard University Press, 1963), p. 87 (hereafter cited as *EB*).

61. *BH*, 167; cf. *MJ*, 62–63.

62. O'Malley's translation; cf. *MJ*, 221–22, 62.

63. *EB*, 166.

64. *EB*, 147.

65. *EB*, 123.

66. *EB*, 133.

67. *BH*, 20.

68. *EB*, 169.

Marcel's Notion of Person

REPLY TO JOHN B. O'MALLEY

On the whole, Professor O'Malley's characterization of my thought is quite correct. Moreover, it demonstrates a remarkable depth of understanding of what I hoped to accomplish. But I confess that I am not sure I understand the difference between *intensional* and *extensional*. In particular, the meaning of *extensional* is not altogether clear to me.

I am never quite certain of the meaning which is given rather frequently nowadays to *thematising,* a word I personally have never used. By this I do not mean to imply that it is inappropriate in this context.

The expression "bodying forth," untranslatable into French, leaves me a bit doubtful, for if it is possible to speak of a power of embodiment, to what extent can I say that this power is mine? It would seem that this power is active prior to the period when I can validly speak of "myself."

When Professor O'Malley defines the relationship between myself and my situation, I do not see what the word *ritual* corresponds to, although the general idea is correct. I am not merely involved in such situations; the situations help to reveal me to myself. But perhaps one should add that this revelation can also be, to some degree, transforming.

This critique of my thought is of the highest quality. It reveals a thorough knowledge of all my philosophical writings and could be supplemented and supported by an examination of my dramatic works, which are entirely concerned with the question of the personal and its relationship to the impersonal and the suprapersonal. Professor O'Malley was particularly inspired in showing that the idea of the personal enters as a mediator between the ideas of person and of personality. To my knowledge, no one has ever noted this before.

G.M.

Translated from the French by Susan Gruenheck.

10

Leo Gabriel

MARCEL'S PHILOSOPHY OF
THE SECOND PERSON

ACCORDING to Gabriel Marcel, one gains the awareness of being through personal encounter, through experience, and through concrete thinking but not through abstract thinking. Time and again Marcel has stressed that the experience of concrete thinking is based on the subjective (*personhaft*) grounds of the cognition of being. Marcel has radically and categorically separated the truth of being of subjective existence from the truth of being of objects of abstraction. Marcel looks back on his experiences during the First World War, when he had to keep records of those missing in action. He realized then the deep, unbridgeable gulf between the personal fate of an individual and the bureaucratic reduction of that fate to statistics, nowadays handled by computers. This insight may be the most decisive perception in Marcel's philosophical thinking with regard to the concrete and the essential.

The true reality of humankind is in principle inaccessible to abstract objective description; it transcends its own potentiality. We must therefore approach our true reality by way of an existential thinking, namely, a concretization on the level of the subjective. Marcel's thinking centers on the experience of a transcendent and at the same time concrete reality of existence (*Dasein*) that transcends the level of objective understanding. He interprets human existence as a personal, subjective existence. But the subjectivity of existence should neither be equated nor confused with the subjectivity of perception (*Bewußtsein*).

Marcel thinks that in a world of objects the radical threat to human existence—the threat to which we are particularly exposed today—stems

---

Translated from the German by Dr. Hans H. Rudnick.

from a certain modern mental attitude toward the world that orients itself exclusively toward the having (*avoir*) and possessing of objects. Arrested (or, as Heidegger would say, *verfallen*) in this attitude toward the world, we lose our sense of being (*être*); consequently, we lose not only a fundamental potentiality of thought but also a potentiality to stand above objects (Heidegger's *ek-sistieren*, "to enjoy one's freedom"). As a condition of potential existence and potential historical continuation, we have to divorce ourselves from our demonic obsession with the world; we have to find the reason for being ourselves, and, within it, we have also to find being as such. (What will we gain by winning the whole world at the cost of our true nature?)

Marcel does not tire of rejecting the elimination of humankind inherent in the abstraction of purely object-related thinking. Purely object-related thinking addresses itself only to objects in order to rule the world with the category of the impersonal, of the it (*Es*). This thinking not only rules as a subject but also is ruled and determined by this category as an object. Marcel attributes this destructive abstractness to a dissociation between subject and object. "We are never separate from our thinking," says Marcel, and "this thinking is never separate from ourselves." The Cartesian "I think" should rather be "Someone is thinking inside me." In all our thinking we are always "entangled" (*verwickelt*) in the reality we create through our thinking. Thus we are entangled in the abstractions of the "systems" we set up. The abstraction of objects constructs the illusionary reality to which we fall victim at each instance of a historical context. Yet our participation in everything that surrounds us as reality is the presence of being, not the object of being.

The presence of being does not result from abstract and original thought-created objectivity, in which being no longer exists. Rather, this objectivity estranges the presence of being from itself, makes it an object projected by a subject, and therefore limits it to such a projection. The object is the frontier preventing us from understanding being. The object has been placed before being and posited in advance as the idea of being. Therefore the Cartesian "I think," which presents ideas as thoughts with attributed notions, canot explain being but rather obscures and removes the received object from actual perception. Consequently, only the encounter with reality in a concrete thought process will permit access to being.

The reality of concrete thinking has to replace certain preconceived notions (*Vor-stellungen*), and this means that the concept of having, of possessing objects within the preestablished segments of categories, has to be abandoned. In a system rationally founded on objects, being finds no place as the inherent plenitude and wholeness of the real. So we become aware that Marcel is concerned with the concrete inherent plenitude (*inhaltliche Fülle*) of being. He sees that the inherent plenitude of being is claimed by a dimensioned interpretation of reality that cannot fulfill its promise by the mere having or possessing of objects or by attributing a predetermined role to them. This insight is based on a genuine experience of being that we have now become aware of. It is impossible to gain such an experience through analyzing and abstracting notions. It would be futile to try to describe accurately and communicate (*vermitteln*) such an insight with the received methods of abstract explanation.

Likewise it would be impossible to reduce the individual-related experience and the uniqueness of its content to general laws of procedure. Thus death is more than a fact that occurs during the course of a person's existence. Like the life to which it belongs, death is an event of an individual's personal fate. Therefore empiricism and historicism will have to give way before the fate of the human individual and its transcendence. And so far as human reality and human history are executed and fulfilled by such events, which are beyond the reach of object-related experience and description, there must always exist in our being an irrational factor that makes it impossible to posit our future as if it were the object of precise projection and infallible forecasting. Because of rigorously defined laws, projection and forecasting apply only to the events of nature; they do not apply to the human condition. If we speak of "fate" (*Schicksal*), we refer to an interhuman bond in the complicated interplay between freedom and necessity, an interplay that withstands every attempt of purely objectified understanding and description. ("There is something between heaven and earth which the wisdom of our schools cannot dream of.")

It may be that the awareness of the insoluble and of the analytically and notionally indescribable has caused Marcel's aversion to schools as an institution. Early in his career he developed an antipathy toward any systematization of the true and the essential. This is the same antipathy toward "the system of being" (*System des Daseins*) of which Kierkegaard has spoken. Such a system is not possible, because the living content of the real cannot be pressed into a petrified and fixed pattern, nor can it be divided into and communicated in handy parcels of learned information.

But what actually happens during the modern extensive expansion of the sciences and those numerous constructions of systems? The basic approach of the sciences to reality relies on the same method used in questionnaires. The actual occurrences are reduced to a common denominator characterized by certain objectively provable and countable data. These data are technologically objectified for any time and any person, amounting to a greatly expanded sense experience for everybody who is in possession of the identical organization of senses and the identical technological means; hence the possibility of intersubjective testing appears to be guaranteed on technical grounds. In accordance with the positivistic point of view, such a methodical cataloguing of objects becomes the only valid possibility of acquiring knowledge on critical grounds. Yet this possibility is in principle not universally valid for the realm of total reality. In the notion of the critical attitude, established by Kant on the basis of his transcendental philosophy, the subject is the locus (*Ort*) in the critical system where the object is validly constituted in cognition (*Erkenntnis*) and where cognition is conditioned by the "limits of perception" (*Grenzen des Bewußtseins*). The subject has been created so that it posits objects and interprets the coherence of objects as a world within the individual's range of perception. In this context Marcel speaks of the "idealists" who are possessed with the thought "that the mind as such can only function as activity or constructive potentiality."

According to Marcel, the transcendental-critical subject has only one flaw: it cannot exist. Through the transcendence of the subject beyond itself, through its object-related constituting activity in the act of subjection (*subjectio*)—unmasked by Nietzsche as "the will to have power" (*Wille zur Macht*)—the world becomes the subject's counter-creation (*Gegenwurf*) as an object; it becomes a newly created world, which then objectively becomes one with the subject itself.

In this critical perception of objects (*Gegenstandsbewußtsein*), which intentionally takes possession of the world by "attributing" (*machen*) a particular, individual content to it, Marcel discovers the conscious "domination" (*Herrschaft*) of "possessing" in a so-called imperialistic and capitalistic world, which denies being and the perception of being. Here we touch on a problem Marx approached from the economic and social perspective. Marx demanded expropriation ("de-possession") because he wanted to put an end to a society based on inconsiderate possession. But he merely intended to transfer the possession from a certain social level, the class of the "haves," to the level of the class of the "have-nots" (*Habenichtse*). Such a transfer would collectively place the same means and possibilities previously enjoyed only by the other class, the bourgeoisie, into the hands of the organized proletariat. In principle Marx does not intend to abolish the domination of possessing in order to establish the conditions for a breakthrough of being; rather, he wants only to bring about a reshuffling among possessors. He postulates a change of the subjects who possess, but he does not try to overcome "subjectivity." Nevertheless Marx's point of departure leads inevitably to an eschatological conclusion in the idea of the classless society. At first Marx remains faithful to the level of object-related thinking. He supports the world-related dominance of objects, of things, so that he can then refer to the necessary existential relations that concern us as humans only under the final aspect of the classless society, from which his present-day followers are farther away than ever.

In Marcel's view being cannot be possessed and cannot be made. Being is no object, and it cannot be made or constituted by any subject into an object. Therefore being cannot be posited or given in knowledge (*Bewußtsein*) in the subject-object correlation. Rather, it is the concrete foundation of this abstract and system-related correlation; it is the *ground* and not the object. Without being there is no subject and no object. Consequently, no possible relation between subject and object can objectively be established that can be thought, with regard to the ground of being, only as it really is.

In the same way being cannot be investigated or searched for as an object-related datum in the framework of individual scientific disciplines. Being is not a problem. The problem only arises when an object does not "appear" within a certain cognitive context—when a gap is evident in the methodically established continuum of recognized objects. The existence of this problem entails the attempt to close the gap by searching and finding the necessary object, even if the method of search has to be modified. Since being is not an object, it cannot become an object-related problem. Being is therefore metaproblematic.

Since being cannot be proven as an object or found by inquiry it is a "mystery." This does not mean that it cannot be recognized, that it is a mystical aphaton, or, even less probable, that it is "irrational." The contrast between rational and irrational points toward the same area of object-related predications of phenomena that can be not only rational, like logical thinking, but also irrational, like feeling and will.

But which road leads to being? How can being be approached? How does it manifest itself? How does it "reveal itself" (*zeigt es sich*)? It does not reveal itself as a certain phenomenon to our senses (*Bewußtsein*)—as an object in front of a subject. Being can only manifest and reveal itself through itself. There is no alternative. This self-revealing, this manifesting, is the transcendental event of being (*Seinsgeschehen*)—a transcending (*Übersteigen*) of perception (*Bewußtsein*), a transcending of its being bound to an object (*Gegenständlichkeit*), and a transcending of its possibilities and limitations. It is a breaking through.

How can this transcendence beyond perception occur? How does the original abolition of the contrast between subject and object happen in the realm of being? As has already been stated, it occurs out of the self of being, out of a unity that precedes the subject-object separation of perception; it *is* a ground that precedes the subject-object split.

At this point we recognize an insurmountable difference between the characteristics of the ground—as origin—and the characteristics of the object. Ground and object are two completely heterogeneous elements. How can I, the thinking one, gain access to the ultimate fundamental unity of the total ground (*Grundganze*)? How can I recapture the original unity? How can I "concentrate" (*zusammennehmen*) myself into the dissipating center of objects in an ultimate unification transcending all object-related multiplicity? Marcel calls this act "concentration" (*recueillement*), and it is not at all an emotional, volitive, or rational function of the perception of reflection. It is not an individually experienced act of thinking, feeling, or willing. Rather, it is the reflection of reflection; it is effort springing from the acquired unity of existence—of an "original" seizing that appears comparable to the Hegelian "effort" (*Anstrengung*) of the notion to understand itself but that is in fact incomparable because of its metatranscendental origin. Marcel calls this the "act" of fundamental philosophical reflection, or of "secondary reflection."

Let us briefly return to Hegel's distinction between dialectic thinking and being. This distinction is echoed not only in its abstractions (*Begrifflichkeit*) but also in the postulated transcendental split between subject and object and, subsequently, in the spontaneity of the postulations (thesis, antithesis, and synthesis). But being is something original and unpostulated; it is something that gives itself within its own authentic manifestation and revelation in secondary, or existential, reflection. By contrast, primary reflection refers to intentional acts or acts of perception directed toward objects (the intentional structure of perception as developed by Brentano). It represents the stage of possessing objects and, according to Marcel, bars access to being. Secondary reflection leads beyond primary reflection to a ground-related, not an object-related, being. It leads into the fundamental ontological region. In secondary reflection perception opens itself to being in a process of original groundings. One goes back to and re-flects about the ultimate ground in the fundamental processes of thinking. If we make ourselves think back to the ultimate ground, we recreate the beginning, the *arché,* of thinking. Then we perform precisely what Marcel calls an act of concentration, where thinking springs from the reflecting existence specific to humankind and enfolds from the reunion with existence.

This transcendent process of thinking toward the ultimate ground or origin—one could call this process fundamental thinking—differs completely from the thinking directed toward the object. It opens the door to being, which rests at the center of everything; it leads as *methodos,* as the path of thinking, to being; it opens the "space," the *topos,* in which being has housed itself because it can be found only in the ground where it is at home and present and where it has been originally located not as an object but as a ground. Thus in its existential reflection on the ground, the act of concentration discovers the truth of being as such, that is, as concentration's enclosure (*Eingeschlossenheit*) in the ground. Being is the fundamental metaproblematic reality and the truth of the existence developed by thinking.

It is the task of philosophy, as secondary reflection, to penetrate to the ultimate ground of objects; this entails a return to being and thereby gives all sciences their common and sustaining ground in truth and cognition.

Metamethodically speaking, Marcel conceives of secondary reflection as an act of concentration and as the central execution of existence, which emerges from the ground-center of the person during his or her engagement within the world. Being is accessible in this act of concentration only when the person exists in a state of openness toward being and receives in this openness, on an interpersonal basis, the plenitude (*Fülle*) of being in unity with the I-Thou; that is, the person shares the plenitude and thus experiences the fulfillment of being within the "plenitude from which we have all received." This participation in a concrete, personal fulfillment of being is the meaning of an "encounter" (*Begegnung*). When we speak of an encounter, we mean a coming together with another human being, in particular with a human being who comes close to us in this coming-together and with whom we communicate continuously. Thus although the encounter is certainly a personal event, it is not an ego-related event but rather a taking place that occurs through the other person, through his or her touching (where this touching becomes the wellspring of a person's course of life). The encounter is executed and accomplished by the Thou; it is the result of love. At the same time, for me to participate in being is to participate in the personal life and fate of a fellow human who trusts me—in an I-Thou relation—and who has thereby been entrusted to me; from this person I receive a reality—within the encounter—that can be neither answered on questionnaires nor tabulated in statistics, because it cannot be formulated or objectified. It occurs only in the consummated existential being-together—only in the reality of love.

Such an act of communication between humans grants a sharing of the common reality of the totality—the reality of being. This union constitutes itself continuously in the relation of faithfulness between humans. It grants and guarantees both a continuous adaptation to the streaming reality of the person-related living-with-each-other and the continuous participation in being marked by this nonobjectifiable personal unity. Being becomes real as a being-together-with-someone-else.

Thus a connection between the metaproblematic, or the secret nature of being, and the person becomes evident. The reality of being reveals itself in the depths of personal union and harmony. "Faithfulness is the locus of being"; it is the *topos*, the space, in which being reveals itself. Faithfulness supplies the essential ontological relation to existence (*Dasein*). Truth—that is, ontological truth, the truth of being—results from the personal relations of understanding in the communion between humans Where the Thou reigns as a genuine value.

In the end, the source from which reality flows in a personal encounter is the personal archetypal ground of reality, the ultimate primeval and divine Thou, God. God is the Thou from whom, as the final source, the plenitude of being springs and from whom we continually receive so that we can exist, that is, so that we can be specifically human. Thus being becomes a gift from God to the receiving creature out of mercy. Not in the immanence of the perception in which it "constitutes" itself as "a pure and original datum" (Husserl), but only in the transcendence of its origin does being achieve the completely open potentiality of existence (*Dasein*) in which it is "present" (or *anwest*, according to Heidegger). The great adventure—the advent of being, its arrival in the encounter, and its epiphany—occurs today in "the expanding desert" (Nietzsche) and in the devastation of human existence.

The lapidary simplicity of Marcel's description of the illuminating event of epiphany reminds us of Pascal. Marcel's words were addressed to a similar event. On the first pages of *Being and Having,* we find the following entry for 5 March 1929:

> On this morning, wonderful felicity, I have no doubts any more. For the first time I have clearly experienced mercy. Words like these are terrifying, but what I say is true. I have finally been engulfed by Christian belief and I have been inundated. Wonderful inundation, but I do not wish to waste any more words. And yet, I must write. What an impression of stammering. . . . It is probably a birth. Everything looks different.

Marcel receives from the experience of a mercifully designed reality the idea of an integral "becoming human" (*Menschwerdung*). This becoming is incarnation; it is becoming flesh—*incorporation,* as Marcel puts it. The body places us in the concrete situation of our existence. Incarnation represents the integral meaning of being human, which must not be diminished materialistically or idealistically. But how can this integrality avoid being destroyed by the contradictory tensions within its reality? Kierkegaard recognized the contradictions within human existence when he realized that our existence is a paradox—that as finite creatures we can and must orient ourselves toward the infinite but that the human and the divine are both contained within us. This human paradox marks the point at which the abstract humanism of modern times fails because its rational abstractions attempt to formulate a purely natural or a purely historical— or at least a rationally well-balanced—image of humankind that can be incorporated into a system (whether logical or dialectical).

This systematic interpretation is inadequate both for human reality and for the concrete construction of existence (*Dasein*), for an adequate cognition is not possible without a transcendency. The totality of the rational and of the reasonable fails at the threshold of the transcendent. Here begins Kierkegaard's paradox and Marcel's mystery. Only from the perspective of transcendency can we be viewed in our total reality. But Marcel does not agree with Kierkegaard's progressive dialectical destruction of the human self. The self is not destroyed "before God's eyes"; it is remolded into a pure sacrificial basin so that it can hold the content of infinity and the absolute purely and completely. ("Make room so that God may come.") According to Marcel, the I is supported by the Thou; they are both integrated, expanded, and widened into an integral existence. The radical form of "de-selfing" (*Entselbstung*), the destructive dissolution of the human self into the divine, and the merging of ethical existence with the religious are aspects of the Protestant theology of original sin. They devalue the ethical act of the person that is responsible and binding in love and faithfulness to the Thou, where being comes from, where it is housed, and where it is perceived.

By placing the Thou in the center, Marcel gives the notion of person a new content and establishes a philosophy of the second person. The word *person* derives from the Latin *personare*, "to sound through," and once indicated the mask of the actor, through which his voice was sounded. Marcel's philosophy acknowledges this root: the person, the medium of transcendence, is also a medium of transparence. Thus the person as medium becomes, so to speak, a pervious membrane through which a transcendent reality passes and enters. This enables the I to accomplish itself through the sharing relation with the Thou and hence to find fulfillment in being. The person's true self can now unfold. The present nature of this transcendent reality must speak to the person in order to "sound through." Only in this way can the sharing in personal communication with the Thou, the other person, take place; only in this way can the sharing (*Mitteilung*) of being as a common reality *between* persons be accomplished as an interpersonal reality. It is therefore the act of love and ultimately the act of God's love from which every individual receives his or her self-accomplishment (*Selbstverwirklichung*) in personal union with others through sharing.

Only in the *corpus mysticum* of an interhuman and divine-human reality of loving, according to Marcel, can the broken world (*monde cassé*) of today become an unbroken, whole world again.

> It is probable that the belief of human in human, neither the belief in the fellow human alone nor the trust in the individual, has ever before been subjected to such a hard and dreadful test as today. What is threatened with death today is humankind as a whole. This is true for humanity in its entirety; it is true for the individual considered as a concrete entity; and it is true for the development and expansion of a characteristic believed to be typical of the human race.[1]

The significance of the great French thinker Gabriel Marcel can be appreciated next to and in opposition to Sartre in Marcel's statement that he wishes to erect "a metaphysics of belief on the ruins of humanism."[2] Marcel believes in humankind within a personal existence. Did not the abstract humanism of modern times have to end up in the concrete field of ruins of a dehumanized time-reality (*Zeitwirklichkeit*) because of its abstractions, which forced it to sever itself from the foundations of human existence? "The death of God in Nietzsche's sense has preceded the agony of humankind under which we live. God's death has made this agony possible."[3] Therefore we can say in Marcel's words that "God can and must arise again from the ashes of humankind."[4] This is the great hope Marcel expresses in his philosophy of hope. It is a philosophy of the threshold (*la philosophie seuil*). Today we can be less convinced than ever that human existence is a problem of economic, social, and political organization. What good would it do if we were to dominate the entire world? The world is not the problem; the possession and use of things, of objects one can acquire, are not the problem. Having is not the problem; being is. The object is not the problem; existence is. Existence cannot be acquired. It just is to be.

Marcel knows that our presence—not in a thing, not in an object, but in being—is threatened not only by the predominance of things and objects but much more profoundly by the predominance of the ego that posits itself as the absolute, that includes itself in its self, and that isolates itself in its "ego-solitariness" (Ferdinand Ebner's *Icheinsamkeit*) by identifying all things as its objects. If the ego of idealism posits itself as the absolute foundation of valid cognition and reality, it loses its existence in the narrowness and reserve of the *solus ipse*—of the "I alone"—as is evident in Sartre,[5] who holds that absolute freedom is vouchsafed only in self-creative subjectivity (*l'homme se fait*). But Marcel shows how the I receives its accomplishment of existence and freedom from its devotion to the Thou. "You are, therefore I am." The I becomes a person by transcending itself and encountering the Thou in the transcendence. It will finally encounter the absolute Thou, God, and will thus ultimately arrive with this far-reaching reflection (*Rückbezug*) in its absolute ground and origin at the highest and most absolute possibility of its expansion of existence within its relation to being. If we can attribute a philosophy of the first person to Sartre, then we can credit Marcel with a philosophy of the second person, whose personal existence is accomplished within the community or, to speak in Jaspers's terms, in "communication."

The principle of the abstract system of individualism, with its axiom "freedom, equality, brotherhood," has been unable to safeguard freedom and brotherly human behavior; instead it has lost them in a consequential antithesis to collectivism. As Marcel demonstrates, the dialectic of the individual and the collective can only be overcome by a concrete synthesis of the person that places the individual, with the freedom of personal connectedness to others, in the safeguarding and cradling unity of the communicating human community and of humanity. This connectedness within being, shared by all humans, will overcome, through its creative power of love and faithfulness, the present tattered condition of demonic hatred in this world. As the female protagonist in one of Marcel's plays says:

> Don't you feel sometimes that we are living . . . if you can call it living . . . in a broken world? Yes, broken like a broken watch. The mainspring has stopped working. Just look at it, nothing has changed. Everything is in place. But put the watch to your ear, and you don't hear any ticking. You know what I'm talking about, the world, what we call the world, the world of human creatures . . . it seems to me it must have had a heart at one time, but today you would say the heart had stopped beating.[6]

That the timepiece of history shows our new world-hour is the hope and conviction of Marcel's philosophy of belief in humankind. It is a philosophy of hope for our future and of perpetual love; it is a philosophy for each of us as a person—in the second person.

Summary and Prospect

Marcel points to the critical notion of Descartes, to the *sum cogitans*. He demonstrates the contradiction and the dissolution of the *sum cogitans* by recognizing that I am not included in the thinking, that in the act of *cogitare* the relation to myself is dissolved. Thinking is a "transcendency of the self; it is a striving for the other." Therefore Descartes should have said: "Something is thinking inside me" (*Es denkt in mir*).[7] The *cogitare* of Descartes constitutes perception as the modus of possessing, not as the modus of being. I have perception, but I am not perception.

Transcendence in the form of thinking is what Marcel calls "grasping" (*prise*). This grasping is the source of judgment, which expresses a relation toward a situation of facts: "At the root of cognition occurs the grasping for reality."[8] The grasping of thinking—as a logical phenomenon in judgment—leads to the thing, to the object, to the thought-created being, and thus neither to being in its own self nor to the real self in the subject engaged in the process of grasping.

The Cartesian "I think" does not grasp reality; rather, it is an axiomatic notion, a formal demarcation and limitation. "Descartes' *cogito* is not origin but obturation."[9] Just as the way to being is blocked by the object of thinking in its logical grasping of the thing, so too the way to being is blocked by the subject, which defines itself in its self-consciousness as the basis in a limiting and isolating procedure and thus includes itself *notionally* as the "subject." Neither in the subject nor in the object can being achieve its transparency.

With reference to the obturation by the object, Marcel says: "The metaphysical nature of the object as such is perhaps exactly its obturative power."[10] In the *cogito* process (*Bewußtsein*) both a subjective and an objective barrier separate us from real being: perception (*Bewußtsein*) as a principle of "immanence." Being can only be reached by breaking through this barrier. In such a breakthrough the subjective and the objective bonds and preoccupations of thinking must be overcome in the subject-object relation—this last term standing for Jaspers's "fixedness" (*Fixierung*). The goal of thinking is the possibility of arrangement (*disponsibilité*); "the open horizon" (*der offene Horizont*), in Jaspers's terms; "the still open behavior" (*offenständiges Verhalten*), in Heidegger's terms. The occurrence of transcendency means for Kierkegaard an intrusion of existence into the immanence of the I, which is thus dialectically dissolved ("self-destruction before God in religion A"). For Marcel the breakthrough to being comes neither from the I nor from dialectics (that is, from self-destruction) but from dialogue with the Thou. In Marcel's thinking the radical appeal by the Thou and everything connected with it becomes much stronger than in Jaspers's "communication." This appeal is the foundation of the realization of existence ("I am, because you are"). It is a communication not of reason but of love. In my connection with the beloved Thou, being opens itself for me. Being in a lovingly shared plenitude is neither abstract object, like the being as object of thinking, nor subject, like the I of my limited and enclosed perception (*cogito*). In the concrete relation of the I to the Thou, in the "intersubjectivity," being is experienced in the transcending of the I through its mutual sharing with the Thou. Since according to Marcel what is concrete and alive is accessible not through logical and comprehending thinking but only through personal and transcendent experiencing, being is in truth the ontological mystery (*le mystère ontologique*).[11]

Marcel particularly emphasizes the coincidence of mystery and being: "The problem of being is, therefore, only the translation into a language inadequate for mystery."[12] Yet this does not mean we have no knowledge of the problem of being. "Every confusion between mystery and the imperceptible must be carefully avoided."[13] Metaphysical thinking aims existentially at the mystery of being, just as logical thinking aims essentially at scientific objects; hence being is only problematic as a problem. Metaphysical reflection relates to what can become neither an object of a science nor a scientific problem. "The mystery is the metaproblematic."[14] And the metaproblematic is something that lies at the ground of possible problems as the condition of becoming problematic; it cannot become a problem itself, but without it no problem would be possible. This definition does not explain why or from where problems result. The metaproblematic as an answer therefore cannot apply in the area of solvable or solved problems.

Our concern refers instead to what can no longer be objectively recognized or solved; it is the concern on which the above is based. The field of the metaobjective and of the metaproblematic is apparent in the sphere of the ultimate ground for what can become a problem and what can become an object. For this reason the dimension of the original ground is disclosed in Marcel's notion of the metaproblematic. How can this ground be reached other than by the road of object-related cognition? Marcel suggests taking the road of communicating participation in being, where the consummation of the intersubjective relation between the I and the Thou takes place. This consummation means a participation in concrete reality, which is shared by us through being rather than through removed, abstract, and objective thinking. I find myself in being—I participate in it; I exist in its presence—only when I am personally concerned with the Thou and thereby participate in the mutually present reality of the totality, that is, of being. The "presence of the totality" (*Gegenwart des Ganzen*) within this sharing in being has been carefully developed by L. Lavelle. Its continuity is guaranteed by faithfulness. Faithfulness—"being faithful to myself, to my fellow humans, and to God"—is simply a continuous participation in the reality and truth of being. It is a permanent road to and locus of existence: "Faithfulness is the locus of being." Belief is the corresponding attitude to the mystery of being. It is being penetrated by the devotional act of believing. Belief alone can transcend into being. Thus belief in the other, in God, and finally in myself reveals "the metaproblematic as a partnership that lies at the ground of my reality and that constitutes my reality."[15]

Being reveals itself in sharing between person and person as something they have in common, and it reveals at the same time its metacritical orientation toward something metaproblematic.[16] One of Marcel's essential contributions is the discovery of the metaproblematic, even if we could ask whether the thinking of the metaproblematic could only unfold in the presence of responding love and faithfulness. Is thinking as reflection not dissolved by the occurring immediate sharing of being? A new basic dimension of thinking reveals itself existentially in the metaproblematic, because, according to Marcel, the personal interrelation cannot be fulfilled by purely object-related thinking. Marcel meets Buber and Ebner in this decisive idea of a revelation of being within the personal context. Therefore his philosophy can indeed be characterized as a philosophy of the second person. Heidegger, with his "whichever mine" (*Jemeinigkeit*), and Sartre, with his *solus ipse,* refer themselves to the freedom of decision, but neither of them knows the second person. Even Kierkegaard fails to see the second person within the perspective of the becoming of the self (*Selbstwerdung*) of the individual as individual and within the absolute realization of the self. Binswanger has felt "the cold atmosphere of the you-lessness" in Heidegger's thinking, and he has tried to reshape the "structure of caring" (*Sorgestruktur*) in existence into the reality of love.[17] But the condition of love is the central reality of the Thou. We encounter it only in Marcel's Neosocratic dialogues of thought.

LEO GABRIEL

INSTITUTE OF PHILOSOPHY
UNIVERSITY OF VIENNA
JULY 1970

NOTES

1. Gabriel Marcel, *Homo Viator: Philosophie der Hoffnung,* trans. Wolfgang Rüttenauer (Düsseldorf: Bastion-Verlag, 1949), p. 218 (hereafter cited as *HV*).
2. *HV,* 218.
3. *HV,* 218.
4. *HV,* 218–19.

5. See Leo Gabriel, *Existenzphilosophie von Kierkegaard bis Sartre* (Vienna: Herold Verlag, 1951), p. 272.

6. Gabriel Marcel, *The Mystery of Being*, trans. G. S. Fraser (vol. 1) and René Hague (vol. 2), 2 vols. (Chicago: Henry Regnery Co., 1960), 1:26–27.

7. "On ne dira jamais assez combien la formule, 'es denkt in mir' est préférable au 'cogito' qui nous expose au pur subjectivisme" (Gabriel Marcel, *Etre et avoir* [Paris: Aubier, 1935], p. 35 [hereafter cited as *EA*]).

8. "Cette prise est au contraire à la source du jugement lui-même qui prolonge et sanctionne unc appréhension" (*EA*, 64). "Il faut qu'il y ait à la racine de l'intelligence une prise sur le réel" (*EA*, 65).

9. "Le 'je pense' n'est pas une source, c'est un obturateur" (*EA*, 35).

10. "Le problème des rapports de l'âme et du corps est plus qu'un problème: et c'est là la conclusion implicite d'*Existence et Objectivité*" (*EA*, 161).

11. Gabriel Marcel, *Position et approches concrètes du mystère ontologique* (Louvain: Nauwelaerts; Paris: Vrin, 1949).

12. "Le problème de l'être me sera donc qu'une traduction en un langage inadéquat d'un mystère" (*EA*, 171).

13. "Toute confusion entre le mystère et l'inconnaissable doit être soigneusement évitée" (*EA*, 170).

14. "Mais il est de l'essence d'un mystère d'être reconnu; la réflexion métaphysique suppose cette reconnaissance qui n'est pas de son ressort.

"Distinction du mystérieux et du problématique. Le problème est quelque chose qu'on rencontre, qui barre la route. Il est tout entier devant moi. Au contraire le mystère est quelque chose où je me trouve engagé, dont l'essence est par conséquent de n'être pas tout entier devant moi. C'est comme si dans cette zone la distinction de *l'en moi* et du *devant moi* perdait sa signification.

"Le naturel: la zone du naturel coincide avec celle du problématique. Tentation de convertir le mystère en problème" (*EA*, 145).

"La philosophie comme métacritique orientée vers une métaproblématique... Le métaproblématique: la paix qui passe tout entendement, l'éternité" (*EA*, 149).

15. "Il faut voir . . . que le métaproblématique, c'est une participation qui fonde ma réalité de sujet" (*EA*, 165).

16. "La philosophie comme métacritique orientée vers une métaproblématique" (*EA*, 149).

17. "One realizes that the caring being-together, that love, is left freezing in the cold outside the gate of this blueprint of being" (Ludwig Binswanger, *Grundformen und Erkenntnis menschlichen Daseins* [Zürich: M. Niehans, 1942], p. 52).

Marcel's Philosophy of the Second Person

REPLY TO LEO GABRIEL

The commentary I wish to make bears on the question of knowing whether it is really legitimate to substitute *Es denkt in mir* for *Ich denke* ("It thinks in me" for "I think"). In my reaction against the traditional interpretations of the Cartesian *cogito* and even of the Kantian *Ich denke,* I am afraid I have expressed myself several times on this question without due reflection. I would be inclined to state it today in a much more modified way. At my present time of life, thinking appears to me to be the act of a subject and, for that reason, as involving a responsibility that would be inconceivable if I could say that a certain impersonal activity is somehow performed through me. What is true is that this act presents some singular characteristics by which it is opposed to the *Je sens* or the *Ich erlebe*. That is absolutely evident when it is a question of a judgment, and it is, after all, in judgment that the essence of the *Je pense* realizes itself. What enters in here, as the great rationalists have correctly seen, is a direction toward, or a reference to, the universal, it being specifically understood that this universality is not taken or considered as a case of extension. Here aesthetic judgment is of particular interest. If I say, "That is beautiful," I not only mean, "That pleases me," but at the same time know very well that there exist an infinite number of people who would be incapable of recognizing that beauty. Yet what is remarkable is that this statement in no way affects the conviction (*Überzeugung*) expressed in my judgment, which those who oppose me will reduce to the level of a claim ("He thinks that work is beautiful; for my part, it is only so much noise"). The question then arises of finding out who would be able to settle the matter between us. This is another problem that is extremely acute in the world today.

From the viewpoint of morality, the difficulty is—or at least seems to

---

Translated from the French by Dr. Garth Gillan.

be—lessened because one believes it possible to refer to a consensus. Yet experience shows that such a consensus, if it ever existed, is today much less effective than it might have been half a century ago.

In all this we are at the threshold of the Kantian position. But this tends to appear today as an extreme position that can strictly be held only if one abstracts from the data of experience. It must be said, moreover, that experience itself is less and less univocal. It would be appropriate to question oneself in depth about the meaning of this evolution and about the grave dangers to which it exposes us today.

G.M.

11

Richard M. Zaner

THE MYSTERY
OF THE BODY-QUA-MINE

I

G ABRIEL Marcel's philosophical career has revolved about a central
thematic concern. In his early writings he stressed the "meaning and
bearing" of his inquiries: "We are concerned essentially with determining
the metaphysical conditions of personal existence."[1] Over a decade later
he wrote that his concern with the "fundamental experiences inscribed in
our *condition*" had assumed the form of a "philosophical anthropology."[2]

The axial place of humankind, of the "metaphysics of the human condition," in Marcel's thought was fully and clearly recognized in his later
and most mature effort, the Gifford Lectures.[3] But his early concern with
"the personal" was in no way lost or obscured, for as he emphatically
asserted on the occasion of the Gifford Lectures, the central question of
such a metaphysics or an anthropology must be, Who, or what, am I?[4] To
seek the metaphysical conditions of humankind—that in virtue of which
we are what-we-are and without which we would not be what-we-are—is,
Marcel has insistently urged, to inquire into what it is to be a human
person, a self. And this requires a philosophical articulation of what it is
to be "a" self. To seek this, however, plunges the philosopher into *his
own self*—to be "a" self is essentially to be "my" self.

The matter can be approached in another way. "My" self is, after all,
"a" self; I am "a" self, "a" person, "a" human being. But what is it to
be a human being? To know this seems to require that I know what
"being" is. Yet if I then ask about being, an abyss opens beneath me: "*Is*
there Being? *What* is Being? But, I cannot bring my reflection to bear on
these problems without seeing a new abyss open out under my feet: *I*, who
inquire into Being, can I be assured that I am? . . . Who am I, I who

question Being? In what way am I qualified to proceed with these investigations? . . . How can I be assured that I am?"[5]

This brings us back to the original question: Who am I, I who ask these questions? At every point I come up against this question and encounter a fundamental *aporia:* I, who pose the question, am myself necessarily brought into the sphere of the question. As Marcel expresses it, I am involved no longer in a straightforward "problem" but rather in a "metaproblem" or "mystery": the inquirer is essentially within the arena of what is brought into question.

At the same time, this *aporia* is critical: it is urgent that I not only respond to the question but that I also have some assurance that my response is legitimate and trustworthy. Unless the being ("condition") of the asker is capable of disclosure, nothing asked about can be truly disclosed. The issue, then, is essentially complex and dialectical; what is at stake is not only what is sought-for in the act of questioning but also what happens to the seeker. When the "issue" is the self—which means, fundamentally, myself—the seeker and the sought-for are one and the same.

Fully cognizant of the apparently inescapable methodological and epistemological paradoxes here, Marcel has nevertheless been able to clarify the elusive and subtly evasive phenomenon of the self. As W. E. Hocking has stressed, the self is Marcel's native philosophical terrain.[6] For Marcel the human condition is disclosed as a fundamental "ontological exigence"[7] concretely manifested as a quest: we are beings who, in our very being, are in quest of ourselves. As seekers, our condition is that of not-knowing; hence, in Marcel's terms, each of us is a "being-on-the-way" (*être-en-route, être-en-marche*), a "voyager" (*homo viator*), whose quest, however much it may be and frequently is masked,[8] *is* his or her most basic condition.

Realizing this, I (the seeker) am brought up abruptly against myself: I who ask, "Who am I?" *am* that very quest for assuredness about myself. In order to utter the question, I must *be,* and thus I *am* this assuredness, this emphasis I give myself in the affirmation "I exist!" "In every case," Marcel states, "I *produce* myself, in the etymological sense of the word, that is to say, I put myself forward."[9] In my seeking, I manifest myself,[10] in what Marcel later calls an "exclamatory consciousness of self . . . of existing."[11]

Inseparable from a certain "wonder" or "astonishment,"[12] this exclamatory sense of myself is what the philosopher must fasten onto unswervingly.[13] Yet in doing so, I encounter still another *aporia.* At the heart of this sense is a crucial opaqueness: my own body. I find myself in quest of myself and in wonder about myself,[14] and with this move I hit on the "central datum of all metaphysics,"[15] the *donné-pivot* of the quest: my own embodiment (*être-incarné*). What thus is of first importance to Marcel's exploration of the human condition is the meaning of "my body-*qua-mine*." It is to this that I now turn.

II

Marcel's quest for an "existential indubitable" in the human condition is a radical question; it seeks to "go to the roots" or "grounds" of human reality. The radical reality of the human is that without which a human being would not be what it is (that is, its essence). The radical question, then, takes us to these grounds. It places them in question and forces the seeker to encounter and abide with them as essentially problematic; hence it discloses the *problematicalness of the ground as ground*.[16] (In Marcel's terms, the philosopher is faced with the metaproblematic, or with mystery.) Because it is radical, the question forces a foundational impasse: the question cannot be posed without calling into question the seeker's own prevailing ideas, beliefs, values, and the like (the seeker's "knowledge-at-hand"). Hence such a question places me—the one who asks, my "what-I-am"—in question precisely because it makes problematic the ground as ground (including what grounds me as the seeker).

Fundamental to Marcel's quest is his effort to account for the "mineness" of my own animate organism. What does it mean for this specific physical organism to be "mine"? Do I "have" it in the sense that a book has covers, a person has clothing, or a triangle has three sides? Does the "mine" here signify that I *am* my body? Or is it rather that "I" and "my body," though not identical, are in some way "unified"? Such questions, Marcel believes, must motivate a complete break with traditional representations of the mind, a "break, accordingly, once and for all with the metaphors which represent consciousness as a luminous circle around which there would be only shadows. It is, to the contrary, the shadow which is at the center."[17] This "shadow" is my own embodiment, which cannot be made into something objective; it is not an "object" (a *Gegen-stand*). I find that no appeal to physiology, anatomy, or similar natural sciences will avail; what makes my body *my own* is disclosed only within my own experience. Accordingly, I must explicate this organism *as it is experienced by me as mine*. Several illustrations will help clarify this phenomenon.

In Richard Hughes's novel *A High Wind on Jamaica,* an event "of considerable importance'' happens to Emily (a ten-year-old) while she is playing house on the ship *Clorinda:*

> Walking rather aimlessly aft . . . it suddenly flashed into her mind that she was *she*.
>
> She stopped and began looking over all of her person which came within the range of her eyes. She could not see much, except a fore-shortened view of the front of her frock, and her hands when she lifted them for inspection; but it was enough for her to form a rough idea of the little body she suddenly realized to be hers.
>
> . . . Each time she moved her arm or a leg . . . it struck her with fresh amazement to find them obeying her so readily. Memory told her, of course, that they had always done so before: but before, she had never realized how surprising this was.
>
> . . . She began examining the skin of her hands with the utmost care: for it was *hers*. She slipped a shoulder out of the top of her frock; and having peeped in to make sure she really was continuous under her clothes, she shrugged it up to touch her cheek. The contact . . . gave her a comfortable thrill. . . . But whether the feeling came to her through her cheek or her shoulder, which was the caresser and which the caressed, that no analysis could tell her.[18]

Robert Russell's strong and enchanting autobiography, *To Catch an Angel,* captures the phenomenon as well but in a somewhat different context. Blinded at the age of five by an accident, he is lying in a hospital bed trying to see when he undergoes a critical discovery:

> For the first time in my life I had wanted to do something with all my being. I had commanded my flesh, and it had failed me. I was ashamed of my weakness, but, even more, I was indignant at the refusal of my body to do what I had insisted. I realized then that my body could not perform the imperative commands of my spirit. This experience was the door through which I passed out of childhood.[19]

Reflecting on experiences like these, Marcel's analysis reveals a number of distinguishable but inseparable moments, or aspects, to the unitary phenomenon of embodiment: (1) the sense of my body's belonging to me, that is, the bond between my body and me; (2) the experience of ''feeling'' or ''sensing'' pertaining to my body; (3) the disclosure of the ''world'' by means of my body (my body as *être-au-monde*); and (4) my body as the ''landmark'' (*repère*) for all existence. We shall discuss these aspects in order, giving the most attention to the first, since this seems to be the ground for Marcel.

III

What does it mean for my body to be mine? Does it belong to me in the same way my dog belongs to me? Marcel believes that an important analogy will help to determine the limits beyond which my body ceases to be mine.[20]

For my dog to be mine, it must either live with me in my house or be lodged in some place where I have decided it shall reside. Thus I assume the responsibility for seeing that it is cared for. There is, moreover, a reciprocal relation here. However minimally, the dog must in some way manifest a recognition that it belongs to me (it must obey me, show a certain affection for me, and so on).

Like my dog, my body is something on which I have an indisputable claim: it belongs to me and to no one else. Even in the case of the cruelest kind of slavery, Marcel urges, the slave retains at least a minimal sense of his body's being his own. At the limit, the slave must feel his body to be his own, for otherwise it would be highly questionable whether or not one could still consider him human. Marcel sets this example as a lower limit to the sense of belonging.

To continue the analogy, I care for my body as I care for my dog. Since my body is mine alone, I am responsible for providing for its subsistence. I must maintain my body, by feeding, exercising, grooming, and so on. My body is mine in that I look after it. According to Marcel, the limit in this instance would be a kind of total asceticism: if I ceased to care for my body, it is questionable whether I would experience it as mine.

Furthermore, as with the dog, I have an immediate control over my body. My body is that by means of which my "I can" is most immediately actualized—that by means of which I "rule and govern" (particularly regarding the body's organs).[21] If I want to pick up an object, I do so "with" my body. Here as well there is a limiting case (an "inner" one): if I lost control of my body because of illness or injury, I would cease to experience it as mine.

The analogy breaks down, however, when I recognize that my dog is external to me—spatiotemporally distinct from me—but my body is not. Still, the question of possession remains: my body is mine, but in what further sense? In order to answer this question, Marcel raises the more general question of "belonging" or "having." Recognizing the many senses of the word *having*, Marcel focuses on instances in which *having* is taken in the forceful and precise sense in order to distinguish two such dimensions of meaning: "having-as-implication" and "having-as-possession."[22] Devoting very little attention to the former, he fastens onto the latter as the most forceful sense for the issue at hand and delineates three fundamental strata in all having.

First, all having reveals a *qui-quid* relation; that is, having is essentially a relation between what is had and the haver, such that the haver is the center of inherence for the had. The haver has the had and not vice versa (at least for the present level of study). Marcel cites the following model for this relation:

> Every affirmation bearing on a "having" seems indeed to be based in some manner on the model of a kind of prototypical situation in which the *qui* is nothing other than *myself*. It seems, indeed, that the having would be felt in its force, that it takes its value, only from within the "I have". If a "you have" or a "he has" is possible, this is only a virtue of a sort of transfer which, moreover, cannot be effectuated without a certain loss.[23]

The understanding (or experiencing) of another as a haver is thus founded on the more fundamental experiencing of oneself as such. The "I have" is fundamental, Marcel suggests, because having means ultimately "having the power to" (*pouvoir*), in the sense of "having the disposal of" (*disposer de*), and this is something that in the first instance I myself experience.[24] To have something, therefore, is to experience oneself as being able to do something with it, as having disposal of it; if I experience something as belonging to another, I experience it accordingly as within the disposal of the other—a sense it acquires through a "transfer" from my own experience.

Considered as *pouvoir,* the relation of having involves a kind of "containing" (*contenir*): the something possessed is contained or included within the sphere of *pouvoir* and *disposer de,* which constitutes the *qui-quid* relation of having. This containing is not, as Marcel sees, merely a matter of spatiality but rather the idea of potentiality: "to contain is to enclose; but, to enclose is to prevent, it is to resist, it is to be opposed to what can overflow, be spilled, escape, etc."[25] Thus, Marcel continues, through this *pouvoir* we are able to detect a kind of "suppressed dynamism" at the heart of the having relation that clearly shows the meaning of the transcendence of the *qui* over the *quid.* The relation is from the *qui* to the *quid,* and it is a relation effected by the *qui;* the *pouvoir* is inward to, or within, the *qui.* This approaches the central point.

Second, this nonspatial movement from the *qui* to the *quid* is possible, Marcel argues, only where there is an "opposition of what is without and what is within."[26] What is central here is the meaning of *within.* To have is "to have to oneself," "to keep to oneself" (*avoir à soi*), and in this sense "to conceal" (*dissimuler*): the haver has the had to himself or herself and therefore in opposition to the other-qua-other (that is, the other as another potential haver). As such, there is an "inward dialectic" in all having, for something is had only so far as it can be exposed, given away, lost, or disclosed—but also only so far as the had is not actually disposed of.

Marcel regards this tension between a "within" and a "without" as essential, and he defines it by the disposability of what is had. The had can be shown or disposed of, but in order to remain a haver, the haver must keep the had while at the same time maintaining its disposability. Hence having is a relation that is always in need of being recognized or acknowledged by others (who, though they do not maintain this relation to the *quid,* could do so). All havers who have a had, have in addition the possibility of getting rid of it, which means that havers have the had only so far as they manifest themselves as havers before nonhavers.

Third and finally, having is essentially a tensioned reference to the other-qua-other; dialectically this reference to the other is what constitutes the haver as a haver. But the "other," Marcel points out, need not be another person; it may be myself, if I take myself as the one who has something: "In so far as I take myself as having in me, or more precisely, as having *to* myself certain characteristics, certain attributes, I consider myself from the point of view of an Other to which I oppose myself only on condition of first implicitly identifying myself with him."[27]

Precisely to the extent that having is constituted by this tension (between the *qui* and the *quid,* between a "within" and a "without," and, more fundamentally, between the self and the other-qua-other), the relation of having is essentially *threatened.* For so far as what is had is a "without" for a "within" and is maintained constantly as a "without" (as disposable), the had is essentially open to the possibility of being lost, stolen, destroyed, plagiarized, and the like. This threat is intrinsic to having, Marcel believes, and reveals itself as the "hold" of the other-qua-other: "there is in having a double permanence: of the *qui,* and of the *quid.* But this permanence is essentially threatened. . . . And this threat is the hold of the Other qua Other—which can be the world in itself—and in the face of which I feel myself so painfully as *me.* I hug to myself this thing which may be taken from me; I attempt desperately to incorporate it to me, to form with it a unique, indecomposable complex. Desperately, vainly. . . ."[28]

The domain of having thus appears to be the domain of despair.[29] That the had is essentially threatened means that the haver is caught up in constant anxiety over the had; the haver is forever on the lookout for dangers to it and thus seeks to "insure" a permanent relation to it. Dialectically, however, the more the haver seeks to secure the had against threats, the more the haver both becomes cognizant of the threats and seeks to secure against them. As Marcel shows, the haver seeks to establish a privileged realm of being for the had to maintain it as at once something disposable and something secured from all threats. It is almost as if the haver seeks to transcend the domain of having by an even stronger relation of having, to close the gap between the *qui* and the *quid* without forfeiting the relation of having. This dialectical tangle is for Marcel the essence of despair.

IV

What does this analysis reveal for the question of my body-qua-mine? I have my body, but in what sense? Marcel's argument is fundamentally that the "avoir-possession" pertaining to "my body-qua-mine" is neither a relation of *partes extra partes* (as between physical things) nor an instrumental relation. To be sure, just as there is a sense in which I "have" my body, so too there is a sense in which I "use" it as an instrument—the difficulty is to determine in which sense. For something to be an instrument means that it is a means of extending or of strengthening a certain power of or capacity for doing something. The instrument is interposed between what is acted on and what acts (the hammer, for example, is between my hand and the nail).

If my body is purely an instrument, it interposes and extends powers or abilities. Is this so?

> When I say that my body is interposed between me and things, I am only expressing a pseudo-idea, because what I call *me* cannot be identified with a thing or with a term. Of course it is possible to say that my body is interposed between a body A which affects and a body R on which it reacts. But in that case what happens to *me,* to the subject? The subject seems to *withdraw into an indeterminate sphere from which it contemplates*—without existing for itself—*the anonymous play of the universal mechanism.*[30]

In the end, to consider my body as an instrument (and hence as something I have in the delineated senses) involves me in an absurdity. If it were an instrument, Marcel shows, then there would have to be a deep community of nature between it and the things on which it acts and between it and me, the subject who "has" it. But reflection shows that although there is a sense in which my body is an instrument and although my body can indeed become the instrument for another (as in slavery), the object and my body do not share that deep community of nature—they are not of the same being. The user of an instrument, in brief, cannot at the same time be a user and be of the same nature as the instrument used.

Accordingly, Marcel concludes that my body is not something I have. To the contrary, it is the "prototype of having" or of "instrumentality." My body-qua-mine is precisely what makes any instrumental having, and indeed any objective relation, at all possible. It is that by virtue of which, by means of which, there are "objects" (and hence instruments, and hence things possessed) in the first place. Thus the having that pertains to my body-qua-mine is *primordial*.[31] But this does not, Marcel contends, rule out all mediation between me and my body; to deny this mediation, he believes, would be "to undermine the very foundation of spiritual life and pulverise the mind into purely successive acts."[32]

Although he is never quite satisfied with his conclusions, Marcel is forced to say that so far as there is a relation of having between me and my body (however prototypical that relation may be), there must be mediation, although not an instrumental mediation. Mineness is essential, but it is not defined by instrumentality; the closest Marcel can come in his efforts to penetrate this phenomenon is to identify "sympathetic mediation."[33] By this Marcel means to point to what he calls a "felt kernel" (*noyau senti*) essential to all possession as such, "and this nucleus is nothing other than the experience, in itself non-intellectualizable, of the connection by means of which my body is mine."[34] The presence of this felt kernel in all having persuades Marcel that mineness should be understood as a fundamental intimacy. Between my body and me is a unity so intimate and profound that "I *am* my body"[35]—not my body as it is for others, but my body as it is experienced by me as mine. I must say that the body that I am is not the *corps-objet* but the *corps-sujet,* whose core is feeling:

> It can be seen straight away that *my* body is only *mine* inasmuch as, however confusedly, it is felt. The radical abolition of coenesthesia, supposing it were possible, would mean the destruction of my body in so far as it is mine. If I am my body this is in so far as I am a being that feels. . . . I only *am* my body more absolutely than I am anything else because to be anything else whatsoever I need first of all to make use of my body.[36]

In order to feel anything else, I must first of all feel my own body as mine; in this sense I must experience my body prior to anything else. My body is that by means of which there are other objects. This priority is expressed in the formula that my body is the prototype of all having and shows again the central importance of the phenomenon of *sentir* ("feeling") for Marcel's theory of the body-qua-mine. We turn now to this second aspect of Marcel's theory.

V

Marcel develops his views of *sentir* primarily by means of a penetrating and decisive critique of traditional theories of sensory perception.

Essentially, all such theories have the same schema, what Marcel calls the "message-theory." To sense something is to "receive" certain data from it; *sentir* is taken to be a sort of "message" transmitted from one pole (for example, a flower) to another pole (for example, the sensitive membranes of the nose). Something emitted by the one then travels or is transmitted under objectively determinable conditions and is received by the other, which "translates" it into the "language" of sensation (or, in the case of the flower, into "olfactory language"). In this sense, we are inclined to regard the act of feeling as a communication like that between two telegraph poles.[37] To perceive something with the senses is to gather specific information from and about it.

> When we use the terms, "to receive," "to emit," and so on, we compare the organism to a pole to which a certain message comes. More precisely, what is gotten by this pole is not the message itself, but an ensemble of data which can be transcribed with the help of a certain code. The message in the strict sense, indeed, implies a double transmission, the first being produced at the point of origin [the sensed object] and the second at the point of termination [the sensitive organism].[38]

Despite modifications among the various theories, this schema holds true for them all.

Now, Marcel contends, this entire mode of interpretation breaks down in its own terms.

> We are dupes of an illusion when we confusedly imagine that the receptive consciousness *translates* into sensation something which is initially given to it as a physical phenomenon, as a disturbance for instance. What, in fact, is "translation"? To translate is in every case to substitute one group of data for another group of data. But, the term, "data," requires that we take it rigorously. The shock experienced by the organism or by its members is in no way a datum; or more precisely, it is a datum for the observer who perceives it in a certain manner, but not for the organism who suffers it.[39]

For the percipient to be able to translate, it must have both the set of data to be translated and the set of data into which the first set is to be translated. This situation is inconceivable, for according to the theory the first set of data is by definition not given to the percipient. If it were, there would be no need for translation. If we were to say that the physical disturbance transmitted by X to Y is received by Y as an "unconscious" or "unnoticed" datum, we would merely push the same problem back a stage; in order to translate the unconscious or unnoticed datum into a conscious or noticed one (whatever this might mean), the percipient must be given the unconscious or unnoticed as a readily accessible datum, but this is ruled out by the theory at the outset. An unsensed message is not a message at all. And if it is called "irreducible" or "unanalyzable," it is still not a message, since a message must be translatable.

For Marcel this message-theory derives from the assumption that the act of feeling or sensing is not an act at all but passive reception, that it occurs by means of a series of terms or objects, and that hence it can be interpreted as an object; that is, the thing sensed, the sensation, and the sensing organism are all equally objects. Such a view is inevitable. We invariably regard the body as an instrument (however "privileged" we may consider it), and for this reason "it must needs appear to be interposed between us and objects, and we are therefore convinced that it mediatizes our apprehension of objects."[40] Consequently all *sentir* appears to be fundamentally mediatized—conditioned by a series of mediations at the level of objects. Therefore the transmission of messages (that is, any instrumental act) is actually a kind of object-mediation.

To take the body as instrument, however, is to exclude this body of mine and hence to exclude the act of feeling not only as an act but also as my act—the *je sens*. Yet when the situation of *sentir* is apprehended as metaproblematic, Marcel believes it becomes necessary "to recognize that the initial assumption must be placed in doubt, and certainly not be compared to a message. This is the case for the fundamental reason, that every 'message' supposes a sensation at its base—precisely in the same manner as any instrument, as we have already seen actually presupposes my body as pre-existent to it."[41]

As soon as we bring my body back into the sphere of *sentir* by means of second reflection, we are forced "to the affirmation of a *pure* immediate, that is to say an immediate which by essence is incapable of mediation,"[42] and thus, of a "nonmediatizable immediate." The act of *sentir* that inseparably connects me to my body (the *je sens*) is nonmediatizable precisely because it is itself the founding stratum of all mediation; it is the initial act of feeling that makes the feeling of anything else possible, and in this sense it is an *Urgefühl*.[43] As such, it is not itself characterizable in the manner prescribed by the message-theory of first reflection. But being noncharacterizable does not mean that this primal feeling at the basis of all other feeling is indeterminate. It means rather "*that the mind when confronting it cannot adopt without contradiction the attitude that is needed for characterizing something.*"[44]

The body, then, as an *Urgefühl*, cannot be regarded in terms of instrumentalities, messages, or the like. Therefore we must alter our notion of *sentir*. This revision brings us to the third moment of the body-qua-mine.

VI

If a sensation or feeling is neither a communication nor a relation between two poles, then, Marcel believes, "it must involve the immediate participation of what we normally call the subject in a surrounding world from which no veritable frontier separates it."[45] The initial mistake of the message-theory is to presuppose such a frontier: on the "outside" is the world, and on the "inside" is me. But questioning the meaning of "outside" and "inside" is rarely if ever done, for it amounts to an absurdity. Furthermore, by presupposing a frontier, the message-theory must explain how I, on the inside, and some object, on the outside, could ever be related to one another. Since according to the principle of division I can never "get outside my skin," then in order for me to sense such outside objects, they must "come to me"; although variously conceived (from the *eidolon* of the Greek atomists to the "sense-data" of classical and modern psychology), the path traveled is always from the object to the percipient subject. To feel, or to sense, is in this view always to suffer, or to receive passively.

But if the initial assumption is unjustified—especially in its own terms, as Marcel shows—then *sentir* does not mean "to suffer"; it is not a "passive reception" of something supposed to be "out there" impinging on me "in here." On the contrary, *sentir* means "to participate," that is, "to receive" in a quite different sense: "To receive is to bring into one's home someone from the outside, it is to introduce him. . . . To feel is to receive; but it would be necessary immediately to specify that to receive, here, is to open myself, and consequently to give myself to, rather than to suffer, an external action."[46]

In the case of *sentir,* we receive as hosts receiving guests into their home; that is, we must view "reception" and "receptivity" here in terms of a certain prior willingness or ability to make ourselves open to what is to be received. Thus, I sense objects by receiving them into a domain that in essence I feel as my own, that is, only by means of my body felt (*senti*) as mine. Only my body senses; "a" or "the" body does not feel anything; it is the body of "anybody." To perceive is always an "I perceive," a *je sens.* "One receives in a room, in a home, strictly, in a garden (*dans un jardin*): not in a vague place, the countryside or in a forest." To receive, in this sense, is to participate.[47]

This notion of participation allows us to understand the fundamental act of feeling—that it is not a mere enduring or suffering but an act in the sense of the *je sens,* "a non-objective participation." It is clear, however, that there are gradations of participation ranging from, for example, sharing a birthday cake or sharing in a business corporation to the fundamental mode of participation Marcel calls "nonobjective," such as when we "take part" in an event like the marriage of a close friend. In this last case, we cannot define participation merely in terms of the number of persons objectively present at the same time and in the same place. Rather, Marcel argues, the participation depends on an idea (such as the idea of marriage, friendship, or a social "cause") that makes the participation possible; the idea is that in terms of which the participation emerges. But at the level of *sentir* we cannot speak of such participation; we must distinguish the participation emerging on the basis of an event from our willingness to participate in it in the first place, that is, from *participation immergée*.[48] Before we can genuinely take part, we must make ourselves "available" (*disponible*) or "open" to such participation. Moreover, participation is possible only "on the basis of a certain consensus which, by definition, can only be felt."[49]

This level of *sentir* is still not manifested at the level of the body. Rather, it refers to the kind of bond that unites, for instance, farmer and soil, shipmaster and sea, artist and creation, and so on. Thus in this sense we can participate in an undertaking, in a task of some sort, with our whole being only because, or on the the ground of, a feeling that is in reality a bond uniting us to our task and to others who also participate in it. The feeling here is in fact a *coesse*, a *Bei-sich-sein*, an act of feeling that is perhaps best rendered in French by *accueillement* or, even better, by *responsivité*.[50] Only in terms of this responsiveness, this *coesse*, is the undertaking made worthwhile; it is a "being-with" without which we could not endure the trials, risks, and failures of the undertaking.

The question for us at this point bears on the relation of this "feeling-participation" to the "feeling" uniting me to my body. Once we have seen that feeling cannot involve the communication of a message but rather that all communication presupposes feeling, we can no longer interpret feeling in terms of "information." Feeling is not a "sign" or "symbol"; it does not give us information about the world or about objects in the world. To the contrary, Marcel states, "To feel is to be affected in a given manner."[51] Of course we can regard feeling as a sign giving information, but then we must note, Marcel emphasizes, that we have gone a step beyond the immediacy of feeling: we have placed an interpretation on the fact of feeling, and the interpretation fractures that immediacy. Thus it is from the perspective of first reflection, of the body-as-object, that feeling appears as a message.

When by way of second reflection we recapture the immediacy and original unity of feeling, we see that to feel is not to suffer but rather to act and that feeling reveals at its center an activity, a "making oneself open to," a "taking upon oneself" (*assumer*), an *accueillir*. In short, *sentir* is participation, and the ground for this participation is my being-embodied, my embodiment by this body that is mine. Finally, to be incarnate is to be exposed or open to the world and to objects in it; in this sense, to be sensitive to objects is to be present to them, to be "at" them, to belong to the world by participating in it by means of my body. Marcel calls this fundamental stratum of *sentir* my *être-au-monde*.[52] To "ex-ist" as an *altérité d'emprunt*, then, is to manifest myself to the world as embodied by my body and thus is to be exposed to the world—to its seasons, its elements, its course, and its influences. As embodied, I not only become able to engage myself in the world by means of bodily activities, I also and consequently open myself to the world's actions on me. I partake of the world by means of my fundamental *sentir*, which connects me to my body and, by means of my body, to the world itself. In this sense, I can act on the world by means of my body only because I can also be acted on by the world and by its objects. This brings us to the final moment of the body-qua-mine.

VII

When Marcel discovered the "exclamatory consciousness of existing," he believed he had discovered as well the *repère* of all existence as such. We can now see how he came to believe this. To say that my body ex-poses me to the world as such is to say that "my body *is in sympathy with things* . . . that I am really *attached* to and really adhere to all that exists—to the universe which is my universe and whose center is my body."[53] Thus to say that something exists is to say that I maintain relations with it that are of the same type as those I maintain with my body; in other words, "to say that a thing exists is not only to say that it belongs to the same system as my body (that it is connected to my body by certain rationally determinable relations); it is to say that that thing is in some fashion united to me as my body is united to me."[54]

A thing exists for me, he stated earlier, only if it in some way is a "prolonging of my body." In other words, to think of a thing as an object—that is, as being indifferent to me, as not taking account of me—is to alter its character as existent for me. *Existence* and *objectivity* are for Marcel mutually exclusive terms; thus to speak of existence as an object or a datum is self-contradictory. "In reality," he points out, "existence and the thing that exists are obviously inseparable,"[55] and the thing that exists is bound to me in the same type of relation by which I am united to my body. In this sense, Marcel can say that my body is in sympathy with things, that my body is thus the center of all that exists and that a thing is or becomes an object only by being disregarded qua existent.

As Prini points out, "The first indubitable is not thought as a reflection or doubt, but the presence of my corporeal sensibility as anterior to doubt itself."[56] And this presence is at once the prototype of existence and the *repère* of existence. Thus at the center of the universe, my universe, Marcel claims to discover a fundamentally nontransparent and nonmediatizable immediate, one that is presupposed by all mediation precisely because it is absolute, making all mediation possible.

This discovery of "mystery," of the domain of the metaproblematic, makes necessary the

> very important distinction between data that are susceptible of forming the occasion for a problem—that is, objective data—and data *on which the mind must be based* so as to state any problem whatsoever. . . . Sensation (the fact of feeling, of participating in a universe which creates me by affecting me), and the intellectually indefectible bond that unites me with what I call my body, are data of this second kind.[57]

To say, accordingly, that I am incarnate in my body-qua-mine is to say that in some sense I am my body. This signifies, Marcel says, that

> I am my body only in virtue of mysterious reasons which account for my continually feeling my body and because this feeling conditions for me all other feeling. . . . This feeling seems bound up with real fluctuations that scarcely seem to me to be capable of bearing on anything save on the body's potential action, its instrumental value at a given moment. But if this is so my body is only felt inasmuch as it is Me-as-acting: feeling is a function of acting.[58]

Thus as Bergson has earlier pointed out and as both Merleau-Ponty and Sartre will say later, my body is mine only because it is "me-as-acting," and the world exists only because it is there for me to act on, so far as I am embodied as a "felt" system of actions for which objects form a "context" of poles of action. The "feelings" that unite me to my body are thus a "function of acting"; were my body not the most immediate manifestation of my fundamental "I can," I would not experience my body as mine.

In sum, through the four moments of my body-qua-mine, Marcel believes he has at least circumscribed the fundamental meaning of "my body."

VIII

Marcel's is an unquestionably seminal body of work. Tentative and cautious though he is, he is also a subtle and tenacious philosopher whose writings include many lasting insights into the human condition. What is most impressive about his work, its greatest strength, is precisely its focal theme, its "Ariadne's thread," which gives it its remarkable unity. This theme—the self in its ontological exigence seeking its own authenticity among other selves[59]—which Marcel has studied with rare penetration and compassion throughout his long career, has been decisively shown to be not only philosophically legitimate but in truth, as Hocking clearly saw, a genuine ground issue of metaphysics and "an aspect of the broadened and heightened empiricism which may well be, in its completion, the major achievement in epistemology of this present century."[60]

As students of Marcel know, the metaproblematic of the body-qua-mine is central to Marcel's work. It is also clear that the radical question underlying it concerns mineness: Marcel seeks to determine the grounds in virtue of which this body is concretely experienced as mine. The force of such terms as *sympathetic mediation* is that they focus on the "intimate union" or "profound connection" between the self and its own body. As we have indicated, this union is so intimate that Marcel feels forced to say, "I am my body"; at the least, it is false to say "I am not my body." Similarly, his concerted effort to distinguish radically between *existence* and *objectivity, being* and *having, mystery* and *problem, second* and *first* reflection, and so on, is a way of saying, negatively, that the union cannot be expressed (or even "approached") through the second term of each of these pairs. It is also a way of saying positively that the union is approachable only through the first term of the pairs. Thus both have the force of asserting that the fundamental or radical reality in human being is this "union"; following from this, the question of embodiment is a matter of delineating the union in its most immediate and intimate form.

Consequently, we can suggest that Marcel's study of embodiment is essentially in line with one facet of Cartesian philosophy, despite his evident antipathy toward Descartes and the profound differences between them.[61] For what was so impressive to Descartes was not the necessity to bring together what his theoretical bifurcation of reality declared to be distinct and independent but rather the peculiar circumstance that mind and body are *already intimately united*. His problem was to account for this union, but he did so in terms of a generative conception that asserted not the union but the radical difference between the two. The basic impasse in Descartes's problematic, then, is not so much that his dichotomy of substances generated an irresolvable, paradoxical question; it is rather that after clearly and insistently recognizing the "intimate union" between mind and body,[62] he proceeds to determine the respective natures of the two and, finding them essentially distinct, becomes concerned with the different question concerning not the intimacy or union but how and where interaction occurs. Thus what initially struck Descartes (that is, the union), and what was subsequently obscured by his interest in quite different issues, is precisely what Marcel never loses sight of and, indeed, what he succeeds in deepening with great sensitivity.

In so doing, however, Marcel obscures a crucial dimension of embodiment: mineness becomes so focal that the radical strangeness of my body tends to be neglected. Recalling the experiences of Richard Hughes's Emily and of Robert Russell, we note that whereas each reveals a sense of mineness (whether as "mad prank" or "hateful infirmity"), more importantly each discloses the sense of radical otherness, and this dimension is experienced as fundamental.

Julián Marías has expressed this otherness succinctly. Despite the intimate and profound union between me and my body, the specifically human reality designated by the personal pronoun *I* is "literally *something other* than *its* organism—so much *other,* that it is not a thing but a person—although it may, on the other hand, be necessary to underline the *its. . . .*"[63]

Although we will not explore this crucial experience in depth here, a few concluding remarks are necessary. The "union" is indeed intimate and deep—so much so that I am tempted to say, "I *am* my body." Yet my body is so fundamentally other that I feel compelled immediately to qualify that "am": it is not identity, equality, inclusion, or the like. Emphasizing the "am" seems only to deepen the impasse I sought to surmount by affirming that I am my body; paradoxically, emphasizing the "am not" has the same result. So close is the union that experiences of my body's otherness are literally shattering (as in Russell's experience of its hateful refusal to obey), and so other is my body that experiences of its intimacy are equally shocking (as in Emily's experience of her body's happy obedience).

This peculiar set of *aporias* is a phenomenon in its own right; it is itself a fundamental experience: the disclosure of the essence of embodiment. In this sense, embodiment is a fundamentally dialectical experience of oneself as simultaneously "at home" (*heimlich*) and "strange and un-canny" (*unheimlich*), that is, an experience that reveals my being-embod-ied by a body at once "always already familiar" to me and yet radically strange—other-than-me, yet mine most of all.

Inescapably, my "who-I-am" is what it is only in terms of my em-bodiment by this particular body; like it or not, my body has its own na-ture, style, and configuration with which I am irrevocably burdened or blessed. Whether I experience my body as disgusting or pleasing, I must fatefully "be and do" within its limits. Being fatefully mine (and I fate-fully its), I am placed "in" (or "at") the world by means of it and am thereby exposed to the world's threats and dangers as well as to its ben-efits and pleasures. Being subject to conditions and laws proper to ma-terial nature, my body can fail me; it is not at my complete disposal. Thus my body is lived by me as the ground for dread, anguish, and frus-tration.

Since my body is mine, if something goes wrong with it, I will suf-fer; since my body is other than me, I will be in anguish. Events go on within it whether or not I understand them; yet I find myself most di-rectly "in charge" of it. Thus I am confronted with something funda-mentally opaque but most intimately mine—impenetrable and other, but mine. Indeed there are moments when, though mine, it seems to control me; I am at its disposal; I must await it. Contrary to my desires, my body often seems strangely to "go its own way" (as when I grow weary, grow old, or am uncoordinated in a game). Because my body has its own rhythms, style, and nature, I find myself intimately bound to a being whose functions, processes, and structures I must contend with, care for, and attend—without, however, having had anything to do with its selec-tion as mine. Compellingly my own, my body is yet radically strange and other. I experience wishes to "do" that exceed the possibilities intrinsic to my embodiment; my body "grounds" me. And though I "know" these things, I cannot achieve the kind of epistemic distance from my body that would permit me to know it as intimately as I experience it to be mine.

Even though Marcel's analysis of embodiment tends to stress mineness to the exclusion of otherness, the above suggestions do not conflict with but rather seek to extend and complement his study. They propose that embodiment is not only a fugitive and mysterious phenomenon but a pro-found and dialectical *aporia*. Pascal's cutting remark against Descartes ex-presses this incisively: "Man is to himself the most wonderful object in nature; for he cannot conceive what the body is, still less what the mind is, and least of all how a body should be united to a mind. This is the consummation of his difficulties, and yet it is his very being.''[64]

RICHARD M. ZANER

VANDERBILT UNIVERSITY
AUGUST 1968

NOTES

1. Gabriel Marcel, *Journal métaphysique* (Paris: Gallimard, 1927), p. 248 (hereafter cited as *JM*); *Metaphysical Journal*, trans. Bernard Wall (Chicago: Henry Regnery Co., 1952), p. 255 (hereafter cited as *MJ*).

2. Gabriel Marcel, *Du refus a l'invocation* (Paris: Gallimard, 1940), p. 122 (hereafter cited as *DR*); *Creative Fidelity*, trans. Robert Rosthal (New York: Noonday Press, 1964), p. 91 (hereafter cited as *CF*).

3. Gabriel Marcel, *Le Mystère de l'être*, 2 vols. (Paris: Aubier, 1951), 1:54 (hereafter cited as *ME*); *The Mystery of Being*, trans. G. S. Fraser (vol. 1) and René Hague (vol. 2), 2 vols. (London: Harvill Press, 1951), 1:45 (hereafter cited as *MB*).

4. *ME* 1:141; *MB* 1:125. See also Gabriel Marcel, *Etre et avoir* (Paris: Aubier, 1935), pp. 72, 73, 158–59, 180–81 (hereafter cited as *EA*); *Being and Having*, trans. Katharine Farrer (Westminster: Dacre Press, 1949), pp. 52, 53, 109–10, 124–25 (hereafter cited as *BH*).

5. Gabriel Marcel, *Position et approches concrètes du mystère ontologique* (Paris: Vrin, 1949), p. 54 (hereafter cited as *PA*); *The Philosophy of Existence*, trans. Manya Harari (London: Harvill Press, 1949), p. 6 (hereafter cited as *PE*). See also *PE*, 1–31.

6. William E. Hocking, "Marcel and the Ground Issues of Metaphysics," *Philosophy and Phenomenological Research* 14, no. 4 (June 1954): 439–69, especially p. 444.

7. See *ME* 1:47–66; *MB* 1:39–56. Cf. *PA*, 51–53; *PE*, 1–4.

8. *ME* 1:116–17; *MB* 1:98–100. See also *EA*, 129–30; *BH* 89–91; and see Gabriel Marcel, *Les Hommes contre l'humain* (Paris: La Colombe, 1951), pp. 46–49 (hereafter cited as *HH*); *Men against Humanity*, trans. G. S. Fraser (London: Harvill Press, 1952), pp. 41–43 (hereafter cited as *MH*).

9. Gabriel Marcel, *Homo Viator* (Paris: Aubier, 1944), p. 17 (hereafter cited as *HV*); *Homo Viator*, trans. Emma Craufurd (Chicago: Henry Regnery Co., 1951), p. 15 (hereafter cited as *HV* [Eng. trans.]).

10. *DR*, 27; *CF*, 17.

11. *ME* 1:106; *MB* 1:91.

12. *DR*, 88; *CF*, 63; *HH*, 50–58, 68–72; *MH*, 46–56, 67–70.

13. Marcel's happy phrase is "la morsure du réel" (*DR*, 89; *CF*, 64).

14. I have attempted to probe this sense of disclosure and wonder. See Richard M. Zaner, *The Context of Self* (Athens, Ohio: University of Ohio Press, 1981),

pp. 144–80; idem, "Self-Awakening: Toward a Phenomenology of Self," in *Phenomenology in Perspective*, ed. F. J. Smith (The Hague: Martinus Nijhoff, 1970), pp. 171–86.

15. *JM*, 19, 125; *MJ*, 18, 126; *DR*, 27, 31; *CF*, 17, 20; *ME* 1:106; *MB* 1:93.

16. Cf. Julian Marías, *Reason and Life: The Introduction to Philosophy* (New Haven: Yale University Press, 1956), p. 5.

17. *EA*, 15; *BH*, 14.

18. Richard Hughes, *A High Wind on Jamaica* (New York: Random House, Modern Library, 1929), pp. 188–91. Herbert Spiegelberg has confirmed the autobiographical source of this experience in "On the 'I-Am-Me' Experience in Childhood and Adolescence," *Review of Existential Psychology and Psychiatry* 5 (1964): 3–21.

19. Robert Russell, *To Catch an Angel* (New York: Popular Library, 1962), p. 14.

20. *ME* 1:112–14; *MB* 1:95–97.

21. Cf. Edmund Husserl, *Cartesian Meditations*, trans. D. Cairns (The Hague: Martinus Nijhoff, 1960), p. 97.

22. Marcel's study of "having" is found principally in *EA*, 223–55; *BH*, 154–75; *JM*, 297–301; *MJ*, 307–11; *ME* 1:110–15; and *MB* 1:95–102.

23. *EA*, 230–31; *BH*, 159.   24. *EA*, 217–18; *BH*, 150.

25. *EA*, 231; *BH*, 159.   26. *EA*, 232; *BH*, 160.

27. *EA*, 234; *BH*, 160.   28. *EA*, 236–37; *BH*, 162–63.

29. See Marcel's lucid treatment of despair in *EA*, 149–55; *BH*, 103–7; *PA*, 47–51.

30. *JM*, 322; *MJ*, 332.

31. Cf. *ME* 1:112–14 and *JM*, 241; *MB* 1:98–100 and *MJ*, 248.

32. *JM*, 239; *MJ*, 246.

33. Cf. *JM*, 239, and *ME* 1:117; *MJ*, 246, and *MB* 1:101.

34. *ME* 1:113; *MB* 1:97.   35. *ME* 1:116; *MB* 1:100.

36. *JM*, 236; *MJ*, 243.   37. *JM*, 317; *MJ*, 327.

38. *DR*, 37; *CF*, 24.   39. *DR*, 37–38; *CF*, 24–25.

40. *JM*, 251; *MJ*, 258.   41. *ME* 1:124; *MB* 1:108.

42. *JM*, 319; *MJ*, 329.   43. *JM*, 240; *MJ*, 247.

44. *JM*, 320; *MJ*, 330.   45. *JM*, 322; *MJ*, 331–32.

46. *DR*, 122–23; *CF*, 90–91.   47. *DR*, 120; *CF*, 88.

48. *ME* 1:130; *MB* 1:114.   49. *ME* 1:132; *MB* 1:115.

50. *ME* 1:135; *MB* 1:117.   51. *JM*, 185; *MJ*, 187.

52. *DR*, 33; *CF*, 22.   53. *JM*, 265; *MJ*, 274.

54. *EA*, 11; *BH*, 11.   55. *JM*, 311; *MJ*, 321.

56. Pietro Prini, *Gabriel Marcel et la méthodologie de l'inverifiable*, with a letter-preface by Gabriel Marcel (Paris: Desclée de Brouwer, 1953), p. 42.

57. *JM*, 328; *MJ*, 338.

58. *JM*, 252–53; *MJ*, 260.

59. A human being is not only a "being beyond" (*sum* is *sursum*) but a "being with" (*esse* is *coesse*)—a dimension of Marcel's thought we have not touched on here.

60. Hocking, "Marcel and the Ground Issues of Metaphysics," p. 441.

61. I have tried to show this in greater detail elsewhere; see Richard M. Zaner, "The Radical Reality of the Human Body," *Humanitas* 2, no. 1 (1967), pp. 73–87.

62. See, for example, René Descartes, *Descartes' Philosophical Writings,* ed. Elizabeth S. Haldane and G. R. T. Ross, 2 vols. (New York: Dover Books, 1955), 1:118, 255, 345.

63. Marías, *Reason and Life,* pp. 322, 378.

64. Blaise Pascal, *Pensées,* trans. W. F. Trotter (New York: Random House, Modern Library, 1941), pp. 27–28. See also Zaner, *Context of Self,* pp. 23–66.

The Mystery of the Body-Qua-Mine

REPLY TO RICHARD M. ZANER

Zaner's study dedicated to my thinking on "my body" seems excellent to me, particularly with regard to all the problems bound up with "having." And it furnishes me with an opportunity—one I would not care to miss— to return to a difficult question I do not think I touched on anywhere except in my *Metaphysical Journal,* the question of what at that time I called "sympathetic mediation." I would briefly like to clarify the question in the light of the opinions I have subsequently stated. I am likewise aware that the extraordinary development of technology in the world today gives this question an importance of which I was not fully cognizant earlier.

Technology is essentially a series of increasingly sure controls over what we call external reality. I will not return in depth here to what I have so frequently said about the nonproblematic character of this reality: that regardless of what innumerable philosophers have thought, this reality of itself poses no question, and doubts about this reality imply an illusion we can clearly expose.

Nevertheless, these controls are possible only for an incarnated being, that is, for a being who in a certain way partakes of this reality we call external. I belong to the world precisely to the extent that I have(?) a body. The question mark is necessary because reflection shows us that in this case the use of the verb *to have* is open to dispute. This usage is legitimate only to the extent that I can say I possess my body, for experience shows that possession is not a one-way street in this case. There are situations when it would be much more exact to say that I am possessed by my body. This is particularly true in physical suffering, in sickness, and perhaps also in desire or in sexual appetite.

Such examples suffice to show that we cannot be content with an in-

Translated from the French by Colette M. Ferran and Francois R. Ferran.

strumentalist interpretation of the body. The least we can say is that my body is not merely my instrument; it is also—and probably first of all—something else.

On reflection, I find that the words I have just used seem totally inadequate. It would seem that the characteristic of my body—at least its negative characteristic, since it is not an instrument—is the fact that it cannot be thought of as a thing, that it cannot be "objectified" (*chosifié*).

What exactly does this mean? It now seems necessary—something I had not previously realized—to bring language into the picture. In reality it comes down to a question of whether I can really *speak* of my body once I have taken the position of leaving out objective characteristics that make my body one among an infinity of others. This takes on a clear meaning if we think of some pain we feel, for example. Everyone has had occasion to observe the strictly incommunicable aspect of such an experience. At the most, it can give rise to sympathy so far as the other person, by an effort of memory or imagination, is able to empathize with the one who suffers.

It is important to understand that in such experiences my body ceases to be an object to the extent that it tends to become my master and that consequently the self feels trapped or threatened in its very existence.

Yet the essential thing surely is to recognize that what I have called "incarnation" implies the possibility of having more experiences of which we can say the cries of the newborn are the first manifestation. Here we have the first reaction—an affective one, to be sure—of the being that I am on my entry into the world.

In sketching this outline, I feel that I am reflecting on a theme that has been dealt with a hundred times before and that could be termed commonplace. At the same time, I have the vague feeling that if I were in the state of mind required, I might be able to uncover the metaphysical implications of this fact; in particular, I might be able to show, by starting with this fact, how it is possible to give full rights to the phenomena that constitute the object of parapsychology.

G.M.

12

John E. Smith

THE INDIVIDUAL, THE COLLECTIVE, AND THE COMMUNITY

G ABRIEL Marcel has long advocated and has practiced the dialogic
approach to philosophical questions; therefore it seems appropriate to
introduce my topic by initiating a conversation with a basic question. My
concern is to understand Marcel's view of the role played by my relation
to the other (and to others) in my knowledge of myself and in the determination of my being as a person. More specifically, I want to ask, for a
start, whether he regards my being related to the other as essential to my
being as a person or whether that relation is merely a means of developing
or bringing to consciousness my ego in a process that inevitably leads to
egotism. The difference here is of basic importance because relation to the
other should issue in the realization of community; yet if it cannot pass
beyond the awakening and hardening of my ego, the result will be individualism, which is the chief factor working against community. In this discussion the expression "relation to the other" signifies something abstract,
since many particular relations will be involved—loving, understanding,
conversing with, dominating, resenting, and so on. But this abstraction
must not obscure the basic question of whether and how relation to the
other enters into my own being. If we can come to an understanding about
my specific question about the ego, we may then go on to raise a more
comprehensive question about the relation between the individual person
and the community of others as distinct from the collective, or the mass of
others. I take these questions to be quite basic to Marcel's thought, for if
I have understood him correctly, he has, like Royce, a concern for maintaining the reality of the individual, but, again like Royce, he is opposed
to individualism, or the belief that my relation to the other is merely ad-
ventitious and does not count in my constitution as a person.

In order to focus my initial question more sharply, I propose to direct attention to the paper "The Ego and Its Relation to Others," which is the initial essay in *Homo Viator*.[1] Like so many of Marcel's writings, this paper is distinctive because of its roots in actual experience and its careful attention to what happens in the human situation under discussion. In his analysis of the human self, William James long ago spoke of "the craving to be appreciated," and it is with this desire to be noticed and recognized by others that Marcel begins his discussion. A child has picked some flowers and presents them to his mother with a triumphant note expressed in an exclamation: "Look, I picked these!" The child's aim is to direct attention to himself as the one who has picked the flowers. For Marcel the other is implied in both the act and the exclamation, since the desired attention must be elicited from that other. But in this example the other is excluded, since the child desires to call attention to himself as this individual and no other; paradoxically the other is still needed to serve as a witness not only to the child's presence but also to this very exclusion. Stated positively, the other is a witness to the child's *presence,* which stands out in the exclusion. Marcel describes this as the act that establishes myself; the "preexistent" ego prior to this act, he claims, can be described only in negative terms, since positive description presupposes that one has already presented oneself. The desire is for recognition on the part of the other; the specific form of such recognition is, in this case, praise or approbation, but whatever particular form it assumes, the minimum desire is to be noticed.

Here the possession of what is mine—whether a virtue or a thing—is realized at the point where I call to the attention of the other the fact that the item in question is mine. I may claim it, give it, or ask for it back, all of which underline the fact that it is mine. I am, nevertheless, quite literally dependent on the other, since this realization cannot be accomplished through my own self-consciousness merely by my calling to my own attention the fact that something is mine. The recognition must come from a being other than myself. Here I am inclined to agree with Marcel, though I should admit that it is unclear why I cannot realize the "mine" by serving myself as the necessary other. Why may I not recognize my own possession as mine? Is this not to have recognition by another? There arises within the individual consciousness a distinction between "I" and "me" that is surely analogous to, if not isomorphic with, the distinction between two different individuals. But even though the "me" as object self distinct from the "I" as creative subject gives rise to an "other" in my consciousness, perhaps the otherness is not fitted to be a genuine witness because it is still myself that is involved, and in this sense there is no other, as a neighbor or a friend. The recognition in question must come from someone who lies beyond and fails to coincide with my consciousness, my ideas, and especially the control of my will. This degree of otherness is required for the recognition to be something that I cannot command, no matter how fervently I desire it.[2] The importance of this recognition is further seen in Marcel's description of the ego as presence embracing both the sense of being in the world and the urge to be recognized by the other. The other thus integrates the self in the sense that the self has, so to speak, to be collected in order to stand as a unity distinct from this other.

Thus far in his discussion Marcel has been speaking chiefly of the ego and sometimes of the self but not specifically of the person. Later on the discussion shifts explicitly to a consideration of the person,[3] and it is at this point that my original question obtrudes. Does relation to the other enter essentially into the presenting of the person, as it does into the presenting of the ego? I put this question not as a hostile critic but as one who shares Marcel's acceptance of the basic idea that self-consciousness and consciousness of the other are intimately related. Yet as Royce pointed out in his analyses of community consciousness, it is important to know when relation to the other awakens my self-consciousness to the point of individualistic self-assertion and rebelliousness vis-à-vis others and when the social relationship leads to the form of togetherness that is community.

Let us return to the paper we have been considering. Marcel describes the ego as an "emphasis" on that part of my experience that I want to safeguard against attack or infringement.[4] Even though, as he rightly says, the ego is indefinite and not a portion of space, it is nevertheless a concentration or localization that must be regarded as a "highly vulnerable enclosure";[5] that is, as an emphasis, the ego does not coincide with the totality of my experience. It is a commonplace of experience that whenever a source of my identity—a community I belong to, a political or religious belief I hold, a person I love—is attacked, I cannot but feel that I am attacked at the same time. The vulnerable character of the ego leads Marcel to see it as rooted initially in anguish rather than in love. One is torn between, on the one hand, the awareness that one wants to possess and control a multitude of things and even persons and, on the other hand, the awareness that one is nothing in the sense that one harbors in oneself nothing that is timeless and permanent. The precariousness of this situation leads us, as he says, to look for the other's recognition as a source of investiture; hence we end with the paradox of the self-centered ego looking to the other for confirmation. And the need for this confirmation may be so strong that we are led to elicit it in essentially inauthentic or distorted ways. Marcel's analysis of the *poseur* is most acute and seems to me to describe accurately what happens when a "preoccupation" with my effect on the other leads to various forms of simulation on my part.[6] When I view the other as no more than a reflector of myself—when, for example, I express agreement with the other in an exaggerated way merely to receive the other's approval and to show that we agree—the other is being manipulated and ceases to be a real person.[7]

Acutely aware of the aberrations that may follow in the wake of the ego made forcefully aware of itself, Marcel goes on to ask whether there is any limit to our capacity for exposing these aberrations. Are the aberrations in the end the rule? Is there no normal state? Marcel does not really answer his own question but goes on to point out that we should not confuse it with another question—the philosophical question that asks for a principle of unity guiding personal development. At this point Marcel returns to what I take to be the underlying task of the paper: to determine the conditions under which I become conscious of myself as a person. The person is a more comprehensive reality than the ego, and although the enclosure of the ego cannot be ignored in determining my awareness as a person, the two do not coincide.

Here I break the line of exposition to make a proposal. I do not know whether this proposal expresses what Marcel wants to say, but I believe it is implied in his paper, and in any case it represents what I would say about the social dimension of self-consciousness and what I believe one must say. To the extent that my relation to the other is based on my knowledge of and need for the other and demand for the other's recognition, it serves mainly to bring my ego to self-consciousness and to heighten my awareness of what is mine as distinct from what belongs to every other person and thing. The chief logical tool in the process is that of comparison, or of relating two terms to each other by relating each to the same third term. To assert, for example, that this table is longer than that one is to relate the two tables with respect to their occupancy of space in one direction. As soon as I become acutely aware of myself as distinct from the other, I make comparisons involving judgments of more and less with respect to material goods, advantages of birth and social position, talents, capabilities, capacities, virtues, vices, and indeed all the familiar reference points we introduce for such comparisons. Comparisons of this sort cause the ego to stand out in boldest relief not only because they are the major source of knowledge of myself as the individual I am and no other but also because factors of importance and value are involved in every comparison. The fact is that in comparing I am competing and attempting to estimate my value in relation to the other. We say, for instance, "He may have more friends than I do, but I am more conscientious than he is." Such expressions represent the standard form of comparison, which is seen at once to be a form of competition. Here the relation to the other realized in the form of comparison breeds individualism, and various forms of self-assertiveness, together with a sense of self-importance and of self-sufficiency. The relation to the other has the effect of so integrating and hardening the ego that the other as a person is in danger of being crushed by the very ego this other helped to invest.

If the impact of my relation to the other or myself were confined to my ego, social consciousness would not lead to the establishment of human community but rather to its opposite in the form of atomic individualism resisting incorporation into any togetherness of persons. But the ego is not identical with the concrete person, and therefore it is necessary to pass beyond the stage in which social consciousness merely develops the ego— important though this stage is, since it involves, at the least, an awareness of dependence on the other that shows that individualism is not the final truth—and to consider the bearing of my relation to the other when each of us is regarded as a person. I propose that here the relation to the other is again seen as essential, but on a new level. This level is one at which concrete personality is introduced and from which we see not only the incompleteness of the first stage but even the dangers for both persons and civilization stemming from a social consciousness that merely develops the ego. For if social consciousness is to lead to community and not to end in a frenzy of self-conceit and in unchecked individualism, factors constituting the person will have to enter the picture. Three conditions are necessary here: first, there must be the acceptance of myself and the other as continuing or enduring agents answerable individually for our deeds; second, the relation to the other must not be confined to knowledge but must include love, loyalty, and concern; and third, both I and the other must direct knowledge and love to the causes and common concerns forming the basis of the communities to which we belong.

If we consider relation to the other on this higher level, we will see how that relation leads beyond the development of the ego and individualism to an acknowledgment of the reality of and the need for the togetherness of individuals that is community. Though we pass ultimately beyond egoism, we still must pass through it. The initial awakening of myself as this individual follows the pattern previously described. We are in need of the other for the awakening and for what Marcel calls the investiture. But in the immediate relation of the coming to consciousness of myself as ego through the recognition elicited from the other, I am regarding neither the other nor myself as a person. The other is merely "other," and so far as I am only ego, the other appears as no more than ego as well. Yet when I acknowledge the other as a person, as an enduring and answerable self,[8] I see the other no longer as merely other, in the sense that his or her being is exhausted in being the other who recognizes me. On the contrary, the other now appears as an existing person—related to me, to be sure, but also independent of this relation to me.[9] When I and the other are related as two persons, we no longer view each other merely as occasions for the mutual development of our own egos; instead we find that concern and love enter in to supplement and transform our earlier relation, which was based largely on knowledge. Now we become concerned to discover the mutual ground we share, the interests, needs, purposes, ideals, and hopes that unite us in a common bond. Instead of being related as ego to ego, where each of us is dominated by the awareness of what is "mine" and "not the other's," our attention moves away from ourselves and to those "third things" that unite us. Because we are working together for a cause transcending both of us, the concerns we share— the "third things"—take us literally out of ourselves and lead us away from the competitive comparisons of the lower stage of our relationship and toward a loyalty to what unites us. For this reason I singled out as a third condition for being a person our capacity to direct our knowledge and our love to the causes and common concerns that not only unite us as these two persons but that are also at the foundation of all the communities including both of us as members. In fact the penetration of one person into the life of another is precisely the process of discovering the communities of loyalty and concern to which both belong without either's being explicitly aware of this common ground.

Unless I have misread him, I believe Marcel would find himself in agreement with the foregoing analysis. Yet on the basis of the one paper I have been considering, there are perhaps two points at least where he would want to supplement what I have said or even to dissent. First, he would probably place more emphasis than I have on persons being realized only in an act through which they become incarnate and express themselves, for example, in a book, a deed, an address, a piece of sculpture, or an object fashioned. If I am correct, Marcel has not considered the implications of the incarnational form as itself an other for the person expressed in it. And clearly this relationship is fundamental for the whole of modern technological culture, which is essentially a vast network of incarnational acts whereby we literally put ourselves into the world. Our concern is, of course, for what happens to the world when we thus express ourselves in it, but we are no less interested in what happens to us when we find ourselves confronted with this vast other (that is, technological society), which is essentially our own creation. Second, Marcel does not stress as much as I do the extent to which the common concern or cause (we both follow Royce in the use of this term) uniting many individuals into a community actually transcends the individual members. Community is not, to use a spatial figure that in this case is not misleading, a collection of horizontal relations between pairs of members—myself and the other— but a vertical relation holding between all the members (that is, between each individually) and the cause or purpose for which the community exists. The members become related to each other not, as Hegel would say, immediately, but because each one is related to the same cause. This cause stands beyond every individual member and can be realized only through their cooperative endeavor. From a reading of his many works I gather the impression that Marcel is uneasy about what I call the transcendence of the cause; I would be much interested to have his view on the matter, especially if I have misinterpreted him.

Let us turn now to the larger question indicated in the title of this paper. What relations hold between the individual, the collective, and the community? To obtain Marcel's answer to this question, we must glean statements and reflections scattered through many writings. I will state what I take his view to be and will then go on to raise some questions; he alone can say whether I have understood him properly.[10]

To express his position in the most general terms, we must say that Marcel defends the reality of the creative individual in the strongest possible terms; at the same time he rejects as distortions individualism and the competitive society of atomic individuals. Equally to be condemned is the "collective," which for him seems to coincide with mass society.[11] The collective is an external togetherness that, as Marcel says, "exist[s] at a level below that at which individuals deliberately organize themselves into groups."[12] The mass or collective is a loose and ephemeral togetherness; it finds a basis in knowledge and in calculable relations between individuals but not in love and concern. Community is, by contrast, an internal togetherness of persons made possible by their openness to and concern for each other. Community is essential for personality because the intersubjectivity, or relation to the other, on which it is based provides us with a means of discovering ourselves and of finding our bearings in the world. Briefly stated, this is Marcel's view. We may now look more closely at some details.

Marcel understands the individual person as a being of responsibility and freedom. As responsible, I acknowledge my accountability both to myself and to the other. In considering the commitments we make and our fidelity to them, Marcel lays great stress on the force of the other. "Fidelity," he writes, "is never fidelity to oneself, but is referred to what I called the hold the other has over us."[13] And it is clear that by the other Marcel means not only other persons but also God and the pull, so to speak, of the transcendent order. As a responsible person, I feel myself "under orders" not issuing entirely from me but dependent on my relation to others. A similar dependence becomes manifest in the realization of freedom. Standing "against mass society," we cannot be wholly assimilated to the order of things—even if a materialist society seeks to impose that assimilation on us—because we belong to an order of transcendence. Indeed Marcel characterizes freedom as a relating of the self to what transcends the self. In contrast to Sartre this transcendence is not merely self-transcendence, either in the comprehensive sense of the for-itself or in the more specific sense of framing a life project. The transcendence intended is that of a divine reality to which we become related in faith. In this regard Marcel is upholding—and I agree with him here—the doctrine that the self together with its capabilities and talents, including freedom itself, cannot be understood as a private abode of originality and individual self-possession but must be seen as a gift or trust bestowed from beyond us. Hence it cannot be the project of freedom for us to become God, since an acknowledgment of God is necessary in order for us to become persons.

The dialectic is obviously more complex than can be worked out here; nevertheless, Marcel's point focuses one particularly urgent problem concerning our contemporary human predicament. Freedom must have a form, a content, or, as Whitehead would have said, a principle of limitation. Marcel therefore reminds us that in a world of limitless self-development and expression—a world in which we are to develop ourselves "beyond all measure"—the result can only be chaos, frustration, or both unless we have some measure that provides principles and goals for our freedom. Paradoxically, from the modern secular standpoint we as beings in need of a measure are supposed to be able to provide this measure for ourselves without either a law or a love that transcends us.

Marcel claims that individual persons cannot realize themselves as free beings in mass society or in the collective based on the ideal of equality. Similarly, the individual cannot be realized in the individualistic competitive form of existence that excludes cooperative ventures. The chief deficiency in both cases is a lack of community. Mass society is for Marcel an aggregate wherein individuals—to the extent that any survive as such—are no more than externally related to one another and live constantly under the shadow of the belief that the mass itself is more real than any of its constituents taken individually.[14] Moreover, the mass is controlled by the idea of equality, which Marcel sees as a principle whose application leads straight to self-assertion and competition. I assert my equality with you and at the same time against you. In the mass, I am either lost as an individual and degraded to the status of a thing, or I am driven to self-centered existence coupled with the hardening effect of resentment growing out of the competitive situation in which I exist. To maintain myself is to stand against you. Again community fails because it can be neither formed nor sustained by individuals centered exclusively on their own concerns or hardened into impenetrable units that "have no windows," allowing anything to come in or go out.[15]

Marcel's concrete and practical suggestion for helping to overcome the evils of mass society as they affect the individual person and as they impede community is for us to form small communities of concern and service based on love for and openness to each other. "The very notion of intersubjectivity on which all my own most recent work has been based," Marcel writes, "presupposes a reciprocal openness between individuals without which no kind of spirituality is conceivable."[16] Community then stands equally opposed to both individualism and collectivism. Community realizes a unity of persons and is not an aggregate; it requires persons open to each other in a spirit of fraternity, which, unlike the self-assertive spirit of equality, means having a concern for the other; community makes freedom possible because it is a form of life in which persons recognize each other as persons who are to be but who are not to be manipulated. Marcel believes that such communities can save us from the mass only if they remain open to each other and do not degenerate into little closed unities of no more significance than a parochial clique.

So far as I understand him correctly, I find myself in sympathy with what Marcel is saying. Since I believe that the community idea is profoundly important at the present time but also more complex than it appears at first glance, it seems to me essential to clarify the idea further so that it will not be misunderstood or confused with something else. We need in fact a logic of the community, and I propose now to offer a brief and undeveloped sketch of that logic. It is implied in much that Marcel has written, but it is not made explicit.

To begin with we must clearly distinguish between a *collection,* an *aggregate,* and a *community.* A collection is any multitude of items such that each item in it is correctly denoted by a general description determining the collection. Thus the odd numbers form a collection, since each number in that collection is correctly denoted as a number that leaves a remainder of one when divided by two. Insurance statistics furnish an almost endless list of examples of collections: the collection of married women thirty-five years of age with three children, the collection of automobile operators under twenty-five who have been involved in two accidents, and so on. A collection is logically defined by one or more reference classes and is in no way dependent on the actual togetherness or copresence of the items in it.

By contrast, an aggregate requires the copresence of its items or, in some cases, its parts. An aggregate is a unity of items or individuals in which the principle of unity is an abstract selective feature of the items thus collected, and in most cases the relation will be that of conjunction, expressed in such logical terms as *and* (for example, this person *and* this person) and in such existential terms as *with*. A pile of sand fulfills this condition, as does a casually formed aggregate of individuals gathering to witness a street corner incident. Nevertheless, the individuals in the crowd form an identifiable unity, since they can be distinguished from other individuals in the vicinity who pass by but who do not stop to watch the incident. The grade of unity here is low; the crowd is attracted by the passing incident, and individuals may leave and their places may be taken by others who happen by without causing any appreciable change in the total situation. Whereas a community is a closely integrated unity, an aggregate comprises individuals who may be said to be "in" it but who do not belong to it in the sense of being "members of" the aggregate. You are not a member of a crowd—as you are a member of a choral society, a labor union, a church, or a family—because there is no enduring life to which to belong.

The crucial difference between an aggregate and a community then is found in the importance and the durability (or endurability) of the unifying elements—the cause or purpose for which the community exists. This cause functions as a point of identity forming some part of the life and historical career of every member. An aggregate of individual persons is a largely ephemeral unity whose items or parts are copresent; what brings them together is an evanescent event or a passing interest.[17] The individuals in a crowd witnessing the street corner incident (the event that brings them together) are not devoted to that incident; they do not commit themselves to it; they do not love it; they are not called on to perform deeds that realize any purpose or goal.[18] They are simply together on that occasion, and as such they have no common past and no hoped-for future; their togetherness is of a low order of cohesiveness, and they disperse without leaving any trace more substantial than the historical fact that they were there. By contrast, a community has a purpose or reason for being, and this purpose establishes two sets of relationships constituting the life of the community. Neglecting this requirement has given rise to the mistaken belief that community can be understood as some sort of "additive" affair, where we start with this individual and then go on to that individual, hoping in the end to express community as a "sum" of individuals. The correct account of community is quite different. The key concept is that of "member of," and in every community all individuals are members of it by their devotion and commitment to its purpose or cause. The two sets of relationships mentioned above are the relation of each individual to the community and the relation of the individuals to each other. The relations involved are of a different order. Each individual is a member of the community or "belongs to" the community, whereas the converse of this relation does not hold. That is to say, the community is not a member of and does not belong to each individual member. Being a member qualifies and determines the life of each member, and the fact that the purpose or cause is accepted or acknowledged by each member provides all of them with insight into the person of every other member. Thus any two of us know something about each other because we both know that the other is committed to the same cause to which we ourselves are committed.

This fact of mutual knowledge is important for grasping the relations between the members, relations that exist precisely because each is related to the same cause. The members are united in their love and devotion to the common cause; they are related to each other as well in love and devotion because the fact of their membership forms a common item in their individual biographies, regardless of any other differences that may exist between them. But community is not reducible to the "horizontal" relations between the members; they are members of it, but they are not members of each other, nor are they members of themselves. What brings them together and unifies them is the cause, which is not the unique possession of any one of them or any finite number of them taken together. The transcendent element in every community is its purpose, the goal for which it exists, the value or good to which the members are each individually committed. The extent to which any community fulfills or realizes an individual member depends on the nature of the cause. To be engaged in working with a community of persons dedicated to the cause of peace, for example, can never fulfill me as a religious community does. The latter is the redemptive community concerned with my self and my being as a whole; by comparison all other communities are partial and involve only an aspect or part of myself.

It is important to notice that in the foregoing account there is no hint or suggestion of the members' being "swallowed up" or "dissolved" into the community. Community presupposes distinct individuals and cannot exist without them; the important point is how they are together as a whole that is more a constantly unifying life than a static unity. They are together in virtue of their devotion to a cause and the relations of love, concern, and acceptance between the members that arise from the consciousness in each individual that every other individual is devoted to the same cause to which he or she is devoted. Thus the I becomes the We, and the We, though plural, does not cease to be the first person—hence community is never an impersonal affair.

JOHN E. SMITH

DEPARTMENT of PHILOSOPHY
YALE UNIVERSITY
MARCH 1970

NOTES

1. Gabriel Marcel, *Homo Viator,* trans. Emma Craufurd (Chicago: Henry Regnery Co., 1951), pp. 13–28 (hereafter cited as *HV*).

2. In *Being and Having* (trans. Katharine Farrer [Westminster: Dacre Press, 1949], pp. 104–7 [hereafter cited as *BH*]), Marcel claims that we begin by attributing existence to the other—as a genuine other and not merely as my idea of an other—and then come to think of ourselves as *not* being the other. He makes a most perceptive interpretation of the *cogito* as a standing back and seeing myself as other, with the result that I appear as existing.

3. *HV,* 20–23.   4. *HV,* 16.

5. *HV,* 16.   6. *HV,* 17.

7. In his philosophy of hope Marcel speaks of being obsessed with the idea of possessing the other in the sense of complete domination. This drive alienates us from ourselves, he maintains, because we make our other into something less than a person. See *HV,* 59; cf. *BH,* 107.

8. I cannot discuss here at length a related question: In order to regard both the other and myself as persons and as answerable, do I not also have to acknowledge my dependence on a transcendent Other not encompassed in human terms? Here the dependence would take the form of faith that I am acknowledged and accepted as a person by the divine Other.

9. The relation of mutual recognition between two finite selves is always imperfect and subject to corruption. I need the other's recognition, but I may come to resent this clear dependence on the other and to wish that I were free of it, especially if the other were to consider me under an obligation for this recognition or in other ways were to place demands on me because of my dependence. One of the reasons we are led to quests for the transcendent Other is that we look for one who recognizes us in love without our having to make a claim that obliges us in terms of justice.

10. Much of what follows is derived from *Man against Mass Society* (see note 11), but relevant passages can also be found in *Being and Having* and the *Metaphysical Journal.*

11. Gabriel Marcel, *Man against Mass Society,* trans. G. S. Fraser (Chicago: Henry Regnery Co., 1962), p. 143 (hereafter cited as *MM*). Cf. especially *MM*, 200.

12. *MM*, 103.

13. *BH*, 46; cf. *BH*, 56.

14. *MM*, 166.

15. Gottfried Wilhelm von Leibniz, *The Monadology*, trans. R. Latta (Oxford: Oxford University Press, 1898), 7:219.

16. *MM*, 200.

17. I do not undertake here to consider what holds true for every type of aggregate, and therefore I do not attempt to analyze physical objects but rather confine my attention to aggregates of persons in order to bring out the contrast between them and communities of persons. A more complete analysis would include not only physical objects but also organisms that are neither collections, aggregates, nor communities, although they may be said to approximate the community form of togetherness more closely than any other.

18. Although individuals in a crowd witnessing a tragedy may be led to form or join a community devoted to the elimination of the conditions that led to the tragic incident, they do not do so as a crowd of witnesses, which is not itself a community.

The Individual, the Collective, and the Community
REPLY TO JOHN E. SMITH

I would like to extend to you* my deepest gratitude for the penetrating article you wrote on the notion of "intersubjectivity" in my works. Indeed, it was with you, in 1961, that I visited my dear friend Hocking for the second time, was it not? What a pleasure it was for me to make that trip with you.

Because of my failing eyesight, I was only able to make a partial study of your article, but it led me to ask myself what I personally understand by "social consciousness." As always, I proceeded concretely and referred to a specific lived experience. I recalled what I felt during the first days of August 1914, when France entered the war against Germany. I remember that I felt something like a "release" in realizing that I was "vibrating" in unison with my fellow citizens—something that has not happened since then. I was no longer "locked" into the narrow limits of my individuality. We were *all together*. This lived experience of being all together is, in my opinion, social consciousness itself, and I am convinced that in its truth or in its purity it is an exceptional state, at which one arrives only in exceptional circumstances. As an example I might also cite the fantastic unanimity that became a reality in Czechoslovakia when that country was invaded by Warsaw-pact troops—a state of unanimity that still persists today.

Strictly speaking, intersubjectivity is not exactly in the same category. A good illustration of intersubjectivity can be found in the relationship between a musician playing an opus of chamber music, where each musician plays a role and makes a contribution in collaboration with (*en ouver-*

Translated from the French by Dr. Girard Etzkorn.
  *Marcel wrote this response in the form of a letter to Smith, dated 27 April 1970.—ED.

ture à) others. The words *in collaboration with* are grammatically perhaps not completely correct; yet for me they define what I once called a copresence. We are a long way from ''unison'' here. Indeed within a string quartet, the violin and the cello may seem in a certain way to be in contrast to each other; yet such opposition is not conflict. It takes place within a certain unity that is both ascertained and desired by each of the participants.

Please excuse me for offering only these few remarks, I hope they will clarify my thinking for you.

Please believe in and rest assured of my most faithful and devoted sentiments.

G.M.

13

Charles Hartshorne

MARCEL ON GOD AND CAUSALITY

G ABRIEL Marcel writes wisely about the difficulties of taking God as
cause.[1] He suggests that we avoid the concept in thinking about God.
I agree that this concept as it has often been used in theology and philosophy of religion has done great harm. But although I appreciate Marcel's
thoughts on the subject, I have somewhat more faith than he in the possibility and value of a sufficiently careful and imaginative rationalism. At
the least I am less convinced than he or than Bergson that the trouble
comes from concepts carefully defined and systematically and logically
employed; I would rather attribute the trouble to concepts ill-defined, care-
lessly and illogically employed, and above all stubbornly persisted in after
plain indications that they do not fit ordinary, not to mention theological,
uses. More specifically, I believe that French and American philosophers
during the last ten or twelve decades, in contrast to some German and
British philosophers during this period, have shown us how to conceive
causality in a way that illuminates many problems, including theological
ones. I shall not relate my discussion in detail to Marcel's but shall propose for his consideration a way of using causality in philosophy of religion that avoids at least some of the difficulties he has in mind.

I take causality to refer essentially to the influence of the past on the
present. Kant's "reciprocal" causation between contemporaries becomes
in contemporary physics—I believe rightly—a crisscross of past-present
influences. The irreducible causal relations are temporal. Causes are antecedent conditions influencing subsequent events. The word *influence* is in
some ways safer than *cause*, for it is freer from extreme technical commitments. There is some justification for the widespread suspicion in current philosophy of pretentious technical terms.

Since the causal relation is temporal, causes and effects are primarily
happenings, actions, or states rather than enduring individuals. We must

therefore distinguish between cause and agent. The murderer, the agent in a murder, became a murderer by the act, say, of firing a pistol. But behind that act are earlier conditions or influences, including the murderer's earlier states, acts, and decisions. An agent is thus not a single cause but a matrix of causes.

Should not God be conceived as supreme agent rather than as supreme single cause? God said, "Let there be light." The cause of the light was not simply mere eternal identity and necessary essence of God, but the contingent or free fiat or act of decreeing light. To identify this as cause with the eternal divine essence is to agree with Spinoza that God's actions are necessary. On the contrary, though God exists and has eminent attributes by eternal necessity, divine decrees or free decisions are contingent additions to his eternal and necessary nature. A decision in favor of a particular world or world feature is more specific than an attribute. It is a first principle of logic that the more specific or determinate (the "logically stronger") cannot follow from or be contained in the less specific (the "logically weaker").

To escape the Spinozistic absurdity one must suppose that God includes, besides his necessary essence, contingent acts, each of which is a cause. Moreover, to conceive the contingent action of God as coeternal with the divine essence violates the Aristotelian axiom, for me intuitively valid, that only the necessary can be eternal. It also implies that the action cannot, as it should, take temporal events into account. As the famous discussion in the *Summa Theologica* of the problem of omniscience and free will shows, the idea of eternal knowledge of noneternal things implies precisely that "spatializing of time" against which Bergson—and in effect Lequier before him—rightly protested. I shall consider Marcel's misgivings about divine knowledge later.

Royce's version of the eternity of God did not convince Marcel, as it did not me when I read it long ago, but I wonder what Marcel thinks now of divine immutability. In partial agreement with Spinoza, I hold that any contingent action or knowledge of contingent things taken as eternal in God would imply the absurdity of a preeternal state of will or knowledge in which the specific action or knowing was not yet determinate. Aristotle would have agreed with this objection. (Of course Spinoza rejected even temporal contingencies, but on quite different and to me quite fallacious grounds.) It was Marcel's friend and my teacher, W. E. Hocking, who first made clear to me the need to admit change and an open future even in God.

If God does have contingent temporal aspects, there must be a divine analogue to temporal succession. Barth and Berdyaev, among others, have suggested such a thing. And if causality is the influence of the past on the present, then an act of God that influences us must precede the states or happenings in us that it influences. And if, as I shall contend later, we also influence God, then the state in God that expresses this influence will be subsequent to its causes or conditions in us. I shall not discuss these relations in detail. They involve the difficult question of how one interprets relativity in physics theologically, or how one relates worldly time to divine time or supertime. Nothing, I believe, is more superficial than the old idea that time and becoming are what the human mind naturally and easily grasps, whereas eternity and being elude us. Physics has been showing ever more clearly that the temporal aspect of reality is extremely difficult to grasp. On this issue I take Bergson (following Schelling) to have been wiser than Kant. The intellect tends to eternalize the temporal and is most readily at home with the timeless.

Concerning the influence of the past upon the present, that is, causality, there are basically two theories. Each amounts to a way of defining causality as such. One way may be called the deterministic or classical, the other the indeterministic or neoclassical. For the former, think of Democritus, Spinoza, Newton, or Kant; for the latter, Boutroux, Bergson, Varisco, Peirce, James, or Whitehead. Most physicists seem now to have something like the neoclassical view.

According to the classical definition, there is a symmetrical relation of strict requirement between antecedent conditions and subsequent events. Not only did the later events require just those antecedent conditions, but the conditions together required just those subsequent events. This symmetry comes out in the phrase "necessary and sufficient condition." The totality of necessary conditions constitutes a sufficient condition for the outcome, meaning that there is no causally possible alternative to what happens subsequently. In short, conditioning is really biconditioning—an "if and only if," the formula for equivalence in logic. Any difference in the antecedents would mean a difference in the outcome; any difference in the outcome would require a difference in the antecedents. The neoclassical view accepts the first stipulation but admits the second only with certain qualifications. A man must have been a child—and only the child that in fact he was—to become the adult he is, but he could have been that very child and yet have become a qualitatively different adult. Or he might have died before maturity. Every adult has been a child; many children never become adults.

It is too late in philosophical and scientific history to declare, with an air of superior wisdom, that of course the nature of the child plus that of the environment hide in their unfathomable complexity conditions sufficing to guarantee uniquely for the child either premature death or survival to maturity and either the achievement or the nonachievement of each and every adult trait you please. Few scientists and few philosophers of science wish to be counted as claiming to know any such thing to be true. And some of us wish to be counted as knowing that it is false, for it leads to insoluble antinomies and absurdities. Indeed every major change in science in over a hundred years, from Carnot's law and Darwinian evolutionism to quantum mechanics (with the sole exception of relativity, which in this respect has yet to be reconciled with quantum mechanics), weakens the claim that classical or strict determinism is even relevant to science. For all experimental and practical purposes it is at least *as if* nature were not as classical determinism pictured it. Future changes beyond quantum mechanics are more likely to increase the divergence from this picture than to decrease it. Dirac and Wigner are among those who have suggested this. Of course quantum mechanics is not the last word. But for all that, it may have sounded the death knell of classical mechanics.

Naturally no one denies that actual happenings, taken concretely, are always influenced and partly determined by their antecedents. Concrete situations are never in all aspects unpredictable. Causality is always present. But what is causality? It is that which determines not precisely what occurs but the "real" possibilities for what occurs. A real possibility is what can happen here and now, rather than somewhere and somewhen. Causality is what makes real or localized possibility more definite or restricted than unlocalized possibility. Just how definite in principle is localized possibility? This is the sensible issue about determinism. The rest involves forms of straw-man fallacy of which indeterminists are often guilty.

Is real possibility as definite as what actually happens to realize the possibility? Classical determinism answers affirmatively. But one theory about possibility (represented by Bergson and Peirce) denies that the possible can ever be as definite as the actual. Moreover, if real possibility were as definite as what happens, it would not be possibility but necessity. Hence a category confusion arises automatically. Yet just in this way Nicolai Hartmann tries to prove determinism. His argument neatly begs the question. No astute determinists will accept the definition of causality or real possibility that Hartmann's reasoning implies. Rather, with Bergson, Peirce, Dewey, and many others they will hold that there is always a creative leap, however trifling in many instances, between the real possibility constituted by prior conditions and the actual concrete happenings. I take this to be an a priori truth. This is what becoming must be, the determining of the previously not wholly determinate. It is the creation of definiteness.

The statistical laws now employed in science are at least compatible with this view, although there is no good reason to take quantum indeterminacy as the whole extent of the creative freedom in nature. Some distinguished physicists think that the causal leeway goes further in organisms, especially in human beings.

There is a strange notion that classical determinism is the more rational or logical view. Does it not take the causal relation to be analogous in its strictness to logical entailment? The answer, however, is plainly no. Logical entailment is not generally biconditional. Only in special or even degenerate cases does the proposition "*p* entails *q*" combine with "*q* entails *p*." If every entailment were biconditional, all reasoning would be tautological and logical laws would have trivial applications at best. The rational view of causation is that causal as well as logical implications are commonly one-way only. It is therefore indeterminism that logical analogues should lead us to expect. To see that the proposition "*x* is an odd number" does not imply "*x* is the number 5" is as truly rational as to see that the reverse implication holds. Logical independence is just as valid an idea as logical dependence, and neither would make sense if the other did not. The basic logical relation of implication normally involves dependence one way and independence the other way.

Relations in logic are typically "internal" at one end or for one term and "external" at the other. When *p* entails *q*, the truth of *p* depends on that of *q*; yet the truth of *q* is normally independent of that of *p*. *Not symmetrical but one-way requirement* is the ultimate logical idea. Monists and pluralists seem almost in a conspiracy to hide this truth. Determinism is causal monism or tautologism, and when combined with Humian pluralism, as it so often has been, it is, as Whitehead once said, a "wonderfully baseless doctrine." It makes events totally interdependent—and thus analogous to a gigantic tautology—and at the same time denies any basis in the nature of things for any dependence whatever. It is strange how few have joined Meyerson in seeing the implicitly tautological structure of classical determinism. But the logical model for sheer pluralism of the Hume-Russell-Ayer variety is the extreme opposite, a vast chaos of mutually independent propositions. It is time we took seriously, as our ontological key, the asymmetry of dependence that is so obvious in propositional logic.

Consider, then, God as causally influencing what happens in the world. Divine actions are supreme conditions for creaturely acts. Like all such conditions they limit possibilities but still leave the outcome partly unsettled. What finally determines the outcome? Not even the combination of divine and antecedent creaturely actions can do this, for the reasonable view of causality is that the totality of necessary conditions is "sufficient" only for the real possibility of a certain sort of happening, some instance of which must happen. An actual happening, however, is never merely a kind of event but a particular instance of the kind, the instance being more determinate than the kind. This step from determinable kind to determinate instance derives from a creative act only in the event itself, not before.

Perhaps Lequier was the first to speak of himself as "creature, creator of himself." According to Whitehead, each momentary state of a person is self-creative. And he properly generalized this, as Peirce had already done, by taking it to apply to all individuals in nature. True, except in human beings and other animals individuals are too small spatially to be inferred without recourse to scientific data. But everywhere there is some creative freedom, however slight. Bergson's mature view was similar.

If this is what causality in principle is, how can anyone infer from the occurrence of a disease, say, that God has deliberately inflicted that disease on that person? Countless "decisions" (resolutions of indeterminacy) besides God's have combined in the outbreak and course of the disease. Even if God is "one more" (rather, the eminent) cause or agent, concrete details of the world cannot be referred to divine decisions.

But surely, you say, the most general features of nature must be divinely instituted, since the divine agent is incomparably superior in power to all other agents and is cosmic in its influence. Also, do not these general features make it probable or even inevitable that there will be some evils, no matter how the creatures resolve their little indeterminacies? Yes, it seems so. But then, given freedom in the creatures, how could there be a general order that made conflict and frustration impossible? I seriously believe that with even two free creatures, no conceivable God and no conceivable order could guarantee them absolute safety from evil. The risk of evil is the price of any existence and of any order. Yet no particular local evil is made inevitable by the order or by any act of God. God does not will particular evils or particular goods, but he wills an order in which creatures, each in its appropriate measure free, can have optimal opportunities for good in spite of certain unavoidable risks of evil.

The risks are not merely the possibility of wicked choices, for conflicts can arise quite innocently. Although, as so many have remarked, creative freedom is not the same as chance, still multiple acts of freedom will intersect to make a world that at every point is different from what anyone antecedently intended or any set of causes made the only possible outcome. If "by chance" means neither intended nor causally required, then chance must be pervasive not only in our world but in any possible one. Indeed it may be argued that the very idea of possibility (and with it the correlative idea of necessity) implies creativity in the Bergsonian-White-headian sense. Other "possible worlds" are just the alternative courses that the complex divine-creaturely creative process might have taken or may yet take. As Boutroux was among the first to urge, even the laws of nature are contingent and should be thought of as generated and subject to change. They too are created and may be superseded by other creations when their utility has been exhausted. They are the nearest we can come rationally to "acts of God." But they leave wide scope to chance. How wise William James was not to be frightened by any "So you believe in chance, that irrational idea"! It is no more irrational than the correlative idea of the causally (or teleologically) entailed. Both stand or fall together, as Dewey pointed out.

That the divine action always leaves creatures some options seems inherent in the very concept of a creature as a noneminent form of the creativity that in its eminent form is the deity. To pass in thought from ordinary individuals to God means to go not from the zero form of attributes to the eminent form but from positive though noneminent forms to the supreme or eminent (unsurpassable) form.

Gilson says that the renaissance metaphysicians—Campanella, Cardanus, and so on—made no important contribution. Ah, but they did! They began to make explicit the principle I have just enunciated. They saw, for instance, that if there is supreme awareness in the eminent individual there must be nonsupreme but still not zero awareness in every noneminent individual. Every creature expresses divine attributes to some degree. Leibniz developed the thought by bringing out the relevance, in just this context, of the distinction between the individual or singular creature and the aggregate. What even he and everybody missed until the nineteenth century was that by the same principle the creatures cannot be less than noneminently free creators and that God—on the concrete and contingent side of his reality—must be the eminent creature. To Whitehead belongs the honor of having stated these relations more clearly than anyone before him, granted that Lequier and Fechner each made a fine start in this direction.

If creatures are noneminently free creators, God of course is "generous," in Marcel's and Père le Blond's phrase; that is, he permits and indeed fosters freedom in the creatures. The enslaving idea of omnipotence in its conventional form is an unworthy notion of divine power. It not only makes God the deliberate author of every evil, but it also implies that God is capable of depressing all creatures below the minimum of creaturely dignity. The notion of a unilateral divine determining of the details of a created world asserts not too much of God but too little—indeed it asserts nothing definite and intelligible. But I have perhaps shown that the source of the trouble is not in the mere idea of causality but in a special, illogical, and now seemingly outmoded form of this idea, which takes it to be strict biconditioning between earlier and later stages of process.

The renaissance principle that creatures are noneminently what God is eminently does not conflict with the belief that God is primarily "creator" and the lesser realities primarily "creatures." For eminent createdness cannot mean that God's very existence and eternal essence are created. Only nonessential divine qualities are so, whereas the entire individual reality of a noneminent creature is a product of an antecedent state of reality in which that individual did not exist at all.

If God is, on one side of the divine nature, created, who are the creators? As with all individuals, God is first of all self-creative. Each phase in the divine becoming determines itself and thus transcends, but grows out of, the previous phase. (Being unborn, God has no first phase; hence Kant's First Antinomy is relevant here, however its cogency is evaluated.) But as with all individuals, God's self-creation uses influences coming from all other individuals. God is in dialogue with them, and dialogue is mutual self-creation between individuals. The creatures are causes of effects in God. Lequier was quite clear about this over a century ago. The Socinians had implied it much earlier. In cordial agreement with these thinkers, I hold that if we could not influence God, our existence would be simply vain. In "serving" the divine life we should then leave it exactly as it would be if unserved. Any religious sense I have rebels against this as a mockery. Moreover, what could it then mean to speak of divine "knowledge" of the world? In all ordinary cases of knowledge, at least of particular concrete things, it is the things known that make the knowledge possible, not vice versa. Perception in any animal is an effect of which events in the environment or the animal's body are causes. This is admitted in much of the Western tradition, especially in Aristotelianism, including Thomism. Yet scholasticism turned this relation upside down in the eminent case and held that the divine analogue of knowing produces and is uninfluenced by the worldy realities it knows.

This severe paradox (it is a strange "analogue" that is the analogate upside down) can be avoided if we admit that God is influenced by the creatures and that the precise worldly object of a given state of divine knowing is influenced by God's knowing not of *it* but of antecedent worldly states. Thus when two individuals know each other and know that they know each other, what A knows "is" happening in B has already occurred before A knows it, and similarly with what B knows is happening in A. I know, for example, what you have just thought, and this knowing of mine influences not what you have just thought but only what you think later when you come to know what I have thought about what you, still earlier, had thought. Dialogue models these relations. Analogously, the creatures are in dialogue with God. If they do not in the full sense "know," they are at least sensitive to or feel God's knowing of them. This analogy is legitimate only if God interacts with the world. Mutual knowledge cannot mean less than mutual influence.

Every individual other than God is both cause and effect. To take God as eminent cause but zero effect is arbitrary in the extreme and has been a fertile source of skepticism about the legitimacy of theistic belief. It is not surprising that just as Marcel has doubts about "cause" in thinking about God, so he has doubts about "knowledge." For the traditional refusal to admit eminent effect as well as eminent cause makes it impossible to construe divine knowledge. I am convinced that one either has no idea of God at all or is implicitly committed to the view that every generic concept inherent in creaturehood has an eminent analogue. Interaction is inherent in creaturehood; therefore eminent interaction belongs to Deity. To confine this to persons of the trinity is to confine mutual knowledge to them. But religion requires dialogue between God and the worldly individuals.

I agree entirely with Marcel that Royce's eternalistic version of eminent or "absolute" experience is confused. Knowing cannot encompass reality in a totality fixed once-and-for-all. But this is not because of some limitation in knowing as such. Reality itself is essentially creative and protean. Being is wholly included in becoming, as Bergson so courageously and sagaciously declared. There is a new total reality every moment. What can be known from the standpoint of eternity is only what is itself eternal, not any contingent event or final totality of contingent events. (There is no such totality, eternally or at any time.) To be is to become or to be a mere abstract aspect of becoming. That God eternally "is" means that divine becoming, as such, is essential to any becoming and to anything thinkable. Though beginningless, the eminent becoming perpetually acquires additional richness of content. This is the definitive becoming by which all lesser becoming is measured and made possible. To happen is to happen for God, to be taken into the Life from which nothing can be lost, where neither moth nor rust can corrupt nor thieves break through and steal.

Marcel sees a threat to the "substantial" divine unity if God is thought to confront alternative possibilities. Is mere oneness so sacred, compared with diversity and the beauty it makes possible? I believe with all my heart that unity is no more necessary to value or to God than diversity of content or the contrast between the newly acquired and the already possessed. (All possible value cannot be eternally possessed because "all possible value all actualized" is contradictory in view of the incompatibilities between values—the "incompossibles.") Unity alone is nothing wonderful, in spite of Plotinus. A chord is as unified as a symphony. Can we not worship God rather than some abstraction like substantial unity?

It is not enough, at least for the religious feelings of some of us, that we should be able to participate in the divine being. We feel that this being should be able to take into itself the diversity of our experiences. We wish to serve, however humbly, by contributing to that life. But this means that the alternative possible contributions we may make are alternative possibilities for God as receptive to creaturely contributions. In addition, if there is an eminent analogue to creaturely choice and freedom, there must be an indeterminacy of real possibilities for divine decision regarding how to respond, or to contribute in turn, to the creatures. "Let there be light." There might have been something else, also good. Divine potentiality is strictly infinite, but any created actuality must have aspects of finitude. The step from infinite possibility to a finite actuality cannot be uniquely required. True, God infallibly makes good decisions and could not make bad ones. But this does not deprive him of open alternatives of action.

The notion that to each practical problem—whether ordinary and local or eminent and cosmic—there is a uniquely best solution is groundless. World-creating is not the mere application of "sufficient reason," a syllogism of the form "I do what is best; this is best; therefore I do this." Leibniz's doctrine is an excess of rationalism, or rather it is not genuinely rational at all, for it attempts to deduce the particular from the general, the concrete from the abstract. Particularity must be freely created, and each new step is a creative leap beyond any definite requirements of the already actual.

To the idea, mentioned above, that God must be eminent effect as well as cause, patient as well as agent, there will of course be strong, perhaps even violent, opposition from some quarters. Can the creator of all things be also effect? Is it not an old saying, reiterated by countless great writers, that "agent is superior to patient" (Philo)? An odd consequence seems to be that if a mosquito bites a person, the mosquito is thereby shown superior to the person. Or if a moving worm reflects light into a person's eyes and thereby causes the person to perceive the movements of the worm, the person thus influenced is inferior to the worm as thus influencing him or her. All concrete causes we know are also effects of prior causes, and all agents interact as well as act. Indeed one of Kant's antinomies about divine causation derives from the assumption that God must act without interacting. But is this theologically necessary?

There are two senses, different in principle, of effect or patient. Ordinarily an agent is not only influenced by other agents but even produced by some of them out of a world from which it was previously absent. But notice that this second way of being patient or effect excludes interaction. It is a purely one-way action of causes preceding one's own existence and entirely uninfluenced by that existence. In this one-sided sense God cannot be patient. The divine existence, or essential nature (they are inseparable), has no predecessors. But for all that, God may have contingent aspects influenced by creatures antecedent to those aspects. God as cognitive must be effect as well as cause, even though the divine existence cannot be caused.

We should of course insist that just as God, taken as cause or agent, is eminently so—being "unsurpassable by any conceivable other" in scope and quality of power—so too, taken as effect or patient, God has this status in its eminent form. Thus the divine actuality must be influenced not simply by some restricted set of agents but by all, and God's response to influence must be unsurpassably appropriate and adequate. Only God is influenced by all or influences all; only God influences, or responds to influence, in an unsurpassable manner. In this way we renounce not one iota of the requirement that God be the eminent, not the ordinary, form of a universal or "transcendental" category.

In general, given any categorial contrast theists have the choice of two procedures: (1) they may take the eminence of deity to imply the unsurpassable form of one pole of the contrast (for example, cause rather than effect) and the purely negative or zero form of the other pole; (2) they may take eminence to imply the unsurpassable form of both poles. I call the second option the principle of dual transcendence (or of dipolarity). Nearly all the great systems before this century chose the nondual notion of transcendence, without any discussion of the dual or dipolar alternative.

Formally and trivially the two procedures can be brought under the same formula. We need only hold that in each contrast the zero or negative form of one pole is the unsurpassable form of that pole. Thus not being causally influenced at all is taken to be the best possible way of being influenced. But is it? I think not. Yet here again matters are a bit subtler than they may seem. As we have said, the ideal way of being caused is indeed not to be caused at all *if* the eminent agent's very existence and necessary or eternal essence is in question.

Dual transcendence implies both an unsurpassable kind of change and an unsurpassable kind of self-identity, and it applies similarly to other categorical contrasts: unity and internal variety, actual and potential being, definite past and open future, simplicity and complexity, absoluteness and relativity, infinity and finitude, and so on. More than a century ago Fech-

ner, the psychologist and natural theologian (little known in the latter capacity), was almost clear about much of this.

In various writings I have tried to show how contradiction is avoided
in this type of theory. Many traditional antinomies are escaped in this way,
including all of Kant's antinomies save that part of the first referring to
past time. This remains a puzzle, as does the status of set theory in mathematics.

Nonetheless, one contradiction that Kant feared might invalidate the
concept of an *ens realissimum* becomes irrelevant, since the dipolar definition of God does not imply an absolute maximum of actual value in God.
With such a maximum there could be no influence upon God, for what
could it accomplish? Fechner long ago virtually gave the solution: God is
surpassable, but only as God surpasses God. Moreover, the principle by
which God, and only God, can surpass what he (she—God transcends
gender) now is is itself unsurpassable even by God. Or, as Fechner admirably put it, God's perfection is his ideal perfectibility. This concept avoids
the absurd view that all possible value is actual in God. God could not
enjoy as actual the values of all possible worlds, for they are not all com-
possible. But God, and only God, can actually enjoy all actual values and
potentially enjoy all possible ones. This is because of the divine infallible
cognitive power and because to know a value in an unsurpassable way is
to fully possess the value. A century after something like the foregoing
was said by the humble German scientist and unrecognized theologian, it
was noticed that he had said it.

Presumably Marcel will be suspicious of any rationalistic program like
the one outlined above. I should not blame him for this. I only wonder
whether he sees in the scheme some advance over the more usual ones—
waiving the question of whether any scheme can be adequate. Am I wrong
in claiming to have a better conceptual instrument than the more usual ones
for explicating the social structure of all experience, including religious
experience? In the I-Thou situation it seems clear that agency is reciprocal,
that each individual influences the other. Dialogue is mutual creation of
quality in agents. How then could God as pure cause rather than effect be
a Thou? Moreover, if causality were deterministic, how could individuals
have any reality as such? The world antecedent to an individual would
completely determine it. There would thus be but one real created individual, the cosmos. And there would be no genuine becoming. Peirce and
Bergson should perhaps share between them the honor of having been the
first to see this clearly, though Lequier to some degree saw it also.

Marcel suggests that causality be taken as having only empirical rather
than transcendent use. He makes this suggestion with wise hesitation and

misgiving. And indeed it seems to me but one more case of trying to have an idea of God without having one. Of course divine causality will be eminent causality with formally unique implications, just as divine existence or individuality must have such implications. But without some conceptual analogy between divinity and ordinary things, there is no idea of God. And without that influence of the settled past upon the nascent, self-creative present that is causality, there is no adequate idea of ordinary things. Hence for any idea of God, a divine analogue to that influence must be admitted.

What ruined traditional analogical concepts was the monopolar prejudice—a form of which is the supposition that one may take the categorial contrast of cause with effect, raise the one to the eminent form while reducing the other to zero, and thereby produce a proper view of deity—or again the supposition that causality simply excludes chance or disorder and amounts to sheer necessity backward and forward between condition and conditioned, a supposition with no basis in logic. As Berdyaev saw, there must be an eminent form of chance, even for God.

One of my deepest convictions is that since Creator and creature as such, or in abstraction from all further specificity, are correlatives, errors about the one abstraction invariably go with errors about the other. An analogical thought about God that starts from a false idea of the ordinary case is bound to result in a false idea of God, and vice versa, for of course one may read the analogy in either direction. That God's creativity must be free should have warned theologians all along against admitting classical determinism even for the ordinary case. (Philo and Socinus saw this much more clearly than Augustine and the scholastics.) And now it turns out that "mechanical causality," to which Marcel refers, was a myth of the intellect, a myth the intellect in practice is forced to reject.

Above all even if God is in each case one cause, or rather *the* unique, eminent cause, among others, God is, according to dipolarity, just as truly and uniquely the eminent effect. And indeed only as the eminent contingent Creature is God the all-inclusive concrete reality, of which as universal cause he (she) is a mere abstract aspect. Deity is above all the summing up of creative achievement rather than its mere source. And the source is not simply identical with the achievement. Both are God, but in distinct aspects; otherwise there would be contradiction.

I have in common with Marcel a deep interest in Royce, whose *Problem of Christianity* led me (at the age of 19) to see the social structure of reality as *the* philosophical key. I also share Marcel's enthusiasm for Buber's I-Thou. I agree too with the rejection of Royce's theodicy, his monstrous albeit heroic attempt to justify a divine choice of the particular evils in the world as necessary ingredients in the supreme good at which the Absolute aims. This view either turns the creatures' freedom into a sham, reduces the absolute will to the sum of the creatures' wills, or—so confused is the doctrine—somehow manages to do both at once. But on one point I may perhaps be more sympathetic than Marcel to Royce's theodicy. I accept the eloquently expressed Roycean doctrine of divine appropriation of our sufferings. Here Berdyaev and Whitehead, as divergent as they were on many things, were at one, presumably in complete independence of one another. God does not simply "know" of our suffering but takes it into her (his) own life incomparably more completely than the most sympathetic friend among creatures ever could.

It would be splendid to have some further thoughts on these topics from the eminent French thinker.

CHARLES HARTSHORNE

DEPARTMENT OF PHILOSOPHY
THE UNIVERSITY OF TEXAS, AUSTIN
APRIL 1968

NOTE

1. See especially Gabriel Marcel, "God and Causality," in *Religion and Culture: Essays in Honor of Paul Tillich,* ed. Walter Leibrecht (New York: Harper, 1959), pp. 211–16.

Marcel on God and Causality

REPLY TO CHARLES HARTSHORNE

I am glad that reading my writings has given Professor Hartshorne the opportunity to develop his very comprehensive view on causality, on the one hand, and on theism, on the other. But I fear that there is between us a rather fundamental disagreement.

I am not sure that philosophers have ever entirely succeeded in explicating the content of the idea of cause, although I am personally inclined to seek the solution of the problem in the direction indicated by Maine de Biran. Above all I fear that the concept of influence, far from offering clarification, is really even more obscure and, I would venture to say, more confused than that of causality, so that I am scarcely disposed to admit the assertion according to which causality refers essentially to the influence of the past on the present.

It seems to me that the term *influence* applies above all to the relations between persons. I would say, for example, that I underwent the influence of Royce during a certain period of my life. But a somewhat closer analysis of such a fact would show, I think, that its domain is outside the field of causality in the strict sense. Professor Hartshorne mentions Emile Boutroux, whose *Contingency of the Laws of Nature* I too have read with great profit. I would be inclined to say that the further one departs from the zone of mechanism, properly speaking, to immerse oneself in the concrete, the more the word *cause* should be applied with caution. This is quite obvious in the domain of life and so much more so in that of consciousness and interpersonal relations.

Let us note, also, that the use of the word *undergo (subir)*, where it is a case of influence, as in the example cited above, implies a distorted view of what is in question. A certain idea of Royce, as I read his works,

---

Translated from the French by Charles Hartshorne.

commands my respect; that is to say, this idea has *enlightened* me and I have accepted it, so that it is in a certain manner incorporated into the totality of my thought. But we are here far from the elementary relation between cause and effect.

Furthermore, I should add that influence seems characteristically to operate in a twilight zone, so that often it becomes conscious only afterward. In truth, one is here in the presence of a life's work, which is rather the sphere of finality. I speak of course of the internal finality as Kant and his successors defined it.

At the same time I agree, of course, that it is necessary to distinguish between cause and agent and to recognize the specificity of the act as such; I note, too, that it is not always easy to distinguish between a simple homicidal gesture, which is perhaps not strictly speaking an act, and a murder. But in my mind, what is important is knowing whether, in regard to the idea we are able to form of God, the distinction between cause and agent is such that it allows us to overcome the difficulties encountered in the idea of divine causality. I must say in all honesty that I do not think so.

In my *Journal métaphysique*, I wrote that when we speak of God, it is not of God that we speak, and this remains for me fundamentally true. But perhaps we should be more explicit and say more strictly that any speech about God ultimately positing Him as an object of thought and defining Him—in short, attributing to Him certain characteristics—is shown to higher reflection as a concern with something precisely other than God. I said "something," but it would be better to say "someone."

But what is this discovery or this negative evidence? It is a question, certainly, of an evidence that not only is not at all Cartesian but that is at the opposite pole from Descartes. I shall try here to be as concrete as possible; that is, I shall attempt to disclose the meaning of the controversy. The term *rejection* (*récusation*) would be more adequate than *controversy* (*contestation*). The essential thing is to know who makes this rejection. Certainly, it is not consciousness in general, the transcendental ego, or anything of the sort. Rather, it should perhaps be called the adult consciousness that has reached maturity only by taking into completely lucid consideration what in human experience resists all attempts at integration or absorption into an intelligible system, that is, above all, suffering and evil. The adult consciousness passes judgment on what we could call the attempted sugar-coating to which an infantile theology all too often resorts, particularly when it tries to interpret suffering as punishment, but also when it strains itself to minimize the reality of evil by reducing it to the mere status of a lesser form of being or of a mere privation.

The central question in my opinion is to see what position the adult consciousness can adopt concerning the idea of a divine agent in the very sense Mr. Hartshorne seeks to define. When we say "agent," it seems to me we are at the same time saying "responsible agent." But responsible to whom? It is here that we get ourselves into difficulties that to me appear inextricable. To say that God thus conceived of is responsible to himself either signifies nothing or is equivalent to saying that he is irresponsible. There is every danger that it will be as though the adult consciousness took on itself the right to judge God as agent. In that case there would occur in consciousness a debate or a trial between itself as both accuser and exonerator.

The experience of this sort of polemic seems definitely to show that there is no escape; this amounts to saying that the exoneration is never fully convincing. Yet something irresistible in us tends to persuade us that the trial is vitiated in principle or that the accusation in itself implies an error—more precisely, a fraud. But here let us take care to avoid a dangerous equivocation. Professor Hartshorne repeatedly returns to the unsurpassable character of the goodness or the perfection of the divine agent as he conceives of him, adding that it may be the essence of this perfection to surpass itself, thus permitting the avoidance of the idea of a static perfection, immutable and hence devitalized. Leaving aside the purely metaphysical difficulties such a conception involves, I admit that it appears to me in itself preferable to the contrary idea. But I confess that the word *unsurpassable* creates in me a sense of uneasiness in that it implies, in spite of everything, the idea of a measure, of a measuring, which seems to me to have a meaning only in the finite, or, if you prefer, within creation. And there is something much more serious; I quote here the statement that seems to me the most significant but that also might provoke the most vigorous rejection: "God does not will particular evils or particular goods; he wills an order in which creatures, each free in its appropriate measure, can have optimal opportunities for good in spite of unavoidable risks of evil."

It seems to me that the idea Professor Hartshorne expresses here differs from the Leibnizian idea only because Professor Hartshorne—under the influence of Fechner and the contemporary philosophies of becoming, especially Bergsonism—is soft-pedaling metaphysical optimism and trying to harmonize it with the idea of a finite God. (This attempt, I note in passing, is not unlike Renouvier's conception in his later philosophy.) But I do not see that this perspective goes very far beyond the idea of a steward-God—I would almost say, a technocratic God—who in no way appears to fulfill what I would call the requirement of transcendence because of which a God who does his best, a God of Whom one must not demand the impossible, and so on, is but a sub-God, that is, a non-God.

I return to what I said previously concerning the "trial" of God by the adult consciousness: it is surely not the optimist who could silence the accuser; on the contrary, I fear the optimist is in grave danger of aggravating the accusation and, ultimately, of assuring its triumph. Yet here a superior reflection intervenes that, beyond the trial itself or the conditions in which it is instituted, makes dubious the very notion of God as an agent who can at best be cleared of the charges; indeed, in the eyes of one who is moved and inspired by the need for transcendence, the exoneration appears as sacrilegious as the accusation itself.

Sacrilege, I have said—that is, an offence against the very holiness of God. This is for me the fundamental idea, although undoubtedly the word *idea* is improper. Faith is the irresistible élan that bears us toward the Holy God. I meant nothing else when I spoke for the first time, in my *Journal métaphysique,* of the absolute Thou (*Toi absolu*).

Can there be a dialogue here, as Professor Hartshorne thinks? I greatly hesitate to affirm it. If such a dialogue is possible, it is, I think, with the incarnate God, with Christ. If we are Christians, we have to recognize that God, very mysteriously, has willed, has created, Himself all-powerless; I use these words in opposition to omnipotence as conceived of by what I call classical theology.

I would tend, therefore, to acknowledge something like a dipolarity between the Holy God and the God incarnate and suffering. It seems to me that an extreme mistrust is in order with regard to efforts of rationalization that consist of changing the Holy God into a divine calculator or legislator, if not into a divine despot.

I should be the first to admit that this is not a comfortable position and that I am personally far from feeling comfortable in it. But it has at least the advantage of implying or presupposing nothing in conflict with that sense of the sacred apart from which religion seems to me to degenerate into idolatry.

G.M.

14

Kenneth T. Gallagher

TRUTH AND FREEDOM IN MARCEL

WHATEVER else remains in dispute with respect to the meaning of truth, the notion is indisputably correlative to some presumed affirmation. That is, with respect to any purported truth, it should always be legitimate to ask who affirms this truth. Truth, after all, is not a thing, a piece of the furniture of nature; it is an event that comes to pass in the life of mind. Every proposition of the form "Such and such is true" always contains an implicit "*I* affirm that such and such is true." It is therefore inevitable that within every theory of truth is a theory of the self.

We might like to contend that the "I" is simply a ubiquitous common factor that can be conveniently canceled out of the truth-equation at the beginning; but this assumption is not self-evident, and even a cursory inspection reveals that the assumption is itself built on an implicit theory of truth and a theory of the self. Far from prescinding from the reference to selfhood, this belief sets up, as we shall see, one modality of selfhood as the arbiter of the whole range of truth. Yet the really significant question is whether there may not be an analogical range of meaning in the notion of truth correlative to the different modalities of the self that affirms it. This certainly must be entertained as an initial question, whatever our ultimate decision with regard to it.

Marcel's thought might be understood as one long effort to reply to this question. For although in the early pages of the *Metaphysical Journal* he wrestles with the problem of truth within a more traditional idealist framework, he is led almost immediately to the issue of the self by which truth is affirmed. At this stage of his thought we find a mutual reference among the terms *truth, existence,* and *verifiability.*[1] An existent is what can be presented in a spatiotemporal manner to consciousness. It seems to be, as Marcel indicates, an essentially Kantian conception.[2] The notion of truth is restricted to the realm of existence and hence is in its turn correl-

ative to verifiability. Only what is verifiable is susceptible to being denom-
inated "true," and only existents (spatiotemporal presentations to consciousness) are verifiable. He is therefore perfectly consistent when he
begins to wonder whether there is meaning beyond truth.[3] For once having
linked truth to a quasi-Kantian objective verifiability, the search for what
lies beyond this verifiability must appear to Marcel as a search for what
lies beyond truth. With good reason, Prini characterized Marcel's struggle
in the *Metaphysical Journal* as a search for the "methodology of the unverifiable."[4]

In the course of this search, Marcel eventually comes to realize that he
is not only modifying his original Kantian conception of truth but correspondingly being forced to win through to a new notion of the subject that
affirms this truth. For the I that affirms the "objectively valid" is equipped
on the one hand with sensory receptivity and on the other with the logical
categories of thought. Although Marcel speaks of this as the *cogito* subject, he regards the *cogito* as a purely formal a priori, something like a
first step on the road to the transcendental ego. Truth is what is correlative
to this purely epistemological subject-in-general. But what of meaning that
cannot be presented as an object to such a subject? Marcel initially encounters this question by meditating on the philosophical status of faith,
for the believing self is neither a purely formal a priori nor a logico-sensory subject, and hence its assurance of its authenticity cannot be derived
from the area of the verifiable.[5] Significantly, in answer to this early question Marcel takes a stand that continues to be central to his thought half a
century later. Who affirms the self's relation to God? I affirm it. But which
I? Not the *cogito,* but the singular, free subject. The transcendent is posited by freedom and by freedom only.[6] Hence there is a meaning that is
there only for my freedom. Conversion creates a new intelligibility, which
is not there for any other modality of selfhood.[7] That is why Marcel will
repudiate the claim of the objective consciousness, the logico-sensory subject-in-general, to declare to the believer that he is suffering from an illusion. This claim implies that the believer's experience has no ontological,
but only psychological, value—which in turn presumes that he can judge
the believer's mode of selfhood by standards supplied from his own mode.
But this begs the question. Marcel insists that the possibility of an "illusion" simply does not exist here, since for the self that comes to itself in
the act of faith, the distinction between appearance and reality no longer
holds.[8]

We should emphasize the basic character of Marcel's breakthrough
here, for once we realize that this is accomplished from the beginning of
the *Metaphysical Journal,* we can better appreciate the astonishing conti-

nuity in Marcel's completely unsystematic thought. What he has glimpsed is that the charge of "mere subjectivism" does not apply to faith, because the self that is competent to make the charge does not exist. As an onto-logically foundational experience of selfhood, faith is recalcitrant to criti-cism by any subject that does not share this mode of selfhood. It is an original entry into meaning and is a revelation both of the self and of the other. The mode of transcendent otherness delivered to the free self is not to be judged by the standards of that subject-in-general for whom "objec-tivity" is the only available mode of otherness.

It is interesting to observe how much Marcel has in common with Karl Jaspers, for whom the transcendent is also correlative to the self in its ultimate freedom, which he calls *Existenz*.[9] For Jaspers the meaning of *I* cannot have an invariable referent, since experientially its content is drawn from more than one source. First, the I means the empirical individual, which can be located as a bundle of particularities within the world and differentiated from other individuals also found there. (Under this aspect the self is *"empirisches Dasein."*) But second, the I is aware of itself as a knower of the universally valid knowledge of the sciences, not at vari-ance with but rather replaceable by and interchangeable with any other scientific knower; as a "consciousness-in-general" (the Kantian *"Denken überhaupt"*), I am the anonymous correlate of a world of objects. But in neither of these postures of selfhood would I be able to affirm the tran-scendent. The empirical individual is an item within the world, and the consciousness-in-general is a knower of an array of objects. But transcend-ence is not an object among others. It is only, says Jaspers, in virtue of *Existenz,* of my self so far as it is unique and unconditional freedom, that I can be related to the transcendent. In the supraworldly experience of selfhood given in freedom, I stand open to the supraworldly transcendent ground. In the ultimate meaning of the I, the ultimate Other is encoun-tered. *"There where I am most myself,"* says Jaspers, *"I am no longer only myself."*[10] Accordingly Marcel declares, "What is deepest in me is not of me."[11]

Marcel's later notion of "mystery" is in strict continuity with his no-tion of the "unverifiable," except that continual reflection has now en-abled him to give a more positive expression to his view. This progress became possible as he proceeded to spell out for himself the ramifications of his original realization of an intelligibility that is available only for free-dom and not for a consciousness-in-general. At first he sees this in respect to faith. Then it occurs to him that the self is also something we cannot "know" in the usual sense,[12] that love is beyond truth,[13] that in fact the whole I-Thou experience is unverifiable and hence that its meaning cannot be given in an objective fashion,[14] that the meaning of the world is not given ultimately to argumentation,[15] that "theodicy is atheism" (meaning that a "proved" God can only be an object for a consciousness, which is just what God cannot be),[16] and that finally there is "*no objectively valid judgment bearing on being*."[17] What has gradually unfolded is a whole realm of meaning that is simply not there at all for the subject constituting the realm of the verifiable—the subject that must regard all targets of its assertions as "objects" posed over against itself and forming part of a totality of items similarly posed. The realm of the verifiable corresponds very well to the realm of what Marcel comes to call "problems"—data that are both external to and correlates of impersonal, logico-sensory subjectivity.

But once he has disengaged the area of "problems" more adequately, Marcel no longer feels the same need to locate "being" beyond truth. It is now perfectly possible for him to say, "I can no longer accept the idea, in any sense, of something beyond truth," for there has occurred a certain transformation in the meaning of truth.[18] This transformation has been wrought by Marcel's more decisive understanding of what, properly speaking, forms the starting point of all thought and all philosophy: *participation*. For what all the aforementioned instances of "unverifiables" also have in common is that they take thought back to an origin that is there before thought and out of which thought arises. All truth and all assertion arise out of a nonobjectifiable ground and are sustained by the roots they maintain in that ground. This comes to the forefront for Marcel in the essay "Existence and Objectivity," where he distinguishes two ideas he had formerly tended to equate.[19] The primordial experience of existence, he now decides, cannot be expressed in a subject-object framework but rather antedates this framework. It is in the experience of embodied selfhood that the existence of the world is globally and indubitably given to me, an experience from which it would be strictly impossible to divorce myself.[20]

My self is founded on this experience. This is the importance of incarnation in Marcel's philosophy. To say "I am my body"[21] is not to point up merely a prominent, isolated fact; it is to point to the most pervasive level of the experience of participation. That is why incarnation always remains the "central datum of metaphysics" for him.[22] Once I succeed in grasping the impossibility of understanding my relation to my body in terms of the relation between two things—that is, once I recognize the inability of ordinary subject-predicate logic to express this relation—I have retrieved through reflection the exemplar of what a participated experience of selfhood means. Marcel goes on to expand the field of my participated subjectivity—the participation afforded in communion becoming his most important concern—but every level is marked by the same discovery: participation founds the being of the participant. When Marcel emphasizes that our being is a being-in-a-situation, he is indicating that the only experience we have of existence is as participating-in-existence. Let there be no mistake about this. The crucial aspect of participated subjectivity is that it is never *merely* an experience of subjectivity. Every participation is a revelation not only of self but of other. It is nonsensical therefore for a self founded on participation to be mired in a problem of subjectivism. The Cartesian difficulty presupposes an experience of subjective existence *prior* to the experience of the other, and this is just what Marcel denies. If I were to divorce myself in thought from every mode of participation, what I would have left would not be a privileged self, but nothing at all; apart from participation, the self is nothing but an abstraction; for the concrete self, *esse est co-esse*.

Once we recognize that participation has the primary role, the notion of truth is transformed. Truth can no longer be exclusively identified with one of its forms, "verifiability." For if all assertion lives off a prepredicative experience of participation, then the criterion for the value of assertion is shifted toward this participation. It is inevitable that if participation founds the content of experience, it founds evidence and therefore founds truth. How wide this content is, how much truth can be affirmed, can no longer be considered decidable by a subject that arrogates a privileged status to itself. For all participation is equally foundational experience and hence cannot be judged by a subject that does not share it. Henceforth, then, the question of truth becomes the question of the scope and depth of participation.

"Mystery" is simply Marcel's name for truth so understood.[23] It is the epistemological side of a metaphysics of participation. For the fundamental question in Marcel's philosophy is bound to be, How do I think participation? To think participation is not, of course, just to think the self. But neither is it to think of something set over against the self. Obviously a participated datum is a datum in which my self is involved and from which I cannot separate my self. It is not something I have but something through which I am. That is why in questioning the datum I call my self into question. Marcel has found a prominent instance of this in his meditation on the body as "mine," but he encounters it whenever thought attempts to comprehend data that it cannot regard as objects, whether it be the Thou on whose presence communion is founded or such traditional philosophical themes as freedom, knowledge, or being. The difficulty in attempting a philosophical comprehension of these data is apparent: if they really are nonobjectifiable, there seems to be a sense in which they should also be unknowable. Ordinarily, to "know" something is to treat it as an object; not to be able to treat it thus is apparently not to know it. So we are back to Marcel's initial difficulty: Is there anything beyond truth? has now become, How do we affirm a meaning that transcends the subject-object dichotomy?

Marcel calls the thought that accomplishes this "secondary reflection."[24] By this he contrasts it with the "primary reflection" that dissolves the immediacy of participated experience and sets up the world of objectivity in which the scientific consciousness finds its natural habitat. Secondary reflection is the recuperative act by which philosophy comes to recognize the derivative character of primary reflection. In doing so, it reroutes the impetus of thought in the direction of the unity antedating objectification. Often this entails seeing the inadequacies of ordinary ways of speaking about the primordial experience of participation, as in the case of incarnation and communion. But here an additional factor comes to our attention: if there is to be a motive for this rerouting—if the inadequacy of objectified modes of speech is to be recognized—then in some sense the original experience of participation must continue to be present to the thought that is trying to think it. Thought could not recognize the inadequacy of primary reflection if, as thought, it had lost all contact with participated experience. This means that secondary reflection lives off an intuition and that Marcel must assign this intuition a central role in the philosophical enterprise.

Let us see how this works out with respect to the cardinal example of a mystery, the mystery of being. Everything in philosophy turns on the decision whether one may or may not consider speech couched in the language of being to be part of the content side of thought. Kant's critique may be understood simply as a denial that the idea of being was anything more than a purely formal organizing instrument. As such it is an empty idea, unable to contribute anything to an empirical statement, and therefore deprived of the absolute status traditional metaphysics allotted to it. In one sense Marcel agrees with Kant: being is not, strictly speaking, an idea. That is, it cannot function in a logical proposition the way an ordinary idea functions. Its intelligibility is not discernible by an analysis of either subject or predicate—or for that matter, of the copula. Being spans the dichotomy between subject and predicate in a logical proposition, just as it spans the dichotomy between subject and object in knowing. For the Kantian cognitive subject—the logico-sensory subject-in-general—being must appear as an empty notion. This is in Marcel's mind when he says that being neither is nor can be a "datum";[25] it eludes all pointing out, all characterization.[26] Then for what subject is it possible to affirm, as a truth with intelligible content, the statement "There is being"? Logic cannot affirm being as anything more than a convenient counter, a notion that could never be put to metaphysical use. Being is what remains to be said when a language perfectly satisfying to logicians has proceeded to its limit. That is why the Wittgenstein of the *Tractatus* and the logical positivists who thought they took their inspiration from him were, on their own premises, well justified in their denial of metaphysics. If "saying" is understood exclusively from the vantage point of the requirements of the logician, then being is not genuinely sayable, and the region of what Marcel calls mystery is simply the domain of silence.

If we want to maintain that more is sayable than either Kant or the Wittgensteinians will admit, we inevitably face the question of who is to say it. It certainly will not be the knower of the logical sphere as such or the anonymous subject to whom the "objects" of science are present. Being is not such an object. Then to whom is it present? Only to the singular subject, the existing self in all its uniqueness. The presence of being, Marcel tells us, is polar to an "exigence" for being.[27] The subject that is a mere guarantor of general validity cannot be the subject of this exigence, to which the notion of "generality" is foreign. In a way, this exigence is even the ultimate definer of what is meant by the I. There must be being, says the self, and I desire to participate in it.[28] But the being that corresponds to this exigence is obviously not to be construed as an "idea," for the idea of being is only the reflection into the conceptual order of an intelligibility that engulfs and transcends this order. Being signifies not an abstract concept, however defined, but rather a fullness, a plenitude of presence,[29] an inexhaustible concrete to which the self aspires.[30] For a concrete philosophy, Marcel says, the contrast between the full and the empty is much more important than the contrast between the one and the many.[31] Whenever Marcel speaks of being, it is in the direction of this experience or presentiment of plenitude; ultimately, he tells us, the exigence for being coincides with the exigence for transcendence.[32]

Being, then, is not an idea but a presence, and here we meet what may be the richest of all Marcellian terms. If there is any sense in saying that there is being, that sense must, as all affirmations, be founded on *participation*. Only so far as I participate in being can I affirm that there is being; and to affirm this participation is to affirm that I am not only a being-in but a being-beyond my situation. To affirm being is to affirm that my self is not exhausted by the phenomenal. Once again, who can affirm this? Not the impersonal subject but only the singular self that feels the exigence for being. And since freedom is the ultimate seal of such singularity, the meaning of being is only revealed to the free self. My freedom is the organ of the affirmation of the transphenomenal intelligibility of the self and, at the same time, of the presence of the plenitude of being. Finally, if all affirmation lives off participation, then the only correct way to understand freedom must be as the ultimate form of participation. This is exactly what Marcel proposes. Freedom is not an arbitrary option or an exulting in autonomy; rather, he believes, it is the profoundest act of "belonging,"[33] a creative participation that reveals in one stroke the most authentic countenance of self and other.

We must now pose a question that will lead to the final appreciation of Marcel's insight. If philosophical thought is going to be the reflexive affirmation of the self's participation in being, and if being is not given as an object, we must ask: How can being be present for thought otherwise than as being given as an object *to* thought? When we see how Marcel deals with this, the intuitive moment in his philosophy becomes apparent. Being, we have seen, is presence, not object. Man's self emerges within an enfolding absolute presence, and his thought, arising out of that self, is in contact at its source with the presence of being. There is, Marcel says, an assurance underlying all thought,[34] an assertion of which I am the place and not the positer.[35] He speaks of this assurance as a "blinded intuition,"[36] and declares in a passage whose importance cannot be overestimated: "In this sphere everything seems to go on as if I found myself acting on an intuition which I possess without immediately knowing myself to possess it—an intuition which cannot be, strictly speaking, self-conscious and which can grasp itself only through the modes of experience in which its image is reflected, and which it lights up by being thus reflected in them."[37]

This intuition, then, is not an object of vision but a principle of vision. It is like a light thrown on experience, and its presence is then read back out of experience. Human experience is the revelation of man, but it is also the revelation of that plenitude of presence in which man participates. To understand what Marcel contends here, we may make a comparison with the creative idea in art. There are actually so many interesting similarities between Marcel's point and the situation of the creative artist that he might well have spoken of a "creative," rather than of a "blinded," intuition of being. In order to make this clear, let us examine the role the creative idea plays in the artistic process.

We speak of the creative idea as an "exemplar," almost implying there is a model that the artist has in his mind and according to which he proceeds. But even the briefest consideration shows that the relation between the creative idea and the work produced is far stranger than this. The creative idea is not a model in the sense that it exists *before* the process as an objective standard to which the artist may refer. The poet or painter does not possess a mental model that he has only to copy out on paper or canvas. To realize the oddity here, we have only to compare the situation to one in which there is a literal copying. If I copy out the first page of *Paradise Lost,* the page is a literal model, objectively predating my copying; but that is not how Milton wrote it. On the other hand the poet does not write at random; he does not merely find himself, with a pen in his hand, idly jotting down haphazard words. The creative idea precedes the work in some sense, for it accounts for the non-haphazardness of the performance. It is also the criterion to which the efforts of the artist are referred and by which they are judged. But then the full paradox becomes evident: the work of the artist is judged in the light of an intuition that does not even fully exist until the work reveals it to him. The poet only knows what he means when his expression reveals it to him; still, there would be no expression unless there were some prevenient idea calling just this expression into being. Clearly this creative process is almost perfectly parallel to what Marcel proposes: an intuition that is present as a source of meaning, yet present in a non-objectifiable way.

We have said that the creative intuition in art is found in the work it produces; it is the condition for the existence of the very process in which it comes to recognize itself. Likewise, Marcel avows, the blinded intuition of being is present to man's thought. Being is present to the self, and it is only this presence that renders certain experiences possible. These experiences express the self, and the meaning of selfhood may be read back out of them. But in this reflective discernment of the meaning of selfhood there is also the recognition of the presence of being, of the inexhaustible in which the self participates. Thought's recognition of the participation in being, then, is analogous to the artist's recognition of his creative idea. We find the transcendent not in turning away from human experience but in turning toward it at its saturation point. This intuition is not converted into an object of knowledge any more than the creative idea is. Philosophical awareness has nothing in common with a "possession" in the cognitive field; it is much more like a presentiment, or at best a recognition that must be perpetually renewed.

Understanding this work of thought by analogy with the creative intuition also enables us to see freedom as something other than a Sartrean option. The Sartrean notion conceives of freedom as the sheer fiat of a groundless consciousness, producing its arbitrary values in unconditioned autonomy. Marcel rejects this on all counts. Not only does he find this view deficient as a philosophical understanding of freedom, but he can even question whether it would be adequate to analyze the creative process in the usual sense. For the poet or artist does not really experience himself as a producer *ex nihilo* of the work he is engaged in. In the first place the freedom animating the artist is not accurately expressed in terms of freedom of choice. In respect to the idea to which he is trying to give expression, the poet does not feel himself free to "choose" at all. Rather, he is *bound*—he is under the exigence of finding just those lines that will reveal the idea by which he is possessed. The idea itself functions as a compelling exigence that, far from leaving things to his indifferent whim, excludes all elements of the arbitrary. Second and for the same reason, not only arbitrary "choice" but even the very notion of "autonomy" is inappropriate in the present situation. Here we may apply language that Marcel uses in respect to the ontological situation generally: we are in a region where invention and discovery coincide.[38] That is doubtless what the hackneyed notion of "inspiration" aims at. Does the poet produce his poem of himself or is it imposed on him? The right answer seems to be that these are false alternatives. A hallmark of a process properly called creative seems to be that the process cannot be described in these either-or categories. The poem is not something that the poet first has and then bestows. He receives it in giving it. Or as Marcel says, this is a case where giving and receiving coincide.[39] It is an instance of what he says of ontological experience: it transcends the distinction between autonomy and heteronomy.[40] Is the poem in the poet's power, or is it imposed on him? Surely it is not in his power to find the right word, as it is in his power to refill his pen when he runs out of ink. But neither is it beyond his power, in the manner that an increase in the number of white corpuscles in his bloodstream is beyond his power. The inapplicability of these hard and fast distinctions is just one more sign that we occupy a realm of originial intelligibility. There is, says Marcel, a receptivity that is another name for creativity,[41] where the distinction between what is "in me" and what is "before me" breaks down.[42] The presence of being is given to the self that inhabits this realm; the thought that thinks being is creative thought, supremely free and supremely bound.

If we think of the freedom involved in the affirmation of being by analogy to the situation of the creative artist, the paradigm meaning of freedom becomes not choice but *response*.[43] For the creative idea is present to the artist precisely as appeal, and his affirmation that it is present is inextricably bound up with his response to it; his response *is* his affirmation that an appeal is present. An appeal is not something that is either imposed or asserted "automatically," independent of the one to whom it is sounded. An appeal is uttered to the singular subject, and that he hears this appeal can only be affirmed by him as a singular subject. Just so, the creative intuition of being is an appeal sounded in the depths of singularity, and the only way the subject can affirm that he hears this appeal is by responding to it. Thought's affirmation that there is this presence *is* its response to it. Here we cannot divorce affirmation and response. That is why Marcel so often uses the qualifier *creative* when he approaches the realm of the ontological. He speaks of "creative belonging," "creative testimony," and "creative fidelity."[44] None of these is intended as a mere honorific adjective. The point is that in the ontological realm it is not an autonomous subject that is operating but a self founded on the very participation it affirms.

On this basis Marcel could easily accept Sartre's verbal formula that man "creates his values"—but he would immediately go on to specify that to create is not the same thing as to produce.[45] Sartre rightly discerns that values are not an inertly objective *en soi* that simply confront consciousness. But he is led too swiftly to locate them on the "subjective" side of a consciousness conceived of as a pure spontaneity. He is led, in short, to pose the alternatives in terms of inventing *or* discovering, subjective *or* objective, when the point here is that the ontological realm is not thinkable according to these distinctions. Values are, in Marcel's view, thoroughly ontological heralds of being; although not objects, they are not "merely subjective" either.[46] They are present precisely as appeals, as invocations. An appeal does not have the existence of a mere fact external to my self, but neither is it thinkable only as something subjective. The hearer of an appeal has already broken through the circle of subjectivism. The subject who hears the appeal is not autonomous: the appeal founds one mode of his subjectivity. The value is neither "in him" nor "before him," since, in respect to this appeal, there is nothing prior in himself for the word *him* to apply to. That is why the experience of value can be regarded as a creative experience; like all creative experience, however, it is thinkable only as participation, and the self involved in it is not spontaneous but responsive.

Because the affirmation of being can only be conceived of as a response to a nonobjectifiable appeal, the affirmation may not be forthcoming, for it is of the very nature of an appeal that it can be refused or rejected. In no way can the affirmation of being be imposed on me, just as no external assurance can guarantee to the artist that he really is an artist. This conviction is present in Marcel from the very beginning of his thought. When he declares, in the *Metaphysical Journal,* that a world in which despair is possible is one in which argument does not have the last word, he is to be understood in this way.[47] Despair is possible only for a self that feels a bottomless exigence for being but at the same time feels that there is nothing that can guarantee the presence of being. Albert Camus speaks of such a soul in *The Myth of Sisyphus,* when he says that the only genuine metaphysical problem is the problem of suicide.[48] Camus is echoing Marcel exactly with respect to the centrality of the problem of the full and the empty. The only difference is that Camus, being able at this stage of his thought to avail himself only of a rationalist, Cartesian conception of truth, was precipitated into the absurd. But rationalism and objectivism cannot deliver the reply to this exigence. There is, in Marcel's view, no objective counterweight to despair.[49] The question is simply, Who affirms being? Or in Camus's words, Who affirms that my life has meaning? Marcel replies that the organ of ontological truth is freedom. Metaphysics is a "logic of liberty."[50] Liberty, in turn, must be understood not as an occurrence in the void but as participation—as a response to the invocation of being.

This means, of course, that the two questions—Is there being? and Who am I?—cannot be separated. In affirming being I affirm myself in a uniquely intelligible way. Apart from this self-affirmation, there is no possiblity of affirming being. This is not an unfortunate shortcoming or a liability of metaphysical thought. Rather it is part of the meaning I am affirming. It is not external to the truth of being, but an element of it, that it can only be affirmed by the self in its freedom. It would be idle to wait for the ontological question to be settled for me by an impersonal and objectively validating thought that left my freedom to one side. No impersonal standard can guarantee for me that my self is open to the presence of being. This consequently rules out any possibility of thinking of metaphysics as a "science" like others, in the manner of traditional metaphysics, for a science is constituted precisely by leaving singularity to one side, and the realm of the ontological is possible only as polar to the absolute singular, to freedom.

We must now consider an objection that not only his antagonists but also honest expositors of Marcel's method inevitably raise: Does not his approach run the risk of retreating to a kind of philosophical fideism and of taking for truth what may be simply illusion? If his assertions are objectively unverifiable, what rules out the possibility of deception? This is a difficulty Marcel has been conscious of as far back as the beginning of the *Metaphysical Journal.* Essentially his answer to it has not varied: The metaproblematic can only be thought of as indubitable.[51] That is, for one who actually occupies this terrain, the distinction between appearance and reality does not apply. We may enlarge on this. What, after all, is the epistemological status of the notion of "illusion"? Who can legislate with regard to illusions? The attempt to do so seems to assume the application of criteria and awakens the very controversy it presumes to settle: Who supplies the criteria? To award this right in advance to an autonomous subject-in-general is to beg the question. If, on the other hand, participation supplies the criteria, then there is no way to specify in advance the limits of meaning. Participation itself functions as the creative criterion of all talk *about* participation.

Proceeding along these lines, we may fear that we surrender all possiblity of mediating between the contentions of the different parties to the philosophical dispute and simply resign ourselves to an irreducible melee of diverse assertions. But Marcel does not leave us in quite so bad a state as this. First, the indubitable assurance of the metaproblematic refers to the primordial moment of participation itself and not to the particular language in which we frame it for ourselves in communicating it; this language always partakes of the nature of objectification and is always open to continual emendation and clarification. What Marcel offers us should not be confused with refurbished dogmatism. Second, we must recall the role he assigns to reflection in his thought. The intuitive element always remains "blinded." It is never something we "possess," for this would allow philosophy to lapse into assertions like: "I see what I see, and if you don't, so much the worse for you." Participation is never "something which" I see. Its role is always that of a nonobjectifiable presence, and the assurance of it more like a presentiment than an apprehension.

We may go still further. We need only recall that the creative intuition of being is related to experience as the creative idea in art is related to the aesthetic process: the presence of being is read back out of the very experiences it makes possible. Reflection in this sense is also crucial to the ontological mystery. But we have not yet emphasized which human experiences reflectively manifest the transcendent plenitude. Certainly for Marcel it is unquestionably the life of communion that most unmistakably manifests being: "The concrete approaches to the ontological mystery should not be sought in the scale of logical thought, the objective reference of which gives rise to a prior question. They should rather be sought in the elucidation of certain data which are spiritual in their own right, such as fidelity, hope and love."[52] Marcel concentrates on such experiences as fidelity, hope, and love because the nonobjectifiable Thou copresent in such experiences is as far removed as possible from a characterizable structure or "essence."[53] The Thou is beyond all inventory; his reality can never be reached by a summation of traits or attributes.[54] The other person is thus a concrete crystallization of a presence that is meaningful but not reachable from the standpoint of objectivity. In the presence of the Thou,

the exigence for being comes to recognize itself as meaningful and finds
an intimation of the promise of fulfillment as it turns toward communion.
Thus communion serves not as a verification of the participation in being—
this would be nonsense—but as a manifestation of that participation. Although itself a free and original form of participation, communion also
mediates our metaphysical reflection on the transcendent. Hence the reality
of human communion is the axis upon which Marcel's ontology turns; it
is the manifestation of an intelligibility founded on freedom and transcending objectivity. Reference to its indubitable reality may thus help to mediate the confusion of voices in respect to the issue of the right to affirm
the transcendent.

Actually, the charge that Marcel is taking us into an area where his
statements cannot be verified or checked is only partially correct. All statements about being or about communion can be confirmed—although not
by the logico-sensory subject. Marcel rules out this confirmation only if it
is conceived of exclusively in terms of this subject. It remains true that
any self, just as singular and free, just as belonging through the appeal-
response relationship to the free intelligibility of communion, is able to
hear and assent to the presence of being. The very existence of communion, then, is like a living confirmation of the transcendent presence of
being. That is why Marcel invariably links these two affirmations, declaring that his thought has been ceaselessly impelled by a double exigence:
the exigence for being and the exigence for beings in their singularity.[55]

Furthermore, although communion is a living assurance of thought's
right to affirm being, communion itself as an existential reality is also the
work of freedom. Communion is not a fact of nature, an automatic given.
The I-Thou relationship is an appeal-response relationship and is thus
thinkable only as a dialogue in freedom. This means that the communion
from which thought draws its discernment of an opening to transcendence
is also the work of liberty. We come to realize that in this case we are
confirming a freedom through a freedom. The existential response through
which the self replies to the Thou and belongs to communion is a participation: the creative act by which my thought affirms the irreducible cognitive value of this participation is a new mode of participation. Both are
thinkable only as freedom.

Truth is habitually associated with universality; hence many are reluctant to permit any intrusion of truth by subjectivity, for they assume that
the subjective is the source of division. If, however, we understand by the
"universal" not what is abstract and general but what is opposed to the
arbitrary and "merely individual," we can say that Marcel's approach
opens up a whole new area of the universal. The universal is opposed to

the indifferent and contingent; it is that in which the individual is bound over to an other. The usual abstract or consensus universal is only one rather meager instance of this. A moral value, as Kant saw, is a peremptory universal without being abstract. Marcel invites us to the universal inherent in the life of freedom as it relates to personal life and to transcendence. His message is that the universal is not opposed to the singular and that the concrete universal is spirit.[56] There is a universal meaning in "love," for example, but that meaning is surrendered only to the self that comes to it in absolute singularity. The I in its freedom is thus not something that separates but something that unites. A whole region of meaning opens up as the free subject responds to an invocation of otherness inaccessible to objective thought.

To belong to this realm of truth is to sustain myself in it by my response. The truth here is something that can be lost or surrendered. My presence to it must be renewed and clung to, as an artist clings to his vision. My response is thus a testimony, a creative testimony. Marcel cites religion, art, metaphysics, communion, and the experience of value as examples of such testimony.[57] We are now at a considerable distance from the initial association of truth and verifiability in the *Metaphysical Journal*. In one way Marcel is engaged in a task similar to that of other post-Kantian and especially contemporary philosophers: the task of providing a more satisfactory account of human experience than Kant's dichotomy of knowledge versus belief made possible. Only Kant's restriction of the term *knowledge* to what could be presented to a logico-sensory knower made this dichotomy inevitable (and incidentally caused Kant's ambivalence with respect to the status of moral and aesthetic experience). Certainly part of Marcel's task can be understood as an attempt to broaden the conception of the range of cognitive experience and thereby to bring to light the transcendent dimension of experience.

Proceeding in this way, Marcel goes much further than Jaspers (who is otherwise so similar) in vindicating language about the transphenomenal. Jaspers tends sharply to oppose the subject-object structure he feels all human knowledge is locked into and the direction to transcendence accomplished by cipher readings that do not qualify as knowledge. Marcel is able to proceed with less hesitation in the direction of an analogy of knowledge, apparently because he does not feel that all knowledge, even on this side of the limit-situation, exhibits a subject-object structure. Wherever participation plays a role, there is nonobjectifiable awareness and, reflexively, creative knowledge. Therefore we do not start from inside the subject-object dichotomy and then attempt to get beyond it but move from a nonobjectifiable awareness of the finite to a nonobjectifiable discourse about the transphenomenal. It is perfectly clear that there is no question of demonstration. A "proof" of the immortality of the soul, for example, is a misguided undertaking. Even the assertion of immortality may, as an objective formulation, be only a somewhat halting attempt to translate into transmittable terms the experience of transcendence. But Marcel will not give up the truth claim of such utterances or swallow them up into apophatic symbols. On the contrary, for him the self even in its ultimate freedom is always continuous with the man of flesh and bone for whom immortality as a mere cipher would be a hollow consolation.

Similarly Marcel encounters no basic theoretical difficulty in affirming God as the absolute Thou. For even in speaking of a finite Thou, our language is both nonobjectifiable and somehow true. There is what has been called an analogy of "presentiality" here rather than a leap from one mode of being or one mode of knowledge to another.[58] Animating the whole process, no doubt, is the creative intuition of inexhaustibility; therefore we might say Marcel's thought gives credence to the ontological argument for the existence of God as the fundamental form of thought with respect to the transcendent. The important proviso, however, is that his intuition is by no means an "idea" from which anything whatsoever could be deduced; rather, it is an underivable truth that comes to recognition only in the presencings it makes possible.

In the last analysis Marcel rejoins the Platonic-Augustinian conception of truth, restating in a more contemporary and existentialist manner their perennial insight: To know the truth, one must be in the truth. That is the philosophical import, surely, of Plato's myth of reminiscence. "To learn is to remember" signifies that to learn is to call to mind a meaning that is present at the depth of the self. This recalling is also a re-calling, a calling of the self back to itself. Marcel too assigns recollection an important role in ontology.[59] At the same time the Platonic-Augustinian approach holds that truth can be sought only by a conversion of the whole self, not by a compartmentalized cognitive faculty. Plato's myth of the cave is the symbol of this existential conversion. It says that the instrument for the revealing of truth is nothing less than the movement by which the whole self turns to the source from which all illumination proceeds. All these features are present in Marcel's approach. Moreover—and this is an area where one without thorough knowledge should speak with the utmost hesitation—there seems reason to think that in this aspect Marcel's thought has some affinity with the great tradition of Indian philosophy, for which a unique species of self-knowledge is inseparable from an awareness of the ultimate truth of being.

That is undoubtedly why the myth of Orpheus and Eurydice has come to be regarded by Marcel as epitomizing the condition of his own existence and, inferentially, of his thought.[60] For this myth symbolically expresses the same paradoxical coincidence of the near and the far found at the heart of the Platonic doctrine of reminiscence. Being is at the same time the nearest and the farthest of all things. As the absolute presence at the core of the self, it remains something I can never make "mine" in a facile objective sense. Just as Orpheus can be confident of the presence of Eurydice only so long as he docs not turn and behold her full in the face, so being is only present to me so long as I do not try to behold it as an object. Present precisely as that which cannot be beheld, it founds my nonobjectifiable presence to myself. The affirmation of this twofold presence as truth is both the accomplishment and the profoundest meaning of freedom.

KENNETH T. GALLAGHER

DEPARTMENT OF PHILOSOPHY
FORDHAM UNIVERSITY
JUNE 1969

NOTES

1. Gabriel Marcel, *Metaphysical Journal*, trans. Bernard Wall (Chicago: Henry Regnery Co., 1952), pp. 113–30, especially p. 26 (hereafter cited as *MJ*).
2. *MJ*, 29.
3. *MJ*, 29–30.
4. Pietro Prini, *Gabriel Marcel et la méthodologie de l'invérifiable* (Paris: Desclée de Brouwer, 1953), p. 63.
5. *MJ*, 40.   6. *MJ*, 57.
7. *MJ*, 51.   8. *MJ*, 51–52, 60.
9. Convenient sources for this in Jaspers are the second lecture in *Reason and Existenz* (trans. William Earle [New York: Noonday Press, 1955]) and part 3, section A, of *Philosophical Faith and Revelation* (trans. E. B. Ashton [New York: Harper & Row, 1967]).
10. Karl Jaspers, *Philosophie*, 3 vols. (Berlin: Springer Verlag, 1956), 2:99.
11. Gabriel Marcel, *Being and Having*, trans. Katharine Farrer (Boston: Beacon Press, 1951), p. 227 (hereafter cited as *BH*).
12. *MJ*, 117.   13. *MJ*, 64.
14. *MJ*, 217–22.   15. *MJ*, 96–98.
16. *MJ*, 64.   17. *MJ*, 98.
18. *BH*, 21.
19. Published as an appendix, *MJ*, 319–39. The essay originally appeared as "Existence et objectivité," *Revue de métaphysique et de morale*, April–May 1925.
20. *MJ*, 322.
21. Gabriel Marcel, *The Mystery of Being*, trans. G. S. Fraser (vol. 1) and

René Hague (vol.2), 2 vols. (Chicago: Henry Regnery Co., 1950), 1:100 (hereafter cited as *MB*).

22. See the essay by that title in Gabriel Marcel, *Creative Fidelity*, trans. Robert Rosthal (New York: Noonday Press, 1964; hereafter cited as *CF*), a translation of *Du refus a l'invocation*.

23. See *BH*, 100–103, 117–23; and see Marcel's essay "On the Ontological Mystery," in *The Philosophy of Existence*, trans. Manya Harari (New York: Philosophical Library, 1949; hereafter cited as *PE*).

24. *MB* 1:93–94.

25. *MB* 2:37.

26. *BH*, 151, 168–69.

27. *MB* 2:33–51.

28. *PE*, 5.

29. *BH*, 102.

30. *CF*, 66.

31. *PE*, 3.

32. *MB* 2:128.

33. *CF*, 96.

34. *BH*, 119.

35. *BH*, 171.

36. *MJ*, x; cf. *MB* 1:13.

37. *BH*, 118.

38. *CF*, 88.

39. *CF*, 91–92.

40. *BH*, 173–74.

41. Gabriel Marcel, *Homo Viator*, trans. Emma Craufurd (Chicago: Henry Regnery Co., 1951), p. 264.

42. *BH*, 149.

43. *CF*, 10; *BH*, 174.

44. *CF*, 96; *MB* 2:139; *BH*, 96.

45. *MB* 2:45.

46. *MB* 2:44; cf. Gabriel Marcel, *Man Against Mass Society*, trans. G. S. Fraser (Chicago: Henry Regnery Co., 1951), p. 122 (hereafter cited as *MM*).

47. *MJ*, 96–98.

48. Albert Camus, *The Myth of Sisyphus*, trans. Justin O'Brien (New York: Knopf, 1958).

49. *BH*, 95.

50. *CF*, 26.

51. *PE*, 11–12.

52. *BH*, 119.

53. *BH*, 80.

54. *MB* 2:176; *MJ*, 158, 165.

55. *CF*, 147.

56. *MM*, 7.

57. *BH*, 175.

58. Prini, *Marcel et la méthodologie*, p. 117.

59. *BH*, 113.

60. Gabriel Marcel, *Presence and Immortality*, trans. Michael Machado (Pittsburgh: Duquesne University Press, 1967), p. 7.

Truth and Freedom in Marcel

REPLY TO KENNETH T. GALLAGHER

In itself Mr. Gallagher's study is excellent. He deserves great credit for showing clearly how the notion of the unverifiable, as presented in my early writings, was subsequently re-incorporated into a more flexible conception of truth. At the same time, his study could be brought up to date in the light of my essay on "Truth and Freedom," published in *Pour une sagesse tragique*,* where the existential aspect of the problem is dealt with more precisely.

It seems obvious to me today that the powers attacking liberty, whether in a dictatorship like the one winning out in the Soviet Union or in openly anti-communist countries like Greece or Brazil, are unavoidably driven to betray truth. Yet the words *betray truth* are too abstract for my liking; what is involved is concrete situations that must be recognized as such. From many possible examples I take one: when the Soviets decided on a military intervention in Czechoslovakia in August 1968, they were inevitably led to justify this indefensible intervention by deceitfully proclaiming the existence of a collusion between the promoters of the Reform Movement in Prague and the American imperialists. Here we have an example of a clear-cut lie. But, of course, we must go much further to prove that the so-called popular democracies are all built on a lie, since they rest on a refusal of free elections, and such a refusal is the very negation of democracy.

Reflection reveals, on the one hand, that freedom can survive only in a climate of truth and, on the other, that the search for truth can be worthily pursued only where no external constraint (particularly from the state) is used against it.

Translated from the French by François R. Ferran and Colette M. Ferran.
*"Truth and Freedom" first appeared in *Philosophy Today* 9 (1965), translated by Rosemary Lauer. It later appeared in *Pour une sagesse tragique* (Paris: Plon, 1968).—ED.

Unfortunately, such remarks lead us to recognize that the so-called free world is itself infected by the destructive consequences of the uncontrolled power of oppression it is forced to put up with if it wants to avoid a planetary conflagration. I refer here in particular to the fact that the brutally imperialistic means used by the Soviet Union in the Baltic countries, for instance, could never be denounced in the United Nations as they should have been. On this point, as on many others, the triumphant force is hypocrisy—that is to say again, falsehood.

Some readers might wonder about such outspoken references to the contemporary political situation. By making them I intend to show that philosophical thought as I understand it must not indulge in the hedging tactics so often used by opportunism, which is the opposite of any philosophical thought worthy of the name.

G.M.

15

John V. Vigorito

ON TIME IN THE PHILOSOPHY
OF MARCEL

IN a number of references throughout his works, Gabriel Marcel acknowledges the importance of some notion of time or temporality to his philosophy, and in a journal note included in *Presence and Immortality*, he has alluded to a study, "long since in progress, on time and eternity."[1] Yet Marcel does not appear to have given us any extended statement of the notion of temporality he says his philosophy demands. The subject is certainly important in itself, and an attempt to work out the implied theory of time in Marcel's work may provide a fresh point of view from which to appreciate other facets of his thought. Of course, in a brief essay we can hardly do justice to the complexity of Marcel's concept of time; we will therefore limit this discussion to those features of temporality that center on Marcel's notion of "my past" as "my life" and "my incarnation."

I

According to Marcel, in order to answer any metaphysical question we must address ourselves to and take our bearings from *the* fundamental question on which "all the other questions hang": What or who am I?[2] "It is probably true," he writes, "to say that the only metaphysical problem is that of 'What am I?,' for all the others lead back to this one."[3] If we examine the many inquiries suggested to Marcel by this most basic of questions, we find that initially, at least, they appear to move in two different, though integrally related, dimensions we shall call the "vertical" and the "horizontal." In the vertical order Marcel has delineated three moments within the structure of the self: the level of incarnation or existence, the level of intersubjectivity, and the level of ontological exigence—

none of which, of course, is separable in fact. Of equal importance to an adequate appreciation of Marcel's notion of the self is that dimension given to us as horizontal. Here the perennial question "Who am I?" has suggested to Marcel dialectics of the form "Am I my life?" "Am I my past?" and "What is my past?"—questions that implicate some notion of the temporal. It is with this dimension that our analysis will begin. Nevertheless, as we have already noted, the two orders are integrally related. For one thing, Marcel soon goes beyond the simplistic and objectified notion of time that the horizontal dimension, taken by itself, presupposes. For another, such notions as "my life" and "my past" increasingly revolve around and acquire their meaning, their *sens*, from the vertical, undergoing a transformation Marcel calls supra-temporalization. Yet in spite of this orientation toward the vertical, the two orders never coincide. And it is this inevitable non-coincidence of the two orders that has led Marcel in another context to speak of the ever present "gap between me and my being."[4]

II

In one of his analyses of the question "Who am I?" Marcel is led to what he calls the "mystery" of embodiment: "I am my body." And my body obviously seems to be the ground for my experience of spatiality. Is there not, though, some analogous category we can use to interpret our experience of lived time? Marcel seems to suggest as much when he queries, "Is not my life . . . related to time as my body is related to space?"[5] What, then, is my life?

My life! I no sooner utter the words than an ambiguity seems to arise within the phrase itself. Do I mean by my life the whole extent of my past right up to the immediate present, perhaps too with some vague reference to my future, the time I anticipate having left to me? Or do I mean by the phrase "my life" to indicate what emerges in the pulsating Now, the immediate present?[6] Since Marcel asserts as early as in his *Metaphysical Journal* that "time has not and cannot have any origin save the present which is the only boundary that can be assigned to it," we might first be tempted to locate the meaning of "my life" in the immediate present of the pulsating now.[7] But this choice leads to instantaneism, a view espoused by such writers as Gide, perhaps partially in protest against the inability of nineteenth-century historicism and idealism to recognize the demands of the lived present. The protest in effect went to the opposite extreme by repudiating all thought and mediation and by reveling in the immediacy of felt present experience. To recognize the rights of the past and of thought, instantaneism maintained, was to betray the present instant; honesty, sincerity, and spontaneity—the impulsive aspect of which was often naïvely identified as creativity—were defined in terms of fidelity to the pulsating Now.[8]

But, Marcel says, if we examine this thesis, we find it totally untenable. The very statement of the thesis contradicts itself, for we can only assert the principle of fidelity to the instant by in some way transcending the instant. Still, this is "merely a dialectical refutation," lacking force against the anti-intellectualist position at which it is directed.[9] More to the point are arguments showing that anything resembling an enjoyed experience of the present presupposes a notion of a past, for the novelty of the moment "cannot be savoured except by the unconscious reference to a past with which it is contrasted."[10] Furthermore, there is such a thing as a satiety of novelty.[11]

Beyond these arguments against instantaneism, Marcel's works reveal other refutations of this theory, refutations that acquire their thrust from the notion of "my life." For example, so far as I am a body, the body at my death may be considered an object to be analyzed—that is, subjected to an autopsy—which, within certain practical limitations, decides on my physical state at the instant of death. But as soon as I apply the notion of an autopsy to my mental or spiritual life—particularly to "the more fundamental modes of [my] personal existence"[12]—an absurdity appears. Take the case of a man who, in a trivial argument with his wife, has told her that he cannot stand her any more and angrily walks out of the house. Even after years of intimacy and love, *at that moment* he feels unable to open himself to her. Suppose he then meets a fatal accident. Could we consider his last outburst the definitive statement of his feelings for his wife? Of course, ultimately the question is unanswerable, for what is involved here is not only a personal relationship, which cannot be objectified,[13] but more precisely a personality, and this infinitely transcends the state of the person at any particular moment.[14] How is it possible to evaluate the latent dynamism of his wife's presence that has become a part of this man's being? Here the notion of a mental or spiritual autopsy, presuming to capture a personality at a certain instant, reveals itself as ludicrous.

Underlying instantaneism is a notion that time is a series of discrete moments, each jealously demanding that its unlimited claims be recognized and met. Precisely to the extent that I proceed to identify myself with my state at this very moment, my state at any other moment inevitably appears to me as radically "other" than what I am. But this discrimination against my past, simply because it is past, bears deleterious consequences for this past. Having orphaned my past, it is no longer *my* past, and I am forced to view it as an object. Hence "it is plain that in immediacy, the pure 'now', a being does not realize the 'fullness of what he is'. . . . The more a *being* is, the less he is reduced to a simple succession of determinations."[15]

But if what I am cannot be reduced to the present now, what else am I? Am I my past? And if so, what is my past, particularly since Marcel has asserted that the present is the origin of time? Perhaps I am my history, that is, the past that from the point of view of the present I can narrate as a story. Of course we need not insist that my past as a story be narrated to another person, who may not be able to appreciate it because he or she did not live it. I may relate the story of my life to myself. But I can do this only if in some sense I detach myself from my life; hence although I may be a most empathic listener to my life story, there is a certain degree of objectification present in all such narrative accounts. Moreover, once I begin to narrate this story, I find much of it monotonous and wearisome detail, even for me whose story it is, and most of what I did experience I have inevitably forgotten.[16] What results, then, is only a summary, and even the summary is distorted. For as I relate the events after they have taken place, my perspective on them is necessarily colored by what subsequently happened. For example, if I relate my experiences of a journey, my narration of what happened at the beginning of the journey—when I could only have been open to what might subsequently happen—is colored by my later experiences of what did in fact happen. In short, "it would be an illusion to claim that my life, as I turn it into a story, corresponds at all completely with my life as I have actually lived it."[17]

Although the sterile factor in any such approach to my past is the objectification invariably attending it, perhaps we gain something from these considerations. For even if my recollections of my past experiences are necessarily colored by subsequent events in my life, there is a sense in which the coloring does not in itself betray the original experience. In fact it is a condition that the original experience leave itself open for subsequent development if it is to be significant at all, that is, if it is truly to be an event in my past. As Marcel has said: "The belief in an immutable past is due to an optical error of the spirit. People will say, 'The past taken in itself does not move, what changes is our way of thinking about it.' But must we not be idealists here and say that the past cannot be separated from the considerations of the past."[18] Indeed, if the past to which I refer as my past is to be *my* past, it can be so only to the degree that it is creative in my present. Or, to resort to one of the musical metaphors of which Marcel is fond, we can say that the original experience is much like a chord or measure in an improvisation. Precisely because we are dealing with an improvisation, at the moment the chord is played its future significance is still open. If the chord could be completely ignored and could retain its pristine quality apart from the improvisation, then there would be a real sense in which it would not be *of* the improvisation. But should the chord or measure be taken up and developed in any one of innumerable possible ways, then it gains significance in the improvisation, its significance being directly proportional to the degree to which it in-forms the whole by giving itself to the coloration of the whole.

Suppose, therefore, that in order to catch the day-to-day vitality of my past with its problems and aspirations, I keep a diary. Soon I have notebooks full of entries lying on the shelf. Can I now say, "There on that shelf lies my life"?[19] Surely this would be absurd. Anyone who knew me well but who was illiterate could see absolutely no relation between me and this stack of papers. In fact, even I, as I reread the earlier entries, am utterly bored by most of them. Suppose, though, that I have literary ability; might I not have been able to inspire these entries with a poetic quality enabling me to recapture the vividness of the original situation? Perhaps, but to the extent that I am so poetically inclined, I should suspect the reshaping that I might have done to achieve this level of readability, bestowing on the lived experiences a significance they did not have. For even here I am writing my experiences after they have occurred. Moreover, as I reread the entries I am overwhelmed by the chaotic impressions they produce, the disconnected details, the convictions that constantly shift and even contradict one another. Surely this is not my life, my past.[20] For "inasmuch as my memory can be likened to a diary we can say that my past is given as a datum; but . . . the more my past is really and intimately mine (the more it is at one with my being) the less it is a datum given."[21]

Although I am wisely reluctant to accept my diary as in any sense my past life, I may be able to salvage something from these considerations. Regarding my past as a narrative, I saw that I must not conceive of my past experience as immutable, as cut and dried. Yet now, regarding my diary, I feel rightfully resentful of any distortion I may subject my experiences to in order to impregnate them and inspire them with significance. Perhaps the past that is most truly mine must be present to me as something mysteriously full of value, as if harboring within it a promise or a secret. Furthermore this value cannot be something I bestow on my past, or rather, I bestow this value on my past only by choosing to acknowledge and welcome it. I do not give it value by imposing on my past experiences a significance that forces them to accord with my own immediate needs or my ideas of myself. Here we come across two themes connected with intersubjectivity:[22] the being of my past is acknowledged as felt, and its value finds its source in a "beyond-of-which-I-am."[23]

Finally, when I say, "I am my past," can I not mean by this my works, the acts or deeds I have performed, or the way these were realized? To be sure, once I begin to consider my acts, I seem to leave behind all objectivity, but here I must be cautious lest I begin talking about the reality of acts as if they were things. Only in the case of the artist, perhaps, do a person's acts come close to being realized in such a concrete fashion, and even here we may be on shaky ground. If I am an artist in the act of creating, in some sense I may be said to "be" my work. But as soon as the work is finished, if I in any way allow it to become a definable center of my world, it becomes something I "have."[24] This is not simply because the product of my creation is an object in such a tangible sense as, say, a painting. It is because it is impossible for me to recognize myself in my act once it has been committed. The very fact that the act is irrevocably over and done with makes it something that I cannot know completely, at least not in the sense in which I realized myself in the act at the time I performed it.[25] But if I can never realize in my past acts the intimacy I had with them when I performed them, then how can I identify myself with them? Does is not become meaningless to say, "I am my past"?

If there is any sense in which I can say I am my past—no matter how loose or incomplete this "identification" may be—it must be directly proportional to the degree of intimacy I can achieve with my past. Such a realization of intimacy can never be a complete identity; in any case, even to try to think of this intimacy in terms of identity would be to adopt in the realm of presence a concept whose only legitimacy is, strictly speaking, in the realm of objectivity.[26] Rather, the intimacy demanded of my past is that it be felt as an at-one-with-ness of presence, as in an intersubjective union.

III

In the *Mystery of Being* Marcel tells us that his concept of time, although not quite the same as Proust's, is "certainly akin to his . . . as expounded by Georges Poulet in his wonderful *Études sur le Temps Humain*."[27] Since Proust's descriptions are essentially concerned with the recovery of one's past, let us follow up this lead, developing Poulet's ideas in order to emphasize certain aspects of Proustian time. Our main interest will be to discern how, for Marcel, one's past is experienced through memory.

Before seeking similarities between Proust's notion of time and Marcel's, we might note, as a word of caution, that there are profound metaphysical differences between Proust and Marcel, and these differences signal some real contrasts even in the areas where Proust and Marcel seem to agree. Above all, *Remembrance of Things Past* is in many ways a monumental expression of the naturalistic empiricism widespread at the *fin de siècle*. Only on rare occasions do we sense there any appreciation for transcendent being underlying the experiences of the main character. In fact Marcel has noted that only "at certain great moments" does Proust recognize "the existence of fixed stars in the heaven of the soul," and he suggests that possibly these moments give rise in the novel to "internal contradictions" with its "usual empiricism inspired by nihilism."[28]

This difference between Proust and Marcel manifests itself in the following way. For both the fundamental question is, Who am I? But for Proust, since there is no transcendent being, the answer to this question invariably lies hidden in the past that memory gives me. For Marcel this is true only if memory is acknowledged as "an ontological sign" that ultimately orients me toward transcendent being.[29] So Marcel might account for the difference between himself and Proust on this issue by saying that Proust gives us an incomparable description of the *way* my past is experienced but does not appreciate the significance—the ontological significance—of the experience he describes. As a consequence of this initial difference, Marcel might further have to maintain that in Proust other aspects of the human condition, some of them bearing on our temporality, become distorted. For example, given this naturalized being that has been subverted to the past—or rather to the rapport between past and present[30]—belief, faith, and hope ultimately become deflated in Proust into a form of desire that can only find substance by returning to the past. For Marcel, though, a metaphysics of hope grounded in faith in transcendent being is a vital option, and this opens up to us what I shall here very loosely call "a future."[31] Or again, since Proust has ignored the ontological significance of memory, the exigence he feels for transcendence tries to find the eternal by somehow transcending time. We refer here to the long exegeses in *The Past Regained*. If Proust cannot regain time completely, he can somehow conquer it.[32] "Time regained is time transcended."[33] But transcendence here has none of the meaning Marcel gives the term (a meaning we shall discuss later); it is, in fact, the privileged state of primary reflection. Thus Marcel writes: "There is no privileged state which allows us to transcend time; and this is where Proust made his great mistake. A state such as he describes has only the value of a foretaste."[34] Immediately after this note, Marcel goes on to discuss fidelity—

a fidelity that is a witness-bearing, that is ultimately grounded in faith in transcendent being, and that forms the basis of hope.[35]

Having noted these differences, let us now turn to memory in Proust to see how it reveals my past to me. For Proust and for Marcel, memory is of two kinds: debased and affective. In the former, memory finds itself reduced to mere servitude to the intelligence;[36] it is what I "use," the "container" of the facts I "have" at my disposal. This "memory of facts, which tells us 'You were such' without allowing us to become such again,"[37] amounts to nothing more than the three inadequate approaches to the past we have just rejected; it is comparable to the answers I give on a questionnaire. But my past is not something I can have in this fashion. Rather, just as all "having" presupposes the union between me and my body, which is its felt model,[38] so too this past that I have, these facts at my disposal in my debased memory, presuppose the union between me and my past that is affective memory. Thus Marcel writes, "to recall does not mean to reread a note."[39] "To recall means to re-live."[40] For my past experience survives and is mine only so far as I assimilate it into my being, that is, only so far as my past becomes "a living accretion."[41] This memory that I relive, or live *with,* is affective memory.

Two features of Proustian memory need to be emphasized in connection with Marcel's theory of time: first, the sense in which my discovery of my past in affective memory is akin to intersubjective presence; and second, the sense in which affective memory is an "act" of receiving. Although Poulet's discussion brings out both these points, we shall undertake here to discuss them in Marcel's terminology.

At the outset of the novel, Proust tells us:

> I feel that there is much to be said for the Celtic belief that the souls of those whom we have lost are held captive in some inferior being, in an animal, in a plant, in an inanimate object, and so effectively lost to us until the day (which to many never comes) when we happen to pass by the tree or to obtain possession of the object which forms their prison. Then they start and tremble, they call us by name, and as soon as we have recognized their voice the spell is broken. We have delivered them: they have overcome death and return to share our life.
> *And so it is with our own past.*[42]

My past, then, is lost; yet I often find myself invaded by a smell, a taste, a color, or a shape that conceals within itself a presence from my past. This presence from a distance (which generally I am unable to recognize) calls to me from both within and without my being, invoking me to seek the transfiguration of this felt dichotomy so that this presence from my past can be with me, can live with me. More often than not, the pressing concerns of the present moment distract me from the task of realizing such presences, and so I falter before I even acknowledge them. But if I persist in laying myself open to such invasions and in trying to realize myself in them, I can regain the past that is most truly mine. Here let us quote extensively from a single passage that, when analyzed, clearly reveals the intersubjective nature of these experiences. The incident takes place on the road to Balbec.

> We came down towards Hudimesnil; suddenly I was overwhelmed with that profound happiness which I had not often felt since Combray; happiness analogous to that which had been given me by—among other things—the steeples of Martinville. But this time it remained incomplete. I had just seen, standing a little way back from the steep ridge over which we were passing, three trees.
> . . .
> I looked at the three trees; I could see them plainly, but my mind felt that they were concealing something which it had not grasped . . . ; I choose . . . to believe that they were phantoms of the past, dear companions of my childhood, vanished friends who recalled our common memories. Like ghosts they seemed to be appealing to me to take them with me, to bring them back to life. In their simple passionate gesticulation I could discern the helpless anguish of a beloved person who has lost the power of speech, and feels that he will never be able to say to us what he wishes to say and we can never guess. Presently, at a cross-roads, the carriage left them. It was bearing me away from what alone I believed to be true, what would have made me truly happy; it was like my life. I watched the trees withdraw, waving their despairing arms, seeming to say to me: "What you fail to learn from us today, you will never know. If you allow us to drop back into the hollow of this road from which we sought to raise ourselves up to you, a whole part of yourself which we are bringing to you will fall forever into the abyss."[43]

We need only refer to the three moments of "having"[44] that are negated in an encounter to appreciate how Proust's experience comes to him in the first instance with all the potential of an intersubjective presence, even though in this incident the union is never realized. First, nowhere in the experience are the trees treated as mere things, as objects. They immediately present themselves as persons, and Proust refers to them throughout as "dear companions," "vanished friends," "ghosts," and "beloved persons." Moreover, all their activities are humanized: they passionately gesticulate to him, for although they are speechless beings, it is only because they have lost the power of speech. And as the carriage draws him away from them, they wave their arms in despair. This farewell can hardly fail to suggest a contrast with the farewell from Martinville, where the experience of the twin steeples, which also took on the character of persons, was happily resolved. For there, as Proust and his party drove away from the village, the church "steeples and that of Vieuxvicq waved once again, in token of farewell, their sunbathed pinnacles. Sometimes one would withdraw, so that the other two might watch us for a moment still. . . . "[45] Second, although on the road to Balbec the presence is not realized, the intent of the appeal is clearly to overcome a within-without dichotomy. The trees conceal from Proust a presence not just their own, for he says, "I could see them plainly." More specifically, they conceal a presence from a past that is no longer his past. The lack is felt within him because he is unable to open himself to his past. Proust says "They seemed to be appealing to me to take them *with* me." But this would only be possible if he could find within himself the resourcefulness to overcome the dichotomy. Finally, although the trees might have revealed to him a whole part of himself and thus have ceased to be other than he (since the appeal has been refused), they will remain "other," dropping "back into the hollow of this road." Moreover, had he creatively realized himself with them in a meaningful experience, he would have enjoyed the fulfillment that attends an intersubjective encounter. But since he was unable to respond, the carriage "was bearing me away from what alone I believed to be true, what would have made me truly happy," and, he adds, "it was like my life."

Let us examine the act involved in such Proustian "invasions." Since I feel myself invaded by a sensation, and since this initial experience takes me unawares, or at least is not anticipated, it would seem that during affective memory I am essentially passive. Certain passages from the novel seem to confirm this view. Hence Proust writes that "all the efforts of our intellect must prove futile"[46] in recapturing this vital past. Later he says, "Despite all my efforts, I never managed to discover" the presence concealed in certain sensations.[47] Yet even though Proustian affective memory has an involuntary character, attempts to explain these experiences in terms of either passive receptivity or psychological laws of association, passively conceived, are totally inadequate.[48] On the contrary, what we find exemplified in Proust's descriptions are many facets of openness and *disponibilité*, as Marcel conceives of these on the levels of existence and intersubjectivity.

For Marcel feeling itself must be acknowledged as a form of participation, as an "act" of receiving.[49] Thus since the subject is never entirely passive in sensation, these invasions do not just come to or happen to anything whatsoever. Of greater significance, though, is the fact that these invasions, far from revealing a passive state of mind, demand an openness on the part of the person receiving them. Some people are more susceptible to them than others. And perhaps this openness is something I might encourage, even if it is not entirely up to me. Poulet has likened these invasions in Proust to grace;[50] he might even have likened them to the revelation one receives from a work of art. None of these—neither memory, grace, nor aesthetic experience—can be regarded as an external cause operating on a passive subject. In such experiences the invasion comes to me as an appeal. And precisely because it is an appeal, it can be either accepted or rejected, with varying degrees of enthusiasm. In the experience of the *petites madeleines*, for example, Proust fully accepts the invitation, trying again and again to recapture the presence. Far from passivity, what the acceptance of the appeal demands is the most intense spiritual activity if the presence is ever to be realized in its fullness: "Ten times over I must essay the task, must lean over the abyss. And each time the natural laziness which deters us from every difficult enterprise, every work of importance, has urged me to leave the thing alone, to drink the tea and to think merely of the worries of today."[51] In one sense Proust is right to disparage the role of the intellect in such experiences, if the intellect is regarded as a "faculty" of reason. Since reasoning is carried out on the primary level of reflection, the intellect is futile, for the desired presence cannot be *reasoned to;* it can only be invoked. Moreover, since the presence comes to me from a beyond, I cannot willy-nilly put myself by some intellectual act in the proper frame of mind from which the realization of presence necessarily follows. Thus the spiritual activity demanded is not the type to which I am spurred in attempting to solve a problem. What is demanded is the openness and *disponibilité* of secondary reflection.

We are now in a position to see how this discussion of Proustian affective memory furthers our inquiry into Marcel's notion of "my past." Affective memory so obviously fulfills what was lacking in the past as my history, as my diary, and as my deeds that we now need only allude to these requirements, developing at the same time other relevant features of the experience.

First, we have seen that my past is mine only if it is vitally significant for me, harboring within itself a mystery, a secret. Its significance, though, is in no way determined by its functional usefulness; it is not my past simply because it helps me "get around in the world." Nor can we say that it becomes significant *because* it yields me the power to be creative. In the realm of being, such a means-ends dichotomy and such a causal relationship are totally misplaced; indeed, what such a statement reveals is a basic misconception of what is involved in creativity. We should rather say that the significance of my past blossoms in my creativity. Second, the value of my past is not a value I impose on it. This is but a corollary of the denial of any means-end dichotomy and of any cause-effect relationship. If I were to assign a value to my past in the light of my present, I would, in effect, be using my past as a resonator to confirm my egocentric present or to further its purposes. Instead, the value of my past transcends all such manipulation. Value is not given to my past; it can only be acknowledged as being of my past. Third—and this follows fast on the above two features—my past is mine only so far as I realize an intimacy with my past yielded by its presence.

Now the essential feature of affective memory is that "the remembered" is not regarded as the content, the "what"; indeed, the remembered is first and foremost felt as presence. This character of feeling is so fundamental to such memories that the felt presence often pervades me long before I recognize the presence. According to our understanding of Marcel on this point, we cannot stress too strongly the subordinate role a definable content plays in affective memory. For "my past, insofar as I consider it, ceases to be my past"; it is then only a past I have.[52] To be sure, if I am intent on pursuing self-knowledge I will often, like Proust, lean over the abyss ten times to invoke this past that beckons to me; and in certain glorious moments I will find fulfillment in a remembrance that, when objectified, seems oriented toward a content. Likewise some few of my most vital experiences that lend themselves freely to affective remembering seem centered on specific data—for instance, experiences I feel capable of recalling at will in reminiscing, an activity that lovers and friends enter into with such fulfillment, reliving and recreating themselves from the past they are. But the charm of reminiscing lies not in the data of the experience remembered but rather in the felt presence that pervades and gives substance to these data. We might even say, then, that to the very extent a remembered experience centers on an identifiable content, to this extent it degenerates into frozen memory.

The primacy of felt presence over content also finds full testimony in Proust. For example, in the experience with the three trees and again at Martinville, what Proust realizes is not a memory in the usual sense but the creative fulfillment of presence. This line of thought reveals in another way the inadequacies of the initial interpretations of my past as my history, my diary, and my deeds. For as soon as I think of my past as something composed of contents of experience, it can only appear as a totality of juxtaposed elements. And "to suppose such a multiplicity [of elements] is to make it extraneous to me, to disrupt the whole intimacy between it and me,"[53] for I would then be attempting to treat as patient of "juxtaposition what should not have been juxtaposed at all."[54] The fullness any such account—even a theoretically exhaustive one—achieves "is a fullness which is nothing but emptiness."[55] My past is fundamentally acknowledged only in a felt beyond-of-which-I-am in the plenitude of presence.

At this point I believe we reach the heart of Marcel's concept of time, particularly as this concerns the past—that is, my past. When Marcel claims, as mentioned above, that the present is the origin and boundary of time, he does not mean that the present is some ideal point of an objective time schema that vanishes as soon as it comes into being. Rather, the very source of time is the presence I am, the felt fullness of my being or the lack of it.[56] And from this we can see clearly the root error of instantaneism. So far as Gide and others attempted to preserve an appreciation for my lived presence, they were on the right track. But they proceeded by first adopting an inadequate empirical thesis—time as a series of discrete moments—and then tried to locate my presence in the present of this objectified time. Yet presence thus strait-jacketed ceases to be presence in any real sense; this is why instantaneism is unable to appreciate what is involved in fidelity. The truth reads in the opposite direction: the pulsating now, conceived of as this moment, is merely the objectification of what is fundamentally the felt presence of my life.

It now remains for us to cull some of the important features of this notion of temporality grounded in presence, to relate the dialectics of "I am my past" and "I am my life," to the datum of my incarnation, and to show that the emerging concept of time enables Marcel to address the problem of temporal successiveness.

First of all, my past, which I experience as a felt presence in affective memory, is for Marcel essentially indifferent to a before-after temporal sequence—that is, to any sense of successiveness—and must therefore be said to be discontinuous. Precisely because it is presence, it resists being chained to any here and now; indeed, in the presence achieved in an encounter, a person is "lifted right out of the here and now."[57] In this regard, then, both Marcel and Proust would seem to disagree with Bergson, to whom both otherwise owe so much. For Bergson time as pure *durée* presents itself as a continuous flow, but for Marcel and Proust this even movement is by no means apparent in my most fundamental experience. My past lives with me; it comes to me in flashes appealing to me to bear witness to it. Only on a superficial level does time appear as a mere chronological succession, and I shall try to show later how Marcel accounts for this aspect of our experience.

Second, once I stop regarding my past as something I cognize or recognize and instead acknowledge it as the presence I relive, I find that the concept of memory undergoes a transformation from its usual sense. Since memory yields me my past as presence—the beyond-of-which-I-am, as I called it above—it is now seen as "inseparable from witness."[58] Here Marcel's concept of creative fidelity finds its roots, for presence emerges in an I-Thou relationship, in an intersubjective union, and "fidelity . . . [is] clarified beginning with the *thou,* with presence itself construed as a function of the *thou.*"[59] It is at this juncture too, we believe, that we can locate the internal relationship between my past and my life, for although my past as presence bequeaths to me the interiority that is the source of my creativity, it is not itself that creativity. Thus although in some sense I may say that I am my past, I must also acknowledge that I am not essentially my past, for "when I talk about my life, I am still caught up in my life. I am still committed to living."[60] To live a commitment is to bear testimony to my past as this is realized in affective memory.

It is not my purpose here to attempt an extended discussion of Marcel's notion of creative fidelity and the many ways it is bound up with my past; yet I might briefly indicate one point of mutual relevance that creative fidelity enjoys with the notion of my time. To be created by the presence of another in an intersubjective union is to love, and Marcel says that to love means "You, at least, shall not die."[61] Needless to say, this may appear as a rather unlikely way to express what one feels in the presence of the beloved; yet the statement points toward a truth that poets and philosophers alike have long recognized. On the one hand, the terrible reality of death can only be felt by a lover; indeed, death appears as *the* threat to love. On the other hand, as Kierkegaard has so forcefully put it, the real challenge to love is time: "He [the married man] has not fought with lions and ogres, but with the most dangerous enemy—with time."[62] In the love that emerges in presence, these two observations are closely linked, and "the problem of death . . . coincides with the problem of time considered in its most acute and paradoxical form."[63] Death is only possible to a being on whom time has some grip. To a lover, it is felt as an absence— an absence of what the lover in his or her being demands should be felt as presence. Temporality as the condition for this absence is death, and creative fidelity is our only hope for transcending and conquering time.[64]

IV

We must now relate the dialectics "I am my past" and "I am my life" with the dialectic "I am my body." Marcel could hardly maintain that my incarnation is "the central 'given' of metaphysics"[65] if this "mystery" could be ignored in a discussion of my life. It is all well and good to speak of my past as a felt presence of a beyond, but how is this experience possible? Is not Marcel's theory, as developed here, on the verge of denying all reality to lived temporality? How does he account for the fact that my body seems to exist only in the present? Or, to make the point of this question more concrete by borrowing an incident from Proust's novel, does the eight-year-old boy I am—thanks to affective memory—have any incarnate reality?

So far as we know, Marcel has nowhere treated extensively the relationship between my past, my life, and my body; nevertheless a number of short entries in his metaphysical diaries point to such a correlation and even indicate some of the approaches to be taken. Let us begin by taking our bearings in the realm of objectivity.

There is, Marcel says, a close affinity between the notions of "being given as an object," "past-ness," and "being successively given": "The two facts of (a) being thought of or treated as object and (b) possessing a past that can be reconstructed [unfolded successively], are essentially connected. The simplest and clearest example is that of a person empirically given."[66] So far as I consider my body something I have as an object, I can conceive of its possessing a past, a history. In fact, corporeity and history in the objective sense imply one another. "A body is a history, or more accurately it is the outcome, the fixation of a history."[67] Thus to the extent that I persist in treating myself as an object, my corporeity and my history (both records of events) dovetail nicely, "for my body has registered all my former experiences."[68] But my body is not an object or an instrument that I have, nor is my past an object—a history, a diary, or an inventory—that I have.

One moment of the mystery of my incarnation as Marcel discusses it is that at the center of my existence there is a basic nontransparency. Consciousness is not a "luminous circle," the Cartesian transparency of the self to itself, with "shadows" surrounding it; instead, "the shadow . . . is at the center." This core of opacity, "my own obscurity to myself" that is my incarnation, is precisely the mystery of my body felt as presence.[69]

Perhaps we can clarify the significance of these remarks for our present purposes by indicating what Marcel means by transparency and nontransparency. The transparent is what can enter into or relate itself as a problematic term to "my system." Now the "continuity implied in all problematisation [and here we may add, objectification] is the continuity of a 'system for me'."[70] But it is the nature of a mystery and the presence implicit in mystery that "I am carried *beyond* any 'system for me'."[71] Any system for me is only conceivable as an extension of my body—not my body as it is felt as presence, but my body so far as it can be treated as an object. Of course, subtending all such objectification is the *percipio;* I feel or I perceive my body as presence. Although this is the ground of all transparency, it is nontransparent. What this seems to mean is that the

embodied presence I am resists all attempts to reduce it to a state of consciousness or, for that matter, to any such terms that lend themselves to
objective treatment. But my life and my past as my life are equally nontransparent to me, for "it is essential to life not to let itself be displayed";
and my past, so far as it is mine, "cannot become a part of my system
and perhaps even breaks up my system."[72] To the extent that my past
enters into my system, it takes on the continuity of the system itself, and
what we end up with is my past as my history. But because it is felt as
presence my past is nontransparent. This serves to show that my life, my
past, and my body are felt as presence. Can we go on to say that they are
the same presence?

The bond uniting me with my body is a feeling, a sympathetic mediation, or an "unmediatizable immediate."[73] My relation with my past is
precisely this bond: "I am my past. Does not that mean that between my
past experiences and my actual experience there is a relation of sympathy?"[74] Yet this relation of sympathy is none other than my union with
my body, for the impossibility of defining my relation to "my past-as-
subject which makes memory possible is only another way of expressing
the impossibility of treating the mediating element [my body] as an object
and of forming an idea of it."[75] So far as I persist in objectifying my body,
my past, given to me in affective memory, becomes a totally unintelligible
notion—the container I carry around with me. But this image of a self
reading a note inscribed in the past and recognized as past presupposes a
self who, created of a presence, is at-one-with his or her past in the plenitude of the felt presence, a presence that resists any possible reduction to
an objectified present instant. The nontransparency I feel in my past and
my life is nothing other than the felt presence of my body submerged
below the surface of all my attempts to objectify them. And my union with
my past, as with my body, is one of love.[76]

At this point I can raise the perplexing question suggested above: since
I am the eight-year-old boy I was, thanks to affective memory, am I also
my eight-year-old-boy body?[77] It would seem, at any rate, that since I can
say I am my past and I am my body, I should also be able to say I am my
eight-year-old-boy body. The real difficulty is that I must struggle to acknowledge both my past and my body as, in a sense, the same presence,
or at least not as different presences. There is always the temptation to say
that I am my present body and then to read into the meaning of "present"
an objective, atomistic concept of the present, as if the eight-year-old boy
I am were a different body so many years behind me on the road I have
traveled. But since there is a correlation between the extent to which I
objectify the present and the extent to which my past is objectified, I have

then only smuggled in an objective representation of the eight-year-old boy I am. So far as I am that eight-year-old boy, if I go on to ask in what body that boy realizes his incarnation, the answer can only be my body. If this seems strange, the strangeness seems to reduce itself to my persistence in treating the boy I am as "that" boy, perhaps even "that other" boy. But when I am now invaded by the same anxiety the boy felt over whether his mother will kiss him good-night, in what body does this relived anxiety tremble? Mine, of course. Can we say then that the eight-year-old boy's body is identical to my present body? Here the notion of identity is illegitimately purloined from its rightful place in objective discourse. The only "identity" we can accept in this realm is the felt personal intimacy of presence. Ultimately Marcel must answer the question confronting us here—that is, whether the presence of my past is the same as the presence of my body—the same way he answers the question of whether I am identical with my body: it is neither meaningful nor correct to say that the body of the eight-year-old boy I am is other than my body.[78]

Thus far the emphasis in this discussion has been on the relation of my past and my body; now let us consider my life and my body. At the outset of this essay we saw that for Marcel my body is the ground for my spatiality, and we then proceeded to follow up his suggestion that perhaps my life could reveal to me the nature of my temporality. Now, since I acknowledge my life and my body as the same presence, my body is also the ground for my temporality. For my body, so far as I feel it as a presence, is my life; so far as I differentiate it from my life, it is just "a" body, perhaps a corpse. But "my corpse is essentially what I am *not*."[79] The extent, then, of my claim that my body has merely spatial implications—that it is the ground for *only* my spatiality—is precisely the extent to which I treat my body as an object that I have. In such a case, the only career this body could claim is that of an objective continuity. But this continuity, the historicity implied in any body whatsoever, is the historicity of "my system," which as we saw presupposes a lived body. And if this lived body were the ground for only my spatiality, it would likewise presuppose another lived body, and so on *ad infinitum*. On the contrary, though, to the extent that my body is *my* body, its presence to me is not other than my life and my past—my time.

This line of thought points to a priority of my lived time over my spatiality in the datum of my incarnation, and I believe this is what Marcel saw when he wrote in his diary on 15 September 1915, "Would it not be true to say that time is only in act and space only in potency?"[80] The terminology, of course, is Aristotelian, and for Aristotle act is prior to potency in the order of being.[81] In the following entry Marcel continues:

"Time cannot be thought of *as an object* without space; but space can only be a datum given in time. We symbolize time by movement—and movement is itself symbolized by space traversed. But in that way we are setting aside the essential element which, for lack of a better word, I call *actuality* (corresponding to *hicceity*)."[82] Here again Marcel seems to be saying that space is the field of objectivity. This interpretation is borne out by a reference in *Being and Having* that links having and spatiality: "Having relates to taking but it seems that there no hold is offered except by things that are in space or can be compared with something spatial."[83] And although time cannot be thought of as an object without space, it is primarily felt as a lived presence—that is, as my body. What subtends all attempts to symbolize or objectify time is the actuality of existential presence, and lived time is this presence subtending spatiality and objectified time.

Moreover, the "relation" between space and potency, on the one hand, and lived time and act, on the other, can be appreciated in these terms. Space is that field of becoming in which we bring about various patterns of external relations, made possible because space is what can be traversed; it comes to us full of this potentiality. But there is no analogue between this and lived time. For a presence can only be; and it is pure nonsense to speak of traversing lived time, for time is not a field. To speak this way would be to objectify time.

To follow up this line of reasoning we might say that for Marcel the datum of my incarnation is not only relevant to my life and thus to my lived time, but also, in the final analysis, it is not other than my life. For my bond with my body is a felt presence, and this presence is the presence to me of my past and of my life—in short, of my temporality. This is not to deny that my body is also the ground for my spatiality, but perhaps what Marcel means (and I shall pursue the implications of this later) is that my temporality enjoys the same priority over my spatiality, in the order of my mode of being, as existence enjoys over objectivity—a priority, of course, that cannot itself be objectified.

We must now consider our experience of temporal successiveness. The need to raise this question is dictated primarily by the recognition that for Marcel my fundamental experience of my temporality is rooted in my presence, and presence resists chronological limitations. Does Marcel mean, then, to deny the successive moving character of time? I think not. In fact, the reason this question has been postponed until now is that this successiveness is directly related to the mystery of my embodiment.

If this essay has emphasized the role of presence, it is because the presence I am seems to be, for Marcel, the origin and ground of my temporality. But my self-presence[84] is not complete and absolute; rather, the same mystery of my incarnation by which I feel my body as a presence provides the boundaries in which this presence is felt. This acknowledgment of my necessarily partial presence gives rise to a "duality,"[85] as Marcel calls it, in my experience—a duality that finds expression in a number of ways. For example, he says that although my body is not primarily my instrument, my object, it "shares a deep community of nature" with objects, enabling them to be instruments and objects for me.[86] Likewise, although my body is not primarily my object, it is precisely because I can to some extent abstract from my situation, treating my body as an object, that thought and science are possible.[87] Moreover, although I do not "have" my body, the bond between me and my body provides the prototype relationship toward which all having is oriented.[88] And in another context, being-in-a-situation means that although the situation is in some sense "given" to me, it is mine only so far as I am permeable to it.[89] It would be easy to enumerate other instances of this sort of duality, a duality, let us note, that emerges only within my existential grip on a world; the important point is to recognize that the duality stems from the very mode of my existence as an incarnate being. I can only acknowledge and humbly accept it as "part of the very nature of man's metaphysical condition. . . . It is the ontological deficiency proper to the creature."[90] Here we can see the import of Marcel's suggestion that perhaps questions of the full and the empty are more relevant to philosophical discussion than is the problem of the one and the many,[91] for the ontological deficiency with which we are dealing is nothing other than my partial presence suspended between the full and the empty. At any rate, my partial self-presence—rooted in my embodiment, which gives rise to the dual "aspects" of my experience—is precisely what calls forth both the possibility and the necessity of my temporality. My temporality is possible because I appear to myself as a felt presence embodied; it is necessary because, as incarnate, my presence is only a partial one and my situation is always to some extent given to me as objective.

We can now discern why successiveness appears to be a feature of my temporality. We noted above that Marcel closely relates the two data of having a past that can be unfolded successively and of being given as an object. So far as my situation appears given to me, time appears reducible to mere succession. Here the images empiricists are so fond of—namely, time as a film or a stream—seem to have a point. But we can readily see the inadequacy and indeed the unintelligibility of such images as soon as they pretend to speak to *my* temporality, to *my* time. For I can only recognize the successive character depicted by these images if I am outside the flow—that is, if I am the spectator watching the film or sitting on the

bank of the stream. But then the succession does not apply to me.[92] That
a succession can be acknowledged as such only from a point transcending
the succession is indeed the idealist criticism of such empirical time concepts, and it leads the idealist to maintain the atemporal character of Mind
or of consciousness. Marcel evidently agrees with the logic of this idealist
criticism here;[93] what he objects to is the idealist notion of transcendence.
For the idealist, to transcend means to move to a higher level objectively
regarded as other than the lower level and from which the inadequate level,
again taken objectively, can be synthesized. Yet since my temporality concerns my lived experience, it is never something apprehended in this way.
The higher level of the idealist, therefore, is merely the privileged vantage
point of primary reflection. For Marcel, though, to transcend means to
participate in a fuller, purer experience of the plenitude of presence.[94] Limiting ourselves to that level on which my experience seems given to me in
chronological succession, we can see that the locus from which the succession is recognized as such is always available to me; it is merely that
presence that I am by virtue of my incarnation and that subtends all forms
of objectification. Thus the level of experience that regards time as a
succession is a limited or at best a limiting one. Chronological succession
is not illusory, as some idealists might maintain; rather, it is merely superficial and seen to be increasingly inadequate as I participate more meaningfully in my situation.

> To transcend time is not to raise ourselves . . . to the actually empty idea of
> a *totum simul*—empty because it remains outside us and thereby becomes in
> some way devitalized. By no means. It is rather to participate more and more
> actively in the creative intention that quickens the whole: in other words, to
> raise ourselves to levels from which the succession seems less and less *given,*
> levels from which a 'cinematographic' representation of events looks more and
> more inadequate, and ceases in the long run to be even possible.[95]

V

I will now attempt to summarize some of the important features of this
essay by sketching in broad strokes the concept of time that is beginning
to emerge. In the process, I will also make at least passing reference to
other themes in Marcel, which in any full study of his notion of temporality would bear on what my own restricted analysis has revealed. According
to Marcel, the concept of "my life" provides the lever with which I can
uncover the basic structure of my temporality, but it does so only so far as
my life and my past as my life are felt as presences. Taken as such, they
are not other than the felt presence of my body. Throughout this essay,

too, we found that Marcel's notion of presence was the key category. Now if we refer to the three moments of the vertical dimension noted at the outset, we can see how presence, which is the source of my temporality, plays itself out on each level. First, on the level of incarnation or existence, my body is felt as my presence, although the mode of presence that my body as feeling achieves is only that of nonobjective *participation immergée*.[96] Second, on the level of intersubjectivity, presence blossoms into my presence—my presence to myself—for it is in intersubjectivity that I am opened to myself,[97] and in the last analysis subjectivity is always intersubjectivity.[98] Finally, on the level of ontological exigence (which we only alluded to in our discussion of Proust), presence is all-pervasive. Here my demand for being is oriented toward absolute Presence, the eternal, greeted—if at all—in contemplation as my "being," the ground on which I can firmly rest.[99] Yet these three moments or levels must not be regarded as in any way neatly distinguishable, much less separable, in my experience. The higher levels are virtual in the lower and presuppose the lower. Thus, for example, although thought is realized on the second level, Marcel insists that thought is grounded in existence.[100] And whereas faith in God or in absolute Presence is realized on the third level, faith itself partakes of feeling.[101]

We can see the relevance for Marcel of my incarnation for my temporality by considering the implications of my embodiment as a being-in-a-situation. Because I am a being-in-a-situation in the way my incarnation makes possible and demands, I am a temporal creature. Within a zone of feeling for existence,[102] my experience of temporality may fluctuate, but invariably this datum of my being-in-a-situation bears with it temporal demands. On the one hand, because I feel my body as a presence subtending an objective world for me, my situation is never "just given" to me. On the other hand, because I am an embodied being—that is, because my being-in-a-situation demands that my situation be given to me as objective—my felt presence is never complete and absolute, never an omnipresence.[103]

On the level of intersubjectivity, the openness and permeability characterizing my felt being in the world takes the form of a personal openness, or *disponibilité*. *Disponibilité* is usually translated as "availability," but, like feeling, such availability cannot be construed as a merely passive openness. A person open as a sieve would not be the most *disponible*.[104] Instead, Marcel tells us in the Gifford Lectures, *disponibilité* must be thought of as a form of handiness or of resourcefulness, the ability to have one's resources at hand to meet the demands of life.[105] He seems to insist that *disponibilité* be seen as an expression of what he elsewhere calls "interiority" or "inwardness." If I am *disponible* I can open myself to the presence of another and can respond by being created and creative in the union. As such I am open to myself. In *Homo Viator,* Marcel says that *disponibilité* is the ability "to give oneself to anything which offers and to bind oneself by the gift,"[106] a definition that might likewise express what is involved in creative fidelity.

We have dwelt on the concept of *disponibilité* because it discloses in a number of ways Marcel's notion of temporality. In his analysis of hope, for example, Marcel insists that hope demands a concept of open time;[107] but one's ability to appreciate time as open is, I believe, inseparable from one's *disponibilité. Disponibilité* is this openness. Likewise, the creative participation of the *disponible* person is the fulfillment of the exigence to transcend mere temporal succession.

On the level of intersubjectivity, the way my presence is realized both makes possible and demands my temporality. On the one hand, because my mode of being yields me a sense of self-presence that assures me at least a minimum of interiority, my situation is never entirely given to me, and my time is never experienced as mere succession.[108] On the other hand, because my self-presence is inevitably partial, I can never escape time. All this only serves to delineate a zone within which I am capable of a greater or lesser degree of *disponibilité,* and this capability determines the degree to which my time is experienced either as what I seem only to undergo or as an appeal—an appeal that is the gift of my life to be realized in creativity. So far as my temporality orients itself toward an appeal, my experience undergoes that transformation toward being that, as the source of all value,[109] bestows the ultimate *sens* on my life. Marcel calls this inner transformation "supratemporalization." It is this need for supratemporalization that Marcel has in mind when he speaks of vanquishing time through creative fidelity and again when he says that faith becomes clarified through creative fidelity.[110] And although faith in absolute Presence can never be realized by reason or even brought about automatically by a change of will on my part, Marcel wonders "whether in the last analysis it is not with a supra-temporalization of [my life] that we have to deal."[111] Of course,

> it cannot be a question, strictly speaking, of our over-stepping the bounds of time; that would be an escape into pure abstraction. What we have to do, I think, is rather to get rid of a certain temporal schematization, which in reality is applicable only to things and to ourselves only in so far as we can be assimilated to things. We must maintain that in so far as we are not things, in so far as we refuse to allow ourselves to be reduced to the condition of things, we belong to an entirely different world-dimension, and it is this dimension which can and must be called supra-temporal.[112]

.   In concluding this essay I would like to pursue the implications of a question raised earlier in relating the notions of my life and my body. There we were led to the conclusion that perhaps my body as my temporality enjoys the same priority over my spatiality as existence enjoys over objectivity. One of the references used to argue this position was Marcel's suggestion that spatiality and having are closely linked. I wonder whether Marcel would wish to maintain this position as stated here or whether he would prefer to hold that the spatiality linked with having concerns only objective space—that is, that space where the distinction between the within and the without, the internal and the external, retains its force. Taking the second alternative, Marcel might maintain—and a number of references seem to imply this—that my fundamental sense of temporality, grounded in presence, is intimately related to, and indeed cannot be divorced from, my sense of inner space. A full discussion of Marcel's notion of time would have to uncover the link between my temporality and my sense of inner space, for a number of Marcel's most important concepts—for example, those of inwardness, interiority, *disponibilité,* and profundity—seem to cluster around this notion of inner space, and all seem likewise to be related to my temporality. Following this line of thought, I wonder if we might take Marcel's account of profundity[113] as a description of what is involved in my acknowledgment of my being as a presence greeted from a distance,[114] with the eternal present as the ground of my temporality. Taken in this way, Marcel's categories of creative fidelity and hope become the basis for my sense of the past and the future respectively, both finding their source in the present of presence, both ultimately grounded in my faith in absolute Presence, and both, because they are but different aspects of the same act of love, revealing "the future as somehow mysteriously in harmony with the most distant past."[115]

JOHN V. VIGORITO

DEPARTMENT OF PHILOSOPHY
UNIVERSITY OF SOUTHWESTERN LOUISIANA
MARCH 1969

NOTES

1. Gabriel Marcel, *Presence and Immortality,* trans. Michael A. Machado (Pittsburgh: Duquesne University Press, 1967), p. 51 (hereafter cited as *PI*). Con-

temporary philosophical parlance recognizes a distinction between time and temporality. Marcel is well aware of this distinction, since he never confuses his own questions concerning temporality with those of objective time; yet he employs the terms synonymously. In this essay I shall also take this freedom.

I might here make a related terminological observation. Perhaps one reason why the subject of temporality has been generally ignored by Marcel's commentators is that he often disparages time, speaking of the need to vanquish and transcend time and of the need for supratemporalization; indeed, in an early entry in his *Metaphysical Journal* he speaks of the "irrelevancy of time." However, elsewhere he insists that there can be no possibility of our transcending or escaping from time. I hope this essay will show that the apparent contradictions between such statements can be easily resolved once we distinguish between Marcel's concept of temporality and what he takes to be inadequate theories of time.

2. Gabriel Marcel, *The Mystery of Being,* trans. G. S. Fraser (vol. 1) and René Hague (vol. 2), 2 vols. (Chicago: Henry Regnery Co., 1960), 1:103 (hereafter cited as *MB*).

3. Gabriel Marcel, *Homo Viator,* trans. Emma Craufurd (New York: Harper & Row, Harper Torchbooks, 1962), p. 138 (hereafter cited as *HV*).

4. *MB* 2:35; see also *MB* 1:168.

5. Gabriel Marcel, *Creative Fidelity,* trans. Robert Rosthal (New York: Noonday Press, 1964), p. 92 (hereafter cited as *CF*).

6. Gabriel Marcel, *Being and Having,* trans. Katharine Farrer (New York: Harper & Row, Harper Torchbooks, 1965), p. 40 (hereafter cited as *BH*).

7. Gabriel Marcel, *Metaphysical Journal,* trans. Bernard Wall (Chicago: Henry Regnery Co., 1952), p. 129 (hereafter cited as *MJ*).

8. *BH*, 15; see also *MB* 1:99–102.   9. *BH*, 110–111.

10. *BH*, 195.   11. *BH*, 195.

12. *CF*, 161.

13. Anyone acquainted with the writings of modern existentialists and phenomenologists will be familiar with Marcel's use of the term *object* and its derivatives. But since the term is technical, perhaps it would be appropriate to specify briefly what Marcel means by it. "The object," Marcel says, "is defined as being independent of the characteristics that make me be this particular person and not another person. Thus it *is essential to the very nature of the object not to take 'me' into account;* if I think it is having regard to me, in that measure I cease to treat it as an object" (*MJ*, 261; Marcel's italics).

14. *CF*, 161–62.   15. *MJ*, 198.

16. *MB* 1:190–91.   17. *MB* 1:192.

18. *BH*, 129. See also *BH*, 72; *PI*, 55.

19. *MB* 1:192.   20. *MB* 1:192–95.

21. *MJ*, 165.   22. *MJ*, 165.

23. I will occasionally use such odd locutions to express what is involved in presence. What I am trying to express in this phrase is that the internal relationship in an intersubjective experience finds its source neither in the persons considered in their individuality nor in the resulting union taken in some objective, reified sense.

24. *CF*, 53.

25. *MB* 1:198.

26. *MB* 1:228–29.

27. *MB* 1:232 and footnote. Georges Poulet's *Études sur le temps humain* has been translated into English by Elliott Coleman under the title *Studies in Human Time* (Baltimore: Johns Hopkins Press, 1956). Poulet's essay on Proust also appears in a collection of essays entitled *Proust,* edited by René Girard (Englewood Cliffs, N.J.: Prentice-Hall, 1962), pp. 150–77.

28. *HV,* 8–9.

29. *BH,* 97.

30. Poulet, *Studies in Human Time,* pp. 313–14.

31. See Marcel's "Sketch of a Phenomenology and a Metaphysic of Hope," in *HV,* 29–67. For what I mean by calling this "a future," see *PI,* 33–37, and *MB* 1:238.

32. Poulet, *Studies in Human Time,* p. 315.

33. Ibid., p. 320.

34. *BH,* 14.

35. Any full account of Marcel's notion of time would have to concern itself extensively with his concept of transcendent being. Where there is transcendent being, there is the eternal (*MJ,* 184); this notion of eternity is, needless to say, of the utmost importance for temporality. Here, at least, Marcel stands squarely within the Platonic-Augustinian tradition, where time can only be appreciated in its relation to the eternal. In this essay, we will only locate, so to speak, the relevance of eternality to temporality in Marcel's thought.

36. Poulet, *Studies in Human Time,* pp. 297–98.

37. From Marcel Proust, *Pastiches et mélanges* (1919), p. 197, as quoted by Poulet in *Studies in Human Time,* p. 298.

38. *MB* 1:119.

39. *MJ,* 164.

40. *MJ,* 164.

41. *MJ,* 178.

42. Marcel Proust, *Remembrance of Things Past,* trans. C. K. Scott Moncrieff, introduction by Joseph Wood Krutch, 2 vols. (New York: Random House, 1934), 1:34; italics mine.

43. Proust, *Remembrance of Things Past,* pp. 543–45.

44. For a discussion of the three moments of "having," see Marcel's "Outlines of a Phenomenology of Having" and the accompanying preparatory notes, in *BH,* 143–74.

45. Proust, *Remembrance of Things Past,* p. 139.

46. Ibid., p. 140.

47. Ibid., p. 34.

48. Poulet, *Studies in Human Time,* pp. 297–98.

49. *MB* 1:145.

50. Poulet, *Studies in Human Time,* p. 297.

51. Proust, *Remembrance of Things Past,* p. 35.

52. *BH,* 40.

53. *PI,* 63.

54. *PI,* 53.

55. *PI,* 52.

56. According to my interpretation of Marcel, the notion of my presence is the origin of my temporality. Marcel's works appear to leave open the possibility of an alternative interpretation—namely, that while my presence is presupposed by

my temporality, it should not itself be regarded as the origin and source of this temporality. This view might argue that in Marcel, presence is by nature atemporal and indeed is the vanquisher of time. I believe that my interpretation takes into account, as we shall see, the real point of these and other such objections and avoids the disastrous implications of the alternative view, which leads to idealism by deflating my existential precognitive grip on the world into a subject-object dichotomy.

57. *MB* 1:218.   58. *BH*, 97.
59. *CF*, 149.   60. *MB* 1:199.
61. *MB* 2:171. This can be directly related to Marcel's thoughts on immortality.
62. Søren A. Kierkegaard, "Either/Or," trans. David F. Swenson, Lillian Marvin Swenson, and Walter Lowrie, in *A Kierkegaard Anthology*, ed. Robert Bretall (New York: Random House, Modern Library, 1946), p. 88.
63. *CF*, 152.   64. *CF*, 152.
65. *BH*, 11.   66. *BH*, 19.
67. *BH*, 84.   68. *MJ*, 259.
69. *BH*, 14.   70. *BH*, 127.
71. *BH*, 128; Marcel's italics.   72. *PI*, 53; *BH*, 129.
73. *MB* 1:135.   74. *MJ*, 249.
75. *MJ*, 250.   76. *MJ*, 164.
77. Here the question of temporality cuts right to the heart of any discussion of personal identity, and indeed in his discussion of personal identity in *The Mystery of Being*, Marcel uses this example from Proust. Marcel's notion of personal identity has not received anywhere near the attention it deserves from his commentators.
78. See *CF*, 19.   79. *BH*, 87; Marcel's italics.
80. *MJ*, 129.   81. Aristotle, *Metaphysics*, 1049 b5.
82. *MJ*, 129; first italics mine.   83. *BH*, 144.
84. I use the term *self-presence* even though Marcel, in one of his diary entries, suggests that the expression is misleading (see *PI*, 158). He objects that the term connotes an "idleness," an inactivity, or even a self-complacency. If we avoid the temptation to construe the expression in this way, I believe we can use the term (for which it would be difficult to find another) to point to my obvious felt presence, which is the ground of my objectivity.
85. *BH*, 174. "Duality" does not quite express the relationship here, for the two features that emerge in this so-called duality are not of the same order.
86. *MJ*, 333; see also *MB* 1:122.   87. *MB* 1:113.
88. *MB* 1:119.   89. *MB* 1:178–79.
90. *BH*, 174.
91. Gabriel Marcel, "On the Ontological Mystery," in *The Philosophy of Existentialism*, trans. Manya Harari, 4th paperbound ed. (New York: Citadel Press, 1964), p. 12.
92. *MB* 1:232–33.   93. *MB* 1:233.
94. *MB* 1:68.   95. *BH*, 18.
96. *MB* 1:140.   97. *MJ*, 147.
98. *MB* 1:224.   99. *MB* 2:35.
100. *BH*, 27.   101. *CF*, 169.
102. *MB* 1:118–19.   103. *MB* 1:164.

104. *MB* 1:179.
106. *HV*, 23.
108. *MB* 1:233.
110. *CF*, 149.
112. *MB* 2:207–8.
114. *MB* 2:36.

105. *MB* 1:201.
107. *MB* 2:181.
109. *MJ*, 151.
111. *MB* 2:207.
113. *MB* 1:236–41.
115. *MB* 1:238.

On Time in the Philosophy of Marcel
REPLY TO JOHN V. VIGORITO

I would like to tell you* that I found the study you dedicated to "time" in my writings truly remarkable. It will certainly be among the better and more useful contributions in the volume devoted to my work in the Living Philosophers series. I especially congratulate you on the comparison you made between Proust and myself. I believe you are absolutely correct in thinking that Proust is closer to me than Bergson. It seems to me that Bergson gave far too little attention to the aspect of discontinuity that, in my opinion, we cannot overlook.

I was particularly interested in the question you asked regarding the relationships between "incarnation" and "temporality." You ask in what sense I can say that I am (to give the details) the child who, on the wharves of Stockholm, watched with nostalgia the ships sailing away toward the Gulf of Bothnia; it is certain that the fact of smelling the peculiar aroma of coal can make me relive this experience in Sweden. You ask legitimately whether my body has remained the same as the body of that child. Here is how I would answer. It is all too clear that if I concentrate on the body-object, the question seems meaningless. It is not the same if I direct my attention to what I call the body-subject in my *Metaphysical Journal,* and you know as well as I that it is solely in the perspective of the body-subject that the term *incarnation* has meaning.

Naturally you are one hundred percent correct to say that the notion of "presence" is central to my thought. With respect to the relationship that joins the octogenarian that I am to the child in Stockholm, we ought to speak of a copresence. I might add that this term *relation,* from which, unfortunately, it is difficult to abstain, actually misrepresents what we are

Translated from the French by Dr. Girard Etzkorn.
*Marcel wrote this response in the form of a letter to Vigorito, dated 27 April 1970.

dealing with; a relation presupposes terms, and the child in Stockholm and the old man who finds himself again in the child cannot in any way be reduced to terms. On this point, I rather identify with Bergson, who denounced in an admirable fashion the materializing role of language. Here it would be better to refer to musical experience in order to *hear* or *understand* (*entendre*) the meaning of this copresence. This amounts to saying that we must acknowledge a very profound metaphysical sense in which it is not true to say that the old man has replaced the child or, if you prefer, that they are two links separated by many others in a certain chain.

Naturally, I won't argue that this representation of the "chain" is inevitable or even practically necessary. For example, under certain circumstances I am led to wonder what I did between two given dates, or, in other words, what links I can find between the two. Here I am dealing with my life as I would deal with any life other than my own; in the strongest sense of the term, I make *someone* of myself. More profoundly, I am someone for another or for myself to the extent that I make myself another, or, if you prefer, to the extent that I constitute myself as another. But this is precisely the opposite of what happens, for example, when Proust relives Combrai on the "magic occasion" of the *madeleines*.

I hope to take all this up again and clarify it in a book, requested of me by a publisher, that I intend to call *My Life and I*.* It will be a kind of meditation and in no way a duplicate of the autobiography I gave to Professor Schilpp, which I find hardly satisfactory.

I sincerely hope, my dear sir, that life will give me the chance to meet you and to tell you of my gratitude for your noteworthy contribution. If you come to France, please do not fail to let me know; we must meet one another.

Be assured of my most sincere and devoted sentiments.

G.M.

---

*Published under the title *En chemin, vers quel éveil?* (Paris: Gallimard, 1971).

16

Hans A. Fischer-Barnicol

SYSTEMATIC MOTIFS IN THE THOUGHT OF GABRIEL MARCEL: TOWARD A PHILOSOPHICAL THEORY OF COMPOSITION

I

IT may at first appear strange to investigate a system underlying the work of Gabriel Marcel. One can hardly find a philosopher whose work seems less suited to this task. No philosophy of our time has been conceived less systematically; none reveals less structure, let alone architectural design. No other philosophy resists so obstinately a systematic approach and a subsequent systematization. Marcel could promptly dissuade us from what since the seventeenth century has been meant by system,[1] and he could consequently persuade us to avoid this task. In agreement with the irony of Novalis and the Romantics[2] and also with the critical decisiveness of Nietzsche,[3] Marcel resists the enticements of systematic philosophizing with arguments that remind us biographically of his growing opposition to Hegel as well as formally of Søren Kierkegaard, whose writings Marcel had not yet read at the time of his critical conversion. Nevertheless Marcel's dispute with the British neo-Hegelians led him to formulate questions similar to Kierkegaard's. He also drew conclusions like those of the great Danish philosopher; but Marcel's questions reach further, and they never leave the dimensions of philosophical inquiry. In the Frenchman's methodology Kierkegaard's leap into paradox remains questionable, if not

Translated from the German by James S. Morgan and revised by Dr. Hans H. Rudnick, with the assistance of Mrs. Dora Fischer-Barnicol.

slightly suspect; Marcel's "breakthrough" (as he calls the decisive turn of
his thought) occurred under different constellations, namely, under the
stars of Pascal, Maine de Biran, Henri Bergson, Maurice Blondel, and
Louis Lavelle. It occurred in Paris at the time of the catastrophe we call
the First World War, which Marcel first characterized correctly as the suicide of Europe. At that time his breakthrough did not drive him into a
hopeless isolation.

Nevertheless such a decisive turn could not and cannot attain general
validity; the recognition it received remains both equivocal and self-contradictory. This corresponds to our present situation, which forbids in the
tangle of ideologies a clear, methodically and systematically founded confrontation like that between Kierkegaard and Hegel. Numerous factions try
to embrace an influential mode of thinking for their interests. In Marcel's
case most parties seem to be irritated by the freedom his philosophy maintains. Even professional critics of ideology are displeased, for this thinker
has offered them at best sympathy and not the unconditional support they
expect, because he knows how rapidly a critique can begin to resemble
that of its opponents and because he sees through the temptations of dialectic. In a kind of naïve innocence Marcel is immune to the lure of
ideological commitment; indeed we hardly know how to relate this attitude
to the never tiring vigilance of enlightening reflection. Marcel's thought
seems not to react at all to the magnetic currents of his age. If he did not
register its tensions and tendencies so precisely, we might think him almost
insensitive toward issues whose ideological attraction captivates others in
the form of "ideas" or Weltanschauungen. This holds true also for the
scarcely controllable inner laws of systematics in the traditional sense and
for the magic suction of concepts about which he is skeptical. Such a style
of thinking is full of risks and neglects the efforts of the professional philosophers who are subjects of Marcel's ridicule in their search for a scientific security in "systems" and in their resistance to radical inquiries.
The easiest way out in academic disputes in such a case is to deny the title
of serious philosophy to one's adversaries. This was not possible in Marcel's case, for critics could not even agree on which stream of modern
thought he belonged to or whether indeed he belonged to modern thought
at all.

Marcel resists all classification, not to mention such obviously wrong
characterizations as that by Paul Tillich, who placed Marcel in the Thomist
tradition.[4] He objects to being classified as an existentialist, as a Christian
humanist, as a thinker of the transcendent in Karl Jaspers's sense, as an
ontologist or a metaphysician, not to mention all the other labels dictated
by theology. These theological misclassifications result from the failure to

recognize that Marcel constantly prefers religious terms like *mystery, sin, belief, hope, love, prayer,* and *communion* to philosophical concepts. At the same time, methodologically he appears to be incapable of thinking in theological concepts. Yet we scarcely know what to do with Marcel's characterization of himself as a Christian Socratic. In short, Marcel's thought cannot be classified in terms of academic schools and trends, and he never wanted to lay the basis of a philosophical system.[5] Although his early works show that he learned to ride in the saddles of all systems, he evidently mistrusts such horses.

Marcel's disclaimers of systematic thought, together with the inability of systematic philosophers to recognize him and his kind as philosophers without systems and also with the failure to somehow integrate him, do not encourage a search for systematic moments or motifs in Marcel's thought. But this is characteristic of the present state of philosophy. We should at least have learned from the philosophical efforts of this post-Nietzschean century that any systematic considerations that disregard the historical situation of the problem and ignore their presuppositions are nothing more than abstract intellectual games leading literally to nothing;[6] they are symptoms of an enlightened nihilism.

If our situation no longer allows elementary questions of life and of human existence to be comprehended and clarified in terms of systematic points of view, because such questions are simply no longer put forward within the framework of a conceptual order to which we can concede the character of a system, then to which consequences must criticism direct itself? And to which consequences must criticism direct itself if the thinkers who raise such questions renounce systematics without exception—because they are skeptical about its possibilities—although they themselves evidently possess all conceivable capacities for the development of a system as well as the sense for constructive connections, which submits their critiques of systems to proof? Since I cannot develop this question in detail here, I will simply eliminate two short circuits that are as simple as they are widespread. The first concerns philosophical positivism; the second, possibly resulting from the first, concerns certain forms of the art of essay writing—of a partially literary, partially philosophical (or sociological and psychological) literature in which little is thought, but much is sensed, guessed, conjured, and rhetorized. Positivism simply excludes such elementary questions from consideration. For the sake of the formal precision of its language and its categories, it leaves such questions to other types of thinking and removes them from the area of philosophical tasks. In the final analysis the entire stock of metaphysical problems is thereby eliminated for reasons of exactness that could easily have been prompted by indolence. The art of essay composition and of aphorism also takes the easy way out. It declares all systematics abstract and unsuitable and resigns itself to a philosophical pointillism, which may all too easily degenerate into a colorful irrationalism. If anything fills Marcel with disgust, it is these forms of the dehumanization of philosophizing: rationalistic desiccation and analytic silting, along with all irrationalistic beclouding, the morass of mere approximation.

Unfortunately I must also forgo a careful perusal of Marcel's way of thinking to show, step by step, that his philosophical discipline forbids not only these cheap evasions but also those maneuvers placing higher demands on the capacity of thinking, namely, those more subtle digressions from the a priori by which we permit ourselves to make conceptual and logical efforts. Such an investigation would be indispensable for an understanding of what philosophical discipline means for Marcel and of the relentlessness with which he adheres to it. Marcel's way of thinking and his style of writing are everything except arbitrary or accidental. Characteristic and apparently unmediated transitions from one subject to another, obvious omissions, the always apparent refusal to follow the evident course from one thought to another even at the cost of system-related repercussions, and Marcel's covert silence are methodically significant and informative. No less a systematist than Karl Rahner once characterized this style in an interview as an almost infamous philosophical understatement. In this respect even Marcel has not escaped the fate of Western thought by being sufficiently understood only within his own field. It requires a far-reaching knowledge and some philosophical ability to notice that this thinker knows what he is doing and that he is also well aware of why he omits something.

These preliminary considerations may suffice to make the question of systematic moments or motifs in Marcel's work appear more sensible. At the same time these considerations pose the question more correctly by basing it on Marcel's own prephilosophical questions, on the critical analysis of his method (which throughout can be said to be systematic), and on his determination not to reject or escape the a priori. From the standpoint of method this would assure him of rarely contradicting the criteria of philosophical systematics, which have proved themselves both clearly and painfully a priori. Marcel has never disregarded or disputed them. However rash the question might sound, it could perhaps be properly stated if it were guided by Marcel's skepticism regarding the very possibility of systematic thought.

In examining these preliminary considerations, their conditions, and their reasons, one must therefore be prepared to discover in the various kinds of systematics as well as in the idea of system itself something quite different from what has usually been conceived of and understood by these concepts. It is easy enough to yield to the internal laws and directions of a system, and it is just as easy to ignore the system and reject the usefulness of its method. There remains only the question of how one can meaningfully conceive of a pattern of the whole without a perception of the original and ultimate unity of knowledge, however uncertain this knowledge may be. How then can thought methodically proceed if not somehow systematically, even if the object of thought is a mirage or Fata Morgana, a vitally important delusion, a necessary Utopia, a recollection, a premonition, or all of these simultaneously, by which our thinking is being spurred on without despairing of its goal and truth?

Marcel has asked himself this question implicitly and indirectly.[7] He speaks repeatedly of an inner coherence of thought and of the communication of ideas, and he means more than a merely external network. In the *Journal métaphysique* he follows with remarkable, amazed awareness the involuntary economy of his thought. His thought takes shape without intention, without constructive rules, and within the realm of the impalpable—very much like a work of art. He noticed rather early how his philosophy was fundamentally influenced by his artistic experience with music and with his dramatic creations. He confesses that the themes and motifs of his thinking announced themselves first in these experiences.[8] In my opinion, such observations actually represent a systematic approach to genuinely philosophical experiences.

II

In section three of his transcendental doctrine of method Kant not only formulated the classical concept of system under the title "Architectonic of Pure Reason" but also anticipated our questions about this concept.[9] The historically conditioned intentions of all systematics are immediately shown to correspond to the prehistory of the problem. Kant defines architectonics, "the art of constructive systems," as the doctrine of the scientific in our knowledge, and he says it belongs necessarily to the doctrine of method because "the systematic unity is that which first raises ordinary knowledge to the rank of science." This is so, Kant observes parenthetically, because it allows "a system" to arise "out of a mere aggregate" of knowledge.[10] Kant is thus fully aware of the derivation and the original intention of systematic thought, namely, that it must now as ever relate philosophy to the sciences and demonstrate philosophy to be a science. This involves "establishing a science," and this is impossible unless it is based on an idea.[11] Kant remarks ironically that the schema and even the definition initially given of a science do not usually correspond to this idea.

> For this idea lies hidden in reason, like a germ in which the parts are still undeveloped and barely recognisable even under microscopic observation. Consequently, since sciences are devised from the point of view of a certain universal interest, we must not explain and determine them according to the description which their founder gives of them, but in conformity with the idea which, out of the natural unity of the parts that we have assembled, we find to be grounded in reason itself. For we shall then find that its founder, and often even his latest successors, are groping for an idea which they have never succeeded in making clear to themselves, and that consequently they have not been in a position to determine the proper content, the articulation (systematic unity), and limits of the science.[12]

Kant's following description of the discovery of systems shows how he deplored these tragic misrepresentations of the idea. After stressing that of all a priori sciences of reason only mathematics, but never philosophy, can be learned—"at best one may learn only to philosophize"—Kant risks formulating the following simple axiom: "Philosophy is the system of all philosophical knowledge." But if this system is, as he at once explains, "a mere idea of a possible science which nowhere exists *in concreto,* but to which, by many different paths, we attempt to approximate," then, he asks, who possesses this science, and how shall we recognize it?[13]

We must let ourselves be confronted by these questions posed by one of the greatest "systematizers" in the history of philosophy so that we do not completely misunderstand his previously given definition of system:

> In accordance with reason's legislative prescriptions, our diverse modes of knowledge must not be permitted to be a mere rhapsody, but must form a system. Only so can they further the essential ends of reason. By a system I understand the unity of the manifold modes of knowledge under one idea. This idea is the concept provided by reason—of the form of a whole—in so far as the concept determines *a priori* not only the scope of its manifold content, but also the positions which the parts occupy relatively to one another. The scientific concept of reason contains, therefore, the end and the form of that whole, which is congruent with this requirement.[14]

With the help of an informative analogy, Kant explains that this entire argument "is thus an organised unity (*articulatio*) and not an aggregate (*coacervatio*). It may grow from within (*per intussusceptionem*), but not by external addition (*per appositionem*). It is thus like an animal body, the growth of which is not by the addition of a new member, but by the rendering of each member, without change of proportion, stronger and more effective for its purposes.[15]

This comparison is significant. It anticipates what has been established in detail in subsequent explanations, namely, the peculiar presence and inaccessibility of what Kant means by a system.[16] It is not a later construction bolting and riveting forms of knowledge to each other. Grown out of the nucleus of an original idea, it is rather an organism the philosopher knows and understands only insufficiently, and yet, as the living law of his thought, it articulates all forms of knowledge by bringing them into a rational pattern. The principle of such a living order is the idea, the highest concept of reason, which forms and determines the entire organism of knowledge. When Kant subsequently outlines the "architectonics of all knowledge arising from pure reason" (whereby he is forced from the start to oppose reason as "the whole higher faculty of knowledge . . . with the empirical"), then tectonic as well as constructive perceptions and concepts again become dominant in his critical reflections.[17] But the determination of the system as an organism remains fundamental. It assures the transcendental dignity of the concept of system. If the concept of system loses this determination, it reduces to a meaningless schema.

It may not be necessary to establish in detail how far Marcel's philosophy and the current formulation of philosophical questions diverge from the position of the Kantian critique. More important is an attempt to describe the direction and character of this divergence. Relevant to our concern is the formal proximity of the problems that the concept of system raised for Kant. Above and beyond all differences in approach and intentions in the course of thought, Kant's explanations offer some fundamental insights into the essence of the systematic and first brought the problem into focus on the proper level. These same insights are substantially confirmed by Hegel's understanding of system[18]—again disregarding all differences in the form of thought and in the intent of philosophy. Of course it cannot be overlooked that system means perfection for Hegel, whereas for Kant it is the original determination of all forms of knowledge, organizing thought by the underlying idea. But this difference is in itself problematic. Hegel stresses explicitly that the result of the dialectical process restores the original immediacy:

> Now more precisely the *third* is the immediate, but the immediate *resulting from sublation of mediation,* the simple resulting from *sublation of difference,* the positive resulting from sublation of the negative, the Notion that has realized itself by means of its otherness and by the sublation of this reality has become united with itself, and has restored its absolute reality, its *simple* relation to itself. This *result* is therefore the *truth*. It is *equally* immediacy *and* mediation; . . . precisely as this unity [it] is self-mediating movement and activity.[19]

What begins as universal now becomes "the *individual,* the *concrete,* the *subject''*—now as much *for itself (für sich)* as it was formerly *in itself (an sich)*. As a result of this interpretation, the whole that has withdrawn into and is identical with itself regains the form of immediacy it determined for itself in the beginning. This means that the original immediacy "is only a *form*, since it was a result as well; hence its determinateness as content is no longer something merely picked up, but something *deduced* and *proved*." Hegel also stresses this assertion. Only as derived and demonstrated may "the *content* of cognition as such" enter "into the circle of consideration," because it now belongs entirely to the method that has titanically made itself independent: "The method itself by means of this moment expands itself into a *system*."[20]

The mere juxtaposition of these two classical conceptions of system illuminates the question posed above. Juxtaposing them at least frees us from the constrictions of the almost mechanical constructive ideas attached to the concept of system. That a computer cannot derive a philosophical systematics need no longer be discussed.

To search for systematic moments in Marcel's thought no longer seems absurd. For an understanding of the motifs and methodological principles of such an apparently unsystematic philosophizing, the differences between the Kantian and Hegelian concepts of system are less important than those points where they correspond to and agree with one another.

Trivial constructions, subject to carrying out only rational calisthenics, have so often been introduced as systems that I cannot state often or emphatically enough how external or even superficial the static, technical aspects of calculation, consistency, and stringency are for genuine systematic concepts. These concepts are crudely misunderstood when they are conceived of as alleged blueprints, as more or less complicated switchboards of problems, or as directions for logical jigsaw puzzles in which thoughts already present are to be bolted, knotted, or glued together. The problem posed by the concept of system had already been understood and considered all along in other, higher dimensions of thought by Aquinas, Cusanus, Descartes, Pascal, Spinoza, and Leibniz and was by no means the discovery of Kant and Hegel. Beyond all possibilities of intervention and manipulation, the method (and what leads to its constitution) arises from the inaccessible as an inquiry into the constitutive principles of our thinking and as a definition and attribution of our potentialities of thought and their significance.

Accordingly the same idea that bestows pattern and unity on the multiplicity of forms of knowledge may, as Kant has shown, remain concealed to the kind of thinking that blindly follows it so that even those who take up such a systematic thought and memorize it nevertheless "wander about the idea'' but fail to discover it. Thus all such systematic zeal is, under certain circumstances, incapable of precisely comprehending the matter at hand. It is the system itself that cannot be learned. Philosophy can never be learned; we can learn at best only how to philosophize. Beyond all mechanical skills of logical connection and every rational technique, philosophizing is understood as a discipline of method demanding the strictest standards, since it is on the way toward philosophy, only a method in the original Greek meaning of this term: preparing the way to ''a possible science which nowhere exists *in concreto,* but to which, by many different paths, we attempt to approximate.''[21] Those who believe they possess it, those who think they ''have'' a philosophy, that is, ''the system of all philosophical knowledge,''[22] have subjected themselves to the ironic smile of Kant's critique.

Philosophical method in this sense—triumphantly totalized and made into a criterion by Hegel—can thus never be confined to what a more vulgar terminology calls ''a system,'' and it can never subject itself to an existing structure of thought. Its dynamics arise from and aim at a final unity of the whole. It seeks to understand itself as the final unity's concretion into form. To its disciplines belongs therefore a particular inner awareness unique to all genuine philosophy—an awareness capable of perceiving the process by which the uniform structure of knowledge gradually discloses itself not only in the never tiring reflection on the presuppositions and foundations of one's own thinking and the observation of its wondrous changes, transformations, and mutations, but still more so by a perceiving with ears or by a process of insight that indeed makes one aware.[23]

The elements of a system do not lie at hand like beams for the construction of a roof. In a way enigmatic to reflection, they are included and incorporated into the whole of the systematic view as it forms and develops. Like every genuine transcendence, this view has two temporal aspects for reflexive thinking. Kant describes them by explaining his concept of system; Hegel links them as the potential foundation of the system into which the method expands and as the result that constitutes the truth in the concept that has found ''its absolute reality, its simple relation to its self.'' Hegel does not hesitate to call this event, which he wants understood as the true concept, the mystical event. Kant's sobriety forbids such exuberance, but he means the same, namely, that the idea, as the rational concept of the form of wholeness, determines a priori the extent and coordination of the multiplicity, which already bears within itself the rational concept of the form of wholeness in the sense and form of the whole. Consequently all developments within the multitude of potentiality corresponding to this ideal predetermination must be formally congruent with it. As a motif and as an intention, this "idea" forms the basis for the systematic approach to the manifest unity and structure of the whole. Systematics is a discipline of obedient attention to this principle by which it is induced and judged from beginning to end, from the ἀρχή to the ἔσχατον.

What appears most important however is that the concept of system constantly incorporates the temporality of thought. Kant emphasizes the history of individual thinking, and this allows him to observe that individual thinking can hardly perceive the significance of its own fate, whereas Hegel identifies the history of thought with world history and subjects it with overwhelming pathos to the idea of a system in which it completes itself.[24] Kant interprets systematics by the image of organic growth; Hegel sees it as an almost "mystical" process in which the world spirit wishes to come to itself. Kant expressly condemns the simplistic conceptions of systematics used by school philosophy.[25] He declares that system is "organized into *articulatio*" and not "accumulated by *coacervatio*"; the system grows outward from the inside, but not from the outside *per appositionem* ("by addition").[26] This clarification of the concept of system is unnecessary for Hegel, whose abstract thought does not permit such externals. Nevertheless both concepts are essentially determined by temporality. Simply and ambiguously, systematics needs time. Because systematics does not "organize" something externally lifeless and because it represents the living "organization" of the potentialities of thought, in its reflective disciplines it seeks a certainty that cannot be achieved by reflection alone. It always seeks something other than the logical consistency of thought to assure itself of the correctness of its method as such.

Thus the question of the significance of thought must be asked by both concepts of system. Historical contexts may have played a role in this. Since philosophy wishes to establish itself as a science by systematics, it also desires to prove that its disciplines reach beyond the limitations of scientific investigation and not only satisfy those purposes but also extend into what cannot intelligibly be asked of science; philosophy provides all questions and thinking with meaning. Kant stresses the purposefulness of philosophical method in order to justify it scientifically. Hegel allows the question of purposes to melt into and be carried away in the ardor of determining ultimate meanings.

Nevertheless such apologetic explanations do not suffice. Concerning form and content, the question of meaning and the problem of system coincide. Without orienting toward an original and ultimately possible agreement on the manifestation of the many in one, of the multiple in the simple, and of the parts in the whole, every method loses its meaning. In question is only how one inquires into this agreement without blocking it with concepts that lie unavoidably at the inquiry's basis and are prior to it. In question is how—beyond Kierkegaard, Bergson, Husserl, and Whitehead all the way to Wittgenstein, Heidegger, and Marcel—one can inquire into the one, the simple, and the whole without evading or concealing these questions altogether. Kant always, Hegel at least for a long time, and all significant thinkers of the modern era at some point have experienced and known the tragedy that this preliminary question of genuine philosophical investigation inflicts on human thought. Human thought can only ask meaningful questions when it dares to ask the ultimate (or the pristine), whose very nature refuses comprehension by questions—a point most positivists, in contrast to Wittgenstein, do not wish to concede.

Such a fickle simultaneity of revelation and obfuscation, of exposition and concealment, of disclosure and disguise, and of clarity and obscurity has already been incorporated constructively into the structure of the ἀλήθεια from which all Heidegger's ways of thinking are deducible. This has to be kept in mind when thinking about the concepts of system within the category of time. This temporality of thinking corresponds to the unavailability and unapproachability of the system proper, toward which all systematics is aimed like an arrow on a bow. Any systematics that deserves to be taken seriously as philosophy knows this innermost tension, whose slackening is equivalent to the extinction of thought. All problems serve to put tension on the bow whose arrow, to use Marcel's term, aims into the *metaproblematic,* that is, the mystery of being.

It is thus neither accidental nor irrelevant that time gains admission into systematics. Time belongs essentially to the problem of system. Systematics constantly reflects its temporal conditions and at the same time—it could not otherwise be faithful to its nature—rebels passionately against these conditions. Systematics not only intimates but knows that certainty can be attained only from those determinations that appear to precede time and lead beyond time. Simultaneously, as thought in time, systematics cannot satisfy these determinations. It is capable of fulfilling them only insufficiently in a radical critique of its presuppositions. Pascal has described this intermediate state painfully and clearly.[27] He has thereby pushed the problem to its final conclusion more boldly than Kant or Hegel and more profoundly even than Kierkegaard, for he recognized it as an existential problem. He does not hesitate to uncover its roots: "Man is to himself the most insoluble engima in the world. He cannot conceive what body is and even less, what spirit is, and least of all, how a body and a spirit can be united. This is the crux of all difficulties and on top of that it is our own nature: *Modus quo corporibus adhaerent spiritus comprehendi ab hominibus non potest, et hoc tamen homo est.*"[28] This point, which firmly places the problem of system in the so-called body-soul relation, is of decisive importance. The idea of organicism in the philosophy of the eighteenth and nineteenth centuries confirms this as well.

In order not to distort the problem from the beginning by using terms loaded with misconceptions and also in order to show how carefully and vigilantly Marcel formulates his ideas, I should speak of bodily presence.[29] The idea, or original intuition, both challenges truthful thinking and predetermines its course, and it takes shape in the system, frequently and happily acquiring bones if not actually flesh and blood.[30] The system grows to full strength by an embodiment. Not only did Kant use no other image, but no better one could even have occurred to him to explain the essence of system. The image of a living body is worth questioning as a declaration of the temporality of thought, without which neither the growth, the method, nor above all the potentiality for establishing a system is conceivable. Over the life history of a particular thinking, this original or ultimate unity gradually develops into the form Kant describes. This transcendental pattern, which shines through in systematics, is itself a temporal form and not ultimately a method. Kant, from the starting point of his questions, and Hegel, because of the totalitarian claim of his history-swallowing gnosticism, had little to say about this problem. Nevertheless Hegel wished to have the "triad" understood as "the full figure" and attempted to demonstrate this completeness by his dialectics not only as a structure and form but also as a procedure, namely, "the movement and activity mediating itself with itself."[31]

But the question of our time structure may result from superficial and hardly considered preconceptions; for us form and structure are spatially determined experiences. Only in music are we familiar with a perception of temporal formation.[32] Strangely enough, experience has rarely been referred to the question of form or structure as such. One instance, however, may be found in medical anthropology (or what one is forced to regard as such), namely, the efforts of medical anthropologists to understand the nature of physical as well as psychical illness from the biography of a particular person and thus to become aware of the body as the concrete symbol of the time-bound life, representing as "time-gestalt" all experiences of existence in time.[33] Such pressing phenomenological tasks encounter almost insurmountable difficulties; we simply lack categories to describe with sufficient precision temporal relationships such as motion understood as form. We lack, as it were, musical forms of thought.

The problem is not new. Goethe's objection to the Newtonians first passionately raised the issue of the preformation and prejudgment of our forms of thought and our categories by the forms of perception to which they refer. It remained incomprehensible and unbearable to Goethe that the sunlike eye should have to submit itself to the dullest of all our senses, the sense of touch.[34] But his objections were little heeded in the sciences and remained largely ignored. Colors as "acts and sufferings of light"[35] have hardly been deemed worthy of inquiry and discussion, particularly because in optics serious investigations in the experienceable values of color have come to a standstill, as have, for example, investigations of the problem of rhythm as a qualification of periodic sequences.[36]

If optical categories remain uninvestigated, how can acoustic forms of thought be known or even imagined? Conceiving of form in the dimensions of time, conceiving of the configuration of measures and criteria within time, and similar possibilities of thought remain unclear to us. Determinations we can scrutinize are deduced from spatial conceptions or from images of things, usually at intervals. There is an almost poetic effect when concepts such as rhythm, dissonance, consonance, unison, modulation, counterpoint, accord, harmony, or fugue are used philosophically as characterizations of intellectual associations and processes or even as criteria for the composition of thinking.

In the final analysis the concepts of "system" and "systematics" qua method, which philosophy cannot forgo, imply categories borrowed from musical experience. A system could be conceived much more simply in terms of musical notions; the movement proceeds from the first sounding of the motif that develops the theme. The theme-forming motif emerges with germinal simplicity from its prenatal presence in silence in order to enter into the boundless multitude of its possibilities and be taken through all transformations and transpositions up to the end, up to the ultimate harmony, which may become perceivable only in pensive reharkening beyond the conclusion. We could then avoid the endless debates of the mostly evident "closedness" and the rarely substantiated "openness" of systems, because all systematics could then be understood only as preliminary tones, as prestructures, audible only in the perception of a fundamental silence as an articulation of stillness.[37]

III

These hints must suffice to explain the presuppositions on whose basis we can intelligently inquire about Marcel's contribution to the problem of systematics in general as well as about the systematic moments of his own thought in particular. The astonishing proximity of musical associations might provide first insights into the problem of the concept of system. Regardless of how it may appear to sworn systematicists, this problem does not arise solely from the rhapsodical, improvisatory thoughts of a philosopher like Marcel who at the same time is also a musician. The problem has existed for a long time; it always surfaces in the deepest reflections of modern philosophy on its own potential grounds as method. In order to provide such grounds, systematics was initially designed as an answer to the challenge of becoming scientific. In the course of its articulations, systematics had to give up its constructive ambitions in order to determine methodology as its constituting motif; systematics became the transcendental potentiality of methodology with Kant, and with Hegel systematics became the dialectical goal and eschatological mission of methodology. The idea of system itself became the center of methodological dynamics; as a motif it became a challenge.

Therefore systematics is an inevitable charge of responsible thinking. In any case it intends a system. From this it follows that a customary and cheap disrespect for systematics has succumbed to the rigid conceptions with which it reproaches the idea of system. Even relativism can be totalitarian, even a neutral tolerance is sometimes inspired by "a castrated illiberality,"[38] and indifference can be inflexible when it pretends to have a wide range of wisdom. Metaphysical dullness is usually not only boring but also dogmatic. The idea of system, on the contrary, can recreate and preserve openness, an openness that is aware of the limited possibilities of human thought and well prepared in honest and humble patience for foundering; this openness is not a postulate but a constituting motif and a continuing moment of the method. The idea of system enables us to transpose or to modulate these motifs and moments by transforming itself as a problem. And this is what happens in Marcel's thinking.

This transformation has been understood from the beginning as a task every new formation of concepts tries to comply with. A reflection on history has already been implied in this task, and time has from the start trickled down ceaselessly into the inner chambers of the question about the constitution and method of thinking, consequently allowing the problem itself to become fluid.[39] This does not discontinue the problem of systematics but rather transforms it, at the same time demonstrating that the system is existentially and concretely of ultimate relevance. The transformation modifies the methodical element of the basic question concerning existence as such and concerning the intelligibility of incarnate thinking in time. The question of the ultimate structure and form (*Gestalt*) that lends meaning to thinking touches on the question of the meaningful shape (*Sinngestalt*) of our life: of the body I am.

That Marcel has prepared the way for this question and has indeed helped it to break through determines his importance for the history of Western thought, whose credibility will hinge on this question. Non-Western thought blames our philosophies and sciences for their neglect of the body and hence criticizes us for thinking almost without relation to the world. We are said to think in abstract fragmentations of reality that are, although immensely productive in terms of technology, in the final analysis illusionary and inhuman. Precisely because Eastern thought has withdrawn confidence from these abstractions and fragmentations and because it has denied unconditional agreement with the civilization that has sprung from them, Marcel today is respected and honored by Chinese, Japanese, and Indian thinkers.

Marcel himself does not know how to explain this admiration. Just as he has unintentionally made central problems accessible in his apparently personal, almost private ways of questioning, so too and just as unwittingly he has been able—given the radical dubitability of Western thought—to do something more important, more difficult, and more decisive than just give answers; he has been able to reestablish confidence. Of course he could not reestablish confidence in the principles and results of Western thinking—that is and remains impossible—but he could establish confidence in the sincerity of his own questions. Hence according to the criteria Eastern religions have contributed to thought, it is registered in Kyoto as well as in Hong Kong, Jaipur, and Cairo that someone here asks real questions, or better, that someone asks in a manner befitting reality. They are asked not about human existence, as if it were somehow a possible object of questioning, but rather about *Existenz*. *Existenz* is only truthful to the degree that it experiences and understands itself as a question by making the liberation of truth possible and at the same time granting liberation by means of truth.[40]

IV

If we now refer to instances in Marcel's work that may be called systematic, we do so on the basis of the above interpretation of the history of the problem, though we will not refer explicitly to it at every instance. Nevertheless, with regard to form and content the above considerations have determined the following observations: We should no longer ask for exter-

nal, constructive relations but rather—corresponding to the observed transformation of the idea of system—we should ask for the constituting motifs
and intentions of this type of thinking. We should not ask for its logical
framework but rather for the rules of motion determining the dynamic
structures and functions of Marcel's procedure of questioning. A verification that bogs down in outmoded systematic conceptions will not do. It
needs rather to become reaware of the essential themes of this questioning
thought so that we might notice its consonances and thereby realize that in
their multiplicity they are in fact manifestations of a single motif. We must
perceive the distinguishing structure of Marcel's type of thinking and discover from which nucleus of insight it has unfolded, not by additions, but
by a natural, internal growth.

Surprisingly Marcel's general principles of thought can be clearly understood from the history of the problem of system. He has addressed
himself, probably unintentionally but constantly and strictly, to the matter
of thinking in our time; he has done so not only in his untiring disputes
with political, social, and cultural problems but even more so in his reflections on the grounds of his own questioning thinking as well as of human
thought in general. Marcel's significance for future philosophy will rest on
this point. His work will also remain significant with regard to the problem
of system; by his aversion to handed-down systematic temptations he has
driven the problem into its fundamental aporia,[41] out of which he has been
able to draw decisive consequences with less fear and more impartiality
than Heidegger. For Marcel this is a personal consequence that claims
validity not only for him but also for future thinking.

Thus what many observers perceive as a tantalizing enigma may perhaps be solved by recognizing that Marcel has taken in his work only one
single—though from the standpoint of method, decisive—step. He took
this step in full awareness of the problem. He justified his decision over
and over again, always in new and at times lucid analyses of the situation.
All further explanations point only to necessary consequences of this step
and offer mere comments on the original decision based on the reflection
of those consequences.

With regard to the problem of the idea of system, Marcel's philosophy
could be explained as the method of a breakthrough whose systematic principle gains shape in this breakthrough and transforms itself into the controlled dynamism of a motif that will then run through and determine all
further thinking. What bestows a patternlike unity on this thought is neither
an idea nor a sublime supreme motif but rather the metaproblematic concreteness of physical existence itself, removed from all reflection. What
was heralded by the history of the idea of system and what could hardly

ever remain hidden in its problematics has now been recognized as the origin of all potentialities of thinking and as the source of the entire problematics. Pascal calls it the most central enigma; Marcel calls it mystery—the mystery of our bodily existence in time. Like every genuine systematic principle, the ground of Marcel's thought transcends reflection and its inquiries. Marcel's thought is also completely "subjective"; essentially it cannot be objectified, made concrete, or integrated completely into the mysterious unity of the concrete. All differentiations of the objective from the subjective, of the exterior from the interior, and of the world from the ego only prove this as soon as they are questioned about their potentiality. Thus Marcel's thought not only satisfies the systematic disciplines as they have developed in the history of their question but also radicalizes them and allows them to become existential. It forbids once and for all the neglect of the question concerning a possible unity within the whole; it forbids the neglect of the most original of all the givens, namely, my body as the form of my presence, which first and foremost makes thinking possible.

I will now consider whether from this premise one can question and think systematically in a meaningful manner. Is Marcel's rejection of systematics correct after all? We have seen that the very idea of system involves the attempt to abstract meaning, given that the organic pattern and the structure of knowledge are intellectually conceived in full independence and separation from the analogue, according to which the system has tacitly been devised by the organic structure of my being.[42] But philosophically it seems more meaningful not to consider this abstraction essential for systematic thinking. Otherwise the idea of system has to be charged with fraud and self-deception, since it is undoubtedly concerned with regaining the original agreement *in concreto*. And Marcel's thinking complies exactly with this final intention of the idea of system. It does so precisely in that breakthrough where the idea of system is transformed from its roots; hence the idea of system must be investigated in a different way as something else.

The decisive methodical breakthrough in Marcel's thinking takes place in the second reflection, by which all elements of a possible systematics are abolished and brought into suspension.[43] This occurs by questioning the origin of the possibility of inquiry; it asks for the evidently hidden center from which that infinite process of analytic division, disentanglement, and dissolution is prompted and sustained, a process Marcel observed previously in the usual first reflection. One so easily overlooks the consequences of this question for the problematics as a whole because in the second reflection one is transferred seemingly unawares into the metaproblematic. In the meantime, anyone who pursues Marcel's train of thinking attentively will notice that it involves not a leap but rather a thoroughly considered, gradual, and methodically responsible crossover. In Marcel's thought questioning meets with nothing supportive, neither idea nor principle. It meets with nothing like an objectively given anchor to which the raft of certainty—a systematic structure of any kind—could be tied. Marcel's thinking is rather thrown back on something essentially incomprehensible, by which it makes itself possible and experiences itself as irredeemably incorporated into existence as physical being, perceivable only "on the ground of a sunken intuition"[44] absorbed in the concrete and itself entirely concrete, because it is undelimitable. What the idea of system has sought to accomplish—namely, to guarantee the unity and form of all knowledge under one idea or as the principle of a method—can no longer be investigated once the reversal of the inquiry eliminates the problematic. The idea of system then cannot be sought in the realm of the questionable. The point around which all our knowledge is focused can only be found in the metaproblematic. The idea of a whole, which overtly or covertly lies within and at the basis of every systematic thinking, every methodical question, and all meaningful knowledge now turns out to be the refraction of that mysterious unity we call *Existenz*. Its innermost dramatics simulate this unity; it is unharnessed and underway to the identity with itself,[45] which existence has received and given to itself as the impenetrable mystery of its self. Feuerbach's thoughts come to mind, namely, the system as "man projected onto the sky of thoughts." Everything depends on the certainty of not being alone at the moment of being thrown back on oneself. We can be sure that we have already been determined and called by a Thou. Feuerbach considers this simple fact the precondition of the discovery that I am. Marcel, in the immediate proximity of Martin Buber, became aware of this "absolute priority of the Thou," which reveals the ultimate and most concrete form of a non-ego and which can never be objectified completely or made an object.[46]

    This train of thought, as it develops in the *Journal métaphysique,* is generally misunderstood as the personal way, as the private fate of an individual thinker. Its expression in the form of a diary may have contributed to this misinterpretation. Yet this train of thought leads directly into the central problems of modern thinking, for all these problems have been articulated in the idea of system. Certainly we ask relentlessly about the meaning of asking questions as such, and certainly we ask relentlessly about the ground and potentiality of inquiring thought. Such relentless decisiveness, which led to Marcel's breakthrough, belongs to the personal fate of this individual but not to the question. The question arises all by itself; indeed it is the crucial systematic problem.

It almost seems as if Marcel had neither attempted nor accomplished anything other than to face this question in its ultimate radicalness and to prepare the way for future possibilities of answering it. What later turned out to be the not always plausible consequence of this approach hardly agrees with the trends of contemporary philosophizing, nor does it conform with the still valid demarcations of the realm and potentialities of statement in philosophical thinking.

In order not to get lost in a tiring critique of dogmatic prejudices, into which philosophical neutrality tends to indulge whenever confronted with religious questions, I state the following: the consequences of Marcel's train of thought cannot be disputed on the basis of the crucial reflection of the reflecting process; they can lead to explicit religious determinations of existence and of the responsible thinking reflecting on the experiences of being called by a mystery that is not speechless or mute. We should rather ask whether the philosophical thought in the breakthrough of the second reflection has not liberated itself from its reserve against religious experiences and even from its reserve against mystical insight, so that many of the problems now attributed to theology necessarily become questions of philosophical thinking. This becomes all the more probable when we recognize that a more exhaustive investigation of Marcel's work, particularly of his later writings, could easily reveal that both Marcel's philosophically relevant questions and his authentic philosophical discoveries are in a certain way religiously determined. He carried on his work not under the artificial light of the laboratories of secularized thinking but rather under the open sky. Only philosophical naïveté could suspect Marcel of importing theological problems into philosophy or could fail to notice that all the concepts he takes from religious linguistic usage (because there are no others objectively relevant to the matter) are conceived and used in a strictly philosophical sense. This includes not only such terms as *mystery, holiness, incarnation,* and *resurrection* but above all *love, faith, hope,* and *sin.* Unlike Jaspers, Marcel does not evaluate these terms on the basis of a preconceived doctrine of theology, against whose misunderstanding (namely, the idea of revelation) philosophy must rebel in order to maintain the freedom of its art of deciphering transcendence.[47] Rather Marcel uses these terms methodically in his transposition to another way of questioning, which rests on nothing.[48]

The breakthrough has resulted as a methodical consequence without a goal, a tendency, or an intent. Marcel's thinking has constantly pursued this systematic approach; he has persistently followed this course by read-mitting religious motifs and categories to philosophy and by allowing them to acquire validity. In this context his thought has gained a unified struc-ture. Marcel's philosophy itself provides a proof of this interpretation. The nucleus from which the living organization of forms of knowledge germi-nated has remained concealed to Marcel's reflection for a long time. Only in retrospect can the structure be comprehended in a unified manner.

The breakthrough involved in the second reflection was only one pas-sageway, though certainly a decisive one, into the central question of a *philosophie concrète,* which Marcel initially identified as the mission of his thinking. The question was answered only in his reflections on bodily existence. In a peculiar retroaction, the inner necessity, the reversal of questioning in the second reflection, came unequivocally to light for the first time. Only then did it become noticeable that access to the concrete could only be gained through such a methodical reduction. The essential problem had been anticipated in the formal realm. It had to be compre-hended in advance in order to become discernible as a problem in which and through which the thought of the metaproblematic presence, the thought of the mystery, could be assured. For "my body" is both in one. It is open to investigation so far as it is subject to my control and so far as I can say, "I have a body"; it is not open to investigation and unavailable so far as I have to say in the same breath, "I am my body," if I do not want to remain disregarded and do not want to neglect what makes the first statement possible, what substantiates it, and what makes it meaningful.

This is obviously neither an idea nor a principle of systematics in the traditional sense. It is an experience that since Plato has seldom been ac-cessible to Western thought. It has always been considered an unreliable, enchanted, repressed, and subsequently forgotten approach. Yet this ex-perience is the embodiment of human existence in the world; it is the embodiment of all conceivable human reality. When thought becomes aware of its own roots in this experience, it returns home, so to speak, into the concreteness of incarnate existence; it becomes concrete, corpo-real, and existential.

The experience of incarnate presence (*être incarné*) has the same func-tion in Marcel's thinking as the idea, the form-providing principle, or the concept of the Hegelian mystique as the fulfillment of all dialectical me-diations and compensations (*Aufhebungen*), and the like in other systematic philosophies. All methodical directions and all pioneering differentiations in Marcel's work can indeed be derived from this theme, from what he calls thinking in process.[49] Such paired Marcellian concepts as problem and mystery, being and having, technology and metatechnology, and accessibility and inaccessibility are all determined and illuminated from this focal point. Furthermore Marcel's phenomenological investigations of anxiety and love, despair and hope, and betrayal and faithfulness are also determined by this focus. A renunciation is always found on one side, and a recognition of the singularly indisputable, reflexive, but inconceivable givenness of the body on the other. Even Marcel's discovery of the Thou and his concept of intersubjectivity result from and relate to the point where problem and mystery converge. Only as concrete existence, by which I am bodily encountered, does the Thou—or, more accurately stated, dost Thou—gain the untouchable dignity that can reveal or conceal itself to me, that I am capable of loving, and that confirms, answers, and determines me. Marcel's critical remarks about psychoanalysis, about all forms of analytical and technological intervention, and about the manipulation and restriction of human beings are easily explained by this basic thought. He is also hostile to every sort of propaganda and ideology that deprives human beings of their inherent dignity by neglecting or not properly recognizing it. Especially in his later work, which devotes itself in a seemingly incoherent manner to entirely diverse problems (involving political, social, sociocultural, and artistic questions as well as questions about philosophical anthropology), Marcel's central thought develops into a structure of grand multiplicity.

Marcel's thought thus looks like a musical structure in which the determinative theme is carried through multiple modulations and transformations on various levels and in manifold dimensions so that motif and structure become one in the principle of a method providing orderly movement. Marcel's autobiographical explanations and reflections also coincide with this interpretation; they are informative, though admittedly only to those acquainted with his works, as authentic piano scores of extensive compositions. They show how consistently and concretely this thinking has proceeded.

At the same time it is obvious how little Marcel's thought has achieved and how little it could achieve. Indeed Marcel has nothing to show that could compare with a system of the earlier kind, nothing that could serve as a vehicle for forms of knowledge gained or as a receptacle of a doctrine. He is without baggage not only as a human being but also as a philosopher. Surprisingly he is as vigilant and mobile as ever and is still ready to begin anew or go on a pilgrimage with the freedom of true poverty. Beyond any doubt he is a philosopher, but if this requires the possession of insight and knowledge, then he is a philosopher without a philosophy.

V

It would be an embarrassing compliment to say of an existentialist philosopher that he has pondered too much about *Existenz* but that he has not thought existentially. What I have tried to elucidate would be refuted if it were possible to respond to truly existential questions without catching sight of the one who does the asking. If this thought has truly succeeded in breaking through to the concrete and if it can be methodically and thematically understood on the basis of the concrete unity of problem and mystery in the bodily presence, in existence as body, and in its scope as well as its form, then it would not be astonishing if this thought process were corporeally to encounter the one who thinks this way. These closing remarks are directed not to the personality but rather to the matter under discussion, so far as person and statement can be differentiated.

A philosopher without a philosophy, a teacher without a doctrine, may be a paradoxical phenomenon in our day. Nevertheless as a form it is as old as wisdom itself, which is essentially direction and not knowledge. Wisdom does not wish to teach insight or pieces of knowledge; rather it wishes to assist in obtaining perception and insight by becoming critical, patient, and ironic while remaining encouraging, shocking, and taciturn with abundant kindness.

This principle has characterized the self-understanding of thinking people all along, not only as a tradition but also as a symbol of the discipline of selfless inquiry. Kant, for example, obliquely supports this principle when he explains that one can at best learn to philosophize but that one cannot learn philosophy. Hegel as medium and witness maintains an almost simple humility even in the excess of the visionary-speculative demand he claimed for the thought process. When philosophical speculation obtains its final glory, from which an extratemporal light appears to reflect, then it deprives and dispossesses those who recognize it, bear it, and suffer it.

The initiating master in all traditions of philosophy never instructed by reading; he primarily instructed through his life. Such a master appeared at the beginning of the Western history of wisdom in Socrates, who, according to Plato, found successors. Even the oral tradition of Israel, passed from mouth to mouth and from heart to heart, was discarded by Christianity or repressed by ritual and literal traditions. Western religion, and with it Western thinking, have separated from the other cultures. Despite their sublime achievements in theological and later in philosophical orthodoxies, they have lost the disciplines of the orthopraxis. By this Western thinkers not only have lost the sensitivity and many criteria of a possible understanding of people from other traditions but have thereby forfeited much of their credibility for other cultures and finally for our culture too.

Today the symbol of the "master" or *maître* is not even conceivable to us as an image. We do not know what initiation really means. Marcel has spoken in this context of the "decline of wisdom," after which the Western mind, unfortunately in bad shape, is confronted historically with other cultures; uncertain of its own truth, it attempts therefore to spread credibility by force. So our Western civilization with its tremendous scientific and technological power drives the other cultures to the brink of annihilation. Marcel was prepared to give a sober account of this perilous situation.

Earlier than others Marcel recognized that the possibilities of thinking opened up by this break with tradition have now evidently reached their final limits in Western thought. A comprehensible image of our world and the comprehensibility of reality have been scattered into a multiplicity of perspectives, for the methods were disjointed very early and have diverged into ever narrowing paths. The idea of system represents the necessary attempt to bring this process of diversification speculatively under control, to restore it to the sources of its potentiality, or at least to check it with abstractions. Yet the transformations of the idea of system show that this is impossible under the given presuppositions; instead of becoming the method's integration or its longed-for *facit,* systematics has become a principle, if not the transcendental motif of method itself. And however inspired or inspiring systematics may once have been as a structure or as a function, its criteria have succumbed to an increasing abstraction that has taken the breath of life from thinking persons, who now know only how to read masterfully and to live wretchedly.[50]

The question of the individual plunged systematic thinking into a crisis that shook the individual's foundations. This question has finally uncovered the genuine motif of the systematic problem: since Western thinking had lost the disciplines of practical confirmation, it had to try to prove the credibility of its truth from out of itself. It had to think its credibility rather than present it *in concreto.* Western metaphysics' powerful and forced attempt had to founder. Life cannot be replaced by arguments. The question has proved more powerful than all conceivable answers, and the unmitigable problem has overwhelmed the highest, most profound attempts to solve it.

In the end the problem was rejected. The precipitous unreliability that shattered Nietzsche's honesty finally swallowed and disintegrated the problem itself. Because the problem was limited to what could still respond— and even this only according to appearance and against better insight[51]—

thinking had to avoid more and more questions. For narrow and shaky certainties, thought seemed to surrender its last and only authentic virtue: the courage to question. What hope remains may still be found in the following words beyond all confidence: "The nearer we come to danger, the brighter the roads to salvation begin to shine and the more inquisitive we will become. For questioning is the piety of thinking."[52]

Thinking must break with the contradiction within itself. Marcel is one of the few to venture this liberation. More distinctly and more inevitably than the others and with a methodical strictness that directed his thought to pursue "systematic motifs," Marcel has led thought back to its original mission, that of guaranteeing that life agrees with truth. In his personal consistency a universal consistency begins to take shape, namely, the consistency of inquiring thinking, which once again breaks through to the concrete, to the one concrete question. We must discover and recognize it for ourselves if we wish to be truthful, for each of us is that concrete question.

We can now understand why Marcel is one of the few whom Asia's thinkers are willing to recognize. In this sense he is also fully entitled to consider himself a Socratic. His philosophy wishes only to make thinking persons into inquiring and pondering persons, because responsibility and humanity will spring only from inquiring thinking, in which truth is born and acquires life.

HANS A. FISCHER-BARNICOL

INSTITUTE OF INTERCULTURAL RESEARCH
HEIDELBERG
APRIL 1970

NOTES

1. On the development of the concept of system, see Otto Ritschl, *System und systematische Methode in der Geschichte des wissenschaftlichen Sprachgebrauchs und in der philosophischen Methodologie* (Bonn: Georgi, 1906); on the critical understanding of its transformations, see, among others, Heinrich Rombach, *Substanz, System, Struktur: Die Ontologie des Functionalismus und der philosophische Hintergrund der modernen Wissenschaft* (Freiburg and Munich: Alber, 1965). Like most constitutive concepts of modern thought, the concept of system arose from a theological need. This need became most acute in the era of nominalism, which implicitly requires compensation for the loss of dogmatic symbols with doctrinaire approaches and consequences. The theology of the Reformation had to attempt to

develop and understand the entire Christian doctrine anew from the so-called *scopus,* or comprehensive meaning, of the Biblical text, since it had to reduce the influence of dogmatic traditions on the Scripture. It thus had to outline and constitute a systematics with the aid of theological hermeneutics. The philosophy of the seventeenth century responded similarly to the inroads made by the natural sciences into the entire range of scholastic scientific methods. It attempted to understand, justify, and explain the sciences and their autonomous methods through one principle establishing their unity of intellectual analysis. It may be that in opposition to metaphysics and theology and in the transformation of these two basic disciplines into their result, philosophy and theology—on the basis of their own laws and so far as they understand and constitute themselves correctly—demand, set free, and confirm the sciences in their freedom. Without critically reflecting on the preliminary questions of its history, we cannot explain the concept of system as a problem. Thus historically speaking the concept of system has arisen in every case from conflicts between heterogeneous concepts of cognition. It remains a question as long as the tensions between theology and philosophy and between philosophy and science prevail in Western thought, and as long as theories of knowledge and science are dominated by the initially metaphysical or religious issues that generated the earlier conflicts.

2. "The more narrow-minded a system is, the more it will please the astute" (Novalis, *Das philosophische Werk,* vol. 2 of *Schriften,* ed. Paul Kluckhohn and Richard Samuel [Stuttgart: Kohlhammer, 1960], *Vermischte Bemerkungen* [Blüthenstaub], fragment 103, p. 412). Aphorism 6 of this collection characterizes Novalis's closeness to Maine de Biran and those French philosophers who follow him, including Marcel. Their critical reflections concerning "inner" experiences are anticipated to a large degree by Novalis when he says, "We will never be able to understand ourselves completely, but we will be able and are able to do much more than merely understand."

3. See F. W. Nietzsche, *Menschliches, Allzumenschliches,* vol. 1 of *Werke,* ed. Schlechta (Munich: Hanser, 1954), aphorism 31, p. 755: "In the desert of science. —Those resplendent mirages called 'philosophical systems' appear to the scientific person on his modest and tiresome wanderings, which must, often enough, be wanderings into the desert. They show, with the magical power of deception, the solution to all enigmas, and the freshest draught of the true water of life very close in the vicinity. . . . Those who have already frequently experienced these subjective consolations have become extremely discontented and have cursed the salty taste these appearances leave in the mouth, causing a raging thirst without getting even one step closer to the fountains."

4. Cf. Paul Tillich, *Systematic Theology,* 2 vols. (Chicago: University of Chicago Press, 1967), 2:24.

5. With the self-irony peculiar to him, Marcel repeatedly asks himself whether he is incapable of systematic thought or reluctant to think systematically. See the introduction to *Du refus à l'invocation,* which states his critical problem. He cannot keep from yearning for the systematic, but he nevertheless remains distrustful of the outline of any systematics whatever. This distrust predetermines the course of the argument, but it could be overcome. As a consequence of this article I assisted Marcel in writing a "systematic" résumé of his philosophy. The 800-page manuscript, however, developed into a new, far-reaching inquiry under the title "Leib

und Tod—Metamorphosen von Anwesenheit'' (''Body and Death—Metamorphoses of Presence'')—Marcel's last paper, carefully scrutinized and finished in April 1973.

6. See Nietzsche's objection in *The Twilight of the Idols,* trans. R. J. Hollingdale (Baltimore: Penguin, 1968), aphorism 26: ''I distrust all systematizers and avoid them. The will to a system shows a lack of honesty.'' Nietzsche makes his point by forecasting the rise of nihilism. For him nihilism inevitably emerges in any thinking that seeks to avoid nihilism by plunging itself into a system whose regularity devitalizes life and truth by rendering both worthless. Marcel's counterquestion arises precisely at this point. The answer leads toward conversion. The philosophical relevance of this concrete decision cannot be overestimated; as a phenomenon it has to be understood as an unconditional decision toward the concrete. Hence conversion explains Marcel's religious path toward philosophy rather well. During a personal conversation with me, Marcel characterized the ''method'' of conversion by declaring, ''Conversion is no singular event, but rather a way of life.'' With the meaning of this statement in mind, one could summarize Marcel's problem of a systematics in the following question: ''Into which final unity do all principles of life and thought convert or converge?''

7. See, for example, Marcel's ''Existence et objectivité'' (1924), first published in *Revue de métaphysique et de morale* (April–May 1925), and later in the appendix to *Journal métaphysique* (Paris: Gallimard, 1927), pp. 309–29, which posed the question for the first time. Also see his *Metaphysical Journal* (January 1938), in *Presence and Immortality,* trans. Michael A. Machado, revised by Henry J. Koren (Pittsburgh: Duquesne University Press, 1967); his ''Mon Propos fondamental'' (written in 1937), in *Présence et immortalité* (Paris: Flammarion, 1959); and his introductory first, second, third, fifth, twelfth, and thirteenth chapters of the Gifford Lectures, published as *Le Mystère de l'être,* 2 vols. (Paris: Aubier, 1951), and as *The Mystery of Being,* trans. G. S. Fraser and René Hague (Chicago: Henry Regnery, 1960). Here we find the dominating theme of *Du refus à l'invocation* (Paris: Gallimard, 1940) translated as *Creative Fidelity* by Robert Rosthal (New York: Noonday Press, 1964), and it still determines such later discussions as ''L'Etre devant la pensée interrogative'' (''The Questioning of Being''), Marcel's lecture of 25 January 1958 to the Société française de philosophie and the ensuing discussion by members of that organization, as published in chapter 4 of *Pour une sagesse tragique et son au-delà* (Paris: Plon, 1968), translated by Stephen Jolin and Peter McCormick as *Tragic Wisdom and Beyond,* Northwestern University Studies in Phenomenology and Existential Philosophy (Evanston, Ill.: Northwestern University Press, 1973), pp. 45–75. The question is also implicitly asked in *Position et approches concrètes du mystère ontologique,* the highly important appendix to *Le Monde cassé* (Paris: Desclée de Brouwer, 1933).

To refer to Marcel's work in the above fashion is unsatisfactory, but to quote all available bibliographical references is beyond the scope of this discussion. With reference to the central problem of the ontology of the body, I will summarize the systematic principles of Marcel's thought and classify their motifs, but I will forgo referring to the numerous references whose interpretation cannot be given in this context.

8. Cf. Marie Magdeleine Davy, *Un Philosophe itinérant: Gabriel Marcel* (Paris: Flammarion, 1959), for the authorized exposition of this problem. Marcel has compared the relation between his theater and his philosophy with the relation

he sees between the Greek islands and the mainland; for him life arises from the islands.

9. Immanuel Kant, *Critique of Pure Reason,* trans. Norman Kemp Smith (London: Macmillan, 1933), B 860–67. That I investigate Marcel's thought here from Kant's point of view and below from Hegel's seems to impose a strange criterion. Nevertheless a reciprocal illumination of what is called system begins to emerge. When interpreting existential or other "modern" problems, we should at last give up the absurdity of calling them new. Just as existential questions constantly raise essential questions, so essentialist questions have always been existentially relevant. To this extent it is possible not only to interpret Aquinas from Kant's point of view, as Maréchal has shown, but also to understand philosophical modernity better, more thoroughly, and more consistently from the prehistory of the questions it poses. Heidegger's private philosophical-historical interpretations assure him of this understanding. With regard to Marcel and to Buber as well, such an interpretation is demanded.

10. Ibid., B 860.

11. Ibid., B 862. It is self-evident that the frame of inquiry changes in turning away from idealism. Marcel made this change together with Heidegger and close to Rosenzweig, Rosenstock-Huessy, Buber, Scheler, and Tillich.

12. Ibid., B 862.

13. Ibid., B 866.

14. Ibid., B 860.

15. Ibid., B 861.

16. Ibid., B 865. It should be mentioned here that Kant's metaphor of the organism as an animal body can be understood on the basis of a fundamental motif of his time. That it is taken up here is particularly significant.

17. Ibid., B 864. See also B 868–69 for a clearer understanding of the fundamental revolt against the principal distinction between "pure" and "empirical" philosophy, a revolt that surfaces in the early writings of Husserl. Kant's *Opus Posthumum* is informative on this point. It becomes apparent that Kant was aware of the insoluble aporia into which his approach was bound to lead him, especially into problems of religion.

18. See, among others, "On Scientific Knowledge in General," in the preface to Hegel's *Phenomenology of Mind,* 2d ed., trans. J. B. Baillie, Muirhead Library of Philosophy (London: Allen & Unwin, 1949). The essay sets science as the goal of philosophy (p. 73), and it shows clearly what is at stake (p. 85): "Knowledge is only real and can only be set forth fully in the form of science, in the form of system. . . . The really positive working out of the beginning . . . may therefore be regarded as a refutation of what constitutes the basis of the system; but more correctly it should be looked at as a demonstration that the *basis* or the principle of the system is in point of fact merely its *beginning*. That the truth is only realised in the form of system, that substance is essentially subject," allows the conclusion that "the Absolute as Spirit (*Geist*) [is] the grandest conception of all," or the essence, the being as such.

19. G. W. F. Hegel, *The Science of Logic,* trans. A. V. Miller, Muirhead Library of Philosophy (London: Allen & Unwin, 1969; reprint ed., New York: Humanities Press, 1976), p. 837. All italics are Hegel's.

20. Ibid, p. 838. It could only be shown *in extenso* that Kierkegaard's critique of this concept of system succumbs to the magic of dialectical opposition, which

ends up by transforming contradiction into contrast. But what Kierkegaard interpreted as a *philosophie concrète* readily opposes Hegel; see, for example, Marcel's foreword to *Les Hommes contre l'humain* (Paris: La Colombe, 1951). Kierkegaard's theological intention, which blames Hegel for not being in perfect agreement with Christian belief (an argument comparable with objections made against Hegel by Schelling or Baader), causes Marcel's hesitation and reluctance. His renunciation of Hegel resulted from other motives. Marcel thinks less idealistically than Kierkegaard. He remarks like Theodor W. Adorno, in *Kierkegaard: Konstruktion des Ästhetischen* (Frankfurt: Suhrkamp Verlag, 1962), p. 156, that Kierkegaard's attempt to overcome the antinomies of existence in thought systematically or to justify them as truth has exhausted itself in an existential "realism without reality *(Wirklichkeit)*." Kierkegaard does not reach the concretion in the incarnated presence in the world (see Heidegger's *Dasein* as *In-der-Welt-Sein*); he designs a paradoxical system of existence whose interior is purely spiritual, an internal sphere without external connections, a soul without body. This spiritual being moves dialectically through its different constitutions in aesthetic and ethical relations from leap to leap toward its religious status without being liberated from the "constellations" of this spherical system except by its abolition in death, in the abolition of the concrete bodily existence as a problem and as a mystery. Only death redeems from the "sickness toward death" by releasing the subjectivity from its idealistic and spiritual solipsism. Hegel attempted to escape this isolation and wanted to investigate the concrete. The meaning of existence reveals itself—following Kierkegaard—only in the abyss of the paradox, and this becomes just as "systematically" almighty in Kierkegaard's thinking as the dialectical mediation is in Hegel's. Truth breaks through only in exceptional stages, prior to the crucial turn into ethical decisiveness in aesthetic experiences and beyond the leap that leaves autonomy behind in the religious status—here as illusion, there as hope. Marcel could agree with this transposition of existence only hesitantly, because he discovered the fundamental ontological problem precisely in this ethical stage of passage. For Kierkegaard this problem remained incomprehensible and almost irrelevant, if indeed his aversion to metaphysics allowed him to be aware of it at all. Yet in order to avoid the misunderstandings that may result from my reinterpretation of Marcel's thought in the light of Kierkegaard's, we have to be aware that the two philosophers formulated the ontological problem in different ways. Marcel tied it down in the "intersubjective," although he was not fully happy with this term, since it can be misunderstood, for example, by psychologically disregarding the manifoldness of the dimensions of encounter and being together with others. In this context Marcel used the English expression "being entangled with," or in German the *Einbezogensein* ("being universally related to"). His fundamental terms—*love, faith, creative fidelity, confidence* (or "being disposable, i.e. to place myself at the disposal of the other") and so on—are derived from the concreteness of experience regained in second reflection, not from a "system of existence" with idealistically conceived stages. In this connection Marcel's critique of Heidegger's formula *Dasein zum Tode* ("presence-toward-death") is characteristic; Heidegger's phrase, like Kierkegaard's reflection, refers to one's own death, whereas Marcel's thinking was primarily concerned with the death of a beloved person. See, for instance, the famous sentence he often quoted: "I love you—that means: you shall never die."

21. Kant, *Critique of Pure Reason*, B 866.
22. Ibid., B 866.

23. The theory of thought and the anthropology of the Indian tradition are significant in this context, for *manas* is understood as a perceiving organ and as a sixth sense. See "Chândogya Upanishad VI," in *One Hundred and Eight Upanishads,* 4th ed., W. L. Shâstri Panśîkar (Bombay: Pândurang Jâwjî, 1932); and *Yoga-Philosophy of Patañjali,* with commentaries of Vyâsa in original Sanskrit, ed. Swâmi Hariharânanda Âranya, trans. P. N. Mukerji (Calcutta: University of Calcutta, 1963).

24. Kierkegaard's objection to this saving-grace claim of philosophy has retained its lasting significance in the tendencies of contemporary theology to allow Christ to become a "mediating" principle. Marcel's objection by contrast should be interpreted from Franz Rosenzweig's perspective. Marcel shares Kierkegaard's concentration on the existence of the individual, whom he tries to consider in terms of drama and dialogue rather than reflection and dialectics. He shares Hegel's confidence in not being forsaken by God, a confidence arising from the process of thought. One might also see Marcel's Catholicism, in its opposition to Protestant rigorism, as a sign that he—just like Hegel and Buber—is *no* bachelor in Kierkegaard's sense. (See *Either-Or,* trans. David F. Swenson and Lillian M. Swenson, with revisions by Howard A. Johnson [Princeton: Princeton University Press, 1971], p. 347).

25. In the same sense Marcel thinks that "professional philosophers are most suspicious" (observation in the unpublished manuscript "Leib und Tod").

26. See Kant, *Critique of Pure Reason,* B 861: *articulatio* means "formation" (of a body); *coacervatio* means "accumulation, piling up"; *apposition* is similar in meaning to the English word *addition.*

27. See Blaise Pascal, *Thoughts, Letters, Opuscules,* trans. O. Wight (Boston: Houghton, Osgood, 1878), p. 158.

28. Ibid., fragment 72 (following the edition by Léon Brunschvicg). "The manner in which a spirit belongs to a body cannot be understood by man, but it is nevertheless a typical characteristic of man" (Augustine, *De civitate Dei* 11. 10).

29. The term *bodily presence* runs as a motif throughout Marcel's work; note the title *Presence and Immortality.*

30. Marcel has spoken about the *évocation* of thinking by the concrete situation in which we become awake. Philosophy answers not only other philosophers, and a thinking that is not stigmatized by reality, wounded by "the bite of the concrete," cannot be called philosophy. Consequently Marcel astonished the members of an international inquiry on theoretical guidelines for the reform of universities with the statement that the history of philosophy in the conventional sense is as abstract as it is unreal. In reality there is only the concrete historical event with which everybody is faced; philosophers in particular have to accept this challenge, although their answers are often distorted and concealed by their "systems."

31. See Hegel, *Phenomenology of Mind,* p. 97; see also *The Science of Logic,* pp. 36–39, for example: "The content is moving itself, driven by its own dialectics" (my translation). Concerning Hegel's gnosticism, see Eric Voegelin, *Science, Politics, and Gnosticism* (Chicago: Henry Regnery Co., Gateway, 1968).

32. Notice the absence of reflections on music in practically all outlines of aesthetics, even in works by Cassirer and Hans U. von Balthasar's *Theologische Ästhetik: 'Herrlichkeit'* (Einsiedeln: Benziger, 1961). Kierkegaard recognized the problem, as did Karl Barth in his interpretations of Mozart as well as in conversations centered on the "acoustic directive of existential awareness." See also Rudolf

Bultmann and, in his profound ontology of the listener of the word, Karl Rahner's *Hörer des Wortes: Zur Grundlegung einer Religionsphilosophie* (Munich: Kösel-Pustet, 1941).

33. See, among others, Victor Weizsäcker, *Körpergeschehen und Neurose* (Stuttgart: Klett, 1947); *Der kranke Mensch* (Stuttgart: Koehler, 1951); *Pathosophie* (Göttingen: Vandenhoeck & Ruprecht, 1956); Eric D. Wittkower and R. A. Cleghorn, eds., *Recent Developments in Psychosomatic Medicine* (Philadelphia: Lippincott, 1954).

34. "Instead of looking up toward an ideal meaning in which all relations become unified, we transform the seen into the touched, so that the keenest of the senses is reduced to the dullest and thus becomes more conceivable to us" (Johann W. von Goethe, *Zur Farbenlehre, historischer Teil, Naturwiss: Schriften II*, Jubiläums-Ausgabe, ed. Eduard von der Hellen, 40 vols. [Stuttgart and Berlin: Cotta, 1902–1912], 40:133–34).

35. The scientific relevance of this idea will not be discussed here; as a reference to the metaphysics of light the idea comes close to the Marcellian proposition that *being* must constantly be able to be replaced by *light* in a relevant ontology. Marcel doubts whether this is possible with Heidegger, as he states in the unpublished "Leib und Tod" (see n. 5 above).

36. Colors are problematic. From a purely spectral point of view they can be described by different frequencies, but if we consider the multiple interactions or mixtures of frequencies, as in gray and black, they can be described as perception. Frequencies are the result of a quantification. Colors in Goethe's sense are intensive experiences of qualities produced, for example, by the superposition of various frequencies on different amplitudes and phases.

37. Compare the musical terms and criteria of all Chinese metaphysics and categories in cosmology, law and political order, and diagnoses and therapies; see Marcel Granet, *La Pensée chinoise* (Paris: Renaissance du Livre, 1934).

38. Friedrich von Schlegel, *Kritische Schriften* (Munich: C. Hanser, 1964), Athenäums-Fragmente 64, p. 32: "An attitude of general moderation is inspired by a castrated illiberality."

39. See, for example, the history of hermeneutics and its ontological problems in Hans Georg Gadamer, *Wahrheit und Methode*, 3d ed. (Tübingen: Mohr, 1972).

40. The reversal of the Biblical statement of truth as that which makes us free is a determinative thought of the leading Japanese philosopher Keiji Nishitani. The thought corresponds to the other approach of Asiatic doctrines of knowledge. If harm results from the *avidyā*, from not-knowing (or not-willing), then truth as being-true becomes possible only in the abolition of the shackles that determine existence in time; being-true then comes to a *moksa*, to a liberation. Marcel's aversion to untruthful "truths," and to knowledge about the dissolution of truth that is not sustained as a living entity, relates Marcel to Buddhist philosophies. In this context his concept of a "sin committed in thought" becomes comprehensible.

41. The term *aporia* is not as usual in English as in other philosophical languages, but it is crucial to an understanding of the critical reflections on contradictory (and at the same time complementary) structures of thought by such philosophers as Kant, Hegel, Kierkegaard, the neo-Kantians, and Nicolai Hartmann as well as the phenomenologists and ontologists after Husserl. Such unsolvable problems "without bridges" or "ways out" (*poros* means "ford") have to be transposed from each level to another level of reflection. In this respect aporetics

as a discipline ultimately coincides with the critique of presuppositions in "axiomatics."

42. See Gabriel Marcel, *Etre et avoir* (Paris: Aubier, 1935); *Being and Having*, trans. Katharine Farrer (Boston: Beacon Press, 1951). The continuation of the *Metaphysical Journal* directs this problem toward a general understanding of reality. The entry of 10 November 1928 explicitly ascertains, with regard to the idea of system (and thus also with regard to the system), that the idea exists only insofar "as it participates in the nature of my body, in other words, insofar as it is not conceived as an object." This entry points to the beginnings of the phenomenology of having, which concerns palpable and objectifiable reality as such. This reality always confronts us anthropomorphically, and it also confronts us covertly as somatic. Marcel says that the world should be understood not only as the "outermost shell of my bodily being" but as my body itself (unpublished symposium on the "Ontologie der Leiberfahrungen," held at Heidelberg in 1967).

43. This central step is taken everywhere in Marcel's thought. Endless examples could be cited (see n. 7 above), since this subquestioning of the question also determines the train of thought where it is not explicitly elaborated or explained. Marcel's discovery of the second reflection might be viewed as his most important methodological discovery, but it seems even more important to recognize it as a profound reversal of philosophical thought and to investigate its implications for all philosophy, from the simplest critical reversal to a meditative change of the constitution of thinking.

44. This formulation is not translatable into English; the German term *Versunkenheit* characterizes the status of consciousness in the empty and illuminated state of "meditation" or "contemplation" without any disturbance from the outside world. In approximately the same sense Marcel uses the French term *recueillement*, as we have shown in "Leib und Tod" (see n. 5 above).

45. Marcel's *Homo Viator* (Paris: Aubier, 1944), among many other works, shows how little such a thought can be abstracted in the terms of a theory of knowledge or idealism: "This [the authentic being-present, which I desire] is the part of creation that is in me; it is the gift to participate in the universal drama entrusted to me from all eternity" (p. 182; translation by the translators of this contribution). I hesitate to characterize the meaning of this declaration as ontological. It is uncertain how concrete, how real, how bodily, and how worldly these statements are meant to be. Thus the opposition between subjectivity and objectivity is basically transcended, as in all central "concepts" since time immemorial, for example, in *Tao, Te,* and *Li* of the Chinese tradition; in *sāt, cittā,* and *samādhi* of the Indian; and in the Greek λόγος and νοῦς and the ἐνέργεια of Aristotle. What thought transfers to expression can be "instrumentalized" by reflection in a twofold manner, either in quasi-subjective or in quasi-objective statements that are as interchangeable as the theorems of alchemy. Ultimately they can only be understood as symbolizations; see also *Sein* or *Seyn* in Heidegger's works.

46. The always astonishing proximity of and distance between Marcel and Buber can be explained only with difficulty. See Marcel's contribution and Buber's reply in Paul A. Schilpp and M. Friedman, ed., *The Philosophy of Martin Buber*, The Library of Living Philosophers (La Salle, Ill.: Open Court, 1963). Religious and confessional impressions are certainly not essential to Marcel's thought, and genuinely Jewish traits are apparent in his philosophy. But when Paul Tillich (in a conversation) expresses the suspicion that Buber's concept of "I and Thou" gen-

eralizes a little bit the concrete suchness of human existence in being male or female, a child or a very old person, he has perhaps shown a way to a correct differentiation. Marcel the dramatist was much more sensible of the scenic situation and of the predominance of the "in between"; in this respect Buber stood closer to Kierkegaard than to Marcel.

47. See Karl Jaspers, *Philosophical Faith and Revelation*, trans. E. B. Ashton (New York: Harper & Row, 1967), especially pp. 325–29, for his reaction to Karl Barth's critique, a critique that I do not think applies to Marcel at all.

48. That the theological area, even in its negations, remains neglected in the thought of Marcel (as opposed to Bloch, Jaspers, Merleau-Ponty, and Ricoeur) becomes evident when one asks what sort of theology could respond to Marcel's manner of inquiry. Starting with the concrete, that is, with experience, Marcel's means of inquiry cannot trust the specific "logic" of previous theologies. His attempt at a philosophical approach to the mystery of being returns to the original form of theology, the mystical one of pure negation, the *theologia negativa,* and phenomenologically exhibits the negation of signs that do not show themselves and cannot be pointed out. Marcel's great friend Henri de Lubac understood this problem. It is also informative that Marcel's thoughts have not yet been applied to theology, as have Heidegger's thoughts at the expense of the preliminary and basic questions from which they have arisen. See, for example, Karl Rahner's application of Heidegger's concept of the "existential" as a category in the formulation of a so-called supernatural existential situation.

49. The term *thinking in process*—in German, *denkendes Denken* or simply *Denken* (in Heidegger's sense), in contrast to *Nach-denken* (as a type of reflective consideration, or rethinking)—follows the French *pensée pensée* rather than *pensée pensante,* which Marcel borrowed from Maurice Blondel. Thinking in process tries to characterize an *Existenzial* and the continuous movement of existence in spontaneous thinking, in contrast to a reflection that in a sense is limping and always looking behind. By *pensée pensée* one can enter the realm of meditation open to mystery; with *pensée pensante* one remains in the reflexive and problematic sphere that adheres to the reflecting ego (the *cogito*)—here I think; there I have thoughts. This kind of thinking in process has always existed in time, in brokenness, in harm, and in the calamity of religions. It has always been aware of the "sin in thought" denied as a possibility at the beginning of the history of Western thought. See Nietzsche's ecstatic entry of August 1881, which he felt expressed his highest intuition regarding this point: "in Sils-Maria, 6000 feet above the sea, and much higher above all human things!" The entry declares that both are missions under the seal of the symbolic experience of an "eternal return": "1. The ingestion [*Einverleibung*] of the basic errors. 2. The ingestion of the passions. 3. The ingestion of knowledge and of the renouncing knowledge (passion of knowledge). . . . 4. The guiltless. The individual as experiment. Making life easier, humiliation, weakening transition. 5. The new force of gravity. The eternal return of the same. Infinite importance of our knowledge, errors, habits and ways of life preparing for the future. . . . We teach the doctrine, it is our strongest means to ingest it into us." See Ryogi Okochi, *Nietzsches 'Amor fati' im Lichte von Karma des Buddhismus,* vol. 1 of *Nietzsche Studien* (Berlin: de Gruyter, 1972), secs. 36–94.

50. Kierkegaard's criticism of Hegel for building a cathedral and living next door in a hovel comprehends only an external aspect of the tragedy of the system-

atic effort and its temptations. See also Matthew 17:4 and Mark 9:5, which reveal the actual problem in the tradition of Israel.

51. See Ludwig Wittgenstein, *Tractatus logico-philosophicus* (London: Kegan Paul, Trench, Trubner and Co., 1922). Beyond all difficulties of interpretation relating to these concentrated thoughts, Wittgenstein's successors only grudgingly acknowledge that even if 6.432 is true, 6.44 and 6.45 definitely enable 6.5 and the following sections to become intelligible, especially 6.522, which avoids contradicting 5.43 only when 6.4321 is in all seriousness taken for what it manifests. What it manifests is the "mystical," which, along with "facts," belongs to the problem but not to the solution, a point no mystic would wish to dispute.

52. Martin Heidegger, "Die Frage nach der Technik," in *Die Künste im technischen Zeitalter* (Munich: R. Oldenbourg, 1954), pp. 70–108.

Systematic Motifs in the Thought
of Gabriel Marcel:
Toward a Philosophical Theory
of Composition

REPLY TO HANS A. FISCHER-BARNICOL

Mr. Fischer-Barnicol is quite right, of course, in emphasizing the aversion I have always felt toward ideologies. I surmise that this is an almost basic characteristic of my thinking, but I must add that this aversion became explicit, or, more precisely, found its real basis, at a relatively late date, that is, after the Second World War, when I wrote a critique of the spirit of abstraction. There is no ideology in existence that does not imply an excessive emphasis on certain abstract notions at the expense either of the context or of other notions that could act as compensating factors.

One might inquire into the origin of this hostility, of this aversion, and I confess I find it rather difficult to reply. I think my father's influence must have been quite effective in this regard, since my father was the opposite of a political-party man. His political positions were clear, but they were not cut and dried. My father was indeed a moderate in the sense that used to be given to the word but that today is no longer used in the political sphere. In one sense I could say I have always remained a moderate, although today I probably understand much better what certain passions, even political ones, can be like.

Finding myself classified by Tillich as a Thomist philosopher really made me laugh, since at no time in my life have I ever been in the least drawn to that great thinker. Only on reflection was I able to recognize that on certain points I was not as far removed from him as I thought.

What I would like to discuss here is whether or not I have been thinking theologically. I recall with amusement that my friend Father Meydieu, a

Translated from the French by Susan Gruenheck.

Dominican, claimed that I was more nearly a theologian than a philosopher. This remark has always given me something to think about, but the truth is I do not really know what it is to think theologically. In any case I think that one mode of theological thought is absolutely finished today and that theology must pursue other approaches. I have no idea whether I have done so. But I do know that my friend Father Sigfried Foeldz, who is presently living in Dresden, told me that his theological thought owed a great deal and would continue to owe even more to his study of my works. As I attempt to clarify these things, it seems to me that in truth I am more likely to stimulate theologians or to offer them food for thought than to think as a theologian myself. The distinction here would probably merit further examination.

Taking Kant as his particular example, Fischer-Barnicol is indeed correct in suggesting that I may have taken the word *system* in too narrow a sense and that it is after all essential for philosophers to think their thoughts in a connected fashion. It is equally certain that I have always been concerned with this connection. Yet what I have found unacceptable is the idea of having a system (and I would emphasize the word *having*), of being as it were the possessor or the manager of a system I would call "mine"—a system that could be compared to a display of goods at a charity sale, behind which I would stand, no doubt wearing a label so that there could be no mistaking who I was.

I find this sort of possessive pretension entirely incompatible with sound philosophical thinking, and basically it was against this that I reacted. I think it would be a great mistake if one were to infer that I underestimate what I mentioned a moment ago, namely, the connection that must indeed exist among thoughts. These thoughts must not be disconnected; disconnection cannot satisfy the mind.* What was fundamentally at work in my mind was a certain fear in the presence of the excesses of the systematizing spirit as it developed, particularly among the post-Kantians. At first they attracted my admiration, but later I felt they went much too far and thus ran the risk of overlooking certain important aspects of reality.

It is in this sense moreover that I could say my dramatic works appeared almost always under the heading of "yes-but." But it is precisely this "yes-but" that is the negation of the one-sidedly systematic, where the latter is excessive and presents itself basically as intellectual imperialism. Essentially it is intellectual imperialism that I have always abhorred.

G.M.

---

*The words *disconnected* and *disconnection* appear in English in the original French manuscript.—Trans.

17

Robert Lechner

MARCEL AS RADICAL EMPIRICIST

THE phrase "radical empiricist" recalls, of course, William James.
Although what is proposed is not a specific consideration of James
and Marcel together, any consideration of Marcel within the perspectives
of radical empiricism will be a reading of Marcel at least against a background of this tradition of American philosophy. And although the influence on Marcel of American philosophers such as W. E. Hocking and
Josiah Royce is well enough known, not much has been made of it. This
brings to mind one of the tenets of pragmatism: any success that induces
us to settle down is a failure, and any failure that teaches us how to take
up new adventures more wisely and with greater sensitivity is a success.
Marcel would surely recognize here his world of the pilgrim-thinker.

Marcel himself has told us how much the American philosopher Henry
Bugbee influenced his philosophy, especially his philosophy of experience.
He mentions this in his introductory preface to Bugbee's remarkable philosophical journal, *The Inward Morning,* especially noting the distinction
Bugbee makes there between empiricism and experiential philosophy.[1] Although this preface dates from twenty-five years ago, Marcel's remarks
there were not incidental. Ten years later he recalled in an interview with
Paul Ricoeur the distinction between "empirical thought" and "experiential thought," and he said that he felt the terms he had learned from Bugbee were just what he always had in mind when he spoke of fidelity and
other experiences central to his thinking.[2] Marcel wrote: "After weighing
my words carefully, I do not hesitate to say that my encounter with the
thought and personality of Henry Bugbee will prove to have been a noteworthy event in my life. This encounter is reminiscent of my discovery
more than forty years ago of the major works of another American, W. E.
Hocking."[3] There is a bit of irony in Marcel's discovering in an American
thinker a fellow philosopher to whom he feels close because of his mode

of philosophizing, for America is the place where depersonalizing demo-
cratic processes and technology, both sources of horror for Marcel, hold
sway. But beyond the irony, it is a tribute to Marcel's openness to reality
to have made a point of this again and again. He once pointed this out
with a metaphor he may have learned from Bugbee himself, since it is
more reminiscent of the frontier wilderness of Bugbee's America than the
salons of Marcel's Paris. In speaking of people who have been influenced
by his philosophy, Marcel singled out Bugbee as the one he could read
without feeling that he was swallowing something he had already digested.[4]

To begin this paper I will look at some of the things Marcel has said
about what I will call radical empiricism or radical experience. Then I will
make a short inventory of some elements of Marcel's philosophy that relate
it to classical empirical attitudes, or what I would call "the spirit of Empiricism," a phrase Marcel should not look down his nose at, considering
his own coining of the phrase "the spirit of abstraction." Finally I will
consider two instances of this experiential mode in Marcel's philosophy:
first what he has to say about my-body-as-mine and my-body-as-myself,
his theme of incarnation, or what I would call "my meeting with existence," and second what he has to say about the experience of transcendence, what he calls "second reflection" and what I would call "my meeting with being."

I should remark on, if not explain, the use of the word *empiricism* to
describe Marcel's thought, for the word is clearly enlarged and extended
in reference to Marcel. The question is whether it is stretched so far that it
is no longer in touch with the common usage and the traditional meaning
of the term in the history of philosophy. I think not. Surely certain elements of empiricism relate to Marcel's thought, and not all philosophers
of experience restrict the word *empirical* to the time-space dimension of
experience in the narrow sense. The use here of *radical* is of course a bow
in the direction of William James's feeling that his fellow empiricists were
not radical enough. In this sense Marcel is an empiricist in a more radical
way than usual. He is not a philosopher of experience, if that expression
means that all we experience is experience itself. Experience for Marcel
reveals something other than experience. Experience is itself transcendent—or intentional, if you will—not only horizontally but also vertically,
especially for Marcel.

Classical empiricism is like a spectrum along which we can locate various philosophers. If we wanted to specify the "spirit of empiricism," we
would find that it draws on pragmatism, empiricism, and experiential phi-

losophy. The following are some of the things that qualify Marcel for at
least this "spirit of empiricism."

1. A feel for the priority of sense experience, regardless of how it is
   eventually understood, how Marcel handles or analyzes it, or what
   it may lead to. If Marcel's philosophy is anything, it is an incarnational thought.
2. The notion of "receiving" as an essential element of sense experience and of all experience. I am not able to explain all that goes on
   in my experience in terms of my own initiative or in terms of myself as the source.
3. A sense of immediacy in primordial experience. Marcel's sense
   here is against mediational idealistic thought and the whole spectator world.
4. A deep trust in one's own experience.
5. The belief that our knowledge cumulates gradually through what we
   can call testing, as in testing an idea, allowing the free play of
   imagination, following a hunch, or what seems at times almost random questioning.
6. A respect for the singular and individual event.
7. A distrust of anything being finished in a way that would call off
   further research and probing. Marcel's remarks against rigid and
   closed systems and against dogmatism in philosophy sound almost
   pathological at times.

Such a random inventory surely qualifies Marcel for the "spirit of empiricism" without in any way saying that this is all there is to Marcel's philosophy.

John Dewey once remarked that "things are had before they are cog-
nized." Marcel might well have found this use of the word *had* very interesting and might well have asked Dewey what he thought of saying,
"We are had before we cognize." If we leave aside what is revealed by
experience for Dewey and what is revealed by experience for Marcel, we
find that along a certain line their perspectives are not far apart. Both
regarded the "objects" of knowledge as special ways of handling experience. Objective knowledge is derived from experience, but it is experience
itself (re-cuperated and re-collected for Marcel) that puts us in touch with
what is really real. It would be foolish to make simple identifications between Dewey's problems and those that arise in Marcel's thought. But it
would be just as foolish to think that there is no kinship at all between
Dewey's contention that experience in the human organism becomes aware

of itself *in* nature and *of* nature and Marcel's struggle with participation expressing our experience of a kind of being that includes us. One thing is sure: when it comes to our ultimate experience of the really real, neither Dewey nor Marcel considers it a spectator experience.

Marcel has left us some remarks on how he changed his attitude toward empiricism and how he enlarged his notion of experience. We find some of these in one of the six interviews that Paul Ricoeur had with Marcel in 1968. In speaking of what he understands as a higher kind of empiricism in Schelling, Marcel says:

> You go back to a certain kind of experience that first of all you must recognize and that carries with it a guarantee of its own worth. In fact, over the years, if there is a point on which my thought has really been transformed, it is in the way I now appreciate experience. I must say that I smile a bit when I look back and remember the disdain I had for empiricism, and even the very notion of experience, during a certain period of my life. . . . I came to see that I had to rediscover experience, but on a level other than that of traditional empiricism.[5]

In this interview Marcel mentions that he feels Bugbee's term *experiential thought* is quite suited for what he has in mind when he speaks of hope and creative fidelity and other experiences central to his thought. He mentions here too that it was coming in contact with the thought of William James that brought about a revision of his earlier judgments on empiricism and experience. He later adds: "But I do not think it was so much the philosophers who sharpened my thought concerning experience. I think it was life itself, especially life with others, reflections . . . on relations with others."[6]

In 1947 a group of friends published a volume of essays on Marcel's philosophy, and Marcel himself added to this collection some final reflections, called "A Look at the Past."[7] He has some interesting things to say here touching our interests that rival any of the pages of Sartre's autobiographical *The Words*. Here are some of Marcel's recollections:

> When I recall my childhood, so carefully watched over and in some ways so confined, with its atmosphere of moral scruples and of hygienic precautions, I can see the reasons why abstraction was the keynote of my early philosophical thoughts and why I was almost contemptuously hostile towards empiricism. This attitude seems to me the direct reflection of that horror of dirt and germs which had been bred in me from my earliest youth upwards. Experience, as it is mostly conceived by philosophers, was to me impure and profoundly suspect. True, there was something in this also of the need to hit back at the practical world which at every step proved to me my inaptitude and my awkwardness: on the plane of Ideas alone was I able to create a shelter from these wounding contacts of everyday life. Thus to philosophize meant for me at first to transcend. But I must make certain reservations.

Firstly, my reference to Ideas must be taken in the widest—not in the Platonic—sense. I am inclined to think that, if, in some ways, the conception of a super-sensual world influenced my whole spiritual development, it was always deeply repugnant to me to conceive this world as a universe of Archetypes. I would say now that my idea of it tended to become less and less *optical*. It is most likely that my passion for music helped to prevent me from imagining this world, if to imagine is, at least in some sense, to project a form into space; this explains the conviction of profound truth which came to me with the discovery of Schopenhauer's theory of music.

For all that, it would be a mistake to think that abstraction as such ever appeared to me as a habitable place. If ever I dwelt in it, it was rather as on a landing stage from which to embark sooner or later. The idea of an aerodrome comes into my mind now when I try to recapture these early experiments. What I denied, rightly or wrongly, was that experience as it is understood by empiricists could ever be a springboard: it seemed to me that it must suck down the spirit like a quicksand.

Doubtless this explains why I was so deeply impressed by post-Kantian philosophy, particularly by Schelling. Fichte irritated me by his moralising and also by the absence of links (not sufficiently realised by himself) between the absolute and the concrete *ego*. It was this concrete *ego* which I could not help regarding as the veritable *I;* for, when all is said and done, did not the problem consist in understanding its reality and its destiny? From this point of view, Hegelianism inspired me more than the doctrine of Spinoza, to which I was always strangely averse; both seemed to me to immerse the reality and the destiny of the individual into an absolute in which they were in danger of becoming lost. As against this, I seemed to discern, at the end of the immense journey travelled by Schelling, a light which perhaps one day might help me to discover my own path. Was there not an arduous way which might give access to a higher empiricism and to the satisfaction of that need of the individual and the concrete which I felt in myself? In other words, would not experience be for me not so much a springboard as a promised land?[8]

Perhaps we can let William Ernest Hocking sum up for us and verify Marcel's "spirit of empiricism."[9] Hocking we know had an impact on Marcel's philosophical development. And Hocking says that he finds in Marcel's philosophy something akin to his own empirical thought. Hocking finds this experience the dominant element in Marcel's thought, and he would even call the method "empirical" by which Marcel uncovers the presuppositions of human experience. He says that Marcel's philosophy is a philosophy of being in an "experienceable sense." Ask Marcel, Hocking might say, how being is to be defined, and you get no answer. Ask how it is to be described, and you do a bit better. Ask how it is to be experienced, and Marcel becomes eloquent. Hocking says that the experience of being for Marcel is not a datum-pressure or a factual dull thud but a "passion-filled presence." It is a "hearth-fire," and at the same time part of the experience is that it is not just a local blaze. It is in everyone. When we

add to the positive element of empiricism a reflective attention to the supposedly refractory element—the to-be—we are on the way to an ontology
of experience, if not an ontological experience. Hocking finds in Marcel's
Metaphysical Journal just such a broadened and heightened empiricism,
which he feels may well be in its completion the major achievement in
epistemology of the present century. Jeanne Delhomme makes a similar
judgment. She says that Marcel is the only philosopher she knows who
has tried to say what epistemology is like within a serious personalist philosophy.[10]

Let us now look at this two-dimensional experiential world that Marcel
presents to us in terms of incarnation and transcendence, existence and
being. More immediately, let us look at the point where he begins to talk
about this incarnational transcending world. With other existentialists Marcel underlines that all is not well with us where we find ourselves. Marcel's particular image for talking about this commonplace is that we find
ourselves in a broken world. We are dislocated. We are in exile. I do not
think that Marcel would find any objection to Heidegger's image of up-
rootedness. I would separate these symbols of brokenness, dislocation, and
exile from others that Marcel uses, such as "in prison," "being bound,"
and similar notions. Getting closer to our original incarnational condition
is a sort of remedy for our broken world in the rediscovery of the primitive
unity. Yet even experiencing body-as-myself does not totally still a kind
of aspiration (an ontological claim or need) that always remains in dramatic tension with incarnation itself.

Probably one of the better known things in Marcel's philosophy is his
account and description of this dislocated, broken, exiled world. This is
the world of what he calls the first level of reflection. This is the world of
the spectator, of the objectivized, of the problem, of definitions and clas-
sifications and questionnaires, and of the impersonal "he" and the neutral
"it." This is the world where sense experience is a message to be decoded
and where my body is only an instrument. This is the world of the "spirit
of abstraction."

Because of Marcel's deep feelings against the hazards of scientific and
technological enterprises, as expressed in his polemical writings against
science and technology, we easily think of his first level of reflection as an
account of these worlds. This it is. But it is also an account of common-
sense experience, of everyone whose life style is dominated by role playing, by having and possessing, and by the will to power. However, this
world of first reflection where we find ourselves is already something of a
paradise lost. We are called both to return to our archeological, incarnational roots and to get on with it toward our transcendental destiny.

Many of Marcel's writings have as their purpose to alert us to the hazards of this world of abstractions and the impersonal and to make us aware of its fascinations and compulsions. Perhaps we are a bit oversensitive to the word these days, but in his early journals he uses *exorcize* more than once. If the philosopher is something of a psychiatrist for Wittgenstein, he is at times "the exorcist" for Marcel. And even the later Marcel, often in a shrill voice but speaking out of loving concern, is still trying to sensitize us to the ontological weight or gravity of our being. Marcel wants to help us clear away the debris that living and thinking somehow leave with us. And even before that he wants us to recognize this debris for what it is. In a talk given in Dublin, "What Can One Expect of Philosophy," Marcel said that one of our problems today is that we have neglected carrying out our cultural garbage for the last few hundred years.[11] More positively, he is trying to awaken us sufficiently so that we can hear the "call," the "unconditional claim" that something and Someone have on us. He tries to construct our body-person into a high-fidelity ontological structure. And it is all for the purpose of teaching us to relax with being in an incarnational world of fidelity and hope, where your body is closer to you than yourself and where metaphysics turns out to be your neighbor.

Jeanne Parain-Vial sees Marcel's theater, philosophy, and music as three related phases of the journey he maps out for us.[12] Drama is the place where we discover and stumble and fumble around in our broken world and where we sense its ambiguities and tensions. Philosophy for Marcel is the privileged place to reflect and question, to analyze the meaning of all this, and, if you will, to seek out the conditions or possibility of the world drama presents to us. But also to puzzle over its deep intentionalities. And if not for everyone, surely for Marcel music is the nearest we get to an authentic experience of resolution, or of a lived answer. He calls music the promise of another world and the experience of reconciliation and communion, discovered in fragments in drama and puzzled over in philosophy.

The world into which Marcel leads us is basically a two-dimensional world, one of incarnational existence and of transcendent being. Marcel's critique of the experience of objectivity (first reflection) was that it tends to do two things to us: it uproots us from primordial participation in the world and deadens in us a sense of transcendence, which closes us to participation in what Marcel eventually calls "mystery." As is often the case, the diagnosis is clearer than the remedy proposed. Marcel proposes a kind of global movement away from the fragmented world of objectivity toward a greater unity, which itself is not perfectly unified. Marcel calls this movement away from the world of objectivity "second reflection," as everyone knows. Although it is not a very elegant or helpful term in itself, it reestablishes for us a world that is at least two-dimensional. Ricoeur says that there are two "immediates" in Marcel's philosophy: the archeological immediate of existence in terms of feeling, body, and world and the eschatological immediate of being in terms of aspiration, fidelity, and hope.[13] Such key terms in Marcel's thought as *participation, presence, immediacy,* and *density* all apply equally well to one dimension as to the other. And yet we surely cannot reduce one world to the other.

We can establish certain relations between these two worlds in Marcel's thought by establishing some priorities as we approach them from various angles. I think one thing Marcel would say is that until I experience my rooting in body and world, I am not even open to authentic transcendence. For just as my unanalyzable experience of body is a paradigm for an authentic and primordial experience of the world, so my experience of being rooted in the body-world is the paradigm for my experience of transcendence. To be caught up in being or caught down in the world of existence is not so awfully different for Marcel. Ricoeur remarks that the experience of existence for Marcel is like the masked experience of a transcendental call.[14] My body-existence is not only a rooting, it is also a launching pad. Moving from the exile of objectivity to the primordial participation in body and world is but to discover a new kind of tension between incarnation and aspiration or hope. Images of "prison" and "being bound" still apply on this level of authenticity. Perhaps the neatest human trick is to be rooted and at the interior of this incarnational world and still to hear the call of the absolute Thou as deliverance rather than as evasion or escape. This seems to be what Marcel calls the authentically and fully human.

We have distinguished in Marcel's experiential world two dimensions: the incarnational and the transcendent. We have pointed out some things that are common to these two dimensions and shown how we might relate one to the other. Now, along with Ricoeur, we are going to move a bit further into each world to sharpen our impression of how Marcel experiences them.[15] Ricoeur bases his discussion on two early essays by Marcel. The first is "Existence et objectivité," originally published in a French journal and then put at the end of Marcel's *Metaphysical Journal.* The second is better known; "Position et approches concrètes du mystère ontologique" was first published in the same volume with Marcel's play *Le Monde cassé.* Ricoeur reads these two essays as two manifestoes, the first concerning the world of incarnation and the second the world of transcendence or mystery.[16]

We will begin with Marcel's incarnational manifesto. In recovering my rootedness in body and world, I experience felt unity as an act of participation. In the body-world I experience the indubitable character of existence. In Marcel's interviews of 1968 we can already see what he found acceptable in this manifesto of so long ago:

> I believe that what I saw at that time was what I would call the indubitable character of existence. The awareness of the impossibility of reducing existence to anything else whatsoever or even of questioning it. I just have never understood the question of certain philosophers' (most recently Schelling and Heidegger's) questioning how it is that something exists, that there is existence. My response at that time [early in the *Metaphysical Journal*] was that the question just does not make sense. . . . When I said that existence had priority (and I did not say "prior to essence") . . . that priority is very important to me. This is an affirmation that existence is not only given, but perhaps one should say in a somewhat paradoxical way, it is "giving" (*donnante*). . . . This is the very condition for any kind of thought.[17]

Marcel is speaking here of an existential density that is closed not only to objective thought but also to pure description, because this experience is to some degree involved with evaluation and freedom.[18] I exist incarnate; this is Marcel's thought.[19] And while I manifest myself, there is an initiative that is not totally mine. I am an event to myself. Richard Zaner, in his study *The Problem of Embodiment,* gives an excellent presentation of what Marcel is about here and of what he experiences.[20] I taste my own embodied identity being given to me. I sense my body as myself, as my insertion in the world, and as my point of reference for all existence. Marcel is dealing here with the familiar phenomenological theme of active-passive experience. I experience the world by receiving it into a domain that I feel is my own. Marcel says that this is the difference between meeting and greeting someone just anywhere and welcoming someone into your own home. Only *my* body senses. You can meet someone anywhere, Marcel says, but you can *receive* that person only into your own home.[21] He says that in grammatical terms, this is the exclamatory consciousness of existing.[22] And in a larger context, this exclamatory experience always brings with it a certain astonishment,[23] a sense of wonder.[24] We are never fully accustomed to it. And there is also a feeling of "this is where the action is"—a certain bite and sting of the real (*la morsure du réel*).[25]

Now we come to Marcel's manifesto on transcendence. Perhaps the first thing to notice here is the discovery that objective thought (first-level reflection) does not use up all the resources of our intellectual power.[26] We can judge the limitations of this world and then by an act of negation begin to recapture some of the primordial unity of our existential situation. One word Marcel uses for this act of negation is *re-collection*. But even when

I recapture something of this felt world where I experience body-as-myself, I find that I still have resources left and even have certain needs to which I have not yet addressed myself. Just as I cannot totally identify myself with the act of objective thought, I find I cannot totally identify myself with the feeling of incarnation. There is something more. The act of recovery and re-collection (negation of the objective world) was sparked not only by the existential weight of my situation but also by the ontological gravity of my being.[27]

What does this mean? It means that I feel the need for a deeper unity than the experience of incarnation brings me. It means that the decentralization of the *cogito* that comes from situating myself in the world is still too fragile and inadequate. What are the reasons for all this? Why is the experience of unity still unsatisfactory? Let us try a couple of answers, as Marcel might say.

I have found that the most serious obstacle to deep unity is not in my being uprooted from my body and from the world, however serious these may be. The most serious obstacle to deep unity is in myself, in the passion that Marcel calls "having"—the passion for appropriation and the passion for domination. The world cannot challenge these effectively. However much I sense my identity being given to me with my recapturing the feeling of body-as-myself, this decentralization is still inadequate. Only being and being-as-personal can make a claim on me that will radically call into question my passion of having. Only someone who can call out to me in the name of love can do this.[28]

Is there anything I can do about the inadequacy of this unity once I have discovered that the ultimate obstacle to deep unity is within myself, however much I needed to locate myself in the world? For however much I am immersed in the world, my life is still ungathered and unraveled. In looking for an answer here, we are close to Marcel's notion of time, especially in *Being and Having*.[29] What transcending acts are there that would gather up even my future and give a meaning to my whole life, right now? We know that for Marcel these acts are acts of promising, of fidelity, and of loving and hoping. We know that philosophy for Marcel is an effort to describe these acts in such a way that their ontological status will be revealed. And on the other side of the coin, Ricoeur remarks that "the ultimate meaning of concrete philosophy, as Marcel understands it, rests upon the possibility of considering these experiences of transcendence as authentic dimensions of experience, as metaphysical experiences."[30]

Promise, fidelity, hope, and love: these are the stars in Marcel's metaphysical heavens. And he feels no need to talk of concepts or myths or ciphers, for they carry immediately within themselves ontological weight and transcendental clout.[31] If existential consciousness brings with it a sense of wonder and the bite of the real, transcendental consciousness brings with it a kind of détente, a kind of peace, Marcel says. To sense such consciousness as radical empiricism, we need to recall that for Marcel metaphysics is our neighbor and that all philosophizing is for communion. One of the best expressions of this, Marcel says, is, "I hope in you for us."[32]

It might seem that to include the experiences of fidelity and hope under the umbrella of empiricism is already stretching it a bit thin, even when we call it radical empiricism. But if we want to be honest and go all the way with Marcel and see just how radical his notion of experience is, we must include what he says about immortality.[33] For Marcel there is an experience of those who are dead, an experience of their presence, or perhaps more exactly an experience of their absent-presence. This depends on an authentic experience of love. Here Marcel is most existentialist, for what he says of immortality clearly relates to his cultural and historical situation and to his personal history.

We have become accustomed to hearing Marcel called a "Christian existentialist," and we probably think the word *Christian* distinguishes him from the avowed non-Christian, perhaps atheistic, existentialists such as Sartre. Or we might think he is called "Christian" because he uses such categories as "incarnation" and "faith" to specify his radical empiricism and to serve as philosophical tools of understanding. But Marcel merits the name "Christian" in his thought in a deeper sense— in the sense that is revealed when he speaks of immortality. If we follow Marcel's thought we find that metaphysics really is our neighbor. In the end we find that love or charity is the primordial experience.[34] We find that this love—in the presence of another person—gives birth to hope, and this hope continues as an act of creative fidelity. Love as expressed in hope and creative fidelity is the ultimate truth of being. For truth—as the prophets of the Old Testament and as Augustine told us so many times—is a rock; it is what does not give way. Marcel, as philosopher, makes the point for us that the experience of love expressed in hope and fidelity is the only experience that does not give way in the face of death. This is the heart of his "Presence and Immortality." And it is here (if at all, as Marcel would say) that he is most Christian and most existentialist: he insists that the concrete experience of a loving presence is stronger than death itself. If we can manage to call this experience empirical, then Marcel is surely the most radical of all empiricists.*

ROBERT LECHNER

DEPARTMENT OF PHILOSOPHY
DE PAUL UNIVERSITY
AUGUST 1974

NOTES

1. Henry Bugbee, *The Inward Morning* (State College, Penna.: Bald Eagle Press, 1958); the references here are to Marcel's introduction to the paperback edition published by Collier Books in 1961, pp. 25–39.

2. Paul Ricoeur and Gabriel Marcel, *Entretiens: Paul Ricoeur/Gabriel Marcel* (Paris: Aubier-Montaigne, 1968), pp. 44–46; idem, *Conversations between Paul Ricoeur and Gabriel Marcel,* trans. Stephen Jolin and Peter McCormick, part 2 of *Tragic Wisdom and Beyond,* Northwestern University Studies in Phenomenology and Existential Philosophy (Evanston, Ill.: Northwestern University Press, 1973), pp. 228–29.

3. Bugbee, *Inward Morning,* p. 25.

4. Ibid., p. 26.

5. Ricoeur and Marcel, *Entretiens,* p. 45, my translation; cf. idem, *Conversations,* pp. 228–29.

6. Ricoeur and Marcel, *Entretiens,* p. 122, my translation; cf. idem, *Conversations,* p. 253.

7. Etienne Gilson, ed., *Existentialisme chrétien: Gabriel Marcel* (Paris: Plon, 1947). Marcel's contribution to this volume, "Regard en arrière," pp. 291–319, has been published in English as "An Essay in Autobiography," in *The Philosophy of Existence,* trans. Manya Harari (New York: Philosophical Library, 1949), pp. 77–96 (hereafter cited as *PE*).

8. *PE,* 77–78.

9. William Ernest Hocking, "Marcel and the Ground Issues of Metaphysics," *Philosophy and Phenomenological Research* 14, no. 4 (June 1954): 439–69, especially 442–44.

10. Jeanne Delhomme, "Témoignage et dialectique," in Gilson, *Existentialisme chrétien,* p. 139.

11. Gabriel Marcel, "What Can One Expect of Philosophy?" trans. Rev. M. B. Crowe, *Philosophy Today* 3 (Winter 1959): 252–61.

12. Jeanne Parain-Vial, *Gabriel Marcel et les nivaeux de l'expérience* (Paris: Editions Seghers, 1966), p. 8.

13. Paul Ricoeur, *Gabriel Marcel et Karl Jaspers* (Paris: Editions du temps présent, 1947), p. 56.

14. Ibid., pp. 58–59.

---

*Marcel did not reply to this essay; see the Preface for an explanation.—ED.

15. Ibid., pp. 48–61.

16. Ibid., p. 52.

17. Ricoeur and Marcel, *Entretiens,* pp. 20–22, my translation; cf. idem, *Conversations,* p. 221.

18. Gabriel Marcel, *Etre et avoir* (Paris: Aubier, 1935), pp. 127–29, 155–59 (hereafter cited as *EA*).

19. Gabriel Marcel, *Du refus à l'invocation* (Paris: Gallimard, 1940), p. 25 (hereafter cited as *DR*).

20. Richard Zaner, *The Problem of Embodiment* (The Hague: Martinus Nijhoff, 1964). In his presentation of Marcel's "Theory of Body as Mystery," Zaner gives us a sense of Marcel's thought in this area in fresh and excellent English terminology.

21. *DR,* 120.

22. Gabriel Marcel, *The Mystery of Being,* trans. G. S. Fraser (vol. 1) and René Hague (vol. 2), 2 vols. (London: Harvill Press, 1950–51), 1:111.

23. *DR,* 88.

24. *PE,* 4.

25. *DR,* 89.

26. Ricoeur, *Marcel et Jaspers,* p. 350.

27. Ibid., p. 351.

28. *EA,* 24, 244. Both Marcel and Emmanuel Levinas agree that the world of things does not really "decentralize" the self.

29. Ricoeur, *Marcel et Jaspers,* p. 109; *EA,* 21–25, 56–80.

30. Ricoeur, *Marcel et Jaspers,* pp. 82–83.

31. Ibid., p. 366.

32. Gabriel Marcel, "Sketch of a Phenomenology and a Metaphysics of Hope," in *Homo Viator* (Chicago: Henry Regnery Co., 1951), p. 60.

33. See especially Gabriel Marcel, "Presence and Immortality," in *Presence and Immortality* (Pittsburgh: Duquesne University Press, 1967), pp. 227–44.

34. Ricoeur and Marcel, *Entretiens,* p. 123, my translation; cf. idem, *Conversations,* p. 254.

18

Paul Ricoeur

GABRIEL MARCEL AND PHENOMENOLOGY

AS I WRITE the title of this essay, I am inevitably led back to the beginning of the debate that I have pursued for over thirty years with my teachers. Indeed it was in the same year, namely, 1934, that I discovered both Husserl, in *Ideen I*,[1] and Gabriel Marcel, in the *Metaphysical Journal*,[2] the latter of which closed with the philosophical manifesto, "Existence and Objectivity," and the play *Le Monde cassé*, accompanied by the essay entitled "On the Ontological Mystery."[3]

Since that time I have never ceased to repay a twofold debt. I carried out at the same time both the French translation of *Ideen I*,[4] published in 1950, and the writing of the book *Gabriel Marcel et Karl Jaspers*,[5] published in 1948. It was to Gabriel Marcel that I dedicated my first personal work, *The Voluntary and the Involuntary*, in 1950, and in its introduction I called into question the phenomenological reductionism and idealism of Husserl while at the same time making use of his eidetic method of description.[6] However, until now I have never attempted to assess what I have just called my twofold debt. The reason for this is not merely my closeness to both Husserl and Marcel, for that did not prevent me from comparing Marcel and Jaspers, but rather the extreme complexity of the enterprise. Between Marcel and Husserl is an interplay of kinship and discordance that is very difficult to unravel. At first they seem close, and then one discovers an abyss between them; in the end one finds a new proximity at the very point of their widest divergence. I would like to attempt today to disentangle this skein in the hope that veneration combined with lucidity will engender a quality of veracity worthy of my two teachers.

Translated from the French by Susan Gruenheck.

At first glance and in truth rather superficially the kinship between the two thinkers is established not at the level of themes or of method but at the more indefinable level of mood, tonality, and atmosphere. When Marcel opened the Gifford Lectures in 1949, today published under the title *The Mystery of Being,* his first words were directed at placing his style of "research," of investigation, in opposition to that of "system," represented in his view by Hegelianism and neo-Thomism.[7] But in the same breath he welcomed the idea of a discursivity of thought, which the metaphor of the "path" (*chemin*) and "following the path" (*cheminement*) propose at the outset for reflection. Joined to this discursivity and coextensive to the mind itself, a certain "lived spatiality" seemed to Marcel inherent even in the notion of investigation.

Marcel's refusal of system and his avowal of discursivity immediately calls to mind the famous *zu den Sachen selbst* of Husserl, which expressly refuses constructions, or more exactly, the constructivism of neo-Kantianism or the mathematical philosophies of anti-intuitionists that Husserl saw overburdening philosophy. Moreover Marcel's position is reminiscent of the concern for clarity and distinctness that places phenomenology at the opposite pole from all philosophies of feeling and from all apologies for mystical fusion. This refusal of system, corrected by a concern for subtle distinctions, is, I think, what places Husserl and Marcel in the same philosophical light. I find no other explanation for Marcel's use of the word *phenomenology* in the title of a lecture given to the Philosophical Society of Lyon in November 1933, "Outlines of a Phenomenology of Having," which is reproduced in *Being and Having*.[8] (This essay even contains notes dating back to 1923, that is, to the period of the first *Metaphysical Journal*).

What is phenomenological about this outline? The inquiry is launched with a seemingly psychological question: How is it possible to identify a feeling that one experiences for the first time? Marcel answers by stating that the more this feeling can be categorized as something I have, the more realizable its definition; one can then focus on it, define it, and intellectualize it. But then the feeling that I *have* has to be placed at one extreme of a range whose other extreme would be the feeling that I *am*. Here we find the beginnings of a phenomenology used to express distinctions—the distinction between what one has and what one is—and to express them in conceptual form. Like Husserl, Marcel indicates the nonpsychological character of his approach: "It really concerns the content of the thoughts which it is trying to bring out, so that they may expand in the light of reflection."[9]

Again like Husserl, Marcel strives to decipher meanings on the basis of well-chosen examples and significant cases, and this implies that the essence-example relationship is irreducible to any inductive generalization and consists in a direct reading of meaning in a singular fact. Thus he brings to the light of reflection the difference between having-as-implication and having-as-possession. With reference to having-as-possession, he pursues analysis in a genuinely eidetic style. What we have, he remarks, is exterior to us, is added to us, but is also added to other properties in an open-ended enumeration; having is at my disposal and under my power, but at the same time it is threatened, since it can escape me or be subtracted from me. I would add in passing that this eidetic analysis constantly relies on an examination of ordinary language; thus the relation of the question *qui* to the question *quid* and the transitive and irreversible movement of having toward the thing possessed constitute significant relations suggested by language itself. But then a second starting point is proposed. Can I say that I have a body, my body? The analytic vein of the investigation is maintained, but in the process a little word crops up that will shortly signal Marcel's profound divorce from Husserl.

> It now becomes necessary to make an analysis. I must warn you that this analysis will not be a *reduction*. On the contrary, it will show us that we are here in the presence of a datum which is opaque and of which we may even be unable to take full possession. But the recognition of an *irreducible* is already an extremely important step in philosophy and it may even effect a kind of change in the consciousness that makes it.[10]

I am quite willing to grant that *reduction* in this context does not mean what the word signifies for Husserl (as we shall see in a moment). The irreducible is the opaque; that is, it eludes the framework of an idea that one can have and therefore can circumscribe and dominate intellectually. Nevertheless the being-having antithesis begins to move away from the plane of notional distinctions—from the eidetic plane, in Husserl's terms— to a more existential plane. Having designates then a direction of existence, a global way of being in which a certain tension reigns between interiority and exteriority, manifested by the link between the desire to have and the fear of losing. This essential threat to having is especially rooted in corporeity.

> This brings us back to the body and corporeity. The primary object with which I identify myself, but which still eludes me, is my own body. We may very well think that we are here at the very heart of the mystery, in the very deepest recesses of having. The body is the typical possession. . . . It seems that it is of the very nature of the body, or my instruments insofar as I treat them as possessions, that they should tend to blot me out, although it is I who possess them.[11]

Through the mediation of the body, my relation to the world is placed globally under the heading of "having." "Our possessions devour us" is said of things, of ideas, and of opinions.

By the same token, the conditions of an eidetic description, of an analysis that I might control, vanish. If phenomenology is first of all an art of bringing the description of experience to the level of eidetic distinctions, then the phenomenology of having gradually eludes this condition. Indeed it leads to a reflection on the conditions of "characterization" in general, and these appear to be linked to the very grammatical rules governing the use of *to have*. A thing "has" characteristics that can be placed only in an order admitting the use of the word *also,* that is, admitting the juxtaposition of an additional idea. And the thing has its characteristics only for a subject placed on the outside, coming implicitly to a halt, and treating itself like a thing confined by its outlines. The will to characterize thus appears to be linked to the pretension of placing oneself before things both as a disinterested observer and as a dominator who disposes of the object.

> Characterization is a certain kind of possession, or claim to possession, of that which cannot be possessed. It is the construction of a little abstract effigy, a *model* as English physicists call it, of a reality which will not lend itself to these tricks, these deceptive pretenses, except in the most superficial way. Reality will only play this game with us insofar as we cut ourselves off from it, and consequently are guilty of self-desertion.[12]

The idea that being is uncharacterizable brings an end to eidetic phenomenology, which cannot help appearing to be prompted by the will to characterize.

The divergence widens if one connects the theme of the uncharacterizable to the distinction between problem and mystery, introduced in the same period and developed in "On the Ontological Mystery."[13] The conditions of the problematizable are actually those of the characterizable. Wherever I find a problem, I am working on data placed before me; at the same time everything seems to authorize me to proceed as if the "I" at work were not implied. Wherever the inquiry concerns being, reflection that a moment ago was carried on from a distance and taken up in regard to the things under consideration is now discovered "within an affirmation which I *am* rather than an affirmation which I *utter:* . . . an affirmation . . . *of which I am the stage rather than the subject.*"[14]

The chain of correlations between having, the characterizable, and the problematizable, on the one hand, and between being, the uncharacterizable, and mystery or the metaproblematic, on the other hand, does not constitute a notional chain that would itself belong to the characterizable. The development of the analysis marks at the same time its transformation into a style of meditation one might better qualify as an ascending dialectic; from the examination of examples such as "I have ideas about that" and "I have or do not have my body," we have moved on to the recognition of an irreducible—irreducible to characterization—and from there to the sort of ontological deficiency, inertia, and negative activity that work in the opposite direction of creative participation in the mystery of being.

We might well say therefore that Marcel's phenomenology shares with Husserl's a sense of description, a taste for eidetic analysis, and even the art of imaginative variations, but there seems to be nothing on the side of Husserlian phenomenology corresponding to this transcending inward movement from the characterizable toward the uncharacterizable, a movement that makes "a problem [encroach] upon its own data, invading them, as it were, and thereby transcending itself as a simple problem."[15]

Why? This question leads us to inquire about what I will call the initial gesture, the one that assures the *entrée* into philosophy.

The *entrée* into Husserlian phenomenology is defined by a certain threshold that Husserl calls "reduction" and that he compares to the suspension of judgment—to the *epochē*—by which the Stoic philosopher achieves a distance from the opinions holding the subject under the sway of passions. Similarly reduction is an abstention by which I as the subject withdraw my belief in the whole of natural reality, that is, in the reality I believe exists in itself absolutely, independently of the aims of a community of subjects. The positive benefit of reduction is twofold. First the objectivity of the object is revealed for what it is: the very eidetic meaning toward which the numerous intentional aims constituting the flux of consciousness converge. This identical meaning of the object provides a sufficient basis for logical thought, since the intentionality of consciousness does not appear to be an irrational explosion but rather a manifold of experience always polarized toward an identity of meaning that permits the naming of objects as "the same," without the identity of the topics being affected by time. In short, in the place of the thing, or precritical realism, which could in principle be irrational, Husserl substitutes intentional meaning, which is by right homogeneous with consciousness, since it is its other pole, its counterpart, and its point of support. The second benefit of a philosophy inaugurated by reduction is to reveal, along with the objectivity of the object, the subjectivity of the subject, namely, a feature immediately linked to its character of temporal flux. Husserl's *Lessons on the Inner Consciousness of Time,* strictly contemporaneous with the discovery of intentionality, indeed reexamines the central theme of the Kantian transcendental aesthetic, namely, that every phenomenon appears in time. But unlike Kant, Husserl defines time not by a quality of dimensionality again transposed from space (and incidentally represented by a line) but rather by features such as retention and protention, which are immediately discernible in every intention of consciousness. In short, what reduction reveals about time is not at first its successive character—what allows one event to be situated before or after another—but rather the power of consciousness, inherent in the very intending of something, to retain a past impression and to anticipate an experience yet to come. On the basis of this temporal experience Husserl perceives as characteristic of the ego the retaining and anticipating of its own identity in the flux that constitutes it as a manifold of experience for itself.

For the early Husserl at least, such is the twofold benefit of reduction: to reveal at the same time both the objectivity of the object and the subjectivity of the subject. This double discovery persistently characterizes Husserlian phenomenology from the *Ideen* to the *Cartesian Meditations*. Phenomenology is a kind of reflection, a descriptive analysis, applied to the correlations established between the structures of the object and those of the subject. Husserl's vocabulary is significant in this regard; the object taken in all its aspects—perceptual, judgmental, practical, affective, and axiological—is called *noema* to emphasize clearly that it is exhausted in being intended by "the mind," the *Nous*. And the very word *noesis* reminds us that the subjectivity of the subject is exhausted in signifying by intending the other-than-consciousness, that is, by intending meaning. A philosophy of meaning is thus what best characterizes Husserlian phenomenology, at least prior to the earthquake that shook it, beginning with the *Krisis*.

Husserl's first philosophical gesture then is reduction. Marcel's is diametrically opposed. In the Gifford Lectures on *The Mystery of Being,* Marcel embarks on his itinerary by introducing the idea of "situation," provisionally defined as "something in which I find myself involved."[16] From the start, this idea adheres to that of "investigation," since a philosophical investigation must be regarded as the ensemble of approaches by which I am able to move "from a situation experienced as basically discordant . . . to a different situation in which some kind of expectation is satisfied."[17] In many ways this point of departure is opposed to Husserl's.

First and fundamentally, being implied or involved excludes both the distance characteristic of reduction and the promotion of a "disinterested spectator," the very subject of phenomenology. The situation not only affects the subject from without but "also qualifies this I, this myself, from within."[18] The opposition of the outer and the inner loses its meaning in a single stroke, and along with this opposition a fundamental feature of Husserlian intentionality, the very correlation of the noematic and the noetic, is called into question. Let us reconsider each of the following three points: the position of the object, the position of the subject, and their correlation.

The theme of situation contests above all the primacy for reflection of the notion of object. By the word *object* we understand the ensemble of distinctive characteristics underlying things we can name, and these things in turn give to the logical subject a basis for attribution in perceptual judgments and in scientific knowledge. If we had to find a further equivalent within phenomenology of the Marcellian notion of situation, it would more likely be the notion of horizon than that of object. But it is precisely this reversal of priority between the object and the horizon that touches on one of the oldest themes of Marcellian philosophy, the one animating the kind of philosophical manifesto published at the end of the *Metaphysical Journal* under the title "Existence and Objectivity." The movement from objectivity to existence appears to be the opposite of the Husserlian movement from natural belief to the phenomenality of meaning. Existence designates the fund of solid, indivisible, undeniable presence attested to by the sensuous presence of the world at the most radical level of feeling. But to think in terms of objects is to nullify this existential mark and to constitute an outline both of geometrical relations without a privileged point of origin and of intelligible physical relations without reference to the vivid and qualified experience of an incarnate person. Objectivity then tends toward a rationally articulated spectacle from which the presence of "the mysterious power of self-affirmation, thanks to which the object arises before the spectator," has been removed.[19] The anti-Cartesian turn of this essay cannot fail to appear to us as equally anti-Husserlian, precisely because Descartes, even more than Kant, is the inspirer of phenomenology. The return to the foundation looks like a return to something indubitable, not in the sense of something resisting doubt or subsisting after doubt but in the sense of a presence precluding doubt; what is indubitably given to me is the confused and global experience of the world as existing. Reduction henceforth can only be a variety of uprooting, from which all modern thought suffers.

It is striking that both Marcel and Husserl should have questioned themselves about perception, although they were expecting an answer to two opposed questions. Husserl wondered how an identical meaning emerges from the flux of appearances and thus how logic can be constructed on a prelogical experience offering the most primitive features of meaning. What interests Marcel in perception is not that a meaning takes form within it—a meaning that we can place in opposition to ourselves as a thinkable object—but rather that feeling designates our primordial participation in the world. How could one account for participation in a philosophy that begins with reduction? For a philosophy of participation, reduction can only appear as a gain in objectivity at the expense of existence. With an insight not contradicted by the evolution of Husserl from the *Ideen I* to the *Krisis,* Marcel notes as early as the essay on "Existence and Objectivity" that "the more emphasis put on the *object* as object, together with the characteristics that constitute it as object, and the intelligibility with which it needs to be weighted so as to provide a grip for the subject who confronts it, the more philosophers leave the existential aspect—I will not say the existential character—of the object in the shade."[20]

For Marcel the theme of intentionality is insufficient to destroy the reign of objectivity. On the contrary, it confirms it; it even constitutes a privileged example of that "logical situation" Marcel characterized as the insularity that thought confers on objects in relation to itself.[21] The intentional object of Husserl indeed constitutes a transcendence in consciousness; it is thus stripped of "the mysterious power of self-affirmation by which the object confronts the spectator."[22] Husserl's analysis also gives weight to this appraisal. In *Ideen I* the "characteristics of being" (being real, possible, probable, and so on) appear to be correlations of the characteristics of belief (affirmation, doubt, computation, and so on). In this sense being is still another feature of *noema* and therefore a characteristic of objectivity. It is hence legitimate to wonder whether the object is reduced to "a rationally articulated spectacle" and how it will make known its power to affect the very being of the one who contemplates and undergoes it. One must regard existence not as the reduction of being to *noema* but as the nonproblematic itself.

A traditional way of putting this is to recall that existence is not a predicate. This was Kant's way of expressing himself in "The Only Possible Ground for a Proof of the Existence of God": "Existence is position."[23] In the same fashion Marcel declares: "It is essential to the character of the *existant* that it should occupy with regard to thought a *position* which cannot be reduced to the position implied in the fact of objectivity itself."[24] But one can remain at the level of Kantian intuition only by denying the interpretation subsequently given to the notion of existence by critical philosophy. Indeed in a philosophy defined by an investigation of the conditions of the possibility of objectivity, existence can no longer appear to be anything but the thing in itself, that is, a being that philosophy can neither determine nor exclude but must treat as unknowable and hence as free from the conditions that specifically define the object as such. Yet for Marcel existence is not the unknowable. The position of existence challenges the critical question itself as an investigation of the conditions of the possibility of objectivity. This question inserts itself like a divider between the thought of something and its existence, and it is this distance, this split, that constitutes the object as object and at the same time constitutes existence as unknowable. By removing the divider, Marcel adds existence like an X both to the object as object for me and to the whole of what is thinkable. The solid assurance constituting the affirmation of existence rules out its being treated as a characteristic for which there would be fixed criteria. Here we are certainly no longer in the area of demonstration, but neither are we in the area of foundation or of regression toward principles; rather we are in the domain where the classical relation between subject and object remains applicable. It is in this domain that all questions of validity are raised. In the language used above, existence is uncharacterizable. This does not mean that it is indeterminate but that in the face of existence the mind cannot adopt the attitude required to characterize something. It is this attitude that gives rise to the pseudo-question of knowing whether or not the predicate *existing* can be applied first to this, then to that, and gradually to all enumerated things. This question admits only of an answer that does away with the question by depriving it of its initial meaning.

But in this case absolute presence, which is thus acknowledged to be indubitable because it is nonproblematic, could not be the presence of something, not even of the universe, although one might tentatively grant the existence of "the existing universe."[25] It is even less the sum Descartes saw implied in the *cogito*.

Marcel's point of departure appears even farther removed from Husserl's if one considers the very quality of the subject implied in phenomenological reduction, on the one hand, and in the position of being as uncharacterizable, on the other.

As early in his writings as "Existence and Objectivity" and "On the Ontological Mystery," Marcel linked his critique of the *cogito* to that of the primacy of objectivity. The modern philosophy of subjectivity remains dependent, in his view, on fixed criteria of the indubitable. In the famous fundamental proposition of Cartesianism—I think; therefore I am—the "I think" remains the measure of the "I am." This is why the entire proposition draws its force from its character of validity, that is, from its resistance to the test of doubt. In a remarkable shortcut Marcel wrote that the *cogito* "guards the threshold of the valid";[26] in other words it is only the other pole of the subject-object relation. Kant drew from the *cogito* all the consequences for a critical philosophy; being identical with itself, the "I think" is the guarantee of objectivity, and this in turn is grounded in the synthetic operations of judgment.

This theme becomes increasingly explicit in Marcel's work. At the beginning of *The Mystery of Being,* the author calls into question the choice, forever arising in thinking of a purely epistemological orientation, between the individual left to his or her own states of being and incapable of transcending them, and a kind of generalized thinking with a claim to universal validity.[27] In this regard the philosopher does no more than reflect the split and dilemma at work throughout modern culture; in "On the Ontological Mystery" he portrays modern humanity reduced to a mere bundle of vital and social functions, with death itself appearing as nothing more than "a fall into uselessness, a sheer waste."[28] The philosophy born of the *cogito* is powerless to ward off the process of degradation precisely to the extent that the duality of the transcendental subject and the empirical subject reduces the latter to a mere function. This vacillation between the impersonality of the transcendental subject and the depersonalization of the empirical subject is the fruit of a monism of the valid "which ignores the personal in all its forms, eliminates the tragic, denies the transcendent or attempts to reduce it to caricatural expressions that disregard its essential characteristics."[29] Thinking that emphasizes verifying activity can only result in the mutilation of the ontological exigence enveloping both personal existence and the existence of the world.

What must be challenged is the very opposition between a subject of representation and objects entirely defined by their correlation to the self-affirmation of the subject. The primacy of being in relation to knowledge, the admission that "knowledge is enveloped by being, that it is in some way within being," implies a symmetrical critique of the notions of subjectivity and of objectivity, which form a pair.[30]

How far does Husserl fall under this critique of the *cogito*? The I resulting from the reduction is a thinking I. It is at the opposite pole of a thinkable object. This is necessarily so, since the problem dealt with in the *Logical Investigations* and in *Formal and Transcendental Logic* is an enterprise of foundation in the sense of a final legitimation.[31] It chiefly aims at justifying characteristics that are brought to light on the logical plane but that do not find their final justification there. The phenomenological ego must therefore be able to give an account of the enterprise of final justification created by the logico-formal sciences themselves. But unlike Kant's conception, the I born of Husserl's reduction is not the "I think," which cannot be considered an individual, since it is reduced to the very function of identity underlying every synthetic operation; rather the Husserlian I is a singular, temporal flux. Thus for Husserl the concept of subjectivity is divided between a *de jure* universality, which fulfills its epistemological function of final justification, and a de facto singularity resulting from its thoroughly temporal constitution. It is this paradox that gave rise to the question of intersubjectivity. If the subject must be the final foundation and if the subject must be singular, there remains only one possibility: a kind of collegial or ecumenical foundation in which the virtually unlimited community of subjects carries the weight of universality.

Less concerned with founding the sciences than with justifying human existence, Marcellian thinking attempts to escape from the choice between the universal and the particular by adopting an "intermediary level," which is illustrated by aesthetic experience. A great work of music or art is not meant for just anyone; some people will be literally refractory toward it. And yet it is not measured by individual impression or emotion; indeed the revelation of a masterpiece cannot be reduced to a state of mere felt satisfaction. This intermediary level is the level of true questions, though one cannot say at the outset for whom they are true. The subject of philosophical reflection, or better still, of philosophical intention, cannot be characterized either by universality or by individuality; it challenges the very alternatives it has used as guidelines.[32]

This fundamental divergence between Husserl and Marcel concerning the very meaning of subjectivity is sharpened by the difference in their approaches to the question of intersubjectivity. Perhaps this difficulty inheres more fundamentally in what I have called here the philosophical gesture of the two philosophies than in the critique of the *cogito*.

We are familiar with Husserl's laborious reflections in the fifth Cartesian Meditation.[33] Husserl needs a philosophy of the alter ego to complete his philosophy of the ego precisely to the extent that (as we recalled a moment ago) the subject resulting from the reduction, unlike the impersonal Kantian subject, retains its undeniable features of singularity. If the ego is the pole of subjective identity, in opposition to the pole of identity of meaning constituting the object, and if the objectivity of the object must manifest the features of universal validity, then intersubjectivity must necessarily establish this validity, whose weight cannot be carried by the individual *cogito,* or better still, by the singular *cogito,* alone. What is new here in relation to Kant is not only that the *cogito* is singular but also that the work performed by the community of subjects is established beginning at the perceptual level and not only at the level of understanding; it is the perceived world that is fundamentally the world in common. The characteristics of universality displayed by science are therefore grounded in the characteristics of the perceiving community.

This feature might create if not a bond at least a proximity of interest between the phenomenology of Husserl and the meditation of Marcel. But the impression of kinship is quickly dissipated as soon as one goes into

Husserl's argument, which revolves entirely around the duplication of the
I. Indeed the only intuitive and immediate reflexive experience is that of
the subject concerning its own life of consciousness. In this sense solipsism, before becoming an absurd thesis, is an ineluctable problem; it forms
the point, or perhaps the bottleneck, through which transcendental reflection is compelled to pass. Passing through requires a reduction within the
reduction, radicalizing the problem of the ego. This reduction within the
reduction consists in bracketing not only the "natural standpoint," the belief in the existence of things in themselves, but also all the predicates of
the perceived thing that do not rely on my perspective alone, that is, whatever has been seen by another, reported to me, and added to the sum of
my knowledge. Thus reduced to the "sphere of belonging," things gravi-
tate around the nucleus of my personal experience; all that is left is me and
my experience, my *vécu* and the aspects of reality correlative to an experience that can be described as original, intuitive, and immediate. This is
the radical position—the position of philosophical solipsism—starting from
which the existence of the other can be constituted in the form of a philosophical problem. The existence of the other appears then as that which
transgresses the sphere of personal belonging, like an irruption of otherness
within the circle of sameness constituted by the insular relation that I form
with my *vécu,* my experience, my world.

Presented in this way, the problem of the other consists in accounting
for the right to apply the words *I, my,* and *mine,* to a *vécu,* to an experience presenting none of the features of originality that, after the reduction
to the primordial sphere of belonging, characterize one ego only, mine.

But on the other hand, the idea of deducing the existence of the other
from my own existence is meaningless; deduction moreover is alien to all
phenomenology. The existence of the other can only be acknowledged in
a paradoxical experience, since it is neither original nor deducible. It is
with this twofold impossibility that Husserl struggled. On the one hand,
the life of consciousness of the other is not given, in the strong and precise
sense of the word; on the other hand, neither is it supposed or reconstructed. Rather it is "appresented," in a mode that is similar to the "presentation" of the life of the ego to itself yet derivative and nonoriginal.
The meaning I is therefore first understood, felt, and lived in the reflection
of the self on itself and then transposed analogically from I to thou. I-
consciousness remains the model of the meaning that can be attached to
the twin expressions "I think" and "I am." It is true that this analogical
transposition is not a reasoned argument, as if I could arrive at the existence of a psychic life outside myself by means of a comparison between
my behavior and the other's. Husserl takes for granted the critique of this

sort of reasoning by analogy. Although for him the other is grasped at a quasi-perceptual level prior to all reasoning, such a deduction could not even be initiated. Indeed I do not observe my behavior from the outside, as I do the behavior of the other. Furthermore the knowledge without observation that I have of my behavior is heterogeneous with the observation I conduct of the other's behavior. If therefore the experience of the other is analogical, the analogy is not a reasoning by analogy but a "coupling" (*Paarung*), operating at the very level of bodily experience, from body-proper to body-proper. I recognize from the outset the psychic meaning of bodily behavior that answers mine, and thus I can multiply the meaning I as often as this pairing places the body-proper of one in a kind of resonance with the body-proper of another.

Thus Husserl fought with a difficulty resembling that of the squaring of a circle. On the one hand, only the experience of the I is original, whereas the experience of the other is derivative. On the other hand, this derivation has something primitive, though nonoriginal, about it, just as the experience one may have of one's past is primitive, though it can never become present. This paradox makes Husserl's analysis seem alternately like an enterprise of genetic derivation in which the initial solipsism is confirmed more than conquered and like the recognition of an initial presence to which one can only attest under the appearances of a derivation of meaning. The phenomenology of the other suffers from a hesitation between two tasks: to ground the experience of the other and to describe it as a given as undeniable as my own existence.

Here the difference in approach between Marcel and Husserl is so striking that it summarizes all the other discordances. What is challenged is the very position of the problem, that is, to overcome solipsism. This position stems from the general orientation of philosophy toward an investigation of validity. The right to transpose the meaning ego from myself to the other is still another modality, perhaps the most fundamental, as Husserl realized, of the problematic conceptions of philosophy. The impossibility of grounding the existence of the other in the *cogito* has the value of a warning if not of a proof *a contrario*. If one does not start from the undeniable presence of the other, one will never overtake this presence. In a sense this is what Husserl does: in describing what "to appresent" the other means, he goes against the current of a philosophy oriented toward the grounding of the ego.

But what does it mean to recognize the presence of the other? It is something altogether different from holding as valid a certain proposition concerning the other that rests on the prior certitude of my own existence. Recognition is not a modality of knowledge via object; love and the channels belonging to the circle of fidelity are the genuine bearers of the indubitable. Marcel's vocabulary is moreover very significant. He does not say "the other," the other me, as in an epistemological perspective, but "thou"; this beautiful word, borrowed from the vocabulary of the prayer of invocation, is itself an indication of a change of focus. In the *Metaphysical Journal* Marcel writes:

> The being I love is a *third person* in the least possible degree. Moreover, that being discovers me to myself, since the efficacy of his or her presence is such that I am less and less *him* for myself—my interior defenses fall at the same time as the barriers that separate me from somebody else. The being I love comes more and more into the circle in relation to which and outside which there are third parties, third parties who are "the others."[34]

Three ideas are condensed here. First, speech in the third person is powerless to say "thou." Second, the recognition of the other is not a second step preceded by the certitude of the *cogito,* but rather communication is constitutive of my very existence. Finally, attesting to the presence of the other depends on my degree of "defensiveness" and therefore on my "unreadiness" or my "openness."

All of Marcel's reflections that tend to place the Thou in oppostion to the him or the it expand on the first of these three themes. (Numerous passages in the *Metaphysical Journal,* in *Being and Having*, in *Creative Fidelity,* and in *The Mystery of Being* stress this affirmation. The Thou is the one to whom I address myself and who is able to reply; where no answer is possible, there is room only for the him or the it.) If the object is defined as a third party between I and thou, as Royce observed, any reduction of the other to a third party is the beginning of objectification. This is what happens when one treats the other as a *repertoire* of information: "The *repertoire* is the *it*." The other is thus the uncharacterizable par excellence. The opposition between existence and objectivity, which served us a moment ago as a guide, springs up and is most strikingly illustrated here: "*The thou is to invocation what the object is to judgment.*" Henceforth reflection on invocation and on love is beyond all epistemology; the very expression "epistemology of love" loses all meaning.

But then—and this is the second theme—it is necessary to abandon the primacy of the *cogito* and to seek in the presence of the other the first surging forth of existence. Or rather the first ontological position is neither I existing nor thou existing but the *co-esse*—the being-with—that engenders us simultaneously. In this regard "On the Ontological Mystery" speaks of the "influx of being" to indicate the kind of inner contribution realized from the moment presence becomes actual. To put it another way, the Thou "is not only before me, he is also within me—or, rather, these categories are transcended, they have no longer any meaning."[35] The *co-esse* is the nonproblematizable par excellence.

With the third theme, that of readiness (*disponibilité*), we reach the level of what I will call ontological movement, the attitude toward being for which there is no epistemological equivalent. In order to understand this theme, let us go back to the metaphor of influx evoked above. If presence is a certain influx, then "it depends upon us to be permeable to this influx, but not, to tell the truth, to call it forth. Creative fidelity consists in maintaining ourselves actively in a permeable state; and there is a mysterious interchange between this free act and the gift granted in response to it."[36] Presence and readiness are therefore closely linked. The ready person is entirely with me; I am a presence for that person, not an object. By the same token, the problem of solipsism Husserl raises seems to be the epistemological projection of an ethical and ontological problem. The intangible obstacle to be overcome is not the original character of the certitude of self but the unreadiness that characterizes a person who is not only self-occupied but self-burdened. The movement from problem to mystery thus entails the complete reversal of the question. For epistemological reflection the *cogito* precedes (in terms of certitude) the recognition of the other. For ontological meditation this priority bears witness to a "contraction" of the I, which renders it inaccessible to presence, that is, to the readiness proceeding from the Thou toward me.

Through these three themes, the philosophy of communication—to use a relatively neutral word—is more closely related to theater than to epistemology. Here we are touching on a close connection in Marcel's work, one without any conceivable parallel in Husserlian phenomenology (although certainly not within phenomenology as a whole, since the work of Sartre constitutes a later example to the contrary). Philosophy and theater are linked together in a way that is neither anecdotal nor biographical, as if it were a question of alternating between two occupations, one of which would be, in every instance, "the violin of Ingres," or the "hobby"* of the other. The latter is not accidental, whereas the former would be essential. Their connection is substantial. We would not reach the profundity of this bond if we limited ourselves to observing that a given character says, before the philosopher and in metaphorical form, what he or she will say later in a more conceptual fashion. The headstart drama has on abstract thought is certainly an important datum for anyone wishing to understand the spiritual evolution of the author, but it does not yet touch the essential point. What is at stake is not only the relationship between theatrical dis-

---

*The word *hobby* appears in English in the original French text.—TRANS.

course and philosophical discourse but the relationship between dramatic existence, that is, the very confrontation of beings at the heart of theatrical fiction, and the philosopher's meditation on the encounter of beings. Indeed only theater can represent, by staging and offering for our viewing, the fundamental situation of beings in relation to each other "which in drama is represented in its raw and, in the last analysis, inextricable complexity."[37]

In the theater, the *co-esse* is not reflected; it is put into action. At the same time it is revealed as drama in several ways, primarily as the drama between persons. Theater, better than philosophy, is situated at the very point where existences in confrontation are tied together in action. In this regard theater has the supreme virtue of justice that fiction alone allows. Gaston Fessard quotes an admirable Marcel essay, "Spiritual Values in Contemporary French Theater," written in 1937:

> The characters brought forth by the playwright are multiple; each says "I"; it is therefore necessary, through an effort directed against our natural inclination, that the playwright find the means to place himself simultaneously at the deepest level possible in each one, that he adopt at once all their ways of being, of understanding, of appreciating, which oppose each other in practice and may even reveal themselves to be forever incompatible. In real life, I should probably be forced to side with one of these characters against the other or to become disinterested in them. In the privileged domain of dramatic creation, I am spared this choice. . . . For several moments it will be possible for me not only to take in existence more widely, but also to reach a higher justice that resembles charity, promises it, allowing me both to be all the antagonists at once as well as to understand and rise above them, without necessarily being able to work out a formula that can be stated, allowing this act to be expressed in an intelligible synthesis.[38]

Drama is within each being, between the potentialities for being closed and the potentialities for being ready. The theater is this very struggle, not spoken but produced. In drama death is quite often the touchstone in the form of a twofold test, the death of the beloved and the temptation to suicide. In this respect as well theater is ahead of philosophy, once again not at the biographical level but at the level where being itself is act and drama and, more than anything else, a test.

The reflections raised by the meeting of theater and philosophy bring us to the heart of the debate between Marcel's and Husserl's phenomenologies. A phenomenology concerned with epistemological validation rests on the exclusion of drama as a field outside philosophy. In the language of the German philosophy of the early twentieth century, this is the refusal of the *Lebensphilosophie*. Husserl's great text on this subject is the article published in 1911 in the review *Logos* under the title "Philosophy as a Rigorous Science.'' Certainly rigorous science is not exact science, in the sense of a *mathesis universalis;* from this point of view Husserl's position is uncompromising. But the ideal of rigorous science is really quite the same as that of the *Wissenschaft* in Fichte's sense, that of an apodictic and grounding knowledge, synonymous with ''first philosophy.'' But this knowledge can be articulated only if philosophy at the same time abandons wisdom. One must choose between wisdom and knowledge. Wisdom would like to be a philosophy for life, that is, a philosophy that teaches not only how to live but how to ''live well'' and consequently delivers a message to individuals and societies. By contrast the ascetic spirit that sustains the phenomenological reduction implies abstention not only with regard to the position of the natural world but also with regard to the evaluations that follow from that world; to arrive at science or first philosophy means sacrificing wisdom. The ego born of the reduction will be a disinterested thinker and in this sense uninvolved. Nonetheless ethical questions remain; the immense amount of unpublished work Husserl left contains several lectures on ethics. But they are concerned not with preaching an ethical behavior related to empirical situations, whether personal or historical, but rather with describing the axiological constitution of the morally valid as an object of evaluation and of judgmental and volitional *noesis,* of which the valid as such is the correlate. I dare say it is precisely so far as philosophy remains impartial in ethical evaluations that it can describe ethical choice and its relationship to values and norms. It is in this sense that philosophy is, as a matter of principle, nondramatic.

For Marcel philosophy cannot help being dramatic, for the situated being from whom it proceeds includes the revelation of a world in which despair is possible, of a world in which betrayal and suicide are temptations coextensive to the earliest revelation of existence.

> We live in a world where betrayal is possible *at every moment, in every degree,* and in every form. It seems that the very constitution of the world recommends us, if it does not force us, to betrayal. . . . But it seems that at the same time, and correlatively, it is of the essence of despair, of betrayal, and even of death itself, that they can be refused and denied. If the word transcendence has a meaning, it means just this denial; or more exactly, this overpassing. (*Überwindung* rather than *Aufhebung.*) For the essence of the world is perhaps betrayal, or, more accurately, there is not a single thing in the world about which we can be certain that its spell could hold against the attacks of a fearless critical reflection.[39]

Faithful to one of his earliest discoveries, Marcel devoted the second of the Gifford Lectures to the theme of the broken world.[40] It is no accident that here the philosopher returns to the words of one of the heroines in his plays: "You see, the world, what we call the world, the world of human creatures . . . it must have had a heart at one time, but today you would say the heart had stopped beating."[41] What haunts the broken world is not the will to know but the will to power and the state of discord and war it carries with it. Although one may wonder whether the fragmentation of individuals, collectivization, and bureaucratization are really the most irrecusable signs of the division of the world against itself, the essential matter for the present discussion is that the most primordial experience on which philosophy reflects already attests to the existence of a break affecting the integrity and wholeness of human experience. From that moment on the exigence that constitutes the inner motive for philosophical investigation cannot be separated from the effort to overcome the fundamental and primordial threat closing in on it from all sides. This exigence, or urgent need, can be called "the need for transcendence" (in keeping with the title of the third Gifford Lecture)[42] only if philosophy continues to recognize the adversary to which it is joined, which we have called the temptation of despair. The exigence for transcendence is therefore not a movement from the empirical to the transcendental by which reflection would claim to move into the realm of pure thought. For Marcel the very idea of the pure—Husserl speaks of pure phenomenology, of pure phenomenological philosophy—is suspect at the outset. In the face of the invitation to despair, the exigence for transcendence is not an escape but rather a recovery of all vital potentialities in a creative meaning. Creation implies transcendence, since "to create is always to create above oneself."[43] But the inverse must not be forgotten; according to the experience of Ramuz, "one grafts only upon wild stock."[44] Transcending therefore does not mean transcending experience; on the contrary, it must be possible to have an experience of transcending, that is, a movement of experience that climbs uphill out of despair.

Such is perhaps the most profound opposition one can uncover between the two philosophical styles of Marcel and Husserl; it concerns the very relation of human beings and the world. For Husserl this relation may be raised to the rank of spectacle for the disinterested eye of the meditating ego. For Marcel the questions of suicide and of death impose on the human relation to the world the fundamental characteristic of concern. On this point Marcel is incontestably closer to Heidegger than to Husserl.

The comparison I have pursued in several areas has been deliberately conducted from a Marcellian position; indeed the kind of stakes raised by the debate exclude a detached position. This is not to say that "rehearsing" Marcellian themes leaves me without any questions. On the contrary it is precisely the questions suggested to me by a long association with Marcel's work that make me ceaselessly return to the work of Husserl.

The fundamental difficulty that has continually beset Marcel's existential ontology concerns the status of its own statements. In this regard a simple, nondialectical opposition between mystery and problem could not be established without immediately destroying the philosophical enterprise as such, threatened with a shift to a philosophico-religious *fidéisme*. Philosophy, as Marcel has acknowledged over and over in his writings, consists in reflection, that is, in the return to the experiences of transcendence with a view to understanding and articulating them. The very possibility of this reflection rests on a thinking dynamism that is not exhausted in the "problematizable." If the ontological affirmation were in no way an intellectual act, then it could not be elevated to philosophical discourse.

Here one may say that the objection arises precisely from the kind of philosophy one wishes to overcome. I think not; it emanates from the very ontology Marcel professes. Indeed if being is the uncharacterizable, "the unqualified *par excellence*," how is it possible that it is not also the pure indeterminate?[45] In Marcel's work this difficulty assumes a specific form; the global affirmation of existence can indeed be, though indistinctly, the affirmation of my embodiment and of the universe taken in a global and undivided way, that is, the universe of God called the Supreme Thou. Although Marcel has not ignored this difficulty, he attributes it to the affirmation of being in general in neo-Thomism.[46] But could this not be turned around? What distinguishes the immanence of thought to being from the immanence to the whole of the world's existence, which is, as in Heidegger, the horizon of every determined object? Marcel admits: "The uneasiness I feel on these subjects is partly due to my old difficulty in seeing the relation between being and existing."[47] And indeed the same philosophy of the uncharacterizable holds for "my body," for "thou," and for "God." Existence is what reveals feeling as well as fidelity and the recourse to being as opposed to despair.

In order to answer the objection one must admit that each of the experiences jointly bearing the seal of existence has a structure that determines it, distinguishes it, and renders it eminently thinkable. Therefore one must also admit that the work of determining, which constitutes reason, is not identical with the objectification that characterizes understanding; moreover understanding itself is perhaps something altogether different from a technique of fragmentation. Perhaps science and technology already have their irreducible aims, and therefore one cannot hold scientific knowledge responsible for the atomization, leveling, and herding characteristic of advanced industrial societies.

I well understand Marcel's reservations. A rationality that would not be understanding, that would not be the rationality of science—much less that of technology—cannot be found today. The spiritual situation of our time, as Jaspers would put it, consists precisely in the fact that objectivity—in the mathematico-experimental sense—has not developed solely according to its own exigence, as a form of understanding, but rather it is inhabited by an absolutely Promethean or demiurgic ambition. In other words the empire of objectivity has been enlarged by all that modern thought has taken away from the ontological exigency; a spiritually mutilated world, devoid of the capacity for wonder, is the actual condition of the exercise of thought today. This is why any reconquest of the ontological dimension must be made against the tide represented by the propensity to problematize and characterize.

Without denying that this is indeed the present condition of reason, I do not see how one can understand the ontological affirmation without at the same time undertaking the deliverance of reason from its scientifico-technological abasement. In other words the "metaproblematic" must give rise to the working of reason on itself, equal to that of existence on itself. In particular the production of delimiting concepts seems quite inseparable both from the negation of opposites such as exterior and interior, before me and within me, and from positive affirmations such as "To raise the ontological problem is to raise the question of being as a whole and of oneself seen as a totality" and "The I *am* is . . . a global statement which it is impossible to break down into its component parts."[48]

My critique is therefore not outside Marcel's work. I would even say that it has an ally in his work. Indeed Marcel has an expression that, without pointing to a solution, nonetheless well delimits the difficulty we are considering; this expression is "secondary reflection." As we have said, the ontological affirmation is a certain reflexive process within an "affirmation that I *am* rather than an affirmation which I *utter*."[49] This text insists on the primacy of the affirmation as opposed to reflection and on the inclusion of reflection within the affirmation. But at the same time it presents the reflexive character of philosophy. Moreover this reflection is "secondary" in that it reconsiders the very conditions of primary reflection, the critical reflection of epistemological philosophies; a "mastery of our own mastery . . . is obviously parallel to reflection in the second degree."[50] Is not the very definition of mystery—"a problem which encroaches upon its own immanent conditions of possibility"[51]—already the work of secondary reflection? Even more than that, it is the rule of secondary reflection that whatever, absolutely speaking, belongs to the order of affirmation reaches us in the form of a question stated in the following way: "How can something which cannot be reduced to a problem actually be thought?"[52] Still more fundamentally the very expression "metaproblematic" is taken from the vocabulary of secondary reflection, as a note from the second *Metaphysical Journal* acknowledges: "I was tempted to say that the word *mystery* is stuck on like a label saying, 'Please do not touch.' In order to begin understanding again, we are always bound to refer back to the order of the problematic. Mystery is the metaproblematic."[53] The intuition attached to the revelation of being is not one I could dispose of but rather one "whose presence is expressed by the ontological unease which is at work in reflection."[54]

This discussion brings us back to the origin of philosophy; in what sense, we ask with Parmenides, are "to be" and "to be thought" the same thing? Or, in Platonic terms, how can the intuition of what is beyond determinations be reflected in a dialectic? The very expression "reflexive intuition," which appears here and there in Marcel's work, is very significant. A passage in *Being and Having* focuses closely on this difficulty: "The essential metaphysical step would then consist in a reflection upon this reflection (in a reflection 'squared'). By means of this, thought *stretches out* towards the recovery of an intuition which otherwise loses itself in proportion as it is exercised."[55] And again: "Knowledge is within being, enfolded by it. The ontological mystery of knowledge. We can only arrive at it by a reflection at one remove, which depends upon an experience of presence."[56]

Let us go further. The ontological affirmation requires secondary reflection not only in order to be expressed and communicated but also to be constituted and maintained; indeed it is in the nature of this affirmation to be vulnerable to primary reflection. This springs from the very notion of mystery itself: "just because it is of the essence of mystery to be recognized or capable of recognition, it may also be ignored and actively denied."[57] We have hardly finished asking, "Surely it is of the essence of anything ontological that it can be no more than *attested*?" when we must admit the possibility "for pure reason to attack witness *in toto*, and to pretend that no valid witness can really be produced. It is of the essence of particular witness that it should be capable of being doubted."[58] The kind of intuition that constitutes the attestation of being is therefore a blind intuition made known only through the work of reflection on reflection. Secondary reflection recaptures in thought an intuition whose efficiency is spent in resisting resistance.

Existential philosophy cannot therefore limit itself to a critique of objectivity, of characterization, and of the problematic; it must be supported by the determinations of thought and by conceptual work whose resources are exhausted neither by science nor by technology.

It is here that Husserl's work recovers its legitimacy. It is precisely his concern for the valid that leads him to seek the foundation of the sciences not in a set of axioms, which would still be the work of science, but in the prescientific, ante-predicative structures of intentionality.

Is it inappropriate to ask that an investigation of the foundations of objectivity engage in secondary reflection? For even if reflection must finally be discovered within being, it is first necessary to constitute it as reflection. It is perhaps in the nature of the original affirmation that it should engender a second Copernican Revolution, a second naïveté presupposing an initial critical revolution, an initial loss of naïveté.

This hard destiny is perhaps what distinguishes philosophy from poetry and faith.

PAUL RICOEUR

L'INSTITUT DE FRANCE
SEPTEMBER 1972

NOTES

1. Edmund Husserl, *Ideen zu einer reinen Phänomenologie und phänomenologischen Philosophie,* ed. Walter Biemel, vol. 3 of *Gesammelte Werke,* under the direction of H. L. van Breda (The Hague: Martinus Nijhoff, 1950); *Ideas: General Introduction to Pure Phenomenology,* trans. W. R. Boyce Gibson, Muirhead Library of Philosophy (1931; London: G. Allen & Unwin; New York: Macmillan Co., 1952).

2. Gabriel Marcel, *Journal métaphysique* (Paris: Gallimard, 1927, 1935); *Metaphysical Journal,* trans. Bernard Wall (Chicago: Henry Regnery Co., 1952; hereafter cited as *MJ*).

3. Gabriel Marcel, *Le Monde cassé,* followed by *Position et approches concrètes du mystère ontologique* (Paris: Desclée de Brouwer, 1933); "On the Ontological Mystery," in *The Philosophy of Existence,* trans. Manya Harari, Essay Index Reprint Series (1948; Freeport, N.Y.: Books for Libraries Press, 1969; hereafter cited as *PE*). There is no published English translation of *Le Monde cassé.*

4. Edmund Husserl, *Idées directrices pour une phénoménologie,* ed. and trans. Paul Ricoeur (Paris: Gallimard, 1950).

5. Paul Ricoeur, *Gabriel Marcel et Karl Jaspers: Philosophie du mystère et philosophie du paradoxe* (Paris: Editions du temps présent, 1947, 1948).

6. Paul Ricoeur, *Le Volontaire et l'involontaire,* vol. 1 of *Philosophie de la volonté,* Editions Montaigne (Paris: Aubier, 1950); *Freedom and Nature: The Voluntary and the Involuntary,* trans. Erazim V. Kohak, Northwestern University Studies in Phenomenology and Existential Philosophy (Evanston, Ill.: Northwestern University Press, 1966).

7. Gabriel Marcel, *The Mystery of Being,* trans. G. S. Fraser (vol. 1) and

René Hague (vol. 2), 2 vols. (Chicago: Henry Regnery Co., Gateway, 1960), 1:3 (hereafter cited as *MB*).

8. Gabriel Marcel, "Esquisse d'une phénoménologie de l'avoir," in *Etre et avoir* (Paris: Aubier, 1935), pp. 223–55; "Sketch of a Phenomenology of Having," in *Being and Having: An Existential Diary,* trans. Katharine Farrer (New York: Harper & Row, Harper Torchbooks, 1965; hereafter cited as *BH*).

9. *BH*, 158.	10. *BH*, 157.
11. *BH*, 163–65.	12. *BH*, 169.
13. *PE*, 1–31.	14. *PE*, 8.
15. *PE*, 8.	16. *MB* 1:9–10.
17. *MB* 1:10.	18. Cf. *MB* 1:10.
19. *MJ*, 320.	20. *MJ*, 319.
21. *MJ*, 319.	22. *MJ*, 320.

23. Immanuel Kant, "Der einzig mögliche Beweisgrund zu einer Demonstration des Daseins Gottes" (1763), in *Vorkritische Schriften,* ed. Artur Buchenau, vol. 2 of *Werke,* ed. Ernst Cassirer, in cooperation with Hermann Cohen et al. (Berlin: Bruno Cassirer, 1922–23), p. 77; "L'Unique Fondement possible d'une demonstration de l'existence de Dieu," in *Pensées successives sur la théodicée et la religion,* trans. Paul Festugière (Paris: Vrin, 1931), p. 25.

24. *MJ*, 326.	25. *MJ*, 331–32.
26. *PE*, 6; *MJ*, 325.	27. *MB* 1:11.

28. *PE*, 1–3.

29. Susan Gruenheck's translation; cf. *PE*, 5–6.

30. Cf. *PE*, 8.

31. Edmund Husserl, *Logical Investigations,* trans. J. N. Findlay (London: Routledge & Kegan Paul; New York: Humanities Press, 1970); idem, *Formal and Transcendental Logic,* trans. Dorion Cairns (The Hague: Martinus Nijhoff, 1969).

32. Cf. *MB* 1:11–17.

33. Edmund Husserl, *Cartesian Meditations: An Introduction to Phenomenology,* trans. Dorion Cairns (The Hague: Martinus Nijhoff, 1960).

34. *MJ*, 147; the substance of this is reprinted in *Creative Fidelity,* trans. Robert Rosthal (New York: Noonday Press, 1964), pp. 33–34.

35. *PE*, 24.

36. *PE*, 24.

37. From the foreword to Marcel's *Le Monde cassé,* quoted by Gaston Fessard in "Théâtre et mystère," the preface to Marcel's play *La Soif* (Paris: Desclée de Brouwer, 1938).

38. Fessard, "Théâtre et mystère."

39. *BH*, 119.

40. *MB* 1:24–47.

41. *MB* 1:26–27; Marcel is quoting Christiane in *Le Monde cassé.*

42. Translated as "The Need for Transcendence," although the translator notes that the word *need* does not convey the full meaning of the French *exigence* or the German *Forderung* (*MB* 1:48*n*).

43. *MB* 1:55.

44. *MB* 1:55; quoted from Charles Ferdinand Ramuz, *Salutation paysanne* (Paris: Grasset, 1929).

45. *BH*, 36.	46. *BH*, 27–40.
47. *BH*, 37.	48. *PE*, 7.

49. *PE*, 8.   50. *BH*, 125.
51. Cf. *PE*, 8–11.   52. *BH*, 126.
53. *BH*, 112.   54. *BH*, 122.
55. *BH*, 118.   56. *BH*, 115.
57. *BH*, 117–18.   58. *BH*, 99.

Gabriel Marcel and Phenomenology
REPLY TO PAUL RICOEUR

Paul Ricoeur's contribution is obviously important, and I can only thank him warmly for it. I will begin by pointing out that I am barely acquainted with Husserl's philosophy. I remember reading the *Ideen* some months before the beginning of the First World War and not understanding a word of it. I had not yet read the *Logical Investigations*. Much later I listened to the first Cartesian Meditations, when Husserl himself came to deliver them at the Sorbonne. At first I found them interesting, then tiresome.

Ricoeur has, I think, brilliantly presented not only the remote and vague relationship that may exist between my investigations and Husserl's but above all the abyss that separates us. He has conveyed both with unsurpassable precision.

I am anxious to turn to the questions Ricoeur addresses to me at the end of his essay, questions whose importance cannot be overestimated. I am thinking especially of the critical remark he formulates as follows: if being is "the uncharacterizable," "the unqualified *par excellence,*" how is it possible that it should be other than "the pure indeterminate"? My reply, first of all, is *mea culpa*. My error, in the text cited and doubtless in others, was to proceed to what I will call (rather ungrammatically) an undue substantivizing of being and to have attached to being thus substantivized the label "uncharacterizable." This is clearly absurd and renders unrecognizable what both has been and has more explicitly become my essential intention. Instead of "uncharacterizable" one should say "noncharacterizing"; in other words, one should remain at the core of what, after Blondel, I should now call *la pensée pensante*.

What I wished to bring out and what for obvious reasons is difficult to formulate without contradiction is that when we attempt to grasp, or more exactly to come closer to, not "being" but rather "what it is to be" (in contrast, of course, to "what it is to have"), we necessarily move into an

area where there is no longer any question of proceeding according to a
method consisting in enumerating and associating predicates (however that
might be done).

An obvious illustration of this is the "Judge not" of the Christian
ethic. What is it to judge if not precisely to introduce predicates? But if I
do not judge—provided that such nonjudgment is not merely abstention—
I can draw nearer to the being of the other, or of my neighbor, in a way
that would be impossible within the sphere of judgment.

Perhaps we can shed some light, however minute, on what is meant by
"the being of my neighbor." Here it becomes quite clear that *being* is
taken as a verb and not as a noun. In this sense the image to which one
almost inevitably resorts, that of a nucleus, must be absolutely rejected. I
think at this point we are close to the truly admirable work of Pierre Boutang in his thesis *L'Ontologie du secret,* which, although certainly difficult, is perhaps inspired. Furthermore I should note that in speaking of
secret, one runs the risk once again of implying something within, offering
a "nuclear" value (in the etymological sense of the word). But the being
of my neighbor, I repeat, cannot be designated; rather it should be understood as, let us say, a certain risk, a certain way of "beating" (as in the
beating of the heart) or of breathing. I would even allow the word *participation* to be used here in the strict sense, although its use raises objections
to which I have often called attention. Nevertheless I may be able to elucidate my thinking somewhat by saying that here participation evokes the
role of a musician in the performance of a symphony. An observer restricted to the merely visual aspect, saying that this musician appeared as
one among the sum total of performers, would obviously fall short of what
is meant here by the word *participation.* Undoubtedly this remark could
apply equally to the mode of participation of citizens in the life of the
community they form together.

It seems to me that this is the perspective we must adopt in order to
truly understand the meaning of the contrast between problem and mystery, a contrast that has resulted in some deplorable misunderstandings. I
will confine myself here to what I was saying about participation in an
orchestral performance. It is quite clear that for a deaf person, the experience will be reduced to a sort of spatial configuration and at the same time
to a notion of compatibility. The deaf person will be able to observe that
no one is absent, for the one hundred and twenty-five persons composing
the orchestra are in the places assigned to them. He or she will even be
able visually to recognize the different instruments and so on. Nevertheless
the invisible reality for which these people are assembled according to this
determined arrangement will remain beyond comprehension; the deaf per-

son cannot imagine what it is all about, even on the basis, for example, of replies to questions written down by some kind person. Eventually the deaf person might be persuaded that there is a reality here, but the reality is comprehensible only in a confused fashion.

We might also think about those who, without being deaf in the physiological sense of the word, do not understand anything about the music being performed, even though they have to some extent contributed to its being played. It should not be necessary to point out that here we are as far as possible from agnosticism, which remains rigorously imprisoned in the idea of being as a nucleus—an idea I began by rejecting. (Of course I do not pretend that my comparison is strictly adequate; it certainly is not, nor can it be. But it puts us on the right path.)

Furthermore as far as reason is concerned, I am increasingly convinced that its characteristic consists precisely in reflecting on itself and in going beyond the expressions of "self" with which it is at first tempted to identify itself. That is the fatal mistake committed by the rationalists (with a lower-case r). The incomparable merit of Kant and, I might add, of Fichte as well was to be fully aware of the dynamic character of reason, even if they were wrong in trying to fix it within immutable categories or within a dialectic that ultimately risks becoming tyrannical. This is sufficient to explain why I will never allow myself to be called an irrationalist.

I readily admit that all these ideas are probably stated too imprecisely in my writings. These gaps or lacunae are doubtlessly explained by what Ricoeur has so well caught when he says that my philosophical thought is essentially an opening on and toward drama and not at all, like Husserl's thought, an opening on and toward science. Without in the least subscribing to the schemata that satisfy the psychoanalyst, one could rightfully say that the whole of my thought and of my work may have had as its starting point the traumatic experiences I suffered in childhood, which I discussed in *En chemin vers quel eveil*? It seems to me permissible to assert that my existential anguish was gradually transmuted into compassion and that in my life compassion has perhaps played a role comparable to that of intentionality in Husserlian phenomenology.

On reflection and within the very area of Ricoeur's preoccupation, I realize that I must once again reconsider the meaning or perhaps even the legitimacy of the question "What is it to be?" The difficulty is self-evident. To ask oneself what it is to be—is this not to seek the mode of suffering or of acting to which being can be assimilated? But on reflection it seems that this search is contradictory, for is it not advisable to admit that any suffering or acting whatsoever is precisely a mode of being? Primary reflection does not seem to be able to go beyond this observation, and this would tend basically to disqualify *esse* as an extreme indetermination.

Yet something in us protests against this reduction. This protest appears at first perhaps as a reminder that is in truth formulated in terms we would do well to revise. This reminder bears on the fact that we are incontestably led to affirm a certain hierarchy in being, but we are tempted to translate this hierarchy into quantitative language, distinguishing between a lesser-being and a greater-being. Moreover, as I have said, this quantitative language is felt to be inadequate, or in any case capable of arousing a certain suspicion best expressed in saying that in reality this hierarchy is qualitative. Let us not fail to confess that at this point our thought proceeds rather gropingly. But it does reveal a certain assurance that intends, at its own horizon, an identity between *esse* and value. This identity cannot be apprehended precisely because it is at the horizon, but it is nevertheless in relation to it that we find the experiences given to us in life—on our way *toward what awakening*?

G.M.

19

Garth J. Gillan

THE QUESTION OF EMBODIMENT: MARCEL AND MERLEAU-PONTY

T O inquire into the question of incarnation in the thought of Marcel and into the question of corporeal subjectivity, the phenomenal body, in the writings of Merleau-Ponty is to create a philosophical reading of two discourses bearing on an ontological center, the manner in which consciousness is in the world and the manner in which the significance of that world captures consciousness: the facticity of existence and the incorporation of consciousness before the fact of the world. Such a task also entails unraveling the texture of those discourses and noting the discordances and the absences that create asymmetrical relationships between the thought of Marcel and the thought of Merleau-Ponty. A philosophical reading of incarnation in Marcel and Merleau-Ponty is more than a textual exegesis; it is an exploration of meaning and structure.

To disengage the center around which the theme of incarnation revolves in Marcel and Merleau-Ponty is therefore impossible without exposing the structural significance of that theme for Marcel and Merleau-Ponty as a moment in the creation of a philosophical problematic or as a singular starting point bestowing on reflection its momentum and direction. *Structure* and *significance* are pivotal words here, for they signify an interpretation lying beyond philology or philological exegesis and disclosing the relations and intentional implications that form the content and meaning of concepts. Within the totality of a single discourse, those relations and intentional implications form the content of the concepts they underscore as well as the texture of the discourse in which they are embedded. Within philosophical discourse ideas are related to ideas not by association but by intrinsic means, in a relationship of founding and founded, so that to understand the content and meaning of ideas it is necessary to under-

stand both their dependence on one another and the material relations binding them to one another within the structure of a total discourse.

It is in this manner that a philosophical reading is a structural reading—
a disengagement, from the total compass of a discourse, of the "signifying
structure" encompassing what is signified by the discourse in its differentiations, silences, and positive moments, which together create a configuration of meaning, that is, a structure.[1] Within the structure of the text, as
a signifying structure and hence as a thought, lies the sedimented history
that each idea carries within its meaning and that recalls to the present the
originality and origins of each meaning.[2] As a meaning within a signifying
structure, an idea signifies what it is within the history it has accumulated
in its passage through the movements of articulations; hence it signifies not
as a positive content, an ideal existent open to the possibility of positive
definition, but as a continual shifting back and forth, within those ruptured
silences, along the lateral relationships making up the web of discourse.

Only on the basis of such reflections can the ambiguity of the theme of
incarnation be understood in Marcel's thought. If there is one fundamental
given for philosophical reflection, that of incarnation, there are throughout
Marcel's writings other ways to gain access to the fundamental domain of
metaphysics: fidelity, saintliness, love, the presence of others, and transcendence. Yet none of these other modes of introduction to the fundamental problematic of philosophy as an approach to being negates the central position of incarnation. At the same time incarnation may be the
central given without being the central preoccupation of a philosophy of
being. Ontology is not exhausted in the theme of incarnation; the development of its significance immediately throws philosophical reflection beyond incarnation as a self-enclosed theme into the reflections or series of
reflections that it generates. Consequently it is impossible to characterize
Marcel's thought as a philosophy of incarnation, but at the same time it is
possible to characterize it as a philosophy of being. What is the significance then of the theme of incarnation for Marcel within the limits of
impossibility and possibility?

From the searchings and groupings of the *Metaphysical Journal* for the
starting point and foundation for philosophy comes a distinction that is
crucial for determining the place of incarnation for Marcel, namely, the
"general and very important distinction between data that are susceptible
of forming the occasion for a problem—that is, objective data—and data
on which the mind must be based so as to state any problem whatsoever."[3]
Among the latter data are those phenomena forming the horizons of the
question of incarnation: sensation as feeling and participation, and the radical bond between me and "my body." In addition the bond of the self

and the body has the "metaphysical form" of "hicceity." The contingency of the bond of the self and the body signifies that when approaching the question of its meaning, reflection is faced with a fact, or a facticity, that cannot be dissolved into concepts proper to reflection but rather must be recognized as the starting point for reflection. Correspondingly the question of incarnation and the questions of sensation and feeling that form its horizons are not questions in the sense of problems to be solved or problems to which reflection could frame an appropriate or adequate answer; rather they form the question-foundations on which and within which reflection must move. Incarnation and its horizons are the ground-questions and the grounding questions for philosophical reflection.

Because we cannot separate existence from our consciousness of ourselves as existing or from our consciousness of ourselves as bound to a body, that is, as incarnate,[4] the theme of incarnation provides access to existence in a twofold manner. Incarnation delivers over to reflection the sense of the existence of subjectivity and in turn is the basis on which we can say that things exist. Existence has a meaning for consciousness, a density that weighs down consciousness, because each of us is an "incarnate personality" with an intimate relationship to a body such that that body is his or her own. The statement "I am my body" is meaningful not because it is a relation posited between concepts but because it is a "fundamental predicament"; "I am my body" expresses a situation underlying all situations, a fact underlying all facts, because it makes all situations realities and all facts possible.

As a fact beneath all facts, the facticity of incarnation—its manner of being a fundamental predicament—eludes inscription into thought. The fact of existence is obscure, and this prevents the total achievement of self-consciousness and brings the eternal world into its own ambit: "The obscurity of the external world is a function of my own obscurity to myself; the world has no intrinsic obscurity."[5] More figuratively, the shadow is at the centre."[6] With incarnation then the world is given as a situation—as an impenetrable fact with the obscurity and shadow necessary for a fact before the gaze of consciousness—and subjectivity is given as a predicament, as data from which reflection must begin, because they are given as that toward which reflection must turn in order to comprehend existence, be it the existence of the world of things or the existence of that consciousness before the world, incarnate personality. Hence a metaphysics of existence as a philosophy of the sense of being must begin with incarnation, for it is the facticity of incarnation that lays down the fundamental situation for philosophical reflection.[7]

But the problematic of the philosophy of existence as Marcel defines it does not end here. The body as the body of someone, my body or the other's body (what Marcel specifically terms "corporeity"), is "the frontier district between being and having."[8] Things are within my reach and at my disposal because I have a body, and hence the relationship I have toward things as possessions issues from the original contact with them that puts them at my disposal and that gives me power over them. Thus open to me is a sphere of objects and a domain of existence that I can call mine and that is an extension of my body as the fact of this power over things and their manipulation. In the mode of having then the world is "my system," a certain framework of experience that I have and thus identify with the extent of my own existence. In this manner the things of the world and others become problems for me. The concept of problematization depends on the mode of having that issues from the facticity of the body, because in that mode of taking up the existence of things and the lives of others, the things of the world and the lives of others enter into a definite framework of existence, into a "certain continuity of experience which is to be safeguarded *against* appearances."[9]

But at the same time that the body lays down the circumference of the world at the disposal of subjectivity, it escapes that relationship itself. Although it gives the appearance of an absolute having, grounding all other modalities of having, the body is not in the end something that I have. All the modalities of having imply the activity of the body and its power over things; therefore it is not truly at my disposal, for it is the source of the disposability of things. Thus the body finally lies outside of the category of having, because it is not an instrument and because in laying down the conditions of having it escapes that condition.[10] Corporeity consequently does not lie entirely within the dimension of having and the existential relation that it grounds with respect to the world. Since *Being and Having* states that the body is also the locus of history, the movement counter to the dimension of having depends on the analysis of phenomena rooted in the body (feeling, suffering, and sensation) and the mode of being proper to them (participation), which plunge the analysis of the facticity of incarnation into the dimension of the metaproblematic, the realm of mystery. On the other side of this dimension lies the sense of the participation in being, which is also an aspect of the facticity of incarnation. The body as corporeity lies between both as the frontier at which the specific problematic of existential philosophy becomes disclosed as the question of the ontological mystery.

The idea of participation occurs on many levels of Marcel's thought, from the fundamental mode of presence in the ontological mystery to the mode of being that defines the relationship of the senses to the sensible world. Marcel rejects the representational image of the way the senses confront reality because it sees sensation merely as a message; instead he sees the senses as witnesses to being and as an attestation of reality that is for the body-subject an immediate feeling on which translation and interpretation are then based.[11] The fundamental level of sensation is not an objectifying relationship; rather it is an involvement in what is sensed and with reality that is prior to the countermovement of detachment from sensible meaning represented by the activities of translation and interpretation. Essential to this characterization is the analysis of feeling (*sentir*), which brings sensation within the question of the mystery of being and which determines the sense in which the latter must be understood.

As Marcel emphasizes in *Creative Fidelity* and *The Mystery of Being,* feeling is beyond the duality of activity and passivity because it is an act of receptivity and an act of creativity. Feeling cannot be seen as passivity, because to receive something or someone is to be originally receptive, to welcome, and thus to engage in an act "of opening oneself to. . . ."[12] The receptiveness of feeling, whether it occurs on the level of intersubjectivity or on the level of sensation, is more than a mere blind passivity, for it calls for a creative orientation toward what presents itself. This positive orientation implies that what presents itself becomes at home (*chez soi*) with the self because it also signifies an original involvement in the appearing sense, which is the characteristic mark of a creative, positive orientation. In this respect our understanding of participation depends on the depth of the meaning of the expression *chez soi*.[13] But what specifically eliminates the interpretation of feeling as the experience of participation from being understood in an objectifying act, or even as an act in the sense of the *cogito,* is not only creative receptiveness, which is at the foundation of feeling, but also its intersubjective character and the sense of an encompassing involvement that carries subjectivity in its wake.

The importance of these last dimensions of the act of participation can clearly be seen in emergent participation, that is, in participation manifest and clearly structured as participation, such as the act of thanksgiving. But even in submerged participation—the participation that can be reached only through secondary reflection, the free act that turns to the nature of things themselves—the same structure holds sway. The will to participate is based on a sense of community, of a sensed and felt bond issuing into a type of unit; we participate on the basis of a common feeling. Furthermore the sense of participation involves being seized and taken up into what appeals to the act of "opening oneself to. . . ." This act cannot maintain the distance that distinguishes the opposition of subjectivity to objectivity, and it lacks the characteristics of distinct acts, *cogitationes,* emanating from the sovereign gaze of subjectivity. Rather in participation the opposition of subject and object and the nature of subjectivity as *cogito* come into question, and both are lost in a movement that captures subjectivity by involving it in a response that takes it beyond itself.[14]

The analysis of participation does more, however, than locate the intelligibility of feeling; at the same time it defines incarnation as the relationship to the body as *mine*. The phrase "I am my body" is relevant not at the level of the body as an object but only at the level of feeling, whose ambiguous identity rests on the meaning of participation. The body is first of all mine, Marcel says, because it is felt; the identity is one of feeling.[15] In this respect the existence of the body is that of a "nonmediatizable immediate," an immediacy of feeling that is incapable of resolution into other terms or into a process of understanding that would transform its immediacy into a systematic order of concepts. The immediacy of incarnation as a mode of feeling stands as an impenetrable obstacle before the evanescent mediations of conceptual thought. Its immediacy in its irreducible facticity is thus related to another type of consciousness of being, one that is not based on the successive transformations of being into thought but is originally a recognition of fact and of the character of fact, facticity. The recognition of the being of the body and of the ontological dimension of incarnation disclosed in the immediacy of feeling that unites self and body is an "exclamatory awareness of existence."[16] The self provides no escape from the originality of this immediate facticity of the body or from its resultant disclosure of an awareness of existence distinct from the mediations of thought, for the sense of feeling as participation unites the experience of self—the experience of the mine, of my-self—with the experience of the body. The self is an incarnate personality and a certain "thickening, a sclerosis, and perhaps—who knows?—a sort of apparently spiritualized expression (an expression *of* an expression) of the body."[17] It is thus not self or thought that leads reflection into the nature of subjectivity but that "exclamatory awareness of existence" that issues from the recognition of the immediacy of participation in existence, which is signified by the body as mine and by the central fact of incarnation.

The analysis of the facticity of incarnation therefore throws reflection beyond the boundaries of mediating thought into a zone dominated by the reality of participation. Subjectivity is subjectivity in and through participation, through an involvement in existence and not through the isolating nature of the *cogito*. But that means that the reality of subjectivity and the significance of the facticity of the body in its ultimate ontological import lie within the dimension of the metaproblematic, that is, within the dimension of mystery. Participation as the concrete existence of subjectivity signifies that to be a subject is to be caught up in a movement of existence, in a mode of being, that encompasses at the same time that it involves and rests the force of its mode of being on the exigency of appeal: "It may be said at once that this reality gives *me* to myself insofar as I give myself to it; it is through the mediation of the act in which I center myself on it, that I truly become a subject, I repeat, *that I become a subject*."[18]

The problematic in terms of which the sense of subjectivity defines itself on the level of the body, the theme of incarnate participation, thus also reveals an ontological problematic, that of the ontological mystery, which after the *Metaphysical Journal* comes to define the specific reaches and limits of Marcel's thought. Incarnation as the existential center of the disclosure of participation is at the same time then the center of the disclosure of the direction that reflection must take to become aware of the nature of existential thought in the question of the ontological mystery.[19] For the dimension of being is precisely what is grasped through participation in what transcends and encompasses: "A mystery is a problem which encroaches upon its own data, invading them, as it were, and thereby transcending itself as a simple problem."[20] But the theme of incarnation defines the problematic of ontology and of existential philosophy not as the specific content of that singular project of reflection but as the stage, the zone, or the grounding fact that reveals the proper sense in which the question of being in the many modalities of its participation—hope, love, friendship, faith, fidelity, and service—must be breached, namely, the sense of mystery. The content of this existential philosophy issues from the concrete ways in which the drama of existence is realized and from the concrete attitudes in which, across the stage of incarnation, human participation in being is played out.

Because of this role of incarnation, ontology for Marcel does not take the road of an ontology of perception, as it does for Merleau-Ponty, but rather launches that "convergence of the metaphysical and religious,"[21] of the ontological and the ethical, that places philosophy for Marcel on the threshold of religious faith. But this "convergence" brings into question the place of incarnation as the ground of Marcel's philosophy. For Marcel the theme of corporeity or incarnation is at the frontier of the reciprocal question of being and having and at the limit of the problematic and the metaproblematic; this signifies that from the outset the question of the body as mine is an ontological question simultaneously phrased in ethical terms. The place of incarnation within the problematic of existential philosophy thus moves from the center toward another *topos*—the confrontation of the problematic and the metaproblematic, or the dimension of mystery—where faith and love are coextensive with the ontological dimensions of existence and at the same time define the meaning of the person. If incarnation is the existential center of ontology without being the center of its reflection, if it gives to existential thought its typology without being the *topos* in and for itself, then in what sense is this philosophy grounded? If the theme of incarnation does not ground ontology in the radiating significance of its latent meaning, does not this ontology take the framework of its questions from one source and the content and concrete direction of its investigations from another? At a deeper level these questions engage the significance of the idea of participation as the relationship of the body to the world and of subjectivity to meaning. Participation on the level of the body orients existential philosophy away from the philosophy of subjectivity and freedom and toward the question of being, but as it thrusts reflection into the dimension of the metaproblematic, participation reveals a multidimensionality—encompassing the levels of existence from corporeity to love—with a center but not with a grounding moment. Incarnation reveals participation as a mode of being only in a privileged way and not as the source of its intelligibility.

In their critical significance the questions arising from the assessment of the place of incarnation in the problematic of Marcel's existential philosophy enclose a countermovement toward the founding moment in the intelligibility of the body and toward the founding relation binding the body to existence and to the world. For Merleau-Ponty this relation is perception not as a generalized relation but as an original engagement with meaning, whose articulations describe the intersection of the body as a perceiving subjectivity and the world as the general structures of the perceived; this forms the unique problematic of an ontology of dispersed and redoubled meaning, the ontology of the flesh. In the analyses of the *Structure of Behavior* and of its theme, behavior as form, in the *Phenomenology of Perception,* this ontology takes on the hesitant form of a founding and operative perceptual presence of which the body and the world are abstract moments and for which corporeal subjectivity, or the phenomenal body, is not the final term or the object of this phenomenology but rather the path this phenomenology must take toward the founding operation of meaning and of the world it illuminates, that is, toward perception and the world of perception.[22] In the *Structure of Behavior* and in the *Phenomenology of Perception,* the organism and the body gain their significance within the larger problematic, which is not the definition of certain objects but the description of perceptual meaning and the assessment of the orientation it gives to philosophical reflection.

The *Structure of Behavior* moves on two levels that are actually one in their mutual dependence. The first level is the analysis of behavior and consequently the location of the significance of perception within the intelligibility and sensibility of behavior. The second is the analysis, or more properly speaking the description, of the significance of the meaning of behavior for perception and the establishment of perception as the moment where the meaning of behavior as form and as structure originally takes on reality. The meaning of behavior is the perceptual meaning of behavior, since the significance of form originally and in its derived forms refers to its sense within perceptual experience. Thus the two levels come to meet in the theoretical moment that grounds them. In effect the realization of the significance of the structure of behavior is accomplished by awakening reflection to the experience of perception as the primal source of the meaning of behavior and thereby awakening it to the significance of perception itself as symbolic behavior.

In the *Structure of Behavior* symbolic behavior is distinguished from the syncretic and amovable forms of behavior by the manner in which human activity possesses meaning. Syncretic behavior is the organism's response to certain abstract patterns or configurations of particular stimuli. Amovable behavior is enclosed within the material conditions of behavior but finds some possibility of variation with respect to the material content of behavior. The situation to which the organism responds is "simple temporal and spatial contiguity," which are relations for the organism and not punctual stimuli. The signal to which behavior responds in conditioned behavior is a *Gestalt*.

Yet symbolic behavior is not merely a response to a situation within the organic environment but also a response where the relationship of behavior to the environment expresses the relationship of the act to the general signification of the stimuli and is thus mediated through the symbol. The specific experience Merleau-Ponty analyzes to establish the pertinence of this characterization of symbolic behavior is the behavior involved in playing a musical instrument. In this behavior a common experience ties together, through an internal bond, the gestures and the visual and auditory stimuli. Within the total behavior each does not have an isolated significance; rather they communicate with each other. The gestures express on their level the significance of the notation, the notation expresses on its level the significance of the melody, and in turn the melody expresses the manner and execution of the gestures. But what is of theoretical importance within this experience is that each part has expressive value for the other and that this expressive value is realized in the different parts of the total behavior and is thus their internal bond. The internal bond uniting the different responses gives rise to a common signification.

In symbolic behavior then the same theme, the same general signification, is expressed in a variety of modes and captured in a multiplicity of perspectives. The meaning of behavior is not the stimuli to which it is a living response, as a moment of the environment, but rather behavior is signification itself. Behavior is no longer the direct and immediate response to certain typical structures within the environment or to certain typical relations but is the mediated significance of the stimuli, as those stimuli are mediated through the activity of the behavior itself. The act is thus its own signification, since it is freed from the environment, from a direct dependence on vital and natural situations, and thus can signify the environment, can express it in a symbol.[23]

The concept of symbolic behavior provides the basic description from which to extend the description of behavior to perception. In the section on the human order, Merleau-Ponty places the significance of perception within the scope of behavior by rejecting the interpretation of perception as an action working on pregivens. If perception is behavior, it is so more along the lines defined by the concept of work: an action that is the production of its givens and a relationship that moves in the direction of an involvement with its content.[24] Perception is the giving; it is not the reworking of pregivens but the working of givens. Perception then is a moment of the dialectical relationship between the conscious subject and its milieu—a relationship that figures in the expressiveness of behavior, in expressing the signification of the milieu—which defines the concrete subject. Perception is behavior.

Perception, as the work that gives its signifying relation to the world, thus grasps meaning in a manner that transcends the interpretation of perception in terms of pregiven sensations. Perception goes directly to its objects in their expressive meaning; perception grasps meaning as physiognomic, as one can perceive the physiognomy of the face without being conscious of its lines or colors.[25] If behavior is form as a perceptual meaning, so is the object of perception, which is an expressive meaning antecedent and prior to the disassembling of meaning within the analysis of punctual sense qualities, first of all lived as a reality, as a source of involvement, and as the obsession of involvement. An object is first lived as such not within the moment of distance and detachment but in an original involvement as the immanent term of practical intentions that thus, as a manner of behaving, are not a type of knowledge but a type of presence.[26] The question of the object of perception then is a question that refers to the emergence of an irreducible, objective meaning within experience itself. And the description of the behavior of the organism as form, structure, and Gestalt is in turn irreducible, because it arises from an experience that does not translate other experiences but is itself the original text.

Corresponding to these noetic analyses of perception and behavioral (organic) subjectivity is an analysis, a noematics, bearing on the structure of the world and laying the foundations for the later description of the intersection of the body and the world in the moment of perceptual presence. In the *Structure of Behavior* the formulation of this description is the analysis of space. Behavior as a dialectic and equilibrium achieved between action and the field of action demands more than actual directions and spacial localizations among things; rather it demands poles of action that are virtual directions situating and giving shape to the field in terms of bodily movements. The space of bodily behavior is not merely an actual space, a space of the here and now understood in the abstract sense of what is absolutely seen, but a virtual space, traced with lines of indicated directions and with possible lines of action.[27]

But there is a more fundamental structure within perception that grounds the virtuality of space and that is the very structure of perceptual meaning as form. Perceptual meaning takes shape within the structure of figure/ground. If it is impossible to give a physiological interpretation of this structure, as the Gestaltists attempted to do, this is because it is a perceptual structure. The structure, figure/ground, cannot be translated into more elementary elements, since at the moment of translation it would lose the specific rapport of figure to ground. It is in perception that we learn of it, and thus it is only within perception that it retains its significance. Since this structure is uniquely a perceptual structure, it signifies, in the rapport of figure to ground, the sense of depth and virtuality to be found in the perceptual world. Meaning is not actuality; it is achieved within a ground that provides the horizon and context within which what is actual as figure emerges. But then perceptual meaning is not only the figure but precisely the relation, figure/ground, since the figure only takes on significance within its relation to the ground. Perceptual meaning is the configuration that arises from the internal rapport between the two terms of the relation. They cannot be separated at the level of perceptual significance, since each functions in terms of the other and the structure as a whole defines behavior as a total act. The structure that opens up virtuality within the world of behavior is the structure of perceptual meaning. The perceived world is a world of virtuality, and perception possesses a sense within the sense of virtuality.

These themes and analyses only place us within the emergence of perceptual behaviors; it is the specific task of the *Phenomenology of Perception* to install reflection within the unique relation that perception creates between corporeal subjectivity and the world.[28] Installed within that perspective, the analysis of perception in the *Phenomenology of Perception* confronts reflection with a subjectivity that is that of the body in its pre-personal adherence to the world and its manner of living its inherence in space, its own spaciality lived as a motor intentionality. This manner of living realizes a hold on physiognomic meaning, a physiognomic perception that grasps meaning in terms of configuration, a meaning grasped and expressed across the lines, illuminations, and colors that serve as its foundation without being isolatable elements. The motricity of the body is a hold on meaning as a modality of existence and as a modulation of the manner in which the body is present to the world and within the world. Beneath personal existence there is an adherence to the world—in the anonymity and generality of the habitual body—that is already operative in the movement and passage of time and that stands surety for the fragile aspirations of personal existence by making possible their incorporation within being, by lending to them the weight and density of the body and its acts, and by placing them within the perspective of that past of all pasts, the body in its habituality and generality, a past that weighs down the sense of things and gives them solidity.

Beneath the personal consciousness of acts and the personal world of things desired and longed for, there is a prepersonal and preobjective world, which is the result not of an act of consciousness but of the "there," the facticity of an original involvement of the body with the world and the world with the body. The density of things in the world, the "power of fact," which testifies to the particular sense of the world, comes not only from the horizon of the ground in perception but also from the ambiance of the body, from its permanent ability to move around things and encompass them. Neither one is solely responsible for the facticity of things or for the event of meaning that arises from the disruption of the landscape as the body moves from perceptual field to perceptual field. This mutual implication is what Merleau-Ponty terms the paradox of the presence to the world: intentions efface themselves before things in order for things to appear in the solidity of their being, and yet things only appear through the intentions they solicit. The body thus cannot be understood without reference to the world, nor the world without reference to the body, because the meaning of things within the world and the meaning of the actions of the body cross each other and intersect.

The name for the body that intersects with the pathways of the world is the habitual body. In opposition to the actual body, this body is impersonal and exists at the level of generality. The phenomenon of repression makes possible the understanding of this dimension of the body as prepersonal involvement with the world by focusing attention on the structure of temporality. The personal world is constructed on a world already given and thus on a world that is past. The world and the body of the world endure not as substances but as the past on which every present is a present action and achievement; they are the past of every personal action, and they give to that action the density of time and duration. The analysis of repression in the *Phenomenology of Perception* follows this analysis by exposing the enduring of the past in the present and by witnessing not to the submergence of meaning in an eternal forgetting and forgottenness but to a submergence of meaning that provides for the broad outlines of present action by providing their general and impersonal framework. What is repressed is not what the subject consciously intends but what is nonetheless continually there to plague the clarity of consciousness to itself and make it turn back to a period of experience when it could not assume responsibility for itself, when it was more acted on than acting, and when the innocence of its desires was the mask of incest. Repression therefore allows us to see that "my organism, as a pre-personal adhering to the general form of the world, as anonymous and general existence, plays, beneath my personal life, this role of an innate complex."[29]

The specific manner in which the body adheres to the world and the manner in which the body is a perceiving consciousness revolves, for Merleau-Ponty, around the question of the spaciality of the body, of the body as postural schema (a consciousness elaborated within the spaciality of the body), as the anchorage of subjectivity in the world, and as motor intentionality. The general expression of this concrete understanding of the body speaks of the body as movement of existence and the founding layer of consciousness. The body is not an object,[30] and as a consequence its spaciality is of another structure, one involving its opening onto things in perception. It is at the level of the motility or motricity of the body that synthesis is formed in which the spacial body, gestures, and things gain in concrete phenomenal significance by being captured in the same movement of understanding.

The phenomenon of allocheiria, the displacement of sensations from one part of the body to another and specifically from one hand to the other, is impossible without a correspondence between the segments of the body that is founded in principle rather than on the fortuitous association of the members of the body in a total impression. The body must be such that a system of equivalences among the members of the body is an actuality. The equivalence evinced by displacement shows clearly that the members of the body form a system within which they correspond to each other. Thus the consciousness that the body has of itself is a corporeal schema

that is the "law of constitution" of this correspondence. The corporeal
schema is then "a total awareness of my posture in the intersensory world,
a 'form' in a sense used by Gestalt psychology."[31]

But it is insufficient to take this unity of the body in a static sense,
since the unity being spoken of is a unity that arises through the gestures
of the body. To the static understanding of form, Merleau-Ponty states,
there must be added the conception of the corporeal schema as something
dynamic, as a posture in relation to the tasks and actions taken up within
the world. In this sense the corporeal schema is the "spaciality of situation."[32] The body then expresses a "here," an inhabiting of space, that is
not the gradual accumulation of different lines of direction, of different
coordinates in exterior space, but "the laying down of the first co-ordi-
nates, the anchoring of the active body in an object, the situation of the
body in fact of its tasks."[33]

The corporeal schema is therefore not the assemblage of the conscious
indications of the members and points of the body but the background from
which the actions of the body emerge and that thus insures their actuality;
this underscores their coordination with other actions and hence makes
them possible as gestures. To the horizon of exterior space there corresponds the horizon of interior space, and both together compose the double
horizon of perception. The body elaborates through its gestures a space
that is irreducible to objective space, because it is an activity beneath that
space—the laying down of the very dimensions within the perceived world
that are assembled into the explicit coordinates of objective space. The
space of the body is the space that arises through movement and action.[34]

Of crucial importance in understanding the spaciality of the body is the
distinction between *greifen* and *zeigen,* "grasping" and "pointing,"
which is established through the analysis of the motor disturbances of a
patient of Goldstein's. Merleau-Ponty does not accept the distinction as
Goldstein interprets it, that is, as the patient's loss of the abstract attitude
and retention of the concrete attitude. Merleau-Ponty sees it as a retention
of a concrete familiarity with the world in the face of the narrowing of the
virtuality of the world.[35] The patient is in contact only with situations that
have an actual and vital significance for him and with which he is familiar
from past activities. And he is only related to his body in the same manner.
He is related to his body through the vital significance of events within
that body; he can move toward a point on his body bitten by a mosquito,
but he cannot point to the same spot on command. Grasping and pointing
therefore do not have the same significance for him. The experience of
grasping points out that the gestures of the body are already in contact with
the things toward which they move; it is the phenomenal body that we

move and not the objective body. Objects are originally given to the body in grasping as poles of action. The body is therefore given as the potentiality of a certain range of actions within a space that is a totality of things to be handled. For the normal subject this manipulation of space is located not only in what is effectively and actually present but in what is not yet present, in what is possible and virtual.[36]

It is this horizon of virtuality and of the possible—an actual possible—that underscores the spaciality of the body as a consciousness inhabiting the gestural anticipation of things as poles of action, a consciousness realized on the level of motricity; this motor intentionality is the presence of the body at once to itself and to the goal of its act.[37] This horizon of virtuality within the structure of the intentional motricity of the phenomenal body enables Merleau-Ponty to escape the duality of the concrete attitude and the abstract attitude, since it establishes the possibility of objective space—the space of localizable points—within corporeal space and thus the abstract attitude within the movement of grasping,[38] just as the objective body is copossible with the phenomenal body and originates in the same movement.[39] The distinction between grasping and pointing cannot then in all rigor be maintained as two levels of consciousness, as the regions of the in-itself and the for-itself, because for normal consciousness the possibility of each lies in the other. Both are moments of a motor intentionality that adheres to a situation in being open to the virtual dimensions of the perceiving gesture present in the horizon of the body and the horizon of the world.

The disturbances of Schneider are not the lack of specific contents or the impairment of thought but an alteration of his perceptual world and of his contact with it. This world is altered in its structure, in the sense of the virtuality that animates it and that brings with it a sense of correspondence and equivalence between thought and vision and the different organs and senses of the body. The reciprocal virtuality of the body and of the world is the realization of a mutual inherence of one in the other that testifies to an innate familiarity of one with the other on the level of the intentional motricity of the body. It is in this respect that the world of thought becomes an acquired sedimentation and surrounds consciousness as a "physiognomy of questions."[40] This same virtuality inhabits the perceived thing and underscores the intercommunication of its perceptual regions with one another, and this leads to the penetration of its texture by its color and gives to it an immediate signification without the intermediary of language. The signification of the perceived thing is a physiognomic meaning; it suggests in its sensible properties a meaning that is the precise function of a physiognomy. Physiognomic perception is "that dialogue of the subject with the object, that taking up on the part of the subject of the meaning dispersed in the object and on the part of the object of the intentions which is physiognomic perception, [a dialogue that] places around the subject a world which speaks to him of himself and installs his own thoughts within the world."[41]

The theory of the body is already a theory of perception. This affirmation, which prefaces the second part of the *Phenomenology of Perception,* introduces the concrete sense in which we should understand the major direction of the problematic of the *Phenomenology of Perception:* it is the attempt to understand the perceiving subject as the perceived world. The central focus of this problematic is found not in the analysis of the intentional motricity of the body and the related discussions of its expressivity and sexuality but beyond the theme of the body, as Merleau-Ponty informs us, and within the theme of the perceived world.[42] It is as the level of the world, at the level of the type of meaning inhabiting perception, that perception gains its full significance and not within an analysis that would concentrate on its characteristics as an act—or as consciousness in the classical sense of the *cogito,* a consciousness that has a specific function to fulfill as an act—since it is distinct from the objects of which it is conscious and untouched by them and hence must be the process in which their unity and its own unity is assured. Perceiving consciousness has no function because it is inhabited with meaning and modified by it and most importantly because it is not an act, since its unity is assured by the unity of time, that is, by a general spontaneity that is the movement of consciousness without being the product of its active synthesis.

Just as the body is an expressive space and the gestures of the body possess expressive meaning as configurations on the invisible horizon of its postural presence to itself, in its sense of itself as a system of equivalences and in the communication of sensory regions, so the meaning that is realized by the object and within perception is indistinguishable from the act in which it comes to be, because it too, as form and *Gestalt,* is an expressive and gestural unity. It is a physiognomy and an organism not only in the sense that perceptual meaning arises as the resolution of tensions in the field within which it appears, within the structure of figure/ground, but also in another sense, which makes it possible to say that the sky "thinks itself in me" and that perception raises the meaning of the sensible to an existence for itself.[43] This is because the sensible is not a literal meaning but arises from the interrelation of its parts rather than from a signification given once and for all and without internal modulation. It is this internal modulation, which corresponds at the same time to the gestural exploration of the body, that accounts for the unity of the perceived and the act of perception in the sharing of a common meaning and consequently a common being. The tension that lives between the different parts of the sensible and that is the configuration of the thing meant, the sensible perceived, is the "sensibility" of each part to the others and a knowledge of the dynamics of the whole.[44] The sensible thus has a mode of being that does not separate it from the sensing. Both arise in a reciprocal articulation and within the reciprocal virtuality of the horizons of the body and the world. The world is configured within the gestures of the body; the gestures of the body lend themselves to this nascent figuration and surrender themselves to a field of meaning. In this double articulation, which makes perception and the perceived two abstract moments of a singular presence (as Merleau-Ponty notes in the chapter on temporality), the body is, in a phrase that anticipates *The Visible and the Invisible,* the "texture" of the world.[45]

The virtuality of the body as introduced in the *Phenomenology of Perception* through the description of the reversible tangibility and visibility of the body is, in addition to the intersection and double articulation of the body and the world, one of the themes in the *Phenomenology of Perception* that prepares for the idea of the flesh in *The Visible and Invisible.* The space from which the eye issues is always empty and void, and the hand touching is not the same hand that is touched. The one goes out to the object and the world; the other is the inhabitant of a definite point in space. "Insofar as it sees or touches the world," Merleau-Ponty says, "my body can therefore be neither seen nor touched. What prevents its ever being an object, ever being 'completely constituted', is that it is that by which there are objects. It is neither tangible nor visible insofar as it is that which sees or touches."[46] In this capacity it serves, in coordination with the horizon of the world, as the ground that ensures the depth of perception and that constitutes a field of primordial presence as the phenomenal field in which things first appear.

On the surface it would seem that the impossibility of seizing the body in the act of perceiving would be contradicted by the existence of "double sensations." The right hand touching the left hand can reverse its role and become the hand touched by the left hand. The right and left hands are not in the same relation of touching-touched, but there is the experience of the alternation of roles, one hand now being touched and now touching as the other hand lapses into passivity. The term "double sensations" then refers to the identity of the hand touched with the hand touching; the hand touched will be the hand touching, and this reversibility of roles is the anticipation of one role over the other. In its touching, the hand touching feels itself being touched by the hand touched, and the hand touched is in turn a touching of the hand touching. In this reversibility the body touches itself touching, but it does so in such a manner that the two hands do not incorporate the same role at the same time. The relation of touching-touched remains on the threshold of coincidence, an immanence that establishes a reversibility by holding coincidence at bay and that thus instills in the sensibility of the body a "kind of reflection."[47]

The ontology of the flesh in *The Visible and the Invisible* issues from the course of the descriptions launched by what the *Structure of Behavior* took to be its task: the question of the relation between consciousness and nature. But at the same time it also signifies a break with that course of descriptions, even as they take form within the analyses of the *Phenomenology of Perception*. The working notes appended to Lefort's edition of *The Visible and the Invisible* recognize the ontological direction of the latter work, and they also isolate, from the multitude of its directions, two that limit its success: the framework established by the discourse of subjectivity and objectivity and the tacit cogito, a consciousness independent of the movement of words. The movement in *The Visible and the Invisible* away from the philosophy of consciousness ends not in a description of the body at a new level but in a description of being and of its fundamental dimension, the flesh.[48]

The flesh is already present in "Eye and Mind" as the encroachment of the visibility of the world on the visibility of the body—in the reference of the movements of vision back to the latent visibility of the eye for itself—and in turn of the visibility of the eye on the world as a visible thing. But it is also an encroachment that, in thus being the relation not of two positive moments but of one visibility rent by the action of seeing, is underscored by a latent texture. This is the invisible, the background that supports the recognition of the visibility of the eye in the visibility of things, the movement from one to the other, and that as background is what is not seen but what makes see. The flesh encompasses the signification of perceptual meaning as texture, and hence the visual quale gives what is not me because "as texture, it is the concretion of a universal visibility, of a unique Space which separates and which re-unites, which maintains all cohesion. . . . Each visual something, every individual gives itself as the result of a dehiscence of Being. That finally means that the specific character of the visible is to have a double of invisibility in the strict sense, which it renders present as a certain absence."[49] Visibility comes to be in terms of what is not seen: the seeing body and the lines of tension, the light, the illumination, and the shadows that are on the threshold of vision but are never on the other side of vision, are never of the visible, because they are, in coming together in a certain point or in a figure, what makes one see.

The Visible and the Invisible makes this precise: the flesh is the general dimension of being, its texture, in which the body and the world intertwine in one visibility and one tangibility; at the same time the different regions of the sensory, visibility and tangibility, intersect and transfer their values while remaining distinct. The emergent tangible and visible thing has an armature of invisibility that is not the negative of visibility or of tangibility but the latent Tangibility and Visibility that belong to the visible and the tangible and that are the dimensions within which these concretions of what is seen and touched—what we call things—install themselves. By its own reversibility—seeing itself see, touching itself touch—the body is a sensible thing among things and thus recognizes its sensibility in them; they too are as sensible as flesh. In the body is united a redoubling of Being, a seeing sensibility such that the latent, carnal being of the thing and the body are the same Being; each is the archetype of the other. The body belongs to the order of things of the world as universal flesh.[50] But in the end there are not two layers or leaves of Being but a "Visibility sometimes wandering and sometimes reassembled."[51] Thus the flesh is the *Urpräsentierbarkeit*,[52] the primordial field of presence that is latent in the texture of the world and of the reversibility of the body and that is the permanent possibility of visibility and tangibility here, there, and everywhere. The same movement underscores this coming into visibility and tangibility: the ontogenesis of the flesh and its dehiscence in being the seeing and the seen.

There is no name in traditional philosophy, Merleau-Ponty notes, for this dimension of Being, for "the flesh is not matter, is not mind, is not substance. To designate it, we should need the old term, 'element,' in the sense it was used to speak of water, air, earth, and fire, that is, in the sense of a *general thing,* midway between the spaciotemporal individual and the idea, a sort of incarnate principle that brings a style of being wherever there is a fragment of being. The flesh is in this sense an 'element of Being.'"[53] There is no name, for the meaning that the flesh signifies is not positive meaning, not an identity of signification, but *écart:* divergence and differentiation, the congealing of dispersed lines of tension, and the reassembling of a Visibility and a Tangibility spread over the body and the world and interposed between them. And yet, strictly speaking, it belongs to neither, because it belongs to both as the dimension in which both have their being and in which both come to be weighed down with the density and opacity of perceptual meaning as solid things in a fragile and invisible world.

In contrast with Marcel then corporeity for Merleau-Ponty does more than engage a singular philosophical style, that of existential philosophy, for it engages philosophy at the point where corporeity itself is thrown into question in its confrontation with the world. For Marcel the theme of incarnation enjoins philosophy within the problematic and the metaproblematic, that is, in the confrontation of problem and mystery, but not in such a way that incarnation itself forms the problematic of existential philosophy. The theme of incarnation does ground existential philosophy for Marcel in launching the further question of problem and mystery and thus bringing into play the full scope of his ontology, but it itself is on the threshold of that confrontation. The theme of incarnation is a question of the metaproblematic; its ontological reality is mystery, but it does not provide the signifying element from which the other dimensions of mystery take their signification. Incarnation retains its status as situating and grounding fact, without crossing the threshold of its own place, or *topos,* in the typology of existential thought.

In a certain sense then the structure of existential thought for Marcel is largely symbolic; it signifies in an empty manner, as Husserl said the symbol did. But in turn as a symbolic structure it calls for fulfillment. In what direction? Certainly it is important that the idea of participation in Marcel's thought is elaborated much more fully on the level of fidelity, hope, and love than on the level of perception. Yet it is the latter that introduces the relation between subjectivity and the world of others as it situates, within the facticity of incarnation, the direction of a thought mulling over the ambiguities and discordances of human existence. It is here that the similarities between participation for Marcel and the intersection of the body and the world in the *Phenomenology of Perception* come to the surface, only to lapse once again into the asymmetrical relations that ultimately define these two descriptions.

To be captured by the world, to lend oneself to the figuration of meaning—this would seem to be a bond tying together participation and the phenomenology of perception. Thus on this level of description there would seem to be the broad outline of symmetry between these two themes and the philosophies they initiate. Yet for Merleau-Ponty the phenomenology of perception does not initiate an ontology of mystery based on the ambiguity of the body; rather it enjoins the founding dimension of meaning to which the ambiguity of the body introduces philosophy, the world of perception, and the operative and anonymous course of the intentional motricity of the perceiving body. From this dimension of meaning, formulated in the primacy of perception, issue, in the relationship of founding and founded, the questions taken up by history, politics, and painting. As perception founds these perspectives on the world of culture, they in turn problematize themselves, in *Signs, Sense and Non-Sense, Humanism and Terror, Les Aventures de la dialectique,* and "Eye and Mind," to become avenues or archeological stakes that signify and lead back to the questions of that fundamental dimension. At the silent center of the thought of Merleau-Ponty there is an obsession that finally comes to indirect expression as the element of Being, the flesh.

It is finally this archeology of meaning signified by the flesh that creates between the existential philosophy of Marcel and the ontology of Merleau-Ponty a relationship not of symmetry but of asymmetry; the problematic, the philosophical goal, of each leads in a different direction after an engagement on the same ground. In fact for each, incarnation or embodiment is not the same *topos,* because the problematic of mystery and the problematic of the flesh create different typologies; different indices must be assigned to incarnation and perception, as they must be assigned to religious faith, politics, and history. In the *Phenomenology of Perception* Merleau-Ponty takes note of this asymmetry by exchanging the values that being and having have for Marcel and by assigning them different indices. Having does not designate a "proprietary relationship" but "the relation which the subject bears to the term into which it projects itself. . . . Hence our 'having' corresponds roughly to M. Marcel's being, and our being to his 'having'."[54] The ontology of the flesh bears the marks of this exchange, for it situates itself within the question of the having of being, not the question of being and having. But then in traditional philosophy there has been no name for that.

GARTH J. GILLAN

DEPARTMENT OF PHILOSOPHY
SOUTHERN ILLINOIS UNIVERSITY—CARBONDALE
APRIL 1970

NOTES

1. Jacques Derrida, *De la grammatologie* (Paris: Editions de minuit, 1967), pp. 227–29; see also Maurice Merleau-Ponty, "On the Phenomenology of Language," in *Signs,* trans. Richard C. McCleary, Northwestern University Studies in Phenomenology and Existential Philosophy (Evanston, Ill.: Northwestern University Press, 1964), pp. 84–97.

2. For the idea of sedimented history and the type of intentional analysis associated with this idea, see Edmund Husserl, *Formal and Transcendental Logic,*

trans. Dorion Cairns (The Hague: Martinus Nijhoff, 1969); idem, "The Origin of Geometry," in *The Crisis of European Sciences and Transcendental Phenomenology: An Introduction to Phenomenological Philosophy*, trans. David Carr, Northwestern University Studies in Phenomenology and Existential Philosophy (Evanston, Ill., Northwestern University Press, 1970), pp. 353–78.

3. Gabriel Marcel, "Existence and Objectivity," in *Metaphysical Journal*, trans. Bernard Wall (Chicago: Henry Regnery Co., 1950), p. 338.

4. Gabriel Marcel, *Being and Having: An Existentialist Diary*, trans. Katharine Farrer (New York: Harper & Row, Harper Torchbooks, 1965), pp. 10–12, 167 (hereafter cited as *BH*).

5. *BH*, 13.

6. *BH*, 14.

7. "Incarnation—the central 'given' of metaphysic. Incarnation is the situation of a being who appears to himself to be, as it were, *bound* to a body. . . . We are not to object that this experience shows a contingent character: in point of fact, all metaphysical enquiry requires a starting-point of this kind. It can only start from a situation which is mirrored but cannot be understood" (*BH*, 11–12).

8. *BH*, 82.

9. *BH*, 127.

10. *BH*, 84–87; on having within the domain of the problematic see p. 172.

11. Gabriel Marcel, *Creative Fidelity*, trans. Robert Rosthal (New York: Noonday Press, 1964), pp. 24–26 (hereafter cited as *CF*); *BH*, 96.

12. *CF*, 29; Gabriel Marcel, *The Mystery of Being*, trans. G. S. Fraser (vol. 1) and René Hague (vol. 2), 2 vols. (Chicago: Henry Regnery Co., 1960), 1:146 (hereafter cited as *MB*).

13. *MB* 1:146.   14. *MB* 1:141–46.

15. *BH*, 125.   16. *BH*, 135–37.

17. *BH*, 167.   18. *CF*, 182–83.

19. "This philosophy is based on a datum which is not transparent to reflection, and which, when reflected, implies an awareness not of contradiction but of a fundamental mystery, becoming an antinomy as soon as discursive thought tries to reduce or problematize it" (*CF*, 23).

20. Gabriel Marcel, "On the Ontological Mystery," in *The Philosophy of Existentialism*, trans. Manya Harari, 4th paperbound ed. (New York: Citadel Press, 1964), p. 19.

21. Gabriel Marcel, "An Essay in Autobiography," in *Philosophy of Existentialism*, p. 127.

22. Maurice Merleau-Ponty, *The Structure of Behavior*, trans. Alden L. Fisher (Boston: Beacon Press, 1963); idem, *Phenomenology of Perception*, trans. Colin Smith, International Library of Philosophy and Scientific Method (New York: Humanities Press, 1962).

23. Merleau-Ponty, *Structure of Behavior*, p. 122.

24. Ibid., pp. 162, 165.   25. Ibid., p. 166.

26. Ibid., p. 168.   27. Ibid., p. 89.

28. Merleau-Ponty, "An Unpublished Text," trans. Arleen B. Dallery, in *The Primacy of Perception*, ed. James Edie, Northwestern University Studies in Phenomenology and Existential Philosophy (Evanston, Ill.: Northwestern University Press, 1964), p. 4. This passage elucidates if not the divergences between *The*

Structure of Behavior and the *Phenomenology of Perception*, at least the relevance for Merleau-Ponty of the former work to the latter and the basic continuity between the two works in the progressive formulation of the question of perception, which can only be said to come to maturity in *The Visible and the Invisible* because of the strictures placed on the *Phenomenology of Perception* by *The Structure of Behavior*.

29. Merleau-Ponty, *Phenomenology of Perception,* p. 99.

30. Ibid., p. 92.　　　　　　　　31. Ibid., p. 100.

32. Ibid.　　　　　　　　　　　33. Ibid.

34. Ibid., p. 102.　　　　　　　35. Ibid., p. 112.

36. Ibid., pp. 107–15.　　　　　37. Ibid., p. 110.

38. Ibid., p. 123.　　　　　　　39. Ibid., p. 106*n.*

40. Maurice Merleau-Ponty, *Phénoménologie de la perception* (Paris: Gallimard, 1945), p. 151.

41. Ibid., p. 154.

42. Merleau-Ponty, *Phenomenology of Perception,* pp. 72, 206.

43. Merleau-Ponty, *Phénoménologie de la perception,* p. 214.

44. Ibid., p. 215.

45. "With the notion of the corporeal schema, it is not only the unity of the body that is described in a new manner; it is also, through it, the unity of the senses and the unity of the object. My body is the place or rather the very actuality of the phenomenon of expression (*Ausdruck*); in it the visual experience and the auditive experience, for example, are pregnant with each other, and their expressive value grounds the prepredicative unity of the perceived world and hence verbal expression and intellectual signification. My body is the common texture of all objects, and it is, at least with respect to the perceived world, the general instrument of my 'understanding'" (Ibid., p. 272).

46. Merleau-Ponty, *Phenomenology of Perception,* p. 92.

47. Ibid., p. 93.

48. Maurice Merleau-Ponty, *The Visible and the Invisible,* ed. Claude Lefort, trans. Alphonso Lingis, Northwestern University Studies in Phenomenology and Existential Philosophy (Evanston, Ill.: Northwestern University Press, 1968); on the tacit *cogito,* see pp. 170, 175; on ontology in the *Phenomenology of Perception,* see pp. 176, 183; on the discourse of consciousness-object, see p. 183 and especially p. 200: "The problems posed in Ph.P. are insoluble because I start there from the 'consciousness'-'object' distinction." Yet in the 1959–60 course on "Nature and Logos: The Human Body," Merleau-Ponty isolates the ideas of the *Umwelt,* the corporeal schema, perception, and mobility as themes leading to the formulation of the idea of the flesh, and these are precisely the themes that we have disengaged from the descriptions of *The Structure of Behavior* and the *Phenomenology of Perception;* see Maurice Merleau-Ponty, *Résumés de cours* (Paris: Gallimard, 1968), pp. 177–78.

49. Maurice Merleau-Ponty, "Eye and Mind," trans. Carleton Dallery, in *The Primacy of Perception,* p. 224.

50. Merleau-Ponty, *The Visible and the Invisible,* p. 137.

51. Ibid., p. 138.

52. Ibid., p. 135. In the working notes the invisible is the *Nichtürpräsentierbar,* "the invisible inner framework (*membrure*)" of the visible; it is not the coun-

terpart of the visible but its other side, the virtuality of the body and of the world, that is part of the dimension of the flesh. The flesh is then the virtual and actual Being of the Body and the world, a virtuality and an actuality that tend to be distinct in the *Phenomenology of Perception.*

53. Merleau-Ponty, *The Visible and the Invisible,* p. 139.
54. Merleau-Ponty, *Phenomenology of Perception,* p. 174.

The Question of Embodiment: Marcel and Merleau-Ponty
REPLY TO GARTH J. GILLAN

With perception, there is already objectification. This is why I have spoken much more about sensation than about perception or about the sensation of *Erlebnissen*. I am perfectly capable of having a kind of sensory reaction to the world before perception is involved. This is what I call the preobjectivizing situation.

I confess that I do not fully understand what Professor Gillan has written concerning the difference between Merleau-Ponty's conception of embodiment (or the flesh) and mine. The best I can do is to endeavor to clarify once again my basic thinking on this point. It seems to me that I am in agreement with Merleau-Ponty in saying that when I speak of "my body," I am not treating my body as an object, or, to employ my own terminology (which is perhaps not the same as his), as an instrument; since this is connected with the fact that every instrument is actually the prolongation of a certain power of the body, then if this power itself is treated as an instrument, we find ourselves caught in an infinite regress.

In what sense then can I say that this philosophy of the body is the center of my existential thought? (I am not sure that it is immediately necessary to bring in here the distinction between problem and mystery, although it is certainly at this point that the distinction must quickly appear.) What I see as most important is that the body-subject (this expression does not satisfy me completely, but I think it is unavoidable) is really the point where I become rooted in the world; I am in the world and not simply in front of it, as if the world were merely a spectacle.

Perhaps what separates my thought from Merleau-Ponty's lies in the following: he brings in perception at a moment when, for me, perception cannot yet intervene. I mean by that that on the whole I remain more or

Translated from the French by Susan Gruenheck.

less in agreement with Kant in thinking that there is no perception without judgment and furthermore that judgment by itself refers to an object. In this sense perception is already of a scientific order, of an order that becomes scientific. By contrast, the flesh (taking this word to designate the body-subject) is situated in a radically different dimension. One could say, by the way, that this dimension is also that of sexuality. I granted to Julián Marías that one finds here an undeniable lacuna in my thought, namely, that although problems relative to sexuality occupy a large part of my dramatic works, they are, so to speak, absent from my strictly philosophical work. But I would point out that the reference to sexuality clearly shows that incarnation in one of its facets is oriented in a direction different from that of perception and thus, *a fortiori,* of science. I would also point out, in answer to Professor Gillan, that I am not bringing into play here the notions of problem and mystery, though it is certainly obvious that in the back of my mind this distinction retains its value, if only because affectivity as such leads us into a domain in which problematizing is difficult.

G.M.

20

John D. Glenn, Jr.

MARCEL AND SARTRE: THE PHILOSOPHY OF COMMUNION AND THE PHILOSOPHY OF ALIENATION

I N THEIR ultimate tenor and direction, the philosophies of Gabriel Marcel and Jean-Paul Sartre are antithetical; the former is essentially a philosophy of communion, the latter a philosophy of alienation.[1] For this reason they are often contrasted. However, although antitheses require common terms, it is not so often noted that the two philosophies are very similar in the range of questions with which they deal and in some of their basic concepts.[2] Indeed I believe there are many respects in which Marcel and Sartre, despite their profound ultimate differences, are more closely related to each other than to any of the other major "existentialist" thinkers.[3] I suspect that in fact Marcel's sense of the resultant need to clarify the differences between them is one reason for his frequent references to Sartre.[4]

It is difficult to determine the extent to which the similarities between them reflect Marcel's influence on Sartre. Sartre has not acknowledged this influence, and in any case it has been manifested not so much by appropriation as by an "internal negation," a transformation that to a considerable extent perverts the original sense of certain of Marcel's basic insights. Therefore although I will note where influence seems to be suggested, this is not the primary purpose of my comparison of these two philosophers. The philosophical dimensions of their agreements and disagreements are, I

The author wishes to thank the Tulane University Research Council for a grant allowing him to pursue a long-standing interest in Marcel's philosophy during the summer of 1970.

think, well worth exploring apart from any concern with the "history of ideas."

One striking and fundamental instance of the similarities and differences between Marcel and Sartre is found in their discussions of the relation that human beings have to the functions they perform or the roles they play in their daily existence. In his essay "On the Ontological Mystery," written in 1933, Marcel suggests that in modern times "the individual tends to appear both to himself and to others as an agglomeration of functions." In the case of a subway worker, for example, "everything within him and outside him conspires to identify this man with his functions." This must, Marcel suggests, lead to a feeling of "dull, intolerable unease," for life in such a world is empty. Although it is a world in which there are innumerable theoretical and technical *problems,* no room is allowed for *mystery,* for what transcends the level of theoretical and technical objectivity.[5]

What is the ontological significance of this state of affairs? It is that the "ontological need," the need to participate in *being*—Marcel would later speak in a similar context of "the need for transcendence"[6]—is unfulfilled and even forgotten. But what sense does the term *being* have here? Rather than attempt a definition, Marcel follows a kind of *via negativa* by suggesting that "being is what withstands—or what would withstand—an exhaustive analysis bearing on the data of experience and aiming to reduce them step by step to elements increasingly devoid of intrinsic or significant value." The pessimist or nihilist who asserts that "*nothing is*" is thus to be understood as claiming that "there is no experience that withstands this analytical test."[7]

Sartre's well-known discussion of the café waiter is in many ways parallel to these reflections of Marcel's. The waiter, Sartre says, moves a little too precisely and rapidly. He is a bit too eager and solicitous; he seems to be playing at something, playing some sort of game. Just what is he doing? "He is playing *at being* a waiter in a café." There is nothing surprising in all this; the public demands of those who have certain social roles that they be nothing but their roles, fillers of their functions. Yet, Sartre says, the attempt to *be,* in this sense, is always a failure. The "being-in-itself" of a waiter, the coincidence of someone with his being a waiter, escapes him simply by virtue of his consciousness, his "being-for-itself." A waiter cannot be a waiter as a table is a table, for his consciousness of being a waiter separates him from that being, and makes it only a role he assumes. Similarly, Sartre proceeds to argue, an emotion such as sadness perpetually eludes being fully embodied by consciousness. Being sad, like being a waiter, is a pose I assume or divest myself of, according to the occasion. And the very fact that I am free to assume or not to assume this pose shows that I retain a transcendence with respect to it, that I cannot really "be" sad. Consciousness, as the negation of being (in-itself), is thus *original nothingness*.[8]

Marcel has discussed both of these examples and has briefly—and in my opinion decisively—criticized the conclusions that Sartre attempts to draw from them. Surely there is a great difference between the pose of sadness that I may assume on certain occasions and the very real sadness that overwhelms me at the death of a friend. Even if I were to attempt to mask such grief, it would still remain in the depths of my consciousness.[9] This fact alone seems sufficient to discredit the Sartrean notion that human consciousness is a total transparency, completely free of any element of gravity.

Their discussions of an individual's relation to his or her function or role manifest both a significant area of agreement and a profound disagreement between Marcel and Sartre. Both note those situations in which social forces tend to restrict an individual to a definite function or role. Both point to at least the possibility of one's transcending this reduction of oneself. Yet here their analyses diverge. Marcel speaks of this transcendence primarily as a *need* rather than a fact and as a transcendence toward *being*, an overcoming of tendencies that would reduce human existence to a *nothing* devoid of intrinsic significance. Writing almost a decade later, Sartre regards the individual's transcendence of his or her role as an inescapable *fact*. On his analysis, it is only by being in a state of self-deception—of "bad faith"—that one can pretend to identify oneself with the "being-in-itself" of, for example, a waiter. And this transcendence of one's role is not positive, not a transcendence toward *being*, but a transcendence consisting of the very nothingness that is consciousness itself.

What has happened here? How can two philosophers begin with similar analyses of what is fundamentally the same situation and yet reach such divergent conclusions? Why does Sartre posit a transcendence into nothingness where Marcel speaks of a need for transcendence that is also a need for being? The answer seems to lie in Sartre's conception of being, which he tends to equate with "being-in-itself," or the being of a mere thing, as opposed to "being-for-itself," or consciousness. Being in this sense is the being of anything that is just what it is. A waiter is not *just* a waiter but is *conscious of* being a waiter. The transcendence of one's role that is constituted by consciousness is thus a disengagement of oneself from or a negation of being—although, as Marcel notes, disengagement and negation are hardly identical[10]—and thereby a nothingness.

But what does it mean to say that a waiter is not just a waiter, that he lacks the "being-in-itself" of a waiter? Marcel would say that regarding an individual as "just a waiter" is an act of falsifying abstraction that ignores his unique reality, his true being. Even if a waiter has come to regard himself as "just a waiter," this must be considered a kind of spiritual suicide, a forgetfulness or betrayal of his own being. Thus we can see concretely, in reference to human existence, the import of Marcel's "definition" of being as that which resists reduction to elements devoid of intrinsic value. Human beings, so far as they transcend reductive objectification and functionalization, participate in the very fullness of being.[11]

Why does Sartre not accept such a positive characterization of the human ability to transcend functions or roles? The basic reason is, I think, his unquestioning acceptance of the ultimacy of the subject-object dichotomy. He assumes that as a conscious *subject* I am always capable of *objectifying* anything that I am in any positive sense and thus am always capable of making myself *other* than it. In fact for Sartre I am not merely capable of such a negation; my consciousness *is* such a negation of or alienation from what I am, and thus as a conscious being I always *am not what I am*.[12]

Marcel's exposure of the extremely tenuous character of Sartre's analysis of sadness has shown the weakness of the sort of thinking on which this theory of consciousness is based. More positively, by his distinction between a *problem*, which concerns what merely "lies before" me, what is indifferent to me, and a *mystery*, a reality in which I am involved in such a way that I cannot objectify it without falsifying it, Marcel has indicated the nonultimacy of the subject-object dichotomy. The human subject is not, he suggests, essentially alienated from being but is "environed by being."[13] Thus Marcel's account of the human being's transcendence toward being provides the foundation of a philosophy of communion, whereas Sartre's analysis of consciousness as nothingness forms the basis of a philosophy of alienation.

This basic divergence becomes even more marked in the two philosophers' analyses of the fundamental ontological dimensions of interpersonal relations. Here again, however, their ultimate disagreement follows a significant initial agreement. Both recognize that one *may* experience another person simply as an object. Marcel writes:

> When I consider another individual as *him,* I treat him as essentially absent; it is his absence which allows me to objectify him, to reason about him as though he were a nature or given essence. However, there is a presence which

is yet a mode of absence. I can act toward somebody as though he were absent. . . . [E]ven though I am addressing him, he continues to be 'someone,' 'that man there.' . . .[14]

And Sartre writes:

This woman whom I see coming toward me, this man who is passing by in the street, this beggar whom I hear calling before my window, all are for me *objects*—of that there is no doubt. Thus it is true that at least one of the modalities of the Other's presence to me is *objectness*.[15]

Both Marcel and Sartre agree, however, that the experience of the other-as-object does not reveal the true reality of the other. And in contrast even to Heidegger, a philosopher with whom Marcel has many affinities and by whom Sartre is very much influenced, they agree that the other is not "given" to me primarily as part of the meaning of an instrumental complex, as, for example, a coworker in the workaday world.[16] Rather both hold that there must be an experience in which the other is "present in person" and that my primary relation to the other is not the external relation of object to object or subject to object but an internal relation, a relation that touches me in my innermost being.[17]

From this point, however, their analyses diverge. Marcel points to the possibility of an essentially positive relation between myself and the other. Continuing the reflections quoted above, he says:

It can happen, however, that a bond of feeling is created between me and the other person, if, for example, I discover an experience which we have both shared . . . hence a unity is established in which the other person and myself become *we,* and this means that he ceases to be *him* and becomes *thou.* . . . The path leading from dialectic to love has now been opened.[18]

Intersubjectivity, as Marcel later comes to call the bond uniting different persons, involves transcending the attitude that regards the other as alien, as an object, and as "essentially absent." Rather the other is acknowledged as a *presence,* as a *being* whose reality transcends the objectively given. The subject-object dichotomy is surpassed as a We is created or acknowledged.[19] Alienation is overcome in intersubjective communion.

Sartre continues his analysis arguing that the experience of the other as an object, even as a privileged object around which other objects form a sort of ideal grouping (as when I experience a chair as something that "he" sees or that "he" may claim before I do),[20] is not sufficient to reveal the other's "being-for-itself," that is, the other as a "subject." Yet he does not recognize the reality of intersubjectivity in Marcel's sense of the term. Rather his thinking remains within the limits of the subject-object dichotomy. How then does he explain my fundamental relation to the other, the primordial revelation of the other to me? His highly ingenious answer to this question, which is elaborated in his discussion of the "Look,"[21] is that I "make contact" with the other when I am conscious of being an *object* for the other as *subject*. His description of one such encounter is instructive:

> Let us imagine that moved by jealousy, curiosity, or vice I have just glued my ear to the door and looked through a keyhole. I am alone and on the level of a non-thetic self-consciousness. This means first of all that there is no self to inhabit my consciousness. . . . I am a pure consciousness of things. . . .
> But all of a sudden I hear footsteps in the hall. Someone is looking at me! What does this mean? It means that I am suddenly affected in my being and that essential modifications appear in my structure.[22]

What was a pure and transparent consciousness of the world becomes, on experiencing the Look of the other, alienated from itself. In shame or in pride I am conscious of being something—namely, my ego—that eludes my knowledge and of which the other, not myself, is the foundation.

Sartre later analyzes love in the light of this discussion. It is, he says, an attempt to overcome this alienation from myself, to become my own foundation, by possessing the freedom of the other. But like other fundamental attempts to heal the rift in my being that is opened up by the other's alienating Look, love necessarily fails.[23] For according to Sartre the dichotomy of for-itself and in-itself, subject and object, is unsurpassable. My basic relation to the other is not, as Marcel would suggest, positive but is rather an "internal negation." When I have been objectified by the other's Look, I must in turn objectify the other in order to regain my free subjectivity. I must transcend the other's transcendence so that I will not be a "transcendence-transcended."

Sartre's analysis of the Look and its consequences is clearly far removed from Marcel's account of the culmination of intersubjectivity in love, in which two persons acknowledge one another as "transcendences," as beings whose reality transcends the objectifiable. The contrast between the two thinkers can perhaps be seen even more clearly if we consider a conversation that Sartre cites as an example of one's being-as-object for the other:

> "I swear to you that I will do it."
> "Maybe so. You tell me so. I want to believe you. It is indeed possible that you will do it."[24]

This is an excellent illustration of Sartre's theory and of its fundamental deficiency. It is undeniably a good example of one human being's regarding another as an object, of one person's freedom being considered a matter of chance or caprice from the point of view of another. What is misleading is that Sartre takes such a state of affairs to be representative of the essential nature of interpersonal relations. He does not at all acknowledge the possibility of that simple trust, transcending all calculation of objective probabilities, that an I can extend to a Thou.[25] He refuses in short to grant the reality of intersubjectivity, and he tries to account for interpersonal relations within the limitations of the subject-object dichotomy. Within these limitations his thought possesses striking originality, as is evidenced by his whole analysis of the Look and its consequences, but it is nevertheless true that they *are* limitations.

Having posited the Look as the fundamental relation of one consciousness to another and having tried to show that all attempts to bind the wounds resulting from the conflict of the self and the other must necessarily fail, Sartre proceeds to analyze the phenomenon of the We.[26] Again, as might be expected, his analysis contrasts sharply with Marcel's. He says:

> Doubtless someone will want to point out to us that our description is incomplete since it leaves no place for certain concrete experiences in which we discover ourselves not in conflict with the Other but in community with him. . . . And these experiences appear *a priori* to contradict the experience of my being-as-object for the Other and the experience of the Other's being-as-object for me. In the 'we,' nobody is the object. The 'we' includes a plurality of subjectives [*sic*] which recognize one another as subjectivities. Nevertheless this recognition is not the object of an explicit thesis; what is explicitly posited is a common action or the object of a common perception. . . . [The recognition] must be effected *laterally* by a non-thetic consciousness whose thetic object is this or that spectacle in the world.[27]

The primacy of the subject-object dichotomy in Sartre's thought is again evident in his assertion that the recognition of one subject by another must be "lateral"; any "face-to-face" relation must, he assumes, take the form of the Look, in which one being is subject, the other object. Thus he excludes a priori the We that is constituted by the mutual relation of an I and a Thou.

What weight then does Sartre give to the experience of the We? He says that he "had no intention of casting doubt" on this experience but simply of "showing that this experience could not be the foundation of our consciousness of the Other." He continues:

> In addition it is clear that the 'we' is not an inter-subjective consciousness. . . . The 'we' is experienced by a particular consciousness; it is not necessary that *all* the patrons at the café should be conscious of being 'we' in order for me to experience myself as being engaged in a 'we' with them. Everyone is familiar with this pattern of every-day dialogue: "We are very dissatisfied." "But no, my dear, speak for yourself."[28]

Sartre's basic contention then is that the experience of the We is nonprimordial, that it is dependent on the experience of "being-for-others" in the Look. He develops this contention by analyzing what he takes to be the two basic forms of the We—the "us-object" and the "we-subject."[29]

As the term might suggest, the us-object is the "community" that arises when I and the other or others are conscious of being objects together for a "Third" whose transcendence transcends us. Such a situation, Sartre suggests, is at the root of the class-consciousness of an oppressed class, which is constituted as an Us by the objectifying Look of its oppressors.[30] Clearly this doctrine is pessimistic in its implications. It seems that only a partial community among human beings could be possible in principle, since community could only arise from the Look of a Third who remains outside it. Unity would only be possible where there is at least an implicit struggle against "outsiders"; the parallels with the various uses of propaganda are, I think, obvious.

The only condition under which humanity as a whole might be able to form a community would be, Sartre says, the presence of "one who is Third in relation to all possible groups, the one who in no case can enter into community with any human group. . . . This concept is the same as that of the being-who-looks-at and who can never be looked-at; that is, it is one with the idea of God." But if, as Sartre would claim, this idea refers to no real being, all efforts to achieve a comprehensive human unity are doomed to fail.[31]

It is, however, somewhat misleading to stress in this context the pessimistic implications concerning the possibility of human community that follow from Sartre's atheism. Much more significant is his implicit conception of what human community *would* be if the existence of God were a recognized fact. The divine existence, his discussion implies, would involve the absolute and irrevocable reduction of human beings to the status of objects. Human community would be nothing but the awareness of sharing this status with others and could perhaps take on a positive significance only in the context of a rebellion against God.

How far the Sartrean doctrine is from the conception of the "brotherhood of man" under the "fatherhood of God"! Perhaps we might say that Sartre has isolated certain aspects of the idea of God as Judge while excluding even the conceivability of divine love or forgiveness. Another passage in *Being and Nothingness* makes his concept of God even clearer. Speaking of shame before God, he says that it is essentially "the recognition of my being-an-object before a subject which can never become an object."[32] Despite the similarity between this formula and Marcel's affirmation that "God is the absolute 'thou' who can never beome a '*him*' "[33] —a similarity that may reflect Sartre's familiarity with Marcel's thought— the conceptions expressed differ greatly in their implications. For Sartre the existence of God as an absolute subject would involve my total alien-ation from myself, since I would then be an object for a transcendence that I could never transcend. Marcel, however, speaks of an "appeal" to the absolute Thou, the only one who is able, in the final analysis, to know me as I am, as one of the most profound expressions of the need for transcend-ence.[34] Sartre thinks that my relation to any other, whether human or di-vine, alienates me from myself; Marcel acknowledges the possibility of communion not only between human persons but also between the human person and God.

There is accordingly a great difference between Sartre's notions of the us-object and of the kind of human community that would be constituted by the divine Look and Marcel's conception of community in its relation to God. Marcel has suggested that it is only in terms of the idea of the fatherhood of God "that an effective, authentically existing human com-munity is even conceivable."[35] It is clear moreover that for him this fa-therhood and this community are to be understood not in terms of the subject-object relation but as forms of intersubjectivity.

The concrete analysis of intersubjectivity that is perhaps most illumi-nating in this context is found in Marcel's Gifford Lectures. These lectures were delivered long after Marcel first became acquainted with Sartre's thought, and the following passage seems to reflect a concern to present his own alternatives to Sartrean ideas. But I would judge that for the most part the thoughts here differ only in emphasis from thoughts that Marcel developed much earlier. Discussing the ego, he uses the example of a "shy young man" who is making his first appearance in fashionable society:

> He is . . . to the highest degree self-conscious. He feels himself to be a center of attention, and, I might add, an infinitely vulnerable center of attention. . . . Thus he is at the same time preoccupied to a great extent with himself and hypnotized to the highest degree by others, by the opinion of others.[36]

So far Marcel's discussion is clearly very similar to Sartre's account of the Look, the self-alienation attendant on the Look, and the ego. But un-like Sartre, Marcel does not make these phenomena paradigmatic for his conception of interpersonal relations. Rather he says that the "tension" just described is

> precisely the opposite of what I will here call intersubjectivity, and it is im-portant to insist on this opposition. A stranger says something to our young man. The latter at first experiences his questioner simply as *him;* Why does he speak to me? What does he want from me? . . . But suppose that the conversation takes on a more intimate character. "I am happy to meet you," the stranger says; "I once knew your parents." A bond is created and, above all, a relaxation takes place.[37]

Thus both Marcel and Sartre—and here either thinker may have influenced the other[38]—attempt to show how a community can arise between myself and another by virtue of the relation to a third person. But the "community" to which Sartre points is that of objects for a transcending subject, whereas Marcel depicts the emergence of a widening intersubjectivity. There is of course no suggestion on Marcel's part that community only arises on the basis of a relation to a third person. What would seem to be essential is that two (or more) persons become aware of participating together in some reality that is significant for each of them, whether this reality is an intimate relation to another person, the sharing of a common suffering, or something of a similar sort. And it is clear, I think, how Marcel's account of intersubjectivity points in the direction of the recognition of "an effective, authentically existing human community" based on an acknowledgement of the universal fatherhood of God.

Like his analysis of the us-object, Sartre's account of the we-subject does not reach the level of what Marcel calls intersubjectivity. The we-subject, as Sartre analyzes it, would seem to be a phenomenon especially indigenous to a mechanized and impersonal environment. It is exemplified when I encounter a manufactured tool or take a subway, for in such situations "I apprehend myself as interchangeable with any one of my neighbors," each of whom is capable of precisely the same actions and experiences. I do what "They" do, for I am one of this They.[39] I am aware of myself as merely "an ephemeral particularization" of this specific we-subject.[40]

Even this rather empty experience of the We is, Sartre says, nonprimordial; it is "of the psychological order and not ontological." It does not constitute "a real unification of the for-itselfs under consideration." My experience of such a We does not imply "a similar and correlative experience in others." The experience of the We presupposes that the other has already been encountered in some other way. Sartre thus argues that the we-subject, like the us-subject, is dependent on the Look, and does not surpass the alienation that the Look involves. He concludes: "It is . . . useless for human reality to seek to get out of this dilemma: one must either transcend the Other or allow oneself to be transcended by him. The essence of the relation between consciousnesses is not the *Mitsein,* it is conflict."[41]

The disagreement between Marcel and Sartre concerning the reality of community is clearly not one of simple contradiction; the We that Marcel affirms is not identical with the one whose primordiality Sartre denies here. Marcel would apparently agree with Sartre that no very significant community can arise on the basis of sharing the rather abstract relation to something like a tool or a subway. In criticizing rationalistic conceptions of community, Marcel notes that "what brings me closer to another being and really binds me to him is not the knowledge that he can check and confirm an addition or subtraction I had to do. . . ."[42] And to the extent that the mechanized world in which we live approaches the abstract character of mathematics, it too seems to offer little or no basis on which community can arise.[43] Because Sartre takes such an abstract world as his starting point, it should perhaps be no surprise that he fails to arrive at any conception of the we-subject that approaches real intersubjectivity.

Marcel's conception of community is thus quite different from the we-subject as Sartre analyzes it. Marcel's view is perhaps best summed up when he says, "A community is only possible when beings acknowledge that they are mutually different while existing together in their differences."[44] If the only we-subject that Sartre recognizes is best symbolized by "the cadenced march of soldiers,"[45] Marcel's conception is, I think, best exemplified by the family, where the reality of the We is not (as Sartre would have it) particularized in basically undifferentiated individuals but is shared by beings whose differences are acknowledged and respected.[46] The contrast between the two conceptions again derives fundamentally from Marcel's affirmation and Sartre's denial of experiences and realities transcending the dichotomy of subject and object.

Both the similarities and the ultimate differences between Marcel and Sartre are further revealed in their conceptions of the significance of interpersonal relations with respect to death. In profound reflections that defy summation, Marcel has attempted to show how love, the highest form of intersubjectivity, involves the affirmation of the immortality of the loved being. For love knows the beloved not as an object but rather as a presence, a being whose reality transcends the realm of the objectively verifiable and who is thus in some sense immortal.[47] This insight, which was first expressed in Marcel's earliest writings, has remained one of the most basic themes of his thinking.[48] Perhaps he has expressed it best in the lines he often quotes from one of his plays: "To love a being . . . is to say you, you in particular, will never die."[49]

Despite certain similarities, Sartre's view of the significance of interpersonal relations with respect to death is ultimately the polar opposite of Marcel's. Just as a character in *No Exit* exclaims that "Hell is—other people,"[50] so in *Being and Nothingness* Sartre says in effect that *death* is other people: "if there is to be nothingness of consciousness, there must be a consciousness which has been and which is no more and a witnessing consciousness which poses the nothingness of the first consciousness for a synthesis of recognition."[51] That is, without the other who objectifies me, whose Look constitutes me as mortal, my death would be totally unimaginable.[52] In death I come to coincide with my being-as-object for the other; death is thus "the triumph of the point of view of the Other over the point of view *which I am* toward myself."[53]

The term *presence,* which Marcel uses to speak of the nonobjectifiable relation of one person to another,[54] is also employed by Sartre in a somewhat similar manner. Like Marcel—and here again he would seem to be influenced by Marcel—he notes that the presence of one person to another is not a function of spatial distance: "the empirical concepts of absence and of presence are two specifications of a fundamental presence of Pierre to Thérèse and of Thérèse to Pierre. . . . At London, in the East Indies, in America, on a desert island, Pierre is present to Thérèse who remains in Paris; he will cease to be present to her only at his death."[55]

Marcel has understandably criticized this last qualification. He suggests that however far from materialism Sartre's conception of presence may sometimes seem to be, he has in the end succumbed to materialistic thinking and has at the same time ignored certain concrete human experiences. "From the phenomenological point of view," Marcel says, "an experience of communion continuing between a living being and a beloved dead one is enough to take all value and all meaning" from Sartre's assertion that presence necessarily ceases at death.[56] Yet even if Sartre were to grant the validity of Marcel's criticism, there would still be a significant difference between their conceptions of presence. According to Marcel, presence is, or at least can be, mutual. But Sartre interprets presence as the presence of, for example, Pierre-as-subject to Thérèse-as-object or Thérèse-as-subject to Pierre-as-object; he does not grant the possibility of a true intersubjectivity, the mutual relation of subject to subject.

Thus both Marcel and Sartre suggest that one person may provide an essential witness to another's ontological status in relation to death; but they disagree over what that attested status is. According to Sartre, because the other constitutes a negation of the for-itself that I am and because I can only be an object for the other, this other is essentially the witness to my death, the one whose Look constitutes my mortality. According to Marcel, love knows and affirms the one loved as a presence, not an object, and attests that the reality of the beloved in some manner transcends death. The disagreement between the two philosophers again reflects the fact that Sartre considers alienation the ultimate truth of interpersonal relations, whereas Marcel affirms the reality of intersubjective communion.

Marcel and Sartre thus offer two opposed but related conceptions of the nature of interpersonal relations. Each proceeds to a great extent through the presentation and analysis of concrete examples. My own judgment is that Marcel's examples and analyses are more convincing and more faithful to experience. Yet I think it must be asked whether there is a firmer basis for deciding the basic issue between them. Can it be established whether intersubjective communion or the alienation of one person from another is more fundamental in human existence and experience?

If, as I believe, Marcel is correct in suggesting that intersubjectivity is in the strictest sense a mystery,[57] then it is clear that no logically or scientifically rigorous demonstration of its reality is possible. In one of his most illuminating discussions of this topic Marcel suggests that for us intersubjectivity is like the inside of a structure whose outside we are totally incapable of imagining; as something more fundamental than any "given" fact, "the intersubjective nexus cannot be in any way asserted: it can only be acknowledged."[58] Those who, like Sartre, choose to deny the reality of intersubjective communion are thus perhaps not to be directly refuted. Yet I believe it can be shown that Sartre's own analyses of interpersonal relations fail to account satisfactorily for some of the phenomena he discusses and that these can be better understood if the reality of intersubjectivity is granted.

Sartre's basic contention in this context is of course that the Look is the primordial experience of the other, that it manifests the basic relation of one self to another, and that any real "community" is an unstable byproduct of it. I would suggest on the contrary that the experience he describes is nonprimordial and that it presupposes the reality of intersubjectivity. Consider the shame felt by the man in Sartre's example who is seen peeping through a keyhole. The fact that the experience of the Look on this occasion takes the form of shame rather than of pride—another feeling that clearly depends on one's relation to others[59]—would seem to reflect the prior awareness of social "norms." More concretely I would suggest that this person experiences himself as an object in relation to the other because he has *made* himself into an object by betraying intersubjectivity in trying to make objects of others. He has made himself less than what he essentially is—a being of community—and hence feels shame before the other, the symbol or representative of community. Thus we can, with Marcel, grant the power of Sartre's description of the Look and yet judge that it does not constitute the primordial form of interpersonal relations but rather *presupposes* the experience of some sort of community.[60]

As for Sartre's attempts to prove that the We is nonprimordial, I think we have seen that he seldom if ever attains an adequate conception of the We. The We whose primordiality he denies is only a pale shadow of the We that Marcel affirms, which involves the awareness of a real community among unique individuals. Why does Sartre deny any We that goes beyond the awareness of our being together objectified by the same Third (the us-object) or of our being undifferentiated subjects related to a common object or project (the we-subject)? The primary reason of course is that he never really questions the adequacy of the subject-object schema, however original he may be in his interpretation and application of it.

At one point Sartre does attempt to establish directly the nonprimordiality of the We by citing this "pattern of every-day dialogue": " 'We are very dissatisfied.' 'But no, my dear, speak for yourself.' "[61] He apparently believes that such examples of fallibility in the consciousness of the We are sufficient to prove that this consciousness is in general nonprimordial and that the experience of the other in the Look is more basic. Yet it would seem that according to Sartre's own analysis the experience of the Look is no less fallible than the consciousness of the We for he admits that I may have this experience when no other is actually watching me.[62]

Sartre's attempts to save his analysis in the face of this rather embarrassing fact are moreover less than convincing. He first suggests—correctly, I think—that the other's absence is only a mode of his presence and that one retains one's relation to the other even during the other's empirical absence. But he then proceeds to argue that in the first place one encounters not individual others but rather an undifferentiated, prenumerical "Other-as-subject" and that it is only when one turns one's Look toward this other that a multiplicity of individual others arises.[63] Yet if correct this analysis would explain only my relation to a prenumerical Other-as-subject and to a multitude of individual Others-as-objects but not—what is surely the primary *explicandum* in this context—my relation to the individual Other-as-subject. I do not believe that Sartre himself succeeds in avoiding the criticism he directs at Heidegger, namely, that in defining my relation to an "abstract Other," he has not explained but has rather precluded my relation to a concrete individual other.[64]

I think moreover that Sartre's analysis of the conversation he quotes is highly questionable. It does not seem to indicate an absolute disunity of two persons but rather a relative disunity, which could only occur, be expressed, and perhaps be resolved within the framework of some kind of community, however attenuated. Marcel, I think, is right in holding that intersubjectivity is the primordial nature of interpersonal relations and an essential "structure" of human existence.

Thus despite a number of similarities between the philosophies of Marcel and Sartre, there is one fundamental difference: Marcel's reflections have led him to affirm the reality of communion, whereas Sartre would make alienation the most basic truth of human existence. Although this difference is perhaps most evident in their analyses of interpersonal relations, it is also reflected in other aspects of their philosophies, including their theories concerning the nature of the human body. Yet even here, despite their ultimate divergence in orientation, there is a considerable area of initial agreement between them, and this would seem to indicate that Marcel influenced Sartre considerably in this respect.[65]

In opposition to the Cartesian tradition, both philosophers deny, for essentially the same reasons, that *my body* can legitimately be interpreted as an instrument that "I" (regarded as soul or consciousness) use. For an instrument is always an extension of some original power residing in the being that uses it, and my body is thus for me the prior condition of all instrumentality and cannot itself be an instrument. My hand's ability to grip, which can be extended by, for example, a pair of pliers, is not itself the extension of some more fundamental power to grip things. For similar reasons, both philosophers reject as inadequate the interpretation of the senses as some sort of receiving apparatus intervening between myself and the world. On the basis of such reflections both conclude that my body is not primarily a mere "physical body"; my body is myself as I am situated in the world, so that in some sense *I am my body.*[66]

This affirmation, however, is elaborated in somewhat different ways by the two philosophers. Sartre takes a more extreme view of the relation between myself (that is, the for-itself) and my body; for him there is a sense in which I am radically identical with my body but also a sense in which I am radically alienated from my body. In its first mode of being, he says, my body is "wholly consciousness."[67] The body is consciousness, is the for-itself as factically situated in the world; it is the "point-of-view" from which consciousness transcends itself toward the world in sensing and using objects.[68] In another of its modes of being, however, my body is myself *as known by the other,* and in this respect it is radically alienated from my consciousness. When I feel the other's Look on me, my body becomes "*a thing totally outside my subjectivity.*"[69] Sartre qualifies this statement by saying that the body does not cease to be for-itself; rather "the body-for-the-other is the body-for-us, but inapprehensible and alienated."[70]

In his own discussion of the sense in which "I am my body," Marcel suggests that this assertion can only mean that it is incorrect to say that my body is one thing and I another. This distinction presupposes an objectification that—as in the case of the "instrumentalist" interpretation of the body—falsifies the mystery of the body as *my* body, to which I am intimately bound. But it is no less mistaken, he argues, simply to identify myself with my body, for this identification would also presuppose an objectification of my body and would thus amount to a denial of my selfhood. "To be incarnated," he says, is thus "to appear to oneself as body, as this particular body, without being identified with it nor distinguished from it—identification and distinction being correlative operations which are significant only in the realm of objects."[71]

As we have seen, Sartre interprets the body in terms of two extremes; in one of its ontological dimensions, he says, my body is wholly subject, whereas in another dimension it is an object for the other and is thus alienated from my subjectivity. Because he does not attempt to fit all reality to the Procrustean bed of the subject-object dichotomy, Marcel is able to avoid these extremes. Rather he suggests that my relation to my body is a kind of indivisible "community," that it is a relation neither of total identification nor of total alienation.[72] As with my relation to my friends or my family or even my relation to myself, my relation to my body can become one of alienation, but it is not necessarily or originally so. According to Marcel's analysis my capacity to alienate myself from my body by an attempted disavowal of it is only one aspect of my general capacity to reject existence itself by choosing the absurd.[73] He would grant, I think, that the way in which others regard me may lead me to be alienated from my body. But he does not, like Sartre, conceive of this alienation as the inevitable result of my relations with others, because he does not conceive of such relations as inevitably alienated. Rather his analysis suggests—although he does not really develop this theme—that my body can be the "bearer" of my presence to the other, and the other's body the "bearer" of the other's presence to me, in a manner transcending the opposition of subject and object.[74]

In their conceptions of the fundamental relations of the individual to being, to other individuals, and to his or her body, Marcel and Sartre have had certain areas of agreement, despite their ultimate disagreements. But this is not true with respect to their conceptions of human freedom. It is here in fact that the consequences of their fundamental divergence in philosophical orientation become most obvious.

According to Sartre freedom basically consists of a kind of negation; more specifically it is the negation of being-in-itself, which consciousness, the for-itself, comprises. Thus Sartre says that "freedom is not *a* being; it is *the being* of man—i.e., his nothingness of being."[75] I am free because I exist as the negation of everything determinate—of objects, of other subjects, of my present condition, and of my own past. This freedom can be neither gained nor lost, for so long as I exist, I *am* my own freedom; "I am condemned to be free."[76]

Human freedom, Sartre claims, inevitably expresses itself in an attempt to achieve some sort of synthesis between the in-itself and the for-itself, namely, to have the coincidence with itself that is characteristic of non-conscious beings and yet to be conscious of this coincidence.[77] Individual for-itselfs attempt to achieve this impossible synthesis in different ways and in terms of different "initial projects," and it is in terms of these projects that "value" comes into the world. Thus according to Sartre value originates wholly in human freedom. The "spirit of seriousness," which holds that things possess value independent of the projects of human subjectivity, is a form of self-deception, of "bad faith."[78]

Sartre's opposition to the "spirit of seriousness" is most strongly expressed when he says that "for human reality, to be is to *choose oneself;* nothing comes to it either from the outside or from within which it can *receive* or *accept.*"[79] The belief in a value independent of human subjectivity, Sartre apparently thinks, would amount to the alienation of freedom from itself, whereas freedom should take itself to be the primary value.[80] Yet it is not at all clear how freedom could be alienated from itself or what it would mean for freedom to take itself as the primary value, if Sartre is correct in suggesting that all human acts are equally expressions of freedom.

Sartre's position seems to imply that the most adequate expression of freedom consists in a perpetual rebellion against all established order, whether in the world or in oneself.[81] Although this notion too would be inconsistent with his view of freedom as the very *being* of the human being, his thinking nevertheless shows a certain sympathy for it. I refer in particular to his doctrine of "the instant."[82] Sartre suggests that the for-itself, as perpetually negating its past and its present in projecting itself toward its future, is always capable of overthrowing its past initial project and replacing it with a new one. The instant is the time of such a choice; it is the end of the old project and the beginning of the new. He says that "precisely because I am free I always have the possibility of positing my immediate past as an object"; since this possibility is always open to me, I am *"perpetually threatened by the instant."*[83]

I think it is fair to say that in Sartre's view freedom is basically a kind of alienation—an alienation from everything other than one's own consciousness and from one's own past, present, and future, for one cannot coincide with any of these. This conception of freedom has found many critics—Marcel being one of the most incisive—and few defenders. My primary purpose at this point is not to repeat their criticisms but rather to show that a profound critique of some of Sartre's basic assumptions as well as a more adequate and positive conception of freedom is implicit in the concept of "creative fidelity," which Marcel elaborated before the publication of Sartre's *Being and Nothingness.*

Sartre's assertion that nothing comes to human reality "either from the outside or from within which it can *receive* or *accept*"[84] clearly depends— as Marcel was later to note[85]—on an identification of receptivity with mere passivity, an identification that would make it the opposite of all freedom and creativity. It is precisely this identification that Marcel's concept of creative fidelity brings into question. The term *receptivity*, he notes, has a whole "spectrum of meanings," extending from the merely passive undergoing of some change to, for example, receiving a guest into one's home. And this latter sort of receptivity is

> really a *gift*, and in the final analysis, even a gift of *self*, of the person who is involved in the act of hospitality. Actually we are not concerned here with filling up some empty space with an alien presence, but of having the other person participate in a certain reality, in a certain plenitude. To provide hospitality is truly to communicate something of oneself to the other.[86]

There is a kind of receptivity then that is truly a giving, that is creative and free. Marcel adds that this is above all true of the creative artist, who "seems to be nourished by the very thing he seeks to incarnate; hence the identification of receiving and giving is ultimately realized in him."[87] And human existence in general seems to be better understood in this way than in terms of isolated individualities for whom the identification of receptivity and passivity would hold. Marcel adds:

> We may assume that we are deceived by the most obvious appearances when we hypostatize, treat as a self-enclosed, independent reality what is perhaps only the land of a certain indefinable realm whose submerged areas and underwater outcroppings can only be identified by accident or by sudden illumination.[88]

Human freedom and creativity are not then to be understood as opposed to receptivity, as pure *spontaneity*, but rather as *response*—not as alienation from but rather as communion with other beings.

Thus the creative aspect of Marcel's conception of creative fidelity, of the free response to another being, provides the alternative to Sartre's view of freedom as alienation from other beings. And I believe that its aspect of fidelity provides the alternative to Sartre's conception of the temporality of human freedom. Marcel's reflections on this last topic take the form of what might be called an examination of the transcendental conditions for making a promise. He poses the basic question in this way: "How can I promise—commit my future? A metaphysical problem."[89] How, he asks, am I able to make a commitment that can in any way bind me in the future? A view like the one Sartre later developed, whose possibility Marcel clearly recognizes, suggests that I cannot make such a commitment, that the self I will be tomorrow cannot really be bound by any act of the self I am today.[90] We could thus imagine making a rash promise—and such a view would recognize no other kind of promise—and then wondering whether we will keep it in the same way that we might wonder whether it will rain tomorrow. The very absurdity of such a state of affairs shows the inadequacy of Sartre's conception of freedom. It would seem to be a very attenuated sort of freedom, certainly falling far short of the "absolute freedom" that Sartre claims to profess, that would preclude the possibility of my freely committing myself!

Significant freedom then must include, not preclude, the possibility of committing one's future. Marcel expresses the metaphysical conditions of such a commitment by saying: "No act of committal . . . is possible except for a being who can be distinguished from his own momentary situation, and who *recognises* this difference between himself and his situation and consequently treats himself as transcending his own life-process, and answers for himself."[91] But if the being who commits himself or herself must have an identity that is not dispersed in time, then this identity cannot be merely abstract and cannot stem only from a formal unity imposed by the self on itself. It must rather, as has already been suggested, be based on a *response:* "There is no commitment purely from my own side; it always implies that the other being has a hold over me. All commitment is a response. A one-sided commitment would not only be rash but could be blamed as pride."[92]

Moreover, Marcel notes, such a commitment cannot be to a mere object; he clearly agrees with Sartre that objects as such lack intrinsic value. Free commitment can take place only at a level that transcends the subject-object dichotomy; it must be a response to a presence, to a being with whom communion is possible. Marcel says:

> In swearing fidelity to a person, I do not know what future awaits us or even, in a sense, what person he will be tomorrow; the very fact of my not knowing is what gives worth and weight to my promise. There is no question of response to something which is, absolutely speaking, *given;* and the essential of a being is just that—not being 'given' either to another or himself. There is something essential here, which defines spirituality.[93]

Thus whereas Sartre was later to suggest that freedom implies one's alienation from other beings, Marcel had already shown how a more authentic freedom could be achieved in communion with other beings. And whereas Sartre was to hold that freedom involves alienation from one's past, present, and future, Marcel had noted that freedom in any significant sense requires some sort of transtemporal unity of the free being. Yet this unity cannot be a merely abstract identity or the passive unchangingness of an inert substance but must itself—as Marcel was later to suggest explicitly[94]—partake to some extent of the nature of intersubjectivity, taking the form of a kind of communion of one's past, present, and future "selves."

Similarities between the philosophies of Marcel and Sartre other than those that I have discussed here could be noted; Sartre's analysis of "having," for example, bears a considerable resemblance to Marcel's. Yet I think that the preceding discussion has indicated the most significant similarities between them and has also shown the nature of the fundamental divergence in orientation between the two philosophers. The similarities, I believe, suggest that Sartre was considerably influenced by Marcel, although his versions of certain Marcellian themes—such as individuals' transcendence of their functions or roles, the internal relation of one subject to another,[95] the notions of a We and of presence, the significance of interpersonal relations with respect to death, and the body as (in some sense) a subject—must necessarily be regarded, by those who are in fundamental agreement with Marcel, as perversions of them. I would also say that in certain respects—particularly in relation to the idea of freedom—Marcel seems to have anticipated the possibility as well as the essential weaknesses of positions that Sartre was later to take.

I have suggested that the basic divergence in orientation between these two philosophers is best expressed by saying that Marcel's philosophy is a philosophy of communion and Sartre's a philosophy of alienation. Yet in a way this characterization of their relation is somewhat misleading. It seems to imply that the relation is one of simple opposition—and it is apparently such suggestions that have led Marcel to be slightly distrustful of comparisons of his thought with Sartre's.[96] The truth is somewhat more complex, for Marcel's philosophy is in a fundamental way more comprehensive than Sartre's. Sartre construes alienation as the essential human condition—however much he may deny that human beings have an essence—and thus excludes the very possibility of real communion. But Marcel's orientation toward communion has not similarly prevented him from recognizing the metaphysical possibility—and the pervasive factual reality—of alienation. Although consistently holding to the conviction that human beings are most truly themselves in communion, Marcel has not forgotten that "*it may be of my essence to be able not to be what I am;* in plain words, to be able to betray myself"[97] and that to which I am essentially united. He has recognized the temptations that may lead one to despair—to reject being, betray community, become alienated from one's own incarnate existence, and employ one's freedom for its own degradation. Both Marcel's philosophical and his dramatic writings bear witness to such possibilities.[98]

I would suggest then that in recognizing both the possibility of freedom's fulfillment in communion and its abuse in the choice of alienation and despair, Marcel has been a truer witness to the nature of human existence and freedom than has Sartre. We can apply to the Sartrean negativity the words with which Kierkegaard characterized sin and say that it is fundamentally "not a negation but a position."[99] For Sartre describes us not as we universally and inevitably are, but rather as we make ourselves be in attempting to escape our finitude and be our own creator. Marcel, however, saw long before that true freedom is only possible in terms of an act of faith that affirms our finite situation, our status as creatures.[100] Despite his intellectual debts to other philosophers, Sartre is a highly original thinker; his *Being and Nothingness* must surely be regarded as one of the most brilliant elaborations of a philosophical system to appear in this century. Yet in comparing Marcel and Sartre, I think we are justified in believing that the less systematic thinker has shown the more profound, comprehensive, and illuminating vision.

JOHN D. GLENN, JR.

DEPARTMENT OF PHILOSOPHY
TULANE UNIVERSITY
JUNE 1971

NOTES

1. I use both of these terms in a broad, nontechnical sense and not in the narrower senses that they sometimes seem to have in the writings of these philosophers and of their interpreters. That is, I do not use *alienation* in a specifically Marxist sense, as Sartre apparently does in his *Critique de la raison dialectique*, nor do I use *communion* in a sense exclusive of *community*, as Troisfontaines does in his interpretation of Marcel. On this point, see Kenneth T. Gallagher, *The Philosophy of Gabriel Marcel* (New York: Fordham University Press, 1962), pp. 22–23, 59, 166. I do not question the validity of thus distinguishing between a unity that precedes alienation and a higher unity that may follow it, but the term *communion* seems to me to encompass best the various modes of unity.

2. One exception to this statement is my colleague Professor Edward G. Ballard; see his "The Mystery of Being," in *Existential Philosophers: Kierkegaard to Merleau-Ponty,* ed. George A. Schrader, Jr. (New York: McGraw-Hill Book Co., 1967), p. 232. I am indebted to his essay and in particular to his discussion of Marcel's criticisms of Sartre.

3. Marcel has of course repudiated the term *existentialism* as it has been

applied to his philosophy (see the author's preface to the *Metaphysical Journal,* trans. Bernard Wall [Chicago: Henry Regnery Co., 1952], p. xiii [hereafter cited as *MJ*]), but this seems to be primarily because of the extent to which it is today associated in so many minds with Sartre and his school. See also Marcel's suggestion that existentialism is "obliged either to deny or transcend itself" (*The Philosophy of Existentialism,* trans. Manya Harari, 4th paperbound ed. [New York: Citadel Press, 1964], p. 88 [hereafter cited as *PE*]).

4. Chapters of both *The Philosophy of Existentialism* and *Homo Viator: Introduction to a Metaphysic of Hope* (trans. Emma Craufurd [Chicago: Henry Regnery Co., 1951]; hereafter cited as *HV*) are devoted to discussions of Sartre's ideas, .s are numerous briefer passages in almost all of Marcel's postwar writings. Although the overwhelming balance of his examination of Sartre is critical, he has occasionally expressed a qualified admiration of certain features of Sartre's work (see, for example, *PE,* 53). Most of the present essay arose from my reflections on the basis in Marcel's thought for his criticisms of Sartre.

5. *PE,* 10–13.

6. This is the title of chap. 3, vol. 1, of Marcel's *The Mystery of Being,* trans. G. S. Fraser (vol. 1) and René Hague (vol. 2), 2 vols. (Chicago: Henry Regnery Co., 1960; hereafter cited as *MB*).

7. *PE,* 14.

8. Jean-Paul Sartre, *Being and Nothingness,* trans. Hazel E. Barnes (New York: Philosophical Library, 1956), pp. 59–62.

9. See *PE,* 64–69.

10. *PE,* 81.

11. See *HV,* 24–26.

12. See Sartre, *Being and Nothingness,* p. 60.

13. *PE,* 18.

14. Gabriel Marcel, *Creative Fidelity,* trans. Robert Rosthal (New York: Noonday Press, 1964) pp. 32–33 (hereafter cited as *CF*).

15. Sartre, *Being and Nothingness,* pp. 252–53.

16. Sartre explicitly criticizes Heidegger's theory in *Being and Nothingness,* pp. 245–47.

17. Ibid., p. 339; I believe that Marcel first explicitly speaks of an "internal relation" in this context in *MB* 1:222, but such a notion was implicit in his thinking long before.

18. *CF,* 33; the French phrase *lien senti,* which is here translated as a "bond of feeling," might better be translated as a "felt bond."

19. See *MB* 1:222. Marcel's suggestion that a bond may be created by the discovery of a "shared experience" suggests that intersubjectivity in the full sense may arise on the basis of an implicit community that is discovered and acknowledged. This passage may seem to imply that the I is really prior to the We; if this is true with respect to certain examples of the We, however, I must add that Marcel regards intersubjectivity in general as more fundamental than the separateness of individual egos. And it seems that any authentic We must to some extent make different persons out of those who participate in it.

20. See *Being and Nothingness,* pp. 254–56, for Sartre's discussion of this phenomenon.

21. Ibid., pp. 252–302; I will capitalize *Look* hereafter when it is used as a technical term.

22. Ibid., pp. 259–60.

23. According to Sartre these other attempts include language, masochism, indifference, desire, sadism, and hate. His analyses are often brilliant but not always convincing. See *Being and Nothingness,* pp. 361–412.

24. Ibid., p. 265.

25. Marcel discusses trust at various points in his writings, usually in the context of an attempt to clarify the nature of religious belief. See, for example, *CF,* 134–36; *MB* 2:86–92.

26. At one point Sartre does suggest the possibility of an "ethics of deliverance and salvation" in which these conflicts might be overcome, but he does not elaborate on this suggestion (*Being and Nothingness,* p. 412). Indeed his basic ontology would seem to preclude such an ethics a priori, although one may admire his personal willingness to leave such a possibility open.

27. Ibid., p. 413; "subjectives" is an error in translation or typography; it should be "subjectivities."

28. Ibid., p. 414.

29. As Sartre's translator notes, the French *nous* means both "we" and "us" (Ibid., p. 414*n*).

30. See ibid., pp. 415–23, for Sartre's analysis of the us-object.

31. Ibid., p. 423.

32. Ibid., p. 290.

33. *MJ,* 137.

34. See the ending of Marcel's play *A Man of God* (trans. Marjorie Gabain, in *Three Plays* [New York: Hill & Wang, 1958]) and the discussion of it in *MB* 1:187–89.

35. *CF,* 9.

36. Cf. Fraser's translation of this passage, in *MB* 1:217. Because he gives a rather free rendition of the original, I offer here my own translation from Marcel's French.

37. This is again my own translation; cf. *MB* 1:217–18.

38. This idea is already implicit in *CF,* 8–9, although Sartre seems to have been the first to make it explicit. In Marcel's early writings the term *Third person* or *third party* refers to the Him or the It that is excluded from the relation of the I and the Thou; see, for example, *MJ,* 145–47. Only later did he begin to move toward the realization that a being who is a Thou for others may help bring about an I-Thou relation between them. Sartre's notion of the Third may have served as a catalyst in this development, although here Sartre may also owe something to Marcel's earlier analyses. At any rate it is clear that this idea has a somewhat different significance for the two philosophers.

39. The French word *on* is here translated as "They." Sartre's analysis at this point admittedly owes much to Heidegger's discussion of *das Man* (*man* has also been translated as "they") in *Being and Time* (trans. John MacQuarrie and Edward Robinson [New York: Harper & Row, 1962]).

40. Sartre, *Being and Nothingness,* pp. 423–24.

41. Ibid., pp. 424–29.

42. *CF,* 8.

43. See *MB* 1:219–22 for a discussion of the various "levels" of intersubjectivity that may be involved in different sorts of relationships.

44. *CF,* 8.

45. Sartre uses this example in *Being and Nothingness,* p. 424.

46. See Marcel's essay "The Mystery of the Family," in *HV,* 68–97. Here I speak of the family as an ideal that is always only imperfectly realized, although it is certainly not a "mere ideal."

47. Marcel has quite consistently refrained from specifying this immortality in empirical terms. It is clear moreover that for him this belief in immortality does not preempt the Christian belief in the resurrection of the dead. See Gabriel Marcel, *Searchings,* no translator given (New York: Newman Press, 1967), p. 55.

48. See Gabriel Marcel, "Notes on the Problem of Immortality," in *Philosophical Fragments 1909–1914,* trans. Lionel A. Blain (Notre Dame, Ind.: University of Notre Dame Press, 1965), pp. 92–102. Today of course Marcel would speak of a "mystery" rather than a "problem" in this context.

49. *HV,* 147.

50. Jean-Paul Sartre, *No Exit,* trans. Stuart Gilbert, in *"No Exit" and Three Other Plays* (New York: Vintage Books, 1949), p. 47.

51. Sartre, *Being and Nothingness,* pp. lv–lvi.

52. I think I am being faithful to Sartre's use of the phenomenological notion of "constitution" in employing the term here; although Sartre has been criticized for misinterpreting the sense in which Husserl uses this term; see Richard M. Zaner, *The Problem of Embodiment* (The Hague: Martinus Nijhoff, 1964), p. 112.

53. Sartre, *Being and Nothingness,* p. 540. This is really only one aspect of the Sartrean doctrine, for he also says that the death of one person involves the irremediable fixing of another's being-as-object for him (see p. 412).

54. As in his *Presence and Immortality,* trans. Michael A. Machado (Pittsburgh: Duquesne University Press, 1967).

55. Sartre, *Being and Nothingness,* p. 279.

56. *HV,* 178.

57. See above for a brief explanation of Marcel's distinction between *problem* and *mystery.*

58. *MB* 2:12; see pp. 5–20 for the full discussion of this point.

59. As Sartre recognizes; see *Being and Nothingness,* p. 261.

60. *PE,* 71.

61. Sartre, *Being and Nothingness,* p. 414.

62. Ibid., pp. 275–77.

63. Ibid., p. 281.

64. Ibid., p. 249.

65. A detailed consideration and comparison of Marcel's and Sartre's analyses of the body can be found in Zaner, *The Problem of Embodiment.* I am indebted to his discussions of certain points, although the main lines of my summary treatment of this topic—which has a purpose different from that of his study—were determined before I became aware of his work. He suggests that both Sartre and Merleau-Ponty owe an unacknowledged debt to Marcel's analysis of the body (p. 147). It is interesting then that Desan, one of Sartre's more perspicacious interpreters, says that his account of the body is "one of the most original of Sartre's views, and probably the one that history will consider as the most valuable" (Wilfrid Desan, *The Tragic Finale,* rev. ed. [New York: Harper & Row, 1960], p. 74).

66. Marcel's development of these ideas begins in his *Metaphysical Journal,* and he repeats and elaborates on them in most of his subsequent major works. A brief exposition of his position can be found in "Incarnate Being as the Central

Datum of Metaphysical Reflection," in *CF*, 11–37, especially 18–26. For Sartre's parallel treatment of these topics, see *Being and Nothingness*, pp. 310–24.

67. Sartre, *Being and Nothingness*, p. 305.

68. Ibid., pp. 326–27.

69. Ibid., p. 353.

70. Ibid. Sartre actually discusses three, rather than two, ontological dimensions of the body, but one of these is a hybrid of doubtful legitimacy; see Zaner, *The Problem of Embodiment*, p. 123.

71. *CF*, 19–20.

72. Gabriel Marcel, *Being and Having: An Existentialist Diary*, trans. Katharine Farrer (New York: Harper & Row, Harper Torchbooks, 1965), p. 14 (hereafter cited as *BH*).

73. See *CF*, 20–23; this notion of the choice of the absurd seems to predate Marcel's acquaintance with Camus's thought.

74. The term *bearer* is inadequate in this context; yet it perhaps suggests as well as any the nature of this everyday experience, which is nevertheless not fully transparent to reflection. Marcel does not of course believe that "presence" is necessarily dependent on bodily incarnation; see *The Influence of Psychic Phenomena on my Philosophy* (London: London Society for Psychical Research, 1956).

75. Sartre, *Being and Nothingness*, p. 441.

76. Ibid., p. 439.

77. Sartre does suggest in the concluding section of *Being and Nothingness* that freedom might "turn its back on" the ideal of the in-itself for-itself (p. 627). But on this point, as on others, the concluding section seems to reveal Sartre's struggling with a host of possibilities, not all of which are consistent with the ontology presented in the main portion of his work.

78. Ibid., p. 626.

79. Ibid., p. 440.

80. Again see the puzzling final paragraphs of *Being and Nothingness*.

81. Marcel has suggested that "Sartre ends up with an *ethic of unconstraint*" (*Problematic Man* [New York: Herder & Herder, 1967], p. 118).

82. Here Sartre seems to owe much to Kierkegaard. His position regarding the relation of freedom and temporality is much like that of the Kierkegaardian aesthete, whereas Marcel's is similar to that of the ethical and religious ";stages." See especially the quotation from Kierkegaard's papers in the editor's introduction to Kierkegaard's *Repetition*, trans. Walter Lowrie (New York: Harper & Row, 1964), pp. 11–13.

83. Sartre, *Being and Nothingness*, pp. 466–67.

84. Ibid., p. 440.

85. *PE*, 82–83. Marcel traces this identification to "Kant and his followers." Although this is not inaccurate historically, it might be noted that in his aesthetic theory Kant began to surpass such an identification.

86. *CF*, 91.

87. *CF*, 92.

88. *CF*, 92.

89. *BH*, 41.

90. Sartre does not, it is true, adopt an atomic conception of the different "moments" of the self, since he considers the self at one moment to be a relative (not an absolute) negation of its past. But his view would seem to have the same

ethical implications. And of course Marcel does not deny that one may come to repudiate a commitment (see *BH*, 44–46), but he wants to show that obligatory commitments can be made.

91. *BH*, 42.

92. *BH*, 46

93. *BH*, 47.

94. See *MB* 1:224ff.

95. Sartre was the first, I think, to speak explicitly of an "internal relation" in this context, although the idea was implicit in Marcel's thought before that time; see note 17 above.

96. See Marcel, *Searchings*, p. 117.

97. *BH*, 106.

98. See, for example, *BH*, 95–97.

99. Søren Kierkegaard, *The Sickness unto Death,* bound with *Fear and Trembling,* trans. Walter Lowrie (Garden City, New York: Doubleday and Co., 1954), p. 227.

100. See *MJ*, 44–45.

*Marcel and Sartre: The Philosophy of Communion
and the Philosophy of Alienation*

REPLY TO JOHN D. GLENN, JR.

If there exists a common denominator—which I could not deny—between
Jean-Paul Sartre's thought and mine, I have every reason to believe that it
reduces itself to very little and that on this score, as indeed on others, the
use of the term *existentialism* has created much confusion.

At the same time, I was interested in the comparison that John Glenn
drew between the text of 1932, where I discussed the relation between
individuals and their functions, and Sartre's remarks on the café waiter in
Being and Nothingness. But I believe that in reality the perspectives are
completely different. What enters into Sartre's thought is the idea of a role
rather than of a function. One could even say that the café waiter plays at
being a café waiter, whereas one could not say that the employee of the
metro plays at being an employee of the metro. A function is something
altogether different from a role. Moreover it could be shown in detail that
the word *transcendence* has in no way the same meaning in Sartre's
thought as in mine.

But above all it must be said that our respective points of view concerning consciousness and freedom, on the one hand, and being itself, on
the other, are so completely different that it does not even make sense to
say that they are opposed. As far as being is concerned, everyone today
knows or should know that on the whole I am infinitely closer to Heidegger than Sartre is. I do not know what the author of *Sein und Zeit*
now thinks of Sartre,* whom he had occasion to see again a few years
ago, but I recall distinctly the very negative opinion, it seemed to me,
that Heidegger had of him at the time of our first conversation in 1946 at

Translated from the French by Dr. Garth J. Gillan.
*We received Marcel's reply to Glenn in June 1971.—Ed.

Freiburg.* He absolutely rejected the idea of existence's priority over essence, an idea that I, for my part, have never admitted as such.

It can generally be said that Sartre's sources never coincide with mine. In the end he remains radically in the tradition of the Cartesian *cogito,* which has never been the case with me. If Kierkegaard has influenced him, it seems to be only to the extent that in his thought he has developed a kind of anarchism, which he later, moreover, had the greatest difficulty keeping in check because of his hopeless effort to cling to Marxism for dear life. But the point where I diverge from him in the most incontrovertible fashion is in his concept of consciousness, taken almost as a lack or emptiness, and in his concept of freedom, conceived entirely negatively. In addition I think that he has certainly often contradicted himself on these scores.

We had cordial relations before the war and even at the time of the publication of *Being and Nothingness.* Later our paths separated to such an extent that there was no longer any question of our meeting. Personally I have, however, regretted that, and I asked him on at least two occasions whether he would not be willing to have a discussion on some of the most important issues. He refused. Furthermore I surmise that it was Simone de Beauvoir who helped to persuade him to adopt such an almost aggressively negative attitude. Has she not been persisting in seeing me as a man of the extreme right, without being willing to take account of all that separates me from the conservatives? All this is certainly regrettable, but there is nothing I can do about it. Moreover Jean-Paul Sartre has become so much of a demagogue, an attention seeker, and a scandal monger that a meeting between us could no longer be meaningful.

G.M.

---

*Marcel's manuscript has ''Fribourg'' at this point, but the editor feels confident that that is a typographical error and that the conversation took place in the German university city of Freiburg, where Heidegger taught.—ED.

21

Julián Marías

LOVE IN MARCEL AND ORTEGA

A LIVING PHILOSOPHER

WHEN Professor Paul A. Schilpp asked me to write an essay on Marcel and Ortega, I could not for a moment resist the temptation to accept. I was in the midst of a friendly triangle: besides my friendly bond with Professor Schilpp, I had a long and strong friendship with Gabriel Marcel and an even longer one with José Ortega y Gasset, my best friend for twenty-three years.

I came to know Schilpp indirectly through Ortega in 1954, when Schilpp was preparing a volume on the great Spanish philosopher for his Library of Living Philosophers. Ortega mentioned my name in his letters, and since I was on my way to Los Angeles to teach at UCLA during the second semester of 1954–55, Schilpp asked me to stop by Chicago to discuss the project. At Northwestern University during a cold Evanston January, Schilpp and I made plans for the volume *The Philosophy of Ortega y Gasset,* announced for some time by the Library of Living Philosophers. Unfortunately Ortega died on 18 October 1955, when the book was just beginning to take shape. Schilpp at once ended the project, since Ortega was no longer alive. I pointed out to him that a philosopher is alive while his thought is alive; besides, Ortega was still alive as an author because numerous posthumous books of his were in the process of being prepared for publication. Schilpp agreed but told me the Library demanded that the philosopher studied be actually living in order to be able to answer observations, objections, or comments. This means that the philosophers dealt with in this admirable series are studied as living men, personally, and that their ideas are viewed as nothing less than a part of their whole reality,

Translated from the Spanish by Josefina I. Frondizi.

since their presence in the replies gives a personal character to what is said in these pages. This gives me the opportunity—and in truth compels me—to speak personally of Gabriel Marcel.

When in 1947 Marcel paid a visit to Madrid, I received an invitation to lunch at an official institution as one of several persons Marcel wanted to meet. My wish to meet him was even greater, but I was afraid the luncheon would be extremely "official." To express my admiration for Marcel, I sent him a copy of my *Introducción a la filosofía,* which had just appeared, but I declined the invitation.

Unexpectedly in the evening my doorbell rang, and a card was brought to me: Gabriel Marcel. Without previously notifying me and not even knowing if I would be home, Marcel had come to pay me a visit. He told me he had received the book and after lunch had gone to his room at the hotel and started to read it. When he got to page 70 or 80, he got up, took his hat, and came to my home.

I am telling this because I think it shows who Gabriel Marcel is: his spontaneity and his personal feelings about everything and particularly about philosophy. We talked for several hours, discovering a great understanding of the surprising nearness of our respective points of view. The next day I attended his lecture at the Institut français, and we conversed again. We renewed our friendship in Paris in 1949, during my first visit to that city, and once again the next year. But it was bound to intensify at various special occasions.

In 1951 we met in Peru at a Congress of Philosophy sponsored by the University of San Marcos of Lima, which was celebrating its four hundredth anniversary. There again we talked endlessly—in Lima, Cuzco, and Machu Picchu. I still remember it as an extraordinary occasion. As guests of the French Ambassador, some friends and I lunched together at the Palace of the Embassy in Lima. After lunch Marcel went up to a piano and started improvising. A peacock from the garden approached the room, entered silently through the open door, and stood still. Marcel, bent over the piano, his hair almost white, continued with his music. The peacock listened as if in reverence.

During the trip from Cuzco to Machu Picchu, in a tiny train that twisted along the Andes, Marcel and I talked for a long time. With unusual candor he told me of his personal life. We shared some profound beliefs, a common way of seeing human life rendered by two different philosophies that were all the same compatible and friendly. On that trip our friendship was sealed, and I was able to understand Marcel's ideas much better.

There came yet another significant encounter, this time in France, at the Castle of Cérisy, in Normandy, where a group of philosophers from various countries had gathered with Martin Heidegger. He began the meetings and seminars with the lecture "Was ist das, die Philosophie?" which he later published. Heidegger wanted the discussions to be carried on with brief "counter-lectures," if I may call them so, in which participants would express their views on the same subject, as Marcel, Paul Ricoeur, Lucien Goldmann, and I did.[1] Marcel was particularly interested in the problem of communication. In that gathering, along with the great philosopher Heidegger, one of the most profound minds of our time—Gabriel Marcel—found his ideas confronted by others, and in this process his ideas became more clearly defined. They ripened in the dialogue, a result to be expected of a man who is both playwright and philosopher in equal creative tension.

Since then my readings of Marcel's work have gone hand in hand with our frequent meetings in Paris or Madrid. We have always been in accord, many times in full agreement. We look at the same reality from different levels and perspectives. For me his pages are always mingled with the sound of his voice, with the expressions of his face, and even with his silences—those pronounced silences when he says he doesn't know, when he is in search of something, corresponding to the frequent appearance in his writings of "Il faut creuser" and "Il faut approfondir." Only from this perspective am I able to talk about him; I can only understand him in dialogue, precisely as a living philosopher.

REFLECTION

Marcel's double method is concerned with reflection in both senses of the word: the operation by which something bends over itself and views itself as if from the inside, and the operation by which something returns after having reached the other object. In Spanish we distinguish the two meanings as *reflexion* and *reflejo*. In Marcel's work they correspond to the two realms to which he has given himself: his philosophical writings and his plays.

Marcel never aimed at a system, in the sense of a body of doctrines. It is no accident that when looking for a name for his ideas, after refusing "Christian existentialism" (which he once accepted in a moment of weakness and relative inauthenticity), he adopted "Socratism," although this does not seem to be very fortunate either. If the spirit of inquiry and research, of permanent questioning, fits both Socrates and Marcel, let us not forget that the former was looking especially for the *tí*, the "what," definition, whereas Marcel probably suspects that the really interesting things cannot be defined.

Marcel's philosophical thought has always been explained in hesitating and vague ways, full of reservations. He has always been conscious that something more should be added, that some other qualifying fact should be taken into consideration. Of his two main books, *Journal métaphysique* and *Le Mystère de l'être,* the first is an intimate reflection, carried on in fragments over many years, and the second is a course (the Gifford Lectures), that is, an effort of verbal communication. It is surely meditation—thought carried on in solitude, reflecting back on itself—but a meditation obsessed by communication; this accounts for Marcel's essential objection to Heidegger, despite his admiration for him, and for what made him satirize if not Heidegger himself then certainly "Heideggerism" in his play *La Dimension Florestan,* whose better German title, *Die Wacht am Sein,* is its original name. It is this concern for communication—a concern not limited to ideas—that made Marcel a playwright.

Both on the stage and in their dialogue, Marcel's characters keep reflecting each other. The dialogue, more than a *diá-logos* (a saying "through," *diá*) as in Plato and Socrates, is a stage reflection, a reciprocal reflex of the characters among each other by means of words and presence. This is why Marcel's plays are neither an "application" of his philosophical ideas nor an "exposition" of them; his is not a theater *à thèse* but a research method parallel to philosophy, simultaneous with it, and complementary to it. When Marcel read my book *Miguel de Unamuno,*[2] he was surprised to realize that from 1897 Spanish authors had done something similar with the novel and that since 1938 I had proposed the theory of the "existential novel," or "personal novel," defined as a way of knowing.[3] The fundamental difference (which I cannot discuss fully here) is that Unamuno was primarily a novelist and not a playwright. His plays can be "reduced" to his novels, that is, he studies human life in narrative form, not through dialogue, whereas Marcel never wrote novels, and his dramatic representation of human life is based in the scenic and verbal confrontation of intimacies rather than in the "reflection" of imagination.

Love as a subject appears in Marcel in a strictly personal perspective, this being his main achievement. It is not by chance that he prefers to use the personal pronouns *I* and *thou* rather than the impersonal *one*. On the other hand, from the beginning there is a close approximation between love and faith. In his *Metaphysical Journal,* at the point of considering love, Marcel writes:

I can say no more than that between God and me there is the relation of one freedom with another. That relation is involved in the act of faith—as affirmation. In other words, between God and me there must be a relation of the kind that love establishes between lovers.

And so, side by side with faith we posit love. I have said elsewhere that love is the condition of faith, and in a sense this is true. But it is only one aspect. I believe that in reality love and faith cannot be dissociated. When faith ceases to be love it congeals into objective belief in a power that is conceived more or less physically. And love which is not faith (which does not posit the transcendence of the God that is loved) is only a sort of abstract game. Just as the divine reality corresponds to faith (the former can only be thought in function of the latter) so divine perfection corresponds to love. And the union of reality and perfection in God, far from needing to be understood in the old intellectualist sense (*ens realissimum*), can only be grasped in function of faith and of the union of faith and love that I have just emphasised. I cease to believe in God the moment I cease to love him; an imperfect God cannot be real.[4]

Further on he calls love "spiritual communication," in opposition to "all mechanical and external" (that is to say, impersonal) communication,[5] and he relates love and individuality:

What I have elsewhere called real interiority is thus involved in every act of love—and, inversely, real individuality is essentially defined through love (or, strictly speaking, in aesthetic creation which makes possible the communication of individualities). Hence the meaning of my statement that love creates its object can be seen more clearly. It must not be understood in a superficially subjectivist and solipsist sense. The reality of the beloved one is essential to love—no (subjective) truth can transcend that reality. In this sense it is perhaps true to say that only love is real knowledge and that it is legitimate to associate love and adequate knowledge, in other words that only for love is the individuality of the beloved immune against disintegration and crumbling away, so to speak, into the dust of abstract elements. But it is only possible to maintain the reality of the beloved because love posits the beloved as transcending all explanation and all reduction. In this sense it is true to say that love only addresses itself to what is eternal, it immobilises the beloved above the world of genesis and vicissitude. And in that way love is the negation of knowledge, which can only ignore transcendence.[6]

This gives rise to some especially interesting points. On the one hand is the theoretical root of Marcel's statement: "Thou, whom I love, shalt never die" (*Toi que j'aime, tu ne mourras pas!*). This assertion is the discovery of the other self as a person beyond the perishable condition of an organism. On the other hand is Marcel's use of the words *explanation* and *reduction,* which in other contexts I have used many times to interpret the genesis of irrationalism in nineteenth-century philosophy, starting with Kierkegaard. The idea of reason from the eighteenth century on in all German idealism, and the idea Kierkegaard criticizes, has been that of scientific reason, since what Kant had in mind in his *Kritik der reinen Vernunft* is Newton's physics. Now for the scientist to know rationally means to explain—*ex-plicare,* "to unfold"—what is implicit or folded and at the same time to reduce a reality to its elements, causes, or principles. All this is admissible when we deal with manipulations, mental or physical, of realities uninteresting in themselves. But when it is not so, when we are interested in the realities themselves—as we are in human life or history—then they are irreducible. And it seems that reason is useless, for it cannot know these realities, which are precisely the most interesting ones. Moreover Marcel uses a dangerous expression; love "immobilizes" the beloved beyond the changing world. Can we accept this immobilization? Does it not affect the dramatic condition of human life? And is it not precisely in that condition that the singular "eternalization" of the beloved has to be sought? In my latest book I have dealt at length with these problems.[7]

After the last passage quoted above, Marcel makes an important statement. He warns us against the error of attributing "blindness" to love. Pascal had already opposed this. It is usual to quote—as Ortega does—the passage that reads: "Therefore the poets were not right in painting Love blind; we must take off his blind and restore to him henceforth the enjoyment of his eyes."[8] But that *therefore* is warning us that we are dealing with a consequence, and this is even more important. In the preceding paragraph, Pascal writes:

> We have unaptly taken away the name of reason from love, and have opposed them to each other without good foundation, for love and reason are but the same thing. It is a precipitation of thought which is impelled to a side before fully examining everything, but it is still a reason, and we should not and cannot wish that it were otherwise, for we would then be disagreeable machines. Let us not therefore exclude reason from love, since they are inseparable.[9]

What Marcel says is especially significant if we keep Pascal's words in mind:

> Of course we need not conclude that love is necessarily blind, that to love means to exclude judgment. As soon as love is knowingly dissociated from knowledge it ceases to be love—from that moment love is no more (for itself) than an illusory and voluntarily idealised knowledge. Love needs to appear to itself as perfect knowledge, and in the measure in which it is now no longer permissible to dissociate being from appearances we can say that it *is* perfect knowledge.[10]

Ortega, meanwhile, emphasizes the insight of love, its ability to discover the qualifications of the beloved. He is opposed to Stendhal's "crystallization" theory, according to which "the real image of a woman falls within the masculine soul and little by little gets embroidered with imaginary superpositions that add to the nude image all possible perfection."[11] For Ortega "crystallization" is not something unique in love. All mental life is crystallization in one way or another. Throwing imaginary elements over real objects is done constantly, for to see things and to appraise them is to complete them.

> All that one has to do to shatter the theory of crystallization is to examine the cases in which it evidently does not appear: they are the exemplary cases of love in which both parties possess a clear mind and, within human limits, are not liable to be mistaken. A theory of eroticism ought to begin by an explanation of its most perfect forms, and not by an immediate orientation toward the pathology of the phenomenon which it is studying. The fact is that, in those cases, the man, rather than projecting perfections which existed only in his mind, suddenly discovers in a woman certain qualities of a nature which until then were unrecognized by him. Note that these are specifically feminine qualities. If they are at all prototypic, how can they pre-exist in the mind of the male?[12]

Marcel's viewpoint is better clarified if we consider another passage from his *Metaphysical Journal*, where he relates love to essence and judgment. The word *knowledge* is misleading when applied to love. Love is beyond judgment, because judgment refers to essence, and love refers to what is beyond essence, for it implies faith in the perpetual renewal of being, the belief that nothing can be lost. Hence the metaphysical and personal Christian commandment "Judge not!"

> Love, then, is not addressed to what the beloved is in himself, if by what he is in himself we understand an essence. The contrary is the case. As I have already said, love bears on what is beyond essence, love is the act by which a thought, by thinking a freedom, is made free. In this sense love extends beyond any possible judgment, for judgment can only bear on essence—and love is the very negation of essence (in this sense it implies faith in the perpetual renewal of being itself, the belief that nothing ever is—that nothing ever can be—irremediably lost). Doubtless, inasmuch as the lover is a thinking subject, and the beloved is the object for this subject, the lover cannot fail to judge, but he can only judge the beloved inasmuch as object, that is, in the beloved's actions. Inasmuch as he loves (that is inasmuch as he converts the object into subject) he must absolutely forgo making a judgment. The *Thou shalt not judge* of Christian morality must be viewed as one of the most important metaphysical formulae on earth.[13]

From this Marcel derives the particularly important consequence in his philosophy that God cannot either be judged or justified and that every theodicy is to be condemned: "God cannot and must not be judged. For judgment is only possible regarding essence. That explains why every kind of theodicy must be condemned, because a theodicy necessarily implies a judgment, it is a judgment, a justification. Now God cannot be justified. The thought that justifies is the thought that has not yet been elevated to love and to the faith that claims to transcend the mind (belief). Theodicy is atheism."[14]

These subjects return in other places in Marcel's *Metaphysical Journal,* though from rather different viewpoints. The problem about the difference between *toi* ("thou") and *lui* ("him") is raised. Every judgment refers to a *lui.* And this brings him to the conclusion that "to love is not to know adequately; it may be that love gives a privileged knowledge but precedes it as it also precedes evaluation." Love is the liberation of the self; more concretely, it is an invocation, a call from self to self. Love is life that loses its center. He summarizes his ideas thus: "Metaphysically the problem divides up as follows: (1) Does love bear not simply on the idea of being but on being itself? and (2) can it bear on being without affecting being? As regards the first question there can be no doubt whatsoever. But the second question seems to me very doubtful."[15]

In a note dated 24 February 1920, Marcel touches briefly, questioningly, on an important point: the connection between love and freedom and between freedom and choice. He writes: "At first this may seem surprising, but does not freedom mean choice? When we love do we choose to love? But doubtless we must dissociate radically the ideas of choice and freedom. In what measure can I say *me*? That is the real problem."[16]

Finally, one passage in his *Journal* throws a great deal of light on the general suppositions of the Marcellian interpretation of love. Is this tantamount to seeing love as an illusion that when bearing on creatures is hindered by reality, but when bearing on God—"that is, on a pure construction"—has full play and nothing to fear from experience? Marcel writes that "we know full well that genuine love, even when directed towards human beings, does not allow itself to stop at knowledge; it affirms the value of its object beyond the merely relative and contingent order of merit and demerit—for love has partaken of divine mediation."[17] This quotation reveals that although Marcel does not speak primarily of human love, when he speaks of love he includes this latter in it.

Let us compare Ortega's point of view. Here I am not expounding his theory of love but merely making some observations to counterpoint Marcel's ideas on the same subject. Ortega is fully aware that the use of the word *love* is very wide and applicable to different objects; moreover he says that what "love" strictly is happens to be common to all possible species of love. This at least is what he thinks in 1926. It is advisable to quote some of his passages on this subject.

The word "love," so simple and with so few letters, is used to label innumerable phenomena which differ so widely that it would be well to doubt if they have anything in common with each other. We speak of "love for a woman"; but also of "love of God," "love of country," "love of art," "maternal love," "filial love," etc. One and the same word embraces and names the most varied fauna of emotions. . . .

Is there some important similarity which exists between "love for a woman" and "love of science"? When we examine both states of mind we find that almost every element in them differs. There is, however, one identical ingredient, which a careful analysis would enable us to isolate in both phenomena. If we saw it freed and isolated from the remaining factors which make up both states of mind, we would understand that, strictly speaking, it alone deserves the name of "love." By virtue of a practical but inaccurate amplification, we apply the name to the entire state of mind in spite of the fact that many things are involved in the latter which are not really "love," or even sentiment. . . .

Love, strictly speaking, is pure sentimental activity toward an object, which can be anything—person or thing. As a "sentimental" activity, it remains, on the one hand, separated from all intellectual functions—perception, consideration, thought, recall, imagination—and, on the other hand, from desire, with which it is often confused. A glass of water is desired, but is not loved, when one is thirsty. Undoubtedly, desires are born of love; but love itself is not desire. We desire good fortune for our country, and we desire to live in it because we love it. Our love exists prior to these desires, and the desires spring from love like the plant from the seed. . . .

[L]oving something is not simply "being," but acting toward that which is loved. In this regard I am not referring to the physical or spiritual movements which love incites; love itself is, by nature, a transitive act in which we exert ourselves on behalf of what we love. Although we are quiescent, when we are a hundred leagues from the object and not even thinking about it, if we love the object an indefinable flow of a warm and affirmative nature will emanate from us. . . .

Moreover, one might add, leaving aside pure sentimental activity, that all the differing elements in "love of science" and "love of a woman" are not, properly speaking, what love is.[18]

This apparent similarity between Marcel and Ortega shows the difference in posing the problem, because in spite of what I have just quoted, when Ortega speaks of love he is primarily speaking of human love, especially of love between a man and a woman, and this type of love draws the greater part of his attention, though he claims that strictly speaking what it has of love can be found in other very different types.

Theoretically Marcel refers to love without specific determinations, and more frequently he has in mind divine love, taking care that all that has been said can be applied to it. Ortega, on the contrary, bears in mind a man's love for a woman, on which he sets forth a theory that in some way could be "generalized." Nevertheless, human love imposes itself on Marcel when he faces the fictitious representation of human life, that is, when he makes imaginary philosophical enquiries in his plays.

IMAGINATION

In *Pour une sagesse tragique* Marcel writes a paragraph that can explain the transition between both points of view: "Reflection cannot be practiced where imagination fails, and I would add, on the other hand, that without imagination there is no charity, no *agapē* worthy of this name."[19]

I really do not know if Brunschvicg's influence on Marcel has been sufficiently emphasized. The word *influence* is ambiguous. I do not mean to say that Marcel has "received" many of Brunschvicg's ideas but rather the contrary. I think Marcel has always had him "present," and this is indeed an especially strong form of influence. Yet Marcel has done his best to avoid Brunschvicg, not to follow him, because aside from his esteem for Brunschvicg's intellectual gifts, Marcel has felt a kind of danger in his way of philosophizing. On different occasions Marcel has referred to his discussion with Brunschvicg about immortality, during the Descartes Congress, when Brunschvicg hinted that Marcel was more concerned about his own death than Brunschvicg was concerned about his. Marcel replied that he was not interested in his own death but in others', in the death of those whom we love. The problem—or mystery—of death is inseparable from love, and this love demands imagining the other person. This is why the reference to absence, that fundamental way of being, must necessarily be taken into consideration: "To the extent that I create a void around me, it is quite clear that I can drag myself toward death and prepare myself for it as for a sleep of indefinite length. It is quite another matter the moment the 'thou' appears. One can only be certain about fidelity in cases where it defies absence. Specifically, it is the absence that presents itself to us— perhaps or even undoubtedly fallaciously—as an absolute that we call death."[20] And death is associated with love, particularly in one imaginative anticipation: "Eveline, if we could only evoke the haranguing, gesticulating human being from tomorrow's tombstone!"[21]

Death's image here is a deterrent to the miseries, weaknesses, and stupidities of the living person; it is also a deterrent to what makes us hate him. If we think of him as the body in the state in which he will be some day, if we see him *tel qu'en lui-même enfin l'éternité le change* ("so eternity changes him as if into himself"), we shall see him from the proper perspective of meeting the other self: love.

Human love, as expected, is foremost in Marcel's plays, though references to divine love are not missing (for example, in the titles *Un Homme de Dieu, Le Signe de la Croix,* and *L'Emissaire*). Human love includes of course the love between a man and a woman. We may say that love, though generic in our reflection, becomes human, and it is intersexual when imagined, that is, when concretely thought of. Let us not forget that in Marcel thinking leads to the concrete, and to the extent that it gets there, it is as such that thought prevails. Dramatic and imaginative works are never mere "illustration" in Marcel's philosophical thought; they are an essential part of him. I would rather say that they are his most vital part, in the same sense that Unamuno's personal novel is the most efficient and philosophical part of his work. Indeed the most interesting findings about the reality of love are found in Marcel's plays, even more so than in his theoretical studies. It is convenient to examine some of these briefly, even though they suffer a certain abstraction when they are isolated from their dramatic context.

In *L'Iconoclaste* (1923) Abel talks of his "infinite love" for Vivienne. His mother asks him when he began to love her, and Abel answers: "A love like mine has no beginning. When you love that way, you know very well it is forever." Projecting this "forever" of love into the future, Abel proposes the notion to which Marcel holds on most energetically: faithfulness. "It is being faithful to his own limit that makes man worthy. I recognize no other virtue." And later on he adds: "The infidel does not deserve but that the memory is kept intact at the bottom of his heart. Repose of the soul is a privilege; one must deserve it."[22]

Yet somewhat earlier, in a despondent mood, Abel utters certain words that seem like the other side of his basic interpretation of love, a complementary aspect that is also true: "Happy are those who have given vent to their caresses. Pity the man with only one love. Passion is but a fixed idea."[23]

The same pattern reappears in *Le Quatuor en fa dièse,* when Roger says: "Yes, forgiveness is perhaps only possible in hearts without memory. One is always the victim of his own way of loving. You are condemned to remember. That is the opposite of fidelity. Also, what is forgiveness spoken by the lips, then, but a lie by which the soul is not fooled?" And Claire says to Stéphane a little later: "For a long time I have known that you are a persistent soul. And I can't bear it."[24]

Perhaps the passage where Marcel epitomizes the significance of all these statements, as far as death is concerned, is in *Le Dard,* when Werner says: "If there were only the living beings, Gisela, I think the earth would be completely uninhabitable."[25]

Concerning the reality of love, Marcel is extremely cautious. For various reasons love is more hinted at than expressed in his plays; barely announced, it withdraws into privacy or turns into affection—into personal love, though not strictly intersexual love. Among the rare explicit texts is a passage in *Rome n'est plus dans Rome,* a play of political and moral interest, where Esther says to her brother-in-law, Pascal:

> Why would I condemn you, since I love you? Yes, the other day I was cowardly when I tried to retract a confession that a sudden emotion evoked from me. I am guilty by telling you. Perhaps I would be even more so by not telling you. I don't know. It is not for me to choose the guilt that pleases me more. We are at a decisive moment in our lives, and you know it just as well as I do. Discretion and modesty are behind us. I know I am yielding to a feeling of dizziness, and I do so knowingly. Understand that if you can."[26]

Esther understands some qualities of love. It is incompatible with judgment, that is to say, with judging a loved person: "How could I condemn you, since I love you?" It is cowardice to hide love, even if it involves guilt. There is also guilt in not hiding it, and one must "choose" not the most convenient but the most authentic action. The decisive element is the combination of dizziness and awareness. When Esther talks about "yielding" knowingly, she points out that it is a matter not of will but of something deeper, of something independent of herself though not at all passive. It is not a matter of her will; it is her reality that is at stake.

Strangely Pascal never answers Esther's declaration of love. Rather his response is: "It seems to me that you have changed. You used to judge sternly those who went away; you talked of desertion. . . ."[27]

Pascal is ready to leave France and accept a position in Brazil. He is terrified by the possibility of a Communist coup followed by a Soviet invasion. His interest is in the change in Esther's moral judgment, not in the personal loving reason for that change. Indeed in a lecture of the same year, 1951, on "Les Vrais Problèmes de *Rome n'est plus dans Rome,*" Marcel wrote: "Pascal is not a lover; he does not have a lover's nature. He will never be Esther's lover. His 'love' is affection and friendship; he is not in love with her."[28]

This brings us to the real question. For Marcel, love is primarily personal love and, if we look at it more closely, the love of God. Whatever he says about love is conditioned by the requirement that it be "valid" for the love we have for our Creator and, to the extent we can imagine it, the love the Creator has for human creatures. In only a few instances does intersexual love in its strict sense (what I call "the state of being in love") appear in Marcel's work. If we think of the "two dramas of the black years'' (war and post-war)—*L'Emissaire* and *Le Signe de la Croix* (the drama of the Jews), published under the common name *Vers un autre royaume*—we can see to what extent the love that abounds in these is above all personal love rather than the state of being in love. This is especially true of the love between Simon and his aunt Lena.

If we compare this with Ortega we find a great difference. In all the works published under the general title *Estudios sobre el amor* (*On Love*) and in the independent writings where the subject is dealt with, Ortega refers mostly to the love between man and woman, to the love of the state of being in love. However strongly he would insist that the essence of all kinds of love is the same—whether love of God, of science, of country, or of woman—it is evident that for Ortega the epitome of all love is the love of woman. Even though Ortega is an author of theory rather than of fiction, all the "species" of love are preferably concentrated in the love of woman. By contrast the playwright Marcel, for the sake of presenting personal relations, is bound to show intersexual love, but this intersexual love is almost always turned into "merely" personal love. We must now question whether either position is wholly satisfactory.

SOME QUESTIONS

For various reasons I will neither question nor object to Ortega's love doctrine. First, I have not discussed it here but have only mentioned some aspects of it as they bear on Marcel's. Second, I have discussed Ortega at length in several writings and especially in my book *Ortega: Circunstancia y vocación*[29] and in the complementary book I am presently preparing, where I will deal extensively with the role and significance of his love doctrine. Third and most importantly, we would need the philosopher's reply, and Ortega's is now unfortunately out of the question. Hence I will restrict myself to asking Marcel some questions drawn from the already discussed passages and within the context of his philosophy.

One of Marcel's most important writings is an essay entitled "Incarnate Being as the Central Datum of Metaphysical Reflection," which is included in the volume *Creative Fidelity*. In it he states most emphatically the need for a concrete philosophy, a philosophy of thoughtful thinking and one that greatly distrusts what is already done and what is depersonalized.[30] Marcel is looking for an indubitable starting point for his research that is at the same time quite different from the Cartesian *cogito:* "At the inception of this investigation it will be necessary to start with certainty.

Not with a logical but with an existential one. If existence is not at the beginning, it is nowhere. There is no pattern to existence, I think, which does not involve sleight of hand and cheating."[31]

Marcel continues the analysis by expressing his conviction that the looked-for "existent-type" is "our own self." But he has to be cautious, because it is not the "I" (*je*) of a subject. He would like to translate *j'existe* into *ich erlebe*. (As is well known, Ortega in 1913 coined the Spanish word *vivencia* as a translation of the German *Erlebnis,* and since then this term has been incorporated into the Spanish language.) My existence, he adds, is inseparable from the fact that "there is my body" (*il y a mon corps*). This is what he means by "being embodied": "Being embodied is to appear as a body, as this body, without being able either to identify with it or to be distinguished from it."[32]

And he explains that my body is "the nexus which binds me to the universe," adding the relevant passage:

> It is in no way a question of positing the universe as in some way dependent on me. This would be falling into an aggravated subjectivism. What I posit here is first of all the priority of the existential over the ideal, but it must immediately be added that the existential inevitably refers to the incarnate being, that is to say, to the fact of *being in the world.* This last expression, not recognized in philosophy, or at any rate not prior to Heidegger, when adequately translated is, I think, something that ought to be understood as participation, not as relation or communication.[33]

In this respect Marcel was mistaken, because, as is well known, Ortega used the word *circumstance* as early as 1914. "I am myself and my circumstance," he wrote in *Meditaciones del Quijote,* thus naming the radical insertion of the self in the world so that the circumstance is a constitutive element of "my" concrete reality.

This bodily presence as the link with the universe is always present in Marcel's thought. Of the Gifford Lectures, published under the title *The Mystery of Being,* the fifth is dedicated to the "existential fulcrum" and deals with the function of the body as an "act of feeling" that cannot be reduced to the instrumental.[34]

On the basis of these assumptions, we cannot help questioning the small importance Marcel assigned to the body in his doctrine of love. It would seem that he should have paid more attention to such an interesting subject as that of the connection between love and body or, better said, to the corporeal structure of human life. In my already mentioned *Metaphysical Anthropology* I have shown how necessary it is to derive the reality of love from the effective way human life exists, that is, in its empirical structure, one of whose ingredients is embodiment and the other—forever intimately connected with the former, though not reducible to it—is the sexual character. Marcel's keen and significant search is somewhat impaired, I think, by the almost total omission of this human dimension, although it is not entirely absent from the core of his philosophy.

Nevertheless, the small importance Marcel assigned the body in his doctrine of love is not the worst of his errors in treating love. In my estimation the important fact is that human life exists as a disjunction (man-woman) that affects each term of the disjunction. In other words there is not just "human life" but "men" and "women," each defined by the installation in its own sex and in its vectoral projection toward the other. Human need is primarily the need man has for woman and woman for man; in fact they need each other to be man and woman, to be human beings in each of the two concrete ways they actually and not abstractly exist.

This is why love is primarily and originally not "sexual" love but love between persons of opposite sex. I do not mean that all love is a transformation or degeneration of this kind of intersexual love but rather that every love is conditioned by this aspect, by this radical human need for the opposite sex to project itself toward it. This is why any anomaly in intersexual love disturbs all other ways of love, including "love" in the general sense: of God, country, or science.

Recently an invading "sexuality" has tried to reduce to sex what is at most sexual love and more properly sexuate love. It is understandable that Marcel would not fall into this tendency, pivoting his thought and imaginative representation of human life in the strictly personal dimensions of love. But being the representative of concrete philosophy and of the incarnated being of the corporeal person, he might have contributed something important to the comprehension of such a fundamentally human phenomenon. Even more he might have derived the other types of love, including the love of God, from the radical situation in which human beings find themselves and constitute themselves, making an intrinsically dramatic process of the polar disjunction in which human life occurs and which provides a basis for living together.

I have dealt with these subjects in greater detail in my *Metaphysical Anthropology,* and I refer the interested reader to it. As far as Marcel is concerned, my questions—for they are questions rather than objections— are meant as a stimulus; they try to encourage him to complete his theory and his dramatic dealings with love. Marcel is one of the most admirably honest thinkers of our time. He is different from others who may be highly talented but who do not use their talents in a desirable way. All through his life Marcel has remained extraordinarily authentic. He may have been wrong and may not have seen many things clearly, but he has never used deception, never borne false witness, and never substituted an arbitrary construction for reality.

Ortega insisted on a subject not commonly dealt with: the truthfulness of a philosopher. Usually this is taken for granted, but perhaps it should not be. Once Ortega talked about writing on the "Genius and Shamelessness in Transcendental Idealism" ("Genialidad e inverecundia en el idealismo transcendental"). Marcel represents the maximum of truthfulness; in very few instances has philosophy proceeded with more exact respect for reality and for what a person can sense of it. In this regard I consider his work an example to be followed, distinguished as it is by particularly strong features at a time of an all too general lack of respect for truth.

Let us not talk in the past tense about Marcel. His has been a long life, but in 1971 it can be considered mature. We may still expect many thoughtful steps, quietly passionate, coming from his open and hospitable mind, full of love for reality. That is why my doubts and my questions are really desiderata. When expressing a certain dissatisfaction with his treatment of love, I want to say that I am not satisfied with what he has already done; from his theoretical writings and still more from his dramas I expect a deep and effective presentation of human love—personal, between man and woman—for this is the basis of human life in its two concrete characters and the perspective from which we can try to understand it, adding or subtracting any other ways of love.

JULIÁN MARÍAS

ROYAL SPANISH ACADEMY
JULY 1970

NOTES

1. Mine is in the volume *Philosophy as Dramatic Theory* (University Park: Pennsylvania State University Press, 1970).

2. Julián Marías, *Miguel de Unamuno* (Cambridge, Mass.: Harvard University Press, 1966).

3. See Julián Marías, "La obra de Unamuno: Un problema de filosofía," in *Obras* (Madrid: Revista de Occidente, 1969) 5:207–327.

4. Gabriel Marcel, *Journal métaphysique* (Paris: Gallimard, 1927), p. 58 (hereafter cited as *JM*); *Metaphysical Journal*, trans. Bernard Wall (Chicago: Henry Regnery Co., 1952), p. 58 (hereafter cited as *MJ*).

5. *JM*, 62; *MJ*, 62.

6. *JM*, 63; *MJ*, 62–63.

7. Julián Marías, *Metaphysical Anthropology: The Empirical Structure of Human Life*, trans. Frances M. López-Morillas (University Park: Pennsylvania State University Press, 1971).

8. Blaise Pascal, "Discourse on the Passion of Love," in *Works of Pascal* (Boston: Houghton, Osgood, 1878), p. 523.

9. Ibid., pp. 522–23.

10. *JM*, 63; *MJ*, 63.

11. José Ortega y Gasset, "Amor en Stendhal," in *Obras completas* (Madrid: Revista de Occidente, 1947), 5:568–69; "Love in Stendhal," trans. Toby Talbot, in *On Love* (New York: Meridian Books, 1947), pp. 43–44.

12. Ibid.   13. *JM*, 64–65; *MJ*, 64.

14. *JM*, 65; *MJ*, 64.   15. *JM*, 218; *MJ*, 223.

16. *JM*, 228; *MJ*, 234.   17. *JM*, 64; *MJ*, 63.

18. Ortega, *Obras*, 5:569–71; *On Love*, 44–48.

19. Gabriel Marcel, *Pour une sagesse tragique* (Paris: Plon, 1968), p. 195; cf. English translation by Stephen Jolin and Peter McCormick, *Tragic Wisdom and Beyond*, Northwestern University Studies in Phenomenology and Existential Philosophy (Evanston: Northwestern University Press, 1973), p. 133: "Reflection cannot operate where there is no imagination. And I would add that without imagination, there is no charity, no *agapē* worthy of the name."

20. Gabriel Marcel, *Du refus a l'invocation* (Paris: Gallimard, 1940), pp. 198–99 (hereafter cited as *DR*); cf. English translation by Robert Rosthal, *Creative Fidelity* (New York: Noonday Press, 1964), p. 152 (hereafter cited as *CF*).

21. Gabriel Marcel, *Les Coeurs avides* (Paris: La Table ronde, 1952), p. 159.

22. Gabriel Marcel, *L'Iconoclaste* (Paris: Stock, 1923).

23. Ibid.

24. Gabriel Marcel, *Le Quatuor en fa dièse* (Paris: Plon, 1925).

25. Gabriel Marcel, *Le Dard* (Paris: Plon, 1936).

26. Gabriel Marcel, *Rome n'est plus dans Rome* (Paris: La Table ronde, 1951).

27. Ibid.

28. Gabriel Marcel, "Les Vrais Problèmes de *Rome n'est plus dans Rome*."

29. Julián Marías, *Ortega: Circunstancia y vocación* (Madrid: Revista de Occidente, 1960). See also the English translation by Frances M. López-Morillas, *José Ortega y Gasset: Circumstance and Vocation* (Norman: University of Oklahoma Press, 1970).

30. *DR*, 20–21; *CF*, 12.   31. *DR*, 25; cf. *CF*, 15.

32. *DR*, 31; cf. *CF*, 20.   33. *DR*, 32–33; cf. *CF*, 21.

34. Gabriel Marcel, *The Mystery of Being*, trans. G. S. Fraser (vol. 1) and René Hague (vol. 2), 2 vols. (London: Harvill Press, 1950–51), 1:77–102.

Love in Marcel and Ortega

REPLY TO JULIÁN MARÍAS

It is scarcely necessary to say that for a long time now I have not been satisfied with statements on love found in my early writings. In general I would now be reticent to state the proper way of conceiving of the relationship between love and knowledge. I am convinced that in the first part of the *Journal métaphysique* I insisted far too much on the fact that love is creation, and thus I may have given the reader the impression that I strongly supported a subjectivism that since then I have never ceased to avoid.

Obviously this does not mean that today I would be willing to regard love as adequate knowledge. Rather I would prefer to bring to light the process by reason of which genuine love cannot accept any misunderstanding whatsoever in relation to the loved object. Here as always I will use concrete examples. Let us take the case of a woman who becomes aware, after many years of marriage, of a certain unworthiness in the man she lives with. Evidently this unworthiness could arouse such a severe reaction in her that she could no longer bear to live with this individual recognized as unworthy. But were this the case would it not prove that the woman never reached a genuine love, that her feeling was attached to a certain image or conception that did not coincide with the reality of the man? It could happen, on the contrary, that having recognized this unworthiness, she persists in loving the unworthy person deeply enough to live in the hope that she will eventually succeed in redeeming him, in elevating him above what he now is. From this point of view I would say that genuine love implies hope as I have defined it, particularly in *Homo Viator*. It is enough to say that today I could under no circumstances admit that a love worthy of the name could consist in immobilizing the beloved in any man-

Translated from the French by Susan Gruenheck.

ner. I think exactly the opposite is true: that it is rather toward a mobilization, toward a transformation, that genuine love must tend.

Here again it is necessary to distinguish carefully between the investigations and assertions found in the first part of the *Journal métaphysique* and all that followed thereafter. Unfortunately it is only too true that in the beginning I tended (I don't quite know why) to approach the problem of love from a metaphysical or theological perspective, although I actually had no clear notion, no specific reference, to which to allude. But it is no less certain that my dramatic works were altogether different from the beginning. This is apparent in my first published play, *La Grâce,* in which precisely this possible misunderstanding between a man and a woman about the nature of the love that binds them is interpreted quite specifically. Gerard imagines that Françoise, his wife, has only an essentially spiritual love for him, whereas in fact her love is, above all, desire, a carnal desire so strong that she cannot bear the idea that, because of his illness, Gerard might escape from her. Accordingly, I think that to understand what I have thought about love and the uncertainties I have felt regarding it, generally speaking it would be much more advisable to refer to my plays than to my philosophical writings. There is extensive work to be done in this area, particularly involving *Le Coeur des autres* and *Un Homme de Dieu.* In reference to my plays, I do not think I could be accused of having oversimplified the philosophical problem of love. On the contrary, in my dramatic works I think it appears in all its complexity, and the reducibility of a certain kind of human love to divine love is brought to light with great honesty.

In regard to all those characters in my plays who express themselves so differently and who in some cases, incidentally, contradict themselves, I would be tempted to say this: it is useless to search for the one character among all the others who at any given moment coincides with my position. Actually the very term *position* ceases to be applicable. I would say that the activity peculiar to philosopher-playwrights (placing the emphasis on the second term) consists in what would have to be called a progressive decentering. For them it is in reality a question of showing quite concretely, or, if you will, existentially, how the situation of a person in the world, or of a person vis-à-vis the other or others, unfolds in the manner of a vast landscape with varied relief. In saying this I am thinking of the vast, unfolding landscape two or three kilometers from my country house, going down toward Collonges or Meyssac. It seems to me that this comparison with the landscape, considered in its fullness, in its variety, and with all that the changes in light can bring to it, best expresses my own vision as a playwright.

I quite willingly acknowledge that Julián Marías is correct in remarking that I have not devoted any of my philosophical writings to the problem of sexuality. Certainly these problems are presented far more often in my plays than in my philosophical works. It is rather difficult for me to give a reason for this. What I can say is that these problems interested me as a playwright rather than as a philosopher. Perhaps this is because sexuality strictly speaking has not played a decisive role in my life—not at all as decisive as that of affection or tenderness. Nevertheless, I think that by starting with what I have said about the *corps-propre*, about my body, others may be able to draw consequences for the very important question of human sexuality.

G.M.

22

Donald M. MacKinnon

DRAMA AND MEMORY

I

T O RETURN, after one's thought has moved in a somewhat different
direction, to consider the work of a philosopher who earlier in one's
development exercised a considerable influence on one's own work, is a
very strange experience. At first one seems to hear a voice from one's own
past; yet after a little while one comes to realise that the work of the
thinker in question has become woven into the texture of one's own reflections. One may even unconsciously have been guilty of plagiarism; yet at
the same time one can plead that one is bearing witness continually to the
reality of a debt too great to be acknowledged by explicit quotation with
reference duly given. Certainly my study of the writings of Gabriel Marcel, and still more the privilege of hearing him deliver his Gifford Lectures
in Aberdeen in 1949 and 1950 (when he was on both occasions the house
guest of my wife and me), left a permanent impression on my own work
in the philosophy of religion. It is with two closely related aspects of my
debt to him that I wish to deal in this paper.

The student of Marcel's Gifford Lectures and indeed of all his philosophical writings, both his articles and still more his extended diaries, is
quickly made aware of the close interconnection between Marcel's philosophical explorations and his work as a dramatist. To discuss the way the
two aspects of his activity play upon each other would require a study in
itself; at this point in my argument I simply want to stress the extreme
significance for a proper appraisal of Marcel's work of continued attention
to his literary activity.

His first work as a philosopher was a study of the ethical ideas of the
highly individual American idealist Josiah Royce. Undoubtedly Marcel
was always deeply attracted to certain elements in the idealist tradition in

metaphysics, especially in the forms it assumed in the English-speaking world in the nineteenth century and in the first decade of the present century. I stress his attachment to the forms this tradition assumed in the English-speaking world, for these forms are in certain respects decisively different from the classical exposition of metaphysical idealism achieved in Hegel's work. It is important that where the English-speaking idealists are concerned, it was Royce to whom Marcel was drawn and not Bradley or Bosanquet. Important elements in Royce's philosophical work remind readers that he belonged to the new world and not to the old; for instance, his obvious sympathies with pragmatism and the discernible presence in his thinking of the mystique of the "frontier." What Marcel learned from Royce was a continuing sense of human societies as enduring spiritual communities from whom individuals could, and indeed must, derive not only their elementary human formation but also a kind of interior strength powerful enough to sustain them in periods of personal disintegration and catastrophe. Clearly noticeable in this vision of the moral dimension of human societies is an element of optimism that can easily blur the distinction between what ideally should be the case and what actually is the case. Marcel, however, is known as the author of *Le Monde cassé,* and one clearly recalls his famous debate with Teilhard de Chardin, on the occasion of the latter's return to Paris in 1946, in which Marcel argued against the monistic optimism of the Jesuit savant by emphasising the broken character of human existence. Certainly in his development Marcel moved a long way from Royce, but one can still see the extent to which he grasped the lessons he had learned from his American master.

For instance, in a play many would consider his best, *Un Homme de Dieu,* after the pastor's understanding of himself and his world has collapsed in ruins and the very foundations of his personal existence are called into question, he is pulled back from the brink of suicide by being called upon to fulfil an elementary duty of his ministerial office: ensuring the proper provision of the simple human need of an old woman for whom he bears pastoral responsibility. Through this very humdrum demand of another person upon his time and energy, he comes to realise that his personal disintegration does not bring the world to an end. Rather the world goes on curiously oblivious to the turmoil raging within his spirit, taking notice of him only as a man with particular responsibilities that it presumes he will (health and other circumstances permitting) fulfil in the usual way. If I understand Marcel aright, he is at this point emphasising the health-giving quality that belongs to the fulfilment of the simple duties of everyday human life, duties imposed upon individuals by the society to which they belong. If in a moment of crisis we are reminded of the need to fulfil one of them, the reminder may be profoundly therapeutic, arresting the movement in a sheerly destructive direction that our knowledge may sometimes threaten to take. Marcel's play studies the overturning of fundamental falsehood in a person's soul; it is the work of a man who is profoundly convinced we must all come to terms with what we are and discern the masquerades we so quickly assume as we cast ourselves in roles that bear no relation to what we actually are or have done. The pastor in Marcel's play built his life on the assumption that he had in fact forgiven his wife's infidelity. But his forgiveness was a counterfeit forgiveness, concerned not so much to restore his wife as to magnify his self-image and to enable him to see himself in his pastoral role as a virtual Christ figure. He had to learn that the concept of forgiveness simply did not apply to what he had done, and that if his considerable ministerial effectiveness were indeed built upon the self-esteem he had achieved through his treatment of his wife, it was altogether groundless. But as Plato makes clear in his allegory of the cave, the moment of rescue from illusion is the moment of gravest peril, for our deliverance may plunge us into a sheer spiritual nihilism rather than issue us into a world of reality. Certainly by the time Marcel wrote this play, he had left much of the characteristic emphases of the idealist tradition a long way behind him. His work had become exploratory rather than systematic; it was detailed, empirical, and even tantalisingly incomplete, but always circumstantial in its attention to individual cases. In his ethics he would avow himself constantly the enemy of what he regarded as the abstract universalism of Kant. But he still recognised that if one were attempting to write a philosophy of spirit (and this I understand to have been his constant aim), one must never forget that human beings are not solitaries. They may indeed die alone, but their lives are inextricably bound up with the lives of others, and in the context of actual, concrete human society, they may receive, through attachments that are thrust upon them, resources of endurance as well as occasions of disaster. It is part of Marcel's genius that he is prepared to allow divers influences to play upon him and to reject the obvious charge of inconsistency as failing to recollect the twisted complexity of human reality. He is an empiricist in that he always prefers the individual to the general, the concrete occurrence to the universal. Here one can see the influence of his work as a dramatist upon his work as a philosopher. Yet at the same time he never forgets that human societies cannot be treated simply as random aggregates of individuals. To regard them in this way is to substitute another sort of abstract model for the sort one has discarded in rejecting, for instance, metaphysical conceits of a supraindividual absolute. Human life is what it is, and its order defies compact statement in the sort of formula that would satisfy the tidy-minded. We discover ourselves to ourselves, and others to themselves, in the deep and continually testing schools of personal relationship. But these schools are sited in a larger world, less testing, it is true, and often seeming to provide a way of escape for those who would seek to dodge personal self-interrogation by deliberately refusing to allow time for its exercise. Yet that larger world has its duties, makes its demands upon individuals, and indeed supplies them with their very means of livelihood in return for their fulfilment of the roles and of the tasks it lays upon them. And of course we may suddenly find that in a part of life that seems far removed from the searching intimacies of personal existence, we are suddenly confronted with ultimate spiritual emergencies.

It is Marcel's achievement to have written highly individual philosophy, partly as the fruit of reflection on his work as a dramatist. I say highly individual philosophy, for there are many who have had a quite different early philosophical experience from what Marcel enjoyed through his study of Royce and who must yet acknowledge a profound sense of gratitude to Marcel for recognising in his practice the significance for philosophical work, especially where fundamental ethics are concerned, of the kind of exploration of the human situation that is only possible in the theatre. One could imagine a variety of dialectical exchanges comparable to that between Marcel's dramatic work and the kind of philosophical reflection that followed his early work on Royce in the work of a philosopher who turned from a serious study of Kantian ethics to a deep engagement with Shakespearian tragedy. The point of contact is clear enough; tragedy demands the reality of human freedom, and Kant is supremely the philosopher for whom human freedom is the veritable keystone of his whole system. Yet the depth of the playwright's explorations serves as nothing else to set a question mark against the final adequacy of the philosopher's strenuous attempt to delineate once and for all the structure of the moral order. It is as if we were driven to essay a new sort of empiricism, one that certainly does not neglect or disregard Kant's hard-won insight concerning the transcendent import of the moral order, but one that insists we understand that order differently—not more lightly or even more profoundly but rather in a new way that recognises its frightening complexity and the extent to which its pressure upon our allegiance is always against the background of an intractable unknown, partly indeed issuing from our own substance but partly coming upon us from the world without. It is in the achievement of this new-style spiritual empiricism that at least part of Marcel's achievement as a philosopher resides. It is something that demanded in his formation the playing, one upon the other, of the two factors I have stressed: Marcel's early apprenticeship to Royce and his strenuous, if not always successful, essays in drama. There are of course vast riches to be quarried from his diaries; his mind is restless and interrogative rather than systematic. But it is my conviction that a fundamental part of his achievement lies in the combination I have stressed.

II

In the second part of this paper, I wish to indicate some of the bearings of these aspects of Marcel's work on the problem of the possibility of metaphysics, referring especially to considerations that seem to arise from the sort of reflection on memory that Marcel's work encourages. This requires a word on Marcel's own conception of metaphysics.

Although his first major work is entitled *Metaphysical Journal* and although he constantly stresses his rejection of the neo-Thomist intuition of being, Marcel hardly offers a clear account of what he supposes metaphysics to be. Rather he seems to identify it with the kind of profound, always interrogative reflection he practises, through which he sometimes seems to dissolve established securities but by which, with extraordinary perception, he seems at other times to open up the unsuspected depths of the familiar. It is certainly true that so far as his reflection finds its subject matter in personal existence, Marcel remains indebted to the idealists. His mood is Socratic; it is seldom Aristotelian, in that it rarely finds its focus of interest in what there is. Certainly Marcel avows a deep concern with ontological problems; his work also in many places reminds one of the strength on the continent of Europe of the phenomenological school. Yet the being in which he is interested is personal being, and the cosmological dimensions of metaphysical philosophy are left to one side. Here one sees the pervasive influence of the idealists. What Marcel has throughout shared with the idealists is their conviction of the self-transparency of autonomous spirit. Where our interior lives are concerned, we are, as it were, on home ground, and no behaviourist argument can ever rob us of the right to describe these lives in the terms that impose themselves upon us. Of course Marcel does not commit the mistake of supposing that here we have to reckon with the data of an essentially private introspection. We learn what we are through our relationships with other people; we acquire in a common life the concepts through which we bring home to ourselves what our experience is. There is no initial privacy from which we go out to meet the world. Rather the private is something that draws its very shape from the public life by which it is nurtured. Because Marcel will never admit that a human being's personal experience can be reduced to the terms of anything other than itself, the weight in his philosophy continually falls on meditation, on reflection, and on interiorization.

Yet the reflection he stresses is one in which a person's life becomes more a matter of an unanswerable questioning than of an interpretable pattern. Among religious philosophers who acknowledge a debt to the idealists' dogma of individuals' transparency to themselves, there is a continual tendency to seek order, even personal providential design, in the events making up a human biography. Memory becomes more a method whereby we impose a form or shape upon our past than an effort to recapture events as they happened and, if possible, to penetrate more deeply their unnoticed substance. One could claim that the pastor in *Un Homme de Dieu* continually recalls his act of forgiveness and continually reminds himself of the act of infidelity that elicited it, and that he comes in the end (or even more quickly) to regard that act as simply the way provided by divine providence for him decisively to exercise his freedom in a manner that permits him to organise his whole life around the recollection of that mighty act of magnanimity. The experience is continually present to his consciousness; indeed one might say that that continuous presence helps to make him what he is. Hence human beings become in their conceit what they remember themselves doing in some action they have invested with paradigmatic force in their essay at self-definition. In the case of the pastor, his memory, although constitutive of what he is, has betrayed him, for it is not a memory of what actually happened. When the truth is thrust upon his awareness in all its rawness—when he is compelled to come to terms with what his wife actually did, felt, and feels—the object of his pretending memory collapses. He is made to face what in a sense he always knew but ran away from. Under the impact of the actual, the pattern dissolves; the design is gone, and it is never recovered. As I remarked earlier, the pastor is saved from self-destruction by his involvement in other sorts of relationships with other sorts of people. He is forced to accept himself not as a kind of Christ figure but as a useful member of the community, even in his role a relatively indispensable one.

No one could write this way who did not treat spiritual experience as something irreducible, but it is not an experience that contains within itself the promise of its own satisfactory outcome. It is a major mistake to argue from the irreducibility of such experience to a fundamentally optimistic vision of existence. If such experience provides the matter of profound metaphysical reflection, that reflection must never too quickly assume the road of systematic construction. We cannot escape the burden of ourselves. We cannot suppose that now we see what we are. We can only recognise that certain mists of illusion have been dissipated, that this or that construction of our past is revealed as woven more of the stuff of self-regard than of the fruit of attention to what actually happened.

Yet it is profoundly significant that where we are continually tossed between human illusion and human truth, in our efforts to come to terms not only with ourselves but with our human world, we are eager at times to impose pattern or order on the intractable, the disturbing, and the sheerly evil. Yet there we cannot rest in such supposedly consoling interpretation but jettison it in the name of a harsher truth that we can scarcely bear. The phrase "le monde cassé" conveys much of the essential style of Marcel's philosophising. Although irreducibly human, the human world is also a broken world, a world somehow opaque to our understanding because it is what we prove it painfully on our pulses to be. If we ask ourselves how we know it is a broken world, we can do no more than rehearse our experience of living in it by being, in our lives, a part of it. We can do no more than impress on our reflection its intractability and its ultimate obscurity.

In his controversy with Teilhard, Marcel appears the spokesman of a pessimistic or rather a tragic vision of the world, for there is in his thought a continued insistence on the actuality of human achievement, on the significance of the institutional framework of human work, and on the reality of love and communion. Certain of his words convey the inwardness of his metaphysical vision, among them *presence* and *mystery*. The transcendent presses upon us in the concrete of our human existence; indeed one could speak in religious terms of the sudden unexpected *parousia* of the ultimate. One cannot charge such a thought with the reproach of pessimism. It is certainly empirical and equally certainly pluralistic in its refusal to allow distinctions of being to be somehow obliterated in the interests of an almost certainly spurious conceptual unification. But it is alive to the frailty of spiritual perception, to the illusions that beset us in our struggle towards identity, to the extent to which the memories through which we gradually define ourselves are organised to secure that definition at the cost of the ever present threat of the "lie in the soul." For although Marcel's reflection is the very condition of human existence, it is always charged with the necessity to correct—a correction that will come most often when the harsh reality of the other (another person) imposes itself on the delicate construction of a self-regarding imagination. It is in and through relationships that we are made what we are; they are the continuing subject matter of our reflective concern. We may misconceive them and recognise our misconception; yet long after that recognition their secret may still elude us, even though we acknowledge that the secret is there. One could say that for Marcel the metaphysical consciousness itself is the acknowledgment of the existence of that secret and of its presence in and to the illusory interpretation we weave around our dealings with one another.

Only a philosopher who was at the same time an experienced dramatist could show us, as Marcel has done, how the broken human world furnishes a point of departure for metaphysical reflection—indeed so invites such reflection that it is seen as a kind of meditation on that world, eliciting the inwardness of its diverse experience—without plunging into the error of imposing coherence where we have to reckon with contradiction and sense where we have to reckon with the tragically intractable, and without supposing that we have reached our journey's end when we remain *homines viatores*. It is part of our debt to Marcel that he has reminded us of the untidy reality of our broken world, without committing us to irrationality, and of the inescapable conflicts into which our bent and twisted natures thrust us, without allowing us to suppose that life is in the end "a tale told by an idiot, full of sound and fury, signifying nothing." He has suggested with great sublety and with attention to the complexity of human life that if we would approach the mystery of the transcendent, we must let its presence be disclosed to us in our searching, in our effort to discipline our memory to reality, and in the very idiom we learn to use in treating our reflection as a journey wherein we have no continuing city but only a ceaseless going on. He has shown us the extent to which we must treat metaphysical philosophising as a school of receptivity rather than as an essay in speculative construction. It is in the peculiarly Socratic quality of his work that his essential achievement lies: he is at his profoundest when he is most inconclusive, for in his very failure to reach definite, communicable conclusions he is quick to remind us of the hidden heights and depths of the familiar. But we are only so reminded if we allow ourselves to be provoked by his questioning to undertake our own work of self-interrogation.

DONALD M. MACKINNON, F.B.A.

NORRIS-HULSE PROFESSOR OF DIVINITY EMERITUS
UNIVERSITY OF CAMBRIDGE
OCTOBER 1970

Drama and Memory

REPLY TO DONALD M. MacKINNON

Dear friend,* your beautiful study of my thought arrived a few days ago. The day before yesterday I had a friend of mine read your essay to me. My eyesight, more and more deficient, no longer allows me to read a typewritten text.

Thank you, and congratulations on your good work. It has given me pleasure to find that the contact between us and our thinking has continued through all these years. I commend you on having so strongly emphasized the bond between my philosophical thought and my dramatic work. I am all the more happy about this because, with rare exceptions, those persons who have contributed to this grand volume under preparation about me seem to have completely ignored my theater. There is a troublesome hiatus here. The retrospection in which I am now considering my work in its entirety enables me to confirm that this unity between my philosophical and dramatic work describes without a doubt what is most original as well as most essential in my contributions.

As for *Un Homme de Dieu* and the role played by memory therein, I would like to propose some complementary remarks. Edmée's and finally Claude's own fatal error consists in a kind of retrospective mental manipulation of a unique experience and of what one must call the actuality, doubtlessly repugnant, of the treatment he is made to undergo. Under an impulse emanating exclusively from her self-love, Edmée's grave fault is to effect retrospectively a kind of discrimination between the man and the pastor. And Claude's weakness is to allow himself in some way to be contaminated by that indictment.

I do not want to say that the pardon was entirely free from a certain

---

Translated from the French by Dr. Girard Etzkorn and revised by Dr. Hans H. Rudnick.
*Marcel wrote this response in the form of a letter to MacKinnon, dated 20 October 1970.

ambiguity. But this ambiguity in reality has to be respected. At the same time, what those two unlucky souls are imagining as they enter into that sort of post mortem, or retrospective dissection, makes them guilty of a sin against life.

This was not clearly apparent to me when I wrote the piece, and I agree moreover that one is not forced to subscribe to this interpretation. It imposed itself on me only after I had seen the play on numerous stages in France, Germany, and even England.

But here is what may be most important: you are slightly simplifying the import of the ending. In the last scene, to be sure, Claude expresses the gratitude of a faithful servant for having been allowed to serve his family. But he also says that his people see him as a weakling, which does not correspond to the truth. They know him as he is not, and it is much for this reason that the supreme invocation rose from his lips: "To be known as one *is*, and one cannot be that except through God." This is the explanation of what I had previously written concerning the absolute Thou.

I was very pleased with the news from you and Mrs. MacKinnon. I can assure you that the memories of the weeks I spent with you at Aberdeen remain with me, fully intact and very precious.

As for me, as you will already have noted at the beginning of this letter, I am scarcely able to read any more, and I walk with great difficulty, which makes me terribly dependent. A sister of my wife, the only one who is still of this world, has been sharing my life for the past two years. She is also disabled, but her presence is nevertheless beneficial to me because every day she reads to me in a loud voice.

Thank you again, dear friend. I send you my most affectionate regards.

G.M.

PART THREE

A BIBLIOGRAPHY OF
THE WRITINGS
OF GABRIEL MARCEL

Compiled by François H. Lapointe

PREFACE TO THE BIBLIOGRAPHY

G ABRIEL Marcel was one of the most prolific writers of the twentieth century. In addition to his plays and philosophical works, he wrote book and drama reviews for over fifty years. In this bibliography I have listed only those reviews I felt were of philosophical significance. For a complete list of M. Marcel's reviews, see Roger Troisfontaines, S.J., *De l'existence à l'être: La Philosophie de Gabriel Marcel,* 2d ed. rev., 2 vols. (Louvain: Nauwelaerts; Paris: Vrin, 1953), which has a letter-preface by Gabriel Marcel.* I wish to acknowledge here my great indebtedness to Father Troisfontaines's bibliography, particularly for the period 1920–40.

FRANCOIS H. LAPOINTE
TUSKEGEE INSTITUTE

*In the meantime *Gabriel Marcel and His Critics: An International Bibliography (1928–1976),* edited by François H. and Claire C. Lapointe, has appeared in English (New York and London: Garland Publishing, 1977).—ED.

THE WRITINGS OF GABRIEL MARCEL

1912   "Les Conditions dialectiques de la philosophie de l'intuition." *Revue de méta-physique et de morale*, September 1912.

1914   *Le Seuil invisible*. Paris: Grasset, 1914. Includes two plays: *La Grâce* (1911) and *Le Palais de sable* (1913).

1918   "La Métaphysique de Josiah Royce." *Revue de métaphysique et de morale*, May–June 1918. Reprinted in *La Métaphysique de Royce*. Paris: Aubier, 1945.

       Royce's Metaphysics. Translated by Virginia Ringer and Gordon Ringer. Chicago: Henry Regnery Co., 1956.

1919   "La Métaphysique de Josiah Royce." *Revue de métaphysique et de morale*, January–April, 1919. Reprint. *La Métaphysique de Royce*. Paris: Aubier, 1945.

       Royce's Metaphysics. Translated by Virginia and Gordon Ringer. Chicago: Henry Regnery Co., 1956.

       "W. E. Hocking et la dialectique de l'instinct." *Revue philosophique de la France et de l'étranger*, July–August 1919.

1920   "Les Principes psychologiques de J. Ward." *Revue de métaphysique et de morale*, January–March 1920.

1921   *Le Coeur des autres*. Paris: Grasset, 1921. A play.

       "Réflexions sur le tragique." *L'Essor*, December 1921.

1923   *L'Iconoclaste*. Paris: Stock, 1923. A play.

1924   "*Les Problèmes de la philosophie*, par Bertrand Russell." *Nouvelle Revue française*, August 1924.

1925   *Un Homme de Dieu*. Paris: Grasset, 1925. Reprint. Paris: La Table ronde, 1950.

       "A Man of God," "Ariadne," "The Funeral Pyre": *Three Plays with a Preface on the "Drama of the Soul in Exile."* Translated by Rosalind Heywood and Marjorie Gabain. London: Secker & Warburg, 1952. First American edition. *Three Plays: "A Man of God," "Ariadne," The Funeral Pyre."* New York: Hill & Wang, 1958. Includes "The Drama of the Soul in Exile," originally delivered as a lecture at the Institut Français in London, July 1950.

       Le Quatuor en fa dièse. Paris: Plon, 1925. A play.

       "Médiation de G. Marcel en réponse à une enquête sur Dieu." *Philosophies*, January–March 1925.

       "Bergsonisme et musique." *Revue musicale*, 1 March 1925.

"Bergsonism and music." In *Reflections on Art: A Source Book of Writings by Artists, Critics and Philosophers,* edited by Susanne K. Langer. Baltimore: Johns Hopkins Press, 1958.

"Existence et objectivité." *Revue de métaphysique et de morale,* April–May 1925. Reprinted as appendix to *Journal métaphysique.* Paris: Gallimard, 1927.

1926   "Note sur l'évaluation tragique." *Journal de psychologie,* January–March 1926.

"Fragments de *Journal métaphysique.*" *Europe,* 15 January 1926.

"Jacques Rivière et l'idéalisme." *Europe,* 15 April 1926.

"A propos de l'*Esprit.*" *Bulletin de l'Union pour la vérité,* May 1926.

"Fragments du *Journal métaphysique.*" *La Ligne de coeur,* June 1926.

"*La liberté humaine* de Schelling." *Nouvelle Revue française,* October 1926. A review of Schelling's book in the French translation by G. Politzer.

1927   "A propos d'une nouvelle doctrine de la sagesse, sur le livre de M. Bouchet." In *La Philosophie de Hermann Keyserling,* edited by Maurice Boucher. Paris: Rieder, 1927. Reprinted in *La Chronique des idées,* March 1927; and in *Europe,* 15 March 1927.

Journal métaphysique. Paris: Gallimard, 1927. Reprint, 1935. Part 1 contains entries from 1 January 1914 to 8 May 1914, part 2 from 15 September 1915 to 24 May 1923.

Metaphysical Journal. Translated by Bernard Wall. Chicago: Henry Regnery Co., 1950. Reprint, 1952, 1967. London: Barrie & Rockliff, 1952.

Metaphysisches Tagebuch. German translation by Hanns von Winter. Vienna and Munich: Herold Verlag, 1955.

"*Etude sur le Parménide,* par Jean Wahl." *Nouvelle Revue française,* May 1927.

"*Le Journal intime de Maine de Biran,* édité par l'Abbé de la Valette Montban." *Nouvelle Revue française,* November 1927.

"Un Grand Livre: *Les Idées et les âges,* par Alain." *L'Europe nouvelle,* 19 November 1927.

"En marge de *La Trahison des clercs,* par M. J. Benda, et réponse de Benda." *Nouvelle Revue française,* December 1927.

"*Les Origines de l'espirit bourgeois en France. I. L'Eglise et la bourgeoisie,* par B. Groethuysen." *L'Europe nouvelle,* 24 December 1927.

1928   "Séance sur La Querelle de l'athéisme (Brunschvicg)." *Bulletin de la Société française de philosophie,* 1928. With the participation of G. Marcel.

"Autour de *La Trahison des clercs,* par J. Benda: Conversation du 21 janvier, 1928." *Bulletin de l'Union pour la vérité,* February 1928. With the participation of G. Marcel.

"*Critique des fondements de la psychologie,* par G. Politzer." *Nouvelle Revue française,* June 1928.

"*Un destin, Martin Luther,* par L. Febvre." *L'Europe nouvelle,* 30 June 1928.

"Aux frontières du surréalisme: *Les Dernières Nuits de Paris,* par Ph. Soupault; *Nadja,* par A. Breton." *L'Europe nouvelle,* 7 July 1928.

"L'Age du politique, ou *La Trahison des clercs,* par J. Benda." *L'Europe nouvelle,* 14 October 1928.

"De l'être, par Louis Lavelle." *La Chronique des idées,* October 1928; *Europe,* 15 October 1928.

1929   "M. l'Abbé Bremond et la philosophie de la prière (vols. VII et VIII de *L'Histoire du sentiment religieux en France).*" *L'Europe nouvelle,* 26 January 1929.

"Dieu et la culture morale." *Bulletin de l'Union des libres penseurs et des libres croyants,* February 1929.

"Carence de la spiritualité." *Nouvelle Revue française,* March 1929.

"Death of spirituality." In *"La Nouvelle Revue française," from the "N.R.F.": An Image of the Twentieth Century from the Pages of the "Nouvelle Revue Française,"* translated by Angelo P. Bertocci et al., edited by Justin O'Brien. New York: Farrar, Straus and Cudahy, 1958.

"Réponse à une enquête sur le communisme." *Revue marxiste,* 1 April 1929.

"Mort de la pensée bourgeoise, par E. Berl." *L'Europe nouvelle,* 1 June 1929.

"André Gide et le problème spirituel (sur *Le Dialogue avec A. Gide,* par du Bos)." *La Nouvelle Revue des jeunes,* 10 July 1929.

"Le Malheur de la conscience dans la philosophie de Hegel, par J. Wahl." *Europe,* 15 September 1929.

"Notes sur les limites du spiritualisme bergsonien." *La Vie intellectuelle,* 10 November 1929.

"La Piété selon Peter Wust." *Vigile,* 1930. Reprinted in *Etre et avoir.* Paris: Aubier, 1935.

"Amiel ou la part du rêve, par A. Thibaudet." *Nouvelle Revue française,* February 1930.

1931   *Trois pièces: "Le Regard neuf," "Le Mort de demain," "La Chapelle ardente."* Paris: Plon, 1931.

"Catholicisme et humanisme, par J. Maritain." *L'Europe nouvelle,* 24 January 1931.

"Remarques sur *L'Essai d'un discours cohérent* et la réponse de J. Benda." *Nouvelle Revue française,* June 1931.

"Le Devoir, par René Le Senne." *La Vie intellectuelle,* July 1931.

"Remarques sur l'irréligion contemporaine." *La Nouvelle Revue des jeunes,* 15 November 1931. Reprinted in *Etre et avoir.* Paris: Aubier, 1935.

"Le Déclin de l'Occident, par O. Spengler." *La Nouvelle Revue des jeunes,* 15 December 1931.

1932   "Situation fondamentale et situation-limite chez K. Jaspers." *Recherches philosophiques,* 1932–33. Reprinted in *Du refus à l'invocation.* Paris: Gallimard, 1940.

"Dénonciation d'un pacte: A propos de 'L'Examen de l'idéalisme,' article de Louis Dallière dans les *Etudes théologiques et religieuses* de Montpellier." *La Vie intellectuelle,* March 1932.

"L'Esprit de la philosophie médiévale, par E. Gilson." *La Nouvelle Revue des jeunes,* 15 March 1932.

"Henri Bergson et le problème de Dieu: A propos des *Deux Sources de la morale et de la religion,* par H. Bergson." *L'Europe nouvelle,* 30 April 1932.

"Taine: La Formation de sa pensée; La Formation philosophique de Taine, par A. Chevrillon.*" La Nouvelle Revue des jeunes*, 15 May 1932.

"Un Evénement philosophique: Les *Deux Sources de la morale et de la religion*, par H. Bergson.*" La Nouvelle Revue des jeunes*, 15 June 1932.

"Le songe de Descartes, par J. Maritain.*" La Nouvelle Revue des jeunes*, 15 July 1932.

"Méditations sud-américaines, par le comte H. Keyserling.*" La Nouvelle Revue des jeunes*, 15 October 1932.

"Sur 'l'idée du philosophe': Entretien tenu au siège de l'Union, le 19 décembre 1931.*" Bulletin de l'Union pour la vérité*, December 1932–January 1933.

"Ma Première Etape: Conférence prononcée au Foyer International des étudiants, le 13 mai, 1932.*" Le Semeur*, 1 December 1932.

"L'Esprit de la philosophie médiévale, 2e série, par E. Gilson.*" La Nouvelle Revue des jeunes*, 15 December 1932.

1933   *Le Monde cassé* (a play), followed by *Position et approches concrètes du mystère ontologique*. Paris: Desclée de Brouwer, 1933. *See also* separate listing for the latter under 1949.

"Esquisse d'une phénoménologie de l'avoir.*" Recherches philosophiques*. 1933–34. Reprinted in *Homo Viator*. Paris: Aubier, 1935.

"La Condition humaine, par André Malraux.*" L'Europe nouvelle*, 3 June 1933.

"Le Comte Keyserling, théoricien du sens.*" L'Europe nouvelle*, 24 June 1933.

"Une Biographie psychanalitique d'Edgar Poe, par la Princesse Marie Bonaparte.*" L'Europe nouvelle*, 5 August 1933.

"Nietzsche, par Thierry Maulnier.*" L'Europe nouvelle*, 9 September 1933.

"Position du mystère ontologique et ses approches concrètes: Résumé de la communication faite à la séance du 21 janvier, 1933.*" Etudes philosophiques*, December 1933.

"Remarques sur les notions d'acte et de personne.*" Recherches philosophiques*, 1934–35. Reprinted in *Du refus à l'invocation*. Paris: Gallimard, 1940.

"Enquête sur la création d'un homme nouveau par le régime social: Réponse de G. Marcel.*" L'Homme nouveau*, February 1934.

"La Crise de la liberté: Entretien tenu au siège de l'Union à la suite d'un exposé de M. Pierre Berl.*" Bulletin de l'Union pour la vérité*, April–May 1934. With the participation of G. Marcel.

"La Pensée et le mouvant, par H. Bergson.*" L'Europe nouvelle*, 31 May 1934.

"Essai sur la misère humaine, par Brice Parain.*" L'Europe nouvelle*, 14 July 1934.

"De la liberté dans une chrétienté moderne: Entretien tenu au siège de l'Union le 21 avril 1934, à la suite d'un exposé de M. Jacques Maritain.*" Bulletin de l'Union pour la vérité*, October–November 1934.

"Réflexions sur la foi.*" La Vie intellectuelle*, 20 October 1934. Reprinted in *Etre et avoir*. Paris: Aubier, 1935.

Etre et avoir. Paris: Aubier, 1935. Takes up the *Journal métaphysique* from 10 November 1928 to 31 October 1933 and includes reprints of the following four essays and lectures: "Esquisse d'une phénoménologie de l'avoir." "Remarques sur l'irréligion contemporaine," "Réflexions sur la foi," and "La Piété selon Peter Wust."

Etre et avoir. Reprint (2 vols.). Collection Foi vivantes, nos. 85, 86. Paris: Aubier, Editions Montaigne, 1968. Vol. 1, *Journal métaphysique (1928–1933)*. Vol. 2, *Réflexions sur l'irréligion et la foi*.

Being and Having. Translated by Katharine Farrer. Westminster: Dacre Press; Glasgow: University Press, 1949. Boston: Beacon Press, 1951. Reprinted under the expanded title *Being and Having: An Existentialist Diary*. London: Fontana Library; New York: Harper & Row, Harper Torchbooks, 1965.

Sein und Haben. German translation by Ernst Behler. Paderborn: Ferdinand Schöningh, 1954.

"Vers un humanisme théocentrique: *Approximations*, par Ch. du Bos." *L'Europe nouvelle*, 2 March 1935.

"Notes sur la fidélité." *La Vie intellectuelle*, 15 March 1935.

"De l'espérance." *Etudes*, 20 April 1935. Excerpts from the *Journal métaphysique*.

"La Vertu de force et la paix." *La Vie intellectuelle*, 15 May 1935.

"*Obstacle et valeur:* A propos du livre de R. Le Senne." *La Vie intellectuelle*, 25 November 1935.

1936   *Le Chemin de crête*. Paris: Grasset, 1936. A play.

Ariadne. Translated by R. Heywood. In *Makers of the Modern Theater*, edited by B. Ulanov. New York: 1961.

Le Dard. Paris: Plon, 1936. Reprint, 1950. A play.

Le Fanal. In *La Vie intellectuelle* supplement, 1936. A play.

"Aperçus phénoménologiques sur l'être en situation." *Recherches philosophiques*, 1936–37. Reprinted in *Du refus à l'invocation*. Paris: Gallimard, 1940.

"*La Pierre philosophale*, par Bertrand de la Salle." *L'Europe nouvelle*, 28 March 1936.

"*Valeurs*, par A. Suarès." *L'Europe nouvelle*, 31 October 1936.

"Réflexions sur Alain: A propos de *L'Histoire de mes pensées*, par Alain." *L'Europe nouvelle*, 7 November 1936.

1937   "Le Transcendant comme métaproblématique." In *Travaux du IXe Congrès international de philosophie*. Paris: Congrès Descartes, 1937. Reprinted in *Du refus à l'invocation*. Paris: Gallimard, 1940.

"Subjectivité et transcendance (Jean Wahl): Séance du 4 déc. 1937." *Bulletin de la Société française de philosophie*, 1937. With the participation of G. Marcel.

"Sur les *Recherches philosophiques*, tome v." *Nouvelle Revue française*, January 1937.

"*Les Grands Penseurs de l'Inde*, par Albert Schweitzer." *Le Jour*, 1 February 1937.

"*Penser avec les mains*, par Denis de Rougemont." *L'Europe nouvelle*, 6 March 1937.

"Réflexions sur les exigences d'un théâtre chrétien." *La Vie intellectuelle*, 31 March 1937.

"L'Homme est-il humain? par Ramon Fernandez." *L'Europe nouvelle,* 3 April 1937.

"En marge de l'autobiographie de G. K. Chesterton." *La Vie intellectuelle,* 15 September 1937.

"De l'opinion à la foi." *La Vie intellectuelle,* 15 November 1937. Reprinted in *Du refus à l'invocation.* Paris: Gallimard, 1940.

1938   *La Soif.* Paris: Desclée de Brouwer, 1938. A play. Reprinted under the title *Les Coeurs avides.* Paris: La Table ronde, 1952.

"Plaidoyer pour le corps, par le R. P. Poucel." *Le Jour,* January–February 1938.

"Etudes kierkegaardiennes, par Jean Wahl." *Le Jour,* February–March 1938.

"De l'acte, par Louis Lavelle." *Nouvelle Revue française,* February 1938.

"Gedanken zu einer konkreten Philosophie (Pour une philosophie concrète)." *Die Tatwelt,* March 1938.

"Ebauche d'une philosophie concrète." *Recherches de sciences religieuses,* April 1938. Reprinted in *Du refus à l'invocation.* Paris: Gallimard, 1940.

"Liberté et métier." *Civilisation,* April 1938.

"Orthodoxie et conformisme." *La Vie intellectuelle,* 30 April 1938.

"Réponse à Brice Parain." *Civilisation,* June 1938.

"Carnets de Joubert." *Nouvelle Revue française,* July 1938.

"Apartenenta si disponibilitate (Appartenance et disponibilité)." *Revista fundatilor regale,* November 1938. Reprinted in *Revue d'histoire et de philosophie religieuse* 19 (1939). Also reprinted in *Du refus à l'invocation.* Paris: Gallimard, 1940.

"De l'acte, par Louis Lavelle." *Le Jour,* December 1938–January 1939.

1939   "L'Etre incarné, repère central de la réflexion métaphysique." In *Etudes philosophiques,* edited by Gaston Bachelard et al. Annales de l'Ecole des hautes études de Gand. Gand: L'Ecole des hautes études, 1939. Reprinted in *Du refus a l'invocation.* Paris: Gallimard, 1940.

Preface to *Diagnostics,* by G. Thibon. Paris: Librairie de Medicis, 1939.

Preface to *Incertitudes,* by Johan Huizinga. Paris: Librairie de Medicis, 1939.

"Notes pour une philosophie du risque." *La Vie réelle,* 1939.

"Déclaration de G. Marcel à propos de l'antisémitisme." La Revue juive de genève, January 1939.

"La Nausée, par J.-P. Sartre." *Carrefour,* January 1939.

"Méditation sur l'idée de preuve de l'existence de Dieu." *Le Semeur,* February 1939. Reprinted in *Du refus à l'invocation.* Paris: Gallimard, 1940.

"Rilke, par R. Pitrou." *Le Jour,* 10 March 1939.

"Le Mur, par J.-P. Sartre." *Carrefour,* June–July 1939.

"Désespoir et philosophie: Etudes kierkegaardiennes, par J. Wahl." *Nouvelle Revue française,* June 1939.

"Phénoménologie et dialectique de la tolérance." *Tijdschrift voor Philosophie,* August 1939. Reprinted in *Du refus à l'invocation.* Paris: Gallimard, 1940.

"La Fidélité créatrice." *Revue internationale de philosophie*, 15 October 1939.

"*L'Amour et l'Occident*, par Denis de Rougemont." *Le Jour*, 6 November 1939.

1940   *Du refus à l'invocation*. Paris: Gallimard, 1940. Reprint. Paris: Aubier, 1945. Contains reprints of the following articles and lectures: "L'Etre incarné: Repère central de la réflexion métaphysique," "Appartenance et disponibilité," "Ebauche d'une philosophie concrète," "Aperçus phénoménologiques sur l'être en situation," "Remarques sur les notions d'acte et de personne," "De l'opinion à la foi," "Le Transcendant comme métaproblématique," "La Fidélité créatrice," "Méditation sur l'idée de preuve de l'existence de Dieu," "L'Orthodoxie contre les conformismes," "En marge de l'oecuménisme," "Phénoménologie et dialectique de la tolérance," and "Situation fondamentale et situation-limites chez Karl Jaspers."

Reprinted in a new edition under the title *Essai de philosophie concrète*. Collection Idées, no. 119. Paris: Gallimard, 1967.

Creative Fidelity. Translated by Robert Rosthal. New York: Farrar, Strauss, Cudahy, Noonday Press, 1964.

Schöpferische Treue. German translation by Ursula Behler. Paderborn: Schöningh Verlag; Zurich: Thomas Verlag, 1963.

"Considérations sur l'égalite: Les Hommes sont-ils égaux?" *Etudes carmelitaines*, February 1940.

1941   "Grandeur de Bergson." In *Henri Bergson: Essais et témoignages*, compiled by Albert Béguin and Pierre Thévenaz. Neuchâtel: Editions de la Baconnière, 1941.

1942   "Le Mystère familial." Lecture delivered to the first general assembly of the Ecole catholique des sciences familiales, Lyons, June 1942. Reprinted in *Homo Viator*. Paris: Aubier, 1945.

"Moi et autrui" *Cité nouvelle*, 10 April 1942. Lecture given at Lyons, December 1942. Reprinted in *Homo Viator*. Paris: Aubier, 1944.

"Remarques sur une interdiction: A propos de Bergson." *Confluences*, October 1942.

1943   "*Les mouches*, par J.-P. Sartre." *Chercher bien*, 1943.

"*Les mouches*, par J.-P. Sartre." *Rencontres* (Editions du cerf), 1943. Reprinted in *L'Heure théâtrale*. Paris: Plon, 1959.

"Le Mystère familial: Comment il se définit." *Revue des jeunes* (new series), January–February 1943.

"*Journal métaphysique*, III: Fragments." *Confluences*, January 1943.

"Le Mystère familial: Comment on l'a dégradé." *Revue des jeunes* (new series), March 1943.

"Le Mystère familial: Son Caractère sacré." *Revue des jeunes* (new series), April 1943.

1944   *Homo Viator: Prolégomènes à une métaphysique de l'espérance*. Paris: Aubier, Editions Montaigne, 1944. Paris: Aubier, 1945. Contains reprints of the following articles and lectures: "Moi et autrui," "Esquisse d'une phénoménologie et d'une métaphysique de l'espérance," "Le Mystère familial," "Le Voeu créateur comme essence de la paternité," "Obéissance et fidélité," "Valeur et immortalité," "Situation périlleuse des valeurs éthiques," "L'Etre et le néant," "Le Refus du salut et l'exaltation de l'homme absurde," and "Rilke, témoin du spirituel."

Homo Viator: Prolégomènes à une métaphysique de l'espérance. Rev. ed. Paris: Aubier, Editions Montaigne, 1963. New, revised, and enlarged edition with a preface by the author and, as an appendix, his lecture on *L'Homme revolté,* by Albert Camus.

Homo Viator: Introduction to a Metaphysic of Hope. Translated by Emma Craufurd. London: Victor Gollancz, 1951. Chicago: Henry Regnery Co., 1951. New York: Harper & Row, Harper Torchbooks, 1962.

Homo Viator: Philosophie der Hoffnung. German translation by Wolfgang Rüttenauer. Düsseldorf: Bastion-Verlag, 1949.

"*L'Etre et le néant,* par J.-P. Sartre." *Rencontres* (Editions du Cerf), March–April 1944. Reprinted in *Homo Viator.* Paris: Aubier, 1944.

"Le Voeu créateur comme essence de la paternité." *Chronique sociale de France,* March–April 1944. Reprinted in *Homo Viator.* Paris: Aubier, 1944.

"Spectroscopie de la trahison." *Temps présent* (new series), 1 September 1944.

"Hierarchie des fidélités." *Temps présent* (new series), 15 September 1944.

"Mise au point." *Carrefour,* 28 October 1944.

1945   *L'Horizon.* Paris: Aux étudiants de France, 1945. A play.

La Métaphysique de Royce. Paris: Aubier, 1945. Reprints, with minor changes, the four articles from *La Revue de métaphysique et de morale,* 1918–19.

Royce's Metaphysics. Translated by Virginia and Gordon Ringer. Chicago: Henry Regnery Co., 1956.

"En mémoire d'Henri Bergson." *Temps présent,* 12 January 1945.

"Il n'est pas mort pour nous: Phrase d'A. Camus." *Temps présent,* 19 January 1945.

"Le Refus du salut et l'exaltation de l'homme absurde." *La Table ronde,* March 1945. A review of G. Bataille's *L'Expérience intérieure.* Reprinted in *Homo Viator.* Paris: Aubier, 1945.

"*Le Sens du dialogue,* par Jean Lacroix." *Temps présent,* 18 April 1945.

"*Huis clos,* par J.-P. Sartre." *Les Nouvelles littéraires,* 26 April 1945.

"*Huis clos,* par J.-P. Sartre." *Horizon,* July 1945. Reprinted in *L'Heure théâtrale.* Paris: Plon, 1959.

"Autour de Heidegger." *Dieu vivant,* August 1945.

"Devoir du philosophe." *Temps présent,* 24 August 1945.

"Responsabilités." *Eaux vives,* September 1945. Note on de Beauvoir and Sartre.

"*Le Sang des autres,* par Simone de Beauvoir." *Temps présent,* 5 October 1945.

"*Les Bouches inutiles,* par Simone de Beauvoir." *Les Nouvelles littéraires,* 8 November 1945.

"Le Phénomène Sartre." *Temps présent,* 9 November 1945.

"J.-P. Sartre: *Les Chemins de la liberté.*" *La Nef,* December 1945.

"La Science inhumaine." *Terre des hommes,* 8 December 1945.

1946   "L'existence et la liberté humaine chez J.-P. Sartre." In André George et al., *Les Grands Appels de l'homme contemporain: Six Conférences prononcées au Centre de culture de l'amitié française*. Paris: Editions du temps présent, 1946.

"Existentialism and Human Freedom." In *The Philosophy of Existence*, translated by Manya Harari. London: Harvill Press, 1949.

Preface to *La Pierre Philosophale*, by A. Larsen. Paris: Albin Michel, 1946.

"Les Débuts de la saison théâtrale (de Beauvoir, Sartre, Camus)." *Etudes*, January 1946.

"Science et humanisme." *La Nef*, February 1946.

"Le Témoignage comme localisation de l'existentiel." *Bulletin de la Société de philosophie de Bordeaux*, March 1946. Also in *Nouvelle Revue de théologie*, March–April 1946.

"Testimony and Existentialism." In *The Philosophy of Existence*, translated by Manya Harari. London: Harvill Press, 1949.

"La Propagande comme technique d'avilissement." *Les Nouvelles Paroles françaises*, 9 March 1946.

"Un Existentialisme tronque." *Diogène*, April 1946.

"Le Sens du profond." *Fontaine*, April 1946.

"Vers une conscience planétaire? Sur la conférence du P. Teilhard de Chardin." *La France catholique*, 28 April 1946.

"Existence et liberté." *Ombre et lumière*, May 1946.

"*Existentialisme et humanisme*, par J.-P. Sartre." *J'ai lu*, May 1946.

"Aperçus sur la liberté" *La Nef*, June 1946. Excerpts from "Etre, valeur, liberté," a lecture given in Belgium, February 1946.

"Josiah Royce." *Une Semaine dans le monde*, 7 August 1946.

"Ultima Verba: *Mon Faust*, par Paul Valéry." *Une Semaine dans le monde*, 17 August 1946.

"*Introduction à une connaissance de la famille*, par L. Doucy." *J'ai lu*, September 1946.

"*Le Tableau de la philosophie française*, par J. Wahl." *Une Semaine dans le monde*, 7 September 1946.

"Caractère et personalité: *Traité du caractère*, par E. Mounier." *Une Semaine dans le monde*, 16 September 1946.

"Fascistes sans le savoir." *Une Semaine dans le monde*, 30 September 1946.

"Retour à Bergson?" *Une Semaine dans le monde*, 12 October 1946.

"Le Théâtre." *Hommes et mondes*, November 1946. Mostly on Sartre.

"Deux Pièces nouvelles de J.-P. Sartre: *Morts sans sépulture; La Putain respectueuse*." *Les Nouvelles littéraires*, 10 November 1946. Reprinted in *L'Heure théâtrale*. Paris: Plon, 1959.

1947   "Regard en arrière." In J. Delhomme et al., *Existentialisme chrétien: Gabriel Marcel*, edited by Etienne Gilson. Paris: Plon, Présences, 1947.

"Essay in Autobiography: 'Regard en arrière.' " In *The Philosophy of Existence*, translated by Manya Harari. London: Harvill Press; New York: Philosophical Library, 1949.

Christlicher Existentialismus: Gabriel Marcel. German translation by Charlotte Horstmann. Warendorf, Westfalen: Verlag J. Schnellsche Buchhandlung (C. Leopold), 1951.

Théâtre comique. Paris: Albin Michel, 1947. Includes *Colombyre ou le brasier de la paix, La Double Expertise, Les Points sur les i,* and *Le Divertissement posthume.*

"De l'audace en métaphysique." *Revue de métaphysique et de morale* 52 (1947). Reprinted after commentaries by Father Belay in *Percés vers un ailleurs: Théâtre: "L'Iconoclaste," "L'Horizon."* Paris: Fayard, 1973.

"Le Théâtre (Sartre, G. Neveux)." *Hommes et mondes,* January 1947.

"Humanisme tragique: A propos d'André Malraux." *J'ai lu,* February 1947.

"Réflexions du critique: *Huis-clos, Morts sans sépulture, La Putain respectueuse.*" *La Revue théâtrale,* February 1947.

"Sartre and Barrault: The Paris Spotlight." *Theatre Arts,* February 1947.

"Le Théâtre (Anouilh, Salacrou, Stève Passeur, Cocteau)." *Hommes et mondes,* February 1947.

"*Sartre est-il un possédé?* par Pierre Boutang et Bernard Pingaud." *J'ai lu,* March 1947.

"Le Théâtre (O'Neill, O'Casey, Duran)." *Hommes et mondes,* March 1947.

"Existentialisme et pensée chrétienne." *Témoignages* (Cahiers de la Pierre-qui-vire), May 1947.

"*Karl Jaspers et la philosophie de l'existence,* par Dufresne et Ricoeur." *J'ai lu,* July–August 1947.

"Un Penseur suisse-allemand: Max Picard." *Ici-France,* 25 July 1947.

"*La Peste,* par A. Camus; et *Théâtre,* par J.-P. Sartre." *J'ai lu,* July 1947.

"Technique et péché." *Le Cheval de Troie,* July 1947. Reprinted in *Les Hommes contre l'humain.* Paris: La Colombe, 1951.

"Réfutation de J.-P. Sartre." *Ici-France,* 18 September 1947.

"Désaccord avec Mounier: Sur le no. d'*Esprit* consacré à la justice." *Carrefour,* 22 October 1947.

"Don et libertè." *Giornale di metafisica,* November 1947.

1948   Jean Cassou, G. Marcel, et al. *Débat sur l'art contemporain.* Vol. 3 of *Rencontres internationales de Genève.* Neuchâtel: La Baconnière, 1948. Eight public addresses, followed by discussions of each.

Dibattito sull'arte contemporanea. Vol. 3 of *Rencontres internationales de Genève.* Milan: Edizioni di Comunità, 1954. Eight public addresses.

"Les Techniques d'avilissement." In Paul Claudel et al., *Le Mal est parmi nous.* Paris: Plon, Présences, 1948. Reprinted in *La France catholique,* 15 April 1949.

"Pessimisme et conscience eschatologique." *Dieu vivant,* 1948. Reprinted in *Les Hommes contre l'humain.* Paris: La Colombe, 1951.

"Les Rencontres internationales de Genève." *La Vie intellectuelle* 16, no. 11 (1948).

"*Introduction à Proudhon,* par Ed. Dolléans." *J'ai lu,* April 1948.

"Pour une définition de l'homme de bonne volonté." *Les Cahiers des hommes de bonne volonté*, April 1948.*

"Note pour une métaphysique de l'acte de charité." *Jeunesse de l'Eglise*, May 1948.

"*Les Mains sales*, par J.-P. Sartre." *Les Nouvelles littéraires*, 13 May 1948. Reprinted in *L'Heure théâtrale*. Paris: Plon, 1959.

"Problème et mystère." *Revue de Paris*, 7 July 1948.

"Max Picard ou le retour à l'originel." *La Nef*, September 1948.

1949   "Ontologie et axiologie." In *Esistenzialismo cristiano*, edited by Enrico Castelli. Archivio di Filosofia. Padua: Editoria Liviana, 1949.

Position et approches concrètes du mystère ontologique. Introduction by Marcel de Corte. Louvain: Nauwelaerts; Paris: Vrin, 1949. 2d rev. ed. Collection Philosophes contemporaine: Textes et études, no. 3. Louvain: Nauwelaerts; Paris: Beatrice Nauwelaerts, 1967.

"On the Ontological Mystery." In *The Philosophy of Existence*, translated by Manya Harari. London: Harvill Press; New York: Philosophical Library, 1949. Reprint. Essay Index Reprint Series. Freeport, N.Y.: Books for Libraries Press, 1969.

"On the Ontological Mystery." In *The Philosophy of Existentialism*, translated by Manya Harari. New York: Citadel Press, 1961. 4th paperbound ed., 1964.

"On the Ontological Mystery." Translated by Manya Harari. In vol. 3 of *Philosophy in the Twentieth Century: An Anthology*, edited by W. Barrett and H. D. Aiken. New York: Random House, 1962.

Preface to *La Vingt-cinquième Heure*, by Constantin Virgil Gheorghiu, in the French translation by Monique Saint-Come. Collection Feux croisés. Paris: Plon, 1949. Reprints. Collection Racine, no. 6. Paris: Plon, 1961. Collection Feux croisés. Paris: Plon, 1966.

G. Marcel et al. *Recherche de la famille, essai sur "l'être familial."* Paris: Editions familiales de France, 1949.

Vers un autre royaume. Paris: Plon, 1949. Contains the plays *L'Emissaire* and *Le Signe de la Croix*.

Le Signe de la Croix: Pièce en trois actes et quatre tableaux, suivie d'un épilogue. Paris: Plon, 1960. Reprint, 1961.

"Existentialisme et humanisme: Esquisse d'une interprétation existentialiste." *Archivio di Filosofia* 18 (1949).

"L'Homme et les techniques." *La France catholique*, 1 April 1949.

"L'Aventure technocratique." *La France catholique*, 8 April 1949.

---

*This publication was established by André Cuisenier to present articles and correspondence on Jules Romains's multivolume novel *Les Hommes de bonne volonté* and its themes. It was published in Paris by Romains's publisher, Flammarion. Marcel's article appeared in the first issue, and only three other numbers came out, the last one in 1950. Cuisenier contributed to *Les Cahiers* himself, but he does not appear to be officially listed as an editor.— ED.

"De Jézabel à Médée: Le Tragique chez Jean Anouilh." *Revue de Paris,* June 1949.

"L'Esprit d'abstraction comme facteur de guerre." *Cahiers du monde nouveau,* December 1949.

1950   *La Chapelle ardente.* Paris: La Table Ronde, 1950. A play.

La Fin des temps. Paris: Réalités, 1950. A play.

Preface to *G. Marcel e la metodologia dell'inverificabile,* by Pietro Prini. Rome: Studium, 1950.

"Y a-t'il une nature humaine?" *Recherches et débats,* March 1950.

"The Malady of the Age: A Fanaticized Conscience." *Dublin Review,* 3d Quarter, 1950. First published in English.

"La Conscience fanatisée." In *Les Hommes contre l'humain.* Paris: La Colombe, 1951.

1951   *Les Hommes contre l'humain.* Paris: La Colombe, 1951. Reprint. Paris: Fayard, 1968.

Men Against Humanity. Translated by G. S. Fraser. London: Harvill Press, 1952.

Man Against Mass Society. Translated by G. S. Fraser. Foreword by Donald MacKinnon. Chicago: Henry Regnery Co., 1952. Reprint. Chicago: Henry Regnery Co., Gateway, 1962.

Die Erniedrigung des Menschen. German translation by Herbert P. M. Schaad. Frankfurt: Verlag Josef Knecht, 1957.

Le Mystère de l'être. Vol. 1, *Réflexion et mystère.* Paris: Aubier, 1951. Contains the Gifford Lectures of 1949.

The Mystery of Being. Vol. 1, *Reflection and Mystery.* Translated by G. S. Fraser. London: Harvill Press, 1950. Chicago: Henry Regnery Co., 1950. Reprint. Chicago: Henry Regnery Co., Gateway, 1960.

Das Geheimnis des Seins. German translation by Hanns von Winter. Vienna: Herold Verlag, 1952. Contains both vols. 1 and 2.

Le Mystère de l'être. Vol. 2, *Foi et réalité.* Paris: Aubier, 1951.

Foi et réalité. Collection Foi vivante, no. 38. Paris: Aubier, Editions Montaigne, 1967.

The Mystery of Being. Vol. 2, *Faith and Reality.* Translated by René Hague. London: Harvill Press, 1951. Chicago: Henry Regnery Co., 1951. Reprint. Chicago: Henry Regnery Co., Gateway, 1960.

Rome n'est plus dans Rome. Paris: La Table ronde, 1951. A play.

"El filosofo ante el mundo de hoy." *Cuadernos hispano-americanos,* 1951.

"Structure de l'espérance." *Dieu vivant* 19 (1951). Also in *Espoir humain, espérance chrétienne.* Semaine des intellectuels catholiques. Paris: Pierre Horay, 1951.

"Etienne Gilson." *Aspects de la France,* January 1951.

"*Les Mouches,* par J.-P. Sartre." *Les Nouvelles littéraires,* 18 January 1951. Reprinted in *L'Heure théâtrale.* Paris: Plon, 1959.

"*Le Diable et le bon Dieu,* par J.-P. Sartre." *Les Nouvelles littéraires,* 16 May 1951. Reprinted in *L'Heure théâtrale.* Paris: Plon, 1959.

"Sartre, Anouilh et le problème de Dieu." *La Nouvelle Revue canadienne*, September–October 1951.

"Jaspers et la situation spirituelle du monde contemporain." *Preuves*, December 1951.

1952   *Les Coeurs avides (La Soif)*. Paris: La Table ronde, 1952.

"Don et liberté." In *Mélanges d'esthétique et de science de l'art: Offerts à Etienne Souriau*. Paris: Librairie Nizet, 1952.

"L'Homme moderne est-il libre?" In *L'Eglise et la liberté*. Semaine des intellectuels catholiques. Paris: P. Horay; Editions de Flore, 1952.

Preface to *The World of Silence*, by Max Picard. Translated by Stanley Godman. Chicago: Henry Regnery Co., 1952.

"Le Primat de l'existentiel: Sa Portée éthique et religieuse, réflexion et mystère, crise des valeurs." In vol. 2 of *Actas del Primer Congreso Nacional de Filosofia*. Mendoza, Argentina: Universidad Nacional de Cuyo, 30 March–9 April 1949.

"Rilke et la philosophie de l'existence." *La Table ronde* 49 (1952).

"Remarques sur la dépersonnalisation de la médecine." *La France catholique*, 18 January 1952.

"Théâtre et philosophie dans le théâtre contemporain." *Recherches et débats*, September 1952. Introduction to the debate on atheism in contemporary theater.

"Méditation sur la musique dans ma pensée." *Revue musicale*, November 1952.

Speech to the Réunion sur la phénoménologie, C.C.I.F. (Catholic Center of French Intellectuals), 20 November 1952.

1953   Appendix to *Gabriel Marcel et la méthodologie de l'invérifiable*, by Pietro Prini. Paris: Desclée de Brouwer, 1953.

"Civilisation et christianisme." In *Civiltà e pace*. Florence: Tipografia l'Impronta, 1953. Proceedings of the First International Meeting for Civilization and Christian Peace, in Florence, 23–28 June 1952.

"L'Eclattement de la notion de sagesse." In *Cristianesimo e ragio de stato*, edited by Enrico Castelli. Rome and Milan: Fratelli Bocca, 1953. Proceedings of the Second International Congress of Humanistic Studies, in Rome, 1952; sponsored by the International Center for Humanistic Studies. Reprinted in *Le Déclin de la sagesse*. Paris: Plon, 1954.

Filosofia della speranza. Edited by Angelo Scivolette. Florence: Philosophia, 1953.

"Glaube and Wissen." *Wissenschaft und Weltbild* 6 (1953): 313–18.

"Irruption de la mélodie." Filosofia dell' arte. *Archivio di Filosofia* 1 (1953): 77–79.

"*Huis-clos* et *La Putain respectueuse*, par Jean-Paul Sartre." *Les Nouvelles littéraires*, 21 May 1953. Reprinted in *L'Heure théâtrale*. Paris: Plon, 1959.

1954   *Le Déclin de la sagesse*. Paris: Plon, 1954. Includes "Les Limites de la civilisation industrielle," "La Notion d'héritage spirituel," and "L'Eclatement de la notion de sagesse."

The Decline of Wisdom. Translated by Manya Harari. London: Harvill Press; Toronto: Collins, 1954. New York: Philosophical Library, 1955.

Der Untergang der Weisheit; Die Verfinsterung des Verstandes. German translation by Herbert P. M. Schaal. Heidelberg: F. H. Kerle, 1960.

Notice sur la vie et les travaux de Emile Bréhier, 1876–1952. Paris: Firmin-Didot, 1954. Presented at a meeting of the Académie des sciences morales et politiques, Institut de France, 27 September 1954.

"Notes pour une philosophie de l'amour." *Revue de métaphysique et de morale* 59 (1954): 374–79.

1955   *Croissez et multipliez.* Paris: Plon, 1955. A play in four acts, with an afterword by the author.

L'Homme problématique. Collection Philosophie de l'esprit. Paris: Aubier, 1955.

Problematic Man. Translated by Brian Thompson. New York: Herder & Herder, 1967.

Der Mensch als Problem. German translation by Herbert P. M. Schaad. Frankfurt: Josef Knecht, 1957.

Mon Temps n'est pas le vôtre. Paris: Plon, 1955. A play, with an afterword by the author.

"Le Scandale vu dans la perspective de René LeSenne." *Giornale di Metafisica* 10 (1955).

"*Nekrassov,* par Jean-Paul Sartre." *Les Nouvelles littéraires,* 15 June 1955. Reprinted in *L'Heure théâtrale.* Paris: Plon, 1959.

"In memoriam (René LeSenne)." *Les Etudes philosophiques,* July–September 1955.

1956   Contribution to *L'Athéisme contemporain,* edited by Edouard Mauris. Geneva: Editions Labor & Fides; Paris: Librairie protestante, 1956.

La Dimension Florestan. Paris: Plon, 1956. A play.

The Influence of Psychic Phenomena on My Philosophy. London: London Society for Psychical Research, 1956. The Frederic W. H. Myers Memorial Lecture, December 1955.

"L'Influence des phénomènes psychiques sur ma philosophie." *Revue française de recherches métapsychiques,* July 1956.

"Témoin de l'absolu." Preface to *Simone Weil,* by Marie M. Davy. Collection Témoin du xxe siècle. Paris: Editions universitaires, 1956. Rev. ed., 1966.

"Existentialismus und modernes Theater." *Wissenschaft und Weltbild* 9 (1956).

"Theism and Personal Relationships." *Cross Currents* 1, no. 1 (1956): 40.

1957   "Schelling fut-il un précurseur de la philosophie de l'existence?" *Revue de métaphysique et de morale,* January–March 1957.

"Universal against the Masses." Translated by G. S. Fraser. In *This Is My Philosophy: Twenty of the World's Outstanding Thinkers Reveal the Deepest Meanings They Have Found in Life,* edited by W. Burnett. New York: Harper, 1957.

"Vers une ontologie concrète." In vol. 19 of *Encyclopédie française,* edited by Lucien Febvre. Paris: Société nouvelle de l'*Encyclopédie française,* 1957.

"L'Idée du drame chrétien dans son rapport au théâtre actuel." *Archivio di Fi-*

losofia 3 (1957): 105–19. Reprinted in *Théâtre et religion*. Lyons: Vitte, 1959.

"Behaviorisme et dualisme." *Bulletin de la Société française de philosophie*, January–March 1957. Statement by Raymond Ruyer. Discussion by Marcel, Berger, Minkowski, Hyppolyte, Wahl, et al. Meeting of 26 January 1957.

1958   *Un Changement d'espérance à la rencontre du réarmement moral: Des témoignages, des faits.* Edited by G. Marcel. Paris: Plon, 1958.

Fresh Hope for the World: Moral Rearmament in Action. Edited by G. Marcel. Translated by Helen Hardinge. New York: Longmans, 1960.

Contribution to *Qu'est-ce que vouloir?* Collection Psychologie. Paris: Editions du cerf, 1958. A collection of addresses delivered at a conference on the will, held at Bonneval in 1956.

"Le Crépuscule du sens commun." In *La Dimension Florestan*. Rev. ed. Paris: Plon, 1958. Afterword to new edition of play.

Preface to *The Inward Morning: A Philosophical Exploration in Journal Form*, by Henry Bugbee. State College, Penna.: Bald Eagle Press, 1958.

"Reintegration of honor." Translated by G. S. Fraser. In *Spirit of Man: Great Stories and Experiences of Spiritual Crises, Inspiration, and the Joy of Life, by Forty Famous Contemporaries.* Edited by Whit Burnett. New York: Hawthorn Books, 1958. Reprinted from *Man Against Mass Society*. Translated by G. S. Fraser. Chicago: Henry Regnery Co., 1952.

"Amédée Ponceau (con un inedito)." *Giornale di Metafisica* 13 (1958).

"Der Mensch vor dem vermeintlichen Tod Gottes." *Wissenschaft und Weltbild* 11, no. 1 (1958).

"L'Etre devant la pensée interrogative." *Bulletin de la Société française de philosophie*, January–March 1958. Statement by Marcel. Discussion by Alquié, Benezé, Berger, Goldmann, Wahl, et al. Meeting of 25 January 1958.

"L'umanesimo autentico e i suoi presuppositi esistenziali." *Il fuoco*, January–February 1958.

"In Memoriam: Amédée Ponceau." *La Croix*, 4–5 May 1958. Also in *Giornale di Metafisica*, November–December 1958.

1959   "Dieu et la causalité." In *De la connaissance de Dieu*, nos. 3 and 4 of *Recherches de philosophie*. Paris and Bruges: Desclée de Brouwer, 1959.

"God and Causality." Translated by Robert W. Flynt. *Religion and Culture: Essays in Honor of Paul Tillich*, edited by Walter Leibrecht. New York: Harper, 1959.

"Fragments du *Journal métaphysique*." Contribution to *La Diriaristica filosofica*. Archivio di filosofia, no. 2, 1959. Edited by Enrico Castelli. Padua: Cedam, 1959.

L'Heure théâtrale de Giraudoux à Jean-Paul Sartre: Chroniques dramatiques. Paris: Plon, 1959. Contains fifty articles, most of which previously appeared in *Les Nouvelles littéraires*, on Giraudoux (nine articles), Henry de Montherland (nine), Jean Anouilh (twenty), Albert Camus (four), Jean-Paul Sartre (eight).

Présence et immortalité: Journal métaphysique (1939–1943) et autre textes.
Paris: Flammarion, 1959. Reprint. Paris: Union générale d'éditions, 1968.
Contains *Mon Propos fondamental* (1937), *Journal métaphysique* (1938–
43), *Présence et immortalité* (1951), and *L'Insondable* (unfinished play,
1919).

Presence and Immortality. Translated by Michael A. Machado. Pittsburgh: Duquesne University Press, 1967.

Théâtre et religion. Collection Parvis. Lyons: Vitte, 1959. Contains two lectures:
"Religion et blasphème dans le théâtre contemporain," and "L'Idée du
drame chrétien dans son rapport au théâtre actuel."

"What Can One Expect of Philosophy? Translated by Rev. M. B. Crowe. *Stud-
ies: An Irish Quarterly Review,* Summer 1959. Reprinted in *Philosophy
Today,* Winter 1959. English translation of an address given at University
College, Dublin, National University of Ireland, 11 March 1959.

"Les Séquestrés d'Altona, par J.-P. Sartre." *Les Nouvelles littéraires,* 1 October
1959.

"Esquisse d'une problématique de la tolérance religieuse." *Choisic,* November
1959.

"Inédit." *Revue Blonde,* November 1959. With an introduction by Marcel de
Corte, "Gabriel Marcel nous ramène à la sagesse."

1960   "Authentic Humanness and Its Existential and Primordial Assumptions." Translated by Pierre de Fontnouvelle. In *The Human Person and the World of
Values: A Tribute to Dietrich von Hildebrand by His Friends in Philosophy,* edited by Balduin V. Schwarz. Orestes Brownson Series on Contemporary Thought and Affairs. New York: Fordham University Press, 1960.
2d rev. ed. Westport, Conn.: Greenwood Press, 1972.

La condición del intelectual en el mundo contemporaneo. Collection ó crece o
muere, no. 144. Madrid: Ateneo, 1960.

"Der Mensch vor dem Totgesagten: Nihilismus oder *'vieillissement'?"* In *Sinn
und Sein: Ein philosophisches Symposium,* edited by Richard Wisses.
Tübingen: Max Niemeyer Verlag, 1960.

"My Life." Translated by G. S. Fraser. In *Modern Catholic Thinkers: An Anthology,* edited with a preface by A. R. Caponigri. New York: Harper,
1960. From *The Mystery of Being,* vol. 1, chap. 8., 1951. With a preface
by A. R. Caponigri and an introduction by Martin Cyril D'Arcy.

Préface to *Monde d'écrivains, destinées d'homme,* by Père Louis Barjon. Paris:
Casterman, 1960.

Preface to *Rives et courants: Récits-témoignages,* edited by André Maurois,
Georges Duhamel, and J. Huguet. Illustrated by Denys de Solère. Collection Rives et courants. Colmar and Paris: Editions Alsatia, 1960.

"Vérité et liberté." In *La Philosophie et ses problèmes: Recueil d'études de
doctrine et d'histoire offert à R. Jolivet.* Lyons and Paris: Vitte, 1960.

"Contemporary atheism and the religious mind." Translated by Thomas Schoen-
baum. *Philosophy Today,* Winter 1960.

"De l'existence à l'être: Introduction." *Philosophy Today,* Winter 1960.

Introduction to *The Inward Morning,* by Henry Bugbee. *Philosophy Today,* Winter 1960.

"Un Septuagénaire cherche à voir clair." *Réalités* (Paris), January 1960.

"Imo corde, en hommage à Albert Camus." *Les Nouvelles littéraires*, 7 January 1960.

1962   "The Finality of the Drama." *Ramparts*, May 1962. Reprinted in *The New Orpheus: Essays Toward a Christian Poetic*, edited by N. A. Scott. New York: Sheed, 1964. Lecture delivered at the University of San Francisco in 1961.

Fragments philosophiques, 1909–1914. Philosophes contemporains: Textes et études, no. 11. Louvain: Nauwelaerts, 1962.

Philosophical Fragments, 1909–1914. Translated by Lionel A. Blain. Published together with *The Philosopher and Peace*, translated by Viola Herms Drath. Notre Dame, Ind.: University of Notre Dame Press, 1965.

Funérailles de Daniel Halévy . . . le 7 février 1962: Discours. Institute de France. Académie des sciences morales et politiques publications, 1962, no. 3. Paris: Firmin-Didot, 1962.

Preface to *Le Message d'Amédée Ponceau*, by Jean Barraud. Paris: Rivière, 1962.

"Philosophical Atheism." *International Philosophical Quarterly* 2, no. 4 (1962): 501–14.

"Le Philosophe en présence du savant." *Les Nouvelles littéraires*, 21 March 1962.

"My Death and Myself." Translated by Michael A. Machado. *Review of Existential Psychology and Psychiatry* 2 (Spring 1962): 105–16.

"Participation." *Review of Existential Psychology and Psychiatry* 2 (Spring 1962): 94–104. Prepublication of chap. 2 of *The Existential Background of Human Dignity*. Cambridge: Harvard University Press, 1963.

"Sacred in the Technological Age." *Theology Today*, April 1962.

1963   *The Existential Background of Human Dignity*. Harvard University: The William James Lectures, 1961–62. Cambridge, Mass.: Harvard University Press, 1963.

La Dignité humaine et ses assises existentialles. Collections Présence et pensée. Paris: Aubier, Editions Montaigne, 1964.

"On the Concept of Love and Peace: An Exchange of Letters between Daisetz T. Suzuki and Dr. Gabriel Marcel." *France-Asie*, January–April 1963.

"Imago Dei: Introduction à la lecture de Max Picard." *La Table ronde*, April 1963.

1964   *Auf der Suche nach Wahrheit und Gerechtigkeit*. Edited by Wolfgang Ruf. Frankfurt: Verlag Knecht, 1964.

Searchings. New York: Newman Press, 1967. This edition contains "In Search of Truth and Justice," "Science and Wisdom," "The Sacral in the Era of Technology," "Death and Immortality," "Martin Buber's Philosophical Anthropology," and "My Dramatic Works as Viewed by the Philosopher." Chap. 5, "Martin Buber's Philosophical Anthropology," has been substituted for the original chapter, "I and Other."

Preface to *La Droite cette inconnue*, by Jean Jaélic. Paris: Les Sept Couleurs, 1964.

Preface to *Hippocrate et la médecine*, by Dr. Marcel Martiny. Collection Le Signe. Paris: Fayard, 1964.

Preface to *Histoire de la philosophie européenne,* by Alfred Weber and Denis Huisman. 3 vols. Paris: Fischbacher, 1964.

Preface to *J'ai subi le lavage de cerveau,* by Dries van Coillie. Collection Les Attentats contre l'homme. Paris: Desclée de Brouwer, Mobilisation des consciences, 1964. Rev. ed. Collection Les Tresors du livre, no. 109. Geneva: Editions Sari, 1968.

Preface to *La Pierre philosophale,* by J. Anker Larsen. Nouvelle Bibliothèque, no. 99. Neuchatel: Nouvelle Bibliothèque, 1964.

Regards sur le théâtre de Paul Claudel. Paris: Editions Beauchesne, 1964. Preface by the author with a discussion on "L'Insertion de la grâce dans le théâtre français du xxe siècle."

"Some Reflections on Existentialism." *Philosophy Today,* Winter 1964.

"The Philosopher Meets the Scientist." *Philosophy Today,* Fall 1964.

"Prise de position." *Les Nouvelles littéraires,* 29 October 1964.

1965   Foreword to *Ascent to Being: Gabriel Marcel's Philosophy of Communion,* by Vincent P. Miceli. New York: Desclée, 1965.

"La Musique, patrie de l'Ame." Inaugural speech, Festival of Music of Salzbourg, 1965.

Musik, Heimat der Seele. Salzburg: Festungsverlag, 1965.

Paix sur la terre: Deux Discours, une tragédie. Paris: Aubier, Editions Montaigne, 1965. Contains "*Laudatio,* de Carlo Schmid," "Le Philosophe et la paix," and *Un Juste.*

Philosophical Fragments 1909–1914. Translated by Lionel A. Blain. Notre Dame, Ind.: University of Notre Dame Press, 1965.

Three Plays. Translated by Marjorie Gabain and Rosalind Heywood. New York: Hill & Wang, 1965.

Introduction by Richard Hayes. Contains *A Man of God, Ariadne,* and *The Votive Candle.*

"Truth and Freedom." Translated by Rosemary Lauer. *Philosophy Today,* Winter 1965.

"Dieu n'est pas une idole." *Janus,* February–March 1965.

"Pourquoi j'ai écrit *Un Juste.*" *Les Nouvelles littéraires,* 25 March 1965.

"Aperçus sur la musique dans ma vie et dans mon oeuvre." *Livres de France,* August–September 1965.

"Tenir Compte." *Nation française,* 30 December 1965.

1966   *Die Französische Literatur im 20. Jahrhundert.* Freiburg, Basel, and Vienna: Herder, 1966. Eight lectures by Marcel.

Gabriel Marcel et les niveaux de l'expérience. Edited by Jeanne Parain-Vial. Paris: Seghers, 1966.

Preface to *De la mort à l'espérance,* by Jean Loisy. Collection Beauchesne, no. 13. Paris: Editions Beauchesne, 1966. Commentary by le Père Carré, O.P.

Preface to *Une Voyante Témoigne,* by Hélène Bouvier. Notes collected by Simone Saint-Clair. Paris: Fayard, 1966.

"Solipsism Surmounted." Translated by Leroy S. Rouner. In *Philosophy, Religion, and the Coming World Civilization: Essays in Honor of William Ernest Hocking*, edited by Leroy S. Rouner. The Hague: Martinus Nijhoff, 1966.

"Le Viol de l'intimité et le dépérissement des valeurs." In *Le Fondement des droits de l'homme*. Florence: La Nuova Italia, 1966. Proceedings of the International Institute of Philosophy Conference at Aquila, 14–19 September 1964.

"Sartre, Camus, Malraux: Philosophie und Dichtung des Existentialismus." *Universitas: Zeitschrift für Wissenschaft, Kunst und Literatur* 21, no. 10 (1966).

"Philosophie négative, théologie, athéisme." *Wissenschaft und Weltbilde*, March 1966.

1967   "A mes amis inconnus d'Allemagne de l'Est." Introduction to a book by Siegfried Foelz containing selections from Marcel's writings. 2 vols. Leipzig: St. Benno Verlag, 1967.

"Desire and Hope." Translated by Nathaniel Lawrence. In *Readings in Existential Phenomenology*, edited by Nathaniel Lawrence and Daniel O'Connor. Englewood Cliffs, N.J.: Prentice-Hall, 1967. A previously unpublished lecture from 1963.

Essai de philosophie concrète. Collection Idées, no. 119. Paris: Gallimard, 1967. Previously published under the title *Du refus à l'invocation*, 1945.

"I and Thou." Translated by Forrest Williams. In *The Philosophy of Martin Buber*, edited by Paul Arthur Schilpp and Maurice Friedmann. The Library of Living Philosophers, vol. 12, LaSalle, Ill.: Open Court, 1967.

"Intersubjectivity." Translated by G. S. Fraser. In *The Human Dialogue*, edited by Floyd W. Matson and Ashley Montagu. New York: Free Press, 1967. Reprinted from *The Mystery of Being*, vol. 1, 1951.

Le Secret est dans les îles: Théâtre. Paris: Plon, 1967. A collection of plays, including *Le Dard*, *L'Emissaire*, and *La Fin des temps*.

"A propos de *Partage de Midi*, de Paul Claudel." *Bulletin de la Société Paul Claudel*, April 1967.

"Pour Israël." *La Nation française*, 8 June 1967.

"Des Comptes séparés." *Exil et liberté*, December 1967.

"Remarques pour une problématique de la foi." *La Table ronde*, December 1967–January 1968.

1968   "L'Anthropologie philosophique de Martin Buber." In *Martin Buber: L'Homme et le philosophe*. Brussels: Editions de l'Institut de sociologie de l'Université libre de Bruxelles, 1968. Introduction by Robert Weltsch. Other contributions by E. Lévinas and André Lacocque.

Entretiens: Paul Ricoeur, Gabriel Marcel. Collection Présence & pensée, no. 10. Paris: Aubier-Montaigne, 1968.

Pour une sagesse tragique et son au-delà. Paris: Plon, 1968. A collection of lectures, with a preface by the author.

Tragic Wisdom and Beyond. Translated by Stephen Jolin and Peter McCormick. Northwestern University Studies in Phenomenology and Existential Philosophy. Evanston, Ill.: Northwestern University Press, 1973.

Tragische Weisheit: Zur gegenwärtigen Situation des Menschen. German translation by Peter Kampits and Liselotte Urbach. Vienna: Europaverlag, 1974.

Preface to *Au delà de l'urbanisme,* by Georges Meyer-Heine. Paris: Centre de recherche d'urbanisme, 1968.

Preface to *La France étrangère,* by Banine. Paris: Desclée de Brouwer, 1968.

Preface to *Im Kraftsfeld des Christlichen Weltbildes,* edited by Andreas Resch. Imago Mundi. Munich: Ferdinand Schöningh, 1968. A collection of partly revised papers by various authors presented at the First International Congress of Imago Mundi, Munich, September 1966.

Preface to *Les Reins et les coeurs,* by Paul Lesort. Collection Le Livre de poche, no. 2471. Paris: Editions du Seuil, 1968.

"La Foi aujourd'hui." *Cahiers de La Table ronde,* 1st Trimester, 1968.

"Une Anomalie révélatrice." *Journal Fédération XXième siècle,* January 1968.

Notes on the *Journal,* by Jean Colin d'Amiens. *Preuves,* May 1968.

"La responsabilidad del filosofo en el mundo actual." Spanish translation by Pedro Lluis Font. *Convivium* October–December 1968. Text of the lecture given in the Faculty of Letters and Philosophy of the University of Barcelona, 1968.

"Le Tragique éternel." *Les Nouvelles littéraires,* 17 October 1968.

"Théâtre et Révolution." *Les Nouvelles littéraires,* 21 November 1968.

"Au coin du sacrilège." *Les Nouvelles littéraires,* 26 December 1968. A review of *Le Diable et le bon Dieu,* by Sartre, on the occasion of the return of the play to the Théâtre nationale populaire.

1969   *Dialog und Erfahrung.* Edited by Wolfgang Ruf. Frankfurt am Main: Knecht, 1969. Lectures in German. Contains "Der Glaube als geistige Dimension," "Weisheit und Pietät in der heutigen Welt," "Der Mensch vor dem totgesagten Gott," "Die philosophische Anthropologie Martin Bubers," "Die geistige Entwicklung Ferdinand Ebners," and "Mein Leib, mein Leben, mein Sein."

Discours de remerciements de Gabriel Marcel à S.A.R. Le Prince Bernhardt des Pays Bas, à l'occasion de la remise du Prix Erasme (à G. Marcel, Oct. 27, 1969, à Rotterdam). Amsterdam: Stichting Praemium Erasmianum, 1969. Speech published as a pamphlet.

"La Dominante existentielle dans mon oeuvre." In *Metaphysics, Phenomenology, Language and Structure.* Vol. 3 of *Contemporary Philosophy: A Survey,* edited by Raymond Klibansky. International Institute of Philosophy. Florence: La Nuova Italia, 1969.

Preface to *Au diapason du ciel: L'Invisible et le réel,* by Marcelle de Jouvenel. Geneva: La Palatine, 1969.

"Hommage à Xavier Léon." *Bulletin de la Société française de philosophie,* January–March 1969.

"Un Homme vieillissant livré aux femmes." *Les Cahiers littéraires de l'O.R.T.F.,* 19 January–1 February 1969. On *Mon Temps n'est pas le vôtre.*

"Claudel Inégalé." *Les Nouvelles littéraires,* 30 January 1969.

"Carta a un amigo sueco." *La estafeta literaria,* 1 February 1969.

"Lettre à un ami suédois." *La estafeta literaria*, 1 February 1969.

"La Tragédie de l'auteur." *Les Nouvelles littéraires*, 13 March 1969.

"Dios ha muerto." *Tribuna medica*, 21 March 1969.

"Le Sel de la terre." *Les Nouvelles littéraires*, 22 May 1969.

"Mein philosophisches Testament." *Wissenschaft und Weltbild*, June 1969.

"Mon Testament philosophique." *Revue de métaphysique et de morale*, July–September 1969.

"De la ville aux conversations dans le Loire et Cher." In *La Pensée religieuse de P. Claudel. Recherches et débats*, September 1969. Special issue dedicated to Paul Claudel.

"Le Préternaturel chez Padre Pio et sa portée pour le philosophe." *Ecclésia*, September 1969.

"L'Alibi des oppresseurs." *Les Nouvelles littéraires*, 18 December 1969.

"La coartada de los opresores." *L'A.B.C.*, 5 September 1971.

"Le Mystère Marivaux." *Les Nouvelles littéraires*, 30 October 1969.

1970   "En pensant à Carmel." *Pourquoi n'êtes-vous pas hippies?* by Bernard Plossu. Paris: La Palatine, 1970.

"Mon Testament philosophique." In *D'Hommages à Xavier Zubiri*. Vol. 2. Madrid: Editoria Moneda y Crédito, 1970.

Preface to *Cet Ardent Sanglot: Pages de mon journal*, by Jacques Brezolles. Paris: Editions Beauchesne, 1970.

Preface to *Les Croyants en U.R.S.S.: L'Eglise orthodoxe officielle contestée: Persécutions et procès des croyants*, by André Martin, Paris: Fayard, 1970.

"Hommage à Léon Brunschwicg." *Bulletin de la Société française de philosophie*, January–March 1970.

"Remarques sur l'avenir de la médecine." *Tribuna medica*, 5 January 1970.

"La Seule Sanction efficace." *Exil et liberté*, February 1970.

"Les Racines de la contestation." *Les Nouvelles littéraires*, 12 February 1970.

"Les Racines de la contestation." *l'A.B.C.*, 1 March 1970.

"A Louis Massignon, dans l'Invisible." *Les Cahiers de l'Herne*, 2d. Trimester, 1970.

"Esquisse d'une méditation sur l'essence et le destin de l'homme." *Mainichi*, May 1970. On the occasion of the Osaka Exposition, 1970.

"Mauvaise Conscience ou mal-être." *Nouvelle Table ronde*, May 1970.

"Hommage à Gabriel Marcel, à l'occasion de ses 80 ans en 1969." *Revue Métapsychique*, June 1970. G. Marcel is one of several contributors.

"*Cet Ardent Sanglot*." *Les Nouvelles littéraires*, 2 July 1970. A review of the book by Jacques Brezolles.

"Un Aerolithe." *Revue de la renaissance de Fleury*, October 1970. Article on Julien Green, in the journal edited by the Bénédictins de St.-Benoit-sur-Loire.

"L'Eclipse des valeurs fondamentales." *France catholique*, 13 November 1970.

1971   "Avant Propos." In *Plus décisif que la violence: Actualité du réarmement moral*, by G. Marcel, in collaboration with Rajmohran Gandhi, Mohamed Masmoudi, Katleen Vundla, Fred Ladenius, et al. Paris: Plon, Tribune libre, 1971. In addition to the introduction, Marcel wrote chap. 11 and collaborated with four others on chap. 1.

Coleridge et Schelling. Paris: Aubier-Montaigne, 1971.

"Le Courage de l'esprit." In *Science et conscience de la société: Mélange en l'honneur de Raymond Aron,* edited by Jean-Claude Casanova. Vol. 2. Paris: Calmann-Lévy, 1971.

En chemin, vers quel éveil? Paris: Gallimard, 1971.

"Une Expérience qui fut une clé." *Communication avec les morts,* by Martin Ebon. L'Expérience psychique. Paris: Fayard, Brosse, 1971.

"Mise en place de la subversion." *Les Nouvelles littéraires,* 4 February 1971.

"Réflexions sur le couple." *L'A.B.C.,* 14 February 1971.

"Un Englobant mortel." *Tribuna medica,* 15 February 1971.

"Du fond des catacombes." *Le Figaro,* 14 April 1971.

"A la recherche de l'humain dans l'homme." *L'Homme nouveau,* 16 May 1971.

"En busqueda de lo humano en el hombre." *L'A.B.C.,* 25 July 1971.

"Regarder hier," *Les Nouvelles littéraires,* 10 September 1971. Extract from *En chemin, vers quel éveil?*

"Prise de position." *Catacombes,* 15 October 1971.

"Vaincre la peur." *France catholique,* 15 October 1971.

"Allocution pour le colloque précédant l'Assemblée des silencieux de l'Eglise à Strasbourg le 7 novembre 1971." *Carrefour,* 17 November 1971.

"Non ingérence ou complicité." *Le Monde,* 30 November 1971.

1972   "Note sur l'attestation créatrice dans mon oeuvre." In *La testimonianza. Archivio di filosofia,* January 1972. The acts and proceedings of a meeting sponsored by the International Center for Humanistic Studies and the Institute of Philosophical Studies of the University of Rome, 5–11 January 1972. Also published as *La testimonianza,* by Enrico Castelli et al. Padua: Cedam, 1972.

"L'Ame de la culture." *Les Nouvelles littéraires,* 17 July 1972.

Reply by G. Marcel to "Marcel, philosophie de la transcendance," by Jacques Rueff. *Les Nouvelles littéraires,* 17 July 1972.

"J'ai horreur de la dictature." *Figaro littéraire,* 20 October 1972. Interview with Frédéric de Towarnicki.

1973   "Geleitbrief." In *Das Wagnis der Treue: G. Marcels Weg zu einer konkreten Philosophie des Schöpferischen,* by Vincent Berning. Freiburg: Karl Alber, 1973.

"Ionesco." In *Ionesco,* edited by Raymond Laubreaux. Paris: Garnier, 1973.

Percées vers un ailleurs. Paris: Fayard, 1973.

Includes two plays: *L'Iconoclaste* and *L'Horizon.* Commentaries by Father Marcel Belay, followed by "L'audace en métaphysique," by G. Marcel.

"Thomas Mann et Nietzsche." *Les Cahiers de l'Herne* 23 (1973).

1974   *The Existentialist Drama of Gabriel Marcel.* Edited by Francis J. Lascoe. West Hartford, Conn.: McAuley Institute of Religious Studies, St. Joseph's College, 1974.

"Vers un humanisme théocentrique: Deux Etudes de G. Marcel consacrées à Charles Du Bos." Edited by Michèle Leleu. *Cahiers Charles Du Bos,* May 1974. The studies concern Du Bos's texts of 1935–1960.

"Vingt et une lettres inédites de Gabriel Marcel et Charles Du Bos." *Cahiers Charles Du Bos,* May 1974.

"Commentaires des réponses données par Gabriel Marcel." *Revue de métaphysique et de morale,* July September 1974. From the Dijon discussions, March 1973.

"Dialogue entre Gabriel Marcel et Mme. Parain-Vial." *Revue de métaphysique et de morale,* July–September 1974.

"Dialogue entre Gabriel Marcel et Marcel Belay." *Revue de métaphysique et de morale,* July–September 1974. A discussion of *Le Monde cassé.*

"Notes sur le mal." *Revue de métaphysique et de morale,* July–September 1974. From the Dijon discussions, March 1973.

1975   "La Liberté en 1971." *Etudes philosophiques,* January–March 1975.

1976   "De la recherche philosophique." In *Entretiens autour de G. Marcel,* by Marcel Belay, Vincent Berning, Joseph Chenu, Henri Gouhier, Jeanne Parain-Vial, René Poirier, Paul Ricoeur, Baldwuin Schwarz, and Gabriel Marcel. Neuchâtel: Editions de la Baconnière; Paris: Diffusion Payot, 1976.

[Conference organized by the] International Cultural Center of Cerisy-la-Salle, 24–31 August 1973. Published with the concurrence of the European Foundation of Culture (Languages).

1977   "Gabriel Marcel interrogé par Pierre Boutang." Followed by *Position et approches concrètes du mystère ontologique.* Archives du xxe Siècle, no. 1. Paris: J. M. Place, 1977.

1979   Henri G. Gouhier, G. Marcel, Emmanuel Levinas, et al. *Gabriel Marcel et la pensée allemande: Nietzsche, Heidegger, Ernst Bloch.* Paris: Présence de Gabriel Marcel, 1979. Includes three works by G. Marcel: "Nietzsche: L'Homme devant la mort de Dieu," unpublished manuscript; "Ma Relation avec Heidegger," unpublished manuscript; and "Dialogue sur l'espérance," by G. Marcel and Ernst Bloch, with the participation of Hans Fischer-Barnicol and Alfred Schmidt, introduced by Maurice de Gandillac.

INDEX

(by S. S. Rama Rao Pappu)

618 INDEX